John Keay is the author of about twenty books, all factual, mostly historical, and largely to do with Asia, exploration or Scotland. His first book stayed in print for thirty years; many others have become classics. A full-time author since 1973, he has also written and presented over 100 documentaries for BBC Radio 3 and 4, and has been a guest lecturer on tour groups. He travels extensively.

Also available

The Mammoth Book of

TRAVEL IN
DANGEROUS PLACES

Edited by
John Keay

With a Foreword by Wilfred Thesiger

ROBINSON

RUNNING PRESS
PHILADELPHIA · LONDON

ROBINSON

Originally published as *The Robinson Book of Exploration* by Robinson Publishing, 1993

This revised edition first published in the UK by Robinson, an imprint of Constable & Robinson Ltd, 2010

Reprinted by Robinson in 2017

3 5 7 9 10 8 6 4

A CIP catalogue record for this book
is available from the British Library.

UK ISBN: 978-1-84901-311-6

Robinson
An imprint of
Little, Brown Book Group
Carmelite House
50 Victoria Embankment
London EC4Y 0DZ

An Hachette UK Company
www.hachette.co.uk

www.littlebrown.co.uk

First published in the United States in 2010 by Running Press Book Publishers
A member of the Perseus Books Group

Books published by Running Press are available at special discounts for bulk purchases in the
United States by corporations, institutions and other organizations. For more information, please
contact the Special Markets Department at the Perseus Books Group, 2300 Chestnut Street, Suite 200,
Philadelphia, PA 19103, or call (800) 810-4145, ext. 5000, or email special.markets@perseusbooks.com.

US Library of Congress number: 2009929934
US ISBN 978-0-7624-3845-7

10 9 8 7 6 5 4 3 2 1
Digit on the right indicates the number of this printing

Running Press Book Publishers
2300 Chestnut Street
Philadelphia, PA 19103-4371
Visit us on the web!
www.runningpress.com

Printed and bound in Great Britain by CPI Group (UK) Ltd., Croydon CR0 4YY

Papers used by Robinson are from well-managed forests and other responsible sources

for trade with Polo's Cathay, Xanadu and Cipangu (Japan) that Columbus sailed west. When natives in Cuba responded to his queries for gold by mentioning a place called "Cubanacan", he was sure they were referring to Kublai Khan.

The age of discovery, as opposed to the age of exploration, began with Columbus and Vasco da Gama. Da Gama was followed east by Cabral, who en route made the first landing in Brazil, while Columbus was followed west by Amerigo Vespucci who gave his name to the new continent. To ignore them, not to mention the Cabots and the great circumnavigators, Magellan and Drake, in an anthology of exploration may seem perverse. Likewise those indefatigable Dutch and English mariners who attempted to emulate Portuguese and Spanish successes round Cape Horn and Cape of Good Hope by rounding Eurasia by the North East Passage or America by the North West Passage. Their additions to man's knowledge of the earth's surface created the map over which later explorers pored in search of blank spaces and unsolved mysteries. It would be absurd to belittle their achievements simply on the grounds that their motivation was wholly commercial rather than scientific.

The same could be said for another class of pioneers who followed hard in their wake and quickly circumscribed those blank spaces. In South and Central America we know them as *Conquistadors*, in North America as *Courreurs de Bois*, and in Siberia as Cossacks. Pushing east in Asia and west in Canada these pioneers reduced trade to something closer to rank exploitation as they shot and trapped their way ever deeper into the continental landmasses. Furs and hides became the currency of embryonic colonies just as in Mexico and South America did gold and silver. There all pretence at commercial exchange was abandoned as the *Conquistadors*, dazzled as much by religious bigotry as precious metals, butchered their way inland to claim for themselves and Christendom the untold wealth of the Aztecs and Incas.

But to Yermak, Cortes, Pizarro or even Champlain geographical discovery was incidental if not irrelevant. The watershed between exploration motivated by greed and exploration motivated by scientific enquiry falls in the eighteenth century and owes everything to the Enlightenment. Commercial and colonial interests certainly featured in the instructions issued to Vitus Bering by Peter the Great in 1725; but so did purely geographical questions, like whether the Asian and American landmasses were joined. Furs also figured prominently in the plans for Bering's second expedition as, much later, they did in Mackenzie's travels across Canada. Yet Bering's inclusion of a naturalist like Steller, and the latter's remarkable contribution to the expedition's findings and its survival, are more significant. Twenty years later, James Cook's instructions from the Royal Society were wholly scientific. He was to observe a transit of Venus across the sun from the southern hemisphere and to investigate the continuing rumours of a southern continent. In this context it was his interest in the colonial possibilities of New Zealand and Australia which was incidental.

With its rejection of dogma and its emphasis on reason and experiment the Enlightenment had given man a new perspective on his world and a new purpose in it. Primitive societies could no longer be regarded as amongst the raw materials of Christendom. Ignorance of outlandish places represented a slur on civilization. Above all the Enlightenment encouraged the individual to think and act for himself. Better examples than Steller or Cook might be James Bruce or Mungo Park. Their solitary and often hazardous wanderings in Africa were undertaken out of little more than an all-consuming curiosity. Although not scientists like the great Alexander von Humboldt, their range of enquiry was as wide and open-minded as the German polymath's. "Man and Nature – whatever is performed by the one or produced by the other" was how Sir William Jones, another Enlightenment polymath, put it. No one took this definition of scientific enquiry more to heart than those who ventured abroad during the great age of exploration.

CONTENTS

Foreword by Wilfred Thesiger   ix
Introduction   xi

Siberia and Alaska

Georg Wilhelm Steller *Stranded on Bering Island*   1
John Dundas Cochrane *The Walk to Moscow*   11

Central and South Asia

Alexander Burnes *Alarms Amongst the Uzbeks*   23
John Wood *On the Roof of the World*   36
Regis-Evariste Huc *Lhasa Beckons*   47
Henri Mouhot *Exploring Angkhor*   60
Francis Edward Younghusband *Over the Karakorams*   69
Ekai Kawaguchi *Trials in Tibet*   81
Sven Hedin *At the Source of the Indus*   91
Edmund Hillary *Everest by Storm*   98

Arabia

William Gifford Palgrave *Escape from Riyadh*   108
Charles Montagu Doughty *Desert Days*   117
Harry St John Bridger Philby *The Point of Return*   125
Wilfred Thesiger *To the Empty Quarter for a
    Drink of Water*   137

West Africa

Mungo Park *Alone in Africa*   147
Hugh Clapperton *The Road to Kano*   157
Richard Lander *Down the Niger*   165
Heinrich Barth *Arrival in Timbuktu*   175
Mary Kingsley *My Ogowé Fans*   186

East and Central Africa

James Bruce *Among the Sudanese*   202
Richard Francis Burton *Not the Source of the Nile*   213
John Hanning Speke *A Glimpse of Lake Victoria*   226
Samuel White Baker *The Reservoir of the Nile*   242
David Livingstone *Last Days*   254
Henry Morton Stanley *Encounters on the
   Upper Congo*   268
Joseph Thomson *A Novice at Large*   286

Australia

James Cook *Landfall at Botany Bay*   301
Charles Sturt *Escape from the Outback*   310
William John Wills *Death at Coopers Creek*   320
John McDouall Stuart *To See the Sea*   336

North America

Alexander Mackenzie *First Crossing of America*   345
Meriwether Lewis *Meeting the Shoshonee*   357

South America

Alexander von Humboldt *Eating Dirt in Venezuela*   374
Henry Savage Landor *Iron Rations in Amazonia*   383
Hiram Bingham *The Discovery of Machu Picchu*   396

Arctic

John Ross *Four Years in the Ice*   404
John Franklin *Living off Lichen and Leather*   415

Fridtjof Nansen *Adrift on an Arctic Ice Floe*   428
Robert Edwin Peary *The Pole is Mine*   440

Antarctic

Ernest Henry Shackleton *Farthest South*   448
Roald Amundsen *The Pole at Last*   458
Robert Falcon Scott *In Extremis*   469
Sources and Acknowledgments   485

FOREWORD

by Wilfred Thesiger

The concept of exploration has always meant the geographical discovery of areas of the earth previously unknown to the explorer himself and to the society to which he belonged. In the past, important exploration was carried out by the Greeks, Romans, Arabs and Polynesians, for example. In modern times, geographical exploration almost inevitably means exploration by Europeans, who have accomplished this on a vast scale, worldwide. The knowledge of their discoveries has been widely disseminated by modern techniques.

Now, with virtually the whole surface of the world surveyed and mapped, journeys in this sense, however arduous, can no longer be described as exploration.

Except for the South Pole, explorers have usually penetrated areas already inhabited or travelled over by other human beings; this has often constituted the greatest risk to themselves. Others with no previous connection with these regions and their inhabitants may well have been there, which means in a sense that the areas had already been explored.

An example of this was when, in Western eyes, the source of the Nile was unknown and its discovery was regarded as the final challenge of exploration. Credit for this discovery was justifiably given to Speke, though in reality Arabs from a far-distant land had already penetrated there with the object of collecting slaves and ivory. Their knowledge of this land was invaluable to Speke, Burton, Grant and other contemporary explorers.

Until recently, explorers travelled on foot with porters or with animal transport, or in sailing boats and canoes and, throughout their journeys, could only rely on themselves, their very whereabouts at any time unknown to their sponsors until they either returned or failed to do so. Today, such geographical exploration as is left has inevitably been carried out with mechanized transport; radio communication has also enabled the expedition members to keep in continuous contact with their base. In some cases they have even known that, in a crisis, an aircraft might come to their assistance.

It has been my good fortune that, when I travelled in the Danakil country and in the Empty Quarter of Arabia, no other means of travel was possible than that employed by their inhabitants. In Arabia this resulted in the very close personal relationship with my Arab companions which gave me the five most memorable years of my life.

Wilfred Thesiger

INTRODUCTION

It is as well to be wary of the word "exploration". Today all manner of racial, colonial and Euro-centric conceits cling to it; even in its heyday it was used sparingly. Captain Cook, sometimes called the greatest of explorers, made "voyages of discovery", not exploration; Bruce, Speke and Barth also made "discoveries", others were mostly content with "travels", "journeys", or in the case of Doughty and Burton mere "wanderings". Exploration was too big a word; "explorer" was not the sort of title a traveller had printed on his visiting card. It presumed too much; had the world really been so ignorant about the tract he claimed to have explored? Had he performed that exhaustive investigation which exploration implied? And what about the people who inhabited the place? Were they also totally ignorant of their surroundings and incapable of contributing to their topography?

"Exploration" had in fact a greater currency amongst its armchair arbiters in the Geographical Societies of Europe than it did amongst their emissaries in the field. They needed a noun to describe and substantiate the activities of these emissaries and hence the word was adopted. Denoting the "action of exploring foreign lands", it first appears in 1823 according to the Oxford English Dictionary; it was very much an English invention.

By any reckoning the nineteenth-century British contribution – Scottish quite as much as English – to our knowledge of the world's less accessible lands was commensurate with the universal and preponderant character of the British empire. The opportunities for filling in the blank spaces fell almost exclusively to the British in Australia, predominantly to the British in Africa, and generously to the British in North America, Arabia, Antarctica and Central

Asia. All were explored during the period 1815–1914, the great age
of what quickly became known as "exploration" and the main focus
of this anthology. It began with the end of the Napoleonic Wars;
demobilization released a host of young officers like Clapperton and
Cochrane who, despairing of advancement and adventure in the
services, looked elsewhere for a challenge; simultaneously the Admiralty, as it cast about for a peacetime role, hit on ideas like testing
its ships and men in a renewed search for the North West Passage.

So peace in Europe ushered in the age of exploration, and war in
Europe abruptly ended it. By 1914 the main deserts had all been
crossed, the great rivers traced to their sources, and the Poles
conquered. Exploration had practically run its course and so had
the typically officered and expeditionary nature of the British style of
exploration. The Norwegian Roald Amundsen's 1911 defeat of
Captain Scott in the race for the South Pole was seen as demonstrating the triumph of single-minded professionals over excessively
scrupulous all-rounders. Brute strength and a morality bordering
on the sentimental (ponies could be eaten but not dogs) began to
seem pig-headed and arrogant. In the unbearable fortitude with
which Scott and his companions met their subsequent fate there may
be detected a foretaste of the greater tragedy that was about to
unfold as the gentlemanly ideals of a vanishing age were laid to rest
in the fields of Normandy and Flanders.

After both World Wars exploring activity did revive, although
whether crossing that small corner of Arabia known as the Empty
Quarter or conquering the conspicuous heights of Everest really
counted is debatable. They were certainly worthy challenges, but
exploration in the nineteenth-century sense reserved to itself an air of
mystery which these new goals could scarcely boast. No one
suspected more than sand in the Empty Quarter or snow and ice
on Everest. Shackleton had been thwarted in his 1908–9 bid for the
South Pole by the discovery that it lay across a plateau 10,000 feet
above sea-level and so nearly as elevated as Tibet. He was defeated
by the effects of altitude as much as latitude; it was a surprise to
everyone. So was the discovery of an elevated "lake region" in the
highlands of East Africa by Burton, Speke, Livingstone and Baker.
This idea proved so exciting that soon lake regions were being
predicted all over the place. Wood thought his Sir-i-kol source of the
Oxus might be part of another and Hedin insisted on a Tibetan lake
region beside his Transhimalaya range. An inland sea, if not a lake
region, was also confidently predicted for the heart of Australia until
Sturt, Burke and Stuart proved otherwise. But Everest held no such
surprises; even its height was known to within a few feet. And no one

suspected lakes or even forbidden cities in the howling wilderness of the Empty Quarter.

There were no major discoveries left for the post-war explorer and there were, and still are, serious doubts about what exploration is now all about. In 1909 Commander Robert Peary's claim to have been first to reach the North Pole occasioned bitter controversy. Some preferred the claim of a fellow American, Dr. Frederick Cook, to have got there first; others disputed whether Peary, who had insisted on making his polar dash alone but for his black servant and some mystified Eskimos, could possibly have reached the Pole in the time he indicated. Subsequently Cook was largely discredited and Peary, when his pre-arrangements were fully appreciated, vindicated. "It was not, however, exploration" declared a doyenne of the British Royal Geographical Society as recently as 1990. Peary's dash was preceded by the establishment of a chain of elaborately equipped igloos reaching almost to his goal; like the post travellers of old, he could travel light being assured of food and shelter at each halt. Whether it was or was not exploration, it was certainly not cricket.

Exploration assumed a high degree of hardship, risk and uncertainty as well as of mystery. And when, in the twentieth century, these ceased to be self-evident, they had to be contrived. Colonel Fawcett's mysterious disappearance in South America could be seen as a fitting end for one who, insisting on the existence of a lost Eldorado, made a mystery out of his route as well as his goal. Similarly the traveller who elects to go on foot where he could perfectly well ride, or to cycle where there are no roads, is merely contriving hardship. His experiences are only marginally more interesting than those of the adventurer who, failing to contrive a knife-edge situation, feels no compunction about inventing it. To such a rascal no indulgence was extended in the great age of exploration. Incident had to be credible and when it was not, as in the monumental narratives of Henry Savage Landor, the author's bluff would be called, as indeed happened to Landor in both London and Paris.

So to qualify as exploration a journey had to be credible, had to involve hardship and risk, and had to include the novelty of discovery. Thereafter, like cricket, it was somewhat hard to explain to the uninitiated. But one element was absolutely vital; indeed it was precisely that which distinguished the age of exploration from previous ages of discovery and which necessitated the adoption of the word "exploration". It was, quite simply, a reverence for science. This might amount to no more than avowing a curiosity about the unknown and spattering one's narrative with compass bearings and distances; or it might, as with some of the polar expeditions, result in a staff of distinguished researchers generating shelves of observations on everything from meteorology to bowel movements.

The point was that science provided a rationale for travel, and elevated it from mere locomotion to something approaching an academic discipline; hence the need in English for that new noun, "exploration". Science also broadened the scope of travel. Lands which travellers had hitherto found no good reason for visiting were of particular interest to scientists, while those from which political competition or religious bigotry had barred the traveller could now be assailed in the name of science. In Africa and America it would not be uncommon for scientific exploration to be used as a pretext for colonial and commercial expansion; British East Africa owed everything to the likes of Burton and Speke and the sea-to-sea configuration of the United States to Lewis and Clark. In Asia exploration was often a cover for political intrigue, as demonstrated by Alexander Burnes, or for military intelligence-gathering, Francis Younghusband's speciality. But that in no way discredited the new priority accorded to scientific enquiry. It is what distinguishes the explorer from the merchant/navigator, and the age of exploration from the centuries of travel which preceded it.

Travel as the raw material of geography has a pedigree as long as history. An anthology could begin with Harkhuf, "the first recorded explorer", who around 2300 BC reached the land of Yam. An inscription on his tomb near Aswan records that after an absence of seven months Harkhuf returned to Egypt laden with "all kinds of gifts" including a dancing dwarf. He also brought panthers, ebony and ivory; it is presumed therefore that Yam lay somewhere up the Nile in Nubia. As old as history, geography amounted to much the same thing for Greek writers like Herodotus and Xenophon. Along with astronomy and what we would now call ethnology, history-geography provided the physical and human context so vital to self-conscious civilizations. Knowledge of where one stood in relation to other planets, other peoples, other lands and other ages was comforting because it presumed an intellectual supremacy over them.

Where one stood was, of course, at the apex of history and at the centre of the world, ideas which could be graphically embodied in diagrammatic form, especially maps. Thus for the Chinese the world map shaded off from their well-ordered Middle Kingdom into various degrees of barbarism; the Graeco-Roman world, with the

Mediterranean at its centre, was similarly uncomplimentary about outsiders with amphibian monsters and woad-speckled savages lurking round its watery perimeter. Religion-crazed societies like those of Hindu-Buddhist India or medieval Christian Europe often found space in their maps for an additional vignette portraying the bliss of nirvana or heaven; it usually appeared at the top, the dead centre being reserved for the Hindu's Mount Meru or the Christian's Jerusalem. Such complacent centricity survived even scientific enlightenment about the true shape of the earth and the rather arbitrary distribution of its land masses. With no attempt at impartiality conventional maps still show the northern hemisphere, home of the erstwhile colonial powers where such cartography was perfected, at the top of the globe; and conventional projections of the world, centred on the Greenwich Mean, still accord Europe a pivotal prominence. That conceit, implicit in exploration, that any first-hand account of places unfamiliar to a European readership constituted discovery, predates the nineteenth century by at least two millennia.

Familiarity with other lands and peoples also conferred a political edge over them. Gathering knowledge is an acquisitive process, a vicarious form of conquest; and understanding one's environment has always been closely associated with mastery of it. Later explorers were not the only ones who were hard put to disclaim all colonizing intentions. Emerging from the Australian outback after an epic crossing of that continent in 1862, one of John McDouall Stuart's companions climbed a small hill, glimpsed the Timor Sea, and announced journey's end. His croaked cries of "The Sea, The Sea" nicely echoed the lustier shouts of Xenophon's Ten Thousand as they breasted the hills above Trebizond in 400 BC and sighted the Black Sea. Stuart had crossed the heart of his continent and confidently anticipated ranchers, settlers and the transcontinental telegraph line following in his trail. Xenophon was in retreat, hard-pressed and anxious to be home. But the knowledge, not the circumstances under which it was acquired, was what mattered. Thanks to Xenophon, Armenia and Anatolia had become as much a part of the Greek world as, thanks to Stuart, central Australia had of the British world. Seventy years after Xenophon, Alexander the Great turned knowledge into dominion.

Whether Harkhuf, our first explorer, was interested in intelligence-gathering is unclear. But to judge by all those "gifts" he was not indifferent to trade. As well as commerce, probably up the Nile, with Yam and other parts of Africa, the ancient Egyptians pioneered maritime trade. Punt, a land which may correspond to Somalia

but was more probably in southern Arabia, was the Pharaohs' main
source of incense and unguents. To a people obsessed with temple
ritual and preserving their dead these were vital commodities, every
bit as valued and desirable as, much later, were spices by meat-eating
medieval Europe. If Harkhuf never ventured to Punt, contemporaries
and descendants certainly did, thus pioneering the maritime trade of
the Arabian Sea and the Indian Ocean. In their wake followed Greeks
and Phoenicians who reached India and may even have circumnavi-
gated Africa. High value commodities like gold, ivory, precious
stones, and spices now comprised the main stimulus to exploration;
tin even tempted mariners beyond the straits of Gibraltar and up
Europe's Atlantic sea-board to the British Isles. The Romans would
follow but in the Indian Ocean, where long distance maritime trade
supplied Rome with spices and exotica, it was the Arabs who
eventually engrossed the ancient world's most lucrative commerce
and its most extensive field of geographical knowledge.

Navigation is of course a science and without the technical
expertise of the Phoenicians, Greeks and Arabs in astronomy and
instrumentation this steady widening of geographical horizons
would have been impossible. Yet until the eighteenth century science
remained but a means to an end. It was the same for the Vikings
whose remarkable voyages in the tenth and eleventh centuries
extended to Iceland, Greenland and Newfoundland; and it was
even so for Henry the Navigator, the Portuguese prince whose
patronage and encouragement of maritime science in the fifteenth
century led to the famous succession of Portuguese voyages down,
and eventually round, the African coast. For Prince Henry, as for
Harkhuf, trade was the priority. Pious objectives, like carrying the
crusades round Islam's African flank, discovering the mythical
kingdom of Prester John, or winning converts, were quickly forgotten the moment that Vasco da Gama reached India (1498) and
filled his ships with spices.

Trade was also responsible for what was known of Eurasia's
inland geography. Here the backbone of all knowledge was the
famous silk route from China through Central Asia to the Black Sea
and the Mediterranean. Political emissaries and religious propagan-
dists occasionally threaded its deserts and mountain passes en route
to fabled Cathay; but much more typical were merchants like Marco
Polo. His detailed account of the route would come in for careful
examination by nineteenth century explorers like Wood and Burnes,
but to the medieval world it was his descriptions of Kublai Khan's
capital of Xanadu and of his rich and well ordered empire which
were so intriguing. Two hundred years later it was to find a short-cut

STRANDED ON BERING ISLAND

Georg Wilhelm Steller
(1709–46)

As physician and scientific know-all on Vitus Bering's 1741 voyage, Steller shared its triumphs, including landing the first Europeans in Alaska. He also shared its disasters. Returning across the north Pacific to Russian Kamchatka, the crew was stricken with scurvy and the vessel grounded. Bering and half his men would die; the others barely survived nine months of Arctic exposure. They owed much to the German-born Steller whose response to each crisis was invariably right, although no less irksome for being so.

O n November 7 we had again a very pleasant day and a northeast wind. I spent the morning in packing so much of my baggage as I could get hold of near by. Because I could see plainly that our vessel could not hold together longer than till the first violent storm, when it must either be driven out to sea or dashed to pieces against the beach, I, with Mr. Plenisner, my cossack, and several of the sick men went ashore first.

We had not yet reached the beach when a strange sight greeted us, inasmuch as from the land a number of sea otters came towards us in the sea, which from a distance some of us took for bears, others for wolverines, but later on we learned to know, unfortunately, only too well. – As soon as we had landed, Mr. Plenisner went to hunt with the gun, while I investigated the natural conditions of the surroundings. After having made various observations, I returned towards evening to the sick men, and there I also found Lieutenant Waxel, who was very weak and faint. We refreshed ourselves with tea. Among other things I remarked: "God knows whether this is Kamchatka!" – receiving, however, from him [Waxel] the reply: "What else can it be? We shall soon send for *podvods* (horses); the ship, however, we shall cause to be taken to the mouth of the

Kamchatka River by cossacks, the anchors can be had any time, the most important thing now is to save the men." – In the meantime Mr. Plenisner also came back, told what he had seen, and brought half a dozen ptarmigans, which he sent on board to the Captain Commander with the Lieutenant, in order to revive him by means of the fresh food. I, however, sent him some nasturtium-like herbs for a salad. – Later two cossacks and a cannoneer arrived, who had killed two sea otters and two seals, news which appeared quite remarkable to us. When we reproached them for not bringing the meat in for our refreshment, they fetched us a seal, which seemed to them preferable to the sea otter for eating. As evening came I made a soup from a couple of ptarmigans and ate this dish with Mr. Plenisner, young Waxel, and my cossack. In the meanwhile Mr. Plenisner made a hut out of driftwood and an old sail, and under it we slept that night alongside the sick.

On November 8 we again enjoyed pleasant weather. This morning Mr. Plenisner made the agreement with me that he should shoot birds, while I should look for other kinds of food, and that we should meet again towards noon in this place. With my cossack I went at first along the beach to the eastward, gathered various natural curiosities, and also chased a sea otter; my cossack, however, shot eight blue foxes, the number and fatness of which as well as the fact that they were not shy astonished me exceedingly. Moreover, since I saw the many manati near shore in the water, which I had never before seen and even now could not well make out as they lay all the time half in the water, but concerning which my cossack asserted that they were known nowhere in Kamchatka, and likewise since nowhere any tree or shrubbery was to be seen, I began to doubt that this was Kamchatka, especially as the sea sky over in the south indicated sufficiently that we were on an island surrounded by the sea.

Toward noon I returned to the hut and after dinner decided to go with Mr. Plenisner and our cossack westward along the beach in order to search for forests or small timber; we found nothing whatever, but saw a few sea otters and killed various blue foxes and ptarmigans. On the way back we sat down at a small stream, regaled ourselves with tea, and thanked God heartily that once more we had good water and under us solid ground, at the same time recalling how wonderfully we had fared and remembering the unjust conduct of various people.

During the day an effort was made by the disposition of the anchors, large and small, as many as we had, to make the ship secure to the land in the best possible manner, and for that reason the boat did not come ashore. In the evening, as we were sitting around the camp fire after having eaten our meal, a blue fox came up and took away two ptarmigans right before our eyes. This was the first sample of the many tricks and thefts which those animals practiced on us later. – I had to encourage my sick and feeble cossack, who regarded me as the cause of his misfortune and reproached me for my curiosity which had led me into this misery, [thus] making the first step to our future companionship. "Be of good cheer," I said, "God will help. Even if this is not our country, we have still hope of getting there; you will not starve; if you cannot work and wait on me, I will do it for you; I know your upright nature and what you have done for me; all that I have belongs to you also; only ask and I will divide with you equally until God helps." – But he said: "Good enough; I will gladly serve Your Majesty, but you have brought me into this misery. Who compelled you to go with these people? Could you not have enjoyed the good times on the Bolshaya River?" – I laughed heartily at his frankness and said: "God be praised, we are both alive! If I have dragged you into this misery, you have in me, with God's help, a lifelong friend and benefactor. My intentions were good, Thoma, so let yours be good also; moreover, you do not know what might have happened to you at home."

In the meantime I took this as a cue to consider how we could protect ourselves against the winter by building a hut, in case it turned out that we were not in Kamchatka but on an island. That evening, therefore, I started to confer with Mr. Plenisner about building a hut for all eventualities and assisting each other with word and deed as good friends, no matter how the circumstances might shape themselves. Although for appearance's sake, in order not to discourage me, he did not assent to my opinion that this was an island, nevertheless he accepted my plan in regard to the hut.

On November 9 the wind was from the east and the weather rather bearable. In the morning we went out to look for a site and to collect wood and selected during the day the spot where we built later on and where the whole command also set up their huts and wintered. – However, we were far too busy killing blue foxes, of which I and Mr. Plenisner in one day got sixty, partly knocking them down with the axe and partly stabbing them with a Yakut *palma*. – Towards evening we returned to our old hut, where again some of the sick had been brought ashore.

On the 10th of November the wind was from the east; in the forenoon it was clear, in the afternoon cloudy, and during the night the wind whirled much snow about. We carried all our baggage a verst away to the place which we had selected the day before for the building of a dwelling. In the meantime more sick were brought ashore, among them also the Captain Commander, who spent the evening and night in a tent. I, with others, was with him and wondered at his composure and singular contentment. He asked what my idea was about this land. – I answered that it did not look to me like Kamchatka; the great number and tame assurance of the animals of itself clearly indicated that it must be sparsely inhabited or not at all; but nevertheless it could not be far from Kamchatka, as the land plants observed here occur in the same number, proportion, and size as in Kamchatka, while on the other hand the peculiar plants discovered in America are not found in the corresponding localities. Besides, I had found on the beach a poplar-wood window shutter, with cross moldings, that some years ago the high water had washed ashore and covered with sand near the place where we later built our huts; I showed it and pointed out that it was unquestionably of Russian workmanship and probably from the *ambars* which stood at the mouth of the Kamchatka River. The most likely place for which this land might be taken would be Cape Kronotski. Nevertheless, I did not fail to make known my doubts as to this, based on the following experience: I showed, namely, a piece of a fox trap that I had found on the beach during the first day; on this the teeth, instead of being of iron, consisted of so-called Entale (toothshell), of the occurrence of which in Kamchatka I have no information and regarding which it consequently is to be supposed that the sea must have washed this token over from America, where, in default of iron, this invention may well have been made use of, while in Kamchatka, where iron already is plentiful through trade, it would be superfluous. I mentioned at the same time the unknown sea animal, manati, which I had seen, and the character of the water sky opposite in the south. – To all this I got the reply: "The vessel can probably not be saved, may God at least spare our longboat."

In the evening after having eaten in company with the Commander the ptarmigans which Mr. Plenisner shot during the day, I told Betge, the assistant surgeon, that he might live with us if he liked, for which he gave thanks; and thus our company now consisted of four. We therefore walked over to the place of our new quarters, sat by the camp fire, and discussed, over a cup of tea, how we would put our plan into execution. I built near by a small hut which I covered with my two overcoats and an old blanket; the openings on the sides were stopped up with dead foxes which we had killed during the day and were lying about in heaps, and then we retired to rest, but Mr. Betge returned to the Commander.

STRANDED ON BERING ISLAND

Towards midnight a strong wind arose, which was accompanied by much snow, tore off our roof, and drove the three of us from our quarters. We ran up and down the beach in the dark gathering driftwood, carried it to a pit dug like a grave for two persons, and decided to pass the night there. We laid the wood crosswise over it and covered the top with our clothes, overcoats, and blankets, made a fire to warm ourselves, went to sleep again, and thus, God be thanked, passed a very good night.

On the following day (November 11) I went down to the sea and fetched a seal, the fat of which I cooked with peas and ate in company with my three comrades, who in the meantime had made two shovels and begun to enlarge our pit. – In the afternoon the Captain Commander was brought to us on a stretcher and had a tent, made of a sail, put upon the spot that we had originally chosen for our dwelling place. We entertained him, as well as the other officers who had come to our pit, with tea. – Towards evening both officers returned to the ship. Master Khitrov even proposed to Lieutenant Waxel that they should winter on board the vessel in the open sea, because, according to his idea, more warmth and comfort could be had there than on land, where, for lack of wood, one would have to endure the winter in a tent. This proposition was now approved as very sensible, yet three days later the Master, on his own accord, came ashore and could not be brought back on board the vessel by any orders when later he was to haul it up on the beach. – However, we continued to enlarge our underground home by digging and collected everywhere on the beach wood for a roof and inside coating. – This evening we fixed up a light roof and in the person of assistant constable Roselius obtained the fifth member of our party. In the same manner a few others, who still had strength left, began also to dig a four-cornered pit in the frozen sand and covered it over the next day with double sails in order to shelter the sick.

On November 12 we worked with the greatest industry on our habitation, observed also that others, following our example, dug for themselves in the same manner a third habitation which received its name from its founder, the boatswain Alexei Ivanov. – During the day many of the sick were brought from the vessel, some of whom expired as soon as they came into the air, as was the case with the cannoneer; others in the boat on the way over, as the soldier Savin Stepanov; some right on the beach, as the sailor Sylvester. – Everywhere on the shore there was nothing but pitiful and terrifying sights. The dead, before they could be interred, were mutilated by the foxes, who even dared to attack the living and helpless sick, who lay about on the beach without cover, and sniffed at them like dogs. Some of the sick cried because they were cold, others because hungry and thirsty, since the mouths of many were so miserably affected by the scurvy that they could not eat anything because of the great pain, as the gums were swollen like a sponge, brown black, grown over the teeth and covering them.

The blue foxes (*Lagopus*), which by now had gathered about us in countless numbers, became, contrary to habit and nature, at the sight of man more and more tame, mischievous, and to such a degree malicious that they pulled all the baggage about, chewed up the leather soles, scattered the provisions, stole and carried off from one his boots, from another his socks, trousers, gloves, coats, etc., all of which were lying under the open sky and could not be guarded because of the lack of well persons. Even objects made of iron, and other kinds which they could not eat, were nevertheless sniffed at and stolen. It even seemed as if these miserable animals were to plague and chastise us more and more in the future, as actually happened, perhaps in order that we, like the Philistines, might also be punished by the foxes for our eagerness for the precious Kamchatkan fox skins. It even seemed that the more of them we killed and tortured for revenge most cruelly before the eyes of the others, letting them run away half-skinned, without eyes, ears, tails, half roasted, etc., the more malevolent and audacious became the others, so that they also broke into our habitations and dragged out of them whatever they could get hold of, though occasionally, in spite of our misery, they moved us to laughter by their cunning and funny monkey tricks.

November 14. This afternoon, with Mr. Plenisner and Mr. Betge, I went hunting for the first time, or, as we afterwards used to say in the Siberian way, went on the *promysl*. We clubbed four sea otters, half of which we threw into a creek, which therefrom afterwards retained the name Bobrovaya Ryechka [Sea Otter Creek] and the place where we killed them Bobrovoe Pole [Sea Otter Field], but the best meat, together with the skins and the entrails, we carried home, where we did not arrive until night. From the liver, kidneys, heart, and the meat of these animals we made several palatable dishes and ate them gratefully and with the wish that Providence would not deprive us of this food in the future or put us in the necessity of eating the stinking, disgusting, and hated foxes, which nevertheless, out of prudence, we did not want to exterminate but only to frighten. The precious skins of the sea otters we regarded already as a burden which had lost its value to us, and, as we had no leisure to dry and prepare them, they were thrown about from one day to another until finally they spoiled, together with many others, and were chewed to pieces by the foxes. On the other hand, we now began to regard many things as treasures to which formerly we had paid little or no attention, such as axes, knives, awls, needles, thread, shoe twine, shoes, shirts, socks, sticks, strings, and similar things which in former days many of us would not have stooped to pick up. We all realized that rank, learning, and other distinctions would be of no advantage here in the future or suffice as a means of sustenance; therefore, before being driven to it by shame and necessity, we ourselves decided to work with what strength we had still left, so as not to be laughed at afterward or wait until we were ordered. Thus we five introduced among ourselves a community of goods with regard to the victuals we still had left and arranged our housekeeping in such a manner that at the end there might be no want. The others of our party, three cossacks, and the two servants of the Captain Commander, whom we later took over, we managed, though not exactly as before, yet in such a way that they had to obey when we decided anything jointly, since they received all household goods from us. Nevertheless, we began in the meantime to address everybody somewhat more politely by their patronymics and given name, so as to win them over and be able to rely more on their fidelity in case of misfortune later on; and we soon learned that Peter Maximovich was more ready to serve than Petrusha was formerly. This evening we talked over how we would arrange our household affairs in the future, prepare beforehand against all unexpected mishaps, and, as far as possible, try to keep alive the hope of returning to Asia; we also discussed the unfortunate circumstances in which we had been placed in such a short time that, setting aside the decencies of life to which everyone was entitled, we now were obliged to work in this unaccustomed way simply to sustain a miserable existence. Nevertheless, we encouraged one another not to lose heart but with the greatest possible cheerfulness and earnestness to work for our own benefit as well as for the welfare of the others and by our exertions to support loyally their strength and undertakings.

Today I brought the Captain Commander a young, still suckling sea otter and counselled him in every way and manner to let it be prepared for himself in default of other fresh food, but he showed a very great disgust at it and wondered at my taste, which adapted itself to circumstances. He much preferred to regale himself with ptarmigans as long as possible, of which he received from our company more than he could eat.

On November 13 the building of dwellings was continued. We divided ourselves into three parties; the first went on the vessel to work in order to bring the sick and the provisions ashore; the others dragged home great logs a distance of four versts from Lyesnaya Ryechka (Wood Creek), thus named by us; I, however, and a sick cannoneer remained at home, I attending to the kitchen and the other making a sled for hauling wood and other supplies. While thus taking upon myself the office of cook I also assumed a twofold minor function, namely, to visit the Captain Commander off and on and to assist him in various ways, as he could now expect but little service from his two attendants. Furthermore, as we were the first to set up housekeeping, it also became my duty to succour some of the weak and sick and to bring them warm soups, continuing this until they had recovered somewhat and were able to take care of themselves.

This day the "Barracks" were completed, and during the afternoon many of the sick were carried in but on account of the narrowness of the space were lying everywhere about on the ground covered with rags and clothing. No one was able to care for another, and nothing was heard but wailing and lamenting, the men times out of number calling down God's judgment for revenge on the authors of their misfortune. And, truly, the sight was so pitiful that even the bravest might lose courage thereat.

On November 15, at last, all of the sick had been brought ashore. We took one of them, by name Boris Sänd, to be cared for in our dwelling, whom God withal helped back to health within three months. Master Khitrov also implored us for God's sake to take him into our company and give him a corner, because he could not possibly longer remain among the crew, who day and night let him hear reproaches and threats for past doings, but as our dwelling was already filled up and as nobody was allowed to undertake anything without the assent of the others, all of us objected, as all were equally insulted by him, and refused him absolutely, especially because he was mostly sick from laziness and was the chief author of our misfortune.

During the days that followed our misery and work grew apace. Finally Waxel himself was also brought ashore. He was so badly ravaged by the scurvy that we abandoned all hope for his life, but nevertheless we did not fail to come to his help with both food and medicine, without a thought of former treatment. We were all the more anxious for his recovery, as it was to be feared that, after his decease, when the supreme command would fall to Khitrov, the universal hatred would destroy all discipline and delay, or even prevent, the enterprises necessary for our deliverance. We also induced our men to build a separate hut for him and a few other patients, but until it was erected he had to stand it in the Barracks.

In these days we also received the news, which depressed everybody still more, that our men sent out to scout had not found any indication in the west of a connection of this land with Kamchatka or even the slightest trace of human inhabitants. Besides, we were in daily fear that our vessel, in view of the constant storms, might be driven out to sea and that with it we should lose at one stroke all our provisions and our hope of deliverance. Because of the high waves we were often unable for several days to reach the vessel in the boat for the purpose of landing as many of the supplies as possible. In addition ten or twelve men were likewise taken sick who until now had worked steadily and beyond their strength and who until the end of the month often stood in the cold sea water to their armpits. Altogether, want, nakedness, cold, dampness, exhaustion, illness, impatience, and despair were the daily guests.

By a stroke of good luck the vessel, towards the end of November, was finally thrown up on the beach in a storm in a better way than perhaps might ever have been done by human effort. As thereby the hope of preserving the food on hand, scant as it was, as well as materials had been greatly raised, while at the same time the task of wading through the water to the vessel was rendered unnecessary, we began after a few days to give up all work for the present and to recover. Only the necessary household tasks were continued. Three men were again sent out to go into the country eastward and gather information. For all hope had not yet been abandoned that this might be Kamchatka and, since an error in the latitude might have been made, perhaps the region about Olyutora, the large number of foxes there also apparently lending probability to this view. Others believed this to be Cape Kronotski, and, although the error was easy to see, they loved to lull themselves into pleasant dreams with such hopes.

A number of persons died ashore at the very beginning. Among them we were particularly grieved over the old and experienced mate, Andreas Hesselberg, who had served at sea for more than fifty years and at the age of seventy was discharging his duties always in such a way that he carried to his grave the reputation of a preëminently useful man, whose disregarded advice might perhaps have saved us earlier. Besides him there died two grenadiers, one cannoneer, the master's servant, one sailor, and finally, on December 8, Captain Commander Bering passed away, from whom this island was afterwards named. Two days after him his former adjutant, the master's mate Khotyaintsov, died, and on January 8 the ensign Lagunov, the thirtieth in the sequence and the last one of our number [to die].

THE WALK TO MOSCOW

John Dundas Cochrane
(1793–1825)

A naval officer made redundant by the end of the Napoleonic wars, Cochrane offered his services to African exploration. They were declined. He then hit on the idea of making the first solo journey round the world on foot. Heading east, he left Dieppe in 1820 and after some scarcely credible Siberian excursions, reached the Pacific opposite Alaska. There the enterprise foundered when he fell for, and married, a doe-eyed Kamchatkan teenager. In this breathless account of the stages between St. Petersburg and Moscow, the greatest ever "pedestrian traveller" betrays both his extraordinary stamina and his emotional vulnerability.

I was now furnished with all the documents which I had deemed necessary. They consisted of the following: The customary passport, with the substitution of the minister's for the governor-general's signature; a secret letter to the governor-general of Siberia; and two official documents which I shall give at length.

The first of these (addressed – "To all civil governors," and signed by the minister of the interior) states, that "The bearer hereof, Captain John Cochrane, of the British royal navy, purposing to travel through Russia on foot, is now on his departure for Kamtchatka, with the intention of penetrating from thence to America.

"Having, by the command of his Imperial Majesty, provided this traveller with open instructions to the police of all the towns and provinces lying in his track from St. Petersburg to Kamtchatka, this is also to desire all the chiefs of the different governments through which he may travel, to aid Captain Cochrane, as far as possible, to proceed on his journey without interruption, as well as to afford him lawful defence and protection, in case it should be desired."

The other was an "open order of his Imperial Majesty Alexander the First, Autocrat of all the Russias," &c. &c. signed by the same minister and stating, that "The bearer hereof, Captain John Cochrane, of his Britannic Majesty's Royal navy, having undertaken to travel on foot through the Russian empire, is now on his way to Kamtchatka, intending from thence to pass over to America. The police of the towns and provinces lying in his track from St. Petersburg to Kamtchatka, are, in consequence hereof, not only forbidden to obstruct Captain Cochrane in his journey, but are moreover commanded, in case of necessity, to afford him every possible assistance."

I quitted the hospitable habitation of Sir Robert Kerr Porter, on the 24th of May; and, having had a lift in the carriage with four horses of Sir Robert, I, with my knapsack on my back, set out, and trotted over a partially cultivated country. A pretty avenue of birch trees lined the road, as if to accompany me as far as possible on my departure from the precincts of civilized man. Nature here got the better of a tolerably stout heart; and, as I turned round to catch a last glimpse of the capital I had left, and of the friends to whom I had bade, perhaps, a last adieu, I could not suppress my grief, and, had not my honour been committed, should certainly have returned. A sigh escaped me as I ejaculated a last farewell, till, startling at the expression of my weakness, I resumed my journey with slow and melancholy steps.

It was ten o'clock, (for I had now a watch), and I had reached six miles. The night was beautifully clear, though rather cold from the effects of a northern breeze; while the moon was near her full. I looked at the beautiful luminary and actually asked myself whether I were, as had been asserted, under the baneful influence of that planet. Smiling that I received no reply, I then considered my projects and intentions, and the conduct I ought to follow; and, sitting down at a fountain on the Poulkousky hill, I read to myself a few lessons, which the time and the occasion seemed to inspire. "Go," said I, "and wander with the illiterate and almost brutal savage! – go and be the companion of the ferocious beast! – go and contemplate the human being in every element and climate, whether civilized or savage – of whatever tribe, nation, or religion. Make due allowance for the rusticity of their manners; nor be tempted to cope with them in those taunts, insults, and rudeness, to which the nature of thy enterprise will subject thee. Contemn those incidental circumstances which but too often surprise mankind from their good intentions, and deprive the world of much useful and interesting information. Avoid all political and military topics, and remember, that, "The proper study of mankind is man." Should robbers attack thee, do not, by a foolish resistance, endanger thy life. Man may become hardened by crimes, and persist in the practice of them, till, meeting with resistance, he will be urged to murder; but man is still a humane being, even while seeking his subsistence by rapine and plunder; and seldom, from mere wantonness, will he spill the blood of his fellow-creature. It is only by patience, perseverance, and humility, by reducing thyself to the lowest level of mankind, that thou canst expect to pass through the ordeal with either safety or satisfaction." Something like these were my self-dictated precepts, and I pledged their performance in a draught from the cool and limpid fountain.

In company with some carters I resumed my journey; and depositing my knapsack in one of their vehicles, entered into conversation as well as my scanty knowledge of German would allow me.

As we proceeded, there suddenly rose to the south-east a tremendous blaze, the cause of which it seemed difficult to conjecture. At first I imagined it might be, as I had often seen in England, a blazing bonfire, with a group of mirthful rustics revelling round it. But the scene grew soon too terrific to allow of so simple a solution, the flame rising to a prodigious height, and the smoke rolling into a beautiful dark arch on the clear sky. Immense masses of fire, and sparks at intervals, exploded and separated like a rocket.

We continued to gaze as we advanced, till on reaching the beautiful town of Tzarsko Selo, the source was indeed but too apparent; it was the Emperor's favourite palace wrapped in an inextinguishable flame. I had looked forward with hope to enjoy the survey of so celebrated an edifice, and had actually taken a letter of recommendation to Prince Theodore Galitzin, one of its principal inhabitants, that I might with the more facility have my desire gratified. It was midnight; parties of men surrounded the wasting pile. All, however, was order and regularity; not a voice was heard amid the thousands of people employed. The Emperor was present, evidently impressed with extreme regret, and all appeared powerfully to partake the sentiment. His Majesty, however, continued to give frequent directions with perfect coolness.

Tzarsko Selo was the palace in which the Emperor and his brother Constantine had been brought up, and passed their earlier years; it was hither also that the Emperor was accustomed to retire, when the cares of state permitted him, to lose among its beauties the anxieties of a throne and the toils of so great a government. It had been greatly embellished by his Majesty, and was considered one of the most

Capt. Thomas Dundas Cochrane, R.N. From *Narrative of a Pedestrian Journey through Russia and Siberian Tartary, from the frontiers of China to the Frozen Sea and Kamchatka*, London, 1825.

beautiful retreats in Europe. Years of time, and millions of money, I thought, must be expended, to make it what it was but yesterday morning.

Being excessively fatigued, and finding my individual exertions perfectly useless towards checking the progress of the flames, I retired to the gardens, where I passed a couple of restless hours on a bed of moss, amid herbs and flowers, whose sweet perfumes were as yet unvanquished by the fire of smoke. Some demon seemed to hover over me, and my dreams presented the probable incidents of my journey, in all the horrors which imagination could shadow forth. I arose, and returned to the scene of devastation, now evidently increasing, and appearing to defy the numerous engines pouring upon it from all sides.

The dome of the church fell with a tremendous crash; and such was the immense mass of fire that fell with it, and so great the force

Portrait of Mrs Cochrane. From *Narrative of a Pedestrian Journey*.

of the rebound, that in its second descent, and assisted by the wind, it set fire to two other parts of the palace, until then considered safe. At this critical moment his Imperial Majesty gave a strong proof of steady collectedness. While the fire was raging from apartment to apartment, apparently mocking the resistance of man, the Emperor gave direction that the doors should be walled up with bricks. This was instantly done, and by such an expedient alone could the amber, the most valuable chamber, have been wrested from the general destruction.

Having taken breakfast with Prince Theodore, and amused myself with the infantine prattle of his children, whether in the French, English, or German languages, for they seemed anxious to show off the proficiency they had made, I proceeded towards Tosna, where I arrived at seven in the evening. Young firs and birch border the road, which is good; though the country presents but little of interest, and seems to support but a slender population, considering its proximity to the capital.

I passed the night in the cottage of a farmer, resigning myself to the attacks and annoyance of such vermin as generally haunt impoverished dwellings, and was therefore proportionably pleased in the morning to resume my journey. My route was towards Liubane, at about the ninth milestone from which I sat down, to smoke a cigar or pipe, as fancy might dictate; I was suddenly seized from behind by two ruffians, whose visages were as much concealed as the oddness of their dress would permit. One of them, who held an iron bar in his hand, dragged me by the collar towards the forest, while the other, with a bayoneted musket, pushed me on in such a manner as to make me move with more than ordinary celerity; a boy, auxiliary to these vagabonds, was stationed on the road-side to keep a look-out.

We had got some sixty or seventy paces into the thickest part of the forest, when I was desired to undress, and having stripped off my trowsers and jacket, then my shirt, and, finally, my shoes and stockings, they proceeded to tie me to a tree. From this ceremony, and from the manner of it, I fully concluded that they intended to try the effect of a musket upon me, by firing at me as they would at a mark. I was, however, reserved for fresh scenes; the villains, with much *sang froid*, seated themselves at my feet, and rifled my knapsack and pockets, even cutting out the linings of the clothes in search of bank bills or some other valuable articles. They then compelled me to take at least a pound of black bread, and a glass of rum, poured from a small flask which had been suspended from my neck. Having appropriated my trowsers, shirts, stockings, and English shooting shoes, (the last of which I regretted most of all, as they were a present from Sir D. Bailey,) as also my spectacles, watch, compass, thermometer, and small pocket-sextant, with one hundred and sixty roubles, (about seven pounds,) they at length released me from the tree, and, at the point of a stiletto, made me swear that I would not inform against them – such, at least, I conjectured to be their meaning, though of their language I understood not a word.

Having received my promise, I was again treated to bread and rum, and once more fastened to the tree, in which condition they finally abandoned me. Not long after a boy who was passing heard my cries, and set me at liberty. I did not doubt he was sent by my late companions upon so considerate an errand, and felt so far grateful; though it might require something more than common charity to forgive their depriving me of my shirt and trowsers, and leaving me almost as naked as I came into the world.

To pursue my route, or return to Tzarsko Selo, would indeed be alike indecent and ridiculous, but there being no remedy, I made therefore "forward" the order of the day; and having first, with the remnant of my apparel, rigged myself *à l'Ecossoise*, I resumed my route. I had still left me a blue jacket, a flannel waistcoat, and a spare one, which I tied round my waist in such a manner that it reached down to the knees; my empty knapsack was restored to its old place, and I trotted on with even a merry heart.

Within a few miles I passed betwixt files of soldiers employed in making a new road, under the orders of General Woronoff, upon whom I waited to report the situation in which I was placed. The servant, perhaps naturally enough, refused to let me pass without first acquainting his excellency with my business; I, however, steadily persisted in my determination; and at length, hearing the noise and scuffle of turning me out, the general appeared, and listened to my mournful tale. The good heart of his excellency suggested the necessity of first administering me food; some clothes were then offered to me, which I declined, considering my then dress as peculiarly, as well as nationally, becoming. The general then sent an officer with two men back to the village, to make inquiries concerning the robbery. These were, however, fruitless, and I quitted, with many thanks to his excellency, in his own carriage, which was directed to take me to the first station. I soon discovered that carriage-riding was too cold, and therefore preferred walking, barefooted as I was; and on the following morning I reached Tschduvo, a low and uncultivated waste, a hundred miles from St. Petersburg. Thence to Podberezie, and thence to Novgorod. I had passed on the road many populous and neat villages, and numerous tents belonging to the military workmen, which gave additional interest to a fertile and picturesque scenery. To the left was the river Volkhoff, on which Novgorod stands. The approach is grand, and the numerous spires and steeples of the churches and convents, with their gilded and silvered casements glittering in the sun, recalled for a moment the memory of its ancient splendour. Crossing the bridge, I entered at two o'clock, and immediately waited on the governor. He would have provided me with clothing on the instant; I was, however, hungry, and requested food. The governor smiled, but assented, I then accepted a shirt and trowsers.

I was recommended by his excellency to stop at Novgorod a few days, under the promise that he would apprehend the robbers. I told him I felt no doubt they would be discovered; but before that time I should have reached the heart of Siberia. Good quarters were, meantime, provided me in the habitation of a Russian merchant, to whom I had a letter of recommendation from St. Petersburg. He had also the kind consideration to provide me a complete refit; and though this must have been at an expense of thirty or forty roubles, he positively refused my offer of reimbursement – an offer I was enabled to make through the delicate kindness of his excellency the Governor Gerebzoff.

This ancient and celebrated city, which in former days was characterised by the proverb, "Who can resist the Gods and the great Novgorod?" is now only the capital of a province of its own name. In its former glory it was the metropolis of a great republic, with four hundred thousand souls within its walls. The population is now reduced to a fortieth part. Its immense trade had been gradually declining since the cruelties of Ivan Vassilich II., and was completely annihilated by the removal of the seat of government, by Peter the Great, from Moscow to the Gulf of Finland. Many handsome edifices, now in ruins, are lamentable proofs of its former grandeur and present decay. Its archiepiscopal cathedral, small, but very ancient, is filled with superstitious relics, and the ashes of several Russian Grand Dukes.

The steeples of Novgorod present a monument of considerable pride in the estimation of its inhabitants. Their distinction is in the cross at the top standing alone, unaccompanied by the crescent; and this is an emblem, intimating that the Tartars, in all their invasions, never succeeded so far as to enter this city. A distinction which universally holds in Russia; the reconquered cities bearing the crescent, but surmounted by the cross.

The following day, being that of Pentecost, I attended the service in the cathedral; and though I understood nothing of the language, yet was I forcibly struck with the primitive appearance of the clergy in their long beards, longer tresses, and still longer robes. They certainly carried all the appearance of devout ministers of religion.

I had intended, from Novgorod, a visit to Mr. Glenny, at his establishment, eight miles distant, on the banks of the Veshora. Not finding him, however, I put up at a farm-house for the night, having previously drunk kuass at a convent, paid a rouble for charity, and received a blessing upon entering Muscovy – not without a hope that I should find better treatment here than in Esthonia. Next day, passing over a wild dreary waste to Zaitzova, a pleasant town, of fifteen hundred inhabitants, I put up at a civil house, if the admission of both sexes, and of all ranks and dispositions, may deserve such a term; the variety was indeed ludicrous enough, but the conduct and conversation were not of such a nature as to merit description.

The women of Muscovy hitherto appear civil and cleanly dressed, though disfigured by the abominable custom of tying their breasts as low, flat, and tight as possible; they are not, however, quite so ludicrous as some of the creoles and slaves in the West Indies, who often suckle their children behind their backs. The men appear equally civil, obliging, and hospitable, but almost equally disguised by their swaddling coat of cloth or sheep-skin, coloured trowsers, and immense boots, sash round the body, a wide-rimmed hat, and long beard; a mode of dress which certainly gives them something of a ferocious appearance.

On the road to Yedrova I received two roubles as charity from the master of a post-house, from whom also I had received refreshment gratis. Knowing, as I did, that assistance was at hand, I declined the money, although my then distressed state might have warranted my open acceptance of it. I continued my route; and, upon my arrival at the next station, I found the money in my cap. This is, indeed, real benevolence.

The canals are observable to the east, and present a beautiful appearance from the neat town of Yedrova. Reached Vishney-Volotchok late at night, a large scattered but flourishing town, formerly an imperial village, but enfranchised by Catherine, with canals uniting the trades of the Caspian and Baltic seas. I had previously crossed the Valday hills, which are the only elevations between the two capitals. They are in the government of Novgorod, as is also the Valday lake, nine miles in circumference. It has an island in its centre, on which stands a handsome monastery, which, with its steeples glittering through the dark foliage of its intervening woods, forms a beautiful and interesting object. There is also a little town of the same name on its banks. The land here rises into gentle eminences, with a good deal of cultivation.

Torjock was the next flourishing town which I reached, amid rain and thunder. This slight impediment, which broke up my travelling for the day, richly compensated the delay, by introducing me, first, to an excellent supper, gratis; and, secondly, to a beautiful and kind-hearted young widow, sister of the unfortunate Captain Golovnin, who was so inhumanly exposed in a cage at Japan. The master of the public house had civilly received me, and I was enjoying my own meditations, when Mrs. Golovnin entered my room, accosting me in German, French, Russian, and lastly in my native tongue. After the manner of her sex, she got all my secrets out of me – but one – and in return sent me some tea, proffering, at the same time, the assistance of her purse. Had she offered me her hand and heart, I certainly should have replied otherwise than I did, for I felt very affectionately and gratefully towards so kind and lovely a woman, and who although a widow, had yet scarcely passed her teens. Upon getting up in the morning, I discovered that my knapsack had been searched, and my small stock of linen had been taken out and washed; but of course not the smallest article was missing.

I refreshed myself at the fount, (which is always at hand in a Russian cottage, with a tea-kettle or other spouted vessel hanging over it,) breakfasted, and, making my *congé* to the household gods in the near corner of the room, departed from Torjock. I had not proceeded far when I met a carriage, and immediately heard myself addressed in the English language – "How do you do, Captain Cochrane?" On my acknowledging the name, the carriage stopped, and the owner, who proved to be a Mr. Hippius, and had for some time been on the look-out for me, treated me very heartily to a biscuit and glass of wine. I then wished him a pleasant journey, and resumed mine, light as a lark at the unexpected pleasure of seeing English faces, and hearing my own tongue. Those who have been similarly situated, can readily conceive how happy I was to have met with a countryman in such a manner.

My way lay over a country where the Tver is a wandering stream, and where numerous handsome seats and neat villages made their appearance. These, however, but too strongly reminded me of the effects of absenteeship in Ireland, being evidently in a rapid state of decay. I have no hesitation, however, in saying, that the condition of the peasantry here is far superior to that class in Ireland. In Russia provisions are plentiful, good, and cheap; while in Ireland they are scanty, poor, and dear, the best part being exported from the latter country, whilst the local impediments in the other render them not worth that expense. Good comfortable log-houses are here found in every village; immense droves of cattle are scattered over an un-limited pasture, and whole forests of fuel may be obtained for a trifle. With ordinary industry and economy the Russian peasant may become rich, especially those of the villages situated between the capitals, both of which might be supplied by them with butter and cheese; whereas at present not a dairy exists, the peasantry con-tenting themselves with the culture of as much land, and the breeding of as many cattle, as may be sufficient for their immediate wants. The women I have always found engaged in some employ-ment; they make very good coarse woollen cloths and linens, as well as knit stockings and spin thread. The whole work of the house is thrown upon them, while they also partake the labours of the field. I will not certainly recommend, for the adoption of any civilized countries, the treatment they receive from their lordly masters; although I have no doubt the like was the custom of England half a century ago, and may be still in the hard-working countries. Having mentioned Ireland in comparison with Russia, I may remark, that both countries may fairly vie with one another in the ancient savage virtue of hospitality.

Reached Tver the following day, and put up at the habitation of a long-bearded merchant; where, after enjoying a good supper and sound sleep, I employed myself in perambulating the city. It is said to contain fifteen thousand inhabitants, being considerably larger, or at least more populous than Novgorod. Tver is situated at the junction of two small rivers, which empty themselves into the noble Volga; the latter hence taking an easterly course towards Nishney Novgorod, and fertilizing, in its course to the Caspian, some of the finest provinces in the Russian empire.

The first circumstance which attracted my notice upon reaching Tver, was at the gate, where an impost of three large stones is levied upon every horse that passes. These are converted to the paving of the city; nor will the tax appear either slight or useless in a country where stones are not very abundant.

Crossing the river over a fine bridge of boats, of 550 feet in length, I entered the principal part of the city. The public edifices on the banks of the Volga are handsome, and kept in good order, though the archbishop's palace resembles one of our workhouses. There is also a theatre, good barracks, and a beautiful building called the Prince's Palace, rebuilt by Catherine. The cathedral is of plain stone; there are, besides, thirty-four churches and three convents, (one of which is said to contain the ashes of a page, whose prince deprived him of his mistress at the moment of their marriage, and afterwards, when too late, repenting of it, and wishing to expiate his crime, had this convent built,) – two of them are for men and one for women; three hospitals are also established upon a liberal plan, and a bazar, with handsome piazzas, forms the city lounge. The public gardens and walks are certainly susceptible of improvement; but, upon the whole, it has a clean and regular appearance, and bids fair, from its trade and situation, to become an important city. The government exports immense quantities of grain from hence to St. Petersburg, and two hundred barges were now lying off the city loaded with that article, and with several millions of eggs.

Early on Monday, the 5th June, I quitted Tver for Moscow, passing sometimes along the banks of the Volga, at others over a rich grain country, amusing my mind alternately with the contemplation of the promising crops, and the thousands of loaded barges destined to bear them. Reached Davidova (thirty-two miles) at two o'clock, where I stopped to refresh, passing on my way a great number of pedestrian labourers, who, like the Gallegos of Spain, were travelling to the southward to assist the less populous districts in getting in the harvest. An amazing quantity of timber was felled and felling on the road-side, merely for the purpose of keeping the road in repair; nearly the whole distance from Novgorod to Moscow being a wooden causeway. At eight in the evening I continued my route, reaching Klinn at midnight, and Peski at four in the morning. The country had a pleasing appearance, immense herds of cattle and flocks of sheep, with well-peopled villages, greeting the eye in every direction. I was supplied with plenty of black bread, milk, salt, and kuass, which I found very excellent fare. Passing through Tschornaya Graz, I entered Moscow at eight in the morning, the last stage being distressingly fatiguing. Much rain fell, and I was not a little happy to reach the hospitable abode of Mr. Rowan in time to breakfast. The last thirty-two hours I warrant as bearing witness to one of my greatest pedestrian trips – the distance is 168 versts, or about 96 miles: I have, however, done the same in Portugal.

ALARMS AMONGST THE UZBEKS

Alexander Burnes
(1805–41)

Of all the "forbidden" cities (Timbuktu, Mecca, Lhasa, Riyadh and so on) none enjoyed a more fearsome reputation than Bukhara in Uzbekistan. The first British Indian expedition, that of William Moorcroft in 1819–26, had never returned. Moorcroft's disappearance, like that of Livingstone or Franklin, posed a challenge in itself and preyed on the minds of his immediate successors. Heavily disguised and in an atmosphere of intense intrigue, Burnes and Dr. James Gerard crossed the Afghan Hindu Kush in 1832 and approached the scenes of Moorcroft's discomfiture. They would both return; and "Bukhara Burnes" would become the most fêted explorer of his day until hacked to death in Kabul at the beginning of the First Afghan War.

The life which we now passed was far more agreeable than a detail of its circumstances would lead one to believe, with our dangers and fatigues. We mounted at daylight, and generally travelled without intermission till two or three in the afternoon. Our day's progress have no standard of measure; and miles, coses, and fursukhs, were equally unknown, for they always reckon by the day's journey. We often breakfasted on the saddle, on dry bread and cheese; slept always on the ground, and in the open air; and after the day's march, sat down cross-legged, till night and sleep overtook us. Our caravan was every thing that could be wished, for the Nazir and his amusing fellow-traveller were very obliging: there were only eight persons in our party, and three of these were natives of the country: two others were instructed to pretend that they were quite distinct from us; though one of them noted the few bearings of the compass, which I myself could not conveniently take without leading to discovery. We were quite happy in such scenes, and at the

Alexander Burnes, in costume. From *Travels into Bokhara*, London, 1839.

novelty of every thing; it was also delightful to recognise some old friends among the weeds and shrubs. The hawthorn and sweet brier grew on the verge of the river; and the rank hemlock, that sprung up under their shade, now appeared beautiful from the associations which it awakened. Our society, too, was amusing; and I took every favourable occasion of mingling with the travellers whom we met by the way, and at the halting-places.

We continued our descent by Khoorrum and Sarbagh to Heibuk, which is but a march within the mountains; and gradually exchanged our elevated barren rocks for more hospitable lands. Our road led us through tremendous defiles, which rose over us to a height of from two to three thousand feet, and overhung the pathway, while eagles and hawks wheeled in giddy circles over us: among them we distinguished the black eagle, which is a noble bird. Near Heibuk, the defile becomes so narrow, that it is called the "Dura i Zindan," or Valley of the Dungeon; and so high are the rocks, that the sun is excluded from some parts of it at mid-day. There is a poisonous plant found here, which is fatal even to a mule or a horse: it grows something like a lily; and the flower, which is about four inches long, hangs over and presents a long seed nodule. Both it and the flower resemble the richest crimson velvet. It is called "zuhr boota" by the natives, which merely expresses its poisonous qualities. I brought a specimen of this plant to Calcutta, and am informed by Dr. Wallich, the intelligent and scientific superintendent of the Company's botanic garden, that it is of the Arum species. We now found vast flocks browsing on the aromatic pastures of the mountains, and passed extensive orchards of fruit trees. Herds of deer might be seen bounding on the summits of the rocks; and in the valleys, the soil was every where turned up by wild hogs, which are here found in great numbers. The people also became more numerous as we approached the plains of Tartary, and at Heibuk we had to encounter another Uzbek chief named Baba Beg, a petty tyrant of some notoriety.

As we approached his town, a traveller informed us that the chief was anticipating the arrival of the Firingees (Europeans), whose approach had been announced for some time past. This person is a son of Khilich Ali Beg, who once ruled in Khooloom with great moderation; but the child has not imitated the example of his parent. He poisoned a brother at a feast, and seized upon his father's wealth before his life was extinct. He had greatly augmented the difficulties of Mr. Moorcroft's party; and was known to be by no means favourable to Europeans. His subjects had driven him from his native town of Khooloom for his tyranny, and he now only possessed the district of Heibuk. We saw his castle about four in the afternoon, and approached with reluctance; but our arrangements were conducted with address, and here also we escaped in safety. On arrival, our small caravan alighted outside Heibuk, and we lay down on the ground as fatigued travellers, covering ourselves with a coarse horse blanket till it was night. In the evening, the chief came in person to visit our Cabool friend the Nazir, to whom he offered every service; nor did he appear to be at all aware of our presence. Baba Beg, on this occasion, made an offer to send the party, under an escort of his own, direct to Balkh, avoiding Khooloom – an arrangement which I heard with pleasure, and, as it will soon appear, that might have saved us a world of anxiety. Our fellow-travellers, however, declined the proffered kindness, and vaunted so much of their influence at Khooloom, that we had no dread in approaching a place where we were ultimately ensnared. While this Uzbek chief was visiting the Nazir, we were eating a mutton chop by the fireside within a few yards and near enough to see him and hear his conversation. He was an ill-looking man, of debauched habits. He was under some obligation to our fellow-travellers; and we and our animals fared well on the flesh and barley which he sent for their entertainment. Our character was never suspected; and so beautiful a starlight night was it, that I did not let this, the first opportunity, pass without observing our latitude north of Hindoo Koosh. We set out in the morning before the sun had risen, and congratulated ourselves at having passed with such success a man who would have certainly injured us.

Heibuk is a thriving village, with a castle of sundried brick, built on a commanding hillock. For the first time among the mountains, the valley opens, and presents a sheet of gardens and most luxuriant verdure. The climate also undergoes a great change; and we find the fig tree, which does not grow in Cabool, or higher up the mountains. The elevation of Heibuk is about 4000 feet. The soil is rich, and the vegetation rank. We had expected to be rid of those troublesome companions of a tropical climate, snakes and scorpions; but here they were more numerous than in India, and we disturbed numbers of them on the road. One of our servants was stung by a scorpion; and as there is a popular belief that the pain ceases if the reptile be killed, it was put to death accordingly. The construction of the houses at Heibuk arrested our attention: they have domes instead of terraces, with a hole in the roof as a chimney; so that a village has the appearance of a cluster of large brown beehives. The inhabitants adopt this style of building, as wood is scarce. The people, who were now as different as their houses, wore conical skull-caps, instead of turbans, and almost every one we met, whether traveller or villager, appeared in long brown boots. The ladies seemed to select the gayest colours for their dresses; and I could now distinguish some very handsome faces, for the Mahommedan ladies do not pay scrupulous attention to being veiled in the villages. They were much fairer than their husbands, with nothing ungainly in their appearance, though they were Tartars. I could now, indeed, understand the praises of the Orientals as to the beauty of these Toorkee girls.

On the 30th of May we made our last march among the mountains, and debouched into the plains of Tartary at Khooloom, or Tash Koorghan, where we had a noble view of the country north of us, sloping down to the Oxus. We left the last hills about two miles from the town, rising at once in an abrupt and imposing manner; the road passing through them by a narrow defile, which might easily be defended. Khooloom contains about ten thousand inhabitants, and is the frontier town of Moorad Beg of Koondooz, a powerful chief, who has reduced all the countries north of Hindoo Koosh to his yoke. We alighted at one of the caravansarais, where we were scarcely noticed. A caravansary is too well known to require much description; – it is a square, enclosed by walls, under which are so many rooms or cells for accommodation. The merchandise and cattle stand in the area. Each party has his chamber, and is strictly private; since it is contrary to custom for one person to disturb another. All are travellers, and many are fatigued. If society were every where on as good a footing as in a caravansary, the world would be spared the evils of calumny. We here rested after our arduous and fatiguing journey over rocks and mountains; and were, indeed, refreshed by the change. Since leaving Cabool, we had slept in our clothes, where we could seldom or ever change them. We had halted among mud, waded through rivers, tumbled among snow, and for the last few days been sunned by heat. These are but the petty inconveniences of a traveller; which sink into insignificance, when compared with the pleasure of seeing new men and countries, strange manners and customs, and being able to temper the prejudices of one's country, by observing those of other nations.

We had entered Khooloom with an intention of setting out next day on our journey to Balkh; placing implicit reliance on the assertion of our friends, that we had nothing to apprehend in doing so. Judge, then, of our surprise, when we learned that the officers of the custom house had despatched a messenger to the chief of Koondooz, to report our arrival, and request his instructions as to our disposal. We were, meanwhile, desired to await the answer. Our companion, the Nazir, was much chagrined at the detention; but it was now useless to upbraid him for having ever brought us to Khooloom. He assured us that it was a mere temporary inconvenience; and likewise despatched a letter to the minister at Koondooz, requesting that we might not be detained, since his business in Russia could not be transacted without us. The minister was a friend of the Nazir's family; and since we had plunged ourselves into difficulties, matters seemed at least to look favourable for our safe conduct through them. I could not but regret that I had ever allowed myself to be seduced by the advice of any one; and would, even at this late period, have endeavoured to escape to Balkh, had not the Cafila-bashee, and every one, pronounced it headstrong and impracticable. At one time, indeed, about midnight, the Cafila-bashee acceded to our proposals for escaping to Balkh in the course of the next night, and even said the first verse of the Koran as his oath and blessing. I did not, however, understand that the plan was to be kept secret from the

Nazir, to whom I revealed it next day, to the great dissatisfaction and dismay of the Cafila-bashee, who was visited with a due share of his wrath. "Wait," said the Nazir to us, "for a reply from Koondooz, and we cannot doubt its favourable nature." We did wait; and at midnight, on the 1st of June, received a summons to repair to Koondooz with all despatch; while the minister, in reply to our conductor's letter, begged he would not allow himself to be detained on our account, but proceed on his journey to Bokhara! Our surprise may be better imagined than described. It was now too late to make our escape, for we were watched in the caravansary, and the officers would not even allow my horse to be taken into the town and shod. It might have been accomplished on our first arrival, but then it was deemed injudicious, and it only remained, therefore, for us to face the difficulties of our situation in a prompt and becoming manner. I urged an immediate departure for Koondooz, leaving Dr. Gerard, and all the party, except two, at Khooloom. I was now resolved on personating the character of an Armenian, and believed that despatch would avail me and allay suspicion. I had letters from the saint at Peshawur, which would bear me out, as I thought, in the new character, since we were there denominated Armenians; but my fellow-travellers assured me that the very possession of such documents would prove our real condition, and I destroyed them all, as well as the letters of the Cabool chief, which were alike objectionable. I divested myself, indeed, of all my Persian correspondence, and tore up among the rest many of Runjeet Sing's epistles, which were now in my eyes less acceptable than I thought they would ever prove. During these arrangements, I discovered that the Nazir had no relish for a journey to Koondooz, and seemed disposed to stay behind, almost frantic with despair; but shame is a great promoter of exertion, and I begged he would accompany me, to which he agreed.

The better to understand the critical situation in which we were now placed, I shall give a brief sketch of the disasters which befell Mr. Moorcroft in this part of the country, in the year 1824, from the very personage who now summoned us to Koondooz. On that traveller crossing the mountains, he proceeded to wait on the chief, and having made him some presents suitable to his rank, returned to Khooloom. He had no sooner arrived there, than he received a message from the chief, saying, that some of his soldiers had been wounded, and requesting that he would hasten his return, and bring along with him his medical instruments, and Mr. Guthrie, an Indo-Briton, who had accompanied Mr. Moorcroft as a surgeon. Mr. Moorcroft's own abilities in that capacity were also known, for he had already given proofs of great skill to these people. He set out for Koondooz without suspicion, but found, on his arrival there, that his surgical services were not wanted, and it was merely a plan to ensnare him. The chief ordered him to send for all his party and baggage, which he did; and, after a month's delay, he only succeeded in liberating himself, by complying with the most extravagant demands of Moorad Beg. By one means or another, he possessed himself of cash to the value of 23,000 rupees, before Mr. Moorcroft was permitted to depart; and it would have been well had the matter here terminated; but the cupidity of the chief had been excited. It is also said, that he entertained some dread of Moorcroft's designs, from the arms and two small field-pieces, which he carried with him for purposes of protection. The party prepared to quit Khooloom for Bokhara, but, on the very eve of departure, were surrounded by 400 horsemen, and again summoned to Koondooz. It was not now concealed, that the chief was resolved on seizing the whole of the property, and putting the party to death. Mr. Moorcroft took the only course which could have ever extricated his party and himself. In the disguise of a native he fled at night, and after a surprising journey, at length reached Talighan, a town beyond Koondooz, where a holy man lived, who was reputed to possess much influence over the conscience of Moorad Beg. He threw himself at the feet of this saint, seized the hem of his garment, and sued for his protection. "Rise up," said he, "it is granted; fear nothing." This good man immediately sent a messenger to Koondooz, to summon the chief, who appeared in person with the answer. At his peril, he could not now touch a hair of the traveller's head; Moorad Beg obeyed, and the holy man declined to receive the smallest reward for his services. After Mr. Moorcroft's flight, the Uzbeks marched his fellow-traveller, Mr. George Trebeck, with all the party and property, to Koondooz. Their anxiety was not allayed till their arrival at that place, when they heard of the success of Moorcroft, his safety, and their own. After these disasters, Moorcroft pursued his journey into Bokhara, but unfortunately died on his return, in the following year, at Andkhooee, about eighty miles from Balkh. His fellow-traveller, Mr. Trebeck, was unable to force his way beyond Muzar, in the neighbourhood of that city, since the chief of Koondooz was resolved on waylaying the party on its return, and the only safe road to Cabool led by Khooloom, where they had already encountered such difficulties. He lingered about Balkh for four or five months, and died of fever, from which he had been suffering during the whole of that time. The Indo-Briton, Mr. Guthrie, was previously cut off by the same disease, to which most of their followers also fell victims. Thus terminated their unfortunate expedition into Tartary.

On the evening of the 2nd of June, I set out on my journey to Koondooz, which lies higher up the valley of the Oxus, having previously prevailed on the custom-house officer, who was a Hindoo, to accompany me. I did not leave Khooloom under very encouraging circumstances, having just discovered that a Hindoo of Peshawur had *kindly* apprised the authorities of many of our acts, circumstances, and condition, since leaving Hindoostan; adding, indeed, numerous exaggerations to the narration, in which we were set forth as wealthy individuals, whose bills had even affected the money market. When beyond the town, we found our caravan to consist of eight or ten tea merchants, of Budukhshan and Yarkund, who had disposed of their property, and were returning to their country. In our own party there was the Nazir, Cafila-bashee, and myself, with the Hindoo, whose name was Chumundass, who came unattended. I discovered that this latter person had a pretty correct knowledge of our affairs, but I did not assist to fill up the thread of his discourse, and boldly denominated myself a Hindoostan Armenian. The name of Englishman, which had carried us through safely in all other places, was here replete with danger; since it not only conveyed notions of great wealth, but a belief that that can be renewed from the inferior metals. I had, however, discovered that the Hindoo was a good man, for his easy manner in searching our baggage at the caravansary, after our first arrival, left a favourable impression on my mind; and he himself declared to the Nazir, that it was no fault of his that we were dragged to Koondooz, since he was but a custom-house officer, and obliged to report our arrival. It was evident to me, that an impression might be made on such a person by persuasion and gold, and from his very presence with us, I construed that money might be his god. He and I soon fell into conversation, and I found him to be a native of Mooltan, who had long resided in these countries. I spoke much of India, and its people and customs; told him that I had seen his native town, using as much eloquence as I was possessed of to praise its people, and every thing connected with it. It would have been difficult to discover, from the varied topics of our conversation, that the time was one of most anxious suspense. I ran over the gods of the Hindoo catalogue as far as I remembered, and produced almost a fever of delight in my associate, who had long ceased to hear them named in aught but terms of deep reproach. It was now time to turn my persuasion to account, and we talked in the language of India, our conversation was conducted in a dialect foreign to most of our party, and unheeded by them. I pointed out in plain terms to the Hindoo, our forlorn and hopeless condition, when in the power of a person like the chief of Koondooz; and I put it to himself, if our baggage did not testify our poverty. I then showed him, that as I belonged to India, I might one day serve him in that country, and finally offered to give him a reward in money, and conjured him by all his Pantheon to aid us in our difficulties. When about twelve miles from Khooloom, we alighted at a village called Ungaruk, to feed our horses, and it now occurred to me that a truly favourable opportunity to make an escape presented itself. There was no guard or escort to attend us, and the honest Hindoo was far from Khooloom, and without the means of giving an alarm, whilst the most moderate speed would carry us beyond Moorad Beg's frontier, and even to the city of Balkh, before morning. This feasible plan, however, could not evidently be put into execution, since Dr. Gerard would be left at Khooloom, and his safety more than ever endangered; and it could only now be regretted, that the scheme had not sooner presented itself. The tone of the Hindoo had, however, reconciled me in a great degree to my situation, and we again prosecuted our midnight journey, and renewed our conversation. Before the sun had risen, I was satisfied that if more honourable motives had not opened this man's heart, the baser metals had, and I almost then believed, that we should triumph over our misfortunes. A new dilemma, however, now overtook us.

We journeyed till within an hour of dawn by a dreary road, over two low passes among hills, not enlivened by a single tree, nor blessed with a drop of fresh water for forty-five miles. In this dismal waste, our attention was roused by some lighted matches in front, that appeared to cross our path, and which we could not but conclude were robbers, since this country is infested by banditti. One of the tea merchants busied himself in tearing up rags, rubbing them with gunpowder, and lighting them, literally as *demonstrations* of our force; and judging by the number of lights that appeared from the opposite party, they must have done the same, which might have been amusing enough had we not construed them into real matchlocks. We had but one piece, and five or six swords, and could have made but a sorry resistance; but generalship may be shown with a small as well as a large band, and the tea merchant, who seemed accustomed to such scenes, called on us to dismount, and prepare for the attack. I will not conceal my feelings at this moment, which were those of vexation and irritability at so many succeeding disasters. At length we approached within speaking distance, and one forward youth in our party challenged in Persian, but he was instantly silenced by an elderly man, who spoke out in Turkish. The Persian, being the language of commerce, would at once betray our character, and it was proper that we should at least appear as soldiers. The other party gave no reply, but veered off towards Khooloom, and we ourselves took the road of Koondooz, mutually glad, I suppose, to be rid of each other. At the town we discovered that we had drawn up against peaceable travellers, who must have been as glad as we were to escape. About eleven in the forenoon we reached the first fields, and alighted in an orchard of apricots, about twelve miles distant from Koondooz, and stole a few hours' rest after the night's journey. I found myself near a hedge of honeysuckles, a bush that delighted me, and which I had never before seen in the East. We reached Koondooz at nightfall, after performing a journey of more than seventy miles.

We were received on our arrival at the house of Atmaram, the minister, or, as he is styled, the Dewan Begee, of Moorad Beg, and sat in his doorway till he came out. I shall long remember the silent look which passed between him and the Nazir. The reception augured well, for the minister conducted us to his house of guests, and fine beds were brought for our use, but he said nothing on the subject which most interested us, and we were left to think about our own affairs. I was now to personate the character of a very poor traveller, and as it behoved me to act as such, I looked demure, took up my seat in a corner, fared with the servants, and treated the Nazir, my master, with great respect; and evinced, on every occasion, as much humility as possible. It was prudent, however, that when questioned we should all tell the same story, and in a quiet hour, before going to sleep, I gave out my character as follows. That I was an Armenian from Lucknow, Sikunder Alaverdi, by profession a watchmaker, and that, on reaching Cabool, I had procured intelligence from Bokhara regarding my relatives in that country, which led me to take a journey to it, and that I was the more induced to do so from the protection I should receive from the Nazir, to whose brother in Cabool I was, in some manner, a servant. We discarded the subject of my accompanying the Nazir to Russia, as it might lead to unpleasant inquiries. I then went on to state, that Dr. Gerard was a relative of my own, and that he was left sick at Khooloom, and thus brought within a short space as much evasion as my ingenuity could invent. All our party agreed, that it would be most advisable to take the name of an Armenian, and entirely discard that of European; but the Cafila-bashee wished to know how far it was proper to deal in such wholesale lies, which had excited his merriment. I replied in the words of Sady,

Durogh i musluhut amez
Bih uz rastee bu fitna ungez.

"An untruth that preserves peace is better than truth that stirs up troubles." He shook his head in approbation of the moralist's wisdom, and I afterwards found him the most forward in the party to enlarge on my pretended narrative and circumstances. It was agreed that we should first tell the consistent tale to the Hindoo of the custom-house, and then adopt it generally; and the Nazir promised in the course of to-morrow to unfold it to the minister.

The 4th of June slipped away without any adjustment of our concerns, and the Nazir now evinced an imbecility and weakness of intellect, which there was no tolerating. At one moment he was whining out to the visiters a sorrowful detail of our disasters, half in tears; at another time he was sitting erect, with all the pride and self-sufficiency of a man of consequence. In the afternoon he retired to a garden, and returned with a train of followers, as if he had been a grandee instead of a prisoner; nor had he even visited the minister during the day, so that our affairs were no further advanced at night than in the morning. As soon as it was dark, I took an opportunity of pointing out to my friend the great impropriety of such conduct, for which I encountered, at first, a good share of his indignation. I told him that his grief and pride were equally ill-timed and impolitic; that every hour added to the danger of our situation; and, if he acted rightly, he would immediately seek an interview with the minister, and endeavour either to convince or deceive him. You are in the house of a Hindoo, I added, and you may effect any thing by throwing yourself upon him, and sitting in *dhurna*, that is, without food, till your request is granted. Your course, continued I, is now the reverse, as you appear to prefer parading in his gardens, and devouring the savoury viands which he sends us. The earnestness with which I enforced these views produced a good effect, and the Nazir sent a messenger to the minister to say, that if he were the friend of his family, he would not detain him in this manner, for he had not come as a dog, to eat his bread, but as an acquaintance, to solicit a favour. I rejoiced at the decision which he was now displaying, and called out in accents of delight from my corner of the apartment, but the Nazir here requested me to conduct myself with greater discretion, and remain more peaceable. I deserved the rebuke, and was thus glad to compromise matters between us. When the minister received the message, he called the Nazir to him, and a long explanation ensued regarding our affairs, which, as far as I could gather, had left him bewildered as to their reality. It now appeared, however, that we were to have his good offices, for it was settled that we should set out early next morning to the country seat of the chief, where we should see that personage. The Nazir, as being a man of consequence, was instructed not to appear empty-handed, and the minister, with great kindness, returned a shawl which he had presented to him on his arrival, and desired him to give it and another to the chief of Koondooz.

Early on the morning of the 5th, we set out on our journey to Moorad Beg. We found him at the village of Khanu-abad, which is about fifteen miles distant, and situated on the brow of the hills above the fens of Koondooz, enlivened by a rivulet, which runs briskly past a fort, shaded by trees of the richest verdure. We crossed this stream by a bridge, and found ourselves at the gate of a small, but neatly fortified dwelling, in which the chief was now holding his court. There were about five hundred saddled horses standing at it, and the cavaliers came and returned in great numbers. All of them were booted, and wore long knives, stuck into the girdle, for swords, some of which were richly mounted with gold. We sat down under the wall, and had ample time to survey the passing scene, and admire the martial air and pomp of these warlike Uzbeks. None of the chiefs had more than a single attendant, and there was great simplicity in the whole arrangements. A Hindoo belonging to the minister went inside to announce our arrival, and, in the mean time, I rehearsed my tale, and drew on a pair of boots, as well for the uniformity as to hide my provokingly white ankles. My face had long been burned into an Asiatic hue, and from it I feared no detection. The custom-house officer stood by, and I had taken care to have him previously schooled in all the particulars above related. We were summoned, after about an hour's delay, and passed into the first gateway. We here found an area, in which stood the attendants and horses of the chief. Six or eight "yessawuls" or doorkeepers then announced our approach, as we entered the inner building. The Nazir headed the party, and marching up to the chief kissed his hand, and presented his shawls. The Hindoo of the custom-house followed, with two loaves of Russian white sugar, which he gave as his offering; and, in my humble capacity, I brought up the rear, and advanced to make my obeisance, sending forth a loud "sulam alaikoom", and placing my hands between those of the chief, kissed them according to custom, and exclaimed "tukseer", which literally means *offence* or *crime*, and is the usual mode of expressing inferiority. The Uzbek gave a growl of approbation, and rolling on one side, said, "Ay, ay, he understands the sulam." The "yessawul" then gave a signal for my retreat, and I stood at the portal with my hands crossed, among the lower domestics. Moorad Beg was seated on a tiger skin, and stretched out his legs covered with huge boots, in contempt of all Eastern rules of decorum. He sat at the door, for, contrary to the custom of other Asiatic courts, an Uzbek there takes up his position, and his visiters pass into the interior of the apartment. The chief was a man of tall stature, with harsh Tartar features; his eyes were small to deformity, his forehead broad and frowning, and he wanted the beard which adorns the countenance in most Oriental nations. He proceeded to converse with the Nazir; and put several questions regarding Cabool, and then on his own affairs, during which he spoke of our poverty and situation. Then came the Hindoo of the custom-house with my tale. "Your slave," said he, "has examined the baggage of the two Armenians, and found them to be poor travellers. It is in every person's mouth that they are Europeans (Firingees), and it would have placed me under your displeasure had I let them depart; I have, therefore, brought one of them to know your orders." The moment was critical; and the chief gave me a look, and said in Turkish, – "Are you certain he is an Armenian?" A second assurance carried conviction, and he issued an order for our safe conduct beyond the frontier. I stood by, and saw his secretary prepare and seal the paper; and I could have embraced him when he pronounced it finished.

ON THE ROOF OF THE WORLD

John Wood
(1811–71)

In 1837 Alexander Burnes returned to Afghanistan on an official mission. Amongst his subordinates was a ship's lieutenant who, having surveyed the navigational potential of the river Indus, took off on a mid-winter excursion into the unknown Pamirs between China and Turkestan. Improbably, therefore, it was John Wood, a naval officer and the most unassuming of explorers, who became the first to climb into the inhospitable mountain heartland of Central Asia and the first to follow to its source the great river Oxus (or Amu Darya).

After mustering our escort before the door of the Akulchail of Langer Kish, we mounted our sturdy hill poneys, and having received the "God-speed" of the half savage Wakhanis, struck into the durah of Sir-i-kol. While awaiting the Kirghiz arrival, we had made sundry alterations in our dress, which, however expedient, were certainly not to the improvement of our personal appearance; and as we moved out of the village in single file, I could not help smiling at my Esquimaux-looking body-guard. The Munshi, in particular, was so hampered up with worsted cloaks, that his arms were all but useless and his short legs had scarcely action enough to keep him on his horse. In addition to the load of clothing with which each had burdened his steed, the animals carried eight days food for their riders and for themselves, as well as some firewood.

The mountains forming the defile were not very lofty, nor were their sides precipitous; they appeared to have been broken down to abrupt declivities, either by frost and the vicissitudes of weather, or by subterranean convulsions; and amid their dislocated fragments ran the snow-wreathed stream we had come so far to trace.

About three hours after starting we arrived on the brink of a deep chasm that crossed our track, in passing over which we met with considerable delay. Its slippery sides constituted the principal difficulty, and it was not without risk that we got the horses across. The Yarkand caravan is frequently interrupted at this place, and its merchandise is obliged to be transferred from the camel's back to that of the yak. After getting clear of the ravine, we pushed on at as rapid a pace as the depth of snow permitted; and some time before the day closed in, selected a spot on which to bivouac for the night. It was the summit of an unsheltered knoll, free from snow, the only place within sight which was so; in return for which exemption it was swept by every breath of wind that moved either up or down the durah. It was, however, calm when we alighted. The wooden saddles of our steeds and the bags of charcoal were disposed in a circle, within which, with our feet to the fire, each man took his station. The kettle soon sang upon the red embers, and the koor-geens having been opened, we had begun to feast and make merry, when an ill-natured gust came howling down the valley, and destroyed at once our fire and our good humour. The latter we soon recovered, but all our coaxing failed for a long time to rekindle the former. The patient labours of the Kirghiz were at length successful, and before long the tea cup had gone its rounds, infusing a warmth into our frames, and a glow into our hearts, that made us, I dare say, happier than many a party who were at that moment quaffing their claret, and surrounded with all the luxuries of civilised life. But all happiness is comparative, and I must confess, that when at the best we were not lying upon a bed of roses, nor was the moaning wintry wind particularly soothing to the ear, nor the biting cold very grateful to the person. The feet were the great sufferers; they were like lead, and when it is so with the extremities, it is no use caring for the body. So peeling stocking after stocking, we toasted our feet into a comfortable burning warmth, and having settled the necessary dispositions for the night, each made his own arrangements to pass it as best he could. Thanks to my good horse and his furniture, I got through it tolerably well, but Abdal Ghani and two Afghans suffered so severely that I was compelled to send them back to Langer Kish in the morning. Our thermometers were only graduated down to +6° of Fahrenheit; and as the mercury had sunk into the bulb, it was not in my power to register the exact degree of cold; it was, however, intense, and the highly rarified state of the atmosphere caused it to be the more severely felt. The height of this halting place was 12,000 feet above the sea.

In the early part of next day, we continued our route through a narrow, rough valley, resembling in its principal features the

portion traversed the preceding day; but towards noon, we descended to the river, and, taking to its icy surface, held on till
nightfall. The change was indeed agreeable, for though the snow on
the elevated table ridges, of which the sides of the river are here
formed, rarely exceeded two feet in depth, our horses were frequently engulphed in wading through the *drift* which was collected
on the margins of these plateaux. The river in this day's march held
its course for upwards of a mile, through a narrow strait not more
than forty yards across in its widest part, and walled throughout
the whole distance by perpendicular banks eighty feet high. On
emerging from this gut the ravine opened, and resumed its old
character.

In the afternoon, a party of men were descried watching us from a
height, about a mile in advance. A halt was immediately called, and
after the Kirghiz of our party had reconnoitred the strangers
attentively, a scout was sent forward to observe them more narrowly, while we dismounted and prepared our fire-arms. Much to
our satisfaction, the spy made the signal for friends, on which we
pushed forward to meet them. They were a party of Kirghiz, who
had left Langer Kish three weeks before us, charged with letters from
Mohamed Rahim Khan to their brethren on the Khoord, or Little
Pamir. Having executed their commission, they were now on their
way to Wakhan. We found that it was to these men we had been
indebted for the comparative ease with which we had hitherto
journeyed. Their tracks in the snow had been carefully followed
by our party, who were thus saved the disheartening toil of forcing a
path through an unbroken, though imperfectly, frozen surface. After
parting with these strangers, we arrived at a copse of red willows;
and as no other opportunity of procuring firewood would offer
between it and the head of the Oxus, we halted, and cut down, or
rather dug out from under the snow, as much fuel as our already
jaded horses could carry. The bushes were stunted, the tallest not
much exceeding the height of a man, and they extended for a quarter
of a mile along the banks of the river, in a patch of swampy ground.
It was dark before we reached the spot which our guides had selected
for the night's bivouac; but we were now on the Kirghiz ground,
with every inch of which they seemed familiar. Quitting the river,
they struck into a lateral defile to our left, and after winding up it for
another hour, pointed to a cold, ugly looking spot, buried three feet
deep in snow, as our quarters for the night. We remonstrated, at
which the Kirghiz laughed, and, seizing their wooden shovels, soon
drew from the soil below an ample store of firing, in the shape of
sheep's and camel's dung. The eligibility of the place for a night's

lodging was now past dispute; no other recommendation was necessary; and what with the fire we were thus enabled to keep up through the night, and the high and warm snow-walls that soon encircled our wintry habitation, we had all great reason to thank our escort for bringing us to such a favoured spot.

The unmounted portion of our party did not reach the camping ground till near midnight, and then so exhausted and way-worn as to render it evident that they would not be able to proceed on the morrow. It was therefore determined that they should be left behind us, to hunt in this neighbourhood till our return, and to look after a *cache* of provision, which was here formed. The height of this station above the sea was 13,500 feet.

On the following morning we retraced our steps to the river, the icy surface of which offered an admirable road. For a great portion of this day's march, the bottom of the valley was bare of snow, or but partially spotted with it, and this was the more remarkable from its lying so deep, further down the durah. We saw numbers of horns strewed about in every direction, the spoils of the Kirghiz hunter. Some of these were of an astonishingly large size, and belonged to an animal of a species between the goat and sheep, inhabiting the steppes of Pamir. The ends of the horns projecting above the snow, often indicated the direction of the road; and wherever they were heaped in large quantities and disposed in a semi-circle, there our escort recognised the site of a Kirghiz's summer encampment. Our keen-sighted guides again pitched on an old haunt for a resting place, and to their practical sagacity we were indebted for a repetition of the comforts of the preceding night. We here found ourselves to be 14,400 feet above the sea.

When about to resume our journey on the following day, a majority of the escort murmured at proceeding further, and coolly requested to be left behind. I endeavoured in a good-humored tone to reason with the defaulters; failing in this, I next tried the efficacy of upbraiding them with their unmanly conduct; but to such a rascally set shame was unknown, and though I managed to work myself into a towering passion, it produced no corresponding effect on the knaves. The more violent my language, and the more bitter my taunts, the more doggedly did they adhere to their resolution. With those, therefore, of the party who remained true, we were fain to set forward, ere disaffection should have further thinned our ranks. Two of the Kirghiz were among the faithful; and as the object of our search was reported to be only twenty-one miles distant, we cared little about the strength of our party, so that it contained a person qualified to lead us to the goal. The cause of this secession soon became apparent. The snow track which I have mentioned, and in which we had hitherto conveniently enough trodden, struck off, towards the close of the preceding day's march, over the hills on our left to the plain of Khoord Pamir, which lay beyond them, after which we had to force our own way up the main defile, and this labour the coward deserters would not face.

We had no occasion to remark the absence of snow this day, for every step we advanced it lay deeper and deeper; and near as we had now approached to the source of the Oxus, we should not have succeeded in reaching it had not the river been frozen. We were fully two hours in forcing our way through a field of snow not five hundred yards in extent. Each individual of the party by turns took the lead, and forced his horse to struggle onward until exhaustion brought it down in the snow, where it was allowed to lie and recruit whilst the next was urged forward. It was so great a relief when we again got upon the river, that in the elasticity of my spirits I pushed my pony to a trot. This a Wakhani perceiving, seized hold of the bridle, and cautioned me against the *wind of the mountain*. We had, indeed, felt the effects of a highly rarified atmosphere ever since leaving Wakhan; but the ascent being gradual, they were less than what would be experienced in climbing an abrupt mountain of much less altitude.

As we neared the head waters of the Oxus the ice became weak and brittle. The sudden disappearance of a yabu gave us the first warning of this. Though the water was deep where the accident occurred, there fortunately was little current, and, as the animal was secured by his halter to a companion, he was extricated, but his furniture and lading were lost. The kind-hearted Khirakush to whom the animal belonged wrapped him in felts, took off his own warm posteen, and bound it round the shivering brute. Had it been his son instead of his yabu, he could not have passed a more anxious night as to the effects of this ducking. The next morning, however, the yabu was alive and well, and the good mule-driver was most eloquent in his thanks to Providence for its preservation.

Shortly after this accident we came in sight of a rough-looking building, decked out with horns of the wild sheep, and all but buried amongst the snow. It was a Kirghiz burial ground. On coming abreast of it, the leading horseman, who chanced to be of that tribe, pulled up and dismounted. His companion followed his example, and wading through the deep drift they reached a tombstone, the top of which was uncovered. Before this they knelt, all cumbered as they were, and with their huge forked matchlocks strapped to their backs; and offered up prayers to the ever-present Jehovah. The whole of the party involuntarily reined in their horses till the two men had concluded their devotions. The stillness of the scene, the wild and wintry aspect of the place, with the absence of all animated nature save these devotees and ourselves, were not unimpressive to a reflecting mind. They forcibly told us that man must have something beyond this life on which to rest his hopes, and that the sight of a brother's grave should remind him of his own fleeting existence; and that, when surrounded with difficulties and perils, he should appeal to that Being in whose hands he believes his destinies to be.

After quitting the surface of the river we travelled about an hour along its right bank, and then ascended a low hill, which apparently bounded the valley to the eastward; on surmounting this, at five o'clock in the afternoon of the 19th of February 1838, we stood, to use a native expression, upon the *Bam-i-Dúniah*, or "*Roof of the World*", while before us lay stretched a noble but frozen sheet of water, from whose western end issued the infant river of the Oxus. This fine lake lies in the form of a crescent, about fourteen miles long from east to west, by an average breadth of one mile. On three sides it is bordered by swelling hills, about 500 feet high, whilst along its southern bank they rise into mountains 3,500 feet above the lake, or 19,000 above the sea, and covered with perpetual snow, from which never-failing source the lake is supplied. From observations at the western end I found the latitude to be 37° 27′ N. by mer. alt. of the sun, and longitude 73° 40′ E. by protraction from Langer Kish, where the last set of chronometric observations had been obtained; its elevation, measured by the temperature of boiling water, is 15,600 feet – as my thermometer marked 184° of Fahrenheit. The temperature of the water below the ice was 32° – the freezing point.

This, then, is the position of the sources of this celebrated river, which, after a course of upwards of a thousand miles in a direction generally northwest, falls into the southern end of the sea of Aral. As I had the good fortune to be the first European who in later times had succeeded in reaching the sources of this river, and as, shortly before setting out on my journey, we had received the news of her gracious Majesty's accession to the throne, I was much tempted to apply the name of Victoria to this, if I may so term it, newly re-discovered lake; but on considering that by thus introducing a new name, however honoured, into our maps, great confusion in geography might arise, I deemed it better to retain the name of Sir-i-kol, the appellation given to it by our guides. The hills and mountains

that encircle Sir-i-kol give rise to some of the principal rivers in Asia.
From the ridge at its east end flows a branch of the Yarkand river,
one of the largest streams that waters China, while from its low hills
on the northern side rises the Sirr or river of Kokan, and from the
snowy chain opposite both forks of the Oxus, as well as a branch of
the river Kuner, are supplied. When the lake is swollen by the melted
snow of summer, the size of the infant river is correspondingly
increased, and no great alteration takes place in the level of the lake
itself.

The aspect of the landscape was wintry in the extreme. Wherever
the eye fell one dazzling sheet of snow carpeted the ground, while the
sky overhead was everywhere of a dark and angry hue. Clouds
would have been a relief to the eye; but they were wanting. Not a
breath moved along the surface of the lake; not a beast, nor even a
bird, was visible. The sound of a human voice would have been
music to the ear, but no one at this inhospitable season thinks of
invading these gelid domains. Silence reigned around – silence so
profound that it oppressed the heart, and, as I contemplated the
hoary summits of the everlasting mountains, where human foot had
never trode, and where lay piled the snows of ages, my own dear
country and all the social blessings it contains passed across my
mind with a vividness of recollection that I had never felt before. It is
all very well for men in crowded cities to be disgusted with the world
and to talk of the delights of solitude. Let them but pass one twenty-
four hours on the banks of the Sir-i-kol, and it will do more to make
them contented with their lot than a thousand arguments. Man's
proper sphere is society; and, let him abuse it as he will, this busy,
bustling world is a brave place, in which, thanks to a kind Providence, the happiness enjoyed by the human race far exceeds the
misery. So, at least, it has always appeared to me.

In walking over the lake I could not but reflect how many
countries owe their importance and their wealth to rivers the sources
of which can be traced to the lonely mountains which are piled up on
its southern margin. This elevated chain is common to India, China,
and Turkistan; and from it, as from a central point, their several
streams diverge, each augmenting as it rolls onwards, until the ocean
and the lake of Aral receive the swollen tribute, again to be given up,
and in a circuit as endless as it is wonderful to be swept back by the
winds of Heaven, and showered down in snowy flakes upon the self-
same mountains from which it flowed.

How strange and how interesting a group would be formed if an
individual from each nation whose rivers have their first source in
Pamir were to meet upon its summit; what varieties would there be

in person, language, and manners; what contrasts between the rough, untamed, and fierce mountaineer and the more civilized and effeminate dweller on the plain; how much of virtue and of vice, under a thousand different aspects, would be met with among them all; and how strongly would the conviction press upon the mind that the amelioration of the whole could result only from the diffusion of early education and a purer religion!

Pamir is not only a radiating point in the hydrographical system of Central Asia, but it is the focus from which originate its principal mountain-chains. The plain along the southern side of which the lake is situated has a width of about three miles; and viewed from this elevated plateau the mountains seem to have no great elevation. The table-land of Pamir is, as I have already stated, 15,600 feet high, or sixty-two feet lower than the summit of Mont Blanc; but the height of 3,400 feet, which I have assigned to the mountains that rise from this elevated basis, is a matter of assumption only. Where nothing but snow meets the eye it is not easy to appreciate heights and distances correctly; and it is therefore not improbable that the dimensions thus assigned to Sir-i-kol may be subsequently found incorrect. Covered as both the land and water were with snow, it was impossible to tell the exact size; the measurements given were obtained from the Kirghiz, who were familiar with the spot, assisted by my own eye. I regret that I omitted to take the necessary trigonometrical observations for determining the altitude of the southern range of mountains. I estimated their height on the spot and noted down the impression at the moment; but though I had fully intended to have made the measurements on the morrow, it quite escaped me in my anxiety to fix the geographical position of the lake, nor did I discover the omission until our arrival in Wakhan.

The Wakhanis name this plain Bam-i-Dúniah, or "Roof of the World", and it would indeed appear to be the highest table-land in Asia, and probably in any part of our globe. From Pamir the ground sinks in every direction except to the south-east, where similar plateaux extend along the northern face of the Himalaya into Tibet. An individual who had seen the region between Wakhan and Kashmir informed me that the Kunar river had its principal source in a lake resembling that in which the Oxus has its rise, and that the whole of this country, comprehending the districts of Gilgit, Gunjit, and Chitral, is a series of mountain defiles that act as water-courses to drain Pamir.

As early in the morning of Tuesday the 20th February as the cold permitted we walked out about 600 yards upon the lake, and, having cleared the snow from a portion of its surface, commenced breaking the ice to ascertain its depth. This was a matter of greater difficulty than it at first sight appeared, for the water was frozen to the depth of two feet and a half, and, owing to the great rarity of the atmosphere, a few strokes of the pick-axe produced an exhaustion that stretched us upon the snow to recruit our breath. By dint, however, of unwearied exertions and frequent reliefs, we had all but carried the shaft through, when an imprudent stroke fractured its bottom, and up the water jetted to the height of a man, sending us scampering off in all directions. This opening was too small to admit our sounding-lead, and had of necessity to be abandoned; besides, a wet jacket where the thermometer is at zero is a much more serious affair than where it is at summer-heat. We resolved to be more circumspect in our next attempt, and diligent search having revealed to us a large stone upon an islet in the lake, it was forthwith transported to the scene of our labours. When, judging by the depth of the first shaft, we concluded the second to be nearly through, the stone was raised and upheld by four men immediately above the hole. A fifth man continued to ply the axe, and at the first appearance of water the stone was dropped in and went clean through the ice, leaving an aperture its own size, and from this larger orifice there was no rush of water. The sounding-lead was immediately thrown in, when, much to my surprise and disappointment, it struck bottom at nine feet, and we had prepared and brought with us from Langer Kish a hundred fathoms of line for the experiment.

The water emitted a slightly fetid smell and was of a reddish tinge. The bottom was oozy and tangled with grassy weeds. I tried to measure the breadth of the lake by sound, but was baffled by the rarety of the air. A musket, loaded with blank cartridge, sounded as if the charge had been poured into the barrel, and neither wads nor ramrod used. When ball was introduced the report was louder, but possessed none of the sharpness that marks a similar charge in denser atmospheres. The ball, however, could be distinctly heard whizzing through the air. The human voice was sensibly affected, and conversation, especially if in a loud tone, could not be kept up without exhaustion: the slightest muscular exertion was attended with a similar result. Half a dozen strokes with an axe brought the workman to the ground; and though a few minutes' respite sufficed to restore the breath, anything like continued exertion was impossible. A run of fifty yards at full speed made the runner gasp for breath. Indeed, this exercise produced a pain in the lungs and a general prostration of strength which was not got rid of for many hours. Some of the party complained of dizziness and headaches;

but, except the effects above described, I neither felt myself, nor perceived in others, any of those painful results of great elevation which travellers have suffered in ascending Mont Blanc. This might have been anticipated, for where the transition from a dense to a highly-rarified atmosphere is so sudden, as in the ease of ascending that mountain, the circulation cannot be expected to accommodate itself at once to the difference of pressure, and violence must accrue to some of the more sensitive organs of the body. The ascent to Pamir was, on the contrary, so gradual that some extrinsic circumstances were necessary to remind us of the altitude we had attained. The effect of great elevation upon the general system had indeed been proved to me some time before in a manner for which I was not prepared. One evening in Badakhshan, while sitting in a brown study over the fire, I chanced to touch my pulse, and the galloping rate at which it was throbbing roused my attention. I at once took it for granted that I was in a raging fever, and after perusing some hints on the preservation of health which Dr. Lord, at parting, had kindly drawn out for me, I forthwith prescribed for myself most liberally. Next morning my pulse was as brisk as ever, but still my feelings denoted health. I now thought of examining the wrists of all our party, and to my surprise found that the pulses of my companions beat yet faster than my own. The cause of this increased circulation immediately occurred to me; and when we afterwards commenced marching towards Wakhan I felt the pulses of the party whenever I registered the boiling point of water. The motion of the blood is in fact a sort of living barometer by which a man acquainted with his own habit of body can, in great altitudes, roughly calculate his height above the sea. Upon Pamir the pulsations in one minute were as follows:-

	Throbs	Country	Habit of body
My own	110	Scotland	spare
Gholam Hussein, Munshi	124	Jasulmeree	fat
Omerallah, mule-driver	112	Afghan	spare
Gaffer, groom	114	Peshawuree	spare
Dowd, do.	124	Kabuli	stout

The danger we incurred in sleeping literally amongst the snow, in the middle of winter, at the great elevation of 15,600 feet, did not occur to me at the time: we were most fortunate in having done so with impunity. Our escape is, under Providence, to be attributed to the oceans of tea we drank. The kettle was never off the fire when we were encamped; indeed, throughout the whole of our wanderings, except when feasted in Jerm, the Munshi and myself lived almost entirely upon it. We used the decoction, not the infusion, and always brewed it strong. Another preservative was the firing we kept up and the precaution of sleeping with our feet towards it.

LHASA BECKONS

Regis-Evariste Huc
(1813–60)

The 1844–6 journey to Lhasa of Father Huc was the only generally known account of a European visit to the Tibetan capital in the nineteenth century. Huc and his companion Father Gabet, also a French Catholic missionary, launched their assault from Mongolia and so approached Lhasa from the north-east and in mid-winter. They hoped for conversions in the Lamaist Rome which would assist their work in Buddhist Mongolia. Like other trespassers in Tibet, they were soon detected and escorted back to China, but not before reaching their goal.

A few days after crossing the Mouroui Oussou, the caravan began to break up; those who rode camels wished to push ahead, to avoid being held back by the slow pace of the yaks. Moreover the type of country was such that so large a company could no longer camp in the same place. The pasture was so thin and poor that there was not enough to go round. We joined up with the camel riders, and left the yaks behind. Later our party split up again; once unity was broken, a number of petty caravan leaders arose, and there was frequent disagreement about camping sites and departure times.

We were gradually approaching the highest part of Upper Asia, when a terrible north wind, which blew for a fortnight, was an added and near fatal hazard. The sky remained cloudless, but the cold was so frightful that only at midday could we feel any warmth at all from the sun; and even then only when we got out of the wind. For the rest of the day and especially at night we were continually in fear of being frozen to death. Deeply chapped faces and hands were universal. Such cold is impossible to appreciate if one has never experienced it, but we perhaps can give some idea of what it was like by mentioning one small but significant detail. Each morning before setting off we had a meal, and then did not eat again until reaching camp in the evening. As our *tsamba* was not sufficiently appetising to consume enough in one go to keep us going till then, we used to prepare three or four balls of the stuff by kneading it in tea, and keep them in reserve for eating during the day. We would wrap the boiling hot paste in a hot cloth and place it next to the skin of our chests; over this we had our clothes, namely: a thick sheepskin vest, then a lambskin waistcoat, then a short fox-fur coat, then a loose woollen robe. Every day of that fortnight our *tsamba*-cakes froze; when we took them out they were like solid putty, yet they had to be eaten, at the risk of breaking one's teeth, to avoid perishing of hunger.

The animals, weakened by fatigue and privation, found it harder and harder to survive such cold. The mules and horses, being less resistant than the camels and the yaks, needed special care. We had to cover them with large felt rugs which we tied underneath, and we wrapped their heads in camelhair. In other circumstances all these bizarre accoutrements would have excited our hilarity; but we were too miserable to laugh. Despite all these precautions, the caravan's animals were decimated by death.

The many frozen rivers that we had to cross were an additional source of hardship and disaster. Camels are so clumsy, their gait is so unsure, that we were obliged to make a track for them by spreading sand or earth on the ice, or by breaking up the surface with our axes. Then we had to lead them carefully in single file to keep them on the right path: if they tripped or slipped, disaster followed; they would crash heavily to the ground, and getting them up again would be a major task. They would have to be unloaded, then dragged on their sides to the river bank; then carpets would have to be spread on the ice; sometimes even that was useless; you could hit them or tug at them and they made no effort at all to get up. Then they had to be left to their fate, for it was impossible to wait, in that terrible place, long enough for a camel to make up its silly mind to get on its feet again.

So many afflictions together eventually wore down the travellers into a state approaching despair. Now not only the animals were dying; men too succumbed to the cold, and were abandoned, still alive, by the wayside. One day when the exhausted state of our animals had forced us to slow down and we had fallen slightly behind the company, we saw a traveller sitting alone beside the way on a boulder; his head was bent, his arms were tight against his side and he was as motionless as a statue; we called him several times, but he made no reply; there was no indication that he had even heard us. "What madness," we said to each other, "to stop in such weather. He will certainly die of cold." We called again, but still no movement. We dismounted and went over to him. We then recognised him: a young Tartar lama who had often been to visit us in our tent. His face was waxen, and his half-open eyes were glazed. Icicles hung from his nose and the corners of his mouth. There was no response when we spoke and we thought for a moment that he was dead. But then he opened his eyes and fixed them on us with a horrible expression of stupidity. He was frozen stiff, and we realised that he had been abandoned by his companions. It seemed so dreadful to let a man die in this way without trying to save his life that without hesitation we took him with us. We dragged him off that awful stone on which he had been put and hoisted him on to Samdadchiemba's little mule. We wrapped him in a blanket and so led him to the camp. As soon as the tent was up, we went to visit the poor young man's companions. When they learned what we had done they prostrated themselves in gratitude; they praised our kindness, but said that all our trouble would be in vain, for there was no saving him. "He is frozen," they said, "and the cold will soon reach his heart!" We could not share their hopelessness. We returned to our tent, accompanied by one of them, to see if the patient showed any sign of recovery, but when we arrived he was dead.

More than forty members of the caravan were left in the desert, still alive, and it was quite impossible to do anything for them. The sick were mounted on camel or horseback whilst there was still hope; but when they could no longer eat, speak, nor keep themselves in the saddle, they were left by the wayside. How could one stop and tend them in an uninhabited waste, with the menace of wild beasts, brigands and above all lack of food? It was heartrending to see these dying men abandoned by the way; as a final gesture, a wooden bowl and a little bag of flour were left beside each one; then the caravan went sadly on. When we had all passed by, the crows and the vultures which ceaselessly wheeled above us swooped down on these wretches, who no doubt had enough life left in them to feel the talons that tore them.

The north winds made Father Gabet's illness much worse. Each day his state became more alarming. He was too weak to walk and therefore unable to keep warm through exercise; his hands and his face were frozen; his lips were already blue, and his eyes dead; then he became too weak to stay in the saddle. All we could do was wrap him in blankets, tie him like a parcel on to a camel and put our trust in God.

One day when we were winding our way along a valley, our hearts full of sad thoughts, we suddenly saw two horsemen appear on the ridge of one of the surrounding mountains. At this period we were in company with a small group of Tibetan merchants who, like us, had let the main body of the caravan go ahead, in order not to exhaust their camels by keeping up too quick a pace. "Tsong Kaba!" cried the Tibetans. "There are horsemen over there; but we are in deserted country where there are no herdsmen." Hardly were these words out before we began to see other horsemen appearing at various points: and when we saw them bearing down on us at speed all together we could not suppress a tremor of fear. What could these horsemen be up to in this uninhabited region, and what did they want of us? We were soon convinced that we had fallen into the hands of brigands. Their appearance did nothing to reassure us: each had a slung rifle, and two sabres one on either side of his belt; they had long black hair down to their shoulders, their eyes flashed and each man wore a wolf's skin on his head. We were surrounded by twenty-seven of these alarming characters, and there were only eighteen of us, by no means all of whom were experienced warriors. Both sides dismounted, and a courageous Tibetan from our party went forward to parley with the brigand chief, distinguishable by two little red flags fluttering behind his saddle. After a long and animated conversation the Kolo chieftain said, "Who is that man?" pointing at Father Gabet, who, tied on his camel, was the only one who had not dismounted.

"He is a great Lama from the Western Heavens, and the power of his prayers is infinite," replied the Tibetan merchant. The Kolo raised his two joined hands to his forehead and gazed at Father Gabet who, with his frozen face and his bizarre cocoon of motley-coloured blankets, looked not unlike one of those terrifying idols in a pagan temple. After a moment's contemplation of the famous Lama from the Western Heavens, the brigand spoke a few words in a low voice to the Tibetan merchant; then, with a sign to his companions, he and the rest mounted and galloped off over the mountains.

"We'll go no further," said the Tibetan merchant, "let's camp here; the Kolo are brigands, but they are great-hearted and generous; when they see that we are not afraid to stay here, where we are in their hands, they will not attack us. And also, I think that they have considerable respect for the power of the Lamas of the Western Heavens." So, following his advice, we all set about pitching camp.

The tents were hardly up when the Kolo reappeared on the skyline and galloped towards us at their usual speed. The chief alone came into our camp; the others waited a little outside. He addressed the Tibetan he had spoken to before.

"I have come," he said, "for an explanation of something that I do not understand. You are aware that our camp is over that mountain, and yet you dare to pitch your tents here, quite close. How many men have you in your party?"

"We are only eighteen; and you, I think, are twenty-seven. But men of courage never take flight."

"So you want to fight?"

"If there were not a number of sick amongst us, I would answer 'Yes', for I have met the Kolo face to face before."

"You have already fought the Kolo? When? What is your name?"

"Five years ago, at the affray over the ambassador; I still have a reminder of that day," and he bared his arm, marked with a long sabre scar. The brigand laughed and again asked him his name.

"I am Rala Tchembé," said the merchant. "Maybe you know that name?"

"Yes, all the Kolo know it, it is the name of a brave man," said the Kolo and jumped off his horse; he drew a sabre from his belt and presented it to the Tibetan. "Here," he said, "take this sabre, it is my best. We fought more than once; when next we meet, we shall meet as brothers." The Tibetan accepted the gift and gave the brigand chief in exchange a magnificent bow and quiver which he had bought in Peking.

The Kolo who had remained outside the camp, seeing that their chief was fraternising with the headman of the caravan, dismounted, tied their horses in pairs by the bridles and came to drink a friendly bowl of tea with the poor travellers who were at last beginning to breathe again. All these brigands were extremely amiable; they asked for news of the Tartar-Khalkas, whom they were particularly anxious to meet, because during the previous year they had killed two of their men who had to be avenged. Politics were also discussed. The brigands claimed to be great supporters of the Dalai Lama, and bitter enemies of the emperor of China; this was why they seldom failed to plunder the embassy on its way to Peking, since they held that the emperor was unworthy to receive gifts from the Dalai Lama, but normally respected it on its return, because it was right and proper that the emperor should send gifts to the Dalai Lama. After graciously accepting the tea and *tsamba* of the caravan, the brigands wished us a good journey and set off

back to their camp. Despite all these brotherly gestures we slept
with one eye open. The night was untroubled, however, and next
day we peacefully resumed our journey. Amongst the many pilgrims who have taken the road to Lhasa, there are few indeed who
can boast of having seen the brigands so near at hand, and suffered
no harm from them.

We had just escaped one danger, but, we were told, another even
greater, though of a different nature, awaited us. We were beginning
to climb the huge chain of the Tant La Mountains. According to our
travelling companions all the sick would die on the plateau, and even
the healthy would suffer greatly. Father Gabet was condemned to
certain death by the experienced travellers. After six days' painful
climb up a number of mountains, ranged as in an amphitheatre one
above another, we finally arrived on this famous plateau, maybe the
highest point of the world. The snow seemed to form a permanent
crust, to be part of the soil. Although it crackled under our feet we
hardly left the slightest footprint. The only vegetation was a grass,
growing here and there in clumps, short, sharp, smooth, of a woody
texture, hard as iron but not brittle; it would have made very good
upholsterers' needles. The animals were so famished that, willy nilly,
they had to graze on this terrible stuff. We could hear it crunch as
they bit, and they could only get a few mouthfuls of it down after a
fierce struggle which made their lips bleed.

Beyond the edge of this magnificent plateau we could see below us
the summits and peaks of a number of great ranges of mountains,
stretching far away to the horizon. We had never seen anything to
compare with the splendour of this stupendous sight. For the twelve
days that we travelled on the top of the Tant La we had good
weather; the air was windless, and each day God sent a health-giving
warm sunshine that tempered to some extent the cold of the atmosphere. Yet the air, much rarefied by the great altitude, was incredibly bracing. Enormous eagles followed our band of travellers,
and every day several corpses were left behind for them. It was
decreed that Death should also take toll of our small caravan; but it
took only our little black mule. We were sad but resigned. The
gloomy predictions made about Father Gabet proved quite wrong.
Quite the contrary, this plateau did him a deal of good. His health
and normal strength gradually returned. This almost unexpected gift
of Providence made us forget all our past hardships. We regained
our courage, and trusted that God would let us reach our destination.

The descent from the Tant La was long, rough and steep. For four
whole days we went down a kind of giant staircase, of which each

step was a mountain. At the bottom, we found hot springs of great magnificence. Amongst great rocks, many pools had been hollowed out by nature, in which the water boiled as if in a pot over a hot fire. In places it spouted from cracks in the rocks, innumerable little jets shooting in all directions in a most bizarre manner. There were some pools in which the water boiled at times so violently that great columns of water rose and fell intermittently, as if a great pump were at work. From these springs thick steam rose continuously, to condense into whitish clouds. The water was all sulphurous. After churning and leaping over and over again in the pools amongst the granite rocks it finally succeeded in escaping and flowed down into a little valley, forming a wide watercourse which ran over a bed of golden pebbles. These waters, though boiling, did not remain liquid for long. The extreme cold of the air cooled them so fast that at a little over a mile from the springs the stream was frozen almost solid. There are many thermal springs in the Tibetan mountains. The doctor-lamas realise that they have great medicinal properties; they frequently prescribe them for their patients, both for baths and for drinking.

From the Tant La mountains onwards, we noticed a gradual descent all the way to Lhasa. As we went, the cold became less intense and the soil produced stronger and more varied grasses. One day we camped in a great plain where the grazing was marvellously abundant. As our animals had long suffered from terrible starvation, it was decided to stop for two days and to let them enjoy this opportunity.

Next morning, as we were peacefully making tea inside our tent, we saw in the distance a troop of horsemen bearing down on us at full speed. Our blood froze at the sight, and we stood a moment petrified. When we had recovered from the shock, we rushed to Rala Tchembé's tent. "The Kolo! The Kolo!" we shouted. "Here comes a great troop of Kolo!" The Tibetan merchants, who were sitting drinking their tea and dunking their *tsamba*, laughed and asked us to come and sit down.

"Take tea with us," they said. "There are no more Kolo to be afraid of here; these horsemen are friendly. We are beginning to reach inhabited country; behind that hill over there on the right there are a large number of black tents. The horsemen you took for Kolo are local herdsmen." These words brought us comfort, and comfort bringing appetite, we were glad to sit down and share the Tibetan merchants' breakfast. But no sooner had they poured us a bowlful of buttered tea than the horsemen arrived at our tent door. Far from being brigands they were splendid fellows who had come to sell us butter and fresh meat. Their saddles looked like butchers' shops, with numerous joints of mutton and venison hanging along the horses' flanks. We bought eight legs of mutton, which being frozen were easy to carry. They cost us an old pair of Peking boots and the saddle from our little mule, which luckily was also from Peking. Everything that comes from Peking is greatly prized by the Tibetans, especially by those who are still herdsmen and nomads. Hence the merchants who accompanied the embassy had carefully marked all their bales of merchandise "Goods from Peking". Snuff is greatly in demand in Tibet. All the herdsmen asked us if we had any Peking snuff. I, the only snuff-taker of the party, had once had some, but for the past week I had been filling my snuff-box with a horrible mixture of earth and ashes. Inveterate snuff-takers will appreciate the grimness of my situation.

Condemned as we had been for the last two months to live exclusively on barley-meal dipped in tea, the mere sight of our joints of mutton seemed to act as a tonic on our stomachs and to strengthen our scraggy limbs. The rest of the day was devoted to culinary operations. For spice and seasoning we had only garlic, but it was so frozen and dried up that there was next to nothing inside the skin. We took all we had left and stuck it into two of the legs of mutton which we put into our biggest pot to boil. As there was an abundance of *argols* on this happy plain we were able to make a good enough fire to cook our priceless supper. The sun was on the point of setting and Samdadchiemba, who had just inspected one of the joints with his thumbnail, was triumphantly announcing that the meat was done to a turn, when we heard all around us cries of disaster: "*Mi yon*! *Mi yon*! Fire! Fire!" We bounded out of our tent. The fire had started indeed inside the camp, burning the dry grass, and threatening to destroy our tents; the flames spread everywhere with terrifying speed. All the travellers, armed with felt rugs, were trying to beat it out, or at least prevent it from reaching the tents. These, fortunately, escaped destruction. The fire, though pursued in all directions, found a way out and escaped into the wilds. Then, fanned by the wind, it spread over the wide prairie, consuming the pasture as it went. We thought that there was nothing more to fear, but shouts of "Save the camels! Save the camels!" soon made us realise how little experience we had of the dangers of fire in the wilderness. We then saw how the camels stood stupidly waiting for the flames to envelop them, instead of running away from them, like the horses and the cattle. So we tore off to save ours, which were still some way from the fire. But the flames were there almost as soon as we were. Soon we were surrounded by fire. We pushed and

beat those silly camels to try and force them to run, but in vain: they
stood still, turning their heads to look at us coolly, as if asking us
what right we had to come and stop them from grazing. We could
have killed them! The flames ate up the grass at such speed that it
soon reached the camels. Their long thick coats caught fire, and we
had to run at them with felt rugs to put out the flames as they ran
over their bodies. We were able to save three whose coats were only
singed. But the fourth was in a pitiful state; it hadn't a hair left on
the whole of its body; nothing remained but skin, and this too was
horribly burnt.

The area of grazing land that had been destroyed by the fire was
about a mile and half long by three-quarters of a mile wide. The
Tibetans again and again blessed their lucky stars that they had
succeeded in stopping the fire, and we heartily joined in when we
realised the extent of the danger we had run. They told us that if the
fire had gone on much longer it would have reached the black tents,
and that then the herdsmen would have pursued and certainly
slaughtered us. Hell knows no fury like that of these poor dwellers
in the wilds when, by mistake or on purpose, someone reduces to
ashes the pasturelands which are their only means of livelihood. It is
tantamount to destroying their cattle.

When we resumed our journey, the burnt camel was not dead, but
it was unusable; the three others had to fill the gap by sharing the
load of their unfortunate fellow between them. In any case, the loads
were much lighter than when we had left the Koukou Noor; our
sacks of meal were almost empty; and since the crossing of the Tant
La we had been reduced to a ration of two bowlfuls of *tsamba* a day.
We had got our sums more or less right before we left, but we had
not reckoned on the wastefulness of our two camel drivers: the one
out of foolishness and carelessness, the other out of malice. Fortunately we were about to reach a large Tibetan supply base, at
which we would be able to stock up.

For several days now our route took us along a succession of
valleys, with here and there a few black tents and some large herds of
yaks. Then at last we pitched our camp outside a large Tibetan
village. It was on the Na Pichu River, marked on the Andriveau-
Goujon map in its Mongol form of Khara Oussou; both mean
"Black Waters". Na Pichu was the first Tibetan settlement of any
size on the road to Lhasa. It consisted of some adobe houses, and a
large number of black tents. There was no sign of any cultivation.
Although the inhabitants were settled, they were herdsmen like the
nomadic tribes, and cattle-raising was their only occupation. We
were told that long ago a king of the Koukou Noor had made war on

the Tibetans, had conquered a large part of the country and given the Na Pichu area to the soldiers he had brought with him. Although by now these Tartars had merged with the Tibetans, we did see a few Mongol yurts amongst the black tents. This historical event may perhaps also explain why a number of Mongol expressions were in use locally, and had become part of the Tibetan language.

All caravans bound for Lhasa had to stop at Na Pichu for some days, to change their means of transport, because the route from then on was so rocky that camels could go no further. Our first task therefore was to sell ours; they were in such poor shape and so exhausted that nobody wanted them. Finally a man claiming to be an animal doctor turned up: he probably knew a way of improving their condition, for we sold him three of them for fifteen ounces of silver, and threw in the "burnt" one for nothing. These fifteen ounces of silver were just what we needed to hire six yaks to carry our baggage to Lhasa.

Our second task was to get rid of our assistant camel driver, the lama from the Ratchico mountains. After paying him off handsomely we told him that if he intended going on to Lhasa he must choose other companions, and that he could regard himself as freed from any obligations contracted with us. So at last we were parted from this fellow who, by his malice, had so increased the hardships we had had to bear on our journey.

We feel that we have a duty to warn anyone who for any reason might have to stop at Na Pichu that he would do well to be on his guard against thieves. The inhabitants of this Tibetan village are remarkable rogues; they exploit Mongol and other caravans to a shocking extent. At night they adroitly slip into the tents and take what they can lay their hands on; even by day they ply their profession with a cool skill which would be the envy of the cleverest crooks in Paris.

After stocking up with butter, *tsamba* and some joints of mutton, we went on towards Lhasa, which was now only about a fortnight's march away. We had as company some Mongols from the kingdom of Khartchin, who were on pilgrimage to Lhasa, the "Eternal Sanctuary"; they had taken their Grand Chaberon with them, that is, a Living Buddha who was the superior of their lamasery. He was a young man of eighteen; his manners were pleasant and refined, his expression was open and artless, contrasting strangely with the role he was made to play. At the age of five he had been declared a Buddha and Grand Lama of the Buddhists of Khartchin. He was going to Lhasa to spend some years in one of the great lamaseries, in the study of prayers and other knowledge required by his position. A brother of the king of Khartchin and several high-ranking lamas acted as his retinue. To be a Living Buddha was evidently a heavy burden for this young man. We could see that he would have enjoyed laughing and playing; he would have preferred to canter around on his horse, but was forced to proceed solemnly between a guard of honour of two horsemen who never left him. When we camped, instead of sitting all the time on cushions inside his tent, trying to look like an idol in a lamasery, he would much have preferred to be free in the wilds, busy with the tasks of nomadic life, but none of that was allowed. His life-task was to act the Buddha, and he must have no part in the everyday affairs of ordinary mortals. This young Chaberon enjoyed coming from time to time to chat with us in our tent; with us at least he could put off his official divinity and belong to the human race. He was most interested to hear us talk of Europe and the Europeans. He questioned us with artless candour about our religion, and greatly admired it; and when we asked him if it would not be better to be a worshipper of Jehovah than to be a Chaberon, he answered that he did not know. He disliked being asked about his previous lives and continual reincarnations; such questions made him blush, and in the end he told us that he found it painful when we spoke of such matters. This poor boy was clearly caught in a maze of religion of which he understood not a word.

The road from Na Pichu to Lhasa was mostly rocky and very hard going. When we reached the Koiran mountain chain it became extremely difficult indeed. Yet as we went along we were of good cheer, as we saw more and more signs of habitation. The sight of black tents in the distance, of many pilgrims on their way to Lhasa, of frequent inscriptions written on cairns by the wayside, and of many small caravans of yaks which we met from time to time all helped to lighten the fatigues of the journey. At a few days' march from Lhasa, the population ceased to be entirely nomadic. A few cultivated fields appeared in the wilderness, and gradually black tents gave way to houses. Then finally there were no more herdsmen and we were amongst an agricultural people. Fifteen days after we had left Na Pichu we arrived at Pampou, which, because of its closeness to Lhasa, was regarded by pilgrims as the gateway to the holy city. Pampou, erroneously marked on the map as Panctou, was a fine plain watered by a large river, which irrigated the land by means of a number of canals. There was no village as such, but large flat-roofed farmhouses were dotted everywhere, mostly well white-washed. They were all surrounded by large trees, and each one had a little turret like a dovecot from which floated many-coloured pennants covered with Tibetan characters. After more than three months spent in dreary deserts, with nothing to see but wild beasts and brigands, the plain of Pampou seemed to us the most beautiful place on earth. Our long hard journey had brought us so close to the savage state that we were lost in ecstasy at anything connected with civilisation. The houses, the ploughs, even a simple furrow seemed exciting. But what struck us most of all was the extraordinary mildness of the temperature. Although it was the end of January, the river and the canals had only a little thin ice along the edges; and hardly anyone was dressed in furs.

At Pampou we again had to reorganise the caravan. Yaks normally go no further than this; they are replaced by donkeys, very small but strong and trained as pack animals. As it was difficult to find enough donkeys for the baggage of the lamas from Khartchin and for our own, we were forced to stay two days. We used these days in an attempt to do something about our appearance. Our hair and our beards were so shaggy, our faces so sooty from the smoke of the tent, so cracked with the cold, so thin, so misshapen, that we felt sorry for ourselves when we looked at ourselves in a glass. As for our clothes, they were no better than we were.

The people of Pampou were most of them very well off; so they were continually gay and carefree. Each evening they gathered in front of their farms and we saw men, women and children jigging to a voice accompaniment. When the dances were over, the farmer plied everyone with a sourish drink made of fermented barley. It was like beer without the hops.

After two days' search in all the farms of the plain, enough donkeys had been collected to equip the caravan and we started off. One mountain stood between us and Lhasa, but it was undoubtedly the hardest and steepest of all that we had come across in our journey. The Tibetans and the Mongols climb it with great reverence; they believe that whoever has the good fortune to reach the top receives absolution for all his sins. Whether or not this is so, it is certain that climbing this mountain is a long, hard act of penance. We left at an hour after midnight, and it was not until nearly ten in the morning that we reached the summit. We were forced to do almost all the climb on foot, as riding was most difficult owing to the steepness and the rocky terrain.

The sun was just about to set when we had negotiated all the zigzags of the descent. We came out into a wide valley, and on our right we saw Lhasa, capital of the Buddhist world. A multitude of ancient trees; large white houses, flat-roofed and turreted; countless temples with golden roofs; the Buddha La, with the palace of the Dalai Lama on it: all this we saw, an impressive and majestic city.

At the entrance to the city, the Mongols whom we had got to know on the journey and who had arrived a few days before us met us and invited us to put up at a lodging that they had arranged for us. It was 29 January 1846; eighteen months had elapsed since we had left the valley of Black Waters.

View of Lhasa. From *Travels in Tartary, Tibet and China*, London, 1852.

EXPLORING ANGKHOR

Henri Mouhot
(1826–61)

Born in France, Mouhot spent most of his career in Russia as a teacher and then in the Channel Islands. A philologist by training, he also took up natural history and it was with the support of the Royal Zoological Society that in 1858 he set out for South East Asia. From Siam (Thailand) he penetrated Cambodia and Laos, where he died; but not before reaching unknown Angkhor and becoming the first to record and depict the most extensive and magnificent temple complex in the world. His discovery provided the inspiration for a succession of subsequent French expeditions up the Mekong.

On the 29th November I took leave of my amiable fellow-countryman and friend, M. Arnoux, to, I may venture to affirm, our mutual regret, and set off, accompanied by Father Guilloux, who had some business at Pinhalú. They both wished me to remain with them until Cochin China was open, and I could travel through the country in safety: I should have liked to do so, could I have foreseen an approaching termination of the war; but in the then state of affairs that was impossible.

As far as Pump-Ka-Daye, the first village we came to after leaving Brelum, I had the society and aid of the missionaries, and of the old chief of the Stiêns, who furnished me with three waggons for my baggage, while Phrai and M. Guilloux's Annamite attendants took charge of my boxes of insects, which, if placed among my other goods, would have been injured by the jolting.

The rains had ceased for the last three weeks, and I was agreeably surprised at the improvement in the state of the country since August. The paths were dry, and we had no longer to flounder through dirty marshes, nor suffer from the wet nights which we formerly found so unpleasant. When we reached the station where

Henri Mouhot, drawn by M. Rousseau. From *Travels in Central Parts of Indo China (Siam), Cambodia, and Laos, during the years 1858, 1859, and 1860*, London, 1864.

we were to pass the first night, our servants lighted a fire to cook their rice, as well as scare away the wild beasts; but, notwithstanding this, we remarked that our oxen, dogs, and monkey showed signs of great fear, and, almost immediately afterwards, we heard a roaring like that of a lion. We seized our guns, which were loaded, and waited in readiness.

Fresh roarings, proceeding from a very short distance off, completed the terror of our animals; and we ourselves could not help feeling uneasy. I proposed to go and meet the enemy, which was agreed to, and we accordingly plunged into that part of the forest whence the sound came. Although familiar with these terrible creatures, we felt far from comfortable; but before long we came upon recent tracks which were quite unmistakeable, and soon, in a small clearing in the forest, perceived nine elephants, the leader being a male of enormous size, standing right in front of us.

On our approach he set up a roar more frightful than ever, and the whole herd advanced slowly towards us. We remained in a stooping position, half hidden behind the trees, which were too tall for us to climb. I was in the act of taking aim at the forehead of the leader, the only vulnerable part, but an Annamite who stood beside me, and who was an old hunter, knocked up my rifle, and begged me not to fire; "for," said he, "if you kill or wound one of the elephants we are lost; and even if we should succeed in escaping, the oxen, the waggons, and all their contents would be overwhelmed by the fury of these animals. If there were but two or three, we might hope to kill them; but nine, of whom five are very large, are too many; and it will be more prudent to retreat." At this moment, Father Guilloux, who had not much confidence in his powers of locomotion, fired his gun in the air to frighten the elephants; and this plan fortunately succeeded: the herd stopped in astonishment for an instant, then turned round, and marched into the forest.

When we reached Pemptiélan we stopped at the house of the mandarin, whose authority extends over the neighbouring district, and, contrary to the usual custom, he offered us hospitality under his own roof. Scarcely, however, were we installed when he came to me and asked for the best of my guns, and, on my declining to part with it, he begged for something else, intimating that we should have begun by offering a present. Thereupon I gave him a suit of European clothes, a powder-flask and some powder, a hunting-knife, and some other small articles. In return he presented me with an ivory trumpet, and placed at my service two elephants to enable me to continue my route more comfortably: he likewise sent off our people with a letter to the chiefs of the Srokkhner.

We resumed our journey on the following day, the Abbé on one elephant, reading his breviary, and I upon another, both of us greatly enjoying the beauty of the landscape. Thus we traversed the beautiful plains, which, when I formerly travelled this road, were inhabited by the poor Thiâmes; but now, in place of rich harvest, I was astonished to find nothing but large trees: the villages were abandoned, and the houses and enclosures in ruins. It appeared that the mandarin of Pemptiélan, executing or exceeding the orders of his master the king of Cambodia, had kept these unfortunate people in such a state of slavery and oppression that they had even been deprived of their fishing and agricultural implements, and, being left without money or resources, experienced such frightful poverty that many of them died of hunger.

The poor wretches, to the number of several thousands, and under the conduct of a chief on whose head a price had been set, and who had secretly returned from Annam, rose in revolt. Those from Penom-Peuh went to Udong to protect their brethren in that place in their flight; and when all were united in one body, they descended the river, and passed into Cochin China. Orders were issued by the king to arrest their departure, but no one remained to execute them; for the whole Cambodian population, with the mandarins at their head, had fled into the forests at the first news of the rising.

Besides the interest inspired by the misfortunes of these poor people, their conduct, when all fled before them, and left Udong, Pinhalú, and Penom-Peuh defenceless, was so noble as greatly to increase this feeling. "We have no enmity against the people", said they, "if they will but let us pass and respect our property; but we will put to death whoever opposes our flight." And, in fact, they never touched one of the large boats which were moored near the market, and unguarded, but took to the river in their narrow and miserable pirogues.

On the 21st December we at last reached Pinhalú.

Penom-Peuh is about 103° 3' 50" long. of Paris, and 11° 37' 30" north lat. It is the great market of Cambodia, and only two or three leagues from the southern frontier of Cochin China: it is situated at the confluence of the Mekon with its tributary: from this point the river flows first north-east, and then north-west, as far as China and the mountains of Thibet. The arm, which has no name, but which, to distinguish it, it might be well to call Mé-Sap, from the name of the lake Touli-Sap, flows from its source south-east to the point of junction. About 12° 25' north lat. commences the great lake, which stretches as far as 13° 53'. In shape it might be compared to a violin. The whole space between it and the Mekon is a vast plain; while on the opposite side are the great chains of Poursat and its ramifications.

The entrance to the great lake of Cambodia is grand and beautiful. The river becomes wider and wider, until at last it is four or five miles in breadth; and then you enter the immense sheet of water called Touli-Sap, as large and full of motion as a sea. It is more than 120 miles long, and must be at least 400 in circumference.

The shore is low, and thickly covered with trees, which are half submerged; and in the distance is visible an extensive range of mountains whose highest peaks seem lost in the clouds. The waves glitter in the broad sunshine with a brilliancy which the eye can scarcely support, and, in many parts of the lake, nothing is visible all around but water. In the centre is planted a tall mast, indicating the boundary between the kingdoms of Siam and Cambodia.

In the province still bearing the name of Ongeor, which is situated eastward of the great lake Touli-Sap, towards the 14th degree of north lat., and 104° long. east of Greenwich, there are, on the banks of the Mekon, and in the ancient kingdom of Tsiampois (Cochin-China), ruins of such grandeur, remains of structures which must have been raised at such an immense cost of labour, that, at the first view, one is filled with profound admiration, and cannot but ask what has become of this powerful race, so civilised, so enlightened, the authors of these gigantic works?

One of these temples – a rival to that of Solomon, and erected by some ancient Michelangelo – might take an honourable place beside our most beautiful buildings. It is grander than anything left to us by Greece or Rome, and presents a sad contrast to the state of barbarism in which the nation is now plunged.

Unluckily the scourge of war, aided by time, the great destroyer, who respects nothing, and perhaps also by earthquakes, has fallen heavily on the greater part of the other monuments; and the work of destruction and decay continues among those which still remain standing, imposing and majestic, amidst the masses of ruins all around.

One seeks in vain for any historical souvenirs of the many kings who must have succeeded one another on the throne of the powerful empire of Maha-Nocor-Khmer. There exists a tradition of a leprous king, to whom is attributed the commencement of the great temple, but all else is totally forgotten. The inscriptions, with which some of the columns are covered, are illegible; and, if you interrogate the Cambodians as to the founders of Ongeor-Wat, you invariably receive one of these four replies: "It is the work of Pra-Eun, the king of the angels"; "It is the work of the giants"; "It was built by the leprous king"; or else, "It made itself."

The work of giants! The expression would be very just, if used figuratively, in speaking of these prodigious works, of which no one who has not seen them can form any adequate idea; and in the construction of which patience, strength, and genius appear to have done their utmost in order to leave to future generations proofs of their power and civilisation.

It is remarkable that none of these monuments were intended for habitations; all were temples of Buddhism. The statues and bas-reliefs, however, curiously enough, represent entirely secular subjects – monarchs surrounded by their wives, their heads and arms loaded with ornaments such as bracelets and necklaces, the body being covered with a narrow *langouti*. On a sort of esplanade is a statue, said to be that of the leprous king. It is a little above the middle height, and the prince is seated in a noble and dignified attitude. The head, particularly, is a *chef-d'œuvre*, the features perfectly regular, and possessing a manly beauty of a description seen now in very rare instances, and only amongst Cambodians of unmixed race, living in seclusion at the foot of the mountains, where the unhealthiness of the climate condemns them to a solitary existence; or among the savage mountaineers who occupy the border country separating Siam and Cambodia from the kingdom of Annam.

This place was probably chosen for the capital on account of its central position. It is situated fifteen miles from the great lake, in an arid and sandy plain, although the banks of the river would appear to have been a preferable site, more fertile, and offering greater facilities for communication.

Although making no pretension whatever either to architectural or archæological acquirements, I will endeavour to describe what I saw, for the benefit of others interested in these sciences, and, as well as I can, to draw the attention of Eastern *savans* to a new scene. I shall commence with the temple of Ongeor, the most beautiful and best preserved of all the remains, and which is also the first which presents itself to the eye of the traveller, making him forget all the fatigues of the journey, filling him with admiration and delight, such as would be experienced on finding a verdant oasis in the sandy desert. Suddenly, and as if by enchantment, he seems to be trans-ported from barbarism to civilisation, from profound darkness to light.

Before arriving at Ongeor from Battambong, having previously crossed the great lake from the mouth of either of the currents which traverse both those localities, you come upon a stream, which, in the dry season, you ascend for a couple of miles, and reach a spot where it becomes somewhat larger, forming a small natural basin, which serves the purpose of a kind of harbour. From this place a raised causeway, still passable at the present day, and extending as far as the limit which the waters attain at the period of the inundations, that is to say, over a space of three miles, leads to New Ongeor, an insignificant little town, the capital of the pro-vince, and situated fifteen miles to the N.N.W. of the shores of the lake.

If, starting from this point, you follow for about a couple of hours in the same direction a dusty sandy path passing through a dense forest of stunted trees; and having also frequently crossed the river, which is exceedingly sinuous in its course, you will arrive at an esplanade about 9 metres wide by 27 long, parallel to the building. At each angle, at the extremity of the two longer sides, are two enormous lions, sculptured out of the rock, and forming, with the

Halt of the caravan in the jungle between Battambong and Bangkok. Drawn by M. Catenacci, from a sketch by Mouhot. From *Travels in Central Parts of Indo China.*

pedestals, only a single block. Four large flights of steps lead to the platform.

From the north staircase, which faces the principal entrance, you skirt, in order to reach the latter, a causeway 230 metres in length by 9 in width, covered or paved with large slabs of stone, and supported by walls of great thickness. This causeway crosses a ditch 220 metres wide, which surrounds the building; the revetment, 3 metres high by 1 metre thick, is formed of ferruginous stone, with the exception of the top row, which is of freestone, each block being of the same thickness as the wall.

What strikes the observer with not less admiration than the grandeur, regularity, and beauty of these majestic buildings, is the immense size and prodigious number of the blocks of stone of which they are constructed. In this temple alone are as many as 1532 columns. What means of transport, what a multitude of workmen, must this have required, seeing that the mountain out of which the stone was hewn is thirty miles distant! In each block are to be seen holes 2½ centimetres in diameter and 3 in depth, the number varying with the size of the blocks; but the columns and the sculptured portions of the building bear no traces of them. According to a Cambodian legend, these are the prints of the fingers of a giant, who, after kneading an enormous quantity of clay, had cut it into blocks and carved it, turning it into a hard and, at the same time, light stone by pouring over it some marvellous liquid.

All the mouldings, sculptures, and bas-reliefs appear to have been executed after the erection of the building. The stones are everywhere fitted together in so perfect a manner that you can scarcely see where are the joinings; there is neither sign of mortar nor mark of the chisel, the surface being as polished as marble. Was this incomparable edifice the work of a single genius, who conceived the idea, and watched over the execution of it? One is tempted to think so; for no part of it is deficient, faulty, or inconsistent. To what epoch does it owe its origin? As before remarked, neither tradition nor written inscriptions furnish any certain information upon this point; or rather, I should say, these latter are as a sealed book for want of an interpreter; and they may, perchance, throw light on the subject when some European savant shall succeed in deciphering them.

A temple, about 100 metres in height, built of limestone has been erected on the top of Mount Bakhêng, which is situated two miles and a half north of Ongeor-Wat, on the road leading to the town. At the foot of the mountain are to be seen, among the trees, two magnificent lions, 20 centimetres in height, and each formed, with the pedestals, out of a single block. Steps, partly destroyed, lead to the top of the mountain, whence is to be enjoyed a view so beautiful and extensive, that it is not surprising that these people, who have shown so much taste in their buildings, should have chosen it for a site.

On the one side you gaze upon the wooded plain and the pyramidal temple of Ongeor, with its rich colonnades, the mountain of Crome, which is beyond the new city, the view losing itself in the waters of the great lake on the horizon. On the opposite side stretches the long chain of mountains whose quarries, they say, furnished the beautiful stone used for the temples; and amidst thick forests, which extend along the base, is a pretty, small lake, which looks like a blue ribbon on a carpet of verdure. All this region is now as lonely and deserted as formerly it must have been full of life and cheerfulness; and the howling of wild animals, and the cries of a few birds, alone disturb the solitude.

Sad fragility of human things! How many centuries and thousands of generations have passed away, of which history, probably, will never tell us anything: what riches and treasures of art will remain for ever buried beneath these ruins; how many distinguished men – artists, sovereigns, and warriors – whose names were worthy of immortality, are now forgotten, laid to rest under the thick dust which covers these tombs!

OVER THE KARAKORAMS

Francis Edward Younghusband
(1863–1942)

As leader of the 1904–5 British military expedition to Lhasa and as promoter of the early assaults on Mount Everest, Younghusband came to epitomize Himalayan endeavour. To the mountains he also owed his spiritual conversion from gung-ho soldier to founder of the World Congress of Faiths. His initiation came in 1887 when, as the climax to a journey from Peking across the Gobi desert, he determined to reach India over the unexplored Mustagh Pass in the Karakorams – "the most difficult and dangerous achievement in these mountains so far" (S. Hedin).

The Mustagh Pass, which we were now approaching, is on the main watershed, which both divides the rivers of India from the rivers of Turkestan, and also the British from the Chinese dominions. Peaks along the watershed, in the vicinity of the pass, had been fixed by trigonometrical observations from the Indian side at 24,000, 26,000, and in one case at over 28,000 feet in height, so I could scarcely doubt that the pass across the range must be lofty and difficult. It was, therefore, all the more worth conquering, and as it would be the final and greatest obstacle on my long journey from Peking, I set out to tackle it with the determination to overcome it at almost any cost. Every other difficulty had been successfully negotiated, and this last remaining obstacle, though the most severe of all, was not to be permitted at the climax of my journey to keep me from my goal.

These were my feelings as I advanced up the valley, at the head of which lay the Mustagh Pass. But I had little idea of the magnitude of the difficulties which in reality lay before me, and these were soon to commence.

Scarcely a mile from our bivouac of the previous night we came to

a point where the valley was blocked by what appeared to be
enormous heaps of broken stones and fragments of rock. These
heaps were between two and three hundred feet in height, and
stretched completely across the valley. I had gone on ahead by
myself, and when I saw these mounds of *débris*, I thought we might
have trouble in taking ponies over such rough obstacles; but I was
altogether taken aback when, on coming up to the heaps, I found
that they were masses of solid ice, merely covered over on the surface
with a thin layer of this rocky *débris*, which served to conceal the
surface of the ice immediately beneath. And my dismay can be
imagined when, on ascending one of the highest of the mounds, I
found that they were but the end of a series which extended without
interruption for many miles up the valley to the snows at the foot of
the pass. We were, in fact, at the extremity of an immense glacier.
This was the first time I had actually stood on a glacier, and I had
never realised till now how huge and continuous a mass of ice it is.
Here and there, breaking through the mounds of stone, I had seen
cliffs of what I thought was black rock, but on coming close up to
these found them to be nothing but solid dark green ice. I discovered
caverns, too, with transparent walls of clear, clean ice, and long,
tapering icicles hanging in delicate fringes from the roof. It was an
astonishing and wonderful sight; but I was destined to see yet more
marvellous scenes than this in the icy region upon which I was now
entering.

To take a caravan of ponies up a glacier like this seemed to me an
utter impossibility. The guides thought so too, and I decided upon
sending the ponies round by the Karakoram Pass, 180 miles to the
eastward, to Leh, and going on myself over the Mustagh Pass with
a couple of men. This would have been a risky proceeding, for if we
did not find our way over the pass we should have scarcely enough
provisions with us to last us till we could return to an inhabited
place again. Supplies altogether were running short, and the longer
we took in reaching the pass, the harder we should fare if we did
not succeed in getting over. But while I was deciding upon sending
the ponies back, the caravan men were making a gallant attempt to
lead them up the glacier. I rejoined them, and we all helped the
ponies along as well as we could; hauling at them in front, pushing
at them behind, and sometimes unloading and ourselves carrying
the loads up the stone-covered mounds of ice. But it was terribly
hard and trying work for the animals. They could get no proper
foothold, and as they kept climbing up the sides of a mound they
would scratch away the thin layer of stones on the surface, and
then, coming on to the pure ice immediately below, would slip and

Lieutenant Francis Younghusband, photographed in December 1887, immediately after the expedition. From *The Heart of a Continent*, London, 1937.

fall and cut their knees and hocks about in a way which went directly to my heart. I did not see how this sort of thing could last. We had only advanced a few hundred yards, and there were still from fifteen to twenty miles of glacier ahead. I therefore halted the ponies for the day, and went on with a couple of men to reconnoitre. We fortunately found, in between the glacier and the mountainside, a narrow stretch of less impracticable ground, along which it would be possible to take the ponies. This we marked out, and returned to our bivouac after dark.

That night we passed, as usual, in the open, thoroughly exhausted after the hard day's work, for at the high altitudes we had now reached the rarefaction of the air makes one tired very quickly, and the constant tumbling about on the slippery glacier in helping the ponies over it added to one's troubles. My boots were cut through, my hands cut all over, and my elbows a mass of bruises.

At daybreak on the following morning we started again, leading the ponies up the route we had marked out; but a mile from the point where our previous exploration had ended we were confronted by another great glacier flowing down from the left. We now had a glacier on one side of us, mountains on the other, and a second glacier right across our front. At this time my last remaining pair of boots were completely worn out, and my feet so sore from the bruises they received on the glacier I could scarcely bear to put them to the ground. So I stayed behind with the ponies, while two men went on to find a way through the obstacles before us. The men returned after a time, and said they could find no possible way for the ponies; but they begged me to have a look myself, saying that perhaps by my good fortune I might be able to find one.

I accordingly, with a couple of men, retraced my steps down the edge of the main glacier for some little distance, till we came to a point where it was possible to get ponies on to the glacier itself and take them right out into the middle. We then ascended a prominent spot on the glacier, from which we could obtain a good view all round. We were in a sea of ice. There was now little of the rocky moraine stuff with which the ice of the glacier had been covered in its lower part, and we looked out on a vast river of pure white ice, broken up into myriads of sharp needle-like points. Snowy mountains rose above us on either hand, and down their sides rolled the lesser glaciers, like clotted cream pouring over the lip of a cream-jug; and rising forbiddingly before us was the cold icy range we should have to cross.

This, marvellous as it was to look upon, was scarcely the country through which to take a caravan of ponies, but I made out a line of moraine extending right up the main glacier. We got on to this, and, following it up for some distance, found, to our great relief, that it would be quite possible to bring ponies up it on to the smooth snow of the *névé* at the head of the glacier. Having ascertained this beyond a doubt, we returned late in the afternoon towards the spot where we had left our ponies. Darkness, however, overtook us before we reached it. We wandered about on the glacier for some time, and nearly lost our way; but at last, quite worn out, reached our little caravan once more.

That night we held a council of war as to which of the two Mustagh Passes we should attack. There are two passes, known as the Mustagh, which cross the range. One, to the east, that is to our left as we were ascending the glacier, is known as the Old Mustagh Pass, and was in use in former days, till the advance of ice upon it made it so difficult that a new one was sought for, and what is known as the New Mustagh Pass, some ten miles farther west along the range, had been discovered. It was over this latter pass that the guides hoped to conduct our party. They said that even ponies had in former times been taken across it by means of ropes and by making rough bridges across the crevasses. No European had crossed either of them, but Colonel Godwin-Austen, in 1862, reached the southern foot of the new pass in the course of his survey of Baltistan. This New Mustagh Pass seemed the more promising of the two, and I therefore decided upon sending two men on the following morning to reconnoitre it and report upon its practicability.

At the first streak of daylight the reconnoiterers set out, and the remainder of us afterwards followed with the ponies along the route which we had explored on the previous day. We took the ponies up the glacier without any serious difficulty, and in the evening halted close up to the head of the glacier where snowy mountains of stupendous height shut us in on every hand. At dusk the two men who had been sent out to reconnoitre the new pass returned, to say that the ice had so accumulated on it that it would be now quite impossible to take ponies over, and that it would be difficult even for men to cross it. The plan which they therefore suggested was to leave the ponies behind, and cross the range by the Old Mustagh Pass, push on to Askoli, the first village on the south side of the range, and from there send back men with supplies for the ponies and the men with them sufficient to enable the caravan to reach Shahidula, on the usual trade route beteen Yarkand and Kashmir. This was evidently all we could do. We could not take the ponies any farther, and we could not send them back as they were, for we had nearly run out of supplies, and Shahidula the nearest point at which fresh supplies could be obtained, was one hundred and eighty miles distant. All now depended upon our being able to cross the pass. If we were not able to, we should have to march this one hundred and eighty miles back through the mountains with only three or four days' supplies to support us. We might certainly have eaten the ponies, so would not actually have starved; but we should have had a hard struggle for it, and there would still have been the range to cross at another point.

Matters were therefore approaching a critical stage, and that was an anxious night for me. I often recall it, and think of our little bivouac in the snow at the foot of the range we had to overcome. The sun sank behind the icy mountains, the bright glow gently disappeared, and they became steely hard while the grey cold of night settled shimmering down upon them. All around was pure white snow and ice, breathing out cold upon us. The little pools and streamlets of water which the heat of the sun had poured off the glacier during the day were now gripped by the frost, which seemed to creep around ourselves too, and huddle us up together. We had no tent to shelter us from the biting streams of air flowing down from the mountain summits, and we had not sufficient fuel to light a fire round which we might lie. We had, indeed, barely enough brushwood to keep up a fire for cooking; but my Chinese servant cooked a simple meal of rice and mutton for us all. We gathered round the fire to eat it hot out of the bowl, and then rolled ourselves up in our sheepskins and went to sleep, with the stars twinkling brightly above, and the frost gripping closer and closer upon us.

Next morning, while it was yet dark, Wali, the guide, awoke us. We each had a drink of tea and some bread, and then we started off to attack the pass. The ponies, with nearly all the baggage, were left behind under the charge of Liu-san, the Chinaman, and some of the older men. All we took with us was a roll of bedding for myself, a sheepskin coat for each man, some native biscuits, tea and a large tea-kettle, and a bottle of brandy. The ascent to the pass was easy but trying, for we were now not far from nineteen thousand feet above sea-level, and at that height, walking uphill through deep snow, we quickly became exhausted. We could only take a dozen or twenty steps at a time, and we would then bend over on our sticks and pant as if we had been running hard uphill. We were tantalised, too, by the apparent nearness of the pass. Everything here was on a gigantic scale, and what seemed to be not more than an hour's walk from the bivouac was in fact a six hours' climb.

It was nearly midday when we reached the top of the pass, and what we saw there makes me shudder even now to think upon. There was nothing but a sheer precipice before us, and those first few moments on the summit of the Mustagh Pass were full of intensest anxiety to me. If we could but get over, the crowning success of my expedition would be gained. But the thing seemed to me simply an impossibility. I had had no experience of Alpine climbing, and I had no ice-axes or other mountaineering appliances with me. I had not even proper boots. All I had for foot-gear were some native boots of soft leather, without nails and without heels – mere leather stockings, in fact – which gave no sort of grip upon an icy surface. How, then, I should ever be able to get down the icy slopes and rocky precipices I now saw before me I could not by any possibility imagine; and if it had rested with me alone, the probability is we never should have got over the pass at all.

What, however, saved our party was my holding my tongue. I kept quite silent as I looked over the pass, and waited to hear what

Camp on the glacier. From *The Heart of a Continent*.

the men had to say about it. They meanwhile were looking at me, and, imagining that an Englishman never went back from an enterprise he had once started on, took it as a matter of course that, as I gave no order to go back, I necessarily meant to go on. So they set about their preparations for the descent. We had brought an ordinary pickaxe with us, and Wali went on ahead with this, while the rest of us followed one by one behind him, each hanging on to a rope tied round Wali's waist to support him in case he slipped while hewing steps across an ice-slope leading to a rocky precipice which seemed to afford the only possible means of descending the pass. This slope was of hard ice, very steep, and, thirty yards or so below the line we took, ended in an ice-fall, which again terminated many hundreds of feet beneath in the head of a glacier at the foot of the pass. Wali with his pickaxe hewed a way step by step across the ice-slope, so as to reach the rocky cliff by which we should have to descend on to the glacier below.

We slowly edged across the slope after him, but it was hard to keep cool and steady. From where we stood we could see nothing over the end of the slope but the glacier hundreds of feet below us. Some of the men were so little nervous that they kicked the fragments of ice hewed out by Wali down the slope, and laughed as they saw them hop down it and with one last bound disappear altogether. But an almost sickening feeling came on me as I watched this, for we were standing on a slope as steep as the roof of a house. We had no ice-axes with which to anchor ourselves or give us support; and though I tied handkerchiefs, and the men bits of leather and cloth, round the insteps of our smooth native boots, to give us a little grip on the slippery ice, I could not help feeling that if any one of us had lost his foothold the rest would never have been able to hold him up with the rope, and that in all likelihood the whole party would have been carried away and plunged into the abyss below.

Outwardly I kept as cool and cheerful as I could, but inwardly I shuddered at each fresh step I took. The sun was now pouring down and just melted the surface of the steps after they were hewn, so that by the time those of us who were a few paces behind Wali reached a step the ice was just covered over with water and this made it still more slippery for our soft leather boots, which had now become almost slimy on the surface. It was under these circumstances that my Ladaki servant Drogpa gave in. He was shaking all over in an exaggerated shiver, and so unsteady, I thought he would slip at any moment and perhaps carry us all with him. We were but at the beginning of our trials. We had not even begun the actual descent yet, but were merely crossing to a point from which we should make it. And to have such a man with us might have endangered the safety of the whole party; so I told him he might return to the ponies and go round with them. It rather upset me to see a born hillman so affected, but I pretended not to care a bit and laughed it off, *pour encourager les autres*, as the thing had to be done.

At last we reached the far side of the slope, and found ourselves on a projecting piece of rock protruding through the ice. Here we could rest, but only with the prospect of still further difficulties before us. We were at the head of the rocky precipice, the face of which we should have to descend to reach the ice-slopes which extended to the glacier at the foot of the pass. At such heights as those which we had now reached, where the snow and ice lie sometimes hundreds of feet thick, it is only where it is very steep that the bare rock shows through. The cliff we had now to descend was an almost sheer precipice; its only saving feature was that it was rough and rugged, and so afforded some little hold for our hands and feet. Yet even then we seldom got a hold for the whole hand or whole foot. All we generally found was a little ledge, upon which we could grip with the tips of the fingers or side of the foot. The men were most good to me, whenever possible guiding my foot into some secure hold, and often supporting it there with their hands; but at times it was all I could do to summon sufficient courage to let myself down on to the veriest little crevices which had to support me. There was a constant dread, too, that fragments of these ledges might give way with the weight upon them; for the rock was very crumbly, as it generally is when exposed to severe frosts, and once I heard a shout from above, as a huge piece of rock which had been detached came crashing past me, and as nearly as possible hit two of the men who had already got half-way down.

We reached the bottom of the cliff without accident, and then found ourselves at the head of a long ice-slope extending down to the glacier below. Protruding through the ice were three pieces of rock, which would serve us as successive halting-places, and we determined upon taking a line which led by them. We had brought with us every scrap of rope that could be spared from the ponies' gear, and we tied these and all the men's turbans and waist-clothes together into one long rope, by which we let a man down the ice-slope on to the first projecting rock. As he went down he cut steps, and when he had reached the rock we tied the upper end of the rope firmly on to a rock above, and then one by one we came down the slope, hanging on to the rope and making use of the steps which had been cut. This was, therefore, a comparatively easy part of the descent; but one man was as nearly as possible lost. He slipped, fell over on his back, and came sliding down the slope at a frightful pace. Luckily, however, he still managed to keep hold of the rope with one hand, and so kept himself from dashing over the ice-fall at the side of the slope; but when he reached the rock his hand was almost bared of skin, and he was shivering with fright. Wali, however, gave him a sound rating for being so careless, and on the next stage made him do all the hardest part of the work.

The other men got down the slope without mishap, and then came the last man. He, of course, could not have the benefit of a rope to hang on by, for he would have to untie it from the rock and bring it with him. Wali had selected for this, the most dangerous piece of work in the whole descent, the man who had especially troubled me by knocking pieces of ice over the precipice when we were on the ice-slope at the head of the pass. He was one of the slaves I had released at Yarkand; an incessant grumbler, and very rough, but, next to Wali, the best man I had for any really hard work. He tied the end of the rope round his waist, and then slowly and carefully came down the steps which had been hewn in the slope. We at the end of the rope pulled it in at every step he took, so that if he slipped, though he might fall past us, we should be able to haul in the rope fast, and so perhaps save him from the ice-fall. He reached our rock of refuge in safety, and we then in the same manner descended two more stages of the ice-slope, and finally reached a part where the slope was less steep, and we could proceed without cutting steps the whole way.

At last, just as the sun set, we reached the glacier at the foot of the pass. We were in safety once more. The tension of six crucial hours was over, and the last and greatest obstacle in my journey had been successfully surmounted. Those moments when I stood at the foot of the pass are long to be remembered by me – moments of intense relief, of glowing pride and of deep gratitude for the success that had been granted. But such feelings as mine were now cannot be described in words; they are known only to those who have had their heart set on one great object and have accomplished it.

I took a last look at the pass, never before nor since seen by a European, and which, viewed from below, looked utterly impracticable to any human being. Then we started away down the glacier to find some bare spot on which to lay our rugs and rest.

The sun had now set, but, fortunately for us, there was an abundance of light, and the night was marvellously beautiful, so that, tired as I was, I could not but be impressed by it. The moon was nearly full, the sky without a cloud, and in the amphitheatre of snowy mountains and among the icy seracs of the glacier, not one speck of anything but the purest white was visible. The air at these altitudes, away from dust and with no misty vapour in it, was absolutely clear, and the soft silvery rays of the moon struck down upon the glistening mountains in unsullied radiance. The whole effect was of some enchanting fairy scene; and the sternness of the mountains was slowly softened down till lost, and their beauty in its purest form alone remained.

With our senses enervated by such a scene as this, and overcome with delight as we were at having successfully crossed the pass, we pushed on down the glacier in a dreamy, careless way, perfectly regardless of the dangers which lay hidden around us. Under ordinary circumstances we should have proceeded cautiously down a glacier which, beautiful though it was, had its full share of crevasses; and it was only when I turned round and found one man missing, that I realised how negligent we had been. We retraced our steps, and found the poor fellow had dropped down a crevasse, the mouth of which had been covered with a thin coating of ice and snow, which had given way under his weight, so that he had dropped through. Very fortunately the crevasse was not wide, and after falling about fifteen feet he had been wedged in between the two sides by the load of my bedding which he was carrying; so by letting a rope down we were able to extricate him in safety. This taught us a lesson, and for the rest of the way we went along roped together, as we ought to have been from the first, and tested each step as we advanced.

I now kept in the rear, and the man with my bedding was in front of me. As we were closed up during a temporary halt, I detected a strong smell of brandy coming from the bundle of bedding. A distracting thought occurred to me. I tore open the bundle, and there was my last bottle of brandy – broken! Lady Walsham, on my leaving Peking, had insisted upon giving me at least two bottles of brandy for the journey. I had drunk one in the Gobi Desert, and I had made up my mind to keep the other till the day I had crossed the Mustagh Pass, but there it was broken, and the brandy wasted, just when both the men and myself were really needing something to pull us together. The bundle of bedding had been thrown over the pass to save carrying it down, and though the bottle had been wrapped up in my sheepskin sleeping-bag, it had been smashed to pieces.

About eleven o'clock we at last reached a piece of ground on the mountain-side free from snow, and here we halted for the night. There was no wood, and only a few roots of weeds about with which to light a fire, so we had to break up a couple of our alpenstocks to make a small fire, by which we managed to boil sufficient water to make a few cups of tea. We had some biscuit with that, and then I got into my sheepskin bag, and the men wrapped themselves up in their sheepskin coats, and we lay down and slept as if nothing could ever wake us again.

TRIALS IN TIBET

Ekai Kawaguchi
(b. c1870)

By the 1890s the capital of "forbidden" Tibet, unseen by a foreigner since Huc's visit, represented the greatest challenge to exploration. Outright adventurers like the dreadful Henry Savage Landor competed with dedicated explorers like Sven Hedin, all succumbed to a combination of official vigilance and physical hardship. The exception, and the winner in "the race for Lhasa", was a Buddhist monk from Japan whose expedition consisted of himself and two sheep. Ekai Kawaguchi was supposedly a pilgrim seeking religious texts. His faith was genuine and often tested, as during this 1900 excursion into western Tibet; but he is also thought to have been an agent of the British government in India.

The next morning, after traversing the bush-land, I came to the foot of a mountain which I had to climb. When half-way up the slope I saw a mountain stream flowing across my road, and it presented a rather curious sight. For the river, at a very short distance, broadened into a lake, and almost described a right angle when flowing out of this and into another basin. Afterwards I ascertained the name of this river to be Chema-yungdung-gi-chu, and that its waters flowed into the Brahmaputra. I shuddered at the thought of having once more to cross an icy mountain stream, but there was no help.

It was only nine o'clock in the morning when I reached the Chema-yungdung-gi-chu, and I found ice quite thick still along its banks. I waited till the ice began to melt, and I finished the noon-meal before making a plunge into the water, not forgetting of course the anointing process. My intention was to make my sheep carry their shares of the luggage across the river; but to this proposal they strenuously objected, probably knowing instinctively

The Shramana Ekai Kawaguchi photographed in 1909. From *Three Years in Tibet*, Madras, 1909.

the depth of the water. In the end I gave in, relieved the animals of their burden, and, leaving the luggage behind, I led them into the water by their ropes. I tucked up my clothes high, but the water proved to be much deeper than I had judged; it came up to my shoulders, and all the clothing I had on became wet through. The sheep proved good swimmers, and we managed to get to the other side without any accident; of course they might have been washed down and drowned, but for the assistance I gave them by means of the ropes. Once on the bank, I tied one end of the ropes to a large boulder, and after taking off all my clothing to get dry I, stark naked, made a second plunge and returned for my luggage. The second crossing was comparatively easy. After a rest of about half an hour, and a thorough anointing for the second time, I made all my baggage into one bundle to be balanced on my head. With that acrobatic equipment, I entered the stream for a third time. All went well, until, in mid-stream, I lost my foothold, treading on a slippery stone in the bottom, and, what with the weight of the luggage on my head, and more or less exhaustion after the repeated wadings, I fell down into the water, while the bundle slid off my head. I had no time even to bring my staff into service; all I could do was to take firm hold of my luggage, and try to swim with one hand; for I was being fast carried down into deep waters. The thought then occurred to me that, if I tried to save my luggage, I might lose my life. But a second thought made it plain to me that to lose my luggage would mean surer death, because my route lay for ten days, at least, over an uninhabited tract of wilderness, and thus it was wiser to cling to it while life lasted. And cling to my luggage I did, but I was rapidly losing the power of moving my free swimming arm, and, in only one hundred yards down the swift stream, I should be washed into one of the lakes, whence I might never be able to get to dry land. I should have said that the river, at the point where I was crossing it, was a hundred and eighty yards wide, more or less. I had now had quite a course of ice and water – all involuntarily certainly – and a feeling of numbness was quickly coming over me. I began to think that it might be just as well to be drowned then as to die of starvation afterwards. In fact, I had spoken my last desire: "O ye! All the Buddhas of the ten quarters, as well as the highest Teacher of this world, Buddha Shākyamuni! I am not able to accomplish my desires and to return the kindness of my parents, friends, followers and specially the favors of all the Buddhas, in this life; but I desire that I be born again, in order to requite the favors which I have already received from all." At that moment, with a thrill, I felt that the end of one of my staves had

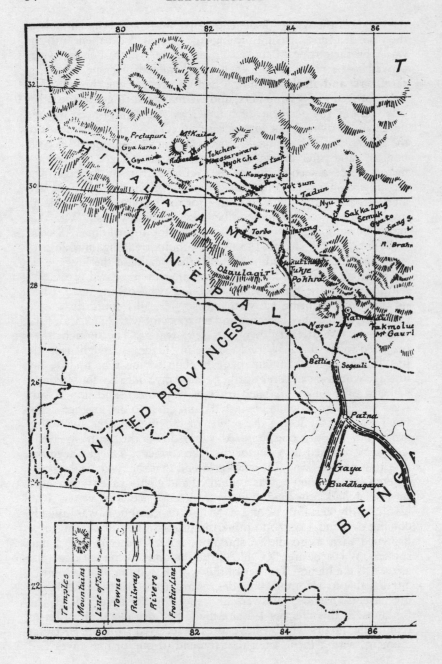

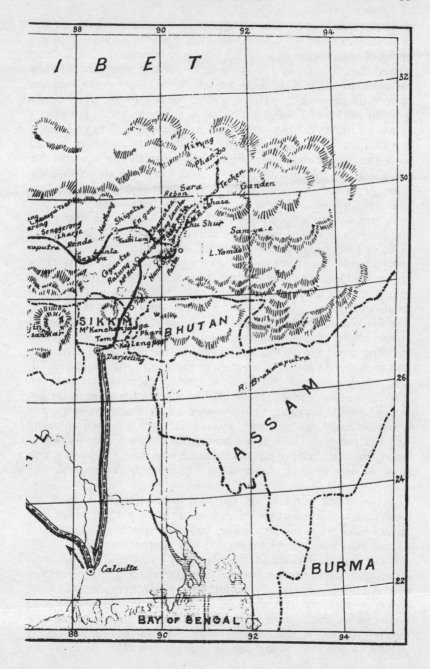

touched something hard. In an instant courage returned to me, and on trying to stand up I found that the water was only up to my breast. I was at that time about forty yards from the bank I had started for. Feeble as I was, with recovered strength I finally managed to reach the "shore of salvation". As for the luggage, heavy with the soaking water, it was impossible for me to rebalance it on my head, and I pulled it along after me in the water; but when I at last got upon the bank, it taxed all my remaining energy to drag it out after me. Arrived on the bank, I found that I had been carried more than two hundred and fifty yards down the stream from the point whence I started to cross it, and I saw my sheep leisurely grazing, perfectly unconscious of their master's sad plight. I had no strength, then, even to crawl up to where my sheep were. My fingers were stiff and immovable, and I rubbed the regions over my heart and lungs with closed fists. After an hour's exercise of this kind, I more or less recovered the circulation of blood in my limbs, and I was just able partially to undo my baggage and to take out hotan – hotan, my life-saving hotan, which Mrs. Ichibei Watanabe of Osaka gave me, when bidding me farewell. A dose of hotan sent me into a fit of convulsions, which lasted for nearly three hours. It was now past five o'clock, and the sun was going down. The convulsions had almost left me. I then made two bundles of my luggage, and in two crawling trips I carried them to where I had left my sheep grazing. It was then that I thought of an ancient method of torture, called *Oi-ishi*, which consisted in making a suspect carry on his back an extremely heavy load – so rackingly heavy I then felt to be the weight of my divided luggage. That evening I had neither courage nor energy to make any fire, and I passed the night wrapped up in my half-wet *tuk-tuk*. The luggage having been done up in hides and skins, the water had not penetrated much into it, and I was thus able to go to sleep dressed, and protected in partially dry apparel.

The sun shone out brightly the next morning, and I dried my clothing and the collection I then had of the sacred Scriptures. The latter I still have in my possession, and every time I take them out, I cannot help wondering how my life was spared when those things got wet. By one o'clock in the afternoon I was ready to proceed, although I had not half recovered from the effect of my experience of the day before, and my things were far from being dry. Consequently even my own share of the luggage proved heavier than before, while circumstances compelled me to relieve my sheep of a part of theirs. To make things worse, I had managed to get a painful cut on one of my feet during my last effort to cross the

Chema-yungdung-gi-chu, and altogether it was an inauspicious start which I made on that afternoon. After all, however, a step forward meant a step nearer to my destination, and with that philosophical reasoning I dragged myself onward. In that way I had proceeded for about five miles, when, to increase my difficulties, snow began to fall thick and fast. When I had arrived near a small pond and stopped to bivouac for the night, fire and tea were entirely out of the question, for the elements were now engaged in a fearful strife – the dazzling lightning, the deafening thunder, the shrieking wind and the blinding blizzard were at war all at once. That which I had managed to dry tolerably the day before became thoroughly wet again, and the whole of the following morning was spent in repeating the process of the preceding morning. No fire was obtainable even then, and consequently no tea; so I allayed my hunger with some raisins before resuming my journey shortly after noon. And little I dreamt of the danger that was in store for me that afternoon and the day following.

I was still heading for the north-west, and in order to adhere to that course I must now climb a snow-clad peak towering into the sky; I saw no way of avoiding the task, and encouraged by an uncertain hope – still a hope – of emerging upon or near Kang Rinpoche, or in the neighborhood of Mount Kailāsa, I began the ascent of that great hill, which I afterward ascertained to be a peak called Kon Gyu-i Kangri, that rises twenty-two thousand six hundred and fifty feet above sea-level. By five o'clock in the afternoon I had made an ascent of about ten miles, and then it began to snow and to blow a gale. I thought it dangerous to continue my ascent under these conditions, and turning first north and then east, I essayed to make a rapid descent. The sun had now gone down, and snow was falling faster than ever. But I had not yet found a shelter and so continued my descent, having made up my mind to go on until I found a hospitable shelving cliff, or some such haven. It was, however, nothing but snow, snow, everywhere and all around and presently there were twelve inches on the ground. By and by my sheep refused to proceed further, whether owing to hunger or not I could not tell, though it was plain that they had not fed the whole afternoon, because of the snow. At first I succeeded in getting them to move on a little as the result of some physical reasoning, but presently even that process of pleading failed. But the prospect of being frozen to death prevented me from yielding to their not unreasonable obstinacy; and putting all my strength into the ropes I dragged them onward. The poor animals reluctantly obeyed me and walked on for about a hundred yards, at the end of which, however, they came to a dead stop and began to breathe heavily. Thereupon I felt no little alarm, thinking that the animals might die that night. But what could I do? I knew that I was many a day's journey at least from the nearest human habitation. A few more miles either way would not make much difference: so let fate decide. Once in that frame of mind, I took out my night-coverings and wrapped myself up and, protecting my head with a water-proof coat, I sat myself down between my two sheep, with the determination to pass the night in religious meditation.

My poor sheep! They crept close to me and lay there in the snow, emitting occasionally their gentle cry, which I thought had never sounded sadder. Nor had I ever felt so lonely as I did then. Wrapped up in the clumsy manner that I have described, I still managed to smear over my body the clove-oil, which seemed to prevent to some extent the radiation of the heat of the body, and I began to feel considerably warmer than I had been before. For all that, the cold increased in intensity after mid-night, and I began to feel that my power of sensation was gradually deserting me. I seemed to be in a trance, and vaguely thought that that must be the feeling of a man on the point of death.

I was now wandering in a dream-land, if I may so describe the mental condition of a man half-way on the road of being frozen to death. Regret, resignation, and the hope of re-birth took turns in my mind, and then all became a blank. During that blankness I no doubt looked exactly like a dead person. Suddenly I awoke, fancying that somebody, something, was stirring about me or near me. I opened my eyes, and saw the two sheep shaking themselves; they were shaking snow off their bodies. That was strange, I dreamily thought. I saw the sheep finish shaking off the snow, and I wanted to shake it off too. But I could not. I was rigid all over. Mechanically I next endeavored to recover the use of my limbs. Presently I became more myself mentally, and I saw the skies still presenting a dismal and threatening appearance, the immense patches of black, black cloud still fleeing or pursuing, and the sun struggling to force his life-giving rays between the intervals of the hurrying vapors. On taking out my watch I found that it was then half past ten of what morning I could not tell. Had I slept only one night, or two in the snow? The question was more than I could just then solve. Nor did I feel that there was any necessity for its instant solution. My immediate desire was for nourishment, and I took some baked flour, helping it down with snow. I gave some also to my sheep, which, by that time, had learnt to feed themselves on flour when green grass was lacking.

I felt that the condition of my health was not equal to the task of making a second attempt to climb over the Kon Gyu-i Kangri, and I continued the descent when I resumed my journey, with the intention of taking a long rest at the foot of the mountain. After going down more than five miles I came to another mountain stream, and at the same time down again came the snow. I almost trembled at a prospect of spending another perilous night in the snow. Just at that juncture I heard some clear, ringing sounds, as of a bird's cry. Turning round, I saw seven or eight cranes stalking along majestically in the shallow part of the river. Never before had I seen a sight so poetically picturesque, so representative of antique serenity. Some little time afterwards I composed an *uta* in memory of that enchanting scene:

> Like feathers white the snows fall down and lie
>   There on the mountain-river's sandy banks;
> Ko-kow, Ko-kow! sounds strange – a melody
>   I hear – I search around for this strange cry.
> In quiet majesty those mountain cranes
>   I find, are proudly strutting – singing thus.

The river was about one hundred and twenty yards wide, and crossing it, I still proceeded down the incline. I had now come to the bottom of a valley, and I saw at a distance what I took for a herd of yaks. But I had before been deceived quite often by exposed boulders and rocks which I had taken for yaks, and I was doubtful of my vision on that occasion. But presently I saw the dark objects moving about, and I was sure that they were yaks. The discovery, wholly unexpected as it was, was delightful, for their presence implied that of some fellow-creatures in the neighborhood. Coming up to the spot, I found that the herd consisted of about sixty yaks, attended by some herdsmen. On my questioning the men, they informed me that they had arrived at the spot the evening before, and that a little further on I should come upon a little camp of four tents. Towards these I forthwith directed my steps.

My arrival in front of one of the tents was, as usual, hailed by a pack of barking dogs. I begged the occupants of the first tent for a night's lodging, but met with a flat refusal. Probably my appearance was against me: I had not shaved for two months, and my unkempt hair and beard no doubt made me look wild, while under-feeding and general exhaustion cannot have improved my features. Still I pleaded for charity, but in vain. Dejectedly I moved to a second tent, but there too I received no better treatment. In fact the treatment was worse: for my urgent pleading, with a detailed account of my sufferings during the previous eight days or so, only seemed to make the master of the tent turn colder, even to the extent of finally charging me with an intention to rob him. That was enough. I turned away, and a great sadness came over me as I stood in the snow. My sheep bleated pitifully, and I felt like crying myself. A third tent stood near, but I could not muster courage enough to repeat my request there. The sight of my sheep was melancholy in the extreme, and with an effort I made an appeal at the fourth and last tent. To my great joy, I met a ready welcome. I was utterly tired out, but a quiet rest near a comfortable fire made me imagine the joys of paradise, and this i was allowed to enjoy all that evening and through the next day. During that stay I occupied my time in writing down the twenty-six desires which I had formulated, with the hope of their accomplishment proving helpful to the spiritual need of others as well as myself.

At five o'clock on the second morning I thanked my host for his hospitality and left him. I now proceeded due north and, after trudging over snow for nearly ten miles, I came out upon a more or less grass-covered plain. By noon I had arrived near a pond, and there took my midday meal. A survey from that point showed me that I had to cross a sandy desert, which appeared to be larger in extent than the one I had traversed after crossing the Chema Yungdung. The thought of another sand-storm gave me new energy, born of fear, and I made no halt until I had walked quite out of the desert.

AT THE SOURCE OF
THE INDUS

Sven Hedin
(1865–1952)

*Hedin's reputation as the greatest Central Asian explorer is unas-
sailable. Over 40 years he criss-crossed Turkestan and Tibet finaliz-
ing their geography. But, born in Stockholm, he had completed his
education in Berlin and thereafter controversially espoused German
hegemonism. Ruthless treatment of his followers and a vainglorious
estimate of his achievements further alienated opinion. In 1907,
having just reached the Tibetan source of the Brahmaputra, he
sought out the nearby headwaters of the Indus and there betrayed
sentiments that contrast unfavourably with Wood's at the source of
the Oxus.*

I mmediately on my arrival in Khaleb I told the old gova, who had
the hopeless and thankless task of watching my proceedings, that
I now intended to take the road past Singi-kabab, or the source of
the Indus.

"If you go thither, Bombo," he answered, "I shall at once send a
courier to the Garpuns, the two chiefs in Gartok."

"I do not think that the Garpuns will have any objection to my
taking a more northerly route."

"Oh yes, the Garpuns received orders from Lhasa five days ago to
watch carefully that you followed no other way but the great high-
road to Gartok. The Garpuns straightway sent couriers to twelve
different places – Parka, Misser, Purang, Singtod, and others – to
make it known that you were not permitted to travel on byroads. If
this letter had not reached me, I would willingly have let you march
northwards, but now I dare not for my own sake."

"What would you do if I quietly disappeared onc night? I can buy
yaks in Tarchen, and then I shall not be dependent on those I have
from you."

Sven Hedin. From *Central Asia and Tibet Towards the Holy City of Lassa*, London, 1903.

"Yes, of course. A man lives in Tarchen who has sixty yaks, and will sell them as soon as he sees silver money. But I shall at once send word to the Garpuns, and they will send men after you and force you to come back. To buy yaks would therefore be useless waste of money. However, if you like to let the main part of your caravan follow the high-road, and make yourself an excursion of a couple of days northwards to the Singi-kabab, and then join your caravan again, I will put no obstacles in your way. But you do it at your own risk, and you will most certainly be caught before you reach the source of the Indus."

I was as much astonished as delighted by this sudden change in the attitude of the gova, and arranged with Robert that he should lead the main caravan in very short day's marches to Gartok, while I made as rapidly as possible for the source of the Indus. I took only as many things as a small leathern trunk would contain, and as companions only five men, among them Rabsang as interpreter and Adul as cook, with our own six animals and three dogs, one of which, a new purchase, ran away on the first day. I had Robert's small tent, and our arsenal consisted of two guns and a revolver, for robbers were said to make the country very unsafe. I could not find a guide, but on the way to Diri-pu, where I encamped once more, I came across an old man from Tok-jalung, who wished to make the round of Kailas thirteen times, and gave me much valuable information. But no money could induce him to accompany us farther.

On the 8th we continued our way through the valley that runs north-north-eastwards from Diri-pu to the Tseti-la. The stream, divided into many arms, was covered in the night by a thin coating of ice, smooth as glass, where the water had run off, but it disappeared when day came. The valley is broad, and the road showed traces of considerable traffic, though we did not meet a soul. The marmots whistled in front of their holes; the summer would soon be over for them. Kang-rinpoche can be seen from many places, and here pilgrims from the north have piled up cairns. Granite predominates everywhere, but crystalline schists occur here and there. We followed the fresh tracks of three horsemen. The gradient became steeper and the scenery assumed more of an alpine character. We mounted up among huge cones of detritus with babbling brooks of melted snow to the pass, which lay at a height of 18,465 feet. Its plateau is singularly flat. On its northern side camp No. 234 was pitched.

In the evening Rabsang reported that our fuel gatherers had heard whistles, and that these signals had been answered from the other side. The men believed that there were robbers here, and did not dare to sit outside by the fire lest they should be good marks for shots out of an ambush. I quieted them with the assurance that no robber would venture to attack a European, but gave orders to the watchmen to keep an eye on our animals.

The night passed quietly and the minimum temperature went down to 16.2°; autumn was come again into dreary Tibet. I had supposed that the Tseti-la was the pass on the main divide, but we had gone far when we saw its brook, which flowed northwards, make a bend to the west, and descend through a well-defined valley to the Dunglung. It therefore belongs to the catchment basin of the Sutlej and not to the Indus, and the Tseti-la is a pass of secondary order. But we soon reached the actual pass, an extremely flat threshold. Here lies a small muddy lake drained by a brook issuing from its eastern side, which we followed all day. This pass is the Tseti-lachen-la, and it is a water-parting between the Sutlej and the Indus. Its height is less than that of the Tseti-la, for it is only 17,933 feet; it lies on the main chain of the Trans-Himalaya. Kailas, therefore, lies a good day's journey south of the watershed of the two rivers, and belongs entirely to the basin of the Sutlej.

From the lake we follow the little affluent of the Indus north-wards. The ground is marshy and rough. Here and there are seen three hearthstoncs. A dead horse lies among the luxuriant grass. It is singular that no nomads are encamped here. At length we see at a far distance quite down in the valley men going downstream with large flocks of sheep. Tundup Sonam and Ishe are sent after them, and by degrees the rest of us come up with the party. They are nomads from Gertse, who have taken salt to Gyanima and are now transporting barley on their 500 sheep. All the valley is dotted over with white sheep, which trip along actively, plucking the grass as they go. In front of us rises a steep purple mountain chain, and along the flank turned towards us the Indus is said to flow. We joined the men of the sheep caravan and camped together with them. There were five of them, all armed with guns, and they said that the district was frequently haunted by robbers, who at times seemed to vanish altogether, and then suddenly came down like a whirlwind, and no one knew whence they came.

Our camping-ground on the bank of the Indus (16,663 feet) is called Singi-buk. Eastwards the valley is broad and open, but the Indus itself is here an insignificant stream. I was therefore not astonished when I heard that it was only a short day's journey to the source, which, I was told, does not proceed from snow or a glacier, but springs up out of the ground. The men called the river the Singi-tsangpo, or Singi-kamba, and the source itself Singi-kabab, though we afterwards heard the word pronounced Senge more frequently than Singi.

It turned out that one of the five men knew all about us. He was a brother of the Lobsang Tsering on the Dungtse-tso who had sold us three yaks the winter before. It was a singular chance that we should fall in with him. He said he had heard how well we had treated his brother, and offered us his services – for a good reward, of course. As he had travelled several times through this region, quite unknown to Europeans, and was acquainted with all the passes, roads, and valleys, I thought he would be very valuable to me, and I proposed to give him 7 rupees a day, that is about half a month's pay of one of my Ladakis. Of course he accepted the terms at once and soon became our intimate friend.

But these business matters were not yet settled. The man had a quantity of sheep and barley. He consented to let us eight sheep on hire, and sell us their loads, which would last our horses for a week. He was to receive a rupee for the hire of each sheep, which was high, for a sheep is worth only 2 to 3 rupees. The old man would therefore receive 18 rupees every evening as long as he was with us; but it was cheap after all, for the discovery of the source of the Indus was involved.

The large sheep-caravan had already started on September 10, when we, with our new guide, whose own *tsamba* was carried on a ninth sheep, followed in its track. After an hour's march we crossed a tributary, the Lungdep-chu, which comes from a valley in the south-east, with flattish mountains in the background.

A little farther up the Singi-kamba expands into a basin containing an abundance of medium-sized fish. As we passed, the fish were darting upstream in compact shoals, and passed a very shallow place with slight swirls. Here Rabsang attacked them, but all his catch was only one small miserable fish. Then we threw up a dam by the bank, with an opening on one side, and the men went into the water and drove in the fish with shouts and splashing. Then the entrance was built up. After we had repeated this diversion three times, we had procured thirty-seven fine fish, and I was eager for my dinner, which I usually looked forward to with some loathing, for the hard dried mutton had become thoroughly distasteful to me. Our old man, who sat and watched us, thought that we had taken leave of our senses. Farther up, the fish were so crowded in a quiet pool that they made the water seem almost black with their dark backs.

We rode up the valley, leaving on our right a red, loaf-shaped mountain called Lungdep-ningri. Opposite, on the northern side of the valley, were seen two fine Ovis Ammon sheep feeding on a conical elevation. They bore splendid horns, and carried their heads royally. They soon perceived us, and made slowly up the slope. But they paid too much attention to our movements, and did not notice that Tundup Sonam, with his gun on his back, was making a detour to stalk them from the other side of the hill. After a while we heard a shot, and a good hour later, when the camp was pitched, Tundup came back laden with as much of the flesh of his victim as he could carry. Thus we obtained a fresh addition to our somewhat scanty rations, and Tundup's exploit enhanced the glory of this memorable day. In the evening he went off again to fetch more meat, and he brought me the head of the wild sheep, which I wished to preserve as a memento of the day at the source of the Indus.

The ground rises exceedingly slowly. Singi-yüra is a rugged cliff to the north, with a large hole through its summit. Singi-chava is the name of a commanding eminence to the south. Then we made through the outflow of the Munjam valley running in from the south-east. Above this the Indus is only a tiny brook, and part of its water comes from a valley in the south-east, the Bokar. A little later we camp at the aperture of the spring, which is so well concealed that it might easily be overlooked without a guide.

From the mountains on the northern side a flattish cone of detritus, or, more correctly, a slope bestrewn with rubbish, descends to the level, open valley. At its foot projects a slab of white rock with an almost horizontal bedding, underneath which several small springs well up out of the ground, forming weedy pounds and the source stream, which we had traced upwards, and which is the first and uppermost of the headwaters of the mighty Indus. The four largest springs, where they issued from the ground, had temperatures of 48.6°, 49.1°, 49.6°, and 50.4° respectively. They are said to emit the same quantity of water in winter and summer, but a little more after rainy seasons. Up on the slab of rock stand three tall cairns and a small cubical *lhato* containing votive pyramids of clay. And below the *lhato* is a quadrangular *mani*, with hundreds of red flagstones, some covered with fine close inscriptions, some bearing a single character 20 inches high. On two the wheel of life was incised, and on another a divine image, which I carried off as a souvenir of the source of the Indus.

Our guide said that the source Singi-kabab was reverenced because of its divine origin. When travellers reached this place or any other part of the upper Indus, they scooped up water with their hands, drank of it, and sprinkled their faces and heads with it.

Through the investigations made by Montgomerie's pundits in the year 1867 it was known that the eastern arm of the Indus is the actual headwater, and I had afterwards an opportunity of proving by measurement that the western, Gartok, stream is considerably smaller. But no pundit had succeeded in penetrating to the source, and the one who had advanced nearest to it, namely, to a point 30 miles from it, had been attacked by robbers and forced to turn back. Consequently, until our time the erroneous opinion prevailed that the Indus had its source on the north flank of Kailas, and, thanks to those admirable robbers, the discovery of the Indus source was reserved for me and my five Ladakis.

We passed a memorable evening and a memorable night at this important geographical spot, situated 16,946 feet above sea-level. Here I stood and saw the Indus emerge from the lap of the earth. Here I stood and saw this unpretentious brook wind down the valley, and I thought of all the changes it must undergo before it passes between rocky cliffs, singing its roaring song in ever more powerful crescendo, down to the sea at Karachi, where steamers load and unload their cargoes. I thought of its restless course through western Tibet, through Ladak and Baltisan, past Skardu, where the apricot trees nod on its banks, through Dardistan and Kohistan, past Peshawar, and across the plains of the western Panjab, until at last it is swallowed up by the salt waves of the ocean, the Nirvana and the refuge of all weary rivers. Here I stood and wondered whether the Macedonian Alexander, when he crossed the Indus 2200 years ago, had any notion where its source lay, and I revelled in the consciousness that, except the Tibetans themselves, no other human being but myself had penetrated to this spot. Great obstacles had been placed in my way, but Providence had secured for me the triumph of reaching the actual sources of the Brahmaputra and Indus, and ascertaining the origin of these two historical rivers, which, like the claws of a crab, grip the highest of all the mountain systems of the world – the Himalayas. Their waters are born in the reservoirs of the firmament, and they roll down their floods to the lowlands to yield life and sustenance to fifty millions of human beings. Up here white monasteries stand peacefully on their banks, while in India pagodas and mosques are reflected in their waters; up here wolves, wild yaks, and wild sheep, roam about their valleys, while down below in India the eyes of tigers and leopards shine like glowing coals of fire from the jungles that skirt their banks, and poisonous snakes wriggle through the dense brushwood. Here in dreary Tibet icy storms and cold snowfalls lash their waves, while down in the flat country mild breezes whisper in the crowns of the palms and mango trees. I seemed to listen here to the beating of the pulses of these two renowned rivers, to watch the industry and rivalry which, through untold generations, have occupied unnumbered human lives, short and transitory as the life of the midge and the grass; all those wanderers on the earth and guests in the abodes of time, who have been born beside the fleeting current of these rivers, have drunk of their waters, have drawn from them life and strength for their fields, have lived and died on their banks, and have risen from the sheltered freedom of their valleys up to the realms of eternal hope. Not without pride, but still with a feeling of humble thankfulness, I stood there, conscious that I was the first white man who had ever penetrated to the sources of the Indus and Brahmaputra.

EVEREST BY STORM

Edmund Hillary
(1919–)

After decades of failure, the first certain ascent of the world's highest mountain was made in May 1953 by a team of 11 climbers, supported by an army of Nepali porters and commanded by Colonel John Hunt. Planned with military precision, each two-man summit attempt was deemed an "assault", and success a "conquest". In this postcript to the age of exploration, individual endeavour was subordinated to the expeditionary esprit. Hunt himself supported the first "assault", by Tom Bourdillon and Charles Evans, and wrote the account of the whole expedition. The second attempt was made by Edmund Hillary, a New Zealander, and Tenzing Norgay, a Nepali, both distinguished climbers in their own right. Their triumph was recorded by Hillary in an unembellished prose and incorporated in Hunt's official narrative. Hillary subsequently led the New Zealand component in the first overland expedition to the South Pole since Scott's, and travelled extensively in Nepal, where he championed educational and social projects.

O n May 22 we again stared at the Lhotse Face. Despite the possibly grave consequences to the assault plan I had sent Tenzing and Hillary up to Camp VII the day before to give encouragement to the Sherpas in their vital mission and support, if it were needed, to Wylie and Noyce, and we watched in amazement as a whole string of seventeen little dots spread out across that great white expanse, creeping gradually – with painful slowness but moving none the less – in Noyce's footsteps of the day before. As the day wore on, it became obvious that they were going to make it and at long last I was able to put an end to the anxiety and suspense by deciding that the assault should start.

The first assault: Evans and Bourdillon

The weather, having done its best to deter us for five weeks, had suddenly turned fine on May 14, just the day before we had planned to be ready to seize any opportunity we might be given. It had succeeded in delaying our readiness for a week, but miraculously – I can give no other explanatiion – the elements continued to smile upon our struggle. Bourdillon, Evans, Da Namgyal, Ang Tenzing and myself went up to Camp V on the evening of May 22, meeting there on arrival some of the most stalwart of the men who had made this possible by carrying loads to the distant Col that day. Among them were Hillary and Tenzing, who, having left Camp IV only the day before, had climbed to the South Col and were now on their way back to Advance Base from 21, 200 to 26,000 feet and back in thirty hours – not only this, but they must now get ready to follow us in the second assault. These facts speak eloquently of the guts and stamina of these two men.

Using oxygen though we now were, we found it a long, hard climb to the South Col. We spent a restless and anxious night at Camp VII, with the great west wind sweeping across the Face of Lhotse in tremendous gusts which buffeted the tents and seemed intent on uprooting us bodily, tents and all, down the mountain-side. We struggled on upwards next day (May 24) heavily burdened and slowed down by the tiresome breakable crust formed on the snow surface by the wind; no traces remained of the large party which had climbed these slopes only two days before. At about 4 p.m. we at last climbed out of the couloir and stood on the top of the Geneva Spur gazing down at the South Col of Everest, a dismal enough scene. We were also looking for the first time at the final keep of the fortress of Everest, the last 3000 feet of the mountain. This was an awe-inspiring sight. A tall slender snow peak, the South Summit (28,720 feet), rose directly above our heads, incredibly close yet somehow depressingly far above; leading to it was the ridge by which we must climb, running down to the south-east, its angle gentle in places but surprisingly steep in others. To reach it was not going to be easy, for we must climb by one of several steep snow-filled gullies in the South Face, which rises above the Col for over 1000 feet. The peak clear, but a great plume of snow dust was as though appended to it – a banner of cloud which is an almost permanent feature of the mountain.

To reach the surface of the Col you have to descend a slope of some 200 feet, so down we went, with the uncomfortable feeling of going into a trap, for this slope, gentle and innocent as it was, must again be climbed to get back to our comrades and safety, at 26,000 feet and very weary, after making our attempt on the summit. It was a dreary, dread scene. There were the tattered remnants of the Swiss tents set up there last autumn, the bare skeletons of them, all but a few shreds of canvas stripped from them by the westerly wind. Around were scattered remains of equipment, a bleached climbing rope, oxygen frames, odd tins of food. A more comforting sight was the mound of stores carefully weighted down with boulders, which had been carried up for the assault. We dragged out two tents, and set to work to put them up. For the next hour and more we were engaged in a struggle which none of us will ever forget. We were trying to put up just one of those two small tents, fighting with the wind, an invisible enemy which pulled the canvas from our hands and made our task all but impossible. Weak as we were after our climb, deprived now of oxygen, we were hopelessly inadequate for the job. We tripped over the ropes, fell over stones, got in each other's way. In the end the tent was up somehow, just before we became completely exhausted and the sun went down. We scrambled in and, amid a confusion of gear, settled down, utterly weary, for the night.

It had been blowing hard during the night; but the morning of May 25 was not only brilliantly clear, the infamous north-west wind, which had so nearly prevented us from getting into our tents, had died away to a stiff breeze: conditions were as favourable for an assault on the summit as they ever can be on Everest. But we quickly decided that we must wait for another day before essaying it. It will be remembered that Evans and Bourdillon were to make their attempt directly from the Col and for this an early start was essential. We had been far too tired the night before to get ready – and getting ready at 26,000 feet is a slow and exhausting business. There remained much to be done, particularly in preparing our oxygen equipment. Moreover, one of the two Sherpas who were to help me in getting a part of the stores for the highest Camp (IX) up on the south-east ridge was in a bad state of exhaustion and we still hoped he might recover with rest. Despite the drawbacks – a possible turn of the wind or weather against us; using up food and fuel not allowed for in the plan; the risk of our own physical deterioration – we stayed through that day on the Col, resting and getting ready for the morrow. On the 26th after some delay and much anxiety over the functioning of the oxygen equipment, both parties set out – Evans and Bourdillon as summit party and Da Namgyal and I as support party. Ang Tenzing was still sick and we two were fairly heavily laden with a tent, fuel, food, in addition to our own oxygen sets and personal equipment – about 45 lb, each. The two "summiters", with the more powerful oxygen soon pulled ahead of Da Namgyal and myself, as we followed very slowly in their tracks up the snow gully we had chosen to lead us to the south-east ridge. Near the top, the angle of the snow steepened uncomfortably and we had to move away on to a slope of rock and snow on the right. A little higher the slope eased suddenly and we found ourselves beside another pathetic relic of the Swiss Expedition: the frame of a small tent just below the ridge, where Tenzing and Lambert had spent a terrible night without sleeping bags almost exactly a year before, during their splendid effort to reach the top. Here we lay to rest and recover from the ordeal of that climb up the gully, fighting and gasping for air for a while; in my case, though I did not realize it at the time, there was a blockage of ice in the tube of my oxygen set which must have added very considerably to the pain and grief of that day's climb. We were both pretty tired by now but decided to struggle on up the ridge as long as we could. Being short of one of our carrying team I had realized that we should probably not be able to lift the stores for the top camp as high as I had planned – I had always intended to place it much higher than any camp established on Everest before and hoped that this might be at 28,000 feet. Now, without Ang Tenzing, it seemed that the best we could do would be to dump the stores and leave the second assault party with their three Sherpas under Gregory, to carry them still higher. Before leaving, I looked round at the view – on the world, in fact, for we were now climbing on its roof. There was Lhotse, for all its 27,800 odd feet not very much higher than we. Away on the western horizon rose another Himalayan giant, Kangchenjunga, third highest in the world, only 800 feet lower than Everest itself. We must have climbed on for another half-hour or perhaps a bit more (it seemed an eternity) until we found a niche in the crest in the ridge where the loads could safely be placed. Here we built a cairn – the height we now reckon to have been 27,350 feet – and leaving our oxygen bottles for Hillary and Tenzing we started down towards the Swiss camp. Even going downhill now seemed a very great effort; every step had to be carefully considered for we were moving on steep ground and a slip would have been serious. We moved one at a time down the couloir, each safeguarding the other with the rope passed over his ice-axe; as we went down, I was relieved to see figures spread out across the great slopes of the Lhotse Face on their way up to the Col. This was of course the second assault party, who had started forty-eight hours after us because of the exhausting feat of Tenzing and Hillary in accompanying the Sherpas to the South Col only a few days before. Here they were, fitting perfectly into the timing of our own attempt. We were both well-nigh at the end of our tether when we reached the level ice surface of the South Col, and without the wonderful help of Hillary and Tenzing, who had got up ahead of the rest of their party, I doubt whether I should have had the strength to crawl back to the tents.

Meanwhile Evans and Bourdillon were climbing strongly and steadily up the south-east ridge – I had last seen them in a break in the clouds – some 300 feet above us, while we rested near the Swiss tent. But those of us who were now gathering on the Col below could not know this, for the weather was by no means good; it was once again blowing hard and the whole of the upper part of the mountain was obscured by cloud.

It might have been half an hour after Da Namgyal and I had got back – I was resting, I remember, in a tent and chatting with Tenzing – when George Lowe shoved his head in through the narrow entrance. He was wildly excited – jubilant. "They're-up!" he shouted. "By God, they're up!" Everyone was overcome with excitement. The Sherpas, believing the slender snow cone of the South Peak to be the summit itself, were even more thrilled than we ourselves. They thought Evans and Bourdillon had climbed the mountain. I remember Ang Nyima, one of the trio forming Gregory's support party for the second attempt saying to me in slang Hindi, "*Everest khatm ho gya, Sahib,*" which in equally slang English might be translated, "Everest has had it."

But we knew that we must await their return for definite news, for from that South Peak there remained a long stretch of ridge which had never before been seen close at hand; we had many times wondered what Everest held in reserve on this final part of its defences. It was an anxious wait, with the lurking question ever in mind: could they come back safely? We could see nothing through the mists swirling around the mountain, tortured by the rising wind.

Then about 3.30 there was a fleeting break at the lower end of it and there, framed in this gap were two little dots at the head of the gully, some 1300 feet above us. I heaved an immense sigh of relief. At least they were safe. They moved slowly and were obviously very tired, but at last they were back among us, telling us of their wonderful first ascent of the South Peak of Everest – 28,720 feet. That they did not continue along the final ridge to the highest point was exactly in accordance with my briefing, for I had been most anxious that they should not take risks with their experimental oxygen equipment. It must have been a tantalizing situation to be up there at 1 p.m. that day, so near to the fulfilment of a life's dream and yet knowing that they had neither the time nor the oxygen to reach the summit along the formidable alpine ridge they now saw stretching before them. To continue would not have been in the interests of the expedition, and in returning safely they not only made a fine mountaineering decision, but gave us all enormous confidence in final triumph.

The second assault: Hillary and Tenzing (Hillary's narrative)

"By May 22 we had made the first great carry to the South Col and fourteen 30-lb loads of vital food, equipment and oxygen were awaiting our use. As we descended to Camp IV after making this lift, we met Bourdillon, Evans and Hunt setting out up the Lhotse Face to make the first assault on the summit. During the next two days we rested and watched their tiny figures on the Lhotse Face climbing steadily to Camp VII and then on to the South Col.

"It was now time for us to move. On May 25 Tenzing and I supported by Lowe and Gregory moved up to Camp VII. The following day we climbed the steep glacier above the camp and then began to cross the great traverse towards the South Col. From here we got our first glimpse of Evans and Bourdillon on the south-east ridge, obviously moving strongly. Just before we reached the South Col, through a gap in the clouds we saw two tiny specks moving on the South Summit. It was a tremendous moment for us.

"We reached the South Col in time to assist Hunt and Da Namgyal back to their tents after their strenuous efforts in carrying food and equipment to 27,350 feet. Much later in the afternoon, two tired figures descended out of the clouds on the ridge and came slowly down the slope towards the Col. They were Evans and Bourdillon. They told us how they had reached the South Summit, the problems they had been faced with and the difficulties they had had with their oxygen sets. They also reported that the ridge leading to the top appeared to be of considerable difficulty.

"We went to bed that night elated over the success of our companions but not particularly happy about our prospects for the summit. The next day the South Col wind at its worst was blowing and no move upwards was possible. We assisted Bourdillon, Evans, Hunt and Da Namgyal to the top of the Geneva Spur and saw them start off on their long and weary descent to the relative comforts of the lower camps. All night it blew fiercely and although we were ready to leave very early, no start was possible before 8.45 a.m. The high-altitude Sherpas chosen to carry our camp high up the south-east ridge had all fallen ill except Ang Nyma, so there was nothing for it but to carry everything ourselves. Lowe, Gregory and Ang Nyma cut a stairway up the firm, steep snow of the couloir. Tenzing and I followed in these tracks and were able to conserve our strength and make faster time. We caught them up on the south-east ridge near the remnants of the Swiss tent of the previous spring. Despite our large loads we were all going very well. The ridge above, although steep, was generously supplied with foot and hand holds and although we moved slowly up it, we were able to climb steadily and rhythmically, taking every care.

"At 27, 350 feet we came to the dump left by Hunt several days previously and reluctantly tied this extra equipment on to our heavy loads. Ang Nyma had just over 40 lb but the rest of us were carrying between 50 and 63 lb. Moving very slowly now, we hauled ourselves up the ridge, all of us breathing oxygen at the rate of 4 litres a minute. A possible camp site would appear deceptively above us, only to vanish as we reached it. We were all very tired, and indeed a little desperate, when we finally reached a snowy ledge, which although uneven was sufficiently roomy to pitch a tent.

"While Lowe, Gregory and Ang Nyma descended to the South Col, Tenzing and I made a very rough platform, tied our tent down as best we could and crawled in for the night. After a somewhat uncomfortable night, I looked out of the tent very early and was greatly encouraged to see every sign of a fine day. We quickly organized ourselves and at 6.30 a.m. set off up the mountain. The first 500 feet was covered very slowly but steadily. We were going well, and were able to overcome without difficulty any problems we met. But then we reached the great 400-foot face running up to the South Summit, and this was a different proposition. Not only was it very steep but I felt the snow was in a dangerous condition. Laboriously beating a track up it, sometimes to our knees and often deeper, we were always conscious of the tremendous drop to the Kangshung Glacier, 11,000 feet below. Half-way up the slope I asked Tenzing his opinion and he replied that he was rather unhappy about it and thought it very dangerous. When I asked him whether he thought we should go on, he gave his familiar reply: 'Just as you wish.' I felt we had a fair chance so decided to persevere. It was a tremendous relief, however, when, 100 feet from the South Summit, the snow became firm and we were able to kick and chip steps up the last steep slopes on to the South Summit itself.

"We sat down and had a drink from our water bottle. We had been using oxygen at the rate of 3 litres a minute and I estimated that this would give us another four and a half hours on our remaining bottle. The ridge ahead looked both difficult and dangerous, heavily corniced on the right, dropping off to enormous rock bluffs on the left. The only possibility was to keep along the steep snow slope running between them. I cut a line of steps down to the saddle between the South Summit and the ridge and was overjoyed to find that the snow, far from being soft and powdery, was firm and hard and that a couple of good blows with the ice-axe would make a step big enough for even our outsize high-altitude boots. We moved slowly and very carefully. I cut 40 feet of steps, then forced my ice-axe into the snow and belayed Tenzing as he moved up to me. Then he in his turn thrust his ice-axe in and protected me as I cut another 40 feet of steps. Moving one at a time and fully conscious that our margin of safety must inevitably be reduced at this great altitude, we forged slowly ahead.

"After an hour's going the South Summit was dropping away beneath us, but I suddenly noticed that Tenzing, who had been going very well, was starting to drag. When he approached me I saw he was panting and in some distress. I examined his oxygen set and, finding that the exhaust outlet from his mask was blocked with ice, was able to give him immediate relief. We moved on again and soon reached the worst problem on the ridge – a great rock bluff which looked far too difficult to tackle directly with our limited strength. There was one possibility: attached to the right-hand side of the rock bluff was a cornice and the ice had peeled away leaving a gap running the full length of the bluff and just large enough to take the human frame. With Tenzing belaying me I moved into the crack and cramponing on the ice behind and using every handhold on the rock in front I wriggled and jammed my way up and pulled myself panting on to the little ledge at the top. I signalled to Tenzing and heaved on the rope until he in his turn struggled up and collapsed exhausted on our little ledge. I really felt now a fierce determination that we would succeed in reaching the summit.

"The ridge stretched on in a never-ending succession of corniced bumps and as I continued cutting the trail round the back of them I wondered just how long we would have to go on. We were starting to tire. I had been cutting steps continuously for almost two hours and wondered rather dully whether we would have enough strength left to get through. I cut around the back of another hump and saw that the ridge ahead dropped away and that we could see far into Tibet. I looked up and there above us was a rounded snow cone. A few whacks of the ice-axe, a few cautious steps and Tenzing and I were on top. The time was 11.30 a.m.

We stayed fifteen minutes, removing our masks and so conserving oxygen. After an hour we were back on the South Summit; moving gingerly down the great snow slope, we were able to shrug off the sense of fear that had been with us all day. At 2 p.m. we were at Camp IX, where we brewed some lemonade before setting off on the long trek down to the ridge. We were both very tired, but not too tired to make the last effort of cutting steps down the couloir where yesterday's tracks had already been blotted out. On the Col we were greeted by Lowe and Noyce; the latter had come up that day in support with Passang Phutar, both making their second trip to the Col." (*End of Hillary's narrative.*)

We waited at Advance Base in vain for news all through May 29. Gregory had come down with the two remaining Sherpas of his support team and had raised our hopes by telling us that he had seen Hillary and Tenzing at 9 o'clock that morning, just as he had watched Evans and Bourdillon on the 26th, approaching the South Peak and going well. This, the early hour that he had seen them, and the glorious weather, apparently with little wind even higher up, had given us great confidence that they might have made it. But by evening we were in the dark about the outcome. I had asked Noyce, who with three Sherpas had gone up a second time after Evans, Bourdillon and I had come down, either to reinforce or rescue the second assault party, to lay up sleeping bags on a certain snow slope just below the Col visible to us below – "T" would mean success: two bags laid parallel would mean they had reached the South Peak; only one would mean failure. But as evening approached, mists drifted across the Lhotse Face, and we stared in vain at the blanket of vapour behind which Noyce and Passang Phutar had, in fact, placed the signal.

Next morning part of our anxiety was removed when we counted five specks high on the Face coming down. They were all there and all were moving independently – they were safe and well. Soon after 2 p.m. they appeared again, much closer this time, only a few hundred yards up the glacier above our Camp. Most of us, unable to bear the suspense, went up to greet them and hear their news. As they came towards us the returning summit party made no sign, just plodded on dejectedly, obviously very tired. My heart sank – this must be failure; I tried to focus my thoughts on that third effort which we had kept in reserve. Then, when they were quite close, George Lowe, who was leading the little group, started gesticulating, making unmistakable jabs with his ice-axe towards the top of Everest, frowning down above us.

ESCAPE FROM RIYADH

William Gifford Palgrave
(1826–88)

A scholar and a soldier, a Jesuit and a Jew, a French spy and a British ambassador – Palgrave was a man of contradictions, all of them highly compromising when in 1862–3, fortified by Pius IX's blessing and Napoleon III's cash, he attempted the first west–east crossing of the Arabian peninsula. To steely nerves and a genius for disguise he owed his eventual success; but not before both were sorely tested when, as a Syrian doctor, he became the first European to enter Riyadh. The desert capital of the fanatical Wahabis, dangerous for an infidel at the best of times, was then doubly so as the sons of the ageing King Feisal intrigued for power.

W e now prepared to start eastwards, but the day of our departure from Nejed was yet to fix, when a sudden explosion of royal ill-will put an end to our indecision, and necessitated more promptitude than we had hitherto intended for our movements.

In one of my medical cases, the nature of the malady had led me to try that powerful though dangerous therapeutic agent strychnia; and its employment had been followed by prompt and unequivocal amelioration. Not that the amendment was, I should think, of a permanent character, but of this point the Nejdeans, who saw no farther than the present effect, were and could be no judges, while the high rank of the patient himself, an old town chief, drew special attention to the fact. Everybody talked about it, and the news reached the palace.

'Abd-Allah had just paid his compulsory visit to Sa'ood, and the mutual rivalry of the brothers, now the more exasperated by vicinity, was very thinly concealed, or rather not concealed, under the formalities of social politeness. Intrigues, treasons, violence itself, were hatching beneath the palace walls, and assassination, whether by the dagger or the bowl, I had better said the coffee-cup, would have been quite in keeping, nor likely to cause the smallest surprise to any one. Maḥboob, too, always odious to 'Abd-Allah, was at this moment more so than ever, and the minister himself could not fail to foresee his own personal peril when time should place undivided and autocratic power in the hands of one whom he had so often browbeaten and kept in abeyance. Hence he sided with Sa'ood, and by so doing heated the furnace of 'Abd-Allah's evil passions one seven times more than it was wont to be heated. The nobles of the town, the very strangers, all sided with the one or the other of the half-brothers, and though Feyṣul's life, like the silken thread round the monsters in Triermain's "Hall of Fear," yet held the tigers back, it might not suffice to restrain some sudden and especially some secret spring.

Now 'Abd-Allah in the course of his amateur lectures had learnt enough to know the poisonous qualities of various drugs, and of strychnine in particular; and though probably unacquainted with the exploits of European criminals, was fully capable of giving them a rival in the East. The cure, or at least the relief, just alluded to, had occurred about the 16th of November, exactly at the time when I had given him to understand our definite refusal of his offers, and when he was in consequence somewhat uncertain what course next to follow. A day or two after he sent for me, expressed his regret at our resolution to quit the capital, and begged that we would at least leave behind us in his keeping some useful medicines for the public benefit, and above all that we would entrust him with that powerful drug whose sanitary effects were now the subject of general admiration.

All that I could say about the uselessness, nay, the great danger, of pharmacy in unlearned hands, was rejected as a mere and insufficient pretext. At last, after much urging, the prince ended by saying that for the other ingredients I might omit them if I chose, but that the strychnine he must have, and that though at the highest price I might fancy to name.

His real object was perfectly clear, nor could I dream of lending a hand, however indirect, to his diabolical designs, nor did I see any way open before me but that of a firm though polite denial. In pursuance, I affected not to suspect his projects, and insisted on the dangerous character of the alkaloid, till he gave up the charge for the moment, and I left the palace.

Next day he renewed his demands, but to no purpose. A third meeting took place; it was the 19th or 20th of the month. Beckoning me to his side, he insisted in the most absolute manner on having the poison in his possession, and at last, laying aside all pretences, made clear the reasons, though not the person for whom he desired it, and declared that he would admit of no excuse, conscientious or otherwise.

He was at the moment sitting in the further end of the Ḳ'hāwah, and I was close by him; while between us and the attendants there present, enough space remained to prevent their catching our conversation, if held in an undertone. I looked round to assure myself that we could not be overheard, and when a flat denial on my part had been met by an equally flat rejection and a fresh demand, I turned right towards him, lifted up the edge of his head-dress, and said in his ear, "'Abd-Allah, I know well what you want the poison for, and I have no mind to be an accomplice in your crimes. You shall *never* have it."

His face became literally black and swelled with rage; I never saw so perfect a demon before or after. A moment he hesitated in silence, then mastered himself, and suddenly changing voice and tone began to talk gaily about indifferent subjects. After a few minutes he rose, and I returned home.

There Aboo-'Eysa, Barakāt, and myself immediately held council to consider what was now to be done. That an outbreak must shortly take place seemed certain; to await it was dangerous, yet we could not safely leave the town in an overprecipitate manner, nor without some kind of permission. We resolved together to go on in quiet and caution a few days more, to sound the court, make our adieus at Feyṣul's palace, get a good word from Maḥboob (no difficult matter), and then slip off without attracting too much notice. But our destiny was not to run so smoothly.

On the evening of the 21st we were sitting up late, talking over the needful preparations of the journey, and drinking coffee with a few good-natured townsmen, who had no objection to a contraband smoke; a practice for which our dwelling had long since become famous or infamous, when a rap at the door announced 'Abd-Allah – not the prince, but his namesake and confidential retainer. "What brings you here at this hour of the night?" said we, not overpleased at the honour of his visit.

"The king" (for such is in common Ri'aḍ parlance the title given to the heir-apparent) "sends for you; come with me at once," was his short and sharp answer. "Shall Barakāt come with me?" said I, looking towards my companion. "The king wants you alone," replied the messenger. "Shall I bring one of my books along with me?" "There is no need." "Wait a few minutes while we get a cup of coffee ready for you."

This last offer could not in common decency be refused. While the ceremony was in performance, I found time to exchange a few words with Aboo-'Eysa and Barakāt. They agreed to dismiss the guests, and to remain on the alert for the result of this nocturnal embassy, easily foreseen to be a threatening one, perhaps dangerous. Yet the fact of my companion's not being also sent for, seemed to me a guarantee against immediate peril.

The royal messenger and myself then left the house, and proceeded in silence and darkness through the winding streets to the palace of 'Abd-Allah. Arrived there, a short parley ensued between my conductor and the guards, who then resumed their post, while the former passed on to give the prince notice, leaving me to cool myself for a minute or two in the night air of the courtyard. A negro then came out, and beckoned me to enter.

The room was dark, there was no other light than that afforded by the flickering gleams of the firewood burning on the hearth. At the further end sat 'Abd-Allah, silent and gloomy; opposite to him on the other side was 'Abd-el-Lateef, the successor of the Wahhābee, and a few others, Zelators, or belonging to their party. Maḥboob was seated by 'Abd-el-Lateef, and his presence was the only favourable circumstance discernible at a first glance. But he too looked unusually serious. At the other end of the long hall were a dozen armed attendants, Nejdeans or negroes.

When I entered, all remained without movement or return of greeting. I saluted 'Abd-Allah, who replied in an undertone and gave me a signal to sit down at a little distance from him but on the same side of the divan. My readers may suppose that I was not at the moment ambitious of too intimate a vicinity.

After an interval of silence, 'Abd-Allah turned half round towards me, and with his blackest look and a deep voice said, "I now know perfectly well what you are; you are no doctors, you are Christians, spies, and revolutionists ('mufsideen') come hither to ruin our religion and state on behalf of those who sent you. The penalty for such as you is death, that you know, and I am determined to inflict it without delay."

"Threatened folks live long," thought I, and had no difficulty in showing the calm which I really felt. So looking him coolly in the face, I replied, "Istaghfir Allah," literally, "Ask pardon of God." This is the phrase commonly addressed to one who has said something extremely out of place.

The answer was unexpected; he started, and said, "Why so?"

"Because," I rejoined, "you have just now uttered a sheer absurdity. 'Christians,' be it so; but 'spies,' 'revolutionists,' – as if we were not known by everybody in your town for quiet doctors, neither more nor less! And then to talk about putting me to death! You cannot, and you dare not."

"But I can and dare," answered 'Abd-Allah, "and who shall prevent me? you shall soon learn that to your cost."

"Neither can nor dare," repeated I. "We are here your father's guests and yours for a month and more, known as such, received as such. What have we done to justify a breach of the laws of hospitality in Nejed? It is impossible for you to do what you say," continued I, thinking the while that it was a great deal too possible after all; "the obloquy of the deed would be too much for you."

He remained a moment thoughtful, then said, "As if any one need know who did it. I have the means, and can dispose of you without talk or rumour. Those who are at my bidding can take a suitable time and place for that, without my name being ever mentioned in the affair."

The advantage was now evidently on my side; I followed it up, and said with a quiet laugh, "Neither is that within your power. Am I not known to your father, to all in his palace? to your own brother Sa'ood among the rest? Is not the fact of this my actual visit to you known without your gates? Or is there no one here?" added I, with a glance at Maḥboob, "who can report elsewhere what you have just now said? Better for you to leave off this nonsense; do you take me for a child of four days old?"

He muttered a repetition of his threat. "Bear witness, all here present," said I, raising my voice so as to be heard from one end of the room to the other, "that if any mishap befalls my companion or myself from Ri'aḍ to the shores of the Persian Gulf, it is all 'Abd-Allah's doing. And the consequences shall be on his head, worse consequences than he expects or dreams."

The prince made no reply. All were silent; Maḥboob kept his eyes steadily fixed on the fireplace; 'Abd-el-Laṭeef looked much and said nothing.

"Bring coffee," called out 'Abd-Allah to the servants. Before a minute had elapsed, a black slave approached with one and only one coffee-cup in his hand. At a second sign from his master he came before me and presented it.

Of course the worst might be conjectured of so unusual and solitary a draught. But I thought it highly improbable that matters should have been so accurately prepared; besides, his main cause of anger was precisely the refusal of poisons, a fact which implied that he had none by him ready for use. So I said, "Bismillah," took the cup, looked very hard at 'Abd-Allah, drank it off, and then said to the slave, "Pour me out a second." This he did; I swallowed it, and said, "Now you may take the cup away."

The desired effect was fully attained. 'Abd-Allah's face announced defeat, while the rest of the assembly whispered together. The prince turned to 'Abd-el-Lateef and began talking about the dangers to which the land was exposed from spies, and the wicked designs of infidels for ruining the kingdom of the Muslims. The Ḳaḍee and his companions chimed in, and the story of a pseudo-darweesh traveller killed at Ḍerey'eeyah, and of another (but who he was I cannot fancy; perhaps a Persian, who had, said 'Abd-Allah, been also recognized for an intriguer, but had escaped to Mascat, and thus baffled the penalty due to his crimes), were now brought forward and commented on. Maḥboob now at last spoke, but it was to ridicule such apprehensions. "The thing is in itself unlikely," said he, "and were it so, what harm could they do?" alluding to my companion and myself.

On this I took up the word, and a general conversation ensued, in which I did my best to explode the idea of spies and spymanship, appealed to our own quiet and inoffensive conduct, got into a virtuous indignation against such a requital of evil for good after all the services which we had rendered court and town, and quoted verses of the Coran regarding the wickedness of ungrounded suspicion, and the obligation of not judging ill without clear evidence. 'Abd-Allah made no direct answer, and the others, whatever they may have thought, could not support a charge abandoned by their master.

What amused me not a little was that the Wahhābee prince had after all very nearly hit the right nail on the head, and that I was snubbing him only for having guessed too well. But there was no help for it, and I had the pleasure of seeing, that though at heart unchanged in his opinion about us, he was yet sufficiently cowed to render a respite certain, and our escape thereby practicable.

This kind of talk continued awhile, and I purposely kept my seat, to show the unconcern of innocence, till Maḥboob made me a sign that I might safely retire. On this I took leave of 'Abd-Allah and quitted the palace unaccompanied. It was now near midnight, not a light to be seen in the houses, not a sound to be heard in the streets, the sky too was dark and overcast, till, for the first time, a feeling of lonely dread came over me, and I confess that more than once I turned my head to look and see if no one was following with "evil," as Arabs say, in his hand. But there was none, and I reached the quiet alley and low door where a gleam through the chinks announced the anxious watch of my companions, who now opened the entrance, overjoyed at seeing me back sound and safe from so critical a parley.

Our plan for the future was soon formed. A day or two we were yet to remain in Ri'aḍ, lest haste should seem to imply fear, and thereby encourage pursuit. But during that period we would avoid the palace, out-walks in gardens or after nightfall, and keep at home as much as possible. Meanwhile Aboo-'Eysa was to get his dromedaries ready, and put them in a courtyard immediately adjoining the house, to be laden at a moment's notice.

A band of travellers was to leave Ri'aḍ for Ḥaṣa a few days later. Aboo-'Eysa gave out publicly that he would accompany them to Hofhoof, while we were supposed to intend following the northern or Sedeyr track, by which the Nā'ib, after many reciprocal farewells and assurances of lasting friendship, should we ever meet again, had lately departed. Mobeyreek, a black servant in Aboo-'Eysa's pay, occupied himself diligently in feeding up the camels for their long march with clover and vetches, both abundant here; and we continued our medical avocations, but quietly, and without much leaving the house. At the palace all were busy about the departure of the Ḥareeḳ contingent, which now set out on its 'Oneyzah way by Shaḳra', but marched, contrary to expectation, without 'Abd-Allah, that prince reserving himself for the arrival of the artillery, which was daily expected from Ḥaṣa, under the charge of Moḥammed es-Sedeyree. Amid all this movement and bustle no particular enquiry was made after us; the tempest had been followed by a lull, and it was ours to take advantage of this interval before a new and a worse outburst.

During the afternoon of the 24th we brought three of Aboo-'Eysa's camels into our courtyard, shut the outer door, packed and laded. We then awaited the moment of evening prayer; it came, and the voice of the Mu'eḍḍineen summoned all good Wahhābees, the men of the town-guard not excepted, to the different mosques. When about ten minutes had gone by, and all might be supposed at their prayers, we opened our door. Mobeyreek gave a glance up and down the street to ascertain that no one was in sight, and we led out the camels. Aboo-'Eysa accompanied us. Avoiding the larger thoroughfares, we took our way by bye-lanes and side passages towards a small town-gate, the nearest to our house, and opening on the north. A late comer fell in with us on his way to the Mesjid, and as he passed summoned us also to the public service. But Aboo-'Eysa unhesitatingly replied, "We have this moment come from prayers," and our interlocutor, fearing to be himself too late, and thus to fall under reprehension and punishment, rushed off to the nearest oratory, leaving the road clear. Nobody was in watch at the gate. We crossed its threshold, turned south-east, and under the rapid twilight reached a range of small hillocks, behind which we sheltered ourselves till the stars came out, and the "wing of night," to quote Arab poets, spread black over town and country.

We drew a long breath, like men just let out of a dungeon, and thanked heaven that this much was over. Then, after the first hour of night had gone over, and chance passers-by had ceased, and left us free from challenge and answer, we lighted our camp-fire, drank a most refreshing cup of coffee, set our pipes to work, and laughed in our turn at 'Abd-Allah and Feyṣul.

So far so good. But further difficulties remained before us. It was now more than ever absolutely essential to get clear of Nejed unobserved, to put the desert between us and the Wahhābee court and capital; and no less necessary was it that Aboo-'Eysa, so closely connected as he was with Ri'aḍ and its government, should seem nohow implicated in our unceremonious departure, nor any way concerned with our onward movements. In a word, an apparent separation of paths between him and us was necessary, before we could again come together and complete the remainder of our explorations.

In order to manage this, and while ensuring our own safety to throw a little dust in Wahhābee eyes, it was agreed that before next morning's sunrise Aboo-'Eysa should return to the town, and to his dwelling, as though nothing had occurred, and should there await the departure of the great merchant caravan, mentioned previously, and composed mainly of men from Ḥaṣa and Ḳaṭeef, now bound for Hofhoof under the guidance of Aboo-Ḍahir-el-Ghannām. This assemblage was expected to start within three days at latest. Meanwhile our friend should take care to show himself openly in the palaces of Feyṣul and 'Abd-Allah, and if asked about us should answer vaguely, with the off-hand air of one who had no further care regarding us. We ourselves should in the interim make the best of our way, with Mobeyreek for guide, to Wadi Soley', and there remain concealed in a given spot, till Aboo-'Eysa should come and pick us up.

All this was arranged; at break of dawn Aboo-'Eysa took his leave, and Barakāt, Mobeyreek, and myself, were once more high perched on our dromedaries, their heads turned to the south-east, keeping the hillock range between us and Ri'aḍ, which we saw no more. Our path led us over low undulating ground, a continuation of Wadi Ḥaneefah, till after about four hours' march we were before the gates of Manfooḥah, a considerable town, surrounded by gardens nothing inferior in extent and fertility to those of Ri'aḍ; but its fortifications, once strong, have long since been dismantled and broken down by the jealousy of the neighbouring capital. In point of climate this town is preferable to Ri'aḍ, because situated on higher ground, and above the damp mists which often gather in the depths of the Wadi; but in a military view it is inferior to the capital, because in a more exposed and less easily guarded position. Passing Manfooḥah without entering it, our road dipped down again, and we found ourselves in Wadi Soley', a long valley, originating in the desert between Ḥareek and Yemāmah, and running far to the north.

After winding here and there, we reached the spot assigned by Aboo-'Eysa for our hiding-place. It was a small sandy depth, lying some way off the beaten track, amid hillocks and brushwood, and without water: of this latter article we had taken enough in the goat-skins to last us for three days. Here we halted, and made up our minds to patience and expectation.

Two days passed drearily enough. We could not but long for our guide's arrival, nor be wholly without fear on more than one score. Once or twice a stray peasant stumbled on us, and was much surprised at our encampment in so droughty a locality. Sometimes leaving our dromedaries crouching down, and concealed among the shrubs, we wandered up the valley, climbed the high chalky cliffs of Ṭoweyḳ, to gain a distant glimpse of the blue sierra of Ḥareek in the far south, and the white ranges of Ṭoweyḳ north and east. Or we dodged the numerous nor over-shy herds of gazelles, not for any desire of catching them, but simply to pass the time, and distract the mind weary of conjecture. So the hours went by, till the third day brought closer expectation and anxiety, still increasing while the sun declined, and at last went down; yet nobody appeared. But just as darkness closed in, and we were sitting in a dispirited group beside our little fire, for the night air blew chill, Aboo-'Eysa came suddenly up, and all was changed for question and answer, for cheerfulness and laughter.

DESERT DAYS

Charles Montagu Doughty
(1843–1926)

*During two years (1875–7) wandering in Central Arabia Doughty
broke little new ground; dependent on desert charity, his achievement was simply to have survived. Yet his book,* Arabia Deserta, *was
instantly recognized as a classic. Its eccentric prose proves well
suited to that minute observation and experience of Bedouin life
which was Doughty's main contribution to exploration. T. E.
Lawrence called it "a bible of a kind"; both syntax and subject
matter have biblical resonances, as in this description of a day's
march, or* ráhla.

I f the ráhla be short the Beduw march at leisure, the while their
beasts feed under them. The sheykhs are riding together in
advance, and the hareem come riding in their trains of baggage-
camels; if aught be amiss the herdsmen are nigh at hand to help
them: neighbours will dismount to help neighbours and even a
stranger. The great and small cattle are driven along with their
households. You shall see housewives dismount, and gossips walk
on together barefoot (all go here unshod,) and spinning beside their
slow-pacing camels. But say the Beduin husbands, "We would have
the hareem ride always and not weary themselves, for their tasks
are many at home." The Fukara women alighted an hour before
noon, in the march, to milk their few ewes and goats. Every family
and kindred are seen wayfaring by themselves with their cattle.
The Aarab thus wandering are dispersed widely; and in the vast
uneven ground (the most plain indeed but full of crags), although
many hundreds be on foot together, commonly we see only those
which go next about us. The Beduins coming near a stead where
they will encamp, Zeyd returned to us; and where he thought
good there struck down the heel of his tall horseman's lance

Sketch of the tents used by the desert people, the Sehamma Aarab.
From *Travels in Arabia Deserta*, London, 1943.

shelfa or *romhh*, stepping it in some sandy desert bush: this is the standard of Zeyd's fellowship, – they that encamp with him, and are called his people. Hirfa makes her camel kneel; she will "build" the booth there: the rest of Zeyd's kindred and clients coming up, they alight, each family going a little apart, to pitch their booths about him. This is "Zeyd's menzil" and the people are Zeyd's Aarab. The bearing-camels they make to kneel under their burdens with the guttural voice, *ikh–kh–kh!* The stiff neck of any reluctant brute is gently stricken down with the driving-stick or an hand is imposed upon his heavy halse; any yet resisting is plucked by the beard; then without more he will fall groaning to his knees. Their loads discharged, and the pack-saddles lifted, with a spurn of the master's foot the bearing-camels rise heavily again and are dismissed to pasture. The housewives spread the tent-cloths, taking out the corner and side-cords; and finding some wild stone for a hammer, they beat down their tent-pegs into the ground, and under-setting the tent-stakes or "pillars" (*am'dàn*) they heave and stretch the tent-cloth: and now their booths are standing. The wife enters, and when she has bestowed her stuff, she brings forth the man's breakfast; that is a bowl of léban, poured from the sour milk-skin, or it is a clot of dates and buttermilk with a piece of sweet butter. After that she sits within, rocking upon her knees the *semîla* or sour milk-skin, to make this day's butter.

As Zeyd so is every principal person of these Beduins, the chief of a little menzil by itself: the general encampment is not disposed (as is the custom of the northern Aarab) in any formal circuit. The nomads of these marches pitch up and down in all the "alighting place" at their own pleasure. The Fejîr or Fukara never wandered in *ferjàn* (*j* for *k* guttural) or nomad hamlets, dispersedly after their kindreds, which is everywhere the nomad manner, for the advantage of pasture; but they journey and encamp always together. And cause was that, with but half-friends, and those mostly outraged upon their borders, or wholly enemies, there were too many reckonings required of them; and their country lies open. Zeyd's Aarab were six booths: a divorced wife's tent, mother of his young and only son, was next him; then the tent of another cast-off housewife, mother of a ward of his, *Settàm*, and by whom he had himself a daughter; and besides these, (Zeyd had no near kinsfolk,) a camel-herd with the old hind his father, of Zeyd's father's time, and the shepherd, with their alliance. Forlorn persons will join themselves to some sheykh's menzil, and there was with us an aged widow, in wretchedness, who played the mother to her dead daughter's fatherless children, a son so deformed that like a beast he crept upon the sand [*ya latîf,* "oh happy sight!" said this most poor and desolate grandam, with religious irony, in her patient sighing] – and an elf-haired girl wonderfully foul-looking. Boothless, they led their lives under the skies of God, the boy was naked as he came into the desert world. The camel upon which they rode was an oblation of the common charity; but what were their daily food only that God knoweth which feedeth all life's creatures. There is no Beduwy so impious that will chide and bite at such, his own tribesfolk, or mock those whom God has so sorely afflicted; nor any may repulse them wheresoever they will alight in the common wilderness soil. Sometimes there stood a stranger's booth among us, of nomad passengers or an household in exile from the neighbour tribesmen: such will come in to pitch by a sheykh of their acquaintance.

Hirfa ever demanded of her husband toward which part should "the house" be built. "Dress the face, Zeyd would answer, to this part," showing her with his hand the south, for if his booth's face be all day turned to the hot sun there will come in fewer young loitering and parasitical fellows that would be his coffee-drinkers. Since the sheukh, or heads, alone receive their tribe's surra, it is not much that they should be to the arms coffee-hosts. I have seen Zeyd avoid as he saw them approach, or even rise ungraciously upon such men's presenting themselves, (the half of every booth, namely the men's side, is at all times open, and any enters there that will, in the free desert,) and they murmuring he tells them, wellah, his affairs do call him forth, adieu, he must away to the mejlis, go they and seek the coffee elsewhere. But were there any sheykh with them, a coffee lord,

Zeyd could not honestly choose but abide and serve them with coffee; and if he be absent himself, yet any sheykhly man coming to a sheykh's tent, coffee must be made for him, except he gently protest, "billah, he would not drink." Hirfa, a sheykh's daughter and his nigh kinswoman, was a faithful mate to Zeyd in all his sparing policy.

Our menzil now standing, the men step over to Zeyd's coffee-fire, if the sheykh be not gone forth to the mejlis to drink his mid-day cup there. A few gathered sticks are flung down beside the hearth: with flint and steel one stoops and strikes fire in tinder, he blows and cherishes those seeds of the cheerful flame in some dry camel-dung, sets the burning sherd under dry straws, and powders over more dry camel-dung. As the fire kindles, the sheykh reaches for his *dellàl*, coffee-pots, which are carried in the *fatya*, coffee-gear basket; this people of a nomad life bestow each thing of theirs in a proper *beyt*, it would otherwise be lost in their daily removing. One rises to go fill up the pots at the water-skins, or a bowl of water is handed over the curtain from the woman's side; the pot at the fire, Hirfa reaches over her little palm-full of green coffee-berries. We sit in a half ring about the hearth; there come in perhaps some acquaintance or tribesmen straying between the next menzils. Zeyd prepared coffee at the hours; afterward, when he saw in me little liking of his coffee-water, he went to drink the cup abroad; if he went not to the mejlis, he has hidden himself two or three hours like an owl, or they would say as a dog, in my little close tent, although intolerably heated through the thin canvas in the mid-day sun. It was a mirth to see Zeyd lie and swelter, and in a trouble of mind bid us report to all comers that 'Zeyd was from home': and where his elvish tribesmen were merry as beggars to detect him. *Mukkarîn el-Beduw*! "the nomads (say the settled Arabs) are full of wily evasions."

The sheykhs and principal persons assemble at the great sheykh's or another chief tent, when they have alighted upon any new camping-ground; there they drink coffee, the most holding yet the camel-stick, *mishaab, mehján* or *bakhorra*, as a sceptre, (a usage of the ancient world,) in their hands. The few first questions among them are commonly of the new dispositions of their several menzils: as, "*Rahŷel*! (the sheykh's brother), *fen ahl-ak?* where be thy people (pitched)? – *Eth-Therrŷeh* (the sheykh's son), *fen ahl-ak?* – *Mehsan* (a good simple man, and who had married Zeyd's only sister,) – *Khálaf* and the rest, where be your menzils? – Zeyd is not here! who has seen Zeyd? – and *Mijwel*, where are his Aarab?" for every new march displaces these nomads, and few booths in the shortness of the desert horizon are anywhere in sight. You see the Beduins silent whilst coffee is being made ready, for all their common talk has been uttered an hundred times already, and some sit beating the time away and for pastime limning with their driving-sticks in the idle sand. They walk about with these gay sticks, in the daytime: but where menzils are far asunder, or after nightfall, they carry the sword in their hands: the sword is suspended with a cord from the shoulder. The best metal is the Ajamy, a little bent with a simple crossed hilt (beautiful is the form), wound about with metal wire; next to the Persian they reckon the Indian blade, *el-Hindy*.

In nomad ears this word, Aarab, signifies "the people". Beduin passengers when they meet with herdsmen in the desert enquire, *Fen el-Aarab*? "where is the folk?" Of the multitude of nomad tribes east and west, they say in plural wise, *el-Arbân*. This other word, Beduin, received into all our languages, is in the Arabian speech Bedùwy, that is to say inhabitant of the waste, (*bâdia*,) in the plural Bedaùwy (*aù* dipth.), but commonly *él-Bèduw*. As we sit, the little cup, of a few black drops, is served twice round. When they have swallowed those boiling sips of coffee-water, and any little news has been related among them, the men rise one after other to go home over the hot sand: all are barefoot, and very rarely any of those Aarab has a pair of sandals. So every one is come again to his own, they say the mid-day prayers; and when they have breakfasted, they will mostly slumber out the sultry mid-day hours in their housewife's closed apartment. I have asked an honest wife, "How may your lubbers slug out these long days till evening?" and she answered, demurely smiling, "How, sir, but in solace with the hareem!"

The héjra, or small flitting-tent, laid out by the housewife, with its cords stretched to the pins upon the ground, before the am'dàn or props be set up under, is in this form: to every pair of cords, is a pair of stakes; there are three stakes to every pair of cords in the waist of the tent. Greater booths are stayed by more pairs of waist-cords, and stand upon taller staves. The Aarab tent, which they call the *beyt* [pl. *byût*] *es-shaar*, "abode, booth, or house of hair," that is of black worsted or hair-cloth, has, with its pent roof, somewhat the form of a cottage. The tent-stuff, strong and rude, is defended by a list sewed under at the heads of the am'dàn, and may last out, they say, a generation, only wearing thinner; but when their roof-cloth is thread-bare it is a feeble shelter, thrilled by the darting beams of the Arabian sun, and casting only a grey shadow. The Arabian tent strains strongly upon all the staves and in good holding ground, may resist the boisterous blasts which happen at the crises of the year, especially in some deep mountainous valleys. Even in weak sand the tents are seldom overblown. Yet the cords, *tunb el-beyt*, which are worsted-twist of the women's spinning, oft-times burst: who therefore (as greater sheykhs) can spend silver, will have them of hempen purchased in the town. In all the road tribes they every year receive rope, with certain clothing and utensils, on account of their haj surra. The tent-stuff is seamed of narrow lengths of the housewives' rude worsted weaving; the yarn is their own spinning, of the mingled wool of the sheep and camels' and goats' hair together. Thus it is that the cloth is blackish: we read in the Hebrew Scripture, "Black as the tents of Kedar." Good webster-wives weave in white borders made of their sheep's wool, or else of their gross-spun cotton yarn (the cotton wool is purchased from Medina or the sea coast).

When the tent-cloth is stretched upon the stakes, to this roof they hang the tent-curtains, often one long skirt-cloth which becomes the walling of the nomad booth: the selvedges are broached together with wooden skewers. The booth front is commonly left open, to the half at least we have seen, for the *mukaad* or men's sitting-room: the other which is the women's and household side, is sometimes seen closed (when they would not be espied, whether sleeping or cooking) with a fore-cloth; the woman's part is always separated from the men's apartment by a hanging, commonly not much more than breast or neck high, at the waist poles of the tent. The mukaad is never fenced in front with a tent-cloth, only in rain they incline the am'dàn and draw down the tent eaves lower. The nomad tents are thus very ill lodging, and the Beduins, clothed no better than the dead, suffer in cold and stormy weather. In winter they sometimes load the back-cloth ground-hem with great stones, and fence their open front at the men's side with dry bushes. The tent side-cloths can be shifted according to the wind and sun: thus the back of the Beduin booth may become in a moment the new front. A good housewife will bethink herself to unpin and shift the curtain, that her husband's guests may have shadow and the air, or shelter.

Upon the side of the hareem, that is the household apartment, is stored all their husbandry. At the woman's curtain stand the few tent-cloth sacks of their poor baggage, *él-gush*: in these is bestowed their corn and rice if they have any; certain lumps of rock-salt, for they will eat nothing insipid; also the housewife's thrift of wool and her spun yarn, – to be a good wool-wife is honourable among Aarab women; and some fathoms perhaps of new calico. There may be with the rest a root of *er'n* or tan wood, the scarlet chips are steeped in water, and in two or three days, between ráhlas, they cure therein their goat-skins for girbies and semílies, besides the leather for watering-buckets, watering-troughs, and other nomad gear. The poorest wife will have some box, (commonly a fairing from the town,) in which are laid up her few household medicines, her comb and her mirror, *mèrguba*, her poor inherited ornaments, the ear-rings and nose-ring of silver or even golden (from the former generations); and with these any small things of her husband's, (no pockets are made in their clothing,) which she has in her keeping. But if her good-man be of substance, a sheykh of surra, for his bundle of reals and her few precious things she has a locked coffer painted with vermilion from Medina, which in the ráhla is trussed (also a mark of sheykhly estate) upon her bearing-camel. – Like to this I have mused, might be that ark of things sacred to the public religion, which was in the nomad life of B. Israel.

Commonly the housewife's key of her box is seen as a glitter-ing pendant, upon her veil backward; and hangs, with her thimble and pincers, (to pluck the thorns out of their bare soles,) by a gay scarlet lace, from the circlet of the head-band. Their clotted dates, if they have any, are stived in heavy pokes of camel-hide, that in the ráhla are seen fluttering upon the bearing-cattle with long thongs of leather. This apparel of fringes and tassels is always to the Semitic humour; of the like we read in Moses, and see them in the antique Jewish sculptures. Of their old camel sack-leather, moisty with the juice of the dates, they cut the best sandals. The full-bellied sweating water-skins are laid, not to fret at the ground, upon fresh sprays of broom or other green in the desert; amongst all stands the great brazen pot, *jidda*, tinned within by the nomad smith, or by the artificer in their market village. They boil in it their butter, (when they have any, to make samn,) and their few household messes; they seethe the guest-meal therein in the day of hospitality.

The Aarab *byût shaar* are thus tents of haircloth made housewise. The "houses of hair" accord with that sorry landscape! Tent is the Semitic house: their clay house is built in like manner; a public hall for the men and guests, and an inner woman's and household apartment. Like to this was Moses' adorned house of the nomad God in the wilderness. Also the firmament, in the Hebrew prophet, is a tabernacle of the one household of God's creation. These flitting-houses in the wilderness, dwelt in by robbers, are also sanctuaries of "God's guests," *theûf Ullah*, the passengers and who they be that haply alight before them. Perilous rovers in the field, the herdsmen of the desert are kings at home, fathers of hospitality to all that seek to them for the night's harbour. "Be we not all, say the poor nomads, *guests of Ullah*?" Has God given unto them, God's guest shall partake with them thereof: if they will not for God render His own, it should not go well with them. The guest entered, and sitting down amongst them, they observe an honourable silence, asking no untimely questions, (such is school and nurture of the desert,) until he have eaten or drunk somewhat at the least, and by "the bread and salt" there is peace established between them, for a time (that is counted two nights and the day in the midst, whilst their food is in him). Such is the golden world and the "assurance of Ullah" in the midst of the wilderness: travelled Beduins are amazed to see the sordid inhospitality of the towns; – but where it were impossible that the nomad custom should hold.

THE POINT OF RETURN

Harry St John Bridger Philby
(1885–1960)

By 1930 the Rubh al Khali, the desolate "Empty Quarter" of southern Arabia, was the only sizeable wilderness which still defied exploration. "Jack" Philby, a rugged individualist, had long set his sights on it. He travelled widely in Arabia, forsook British employ to serve under King ibn Saud of Riyadh, and converted to Islam. But when permission was at last given, it coincided with news that Bertram Thomas, another Briton, had just completed the first crossing. Philby was heartbroken. Asserting that Thomas had chosen the shortest south-north route, in 1932 he set off from the Gulf for Shanna on Thomas's route, and then headed west into the unknown. His followers were horrified, not least because Philby insisted on travelling by day so as to conduct observations. Later evidence showed that, had he not accepted defeat, he would certainly have been murdered. A second attempt fared better, and he became the first to make an east-west crossing of the "Empty Quarter".

W e began the fourth day's march under a sense of combined strain and expectation. During the night the abandonment of our enterprise had been seriously canvassed and my lack of sympathy with our strained camels provided Farraj with an opportunity to read me a lecture. If your beast is well, said he, then you are well; but if she wilts, then you wilt. Very true, I said, but it is you folk that think not twice of increasing the strain. We have to cross this Empty Quarter, and I but ride straight on, neither thinking of retreat nor thinking of diversion. But look for instance at Zayid and Salih, who rode off just now on the trail of an Oryx. All day they may ride their beasts after their quarry and return at nightfall unsuccessful, disheartened and tired. Then they will chide me for my obstinacy and want to return to water. That is always your way.

Soon after starting on the day's march and just passing from the Abal Khadhim tract into the very similar bare rolling country of Hadhat al Qata – indeed the only difference was the scanty appearance of *Hadh* amidst the *Abal* and *Alaq* – we had come upon the tracks of four Oryx, and our men lusted to be off after them. Zayid drew up to me with a cringing request for permission to follow up the tracks, and I was glad enough to think that I might have some hours free of his company. To Salih I replied that he could please himself, and off the pair went at a steady walk which soon took them out of sight on our flank. 'Ali had unsuccessfully pleaded for similar liberty. Look you, he had said untruthfully, we have come to the end of the country I know. Beyond this there is no guidance in me, but Ibn Humaiyid knows it all and I can go and seek out an Oryx for you. I can do without the Oryx, I had replied, and I want your company. So he rode on sulkily far ahead, while Farraj danced attendance on me.

An hour later we passed the spot where the advance-party had prayed and made coffee. It was 9 a.m. and they must have left the spot barely an hour and a half before, yet over their fresh tracks lay the still more recent trail of a full-grown bull Oryx! That was too much for us all. Lovingly they read the message of the tracks aloud – how the great beast had sauntered along from the north cropping a bush here and there as he passed: how he had stood transfixed for a moment as he came upon the ploughed-up channel of our baggage camels: and how finally he had galloped away for dear life from the scent and signs of danger. 'Ali pleaded with tears in his eyes, and I yielded. Farraj strained at the leash, and I acquiesced with the reproach that I would soon be left entirely alone. Off they went, and we went on.

Very soon Farraj came back, protesting that he could not bear to leave me so ill-attended. Look you, he said, we would never have left our dear families and come out on this business but for two reasons: hope of profit and fear of punishment. I have no desire but to serve you, but it is Zayid and 'Ali that are to blame for all our troubles. You will surely not let their behaviour involve the rest of us in loss. Tell me what you want and I will do it. He was the lack-wit of our party – ever resisting but repenting, repenting but resisting – but the frankest of them all in naïve self-seeking. I had appealed to his cupidity the previous evening with some small pecuniary compensation for the trouble involved in capturing the two foxes – and for a bitten finger of which he had made the most, quite shamelessly.

Up hill and down dale we marched on. Here and there a small patch of exposed bluish rock in the bottom of a valley claimed our attention. The vegetation became scantier as we went, and all that there was was dead. Soon the rolling downs became absolutely bare, and the hot sun blazed down on them until the sand glared again into our faces mercilessly. Now and again the higher sands produced a mirage like sheets of glass. Not a bird did we see all that day, though once we heard the piping of an invisible lark. A dragonfly astonished me in such surroundings and thrice we saw a butterfly – flitting shadows that caught my eye for an instant and disappeared into the enveloping sheen of sand-reflected light. Two gargoylish lizards crouched in the sandy fire as we passed and were duly consigned to my ever-ready bottle.

We passed from Hadhat al Qata into Khillat al Hawaya about midday – a vast down-tract of rounded ribs of soft sand lying SW. and NE. as usual, with occasional lofty dunes to vary the monotony. It was easy going, but the heat was intense without relief. At 2 p.m. we halted by an exposed patch of the underlying bedrock for a short rest. I spread my mantle over the branches of a moribund *Abal* bush and scraped away the heated upper layer of sand to make myself a couch in the shade. I slept until I was summoned to coffee, and we disposed of the afternoon prayer before resuming the march.

Far away now to our southward lay the long line of the Hibaka, whose northerly extremity we had traversed the previous day, with the Qa'amiyat uplands beyond it; while to our north the Hawaya ridges extended a day and a half to the Bani Jallab tract, westward of which lies Al Jaladal* (apparently a gravel plain), with the northern Hibaka (or Hibaka Faraja) on its northern side. The downs gradually changed in character to form a series of more or less parallel ridges (always lying SW. and NE.), which we crossed in wearisome succession at intervals of a quarter-mile or more. Very hot it became as the afternoon wore on and our spirits drooped. Yet every now and then a cool zephyr breathed upon us from the east, fragrant reminder of the oncoming night. At the hottest of the day the shade temperature had touched 93°, but at 10 p.m. it was only 65°, and the minimum of the night in camp was 50°. We camped at 5 p.m. near the western edge of Khillat Hawaya and our hunters dribbled in about sunset from their futile hunting. The camels had felt the day's strain, marching through a pastureless wilderness, but there was less talk of giving up. We were now a hundred miles away from Shanna and at least as far from any water, while Zayid and 'Ali had evidently devised a plan for the morrow to their own liking. The baggage-train was started off before 2 a.m., and after the chatter and

*More probably, perhaps, Sahma or Ra'la.

clatter of their starting we slept in peace in the cool desert while the
waning moon went its way over us through an almost starless sky.

I awoke before dawn as usual, and over our morning coffee and
dates after the prayer it was announced that the camels of Zayid and
'Ali were missing! Having come in rather late the previous evening,
they had been left to graze in the moonlight and had strayed away.
An hour was wasted in looking for them – a precious hour of the
day's coolth – and then it was proposed that the rest of us should
start leaving Muhaimid with one camel, carrying water and provisions, in attendance on Zayid and 'Ali, who would track down their
lost beasts and follow in our trail. They might as well have made a
clean breast of their plans, which were too obvious to call for
comment. They would have today for another long pursuit of the
elusive Oryx and – most significant of all – our future plans could be
reconsidered if they failed again. By nightfall we would still be near
enough to water to go back and, viewed in the light of such a pact,
the developments of the day fall into a clearer, if ominous, perspective. Meanwhile there was nothing to be done but to make the best of
a bad situation and hope for the best. But I did privately register the
hope that Zayid and 'Ali might not meet with success in their selfish
quest. So we started off on our fifth day's march with Farraj riding
the animal that carried my boxes, Ibn Humaiyid as guide and Salih
in attendance. All went merrily enough and we joked and laughed,
nominating Parraj to the Amirate, left vacant by the desertion of
Zayid, and Salih as his deputy. And I offered to wager a large sum
that the hunters would return disappointed. Meanwhile we could be
happy without their company. And we were happy enough as we
struck out over the bare, easy, rolling downs, streaked at wide
intervals with ridges of sand so low as to be scarcely perceptible.
Farraj characteristically made the most of his uncomfortable perch
on my boxes as evidence of his will to service; and I chaffed him,
pointing out how he dominated us all as from a throne raised aloft.
How well it would be, I said, if we could always march thus without
Zayid and 'Ali! You and Salih could take it in turns each day to be
our leader and ride upon the throne, as rode the Arab virgins in the
good old days in a litter leading their tribal, warriors into battle. I am
content, Salih interposed hastily, to leave that honour to Farraj, and
I can serve you better catching lizards for you or turning aside with
you to collect rocks and shells – and perhaps flints – from the bare
valley-bottoms on the way. And at intervals when the conversation
flagged, they would strike up their barren singing to break the silence
of the desert.

After an hour we passed into Qasba Hawaya, and they pointed

out to me the dried-up stubble of the *Qasab* grass which differ-
entiates it from what had gone before. After good rains, said Ibn
Humaiyid, this is good grazing country and the Arabs come hither
with their milch-camels to seek the Oryx. And they remain out until
the camels need water, themselves living only on milk and the meat
of the chase. But it is the great ones only who do that – people like
Ibn Nifl and Ibn Jahman and Ibn Suwailim. It is a hard life. But there
has been no rain in these parts for seven or eight years now, and
none come hither these days. Gradually the country had become
more undulating with rounded dunes and low ridges. But it was
amazingly bare.

The light, cool breeze of the early morning dropped, but for an
hour or two the conditions remained pleasant enough though the air
was deathly still. The silence – once broken by the sweet piping of an
invisible lark – was astonishing. And the dunes and ridges merged
into a sea of billows without order, tossed and tumbled by the
conflict of desert winds. A little way off to the southward a group of
lofty pink dunes towered above it all, and we went by the tracks and
dung of a solitary Oryx, which had passed across this wilderness two
days earlier questing for pastures further north.

Suddenly there appeared before us the trough of a great valley-
bottom cleaving the rolling downs from south-west to north-east. In
its bed we saw a long series of exposed patches of the underlying
rock, which we turned out of our way to visit in search of shells. We
found none and climbed up the long and weary slope beyond to
enter, on its crest, the district of Hadhat al Hawaya, a tract of deeper
valleys and higher ridges which extend in uniformly parallel lines for
some 40 or 50 miles westward to the Shuwaikila country. Here the
Hadh bush reappeared after a long absence, dead like everything else
though occasional tufts of green raised hopes that were doomed to
disappointment. As the day drew on to noontide and the sun blazed
down on us without mercy it was easy to believe that never in twenty
years or more had rain fallen in this district. The dry *Hadh* shrubs
had gathered mounds of sand about their half-buried heads and even
the hardy *Abal*, the longest-lived of all the desert plants, had not
survived the strain.

Its long, blackened roots lay spread about the sandy floor round
the perished relics of once great thickets, whose gnarled and
writhing branches proclaimed the agonies to which at last after
a gallant struggle they had succumbed exhausted. Drought and
famine stalked the land with drawn swords of flaming fire, breathing hotly upon us who ventured thus into their domain. It was
impressive but it was depressing, and I was oppressed, maybe, by a

premonition of failure. Grimly and in silence we marched on over
an endless succession of valleys and ridges, hoping that each crest
would gladden our eyes with a vision of pastures ahead, but
hoping in vain. Nevertheless it was a pleasant landscape – these
rolling downs and deep valleys of Hawaya, where Death reigned
supreme, and a single raven waged perpetual war against the little
creatures that dared to live against such odds, larks and lizards and
tiny warblers.

It occurred to me, as we passed through the various belts of this
great sand-desert, that the sharply defined limits of *Hadh* and
Qasba, *Hamra** and *Khilla* and the like must in some way reflect
the chemical character of the sands themselves or of the soils and
waters underlying them. Each plant has a more or less definite life-
period dependent on the frequency of rains, the hardiest coming to
life out of death or dormancy upon the slightest encouragement and
lasting through the years under the greatest provocation, while the
tenderer herbs shrink from rebirth until tempted by copious rainfall
and wilt as soon as the drought resumes its sway. But a systematic
study of the plants themselves and of the sand and bedrock of their
habitat would certainly yield interesting and important results,
especially if correlated with the study of similar or comparable
plant-zones in the Sahara and other great desert tracts of the world.
The untutored eye could detect no outward and visible explanation
of the zone phenomenon. It merely noted the beginnings and the
ends of the *Hadh* belts, outside which all was *Khilla* dotted with
Abal or naked *Hamra*, with minor zones of *Qasba* and *Birkan*.

In a space of about four hours we had crossed as many valleys,
well-marked channels between broad gently sloping ridges. In each
case the wind had scoured out the bed to expose patches of the
calcareous rock below, of which we collected samples while searching in vain for shells and fossils. Here and there in the sandy hollows
we found queer, thin tubes of coagulated sand, which my companions regarded as evidence of subsoil water in the neighbourhood and
which they often find near the known wells. These proved to be
fulgurites or lightning-sticks, formed by the fusing of damp sand by
lightning and the adhesion of sand to the fused mass in such a
manner as to form a thin tube. Our specimens are puny little things
compared with many in the British Museum, but the frequency of
their occurrence in the rainless, or almost rainless, desert is remarkable enough.

Hamra, Hamrur (pl. Hamarir), apparently used only of sand-tracts absolutely
destitute of any kind of vegetation.

Some of these ridges flattened out at the top into broad plateaux of a gentle switchback character with shallow undulations and occasional moraines of low rounded dunes in large groups. Far and wide it was an unimaginably bare wilderness, and our nerves seemed to be at high tension as we faced the prospect of hour after hour of the same desolation, labouring on in the growing sultriness of noon along the furrow ploughed ahead of us by the passage of our baggage-train. Not once had we drawn rein since starting and the time drew nigh for a short halt for a breather, with coffee to cheer the heart of man. We had crossed the third valley and slowly climbed the long slope beyond it to the ridge crest, whence we looked forth on yet another valley with rolling downs beyond. Our general course had been WNW., but now almost due north of us, as we scanned the horizon, we saw a tent silhouetted against the slope of the further ridge. It was evidently one of our own tents, pitched for the first time since leaving Shanna, for we had discarded all unnecessary trouble and comfort to save time. The tent foreboded ill; the sudden change of direction was ominous. It was scarcely past midday and I railed in natural wrath against the transport folk for their wretched marching. The light-headed Farraj took up the challenge with a hysterical outburst. We toil for you in vain; we strain the camels till they break – all in vain. You are ever displeased and critical. Would you have them march on in the fire of this noontide sun? They are perchance resting for an hour or two. Yet he knew, as I felt instinctively, that the tent foreboded more than ill – perhaps disaster. Could one be anything but critical and on one's guard with companions who would readily have sacrificed the whole object of our endeavour to their own miserable comfort? In such circumstances the Arab does not show up to advantage. He clings frantically, desperately, to life, however miserable, and, when that is at risk, loses heart and head. Greed of filthy lucre alone makes him pause from flight, and gradually he may be brought round to a more reasonable attitude if he can be made to feel that all the troubles of the past may have been in vain if he shrinks from those of the future. At Shanna it had been fear of human foes that had produced rebellion, and I had submitted with a good enough grace though not without a struggle. On the way I had frankly, though vainly, tried to bribe 'Ali Jahman to turn south while it was still not too late, but he had shrunk from the prospect of incurring the hostility of his companions. And now it was the waterless desert, the fear of thirst and death, that made women of these men. I could not, would not yield. We had come 140 miles. A third of the journey was behind us and a steady effort would carry us through if only they would play the man. They were, of course, weak and disheartened with hunger for we had had nothing but dates since Shanna. I was famished myself and could sympathise with their condition. I felt like Moses in the wilderness when the multitude clamoured against him, but I could produce neither water nor manna.

So we marched on wrangling towards the distant tent. In half an hour we reached camp to hear that five or six baggage-animals had collapsed from thirst, hunger and exhaustion. One of them was actually sheltering against the sun under cover of the tent at the time, while two or three others were similarly indulged when in due course they were brought in from the desert with the loads of which they had been relieved for a time to let them recover from the strain. The position was just about as serious as it could be and some reconsideration of our plans would obviously be necessary. We were at a crisis of our fortunes, but the battle had yet to be joined that would end at midnight in my own discomfiture.

My tent had been pitched near the other when we arrived but, after depositing my goods and chattels in it, I hastened to join my companions, whom I found in surly mood and openly mutinous, attributing the debacle of the day to my insane insistence both on embarking upon such an enterprise and on marching through the heat of the day. I tried to be conciliatory in the circumstances and pointed out gently that night-marching would have defeated the whole object of our journey. I went on to declare that at Shanna I had strongly urged the division of our forces and the despatch of all our heavy baggage by the comparatively easy route by the wells to Riyadh or Hufuf, so that we might attempt the waterless crossing with a light and well-equipped party. It was therefore they who had brought about the present disastrous state of affairs by neglecting my advice. I had moreover warned them at Shanna that the journey would take at least fifteen days while they had clung foolishly to Ibn Suwailim's optimistic estimate of eleven or twelve, and thus had only themselves to thank for the disappointment of their hopes. We had in fact done exactly one-third of the distance in one-third of the time allowed for by me, and there was no reason to talk of abandoning the enterprise. I certainly would not do that. I would go on alone if necessary and they could go back and tell their master that they had abandoned their guest in the desert. And now, I continued, our course is clear enough. We can send back the baggage-animals to Naifa, whence they may either return to the Hasa or rejoin us at Wadi Dawasir by way of Bir Fadhil and the Aflaj. The rest of us could continue the march direct to Sulaiyil, where we should await the arrival of the baggage. The only course was to be firm and

unyielding with as much conciliatoriness as possible, but my frankness merely fanned the flames of mutiny as they sat silent and
brooding round the embers of the coffee fire. The coffee cups were
passing round.

'Abdul Rahman, the coffee-man, scion of the dour clans of
Dhruma and usually too absorbed in his coffee-making to take
much part in the general conversation, looked up with a snarl and
jerked out some offensive remark about my lack of consideration for
others. I rounded on the assembled company and chid them. I came
over to your tent, I said, to discuss the situation with you that we
may make plans for the future. I did not come to hear expressions of
your ill-temper, and it astonishes me that you should all sit by and let
such a remark as that be made in your presence with impunity. I, at
any rate, will not stand that from any of you. With that I tossed my
untasted cup on the sand and rose to leave the tent. Ibn Ma'addi,
doubtless remembering the Sa'dan incident at Adraj, interposed with
an olive branch. If you wish it, he said, we will give 'Abdul Rahman
a beating for his insolence. No, I replied as I walked away, I do not
wish it; I have forgiven him. But if any of you wish to discuss matters
with me, he must come to my tent. I come no more to yours. At such
a crisis it was obviously undesirable to make enemies gratuitously,
while I also reflected that 'Abdul Rahman had probably had a
gruelling day of it with the breakdown of the camels. He was
perhaps also contemplating death from thirst as a very real possibility. High words and ill-temper were inevitable in such circumstances, and I was full of sympathy for the unfortunate wretches
though by no means disposed to yield to their clamour for an
ignominious retreat. So I left them to their talking, and fragments
of their wild conversation floated over to my ears as I settled down to
plot out our whole march from Shanna to this point. I had had no
time to do such work during the past five days and it was imperative
that I should know roughly without delay our actual position in the
great waterless desert. Sa'dan brought me my customary pot of tea
and the gossip of the enemy camp, whence emissaries came from
time to time to resume negotiations with me about our future
movements. By sunset I had finished my task and, as soon as it
was dark enough, I made and worked out the necessary astronomical observations to check the accuracy of my compass traverse. Our
progress had been certainly a little disappointing though I had
discounted such a contingency in advance. Two-thirds of the desert
journey lay before us – a matter of ten days, though these might be
reduced to eight with a reasonable amount of night-marching. Could
the best of our camels do it? That was the great question, while there

could be no doubt, whatever, that the baggage-animals must make with all possible speed for the nearest water. There was little to choose in the matter of distance between Naifa and Shanna, but wild horses would not have dragged my companions back to the latter. They feared it as the plague, and there was no reason why their preference should not be conceded. For the camels (and to a lesser extent for the personnel) it was literally a question of life and death. And four of the camels lay there before us in a state of complete collapse. Nothing but water would revive them for further marching, and there was no water to spare if all claims had to be considered.

Meanwhile the stream of visitors to my tent had enabled me to devise a scheme which was at least feasible and acceptable though not acclaimed with the enthusiasm demanded by our parlous situation. The absentees, Zayid and 'Ali, were to be encouraged to accompany the baggage back to Naifa, while I insisted that Ibn Suwailim should go with my party as guide for he alone knew the general direction and conditions of the march before us well enough to act in such a capacity, though even he had never traversed the desert on any line southward of Faraja and Maqainama. Sa'dan would, of course, go with me, for he both desired to do so and was indispensable for my work, and that made a nucleus of three, to which Salih adhered unconditionally, thus making four. Farraj hedged, torn between fear and greed – and never have I met an Arab so vacillating and uncertain in temper – but eventually decided to throw in his lot with me. Humaid would not be parted from Salih and that made six, while Suwid, who had publicly denounced the scheme as sheer madness, came to my tent alone and very mysteriously to indicate by wordless signs that he too would be included in my party, which was duly completed by the inclusion of Abu Ja'sha, the indispensable handy man. On my part I agreed readily enough to a reasonable amount of night-marching – a concession that I could scarcely refuse in the circumstances seeing that we should in any case have scarcely enough water to see us through to the end, for we should have to spare some for the weariest of the camels and leave the baggage-party with sufficient to bring them to Naifa.

As the hours passed by with no sign of Zayid and 'Ali we agreed that the desert party should make a start with the first appearance of the moon, due sometime after midnight, as there was clearly no time to be lost. The interval was spent in making the necessary dispositions to give effect to our plans. The available food supplies were divided up and the camels destined for our party selected. In due course everything was ready and I had just completed my star observations when we heard afar off the grunts and chatter that portended the unwelcome return of Zayid and his companions.

As I had anticipated with dread, all our carefully worked out plans collapsed with Zayid's arrival in camp. He was quite naturally furious that any plans should have been concerted in his absence, and neither he nor 'Ali was inclined to be communicative on the subject of the day's hunting, which had at any rate provided no venison. They left it to be understood that they had toiled all day in search of their lost camels and they had a colourable grievance in our decision to relegate them unconsulted to the returning baggage-party. From the first moment Zayid declared himself against our scheme. After the inevitable cup of coffee which enabled him rapidly to take stock of the situation, as I could gather from the privacy of my own tent by the voluble protests made in the other, he came over to discuss matters with me. He was charming as could be and honey-tongued in his protestations of devoted service. Look you, he said, I cannot desert you thus; I will come with you myself, for my face would be blackened for ever if I left you now to your fate. The way is far and there is not sufficient water and the camels are dead. We will, however, do what you wish. We will perish with you. We will take the best camels and all the water that can be spared and what matter? We will put our trust in God. If God so wills, we will reach Sulaiyil alive, but blame not us if we all die of thirst in the desert. You saw today how many of the animals broke down. They cannot march without pastures to fill their bellies. There are but two or three of them that are fit for the journey. Why, even my mount and 'Ali's are more dead than alive. But whatever you wish we will do. I have done my duty in warning you of the danger we shall be running, but the ordering is yours.

The advent of Zayid had clearly changed the situation. He could make or mar our enterprise, and I could not trust him to make arrangements that would give us a sporting chance of success. I felt that I had lost my throw with Fate, and I turned to the only alternative – a faint hope of ultimate success to weigh in the balance against the certain failure of the plans we had made so hopefully. Look you, Zayid, I said, your coming has spoiled my plans and you have turned my companions against me. Either let me go with my men and the camels we have chosen or give me your word of honour here and now. If I agree to go back to Naifa now with all our party intact will you give me your word of honour that, when we have rested and refreshed our camels, you will ride with me again across the Empty Quarter, even to Sulaiyil, as you gave me your word to do at Shanna? That was part of your charge from Ibn Jiluwi, and I warn you that Ibn Sa'ud himself will be wroth with you and the rest of them if you fail in this matter. I cannot go back except across the Empty Quarter. I give you my word of honour to that, oh Shaikh Abdullah, he replied blandly, and the matter is of God's will. For a moment I wrestled with myself and saw that there was no reasonable alternative to putting my trust in any sense of decency that remained in him. The men were all so obsessed with fear of Zayid that they could do nothing on their own initiative. Salih and Farraj, who had solemnly given me their hands in token of loyalty to the afternoon's bargain, cut but sorry figures in their sudden and complete collapse. And in the few moments that remained before a final decision was reached I listened to a loud altercation proceeding in the rival camp. He cannot go, I heard, without a guide; so let Ibn Suwailim tell him straight out that he will not accompany him. Rise Salim and tell him that we may get back to the watering without delay. And a moment later Ibn Suwailim was led into my tent by Suwid, repeated his lesson like a child and went his way.

Thus it was finally agreed that we should all return together to Naifa and that the baggage-train should start off as soon as the moon had risen. Of the whole nineteen of us, I alone was unhappy that evening, while the rest set about their remaining tasks with a good will worthier of a better cause than ignominious retreat. The Empty Quarter had routed us. We had come about 140 miles – a five days' journey – into its inhospitable, drought-stricken wastes, and now we were to flee from its terrors.

TO THE EMPTY QUARTER FOR A DRINK OF WATER

Wilfred Thesiger
(1910–)

Thesiger, like Philby, was drawn to Arabia's Empty Quarter and would make many journeys there. But he embraced the sands less as a geographical challenge and more as a test of the human spirit. After a childhood in Addis Ababa and subsequent wanderings in Somalia, Sudan, Syria and the Sahara, he had come to think of the desert as his natural home. After World War II he welcomed a move to Arabia, initially to work on locust control and then to make a series of remarkable journeys. He was particularly interested in how the beduin (bedu) had adapted to their impossibly harsh surroundings, and he was deeply saddened that this unique lifestyle and its values were about to be eclipsed. More than any of his contemporaries, he lived as a bedu, *suffering the pangs of thirst and hunger with them, enjoying their companionship, and making no concessions to comfort. His first crossing of the Empty Quarter in 1946 was made with just five companions from the Rashid and Bait Kathir tribes.*

After the meal we rode for two hours along a salt-flat. The dunes on either side, colourless in the moonlight, seemed higher by night than by day. The lighted slopes looked very smooth, the shadows in their folds inky black. Soon I was shivering uncontrollably from the cold. The others roared out their songs into a silence, broken otherwise only by the crunch of salt beneath the camels' feet. The words were the words of the south, but the rhythm and intonation were the same as in the songs which I had heard other Bedu singing in the Syrian desert. At first sight the Bedu of southern Arabia had appeared to be very different from those of the north, but

I now realized that this difference was largely superficial and due to the clothes which they wore. My companions would not have felt out of place in an encampment of the Rualla, whereas a townsman from Aden or Muscat would be conspicuous in Damascus.

Eventually we halted and I dismounted numbly. I would have given much for a hot drink but I knew that I must wait eighteen hours for that. We lit a small fire and warmed ourselves before we slept, though I slept little. I was tired; for days I had ridden long hours on a rough camel, my body racked by its uneven gait. I suppose I was weak from hunger, for the food which we ate was a starvation ration, even by Bedu standards. But my thirst troubled me most; it was not bad enough really to distress me but I was always conscious of it. Even when I was asleep I dreamt of racing streams of ice-cold water, but it was difficult to get to sleep. Now I lay there trying to estimate the distance we had covered and the distance that still lay ahead. When I had asked al Auf how far it was to the well, he had answered, "It is not the distance but the great dunes of the Uruq al Shaiba that may destroy us." I worried about the water which I had watched dripping away on to the sand, and about the state of our camels. They were there, close beside me in the dark. I sat up and looked at them. Mabkhaut stirred and called out, "What is it, Umbarak?" I mumbled an answer and lay down again. Then I worried whether we had tied the mouth of the skin properly when we had last drawn water and wondered what would happen if one of us was sick or had an accident. It was easy to banish these thoughts in daylight, less easy in the lonely darkness. Then I thought of al Auf travelling here alone and felt ashamed.

The others were awake at the first light, anxious to push on while it was still cold. The camels sniffed at the withered tribulus but were too thirsty to eat it. In a few minutes we were ready. We plodded along in silence. My eyes watered with the cold; the jagged salt-crusts cut and stung my feet. The world was grey and dreary. Then gradually the peaks ahead of us stood out against a paling sky; almost imperceptibly they began to glow, borrowing the colours of the sunrise which touched their crests.

A high unbroken dune-chain stretched across our front. It was not of uniform height, but, like a mountain range, consisted of peaks and connecting passes. Several of the summits appeared to be seven hundred feet above the salt-flat on which we stood. The southern face confronting us was very steep, which meant that this was the lee side to the prevailing winds. I wished we had to climb it from the opposite direction, for it is easy to take a camel down these precipices of sand but always difficult to find a way up them.

Al Auf told us to wait while he went to reconnoitre. I watched him walking away across the glistening salt-flat, his rifle on his shoulder and his head thrown back as he scanned the slopes above. He looked superbly confident, but as I viewed this wall of sand I despaired that we would ever get the camels up it. Mabkhaut evidently thought the same, for he said to Musallim, "We will have to find a way round. No camel will ever climb that." Musallim answered, "It is al Auf's doing. He brought us here. We should have gone much farther to the west, nearer to Dakaka." He had caught a cold and was snuffling, and his rather high-pitched voice was hoarse and edged with grievance. I knew that he was jealous of al Auf and always ready to disparage him, so unwisely I gibed, "We should have got a long way if you had been our guide!" He swung round and answered angrily, "You don't like the Bait Kathir. I know that you only like the Rashid. I defied my tribe to bring you here and you never recognize what I have done for you."

For the past few days he had taken every opportunity of reminding me that I could not have come on from Ramlat al Ghafa without him. It was done in the hope of currying favour and of increasing his reward, but it only irritated me. Now I was tempted to seek relief in angry words, to welcome the silly, bitter squabble which would result. I kept silent with an effort and moved apart on the excuse of taking a photograph. I knew how easily, under conditions such as these, I could take a violent dislike to one member of the party and use him as my private scapegoat. I thought, "I must not let myself dislike him. After all, I do owe him a great deal; but I wish to God he would not go on reminding me of it."

I went over to a bank and sat down to wait for al Auf's return. The ground was still cold, although the sun was now well up, throwing a hard, clear light on the barrier of sand ahead of us. It seemed fantastic that this great rampart which shut out half the sky could be made of wind-blown sand. Now I could see al Auf, about half a mile away, moving along the salt-flat at the bottom of the dune. While I watched him he started to climb a ridge, like a mountaineer struggling upward through soft snow towards a pass over a high mountain. I even saw the tracks which he left behind him. He was the only moving thing in all that empty, silent landscape.

What were we going to do if we could not get the camels over it? I knew that we could not go any farther to the east, for al Auf had told me that the quicksands of Umm al Samim were in that direction. To the west the easier sands of Dakaka, where Thomas had crossed, were more than two hundred miles away. We had no margin, and could not afford to lengthen our journey. Our water was already dangerously short, and even more urgent than our own needs were those of the camels, which would collapse unless they were watered soon. We *must* get them over this monstrous dune, if necessary by unloading them and carrying the loads to the top. But what was on the other side? How many more of these dunes were there ahead of us? If we turned back now we might reach Mughshin, but I knew that once we crossed this dune the camels would be too tired and thirsty to get back even to Ghanim. Then I thought of Sultan and the others who had deserted us, and of their triumph if we gave up and returned defeated. Looking again at the dune ahead I noticed that al Auf was coming back. A shadow fell across the sand beside me. I glanced up and bin Kabina stood there. He smiled, said "Salam Alaikum", and sat down. Urgently I turned to him and asked, "Will we ever get the camels over that?" He pushed the hair back from his forehead, looked thoughtfully at the slopes above us, and answered, "It is very steep but al Auf will find a way. He is a Rashid; he is not like these Bait Kathir." Unconcernedly he then took the bolt out of his rifle and began to clean it with the hem of his shirt, while he asked me if all the English used the same kind of rifle.

When al Auf approached we went over to the others. Mabkhaut's camel had lain down; the rest of them stood where we had left them, which was a bad sign. Ordinarily they would have roamed off at once to look for food. Al Auf smiled at me as he came up but said nothing, and no one questioned him. Noticing that my camel's load was unbalanced he heaved up the saddle-bag from one side, and then picking up with his toes the camel-stick which he had dropped, he went over to his own camel, caught hold of its head-rope, said "Come on", and led us forward.

It was now that he really showed his skill. He picked his way unerringly, choosing the inclines up which the camels could climb. Here on the lee side of this range a succession of great faces flowed down in unruffled sheets of sand, from the top to the very bottom of the dune. They were unscalable, for the sand was poised always on the verge of avalanching, but they were flanked by ridges where the sand was firmer and the inclines easier. It was possible to force a circuitous way up these slopes, but not all were practicable for camels, and from below it was difficult to judge their steepness. Very slowly, a foot at a time, we coaxed the unwilling beasts upward. Each time we stopped I looked up at the crests where the rising wind was blowing streamers of sand into the void, and wondered how we should ever reach the top. Suddenly we were there. Before slumping down on the sand I looked anxiously ahead of us. To my relief I saw that we were on the edge of rolling downs, where the going would be easy among shallow valleys and low, rounded hills. We have made it. We are on top of Uruq al Shaiba, I thought triumphantly. The fear of this great obstacle had lain like a shadow on my mind ever since al Auf had first warned me of it, the night we spoke together in the sands of Ghanim. Now the shadow had lifted and I was confident of success.

We rested for a while on the sand, not troubling to talk, until al Auf rose to his feet and said "Come on." Some small dunes built up by cross-winds ran in curves parallel with the main face across the back of these downs. Their steep faces were to the north and the camels slithered down them without difficulty. These downs were brick-red, splashed with deeper shades of colour; the underlying sand, exposed where it had been churned up by our feet, showing red of a paler shade. But the most curious feature was a number of deep craters resembling giant hoof-prints. These were unlike normal crescent-dunes, since they did not rise above their surroundings, but formed hollows in the floor of hard undulating sand. The salt-flats far below us looked very white.

We mounted our camels. My companions had muffled their faces in their head-cloths and rode in silence, swaying to the camels' stride. The shadows on the sand were very blue, of the same tone as the sky; two ravens flew northward, croaking as they passed. I struggled to keep awake. The only sound was made by the slap of the camels' feet, like wavelets lapping on a beach.

To rest the camels we stopped for four hours in the late afternoon on a long gentle slope which stretched down to another salt-flat. There was no vegetation on it and no salt-bushes bordered the plain below us. Al Auf announced that we would go on again at sunset. While we were feeding I said to him cheerfully, "Anyway, the worst should be over now that we are across the Uruq al Shaiba." He looked at me for a moment and then answered, "If we go well tonight we should reach them tomorrow." I said, "Reach what?" and he replied, "The Uruq al Shaiba", adding, "Did you think what we crossed today was the Uruq al Shaiba? That was only a dune. You will see them tomorrow." For a moment, I thought he was joking, and then I realized that he was serious, that the worst of the journey which I had thought was behind us was still ahead.

It was midnight when at last al Auf said, "Let's stop here. We will get some sleep and give the camels a rest. The Uruq al Shaiba are not far away now." In my dreams that night they towered above us higher than the Himalayas.

Al Auf woke us again while it was still dark. As usual bin Kabina made coffee, and the sharp-tasting drops which he poured out stimulated but did not warm. The morning star had risen above the dunes. Formless things regained their shape in the first dim light of dawn. The grunting camels heaved themselves erect. We lingered for a moment more beside the fire; then al Auf said "Come", and we moved forward. Beneath my feet the gritty sand was cold as frozen snow.

We were faced by a range as high as, perhaps even higher than, the range we had crossed the day before, but here the peaks were steeper and more pronounced, rising in many cases to great pinnacles, down which the flowing ridges swept like draperies. These sands, paler coloured than those we had crossed, were very soft, cascading round our feet as the camels struggled up the slopes. Remembering how little warning of imminent collapse the dying camels had given me twelve years before in the Danakil country, I wondered how much more these camels would stand, for they were trembling violently whenever they halted. When one refused to go on we heaved on her head-rope, pushed her from behind, and lifted the loads on either side as we manhandled the roaring animal upward. Sometimes one of them lay down and refused to rise, and then we had to unload her, and carry the water-skins and the saddlebags ourselves. Not that the loads were heavy. We had only a few gallons of water left and some handfuls of flour.

We led the trembling, hesitating animals upward along great sweeping ridges where the knife-edged crests crumbled beneath our feet. Although it was killing work, my companions were always gentle and infinitely patient. The sun was scorching hot and I felt empty, sick, and dizzy. As I struggled up the slope, knee-deep in shifting sand, my heart thumped wildly and my thirst grew worse. I found it difficult to swallow; even my ears felt blocked, and yet I knew that it would be many intolerable hours before I could drink. I would stop to rest, dropping down on the scorching sand, and immediately it seemed I would hear the others shouting, "Umbarak, Umbarak"; their voices sounded strained and hoarse.

It took us three hours to cross this range.

On the summit were no gently undulating downs such as we had met the day before. Instead, three smaller dune-chains rode upon its back, and beyond them the sand fell away to a salt-flat in another great empty trough between the mountains. The range on the far side seemed even higher than the one on which we stood, and behind it were others. I looked round, seeking instinctively for some escape. There was no limit to my vision. Somewhere in the ultimate distance the sands merged into the sky, but in that infinity of space I could see no living thing, not even a withered plant to give me hope. There is nowhere to go, I thought. We cannot go back and our camels will never get up another of these awful dunes. We really are finished. The silence flowed over me, drowning the voices of my companions and the fidgeting of their camels.

We went down into the valley, and somehow – and I shall never know how the camels did it – we got up the other side. There, utterly exhausted, we collapsed. Al Auf gave us each a little water, enough to wet our mouths. He said, "We need this if we are to go on." The midday sun had drained the colour from the sands. Scattered banks of cumulus cloud threw shadows across the dunes and salt-flats, and added an illusion that we were high among Alpine peaks, with frozen lakes of blue and green in the valley, far below. Half asleep, I turned over, but the sand burnt through my shirt and woke me from my dreams.

Two hours later al Auf roused us. As he helped me load my camel, he said, "Cheer up, Umbarak. This time we really are across the Uruq al Shaiba", and when I pointed to the ranges ahead of us, he answered, "I can find a way through those; we need not cross them." We went on till sunset, but we were going with the grain of the country, following the valleys and no longer trying to climb the dunes. We should not have been able to cross another. There was a little fresh *qassis* on the slope where we halted. I hoped that this lucky find would give us an excuse to stop here for the night, but, after we had fed, al Auf went to fetch the camels, saying, "We must go on again while it is cool if we are ever to reach Dhafara."

We stopped long after midnight and started again at dawn, still exhausted from the strain and long hours of yesterday, but al Auf encouraged us by saying that the worst was over. The dunes were certainly lower than they had been, more uniform in height and more rounded, with fewer peaks. Four hours after we had started we came to rolling uplands of gold and silver sand, but still there was nothing for the camels to eat.

A hare jumped out from under a bush, and al Auf knocked it over with his stick. The others shouted, "God has given us meat." For days we had talked of food; every conversation seemed to lead back to it. Since we had left Ghanim I had been always conscious of the dull ache of hunger, yet in the evening my throat was dry even after my drink, so that I found it difficult to swallow the dry bread Musallim set before us. All day we thought and talked about that hare, and by three o'clock in the afternoon could no longer resist stopping to cook it. Mabkhaut suggested, "Let's roast it in its skin in the embers of a fire. That will save our water – we haven't got much left." Bin Kabina led the chorus of protest. "No, by God! Don't even suggest such a thing"; and turning to me he said, "We don't want

Mabkhaut's charred meat. Soup. We want soup and extra bread. We will feed well today even if we go hungry and thirsty later. By God, I am hungry!" We agreed to make soup. We were across the Uruq al Shaiba and intended to celebrate our achievement with this gift from God. Unless our camels foundered we were safe; even if our water ran out we should live to reach a well.

Musallim made nearly double our usual quantity of bread while bin Kabina cooked the hare. He looked across at me and said, "The smell of this meat makes me faint." When it was ready he divided it into five portions. They were very small, for an Arabian hare is no larger than an English rabbit, and this one was not even fully grown. Al Auf named the lots and Mabkhaut drew them. Each of us took the small pile of meat which had fallen to him. Then bin Kabina said, "God! I have forgotten to divide the liver", and the others said, "Give it to Umbarak." I protested, saying that they should divide it, but they swore by God that they would not eat it and that I was to have it. Eventually I took it, knowing that I ought not, but too greedy for this extra scrap of meat to care.

Our water was nearly finished and there was only enough flour for about another week. The starving camels were so thirsty that they had refused to eat some half-dried herbage which we had passed. We must water them in the next day or two or they would collapse. Al Auf said that it would take us three more days to reach Khaba well in Dhafara but that there was a very brackish well not far away. He thought that the camels might drink its water.

That night after we had ridden for a little over an hour it grew suddenly dark. Thinking that a cloud must be covering the full moon, I looked over my shoulder and saw that there was an eclipse and that half the moon was already obscured. Bin Kabina noticed it at the same moment and broke into a chant which the others took up.

> 'God endures for ever.
> The life of man is short.
> The Pleiades are overhead.
> The moon's among the stars.'

Otherwise they paid no attention to the eclipse (which was total), but looked around for a place to camp.

We started very early the next morning and rode without a stop for seven hours across easy rolling downs. The colour of these sands was vivid, varied, and unexpected: in places the colour of ground coffee, elsewhere brick-red, or purple, or a curious golden-green. There were small white gypsum-flats, fringed with *shanan*, a grey-green salt-bush, lying in hollows in the downs. We rested for two hours on sands the colour of dried blood and then led our camels on again.

Suddenly we were challenged by an Arab lying behind a bush on the crest of a dune. Our rifles were on our camels, for we had not expected to meet anyone here. Musallim was hidden behind mine. I watched him draw his rifle clear. But al Auf said, "It is the voice of a Rashid," and walked forward. He spoke to the concealed Arab, who rose and came to meet him. They embraced and stood talking until we joined them. We greeted the man, and al Auf said, "This is Hamad bin Hanna, a sheikh of the Rashid." He was a heavily built bearded man of middle age. His eyes were set close together and he had a long nose with a blunt end. He fetched his camel from behind the dune while we unloaded.

We made coffee for him and listened to his news. He told us that he had been looking for a stray camel when he crossed our tracks and had taken us for a raiding party from the south. Ibn Saud's tax-collectors were in Dhafara and the Rabadh, collecting tribute from the tribes; and there were Rashid, Awamir, Murra, and some Manahil to the north of us.

We had to avoid all contact with Arabs other than the Rashid, and if possible even with them, so that news of my presence would not get about among the tribes, for I had no desire to be arrested by Ibn Saud's tax-collectors and taken off to explain my presence here to Ibn Jalawi, the formidable Governor of the Hasa. Karab from the Hadhramaut had raided these sands the year before, so there was also a serious risk of our being mistaken for raiders, since the tracks of our camels would show that we had come from the southern steppes. This risk would be increased if it appeared that we were avoiding the Arabs, for honest travellers never pass an encampment without seeking news and food. It was going to be very difficult to escape detection. First we must water our camels and draw water for ourselves. Then we must lie up as close as possible to Liwa and send a party to the villages to buy us enough food for at least another month. Hamad told me that Liwa belonged to the Al bu Falah of Abu Dhabi. He said that they were still fighting Said bin Maktum of Dibai, and that, as there was a lot of raiding going on, the Arabs would be very much on alert.

We started again in the late afternoon and travelled till sunset. Hamad came with us and said he would stay with us until we had got food from Liwa. Knowing where the Arabs were encamped he could help us to avoid them. Next day, after seven hours' travelling, we reached Khaur Sabakha on the edge of the Dhafara sands. We cleaned out the well and found brackish water at seven feet, so bitter that even the camels only drank a little before refusing it. They sniffed thirstily at the water with which al Auf tried to coax them from a leather bucket, but only dipped their lips into it. We covered their noses but still they would not drink. Yet al Auf said that Arabs themselves drank this water mixed with milk, and when I expressed my disbelief he added that if an Arab was really thirsty he would even kill a camel and drink the liquid in its stomach, or ram a stick down its throat and drink the vomit. We went on again till nearly sunset.

The next day when we halted in the afternoon al Auf told us we had reached Dhafara and that Khaba well was close. He said that he would fetch water in the morning. We finished what little was left in one of our skins. Next day we remained where we were. Hamad said that he would go for news and return the following day. Al Auf, who went with him, came back in the afternoon with two skins full of water which although slightly brackish, was delicious after the filthy evil-smelling dregs we had drunk the night before.

It was 12 December, fourteen days since we had left Khaur bin Atarit in Ghanim.

In the evening, now that we needed no longer measure out each cup of water, bin Kabina made extra coffee, while Musallim increased our rations of flour by a mugful. This was wild extravagance, but we felt that the occasion called for celebration. Even so, the loaves he handed us were woefully inadequate to stay our hunger, now that our thirst was gone.

The moon was high above us when I lay down to sleep. The others still talked round the fire, but I closed my mind to the meaning of their words, content to hear only the murmur of their voices, to watch their outlines sharp against the sky, happily conscious that they were there and beyond them the camels to which we owed our lives.

For years the Empty Quarter had represented to me the final, unattainable challenge which the desert offered. Suddenly it had come within my reach. I remembered my excitement when Lean had casually offered me the chance to go there, the immediate determination to cross it, and then the doubts and fears, the frustrations, and the moments of despair. Now I had crossed it. To others my journey would have little importance. It would produce nothing except a rather inaccurate map which no one was ever likely to use. It was a personal experience, and the reward had been a drink of clean, nearly tasteless water. I was content with that.

ALONE IN AFRICA

Mungo Park
(1771–?1807)

Park's 1795–7 odyssey in search of the Niger first awakened the world to the feasibility of a white man penetrating sub-Saharan Africa. But unlike his illustrious successors, this quiet tenant farmer's son from the Scottish Borders travelled alone; relieved of his meagre possessions, he was soon wholly dependent on local hospitality. In what he called "a plain unvarnished tale" he related horrific ordeals with admirable detachment – never more tested than on his return journey through Bamako, now the capital of Mali.

*18*th August, 1796. By mistake I took the wrong road, and did not discover my error until I had travelled near four miles; when coming to an eminence, I observed the Niger considerably to the left. Directing my course towards it. I travelled through long grass and bushes, with great difficulty, until two o'clock in the afternoon; when I came to a comparatively small, but very rapid river, which I took at first for a creek, or one of the streams of the Niger. However, after I had examined it with more attention, I was convinced that it was a distinct river; and as the road evidently crossed it (for I could see the pathway on the opposite side), I sat down upon the bank, in hopes that some traveller might arrive, who would give me the necessary information concerning the fording place; for the banks were so covered with reeds and bushes, that it would have been almost impossible to land on the other side, except at the pathway; which on account of the rapidity of the stream, it seemed very difficult to reach. No traveller, however, arriving, and there being a great appearance of rain, I examined the grass and bushes, for some way up the bank, and determined upon entering the river considerably above the pathway, in order to reach

Park first setting eyes on the Niger. From *Travels in the Interior of Africa*, Edinburgh, 1860.

the other side before the stream had swept me too far down. With this view I fastened my clothes upon the saddle, and was standing up to the neck in water, pulling my horse by the bridle to make him follow me, when a man came accidentally to the place, and seeing me in the water, called to me with great vehemence to come out. The alligators, he said, would devour both me and my horse, if we attempted to swim over. When I had got out, the stranger, who had never before seen a European, seemed wonderfully surprised. He twice put his hand to his mouth, exclaiming in a low tone of voice, "God preserve me! who is this?" But when he heard me speak the Bambarra tongue, and found that I was going the same way as himself, he promised to assist me in crossing the river; the name of which he told me was Frina. He then went a little way along the bank, and called to some person, who answered from the other side. In a short time, a canoe with two boys came paddling from among the reeds; these boys agreed, for fifty cowries, to transport me and my horse over the river, which was effected without much difficulty; and I arrived in the evening at Taffara, a walled town, and soon discovered that the language of the natives was improved, from the corrupted dialect of Bambarra, to the pure Mandingo.

On my arrival at Taffara, I inquired for the dooty, but was informed that he had died a few days before my arrival, and that there was, at that moment, a meeting of the chief men for electing another; there being some dispute about the succession. It was probably owing to the unsettled state of the town, that I experienced such a want of hospitality in it; for though I informed the inhabitants that I should only remain with them for one night, and assured them that Mansong had given me some cowries to pay for my lodging, yet no person invited me to come in; and I was forced to sit alone under the bentang tree, exposed to the rain and wind of a tornado, which lasted with great violence until midnight. At this time the stranger who had assisted me in crossing the river paid me a visit, and observing that I had not found a lodging, invited me to take part of his supper, which he had brought to the door of his hut; for being a guest himself, he could not, without his landlord's consent, invite me to come in. After this, I slept upon some wet grass in the corner of a court. My horse fared still worse than myself; the corn I had purchased being all expended, and I could not procure a supply.

20th August I passed the town of Jaba, and stopped a few minutes at a village called Somino, where I begged and obtained some coarse food, which the natives prepare from the husks of corn, and call boo. About two o'clock I came to the village of Sooha, and endeavoured to purchase some corn from the dooty, who was sitting by the gate, but without success. I then requested a little food by way of charity, but was told he had none to spare. Whilst I was examining the countenance of this inhospitable old man, and endeavouring to find out the cause of the sullen discontent which was visible in his eye, he called to a slave who was working in the corn field at a little distance, and ordered him to bring his hoe along with him. The dooty then told him to dig a hole in the ground; pointing to a spot at no great distance. The slave, with his hoe, began to dig a pit in the earth; and the dooty, who appeared to be a man of a very fretful disposition, kept muttering and talking to himself until the pit was almost finished, when he repeatedly pronounced the words "dankatoo" (good for nothing), "jankra lemen" (a real plague): which expressions I thought could be applied to nobody but myself; and as the pit had very much the appearance of a grave, I thought it prudent to mount my horse, and was about to decamp, when the slave, who had before gone into the village, to my surprise, returned with the corpse of a boy about nine or ten years of age, quite naked. The Negro carried the body by a leg and an arm, and threw it into the pit with a savage indifference which I had never before seen. As he covered the body with earth, the dooty often expressed himself, "naphula attiniata" (money lost), whence I concluded that the boy had been one of his slaves.

Departing from this shocking scene. I travelled by the side of the river until sunset, when I came to Koolikorro, a considerable town, and a great market for salt. Here I took up my lodging at the house of a Bambarran, who had formerly been the slave of a Moor, and in that character had travelled to Aoran, Towdinni, and many other places in the Great Desert; but turning Mussulman, and his master dying at Jenné, he obtained his freedom, and settled at this place, where he carries on a considerable trade in salt, cotton cloth, etc. His knowledge of the world has not lessened that superstitious confidence in saphies and charms which he had imbibed in his earlier years; for when he heard that I was a Christian, he immediately thought of procuring a saphie, and for this purpose brought out his walha, or writing-board, assuring me that he would dress me a supper of rice if I would write him a saphie to protect him from wicked men. The proposal was of too great consequence to me to be refused; I therefore wrote the board full from top to bottom on both sides; and my landlord, to be certain of having the whole force of the charm, washed the writing from the board into a calabash with a little water, and having said a few prayers over it, drank this powerful draught; after which, lest a single word should escape, he licked the board until it was quite dry. A saphie writer was a man of too great consequence to be long concealed; the important information was carried to the dooty, who sent his son with half a sheet of writing paper, desiring me to write him a naphula saphie (a charm to procure wealth). He brought me, as a present, some meal and milk; and when I had finished the saphie, and read it to him with an audible voice, he seemed highly satisfied with his bargain, and promised to bring me in the morning some milk for my breakfast. When I had finished my supper of rice and salt, I laid myself down upon a bullock's hide, and slept very quietly until morning; this being the first good meal and refreshing sleep that I had enjoyed for a long time.

21st August At daybreak I departed from Koolikorro, and about noon passed the villages of Kayoo and Toolumbo. In the afternoon I arrived at Marraboo, a large town, and like Koolikorro, famous for its trade in salt, I was conducted to the house of a Kaartan, of the tribe of Jower, by whom I was well received. This man had acquired a considerable property in the slave trade, and from his hospitality to strangers, was called by way of pre-eminence jattee (the landlord), and his house was a sort of public inn for all travellers. Those who had money were well lodged, for they always made him some return for his kindness; but those who had nothing to give were content to accept whatever he thought proper; and as I could not rank myself among the monied men, I was happy to take up my lodging in the same hut with seven poor fellows who had come from Kancaba in a canoe. But our landlord sent us some victuals.

22nd August One of the landlord's servants went with me a little way from the town to show me what road to take; but whether from ignorance or design, I know not, he directed me wrong; and I did not discover my mistake until the day was far advanced; when, coming to a deep creek, I had some thoughts of turning back; but as by that means I foresaw that I could not possibly reach Bammakoo before night. I resolved to cross it; and leading my horse close to the brink, I went behind him, and pushed him headlong into the water; and then taking the bridle in my teeth, swam over to the other side. This was the third creek I had crossed in this manner, since I had left Sego; but having secured my notes and memorandums in the crown of my hat, I received little or no inconvenience from such adventures. The rain and heavy dew kept my clothes constantly wet; and the roads being very deep and full of mud, such a washing was sometimes pleasant, and oftentimes necessary. I continued travelling through high grass without any beaten road, and about noon came to the river, the banks of which are here very rocky, and the force and roar of the water were very great. The king of Bambarra's canoes, however, frequently pass these rapids, by keeping close to the bank; persons being stationed on the shore with ropes fastened to the canoe, while others push it forward with long poles. At this time, however, it would, I think, have been a matter of great difficulty for any European boat to have crossed the stream. About four o'clock in the afternoon, having altered my course from the river towards the mountains, I came to a small pathway, which led to a village called Frookaboo, where I slept.

23rd August Early in the morning I set out for Bammakoo, at which place I arrived about five o'clock in the afternoon, I had heard Bammakoo much talked of as a great market for salt, and I felt rather disappointed to find it only a middling town, not quite so large as Marraboo; however, the smallness of its size is more than compensated by the riches of its inhabitants; for when the Moors bring their salt through Kaarta or Bambarra, they constantly rest a few days at this place; and the Negro merchants here, who are well acquainted with the value of salt in different kingdoms, frequently purchase by wholesale, and retail it to great advantage. Here I lodged at the house of a Serawoolli Negro, and was visited by a number of Moors. They spoke very good Mandingo, and were more civil to me than their countrymen had been. One of them had travelled to Rio Grande, and spoke very highly of the Christians. He sent me in the evening some boiled rice and milk. I now endeavoured to procure information concerning my route to the westward, from a slave merchant who had resided some years on the Gambia. He gave me some imperfect account of the distance, and enumerated the names of a great many places that lay in the way; but withal told me that the road was impassable at this season of the year; he was even afraid, he said, that I should find great difficulty in proceeding any farther; as the road crossed the Joliba at a town about half a day's journey to the westward of Bammakoo; and there being no canoes at that place large enough to receive my horse, I could not possibly get him over for some months to come. This was an obstruction of a very serious nature; but as I had no money to maintain myself even for a few days, I resolved to push on, and if I could not convey my horse across the river, to abandon him, and swim over myself. In thoughts of this nature I passed the night, and in the morning consulted with my landlord how I should surmount the present difficulty. He informed me that one road still remained, which was indeed very rocky, and scarcely passable for horses; but that if I had a proper guide over the hills to a town called Sibidooloo, he had no doubt, but with patience and caution, I might travel forwards through Manding. I immediately applied to the dooty, and was informed that a jilli kea (singing man) was about to depart for Sibidooloo, and would show me the road over the hills. With this man, who undertook to be my conductor. I travelled up the rocky glen about two miles, when we came to a small village; and here my musical fellow-traveller found out that he had brought me the wrong road. He told me that the horse-road lay on the other side of the hill, and throwing his drum upon his back, mounted up the rocks, where indeed no horse could follow him, leaving me to admire his agility, and trace out a road for myself. As I found it impossible to proceed, I rode back to the level ground, and directing my course to the eastward, came about noon to another glen, and discovered a path on which I observed the marks of horses' feet; following this path, I came in a short time to some shepherds' huts, where I was informed that I was in the right road, but that I could not possibly reach Sibidooloo before night. Soon after this I gained the summit of a hill, from whence I had an extensive view of the country. Towards the south-east appeared some very distant mountains, which I had formerly seen from an eminence near Marraboo, where the people informed me that these mountains were situated in a large and powerful kingdom called Kong; the sovereign of which could raise a much greater army than the king of Bambarra. Upon this height the soil is shallow; the rocks are ironstone and schistus, with detached pieces of white quartz.

A little before sunset, I descended on the north-west side of this ridge of hills; and as I was looking about for a convenient tree under which to pass the night (for I had no hopes of reaching any town), I descended into a delightful valley, and soon afterwards arrived at a romantic village called Kooma. This village is surrounded by a high wall, and is the sole property of a Mandingo merchant, who fled hither with his family during a former war. The adjacent fields yield him plenty of corn, his cattle roam at large in the valley, and the rocky hills secure him from the depredations of war. In this obscure retreat he is seldom visited by strangers; but whenever this happens, he makes the weary traveller welcome. I soon found myself surrounded by a circle of the harmless villagers. They asked me a thousand questions about my country; and, in return for my information, brought corn and milk for myself, and grass for my horse; kindled a fire in the hut where I was to sleep, and appeared very anxious to serve me.

25th August I departed from Kooma, accompanied by two shepherds, who were going to Sibidooloo. The road was very steep and rocky, and as my horse had hurt his feet much in coming from

Bammakoo, he travelled slowly and with great difficulty; for in many places the ascent was so sharp, and the declivities so great, that if he had made one false step, he must inevitably have been dashed to pieces. The shepherds being anxious to proceed, gave themselves little trouble about me or my horse, and kept walking on at a considerable distance. It was about eleven o'clock, as I stopped to drink a little water at a rivulet (my companions being nearly a quarter of a mile before me), that I heard some people calling to each other, and presently a loud screaming, as from a person in great distress. I immediately conjectured that a lion had taken one of the shepherds, and mounted my horse to have a better view of what had happened. The noise, however, ceased; and I rode slowly towards the place from whence I thought it had proceeded, calling out, but without receiving any answer. In a little time, however, I perceived one of the shepherds lying among the long grass near the road; and though I could see no blood upon him, I concluded he was dead. But when I came close to him, he whispered me to stop; telling me that a party of armed men had seized upon his companion, and shot two arrows at himself as he was making his escape. I stopped to consider what course to take, and looking round, saw at a little distance a man sitting on the stump of a tree; I distinguished also the heads of six or seven more, sitting among the grass, with muskets in their hands. I had now no hopes of escaping, and therefore determined to ride forward towards them. As I approached them, I was in hopes they were elephant-hunters; and by way of opening the conversation, inquired if they had shot anything; but without returning an answer, one of them ordered me to dismount; and then, as if recollecting himself, waved with his hand for me to proceed. I accordingly rode past, and had with some difficulty crossed a deep rivulet, when I heard somebody holloa; and looking behind, saw those I had taken for elephant-hunters running after me, and calling out to me to turn back. I stopped until they were all come up; when they informed me that the king of the Foulahs had sent them on purpose to bring me, my horse, and every thing that belonged to me, to Fooladoo, and that therefore I must turn back, and go along with them. Without hesitating a moment, I turned round and followed them, and we travelled together near a quarter of a mile without exchanging a word; when coming to a dark place of the wood, one of them said, in the Mandingo language. "This place will do"; and immediately snatched my hat from my head. Though I was by no means free of apprehension, yet I resolved to show as few signs of fear as possible, and therefore told them, that unless my hat was returned to me, I should proceed no further. But before I had time to receive an answer, another drew his knife, and seizing upon a metal button which remained upon my waistcoat, cut it off, and put it into his pocket. Their intentions were now obvious; and I thought that the easier they were permitted to rob me of everything, the less I had to fear. I therefore allowed them to search my pockets without resistance, and examine every part of my apparel, which they did with the most scrupulous exactness. But observing that I had one waistcoat under another, they insisted that I should cast them both off: and at last, to make sure work, stripped me quite naked. Even my half-boots (though the sole of one of them was tied on to my foot with a broken bridle rein) were minutely inspected. Whilst they were examining the plunder, I begged them, with great earnestness, to return my pocket compass; but when I pointed it out to them, as it was lying on the ground, one of the banditti, thinking I was about to take it up, cocked his musket, and swore that he would lay me dead on the spot if I presumed to put my hand upon it. After this, some of them went away with my horse, and the remainder stood considering whether they should leave me quite naked, or allow me something to shelter me from the sun. Humanity at last prevailed; they returned me the worst of the two shirts, and a pair of trousers; and, as they went away, one of them threw back my hat, in the crown of which I kept my memorandums; and this was probably the reason they did not wish to keep it. After they were gone, I sat for some time looking around me with amazement and terror. Whichever way I turned, nothing appeared but danger and difficulty. I saw myself in the midst of a vast wilderness in the depth of the rainy season, naked and alone; surrounded by savage animals, and men still more savage. I was five hundred miles from the nearest European settlement. All these circumstances crowded at once on my recollection; and I confess that my spirits began to fail me. I considered my fate as certain, and that I had no alternative, but to lie down and perish. The influence of religion, however, aided and support me. I reflected that no human prudence or foresight could possibly have averted my present sufferings. I was indeed a stranger in a strange land, yet I was still under the protecting eye of that Providence who has condescended to call himself the stranger's friend. At this moment, painful as my reflections were, the extraordinary beauty of a small moss, in fructification, irresistibly caught my eye. I mention this to show from what trifling circumstances the mind will sometimes derive consolation; for though the whole plant was not larger that the top of one of my fingers, I could not contemplate the delicate conformation of its roots, leaves, and capsula, without admiration. Can that Being (thought I) who planted, watered, and brought to perfection, in this obscure part of the world, a thing which appears of so small importance, look with unconcern upon the situation and sufferings of creatures formed after his own image? – surely not! Reflections like these would not allow me to despair. I started up, and disregarding both hunger and fatigue, travelled forwards, assured that relief was at hand; and I was not disappointed. In a short time I came to a small village, at the entrance of which I overtook the two shepherds who had come with me from Kooma. They were much surprised to see me; for they said they never doubted that the Foulahs, when they had robbed, had murdered me. Departing from this village, we travelled over several rocky ridges, and at sunset arrived at Sibidooloo, the frontier town of the kingdom of Manding.

THE ROAD TO KANO

Hugh Clapperton
(1788–1827)

In one of exloration's unhappier sagas two Scots, Captain Hugh Clapperton and Dr. Walter Oudney, were saddled with the unspeakable Major Dixon Denham on a three year journey to Lake Chad and beyond. Clapperton mapped much of northern Nigeria and emerged with credit. Major Denham also excelled himself, twice absconding, then accusing Oudney of incompetence and Clapperton of buggery. Happily the Major was absent when in 1824, after nursing his dying friend, Clapperton became the first European to reach Kano.

O ur servants caught a female rat, or bandicoot, as it is called in the East Indies, which measured two feet seven inches from the nose to the tip of the tail. The colour of the body was light grey, the tail black, and covered with long hairs, and the head much rounder than that of the common rat.

The diarrhoea of Dr. Oudney had ceased, but the cough was no better, and he was otherwise extremely ill: he had himself cupped on the left side of the chest by one of the natives. This operation is dexterously performed by them; they make the scarifications with a razor, and afterwards apply a perforated horn, from which they first extract the air by suction, and then stop the aperture with the thumb.

In the afternoon, I was not a little astonished at a message from the governor, brought us by El Wordee, acquainting us that Hadje Ali had told him we were spies and bad people, and wishing to know from us if it was true. I did not think proper to disturb Dr. Oudney by relating to him this calumny, and merely desired El Wordee to say to the governor, that as we were in his power he could do with us as he pleased; at the same time referring him particularly to the letter of

Henry Clapperton, from a sketch by Manton. Courtesy of the
Mansell Collection.

the sheikh of Bornou. El Wordee came back almost immediately, and assured me the governor was satisfied.

Jan. 10 To-day we left Katagum; the governor having furnished us with a guide. We had a bassoor, or frame of wood, put on a camel, and spread Dr. Oudney's bed upon it, as he was now too weak to ride on horseback; I also felt myself unwell. The governor accompanied us four miles out of town. At half past three o'clock in the afternoon we were obliged to halt, on account of Dr. Oudney's weakness; he was quite worn out, and could proceed no further; the road, too, being crooked and entangled, and lying along a large swamp to the south. We passed a number of villages.

Jan. 11 At eight o'clock in the morning we proceeded on our journey; but, at noon, were obliged to stop at the town of Murmur, on account of the alarming situation of Dr. Oudney, who had now become so feeble and exhausted, that I scarcely expected him to survive another day. He had been wasting away in a slow consumption, ever since we left the hills of Obarree, in Fezzan; where he was seized with inflammation of the chest, in consequence of sitting down in a current of cold air after being overheated.

12th Jan. Dr. Oudney drank a cup of coffee at day-break, and, by his desire, I ordered the camels to be loaded. I then assisted him to dress, and, with the support of his servant, he came out of the tent; but, before he could be lifted on the camel, I observed the ghastliness of death in his countenance, and had him immediately replaced in the tent. I sat down by his side, and, with unspeakable grief, witnessed his last breath, which was without a struggle or a groan. I now sent to the governor of the town to request his permission to bury the deceased, which he readily granted; and I had a grave made about five yards to the north of an old mimosa tree, a little beyond the southern gate of the town. The body being first washed, after the custom of the country, was dressed by my directions, in clothes made of turban shawls, which we were carrying with us as presents. The corpse was borne to the grave by our servants, and I read over it the funeral service of the church of England, before it was consigned to the earth; I afterwards caused the grave to be enclosed with a wall of clay, to keep off beasts of prey, and had two sheep killed and distributed among the poor.

Thus died, at the age of 32 years, Walter Oudney, M. D., a man of unassuming deportment, pleasing manners, steadfast perseverance, and undaunted enterprise; while his mind was fraught at once with knowledge, virtue, and religion. At any time, and in any place, to be bereaved of such a friend, had proved a severe trial; but to me, his friend and fellow traveller, labouring also under disease, and now left alone amid a strange people, and proceeding through a country which had hitherto never been trod by European foot, the loss was severe and afflicting in the extreme.

At day-break, on the following morning, I resumed my journey, trusting to the salutary effects of change of air and abstinence, as the best remedies both for mind and body. The road was swampy, and we crossed a narrow stream called Shashum, that falls into the Yeou, near the town. There were numerous villages on all sides.

14th Jan. Thermometer 52°. Our road lay through a well culti-vated country; at nine o'clock, a.m., we came to the town of Digoo, having an indifferent double wall, and a triple ditch nearly filled up. The town contained very few houses, but date-trees were in great abundance; outside the walls, however, there were several villages, or rather detached clusters of houses. The country afterwards began to rise into ridges, running nearly east and west; our road lying along one of them, gave me an excellent view of beautiful villages all around, and herds of cattle grazing in the open country. In the evening we halted under the walls of a town called Boogawa; this is the last town in the province of Katagum: I did not enter it.

15th Jan. The road to-day was through a thickly wooded country. Before mid-day, we again crossed the Shashum, which here runs nearly due north. The camel-drivers brought me a quantity of wild figs, which they found on the trees by the road side, near the river. We next entered an open, well cultivated country, and in the evening halted at a town called Katungwa, which is surrounded by a wall, and has a number of fine date-trees. This was the first town I entered in the kingdom Haussa proper. I was visited by a Felatah, who had been at Bagdad, Constantinople, Jerusalem, and Mecca, and be-longed to the order of Dervishes. He was a chattering little fellow, and told me he had seen the Wahabees at Mecca, who, he said, were the same people and spoke the same language as the Felatahs. I made him a present of a pair of scissors and a snuff-box, of which he seemed very proud, and sent me a bowl of bazeen in the evening. I here saw a range of low rocky hills, stretching nearly south-west. They are called, in the language of Haussa, Dooshee, or The Rocks, from which a large town on one of the roads leading from Katagum to Kano takes its name. Since we left the Wells of Beere-Kashifery, on the southern borders of the great desert, we had not met with rocks, or even pebbles, till now, the very channels of the rivers being destitute of stones, and the whole country consisting of soft alluvial clay. The camels were missing, and I sent all the servants after them;

they were not brought back before midnight, being found on their return to Bornou.

Jan. 16 The country still open and well cultivated, and the villages numerous. We met crowds of people coming from Kano with goods. Some carried them on their heads, others had asses or bullocks, according to their wealth. All were armed with bows and arrows, and several with swords; the Bornouese are known by carrying spears.

El Wordee and I having advanced before the cavalcade were waiting for it under a tree, near a town called Zangeia, when a man from Katagum went, of his own accord, and told the governor of Zangeia that a friend of the governor of Katagum was close at hand. The governor of Zangeia sent the man to tell us he would come and meet us on horseback, and show us a proper place to pitch our tents. We mounted our horses, and, led by the Katagumite who was so anxious for the honour of the friend of his master, we met the governor, about a quarter of a mile from the tree under which we had reposed ourselves. He was mounted on a very fine white horse, gaily caparisoned, and had seven attendants behind him, also on horseback, besides being accompanied by several men on foot, armed with bows and arrows. He advanced to us at full gallop, and, after many courteous welcomes, placed himself at our head, and rode before us into the town. On reaching his own house, he desired us to pitch our tents before his door, observing, "Here is a place of great safety." The camels arriving with the baggage, I presented him with a razor, a knife, a pair of scissors, and some spices. He sent me, in return, some milk and bazeen, with grass and gussub for the horses. Although a governor, I found out he was only an eunuch, belonging to the governor of Kano. He was in person fat, coarse, and ugly, with a shrill squeaking voice, and kept me awake half the night, laughing and talking among his people.

Zangeia is situate near the extremity of the Dooshee range of hills, and must have been once a very large town, from the extensive walls which still remain. The inhabitants were slaughtered or sold by the Felatahs, and plantations of cotton, tobacco, and indigo now occupy the place where houses formerly stood. Indeed the town may be said to consist of a number of thinly scattered villages. Within the walls there is a ridge of loose blocks of stone, connected with the range of hills in the neighbourhood. These masses of rock may be about two hundred feet high, and give a romantic appearance to the neat huts clustering round the base, and to the fine plantations of cotton, tobacco, and indigo, which are separated from one another by rows of date-trees, and are shaded by other large umbrageous trees, of

whose names I am ignorant. The prospect to the south was bounded
by high blue mountains. It was market day; plenty of beef, yams,
sweet potatoes, &c. for sale.

Jan. 17 The country still highly cultivated, and now diversified by
hill and dale. We passed a remarkable range of little hillocks of grey
granite; they were naked rocks, flattened or rounded at top, and
appeared like detached masses of stone rising singly out of the earth.
We also passed several walled towns quite deserted, the inhabitants
having been sold by their conquerors, the Felatahs. Women sat
spinning cotton by the road side, offering for sale, to the passing
caravans, gussub water, roast meat, sweet potatoes, cashew nuts,
&c. In the afternoon, we halted in a hollow, to the west of a town, or
rather a collection of villages, called Nansarina, where it was also
market day. The governor, when he heard of my arrival, sent me
milk and bazeen. I sent him, in return, a pair of scissors and a snuff-
box.

Jan. 18 When I ascended the high ground this morning, I saw a
range of hills to the south-west, which, I was told, were called Dull,
from a large town at their base. They appeared to be 600 or 700 feet
high, not peaked, but oval topped, and running in a direction nearly
north and south. I could not learn how far southward they extended.
We crossed a little stream, flowing to the north. The country
continued beautiful, with numerous plantations, as neatly fenced
as in England. The road was thronged with travellers, and the shady
trees by the road side served, as yesterday, to shelter female huck-
sters. The women not engaged in the retail of their wares were busy
spinning cotton, and from time to time surveyed themselves, with
whimsical complacency, in a little pocket mirror. The soil is a strong
red clay, large blocks of granite frequently appearing above the
surface.

At eleven in the morning we halted at a walled town called
Girkwa, through which I rode with El Wordee. The houses were
in groups, with large intervening vacancies, the former inhabitants
having also been sold; the walls are in good repair, and are
surrounded by a dry ditch. It was market day, and we found a
much finer market here than at Tripoli. I had an attack of ague, – the
disease that chiefly prevails in these parts, – and was obliged to rest
all day under the shade of a tree. A pretty Felatah girl, going to
market with milk and butter, neat and spruce in her attire as a
Cheshire dairy-maid, here accosted me with infinite archness and
grace. She said I was of her own nation; and, after much amusing
small talk, I pressed her, in jest, to accompany me on my journey,
while she parried my solicitations with roguish glee, by referring me

to her father and mother. I don't know how it happened, but her presence seemed to dispel the effects of the ague. To this trifling and innocent memorial of a face and form, seen that day for the first and last time, but which I shall not readily forget, I may add the more interesting information to the good house-wives of my own country, that the making of butter such as ours is confined to the nation of the Felatahs, and that it is both clean and excellent. So much is this domestic art cultivated, that from a useful prejudice or superstition, it is deemed unlucky to sell new milk; it may, however, be bestowed as a gift. Butter is also made in other parts of central Africa, but sold in an oily fluid state something like honey.

A native of Mourzuk who resides here sent me some kouskousoo and fowls. I received a visit from a black shreef, who informed me he had seen the sea, and that a river I should cross on the morrow communicated between the Kowara and the Yeou. By the Kowara, I understood him to mean the river that passes Timbuctoo, and which, of late years, has been so much talked of in Europe, under the name of Niger. This was a piece of gratuitous information, for on cross-questioning him he could furnish no authority for his opinion. But I soon discovered the whole trick, by El Wordee strongly recommending me to give my informant a present. The country to the south and south-west was very hilly.

19th Jan. We crossed a water-course called Girkwa, from the name of the town in its immediate vicinity.

It is the channel of the same river the black shreef alluded to, but did not now contain a drop of water. Indeed the channel itself is extremely shallow, and only about sixty or seventy yards across. The guide furnished me by the governor of Katagum told me, that the river took its rise in the mountains of Dull, and falling into another river, which we should soon come to, and which rose among the mountains of Nora, their united waters flowed into the Yeou, to the north of Katagum.

The country was much the same as yesterday; clear of wood, well cultivated, and divided into plantations. At noon we crossed the river Sockwa, alluded to above, and forming a junction with the Girkwa. The water was not above ankle deep in the middle of the stream, which did not now fill one twentieth part of the channel, and both rivers, I have no doubt, are at all times fordable, even during the rainy season. About a mile from the banks of the river, we passed the town of Sockwa, which is defended by a high clay wall. Being very unwell, I did not enter the town, but rode on through a clear, open country, to the town of Duakee, where I halted under a tree until the camels came up. This town is also walled, but contains few inhabitants, although the walls, made of clay like all the others, are of great extent, and in good repair. Before four o'clock the camels arrived, and we pitched our tents under the tree where I had lain down. The road was still crowded, from sunrise to sunset, with people going to or coming from Kano.

20th Jan.   By El Wordee's advice, I prepared myself this morning for entering Kano, which was now at hand. Arrayed in naval uniform, I made myself as smart as circumstances would permit. For three miles to the north of Duakee, the country was open and well cultivated. It then became thickly covered with underwood, until we ascended a rising ground, whence we had a view of two little mounts within the walls of Kano. The soil here is a tough clay mixed with gravel, the stones of which appear to be clay iron-stone. The country was now clear of wood, except here and there a few large shady trees, resorted to as usual by the women of the country selling refreshments. The villages were numerous, and the road was thronged with people of all descriptions.

At eleven o'clock we entered Kano, the great emporium of the kingdom of Haussa; but I had no sooner passed the gates, than I felt grievously disappointed; for from the flourishing description of it given by the Arabs, I expected to see a city of surprising grandeur: I found, on the contrary, the houses nearly a quarter of a mile from the walls, and in many parts scattered into detached groups, between large stagnant pools of water. I might have spared all the pains I had taken with my toilet; for not an individual turned his head round to gaze at me, but all, intent on their own business, allowed me to pass by without notice or remark.

DOWN THE NIGER

Richard Lander
(1804–34)

As Clapperton's manservant, Lander attended his dying master on his 1825 expedition to the Niger and was then commissioned, with his brother John, to continue the exploration of the river. The mystery of its lower course was finally solved when in 1831 they sailed down through Nigeria to the delta and the sea. Unassuming Cornishmen, the Landers approached their task with a refreshing confidence in the goodwill of Africans. It paid off in a knife-edge encounter at the confluence of the Benoue, although Richard subsequently paid the price with his life.

M onday, *October 25th.* At one A.M., the direction of the river changed to south-south-west, running between immensely high hills. At five o'clock this morning, we found ourselves nearly opposite a very considerable river, entering the Niger from the eastward; it appeared to be three or four miles wide at its mouth, and on the bank we saw a large town, one part of which faced the river, and the other the Quorra. We at first supposed it to be an arm of that river, and running from us; and therefore directed our course for it. We proceeded up it a short distance, but finding the current against us, and that it increased as we got within its entrance, and our people being tired, we were compelled to give up the attempt, and were easily swept back into the Niger. Consequently we passed on, but determined on making inquiries concerning it the first convenient opportunity. But we conclude this to be the Tshadda, and the large town we have alluded to, to be Cuttumcurrafee the same which had been mentioned to us by the old Mallam. At all events we had satisfied ourselves it was not a branch of the Niger. The banks on both sides, as far as we could see up it, were very high, and appeared verdant and fertile.

The morning was dull and cloudy; yet, as soon as the sun had partially dispersed the mists which hung over the valleys and upon the little hills, we could distinguish irregular mountains jutting up almost close to the water's edge, whose height we were prevented even from guessing at; because their summits were involved in clouds, or enwrapped in vapours, which yet lingered about their sides. A double range of elevated hills appeared beyond them on the south-east side; and on the north-west side a chain of lesser hills extended as far as the eye could discern. They appeared very sterile. Those on the north-west were formed of clumps, very much resembling the shape of those we had seen in Yarriba, which are here called the Kong mountains.

At seven o'clock the Niger seemed free of islands and clear of morasses on both sides, and its banks were well wooded, and much higher than we had observed them for a long time previously; nevertheless, it ran over a rocky bottom, which caused its surface to ripple exceedingly. Just about the same hour, one of the canoes, which we were told of as of different make to our own, passed us. In shape, it much resembled a common butcher's tray, and it was furnished with seats like those used on various parts of the sea-coast. It was paddled by eight or ten little boys, who sung as they worked; and they were superintended by an elderly person who sat in the middle of the canoe. The motion of their paddles was regulated by a peculiar hissing noise which they made at intervals with their mouths; and it was pleasing to observe the celerity with which this little vessel was impelled against the stream. In the early part of the morning, after daylight, we passed a great many villages. The banks of the river were ornamented with palm trees, and much cultivated ground, which extended to the foot of the mountains, and among the avenues formed between them.

At 10 A.M., we passed a huge and white naked rock, in the form of a perfect dome, arising from the centre of the river. It was about twenty feet high, and covered with an immense quantity of white birds, in consequence of which we named it the Bird Rock: it is about three or four miles distant from Bocqua, on the same side of the river. It is safest to pass it on the south-east side, on which side is also the proper channel of the river, about three miles in width. We passed it on the western side, and were very nearly lost in a whirl-pool. It was with the utmost difficulty we preserved the canoe from being carried away, and dashed against the rocks. Fortunately, I saw the danger at first, and finding we could not get clear of it, my brother and I took a paddle, and animating our men, we exerted all our strength, and succeeded in preventing her from turning round.

The distance of this rock from the nearest bank is about a quarter of a mile, and the current was running with the velocity of six miles an hour, according to our estimation. Had our canoe become unmanageable, we should inevitably have perished. Shortly after, seeing a convenient place for landing, the men being languid and weary with hunger and exertion, we halted on the right bank of the river, which we imagined was most convenient for our purpose. The course of the river this morning was south-south-west, and its width varied as usual from two to five or six miles. The angry and scowling appearance of the firmament forewarned us of a heavy shower, or something worse, which induced us hastily to erect an awning of mats under a palm-tree's shade. As soon as we had leisure to look around us, though no habitation could anywhere be seen, yet it was evident the spot had been visited, and that very recently, by numbers of people. We discovered the remains of several extinct fires, with broken calabashes and pieces of earthen vessels, which were scattered around; and our men likewise picked up a quantity of cocoanut shells, and three or four staves of a powder-barrel. These discoveries, trifling as they were, filled us with pleasant and hopeful sensations; and we felt assured, from the circumstance of a barrel of powder having found its way hither, that the natives in the neighbourhood maintained some kind of intercourse with Europeans from the sea.

The spot, for a hundred yards, was cleared of grass, underwood, and vegetation of all kinds; and, on further observation, we came to the conclusion that a market or fair was periodically held thereon. Very shortly afterwards, as three of our men were straggling about in the bush, searching for firewood, a village suddenly opened before them: this did not excite their astonishment, and they entered one of the huts which was nearest them, to procure a little fire. However, it happened to contain only women; but these were terrified beyond measure at the sudden and abrupt entrance of strange-looking men, whose language they did not know, and whose business they could not understand; and they all ran out, in a fright, into the woods, to warn their male relatives of them, who were labouring at their usual occupation of husbandry. Meanwhile, our men had very composedly taken some burning embers from the fire and returned to us in a few minutes, with the brief allusion to the circumstance of having discovered a village. They told us also that they had seen cultivated land, and that these women had run away from them as soon as they saw them. This we thought lightly of; but rejoiced that they had seen the village, and immediately sent Pascoe, Abraham, and Jowdie, in company, to obtain some fire, and to purchase a few yams for us. In about ten minutes after they returned in haste, telling us that they had been to the village, and had asked for some fire; but that the people did not understand them, and, instead of attending to their wishes, they looked terrified, and had suddenly disappeared. In consequence of their threatening attitudes, our people had left the village, and rejoined us with all the haste they could. We did not, however, think that they would attack us, and we proceeded to make our fires, and then laid ourselves down.

Totally unconscious of danger, we were reclining on our mats – for we, too, like our people, were wearied with toil, and overcome with drowsiness – when, in about twenty minutes after our men had returned, one of them shouted, with a loud voice, "War is coming! Oh, war is coming!" and ran towards us with a scream of terror, telling us that the natives were hastening to attack us. We started up at this unusual exclamation, and, looking about us, we beheld a large party of men, almost naked, running in a very irregular manner, and with uncouth gestures, towards our little encampment. They were all variously armed with muskets, bows and arrows, knives, cutlasses, barbs, long spears, and other instruments of destruction; and, as we gazed upon this band of wild men, with their ferocious looks and hostile appearance, which was not a little heightened on observing the weapons in their hands, we felt a very uneasy kind of sensation, and wished ourselves safe out of their hands. To persons peaceably inclined, like ourselves, and who had done them no harm, we could look on their preparations with calmness; but as it is impossible to foresee to what extremities such encounters might lead, we waited the result with the most painful anxiety.

Our party was much scattered; but fortunately we could see them coming to us at some distance, and we had time to collect our men. We resolved, however, to prevent bloodshed, if possible – our numbers were too few to leave us a chance of escaping by any other way. The natives were approaching us fast, and had by this time arrived almost close to our palm-tree. Not a moment was to be lost. We desired Pascoe and all our people to follow behind us, at a short distance, with the loaded muskets and pistols; and we enjoined them strictly not to fire, unless they first fired at us. One of the natives, who proved to be the chief, we perceived a little in advance of his companions; and, throwing down our pistols, which we had snatched up in the first moment of surprise, my brother and I walked very composedly, and unarmed, towards him. As we approached him, we made all the signs and motions we could with our arms, to deter him and his people from firing on us. His quiver was dangling at his side, his bow was bent, and an arrow, which was pointed at our breasts, already trembled on the string, when we were within a few yards of his person. This was a highly critical moment – the next might be our last. But the hand of Providence averted the blow; for, just as the chief was about to pull the fatal cord, a man that was nearest him rushed forward, and stayed his arm. At that instant we stood before him, and immediately held forth our hands; all of them trembled like aspen leaves; the chief looked up full in our faces, kneeling on the ground – light seemed to flash from his dark rolling eyes – his body was convulsed all over, as though he were enduring the utmost torture, and with a timorous, yet undefinable, expression of countenance, in which all the passions of our nature were strangely blended, he drooped his head, eagerly grasped our proffered hands, and burst into tears. This was a sign of friendship – harmony followed, and war and bloodshed were thought of no more. Peace and friendship now reigned amongst us; and the first thing that we did was to lift the old chief from the ground, and to convey him to our encampment. The behaviour of our men afforded us no little amusement, now that the danger was past. We had now had a fair trial of their courage, and should know who to trust on a future occasion. Pascoe was firm to his post, and stood still with his musket pointed at the chief's breast during the whole time. He is a brave fellow; and said to us, as we passed him to our encampment with the old man, "If the *black* rascals had fired at either of you, I should have brought the old chief down like a guinea-fowl." It was impossible to avoid smiling at the fellow's honesty – although we were on the best of terms with the old chief – and we have little doubt that he would have been as good as his word. As for our two brave fellows, Sam and Antonio, they took to their heels and scampered off as fast as they could, directly they saw the natives approaching us over the long grass; nor did they make their appearance again until the chief and all his people were sitting round us; and even when they did return, they were so frightened they could not speak for some time.

All the armed villagers had now gathered round their leader, and anxiously watched his looks and gestures. The result of the meeting delighted them – every eye sparkled with pleasure – they uttered a shout of joy – they thrust their bloodless arrows into their quivers – they ran about as though they were possessed of evil spirits – they twanged their bow-strings, fired off their muskets, shook their spears, clattered their quivers, danced, put their bodies into all manner of ridiculous positions, laughed, cried, and sung in rapid succession – they were like a troop of maniacs. Never was spectacle more wild and terrific. When this sally of passion to which they had worked themselves had subsided into calmer and more reasonable behaviour, we presented each of the war-men with a quantity of needles, as a further token of our friendly intentions. The chief sat himself down on the turf, with one of us on each side of him, while the men were leaning on their weapons on his right and left. At first no one could understand us; but an old man made his appearance shortly after, who understood the Hàussa language. Him the chief employed as an interpreter; and every one listened with anxiety to the following explanation which he gave us: –

"A few minutes after you first landed, one of my people came to me, and said that a number of strange people had arrived at the market-place. I sent him back again to get as near to you as he could, to hear what you intended doing. He soon after returned to me, and said that you spoke in a language which he could not understand. Not doubting that it was your intention to attack my village at night, and carry off my people, I desired them to get ready to fight. We were all prepared and eager to kill you, and came down breathing vengeance and slaughter, supposing that you were my enemies, and had landed from the opposite side of the river. But when you came to meet us unarmed, and we saw your white faces, we were all so frightened that we could not pull our bows, nor move hand or foot; and when you drew near me, and extended your hands towards me, I felt my heart faint within me, and believed that you were '*Children of Heaven*,' and had dropped from the skies." Such was the effect we had produced on him; and under this impression he knew not what he did. "And now," said he, "white men, all I want is your forgiveness." "That you shall have most heartily," we said, as we shook hands with the old chief; and having taken care to assure him we had not come from so good a place as he had imagined, we congratulated ourselves, as well as him, that this affair had ended so happily. For our own parts, we had reason to feel the most unspeakable pleasure at its favourable termination; and we offered up internally to our merciful Creator a prayer of thanksgiving and praise, for his providential interference on our behalf; for the Almighty has, indeed, to use the words of the Psalmist of Israel, "delivered our soul from death, and our feet from falling; and preserved us from any terror by night, and from the arrow that flieth by day; from the pestilence that walketh in darkness, and from the sickness that destroyeth at noon-day." We were grateful to find that our blood had not been shed, and that we had been prevented from spilling the blood of others, which we imagined we should have been constrained to do from irremediable necessity. Our guns were all double-loaded with balls and slugs, our men were ready to present them, and a single arrow from a bow would have been the signal for immediate destruction. It was a narrow escape; and God grant we may never be so near a cruel death again! It was happy for us that our white faces and calm behaviour produced the effect it did on these people – in another minute our bodies would have been as full of arrows as a porcupine's is full of quills.

The old chief returned to the village, followed by his people, whom he addressed by the way from an ant-hill on which he mounted himself. He put himself into a great variety of attitudes, and delivered them a speech which lasted more than half an hour. Whether this was relating to ourselves or not we could not ascertain; but it seemed more than probable. They came back to us again in the afternoon, bringing with them a large quantity of yams and gooranuts as a present, and invited us with urgent importunity to sleep in their huts for the night, promising to treat us as well as their circumstances would permit. We thanked them for their kindness, but for many reasons we did not embrace their offer. However, it seemed as though this refusal on our parts caused them to be mistrustful of our intentions; for the villagers were discharging their muskets from sunset till nearly eleven o'clock at night, when the chief paid us a third visit, and brought with him eight thousand cowries, and a large heap of yams, which he laid at our feet. Poor fellow! his countenance beamed with joy on discovering that we were *really* his friends. At length he was induced to place confidence in us; and, as he wished us good night, he seemed well pleased with the tranquil appearance of things, and went away.

In the course of our conversation with the chief, when all his villagers were assembled around us, we pointed to their guns, and the bits of red cloth they had with them, and made them understand that they all came from our country, at which their admiration and wonder was much increased. The old man who had performed the part of our interpreter so admirably is an old Funda Mallam. He understood the Hàussa language perfectly, and told us he had come here from Funda to attend the market which was held here every nine days. He informed us that many people came from the sea-coast, with goods from the white men to purchase slaves, a great number of which, he said, came from his country. He told us that this place is the famous Bocquâ market-place, of which we had heard so great talk, and that the opposite bank of the river belonged to the Funda country. We now asked the old Mallam the distance from this place to the sea, and he told us about ten days' journey. We then pointed out the hills on the opposite side of the river, and asked him where they led to. "The sea," was his answer. And "where do they lead to?" we inquired, pointing to those on the same bank of the river as ourselves. He answered, "they run a long way into a country we do not know." We then asked him, if he had ever heard of a country called Eyeo or Yarriba. To which he replied, he had never heard of any country of either of those names. Our next concern was about the safety of the river navigation; and we anxiously inquired his opinion of it lower down, and whether there were any rocks or dangerous places. As to the river navigation, he satisfied us by saying, he knew of no dangers, nor had he ever heard of any; but the people on the banks, he said, were very bad. We asked him if he thought the chief would send a messenger with us if we were to request him, even one day's journey from this place. Without the least hesitation he answered us – "No; the people of this country can go no farther down the river; if they do, and are caught, they will lose their heads. Every town that I know of on the banks of the river is at war with its neighbour, and all the rest likewise." We asked him then how far Bornou was from Funda? to which he replied, "Fifteen days' journey." We were also anxious to know the character of the people on the borders of the Tshadda; and he informed us they were all good people, nearly all Mussulmen. There was one bad place to pass, he said, which was Yamyam. Here our conversation was interrupted by the old chief, who wished to return to the village, and the Mallam was obliged to accompany him. He was a fine respectable old man, and answered all our questions with a readiness which evinced the superiority of his class.

We offered up a prayer to the Almighty for his signal protection during this eventful day, and retired to rest.

Tuesday, October 26th   When I awoke in the morning, the first person I saw was our trusty old man, Pascoe, very busy roasting yams for our breakfast. This man has been a most valuable servant to us, and is the only staunch fellow among all our people. In spite of a good deal of rain that had fallen in the night, we got up much refreshed this morning; for our mat awning, although rather a frail covering, had excluded the rain and kept us tolerably dry. Early in the morning the chief of the village, the old man that acted as interpreter, and a number of men and women, visited our encampment, and behaved themselves in the most becoming and friendly manner. Not satisfied with what they had given us yesterday, the villagers offered us another large heap of yams, which, however, we refused to accept without making a suitable recompense. We accordingly gave them some beads in exchange for them, although I believe they would have been contented had we possessed nothing to offer them in return.

We now learnt from the interpreter that buyers and sellers attend this market, not only from places adjacent, but also from remote towns and villages, both above and below, and on each bank of the Niger. A small tribute is exacted by the chief from every one that offers articles for sale at the market, and in this consists the whole of his revenues. All the villagers that came out against us yesterday are his slaves. We were likewise informed, that directly opposite, on the eastern bank, is the common path to the city of Funda, which is, indeed, as we have been told at *Fofo*, situated three days' journey up the Tshadda from the Niger; that the large river which we observed yesterday falling into the Niger from the eastward, is the celebrated *Shar, Shary, or Sharry*, of travellers, or, which is more proper than either, the *Tshadda*, as it is universally called throughout the country. The interpreter said, further, that the smaller stream which we passed on the 19th, flowing from the same direction, is the *"Coodoonia."*

The chief assured us that we had nothing to fear, having passed all those places from which we might have expected danger and molestation during the night. However, he cautioned us to avoid, if possible, a very considerable town lying on the eastern bank, which we should pass in the afternoon, the governor of which, he affirmed, would detain us a considerable time in his territories, though he might treat us well. A little way below Bocquâ, he said, on the left border of the river, resides a powerful king, sovereign of a fine country, called *Attà*, who would force us to visit him, if by any means he were to be forewarned of our approach. He said, that he did not think he would do us any injury, but that the chief was a very extraordinary man, and if he had us in his power would detain us longer than we wished. Perhaps he might keep us in his town two or three months, but he would at least detain us till all his people had satisfied their curiosity, and then he might allow us to depart. As the chief of Bocquâ was decidedly of opinion that it would be in the power of this prince to render us the most essential service if he were our friend, we requested of him a guide and messenger to accompany us to *Attà*, and introduce us to the king; but he answered, without hesitation, that a man from him would be captured and slain the moment he should make his appearance there, but for what reason we are left to conjecture. This did not argue, however, very favourably as to the clemency or merciful disposition of the monarch of *Attà*; and therefore we resolved to keep out of his reach by

running along close to the shore on the opposite side of the water.
The chief concluded by observing that in seven days we should reach
the sea, a piece of intelligence with which we were not a little pleased.
The old interpreter had told us that we should get there in ten days;
therefore we cannot be far from it.

ARRIVAL IN TIMBUKTU

Heinrich Barth
(1821–65)

Born in Hamburg, Barth was already an experienced traveller and a methodical scholar when in 1850 he joined a British expedition to investigate Africa's internal slave trade. From Tripoli the expedition crossed the Sahara to Lake Chad. Its leader died but Barth continued on alone, exploring a vast tract of the Sahel from northern Cameroon to Mali. Timbuktu, previously visited only by A.G. Laing and René Caillié, provided the climax as Barth, in disguise, approached the forbidden city by boat from the Niger.

7th September, 1853 Thus the day broke which, after so many months' exertion, was to carry me to the harbour of Timbúktu. We started at a tolerably early hour, crossing the broad sheet of the river, first in a north-easterly, then in an almost northerly direction, till finding ourselves opposite the small hamlet Tásakal, mentioned by Caillié, we began to keep along the windings of the northern bank which, from its low character, presented a very varying appearance, while a creek, separating from the trunk, entered the low ground. The river a month or two later in the season inundates the whole country to a great distance, but the magnificent stream, with the exception of a few fishing-boats, now seemed almost tenantless, the only objects which in the present reduced state of the country animated the scenery being a number of large boats lying at anchor in front of us near the shore of the village Koróme. But the whole character of the river was of the highest interest to me, as it disclosed some new features for which I had not been prepared; for, while the water on which Koróme was situated formed only by far the smaller branch, the chief river, about three quarters of a mile in breadth, took its direction to the south-east, separated

from the former by a group of islands called Day, at the headland
of which lies the islet of Tárashám.

It was with an anxious feeling that I bade farewell to that noble
river as it turned away from us, not being sure whether it would fall
to my lot to explore its further course, although it was my firm
intention at the time to accomplish this task if possible. Thus we
entered the branch of Koróme, keeping along the grass which here
grows in the river to a great extent, till we reached the village,
consisting of nothing but temporary huts of reed, which, in the
course of a few weeks, with the rising of the waters, were to be
removed further inland. Notwithstanding its frail character, this
poor little village was interesting on account of its wharfs, where a
number of boats were repairing. The master of our own craft
residing here (for all the boatmen on this river are serfs, or nearly
in that condition), we were obliged to halt almost an hour and a half;
but in order not to excite the curiosity of the people, I thought it
prudent to remain in my boat. But even there I was incommoded
with a great number of visitors, who were very anxious to know
exactly what sort of person I was. It was here that we heard the
unsatisfactory news that El Bakáy, whose name as a just and
intelligent chief alone had given me confidence to undertake this
journey, was absent at the time in Gúndam, whither he had gone in
order to settle a dispute which had arisen between the Tawárek
[Tuareg] and the Berabísh; and as from the very beginning, when I
was planning my journey to Timbúktu, I had based the whole
confidence of my success upon the noble and trustworthy character
which was attributed to the Sheikh El Bakáy by my informants, this
piece of information produced a serious effect upon me.

At length we set out again on our interesting voyage, following
first a south-easterly, then a north-easterly direction along this
branch, which, for the first three miles and a half, retained some
importance, being here about 200 yards wide, when the channel
divided a second time, the more considerable branch turning off
towards Yélluwa and Zegália, and other smaller hamlets situated on
the islands of Day, while the watercourse which we followed
dwindled away to a mere narrow meadow-water, bearing the
appearance of an artificial ditch or canal, which, as I now heard,
is entirely dry during the dry season, so that it becomes impossible to
embark directly at Kábara for places situated higher up or lower
down the river. But at that time I had formed the erroneous idea that
this canal never became navigable for more than four months in the
year, and thence concluded that it would have been impossible for
Caillié to have reached Kábara in his boat in the month of April. The

navigation of this water became so difficult, that all my people were obliged to leave the boat, which, with great difficulty was dragged on by the boatmen, who themselves entered the water and lifted and pushed it along with their hands. But before we reached Kábara, which is situated on the slope of a sandy eminence, the narrow and shallow channel widened to a tolerably large basin of circular shape; and here, in front of the town, seven good-sized boats were lying, giving to the whole place some little life. Later in the season, when the channel becomes navigable for larger boats, the intercourse becomes much more animated. During the palmy days of the Songhay empire, an uninterrupted intercourse took place between Gágho and Timbúktu on the one side, and between Timbúktu and Jenni on the other, and a numerous fleet was always lying here under the orders of an admiral of great power and influence. The basin has such a regular shape, that it looks as if it were artificial; but, nevertheless, it may be the work of nature, as Kábara from the most ancient times has been the harbour of Timbúktu, and at times seems even to have been of greater importance than the latter place itself.

A branch of the river turns off to the east, without however reaching the main trunk, so that in general, except when the whole country is inundated, boats from Kábara which are going down the river must first return in a south-westerly direction towards Koróme, in order to reach the main branch. Even at the present time, however, when this whole region is plunged into an abyss of anarchy and misrule, the scene was not entirely wanting in life; for women were filling their pitchers or washing clothes on large stones jutting out from the water, while a number of idle people had collected on the beach to see who the stranger was that had just arrived.

At length we lay to, and sending two of my people on shore, in order to obtain quarters, I followed them as soon as possible, when I was informed that they had procured a comfortable dwelling for me. The house where I was lodged was a large and grand building (if we take into account the general relations of this country), standing on the very top of the mound on the slope of which the town is situated. It was of an oblong shape, consisting of very massive clay walls, which were even adorned, in a slight degree, with a rude kind of relief; and it included, besides two anterooms, an inner courtyard, with a good many smaller chambers, and an upper story. The interior, with its small stores of every kind, and its assortment of sheep, ducks, fowls, and pigeons, in different departments, resembled Noah's ark, and afforded a cheerful sight of homely comfort which had been preserved here from more ancient and better times, notwithstanding the exactions of Fúlbe and Imóshagh.

Having taken possession of the two ante-rooms for my people and luggage, I endeavoured to make myself as comfortable as possible; while the busy landlady, a tall and stout personage, in the absence of her husband, a wealthy Songhay merchant, endeavoured to make herself agreeable, and offered me the various delicacies of her store for sale; but these were extremely scanty, the chief attraction to us, besides a small bowl of milk seasoned with honey, being some onions, of which I myself was not less in want than my people for seasoning our simple food; but fresh ones were not even to be got here, the article sold being a peculiar preparation which is imported from Sansándi, the onions, which are of very small size, being cut into slices and put in water, then pounded in a wooden mortar, dried again, and, by means of some butter, made up into a sort of round ball, which is sold in small pats of an inch and a half in diameter for five shells each: these are called "láwashi" in Fulfúlde, or "gabú" in the Songhay language. Besides this article, so necessary for seasoning the food, I bought a little bulánga, or vegetable butter, in order to light up the dark room where I had taken up my quarters; but the night which I passed here was a very uncomfortable one, on account of the number of mosquitoes which infest the whole place.

Thus broke the 6th of September, – a very important day for me, as it was to determine the kind of reception I was to meet with in this quarter. But notwithstanding the uncertainty of my prospects, I felt cheerful and full of confidence; and, as I was now again firmly established on dry soil, I went early in the morning to see my horse, which had successfully crossed all the different branches lying between Kábara and Sarayámo; but I was sorry to find him in a very weak and emaciated condition.

While traversing the village, I was surprised at the many clay buildings which are to be seen here, amounting to between 150 and 200; however, these are not so much the dwellings of the inhabitants of Kábara themselves, but serve rather as magazines for storing up the merchandise belonging to the people of, and the foreign merchants residing in, Timbúktu and Sansándi. There are two small market-places, one containing about twelve stalls or sheds, where all sorts of articles are sold, the other being used exclusively for meat. Although it was still early in the day, women were already busy boiling rice, which is sold in small portions, or made up into thin cakes boiled with bulánga, and sold for five shells each. Almost all the inhabitants, who may muster about 2000, are Songhay; but the authorities belong to the tribe of the Fúlbe, whose principal wealth consists of cattle, the only exception being the office of the inspector of the harbour, – a very ancient office, repeatedly mentioned by A'hmed Bábá, – which at present is in the hands of Múláy Kásim, a sheríf whose family is said to have emigrated originally from the Gharb or Morocco, but who has become so Sudánised that he has forgotten all his former knowledge of Arabic. On account of the cattle being driven to a great distance, I found that milk was very scarce and dear. The inhabitants cultivate a little rice, but have some cotton, besides bámia, or *Corchorus olitorius*, and melons of various descriptions.

Having returned to my quarters from my walk through the town, I had to distribute several presents to some people whom El Waláti chose to represent as his brothers and friends. Having then given to himself a new, glittering, black tobe of Núpe manufacture, a new "háf", and the white bernús which I wore myself, I at length prevailed upon him to set out for the town, in order to obtain protection for me; for as yet I was an outlaw in the country, and any ruffian who suspected my character might have slain me, without scarcely anybody caring anything about it; and circumstances seemed to assume a very unfavourable aspect: for there was a great movement among the Tawárek in the neighbourhood, when it almost seemed as if some news of my real character had transpired. Not long after my two messengers were gone, a Tárki chief, of the name of Knéha, with tall and stately figure, and of noble expressive features, as far as his shawl around the face allowed them to be seen, but, like the whole tribe of the Kél-hekítan to which he belongs, bearing a very bad character as a freebooter, made his appearance, armed with spear and sword, and obtruded himself upon me while I was partaking of my simple dish of rice; notwithstanding which, he took his seat at a short distance opposite to me. Not wishing to invite him to a share in my poor frugal repast by the usual "bismillah", I told him, first in Arabic and then in Fulfúlde, that I was dining, and had no leisure to speak with him at present. Whereupon he took his leave, but returned after a short while, and, in a rather peremptory manner, solicited a present from me, being, as he said, a great chief of the country; but as I was not aware of the extent of his power, and being also afraid that others might imitate his example, I told him that I could not give him anything before I had made due inquiries respecting his real importance from my companion who had just gone to the town. But he was not at all satisfied with my argument; representing himself as a great "dhálem", or evil-doer, and that as such he might do me much harm; till at length, after a very spirited altercation, I got rid of him.

He was scarcely gone, when the whole house was filled with armed men, horse and foot, from Timbúktu, most of them clad in light blue tobes, tightly girt round the waist with a shawl, and dressed in short breeches reaching only to the knee, as if they were going to fight, their head being covered with a straw hat of the peculiar shape of a little hut with regular thatchwork, such as is fashionable among the inhabitants of Másina and of the provinces further west. They were armed with spears, besides which some of them wore also a sword: only a few of them had muskets. Entering the house rather abruptly, and squatting down in the ante-chambers and courtyard, just where they could find a place, they stared at me not a little, and began asking of each other who this strange-looking fellow might be, while I was reclining on my two smaller boxes, having my larger ones and my other luggage behind me. I was rather at a loss to account for their intrusion, until I learned, upon inquiry from my landlady, that they were come in order to protect their cattle from the Tawárek, who at the time were passing through the place, and who had driven away some of their property. The very person whom they dreaded was the chief Knéha, who had just left me, though they could not make out his whereabouts. Having refreshed themselves during the hot hours of the day, these people started off; but the alarm about the cattle continued the whole of the afternoon, and not less than 200 armed men came into my apartments in the course of an hour.

My messengers not returning at the appointed time from their errand to the town, I had at length retired to rest in the evening, when shortly before midnight they arrived, together with Sídi A'lawáte, the Sheikh El Bakáy's brother, and several of his followers, who took up their quarters on the terrace of my house in order to be out of the reach of the mosquitoes; and after they had been regaled with a good supper, which had been provided beforehand by some of the townspeople, I went to pay my respects to them.

It was an important interview; for, although this was not the person for whom my visit was specially intended, and whose favourable or unfavourable disposition would influence the whole success of my arduous undertaking, yet for the present I was entirely in his hands, and all depended upon the manner in which he received me. Now my two messengers had only disclosed to himself personally, that I was a Christian, while at the same time they had laid great stress upon the circumstance that, although a Christian, I was under the special protection of the Sultan of Stambúl; and Sídi A'lawáte inquired therefore of me, with great earnestness and anxiety, as to the peculiar manner in which I enjoyed the protection of that great Mohammedan sovereign.

Now it was most unfortunate for me that I had no direct letter from that quarter. Even the firmán with which we had been provided by the Bashá of Tripoli had been delivered to the governor for whom it was destined, so that at the time I had nothing with me to show but a firmán which I had used on my journey in Egypt, and which of course had no especial relation to the case in question. The want of such a general letter of protection from the Sultan of Constantinople, which I had solicited with so much anxiety to be sent after me, was in the sequel the chief cause of my difficult and dangerous position in Timbúktu; for, furnished with such a letter, it would have been easy to have imposed silence upon my adversaries and enemies there, and especially upon the merchants from Morocco, who were instigated by the most selfish jealousy to raise all sorts of intrigues against me.

Having heard my address with attention, although I was not able to establish every point so clearly as I could have wished, the sheikh's brother promised me protection, and desired me to be without any apprehension with regard to my safety; and thus terminated my first interview with this man, who, on the whole, inspired me with a certain degree of confidence, although I was glad to think that he was not the man upon whom I had to rely for my safety. Having then had a further chat with his telamid or pupils, with whom I passed for a Mohammedan, I took leave of the party and retired to rest in the close apartments of the lower story of the house.

Wednesday, September 7th   After a rather restless night, the day broke when I was at length to enter Timbúktu; but we had a good deal of trouble in performing this last short stage of our journey, deprived as we were of beasts of burden; for the two camels which the people had brought from the town in order to carry my boxes, proved much too weak, and it was only after a long delay that we were able to procure eleven donkeys for the transport of all my luggage. Meanwhile the rumour of a traveller of importance having arrived had spread far and wide, and several inhabitants of the place sent a breakfast both for myself and my protector. Just at the moment when we were at length mounting our horses, it seemed as if the Tárki chief Knéha was to cause me some more trouble, for in the morning he had sent me a vessel of butter in order thus to acquire a fair claim upon my generosity; and coming now for his reward, he was greatly disappointed when he heard that the present had fallen into the hands of other people.

It was ten o'clock when our cavalcade at length put itself in motion, ascending the sandhills which rise close behind the village of Kábara, and which, to my great regret, had prevented my obtaining a view of the town from the top of our terrace. The contrast of this desolate scenery with the character of the fertile banks of the river which I had just left behind was remarkable. The whole tract bore decidedly the character of a desert, although the path was thickly lined on both sides with thorny bushes and stunted trees, which were being cleared away in some places in order to render the path less obstructed and more safe, as the Tawárek never fail to infest it, and at present were particularly dreaded on account of their having killed a few days previously three petty Tawáti traders on their way to A'rawáin. It is from the unsafe character of this short road between the harbour and the town, that the spot, about halfway between Kábara and Timbúktu, bears the remarkable name of "Ur-immándes", "he does not hear", meaning the place where the cry of the unfortunate victim is not heard from either side.

Having traversed two sunken spots designated by especial names, where, in certain years when the river rises to an unusual height, as happened in the course of the same winter, the water of the inundation enters and occasionally forms even a navigable channel; and leaving on one side the talha tree of the Welí Sálah, covered with innumerable rags of the superstitious natives, who expect to be generously rewarded by their saint with a new shirt, we approached the town: but its dark masses of clay not being illuminated by bright sunshine, for the sky was thickly overcast and the atmosphere filled with sand, were scarcely to be distinguished from the sand and rubbish heaped all round; and there was no opportunity for looking attentively about, as a body of people were coming towards us in order to pay their compliments to the stranger and bid him welcome. This was a very important moment, as, if they had felt the slightest suspicion with regard to my character, they might easily have prevented my entering the town at all, and thus even endangered my life.

I therefore took the hint of A'lawáte, who recommended me to make a start in advance in order to anticipate the salute of these people who had come to meet us; and putting my horse to a gallop, and gun in hand, I galloped up to meet them, when I was received with many saláms. But a circumstance occurred which might have proved fatal, not only to my enterprise, but even to my own personal safety, as there was a man among the group who addressed me in

Turkish, which I had almost entirely forgotten; so that I could with difficulty make a suitable answer to his compliment; but avoiding farther indiscreet questions, I pushed on in order to get under safe cover.

Having then traversed the rubbish which has accumulated round the ruined clay wall of the town, and left on one side a row of dirty reed huts which encompass the whole of the place, we entered the narrow streets and lanes, or, as the people of Timbúktu say, the tijeráten, which scarcely allowed two horses to proceed abreast. But I was not a little surprised at the populous and wealthy character which this quarter of the town, the Sáne-Gúngu, exhibited, many of the houses rising to the height of two stories, and in their façade evincing even an attempt at architectural adornment. Thus, taking a more westerly turn, and followed by a numerous troop of people, we passed the house of the Sheikh El Bakáy, where I was desired to fire a pistol; but as I had all my arms loaded with ball I prudently declined to do so, and left it to one of my people to do honour to the house of our host. We thus reached the house on the other side of the street, which was destined for my residence, and I was glad when I found myself safely in my new quarters.

It had been arranged that, during the absence of the Sheikh el Bakáy, whose special guest I professed to be, my house should be locked up and no one allowed to pay me a visit. However, while my luggage was being got in, numbers of people gained access to the house, and came to pay me their compliments, and while they scrutinised my luggage, part of which had rather a foreign appearance, some of them entertained a doubt as to my nationality. But of course it could never have been my intention to have impressed these people with the belief of my being a Mohammedan; for having been known as a Christian all along my road as far as Libtáko, with which province the Arabs of A'zawád keep up a continual intercourse, although there the people would scarcely believe that I was a European, the news of my real character could not fail soon to transpire; and it was rather a fortunate circumstance that, notwithstanding our extremely slow progress, and our roundabout direction, the news had not anticipated us. I had been obliged to adopt the character of a Mohammedan, in order to traverse with some degree of safety the country of the Tawárek, and to enter the town of Timbúktu, which was in the hands of the fanatical Fúlbe of Hamda-Alláhi, while I had not yet obtained the protection of the chief whose name and character alone had inspired me with sufficient confidence to enter upon this enterprise.

Barth's arrival at Timbuktu. Drawing by J. M. Bernatz, from a sketch by Dr. Barth. From *Travels and Discoveries in North and Central Africa*, London, 1858.

Thus I had now reached the object of my arduous undertaking; but it was apparent from the very first, that I should not enjoy the triumph of having overcome the difficulties of the journey in quiet and repose. The continuous excitement of the protracted struggle, and the uncertainty whether I should succeed in my undertaking, had sustained my weakened frame till I actually reached this city; but as soon as I was there, and almost at the very moment when I entered my house, I was seized with a severe attack of fever. Yet never were presence of mind and bodily energy more required; for the first night which I passed in Timbúktu was disturbed by feelings of alarm and serious anxiety.

MY OGOWE FANS

Mary Kingsley
(1862–1900)

Self-educated while she nursed her elderly parents, Mary Kingsley had known only middle-class English domesticity until venturing to West Africa in 1892. Her parents had died and, unmarried, she determined to study "fish and fetish" for the British Museum. Her 1894 ascent of Gabon's Ogowé river (from Travels in West Africa, *1897) established her as a genuine pioneer and an inimitable narrator. She died six years later while nursing prisoners during the Boer War.*

A certain sort of friendship soon arose between the Fans and me. We each recognised that we belonged to that same section of the human race with whom it is better to drink than to fight. We knew we would each have killed the other, if sufficient inducement were offered, and so we took a certain amount of care that the inducement should not arise. Gray Shirt and Pagan also, their trade friends, the Fans treated with an independent sort of courtesy; but Silence, Singlet, the Passenger, and above all Ngouta, they openly did not care a row of pins for, and I have small doubt that had it not been for us other three they would have killed and eaten these very amiable gentlemen with as much compunction as an English sportsman would kill as many rabbits. They on their part hated the Fan, and never lost an opportunity of telling me "these Fan be bad man too much." I must not forget to mention the other member of our party, a Fan gentleman with the manners of a duke and the habits of a dustbin. He came with us, quite uninvited by me, and never asked for any pay; I think he only wanted to see the fun, and drop in for a fight if there was one going on, and to pick up the pieces generally. He was evidently a man of some importance, from the way the others treated him; and moreover he had a splendid gun, with a gorilla skin sheath for its lock, and ornamented all over its stock with brass nails. His costume consisted of a small piece of dirty rag round his loins; and whenever we were going through dense undergrowth, or wading a swamp, he wore that filament tucked up scandalously short. Whenever we were sitting down in the forest having one of our nondescript meals, he always sat next to me and appropriated the tin. Then he would fill his pipe, and turning to me with the easy grace of aristocracy, would say what may be translated as "My dear Princess, could you favour me with a lucifer?"

I used to say, "My dear Duke, charmed, I'm sure," and give him one ready lit.

I dared not trust him with the box whole, having a personal conviction that he would have kept it. I asked him what he would do suppose I was not there with a box of lucifers; and he produced a bush-cow's horn with a neat wood lid tied on with tie tie, and from out of it he produced a flint and steel and demonstrated. Unfortunately all his grace's minor possessions, owing to the scantiness of his attire, were in one and the same pine-apple-fibre bag which he wore slung across his shoulder; and these possessions, though not great, were as dangerous to the body as a million sterling is said to be to the soul, for they consisted largely of gunpowder and snuff, and their separate receptacles leaked and their contents commingled, so that demonstration on fire-making methods among the Fan ended in an awful bang and blow-up in a small way, and the Professor and his pupil sneezed like fury for ten minutes, and a cruel world laughed till it nearly died, for twenty. Still that bag with all its failings was a wonder for its containing power.

The first day in the forest we came across a snake – a beauty with a new red-brown and yellow-patterned velvety skin, about three feet six inches long and as thick as a man's thigh. Ngouta met it, hanging from a bough, and shot backwards like a lobster, Ngouta having among his many weaknesses a rooted horror of snakes. This snake the Ogowé natives all hold in great aversion. For the bite of other sorts of snakes they profess to have remedies, but for this they have none. If, however, a native is stung by one he usually conceals the fact that it was this particular kind, and tries to get any chance the native doctor's medicine may give. The Duke stepped forward and with one blow flattened its head against the tree with his gun butt, and then folded the snake up and got as much of it as possible into the bag, while the rest hung dangling out. Ngouta, not being able to keep ahead of the Duke, his Grace's pace being stiff, went to the extreme rear of the party, so that other people might be killed first if the snake returned to life, as he surmised it would. He fell into other dangers from this caution, but I cannot chronicle Ngouta's afflictions in full without running this book into an old-fashioned folio size. We had the snake for supper, that is to say the Fan and I; the others would not touch it, although a good snake, properly cooked, is one of the best meats one gets out here, far and away better than the African fowl.

The Fans also did their best to educate me in every way: they told me their names for things, while I told them mine, throwing in besides as "a dash for top" a few colloquial phrases such as: "Dear me, now," "Who'd have thought it," "Stuff, my dear sir," and so on; and when I left them they had run each together as it were into one word, and a nice savage sound they had with them too, especially "dearmenow," so I must warn any philologist who visits the Fans, to beware of regarding any word beyond two syllables in length as being of native origin. I found several European words already slightly altered in use among them, such as "Amuck" – a mug, "Alas" – a glass, a tumbler. I do not know whether their "Ami" – a person addressed, or spoken of – is French or not. It may come from "Anwĕ" – M'pongwe for "Ye," "You." They use it as a rule in addressing a person after the phrase they always open up conversation with, "Azuna" – Listen, or I am speaking.

They also showed me many things: how to light a fire from the pith of a certain tree, which was useful to me in after life, but they rather overdid this branch of instruction one way and another; for example, Wiki had, as above indicated, a mania for bush-ropes and a marvellous eye and knowledge of them; he would pick out from among the thousands surrounding us now one of such peculiar suppleness that you could wind it round anything, like a strip of cloth, and as strong withal as a hawser; or again another which has a certain stiffness, combined with a slight elastic spring, excellent for hauling, with the ease and accuracy of a lady who picks out the particular twisted strand of embroidery silk from a multi-coloured tangled ball. He would go into the bush after them while other people were resting, and particularly after the sort which, when split is bright yellow, and very supple and excellent to tie round loads.

On one occasion, between Egaja and Esoon, he came back from one of these quests and wanted me to come and see something, very quietly; I went, and we crept down into a rocky ravine, on the other side of which lay one of the outermost Egaja plantations. When we got to the edge of the cleared ground, we lay down, and wormed our way, with elaborate caution, among a patch of Koko; Wiki first, I following in his trail.

After about fifty yards of this, Wiki sank flat, and I saw before me some thirty yards off, busily employed in pulling down plantains, and other depredations, five gorillas: one old male, one young male, and three females. One of these had clinging to her a young fellow, with beautiful wavy black hair with just a kink in it. The big male was crouching on his haunches, with his long arms hanging down on either side, with the backs of his hands on the ground, the palms upwards. The elder lady was tearing to pieces and eating a pineapple, while the others were at the plantains destroying more than they ate.

They kept up a sort of a whinnying, chattering noise, quite different from the sound I have heard gorillas give when enraged, or from the one you can hear them giving when they are what the natives call "dancing" at night. I noticed that their reach of arm was immense, and that when they went from one tree to another, they squattered across the open ground in a most inelegant style, dragging their long arms with the knuckles downwards. I should think the big male and female were over six feet each. The others would be from four to five. I put out my hand and laid it on Wiki's gun to prevent him from firing, and he, thinking I was going to fire, gripped my wrist.

I watched the gorillas with great interest for a few seconds, until I heard Wiki make a peculiar small sound, and looking at him saw his face was working in an awful way as he clutched his throat with his hand violently.

Heavens! think I, this gentleman's going to have a fit; it's lost we are entirely this time. He rolled his head to and fro, and then buried his face into a heap of dried rubbish at the foot of a plantain stem, clasped his hands over it, and gave an explosive sneeze. The gorillas let go all, raised themselves up for a second, gave a quaint sound between a bark and a howl, and then the ladies and the young gentleman started home. The old male rose to his full height (it struck me at the time this was a matter of ten feet at least, but for scientific purposes allowance must be made for a lady's emotions) and looked straight towards us, or rather towards where that sound came from. Wiki went off into a paroxysm of falsetto sneezes the like of which I have never heard; nor evidently had the gorilla, who doubtless thinking, as one of his black co-relatives would have thought, that the phenomenon favoured Duppy, went off after his family with a celerity that was amazing the moment he touched the forest, and disappeared as they had, swinging himself along through it from bough to bough, in a way that convinced me that, given the necessity of getting about in tropical forests, man has made a mistake in getting his arms shortened. I have seen many wild animals in their native wilds, but never have I seen anything to equal gorillas going through bush; it is a graceful, powerful, superbly perfect hand-trapeze performance.

After this sporting adventure, we returned, as I usually return from a sporting adventure, without measurements or the body.

Our first day's march, though the longest, was the easiest, though, providentially I did not know this at the time. From my Woermann road walks I judge it was well twenty-five miles. It was easiest however, from its lying for the greater part of the way through the gloomy type of forest. All day long we never saw the sky once.

The earlier part of the day we were steadily going up hill, here and there making a small descent, and then up again, until we came on to what was apparently a long ridge, for on either side of us we could look down into deep, dark, ravine-like valleys. Twice or thrice we descended into these to cross them, finding at their bottom a small or large swamp with a river running through its midst. Those rivers all went to Lake Ayzingo.

We had to hurry because Kiva, who was the only one among us who had been to Efoua, said that unless we did we should not reach Efoua that night. I said, "Why not stay for bush?" not having contracted any love for a night in a Fan town by the experience of M'fetta; moreover the Fans were not sure that after all the whole party of us might not spend the evening at Efoua, when we did get there, simmering in its cooking-pots.

Ngouta, I may remark, had no doubt on the subject at all, and regretted having left Mrs. N. keenly, and the Andande store sincerely. But these Fans are a fine sporting tribe, and allowed they would risk it; besides, they were almost certain they had friends at Efoua; and, in addition, they showed me trees scratched in a way that was magnification of the condition of my own cat's pet table leg at home, demonstrating leopards in the vicinity. I kept going, as it was my only chance, because I found I stiffened if I sat down, and they always carefully told me the direction to go in when they sat down; with their superior pace they soon caught me up, and then passed me, leaving me and Ngouta and sometimes Singlet and Pagan behind, we, in our turn, overtaking them, with this difference that they were sitting down when we did so.

About five o'clock I was off ahead and noticed a path which I had been told I should meet with, and, when met with, I must follow. The path was slightly indistinct, but by keeping my eye on it I could see it. Presently I came to a place where it went out, but appeared again on the other side of a clump of underbush fairly distinctly. I made a

short cut for it and the next news was I was in a heap, on a lot of
spikes, some fifteen feet or so below ground level, at the bottom of a
bag-shaped game pit.

It is at these times you realise the blessing of a good thick skirt.
Had I paid heed to the advice of many people in England, who ought
to have known better, and did not do it themselves, and adopted
masculine garments, I should have been spiked to the bone, and
done for. Whereas, save for a good many bruises, here I was with the
fulness of my skirt tucked under me, sitting on nine ebony spikes
some twelve inches long, in comparative comfort, howling lustily to
be hauled out. The Duke came along first, and looked down at me. I
said, "Get a bush-rope, and haul me out." He grunted and sat down
on a log. The Passenger came next, and he looked down. "You kill?"
says he. "Not much," say I; "get a bush-rope and haul me out." "No
fit," says he, and sat down on the log. Presently, however, Kiva and
Wiki came up, and Wiki went and selected the one and only bush-
rope suitable to haul an English lady, of my exact complexion, age,
and size, out of that one particular pit. They seemed rare round there
from the time he took; and I was just casting about in my mind as to
what method would be best to employ in getting up the smooth,
yellow, sandy-clay, incurved walls, when he arrived with it, and I
was out in a twinkling, and very much ashamed of myself, until
Silence, who was then leading, disappeared through the path before
us with a despairing yell. Each man then pulled the skin cover off his
gun lock, carefully looked to see if things there were all right and
ready loosened his knife in its snake-skin sheath; and then we set
about hauling poor Silence out, binding him up where necessary
with cool green leaves; for he, not having a skirt, had got a good deal
frayed at the edges on those spikes. Then we closed up, for the Fans
said these pits were symptomatic of the immediate neighbourhood
of Efoua. We sounded our ground, as we went into a thick plantain
patch, through which we could see a great clearing in the forest, and
the low huts of a big town. We charged into it, going right through
the guard-house gateway, at one end, in single file, as its narrowness
obliged us, and into the street-shaped town, and formed ourselves
into as imposing a looking party as possible in the centre of the
street. The Efouerians regarded us with much amazement, and the
women and children cleared off into the huts, and took stock of us
through the door-holes. There were but few men in the town, the
majority, we subsequently learnt, being away after elephants. But
there were quite sufficient left to make a crowd in a ring round us.
Fortunately Wiki and Kiva's friends were present, and we were soon
in another world – fog, but not so bad a one as that at M'fetta;

indeed Efoua struck me, from the first, favourably; it was, for one thing, much cleaner than most Fan towns I have been in.

As a result of the confabulation, one of the chiefs had his house cleared out for me. It consisted of two apartments almost bare of everything save a pile of boxes, and a small fire on the floor, some little bags hanging from the roof poles, and a general supply of insects. The inner room contained nothing save a hard plank, raised on four short pegs from the earth floor.

I shook hands with and thanked the chief, and directed that all the loads should be placed inside the huts. I must admit my good friend was a villainous-looking savage, but he behaved most hospitably and kindly. From what I had heard of the Fan, I deemed it advisable not to make any present to him at once, but to base my claim on him on the right of an amicable stranger to hospitality. When I had seen all the baggage stowed I went outside and sat at the doorway on a rather rickety mushroom-shaped stool in the cool evening air, waiting for my tea which I wanted bitterly. Pagan came up as usual for tobacco to buy chop with; and after giving it to him, I and the two chiefs, with Gray Shirt acting as interpreter, had a long chat. Of course the first question was, Why was I there?

I told them I was on my way to the factory of H. and C. on the Rembwé. They said they had heard of "Uguinu," *i.e.*, Messrs Hatton and Cookson, but they did not trade direct with them, passing their trade into towns nearer to the Rembwé, which were swindling bad towns, they said; and they got the idea stuck in their heads that I was a trader, a sort of bagman for the firm, and Gray Shirt could not get this idea out, so off one of their majesties went and returned with twenty-five balls of rubber, which I bought to promote good feeling, subsequently dashing them to Wiki, who passed them in at Ndorko when we got there. I also bought some elephant-hair necklaces from one of the chiefs' wives, by exchanging my red silk tie with her for them, and one or two other things. I saw fish-hooks would not be of much value because Efoua was not near a big water of any sort; so I held fish-hooks and traded handkerchiefs and knives.

One old chief was exceedingly keen to do business, and I bought a meat spoon, a plantain spoon, and a gravy spoon off him; and then he brought me a lot of rubbish I did not want, and I said so, and announced I had finished trade for that night. However the old gentleman was not to be put off, and after an unsuccessful attempt to sell me his cooking-pots, which were roughly made out of clay, he made energetic signs to me that if I would wait he had got something that he would dispose of which Gray Shirt said was "good too much." Off he went across the street, and disappeared into his hut, where he evidently had a thorough hunt for the precious article. One box after another was brought out to the light of a bush torch held by one of his wives, and there was a great confabulation between him and his family of the "I'm sure you had it last," "You must have moved it," "Never touched the thing," sort. At last it was found, and he brought it across the street to me most carefully. It was a bundle of bark cloth tied round something most carefully with tie tie. This being removed, disclosed a layer of rag, which was unwound from round a central article. Whatever can this be? thinks I; some rare and valuable object doubtless, let's hope connected with Fetish worship, and I anxiously watched its unpacking; in the end, however, it disclosed, to my disgust and rage, an old shilling razor. The way the old chief held it out, and the amount of dollars he asked for it, was enough to make any one believe that I was in such urgent need of the thing, that I was at his mercy regarding price. I waved it off with a haughty scorn, and then feeling smitten by the expression of agonised bewilderment on his face, I dashed him a belt that delighted him, and went inside and had tea to soothe my outraged feelings.

The chiefs made furious raids on the mob of spectators who pressed round the door, and stood with their eyes glued to every crack in the bark of which the hut was made. The next door neighbours on either side might have amassed a comfortable competence for their old age, by letting out seats for the circus. Every hole in the side walls had a human eye in it, and I heard new holes being bored in all directions; so I deeply fear the chief, my host, must have found his palace sadly draughty. I felt perfectly safe and content, however, although Ngouta suggested the charming idea that "P'r'aps them M'fetta Fan done sell we." The only grave question I had to face was whether I should take off my boots or not; they were wet through, from wading swamps, &c., and my feet were very sore; but on the other hand, if I took those boots off, I felt confident that I should not be able to get them on again next morning, so I decided to lef 'em.

As soon as all my men had come in, and established themselves in the inner room for the night, I curled up among the boxes, with my head on the tobacco sack, and dozed.

After about half an hour I heard a row in the street, and looking out, – for I recognised his grace's voice taking a solo part followed by choruses, – I found him in legal difficulties about a murder case. An *alibi* was proved for the time being; that is to say the prosecution could not bring up witnesses because of the elephant hunt; and I went in for another doze, and the town at last grew quiet. Waking up again I noticed the smell in the hut was violent, from being shut up I suppose, and it had an unmistakably organic origin. Knocking the ash end of the smouldering bush-light that lay burning on the floor, I investigated, and tracked it to those bags, so I took down the biggest one, and carefully noted exactly how the tie tie had been put round its mouth; for these things are important and often mean a lot. I then shook its contents out in my hat, for fear of losing anything of value. They were a human hand, three big toes, four eyes, two ears, and other portions of the human frame. The hand was fresh, the others only so so, and shrivelled.

Replacing them I tied the bag up, and hung it up again. I subsequently learnt that although the Fans will eat their fellow friendly tribesfolk, yet they like to keep a little something belonging to them as a memento. This touching trait in their character I learnt from Wiki; and, though it's to their credit, under the circumstances, still it's an unpleasant practice when they hang the remains in the bedroom you occupy, particularly if the bereavement in your host's family has been recent. I did not venture to prowl round Efoua; but slid the bark door aside and looked out to get a breath of fresh air.

It was a perfect night, and no mosquitoes. The town, walled in on every side by the great cliff of high black forest, looked very wild as it showed in the starlight, its low, savage-built bark huts, in two hard rows, closed at either end by a guard-house. In both guard-houses there was a fire burning, and in their flickering glow showed the forms of sleeping men. Nothing was moving save the goats, which are always brought into the special house for them in the middle of the town, to keep them from the leopards, which roam from dusk to dawn.

Dawn found us stirring, I getting my tea, and the rest of the party their chop, and binding up anew the loads with Wiki's fresh supple bush-ropes. Kiva amused me much; during our march his costume was exceeding scant, but when we reached the towns he took from his bag garments, and attired himself so resplendently that I feared the charm of his appearance would lead me into one of those dreadful wife palavers which experience had taught me of old to dread: and in the morning time he always devoted some time to repacking. I gave a big dash to both chiefs, and they came out with us, most civilly, to the end of their first plantations; and then we took farewell of each other, with many expressions of hope on both sides that we should meet again, and many warnings from them about the dissolute and depraved character of the other towns we should pass through before we reached the Rembwé.

Our second day's march was infinitely worse than the first, for it lay along a series of abruptly shaped hills with deep ravines between them; each ravine had its swamp and each swamp its river. This bit of country must be absolutely impassable for any human being, black or white, except during the dry season. There were representatives of the three chief forms of the West African bog. The large deep swamps were best to deal with, because they make a break in the forest, and the sun can come down on their surface and bake a crust, over which you can go, if you go quickly. From experience in Devonian bogs, I knew pace was our best chance, and I fancy I earned one of my nicknames among the Fans on these. The Fans went across all right with a rapid striding glide, but the other men erred from excess of caution, and while hesitating as to where was the next safe place to plant their feet, the place that they were standing on went in with a glug. Moreover, they would keep together, which was more than the crust would stand. The portly Pagan and the Passenger gave us a fine job in one bog, by sinking in close together. Some of us slashed off boughs of trees and tore off handfuls of hard canna leaves, while others threw them round the sinking victims to form a sort of raft, and then with the aid of bushrope, of course, they were hauled out.

The worst sort of swamp, and the most frequent hereabouts, is the deep narrow one that has no crust on, because it is too much shaded by the forest. The slopes of the ravines too are usually covered with an undergrowth of shenja, beautiful beyond description, but right bad to go through. I soon learnt to dread seeing the man in front going down hill, or to find myself doing so, for it meant that within the next half hour we should be battling through a patch of shenja. I believe there are few effects that can compare with the beauty of them, with the golden sunlight coming down through the upper forest's branches on to their exquisitely shaped, hard, dark green leaves, making them look as if they were sprinkled with golden sequins. Their long green stalks, which support the leaves and bear little bunches of crimson berries, take every graceful curve imaginable, and the whole affair is free from insects; and when you have said this, you have said all there is to say in favour of shenja, for those long green stalks of theirs are as tough as twisted wire, and the graceful curves go to the making of a net, which rises round you shoulder high, and the hard green leaves when lying on the ground are fearfully slippery. It is not nice going down through them, particularly when nature is so arranged that the edge of the bank you are descending is a rock-wall ten or twelve feet high with a swamp of unknown depth at its foot; this arrangement was very frequent on the second and third day's marches, and into these swamps the shenja seemed to want to send you head first and get you suffocated. It is still less pleasant, however, going up the other side of the ravine when you have got through your swamp. You have to fight your way upwards among rough rocks, through this hard tough network of stems; and it took it out of all of us except the Fans.

These narrow shaded swamps gave us a world of trouble and took up a good deal of time. Sometimes the leader of the party would make three or four attempts before he found a ford, going on until the black, batter-like ooze came up round his neck, and then turning back and trying in another place; while the rest of the party sat upon the bank until the ford was found, feeling it was unnecessary to throw away human life, and that the more men there were paddling about in that swamp, the more chance there was that a hole in the bottom of it would be found; and when a hole is found, the discoverer is liable to leave his bones in it. If I happened to be in front, the duty of finding the ford fell on me; for none of us after leaving Efoua knew the swamps personally. I was too frightened of the Fan, and too nervous and uncertain of the stuff my other men were made of, to dare show the white feather at anything that turned up. The Fan took my conduct as a matter of course, never having travelled with white men before, or learnt the way some of them require carrying over swamps and rivers and so on. I dare say I might have taken things easier, but I was like the immortal Schmelzle, during that omnibus journey he made on his way to Flætz in the thunder-storm – afraid to be afraid. I am very certain I should have fared very differently had I entered a region occupied by a powerful and ferocious tribe like the Fan, from some districts on the West Coast, where the inhabitants are used to find the white man incapable of personal exertion, requiring to be carried in a hammock, or wheeled in a go-cart or a Bath-chair about the streets of their coast towns, depending for the defence of their settlement on a body of black soldiers. This is not so in Congo Français, and I had behind me the prestige of a set of white men to whom for the native to say, "You shall not do such and such a thing"; "You shall not go to such and such a place," would mean that those things would be done.

But to return to that gorilla-land forest. All the rivers we crossed on the first, second, and third day I was told went into one or other of the branches of the Ogowé, showing that the long slope of land between the Ogowé and the Rembwé is towards the Ogowé. The stone of which the mountains were composed was that same hard black rock that I had found on the Sierra del Cristal, by the Ogowé rapids; only hereabouts there was not amongst it those great masses of white quartz, which are so prominent a feature from Talagouga upwards in the Ogowé valley; neither were the mountains anything like so high, but they had the same abruptness of shape. They look like very old parts of the same range worn down to stumps by the disintegrating forces of the torrential rain and sun, and the dense forest growing on them. Frost of course they had not been subject to, but rocks, I noticed, were often being somewhat similarly split by rootlets having got into some tiny crevice, and by gradual growth enlarged it to a crack.

Of our troubles among the timber falls on these mountains I have already spoken; and these were at their worst between Efoua and Egaja. I had suffered a good deal from thirst that day, unboiled water being my ibet and we were all very nearly tired out with the athletic sports since leaving Efoua. One thing only we knew about Egaja for sure, and that was that not one of us had a friend there, and that it was a town of extra evil repute, so we were not feeling very cheerful when towards evening time we struck its outermost planta-tions, their immediate vicinity being announced to us by Silence treading full and fair on to a sharp ebony spike driven into the narrow path and hurting himself. Fortunately, after we passed this first plantation, we came upon a camp of rubber collectors – four young men; I got one of them to carry Silence's load and show us the way into the town, when on we went into more plantations.

There is nothing more tiresome than finding your path going into a plantation, because it fades out in the cleared ground, or starts playing games with a lot of other little paths that are running about amongst the crops, and no West African path goes straight into a stream or a plantation, and straight out the other side, so you have a nice time picking it up again.

We were spared a good deal of fine varied walking by our new friend the rubber collector; for I noticed he led us out by a path nearly at right angles to the one by which we had entered. He then pitched into a pit which was half full of thorns, and which he observed he did not know was there, demonstrating that an African guide can speak the truth. When he had got out, he handed back Silence's load and got a dash of tobacco for his help; he left us to devote the rest of his evening by his forest fire to unthorning himself, while we proceeded to wade a swift, deepish river that crossed the path he told us led into Egaja, and then went across another bit of forest and down hill again. "Oh, bless those swamps!" thought I, "here's another," but no –

not this time. Across the bottom of the steep ravine, from one side to another, lay an enormous tree as a bridge, about fifteen feet above a river, which rushed beneath it, over a boulder-encumbered bed. I took in the situation at a glance, and then and there I would have changed that bridge for any swamp I have ever seen, yea, even for a certain bush-rope bridge in which I once wound myself up like a buzzing fly in a spider's web. I was fearfully tired, and my legs shivered under me after the falls and emotions of the previous part of the day, and my boots were slippery with water soaking.

The Fans went into the river, and half swam, half waded across. All the Ajumba, save Pagan, followed, and Ngouta got across with their assistance. Pagan thought he would try the bridge, and I thought I would watch how the thing worked. He got about three yards along it and then slipped, but caught the tree with his hands as he fell, and hauled himself back to my side again; then he went down the bank and through the water. This was not calculated to improve one's nerve; I knew by now I had got to go by the bridge, for I saw I was not strong enough in my tired state to fight the water. If only the wretched thing had had its bark on it would have been better, but it was bare, bald, and round, and a slip meant death on the rocks below. I rushed it, and reached the other side in safety, whereby poor Pagan got chaffed about his failure by the others, who said they had gone through the water just to wash their feet.

The other side, when we got there, did not seem much worth reaching, being a swampy fringe at the bottom of a steep hillside, and after a few yards the path turned into a stream or backwater of the river. It was hedged with thickly pleached bushes, and covered with liquid water on the top of semi-liquid mud. Now and again for a change you had a foot of water on top of fearfully slippery harder mud, and then we light-heartedly took headers into the bush, side-ways, or sat down; and when it was not proceeding on the evil tenor of its way, like this, it had holes in it; in fact, I fancy the bottom of the holes was the true level, for it came near being as full of holes as a fishing-net, and it was very quaint to see the man in front, who had been paddling along knee-deep before, now plop down with the water round his shoulders; and getting out of these slippery pockets, which were sometimes a tight fit, was difficult.

However that is the path you have got to go by, if you're not wise enough to stop at home; the little bay of shrub overgrown swamp fringing the river on one side and on the other running up to the mountain side.

At last we came to a sandy bank, and on that bank stood Egaja, the town with an evil name even among the Fan, but where we had got to stay, fair or foul. We went into it through its palaver house, and soon had the usual row.

I had detected signs of trouble among my men during the whole day; the Ajumba were tired, and dissatisfied with the Fans; the Fans were in high feather, openly insolent to Ngouta, and anxious for me to stay in this delightful locality, and go hunting with them and divers other choice spirits, whom they assured me we could easily get to join us at Efoua. Ngouta kept away from them, and I was worried about him on account of his cold and loss of voice. I kept peace as well as I could, explaining to the Fans I had not enough money with me now, because I had not, when starting, expected such magnificent opportunities to be placed at my disposal; and promising to come back next year – a promise I hope to keep – and then we would go and have a grand time of it. This state of a party was a dangerous one in which to enter a strange Fan town, where our security lay in our being united. When the first burst of Egaja conversation began to boil down into something reasonable, I found that a villainous-looking scoundrel, smeared with soot and draped in a fragment of genuine antique cloth, was a head chief in mourning. He placed a house at my disposal, quite a mansion, for it had no less than four apartments. The first one was almost entirely occupied by a bedstead frame that was being made up inside on account of the small size of the door.

This had to be removed before we could get in with the baggage at all. While this removal was being effected with as much damage to the house and the article as if it were a quarter-day affair in England, the other chief arrived. He had been sent for, being away down the river fishing when we arrived. I saw at once he was a very superior man to any of the chiefs I had yet met with. It was not his attire, remarkable though that was for the district, for it consisted of a gentleman's black frock-coat such as is given in the ivory bundle, a bright blue felt sombrero hat, an ample cloth of Boma check; but his face and general bearing was distinctive, and very powerful and intelligent; and I knew that Egaja, for good or bad, owed its name to this man, and not to the more sensual, brutal-looking one. He was exceedingly courteous, ordering his people to bring me a stool and one for himself, and then a fly-whisk to battle with the evening cloud of sand-flies. I got Pagan to come and act as interpreter while the rest were stowing the baggage, &c. After compliments, "Tell the chief," I said, "that I hear this town of his is thief town."

"Better not, sir," says Pagan.

"Go on," said I, "or I'll tell him myself."

So Pagan did. It was a sad blow to the chief.

"Thief town, this highly respectable town of Egaja! a town whose moral conduct in all matters (Shedule) was an example to all towns, called a thief town! Oh, what a wicked world!"

I said it was; but I would reserve my opinion as to whether Egaja was a part of the wicked world or a star-like exception, until I had experienced it myself. We then discoursed on many matters, and I got a great deal of interesting fetish information out of the chief, which was valuable to me, because the whole of this district had not been in contact with white culture; and altogether I and the chief became great friends.

Just when I was going in to have my much-desired tea, he brought me his mother – an old lady, evidently very bright and able, but, poor woman, with the most disgusting hand and arm I have ever seen. I am ashamed to say I came very near being sympathetically sick in the African manner on the spot. I felt I could not attend to it, and have my tea afterwards, so I directed one of the canoe-shaped little tubs, used for beating up the manioc in, to be brought and filled with hot water, and then putting into it a heavy dose of Condy's fluid, I made her sit down and lay the whole arm in it, and went and had my tea. As soon as I had done I went outside, and getting some of the many surrounding ladies to hold bushlights, I examined the case. The whole hand was a mass of yellow pus, streaked with sanies, large ulcers were burrowing into the fore-arm, while in the arm-pit was a big abscess. I opened the abscess at once, and then the old lady frightened me nearly out of my wits by gently subsiding, I thought dying, but I soon found out merely going to sleep. I then washed the abscess well out, and having got a lot of baked plantains, I made a big poultice of them, mixed with boiling water and more Condy in the tub, and laid her arm right in this; and propping her up all round and covering her over with cloths I requisitioned from her son, I left her to have her nap while I went into the history of the case, which was that some forty-eight hours ago she had been wading along the bank, catching crawfish, and had been stung by "a fish like a snake"; so I presume the ulcers were an old-standing palaver. The hand had been a good deal torn by the creature, and the pain and swelling had been so great she had not had a minute's sleep since. As soon as the poultice got chilled I took her arm out and cleaned it again, and wound it round with dressing, and had her ladyship carried bodily, still asleep, into her hut, and after rousing her up, giving her a dose of that fine preparation, *pil. crotonis cum hydrargi*, saw her tucked up on her own plank bedstead for the night, sound asleep again. The chief was very anxious to have some pills too; so I gave him some, with firm injunctions only to take one at the first time. I knew that that one would teach him not to take more than one for ever after, better than I could do if I talked from June to January. Then all the afflicted of Egaja turned up, and wanted medical advice. There was evidently a good stiff epidemic of the yaws about; lots of cases of dum with the various symptoms; ulcers of course galore; a man with a bit of a broken spear head in an abscess in the thigh; one which I believe a professional enthusiast would call a "lovely case" of filaria, the entire white of one eye being full of the active little worms and a ridge of surplus population migrating across the bridge of the nose into the other eye, under the skin, looking like the bridge of a pair of spectacles. It was past eleven before I had anything like done, and my men had long been sound asleep, but the chief had conscientiously sat up and seen the thing through. He then went and fetched some rolls of bark cloth to put on my plank, and I gave him a handsome cloth I happened to have with me, a couple of knives, and some heads of tobacco and wished him good-night; blockading my bark door, and picking my way over my sleeping Ajumba into an inner apartment which I also blockaded, hoping I had done with Egaja for some hours.

AMONG THE
SUDANESE

James Bruce
(1730–94)

Bruce reached the source of the Blue Nile in 1771, a century before the search for the source of the White Nile became headline news. His descriptions of the cruelties and orgies at Gondar, the Ethiopian capital, were greeted with disbelief; so was his account of the Sudanese rulers, and their queens, at Sennar. Of independent means and gigantic physique, "Yagoube", as he was called in Africa (or "The Abyssinian" as he became in his native Scotland), was later shown to be an accurate observer as well as the eighteenth century's most intrepid traveller.

The drum beat a little after six o'clock in the evening. We then had a very comfortable dinner sent us, camels flesh stewed with an herb of a viscous slimy substance, called bammia. After having dined, and finished the journal of the day, I fell to unpacking my instruments, the barometer and thermometer first, and, after having hung them up, was conversing with Adelan's servant when I should pay my visit to his master. About eight o'clock came a servant from the palace, telling me now was the time to bring the present to the king. I sorted the separate articles with all the speed I could, and we went directly to the palace. The king was then sitting in a large apartment, as far as I could guess, at some distance from the former. He was naked, but had several clothes lying upon his knee, and about him, and a servant was rubbing him over with very stinking butter or grease, with which his hair was dropping, as if wet with water. Large as the room was, it could be smelled through the whole of it. The king asked me, if cver I greased myself as he did? I said, Very seldom, but fancied it would be very expensive. He then told me that it was elephant's grease, which made people strong, and preserved the skin very smooth. I said, I thought it very proper, but

James Bruce, engraving. Courtesy of the Mansell Collection.

could not bear the smell of it, though my skin should turn as rough
as an elephant's for the want of it. He said, "If I had used it, my hair
would not have turned so red as it was, and that it would all become
white presently, when that redness came off. You may see the Arabs
driven in here by the Daveina, and all their cattle taken from them,
because they have no longer any grease for their hair. The sun first
turns it red, and then perfectly white; and you'll know them in the
street by their hair being the colour of yours. As for the smell, you
will see that cured presently."

After having rubbed him abundantly with grease, they brought a
pretty large horn, and in it something scented, about as liquid as
honey. It was plain that civet was a great part of the composition.
The king went out at the door, I suppose into another room, and

there two men deluged him over with pitchers of cold water, whilst, as I imagine, he was stark naked. He then returned, and a slave anointed him with this sweet ointment; after which he sat down, as completely dressed, being just going to his women's apartment, where he was to sup. I told him I wondered why he did not use rose-water, as in Abyssinia, Arabia, and Cairo. He said, he had it often from Cairo, when the merchants arrived; but as it was now long since any came, his people could not make more, for the rose would not grow in his country, though the women made something like it of lemon flower.

His toilet being finished, I then produced my present, which I told him the king of Abyssinia had sent him, hoping that, according to the faith and custom of nations, he would not only protect me while here, but send me safely and speedily out of his dominions into Egypt. He answered, There was a time when he could have done all this, and more, but those times were changed. Sennaar was in ruin, and was not like what it once was. He then ordered some perfumed sorbet to be brought for me to drink in his presence, which is a pledge that your person is in safety. I thereupon withdrew, and he went to his ladies.

It was not till the 8th of May I had my audience of Shekh Adelan at Aira, which is three miles and a half from Sennaar; we walked out early in the morning, for the greatest part of the way along the side of the Nile, which had no beauty, being totally divested of trees, the bottom foul and muddy, and the edges of the water, white with small concretions of calcareous earth, which, with the bright sun upon them, dazzled and affected our eyes very much.

We then struck across a large sandy plain, without trees or bushes, and came to Adelan's habitation; two or three very considerable houses, of one storey, occupied the middle of a large square, each of whose sides was at least half of an English mile. Instead of a wall to inclose this square, was a high fence or impalement of strong reeds, canes, or stalks of dora (I do not know which), in fascines strongly joined together by stakes and cords. On the outside of the gate, on each hand, were six houses of a slighter construction than the rest; close upon the fence were sheds where the soldiers lay, the horses picqueted before them with their heads turned towards the sheds, and their food laid before them on the ground; above each soldier's sleeping-place, covered only on the top and open in the sides, were hung a lance, a small oval shield, and a large broad-sword. These, I understood, were chiefly quarters for couriers, who, being Arabs, were not taken into the court or square, but shut out at night.

Within the gate was a number of horses, with the soldiers barracks behind them; they were all picqueted in ranks, their faces to their masters barracks. It was one of the finest sights I ever saw of the kind. They were all above sixteen hands high, of the breed of the old Saracen horses, all finely made, and as strong as our coach horses, but exceedingly nimble in their motion; rather thick and short in the forehand, but with the most beautiful eyes, ears, and heads in the world; they were mostly black, some of them black and white, some of them milk-white, foaled so, not white by age, with white eyes and white hoofs, not perhaps a great recommendation.

A steel shirt of mail hung upon each man's quarters, opposite to his horse, and by it an antelope's skin, made soft like shamoy, with which it was covered from the dew of the night. A head-piece of copper, without crest or plumage, was suspended by a lace above the shirt of mail, and was the most picturesque part of the trophy. To these was added an enormous broad-sword, in a red leather scabbard; and upon the pummel hung two thick gloves, not divided into fingers as ours, but like hedgers' gloves, their fingers in one poke. They told me, that, within that inclosure at Aira, there were 400 horses, which, with the riders, and armour complete for each of them, were all the property of Shekh Adelan, every horseman being his slave, and bought with his money. There were five or six (I know not which) of these squares or inclosures, none of them half a mile from the other, which contained the king's horses, slaves, and servants. Whether they were all in as good order as Adelan's I cannot say, for I did not go further; but no body of horse could ever be more magnificently disposed under the direction of any Christian power.

Adelan was then sitting upon a piece of the trunk of a palm-tree, in the front of one of these divisions of his horses, which he seemed to be contemplating with pleasure; a number of black people, his own servants and friends, were standing around him. He had on a long drab-coloured camblet gown, lined with yellow sattin, and a camlet cap like a head-piece, with two short points that covered his ears. This, it seems, was his dress when he rose early in the morning to visit his horses, which he never neglected. The Shekh was a man above six feet high, and rather corpulent, had a heavy walk, seemingly more from affectation of grandeur, than want of agility. He was about sixty, of the colour and features of an Arab, and not of a Negro, but had rather more beard than falls to the lot of people in this country; large piercing eyes, and a determined, though, at the same time, a very pleasing countenance. Upon my coming near him, he got up; "You that are a horseman," says he without any salutation, "what would your king of Habesh give for these horses?"

"What king," answered I, in the same tone, "would not give any price for such horses, if he knew their value?" "Well," replies he, in a lower voice, to the people about him, "if we are forced to go to Habesh, as Baady was, we will carry our horses along with us." I understood by this he alluded to the issue of his approaching quarrel with the king.

We then went into a large saloon, hung round with mirrors and scarlet damask; in one of the longest sides, were two large sofas covered with crimson and yellow damask, and large cushions of cloth of gold, like to the king's. He now pulled off his camlet gown and cap, and remained in a crimson satin coat reaching down below his knees, which lapped over at the breast, and was girt round his waist with a scarf or sash, in which he had stuck a short dagger in an ivory sheath, mounted with gold; and one of the largest and most beautiful amethysts upon his finger that ever I saw, mounted plain, without any diamonds, and a small gold ear-ring in one of his ears.

"Why have you come hither," says he to me, "without arms and on foot, and without attendants?" *Yagoube*. "I was told that horses were not kept as Sennaar, and brought none with me." *Adelan*. "You suppose you have come through great dangers, and so you have. But what do you think of me, who am day and night out in the fields, surrounded by hundreds and thousands of Arabs, all of whom would eat me alive if they dared?" I answered, "A brave man, used to command as you are, does not look to the number of his enemies, but to their abilities; a wolf does not fear ten thousand sheep more than he does one." *Ad*. "True; look out at the door; these are their chiefs whom I am now taxing, and I have brought them hither that they may judge from what they see whether I am ready for them or not." *Yag*. "You could not do more properly; but as to my own affairs, I wait upon you from the king of Abyssinia, desiring safe conduct through your country into Egypt, with his royal promise, that he is ready to do the like for you again, or any other favour you may call upon him for." He took the letter and read it. *Ad*. "The king of Abyssinia may be assured I am always ready to do more for him than this. It is true, since the mad attempt upon Sennaar, and the next still madder, to replace old Baady upon the throne, we have had no formal peace, but neither are we at war. We understand one another as good neighbours ought to do; and what else is peace?" *Yag*. "You know I am a stranger and traveller, seeking my way home. I have nothing to do with peace or war between nations. All I beg is a safe conduct through your kingdom, and the rights of hospitality bestowed in such cases on every common stranger; and one of the favours I beg is, your acceptance of a small present. I bring it not from home; I have been long absent from thence, or it would have been better." *Ad*. "I'll not refuse it, but it is quite unnecessary. I have faults like other men, but to hurt, or ransack strangers, was never one of them. Mahomet Abou Kalec, my brother, is, however, a much better man to strangers than I am; you will be lucky if you meet him here; if not, I will do for you what I can, when once the confusion of these Arabs is over."

I gave him the Sherriffe's letter, which he opened, looked at, and laid by without reading, saying only, "Aye, Metical is a good man, he sometimes takes care of our people going to Mecca; for my part, I never was there, and probably never shall." I then presented my letter from Ali Bey to him. He placed it upon his knee, and gave a slap upon it with his open hand. *Ad*. "What! do you not know, have you not heard, Mahomet Abou Dahab, his Hasnadar, has rebelled against him, banished him out of Cairo, and now sits in his place? But, don't be disconcerted at that; I know you to be a man of honour and prudence; if Mahomet, my brother, does not come, as soon as I can get leisure I will dispatch you." The servant, that had conducted me to Sennaar, and was then with us, went forward close to him, and said, in a kind of whisper, "Should he go often to the king?" "When he pleases; he may go to see the town, and take a walk, but never alone, and also to the palace, that, when he returns to his own country, he may report he saw a king at Sennaar, that neither knows how to govern, nor will suffer others to teach him; who knows not how to make war, and yet will not sit in peace." I then took my leave of him; but there was a plentiful breakfast in the other room, to which he sent us, and which went far to comfort Hagi Ismael for the misfortune of his patron, Ali Bey. At going out, I took my leave by kissing his hand, which he submitted to without reluctance. "Shekh," said I, "when I pass these Arabs in the square, I hope it will not disoblige you if I converse with some of them out of curiosity?" *Ad*. "By no means, as much as you please; but don't let them know where they can find you at Sennaar, or they will be in your house from morning till night, will eat up all your victuals, and then, in return, will cut your throat, if they can meet you upon your journey."

I returned home to Sennaar, very well pleased with my reception at Aira. I had not seen, since I left Gondar, a man so open and frank in his manners, and who spoke, without disguise, what apparently he had in his heart; but he was exceedingly engaged in business, and it was of such extent that it seemed to me impossible to be brought to an end in a much longer time than I proposed staying at Sennaar.

The distance, too, between Aira and that town was a very great discouragement to me. The whole way was covered with insolent, brutish people; so that every man we met between Sennaar and Aira produced some altercation, some demand of presents, gold, cloth, tobacco, and a variety of other disagreeable circumstances, which had always the appearance of ending in something serious.

I had a long conversation with the Arabs I met with at Aira, and from them I learned pretty nearly the situation of the different clans, or tribes, in Atbara. – These were all in their way northward to the respective countries, in the sands to the eastward of Mendera and Barbar. These sands, so barren and desolate the rest of the year, were beginning now to be crowded with multitudes of cattle and inhabitants. The fly, in the flat and fertile mold, which composes all the soil to the southward of Sennaar, had forced this number of people to migrate, which they very well knew was to cost them at least one half of their substance; of such consequence is the weakest instrument in the hand of Providence. The troops of Sennaar, few in number, but well-provided with every thing, stood ready to cut these people off from their access to the sands, till every chief of a tribe had given in a well-verified inventory of his whole stock, and made a composition, at passing, with Shekh Adelan.

All subterfuge was in vain. The fly, in possession of the fertile country, inexorably pursued every single camel till he took refuge in the sands, and there he was to stay till the rains ceased; and if, in the interim, it was discovered that any concealment of number, or quality, had been made, they were again to return in the beginning of September to their old pastures; and, in this second passage, any fraud, whether real, or alledged, was punished with great severity. – Resistance had been often tried, and as often found ineffectual. However great their numbers, encumbered with families and baggage as they were, they had always fallen a sacrifice to those troops, well-mounted and armed, that awaited them in their way within sight of their own homes. Arrived once in these sands, they were quiet during the rains, having paid their passage northward; and so they were afterwards, for the same reason, when they came again to their own station, southward, when those rains had ceased.

It may be asked reasonably, "What does the government of Sennaar do with that immense number of camels, whic they receive from all those tribes of Arabs in their passage by Sennaar?" To this I answer, "That all this tribute is not paid in kind." The different tribes possessing so many camels, or so many other cattle, have a quantum laid upon them at an average value. This is paid in gold, or in slaves, the rest in kind; so many for the maintenance of the king and government; for there is no flesh commonly used at Sennaar in the markets but that of camels. The residue is bought by the merchants of Dongola, and sent into Egypt, where they supply that great consumption of these animals made every year by the caravans going to Mecca.

One thing had made a very strong impression on me, which was the contemptuous manner in which Adelan expressed himself as to his sovereign. I was satisfied, that, with some address, I could keep myself in favour with either of them; but, in the terms they then were, or were very soon to be, I could not but fear I was likely to fall into trouble between the two.

A few days after this I had a message from the palace. I found the king sitting alone, apparently much chagrined, and in ill-humour. He asked me in a very peevish manner, "If I was not yet gone?" To which I answered, "Your Majesty knows that it is impossible for me to go a step from Sennaar without assistance from you." He again asked me, in the same tone as before, "How I could think of coming that way?" I said, "Nobody imagined in Abyssinia, but that he was able to give a stranger safe conduct through his own dominions." He made no reply, but nodded a sign for me to depart; which I immediately did, and so finished this short, but disagreeable interview.

About four o'clock that same afternoon I was again sent for to the palace, when the king told me that several of his wives were ill, and desired that I would give them my advice, which I promised to do without difficulty, as all acquaintance with the fair sex had hitherto been much to my advantage. I must confess, however, that calling these the fair sex is not preserving a precision in terms. I was admitted into a large square apartment, very ill-lighted, in which were about fifty women, all perfectly black, without any covering but a very narrow piece of cotton rag about their waists. While I was musing whether or not these all might be queens, or whether there was any queen among them, one of them took me by the hand and led me rudely enough into another apartment. This was much better lighted than the first. Upon a large bench, or sofa, covered with blue Surat cloth, sat three persons cloathed from the neck to the feet with blue cotton shirts.

One of these, who, I found, was the favourite, was about six feet high, and corpulent beyond all proportion. She seemed to me, next to the elephant and rhinoceros, the largest living creature I had met with. – Her features were perfectly like those of a Negro; a ring of gold passed through her under lip, and weighed it down, till, like a flap, it covered her chin, and left her teeth bare, which were very small and fine. The inside of her lip she had made black with antimony. Her ears reached down to her shoulders, and had the appearance of wings; she had in each of them a large ring of gold, somewhat smaller than a man's little finger, and about five inches diameter. The weight of these had drawn down the hole where her ear was pierced so much, that three fingers might easily pass above the ring. She had a gold necklace, like what we used to call *esclavage*, of several rows of sequins pierced. She had on her ankles two manacles of gold, larger than any I had ever seen upon the feet of felons, with which I could not conceive it was possible for her to walk, but afterwards I found they were hollow. – The others were dressed pretty much in the same manner; only there was one that had chains, which came from her ears to the outside of each nostril, where they were fastened. There was also a ring put through the gristle of her nose, and which hung down to the opening of her mouth. I think she must have breathed with great difficulty. It had altogether something of the appearance of a horse's bridle. Upon my coming near them, the eldest put her hand to her mouth, and kissed it, saying, at the same time, in very vulgar Arabic, "Kifhalek howaja?" (how do you do, merchant) – I never in my life was more pleased with distant salutations than at this time. I answered, "Peace be among you! I am a physician, and not a merchant."

I shall not entertain the reader with the multitude of their complaints; being a lady's physician, discretion and silence are my first duties. It is sufficient to say, that there was not one part of their whole bodies, inside and outside, in which some of them had not ailments. The three queens insisted upon being blooded, which desire I complied with, as it was an operation that required short attendance; but, upon producing the lancets, their hearts failed them. They then all cried out for the Tabange, which, in Arabic, means a pistol; but what they meant by this word was, the cupping instrument, which goes off with a spring like the snap of a pistol. I had two of these with me, but not at that time in my pocket. I sent my servant home, however, to bring one, and, that same evening, performed the operation upon the three queens with great success. The room was overflowed with an effusion of royal blood, and the whole ended with their insisting upon my giving them the instrument itself, which I was obliged to do, after cupping two of their slaves before them, who had no complaints, merely to shew them how the operation was to be performed.

Another night I was obliged to attend them, and gave the queens, and two or three of the great ladies, vomits. I will spare my reader the recital of so nauseous a scene. The ipecacuanha had great effect, and warm water was drunk very copiously. The patients were numerous, and the floor of the room received all the evacuations. It was most prodigiously hot, and the horrid, black figures, moaning and groaning with sickness all around me, gave me, I think, some slight idea of the punishment in the world below. My mortifications, however did not stop here. I observed that, on coming into their presence, the queens were all covered with cotton shirts; but no sooner did their complaints make part of our conversation, than, to my utmost surprise, each of them, in her turn, stript herself entirely naked, laying her cotton shirt loosely on her lap, as she sat cross-legged like a tailor. The custom of going naked in these warm countries abolishes all delicacy concerning it. I could not but observe that the breasts of each of them reached the length of their knees.

This exceeding confidence on their part, they thought, merited some consideration on mine; and it was not without great astonishment that I heard the queen desire to see me in the like dishabille in which she had spontaneously put herself. The whole court of female attendants flocked to the spectacle. Refusal, or resistance, were in vain. I was surrounded with fifty or sixty women, all equal in stature and strength to myself. The whole of my cloathing was, like theirs, a long loose shirt of blue Surat cotton cloth, reaching from the neck down to the feet. The only terms I could possibly, and that with great difficulty, make for myself were, that they should be contented to strip me no farther than the shoulders and breast. Upon seeing the whiteness of my skin, they gave all a loud cry in token of dislike, and shuddered, seeming to consider it rather the effects of disease than natural. I think in my life I never felt so disagreeably. I have been in more than one battle, but surely I would joyfully have taken my chance again in any of them to have been freed from that examination. I could not help likewise reflecting, that, if the king had come in during this exhibition, the consequence would either have been impaling, or stripping off that skin whose colour they were so curious about; though I can solemnly declare there was not an idea in my breast, since ever I had the honour of seeing these royal beauties, that could have given his majesty of Sennaar the smallest reason for jealousy; and I believe the same may be said of the sentiments of the ladies in what regarded me. Ours was a mutual passion, but dangerous to no one concerned. I returned home with very different sensations from those I had felt after an interview with the beautiful Aiscach of Teawa. Indeed, it was impossible to be more chagrined at, or more disgusted with, my present situation that I was, and the more so, that my delivery from it appeared to be very distant, and the circumstances were more and more unfavourable every day.

NOT THE SOURCE OF THE NILE

Richard Francis Burton
(1821–90)

In Burton a brilliant mind and dauntless physique were matched with a restless spirit and a deeply troubled soul to produce the most complex of characters. Contemptuous of other mortals, including Speke, his companion and rival, he found solace only in the extremities of erudition and adventure. The classic accounts of his journeys to Mecca (1853) and Harar (1854) appeared in a more digestible narrative as Wanderings in Three Continents. *Here he also describes his celebrated foray from Dar es Salaam to Lake Tanganyika (1857) in search of the source of the Nile.*

On June 26th, 1857, I set out in earnest on a journey into the far interior.

At Nzasa I was visited by three native chiefs, who came to ascertain whether I was bound on a peaceful errand. When I assured them of my unwarlike intentions, they told me I must halt on the morrow and send forth a message to the next chief, but as this plan invariably loses three days, I replied that I could not be bound by their rules, but was ready to pay for their infraction. During the debate upon this fascinating proposal for breaking the law, one of the most turbulent of the Baloch, who were native servants in my train, drew his sword upon an old woman because she refused to give up a basket of grain. She rushed, with the face of a black Medusa, into the assembly, and created a great disturbance. When that was allayed, the principal chief asked me what brought the white man into their country, and at the same time to predict the loss of their gains and commerce, land and liberty.

"I am old," he quoth pathetically, "and my beard is grey, yet I never beheld such a calamity as this."

"These men," replied my interpreter, "neither buy nor sell; they do not inquire into price, nor do they covet profit."

An extravagant present – for at that time I was ignorant of the price I ought to pay – opened the chiefs' hearts, and they appointed one of their body to accompany me as far as the western half of the Kingani valley. They also caused to be performed a dance of ceremony in my honour. A line of small, plump, chestnut-coloured women, with wild, beady eyes and thatch of clay-plastered hair, dressed in their loin-cloths, with a profusion of bead necklaces and other ornaments, and with their ample bosoms tightly corded down, advanced and retired in a convulsion of wriggle and contortion, whose fit expression was a long discordant howl. I threw them a few strings of green beads, and one of these falling to the ground, I was stooping to pick it up when Said, my interpreter whispered, in my ear, "Bend not; they will say 'He will not bend even to take up beads.'"

In some places I found the attentions of the fair sex somewhat embarrassing, but when I entered the fine green fields that guarded the settlements of Muhoewee, I was met *en masse* by the ladies of the villages, who came out to stare, laugh, and wonder at the white man.

"What would you think of these whites as husbands?" asked one of the crowd.

"With such things on their legs, not by any means!" was the unanimous reply, accompanied by peals of merriment.

On July 8th I fell into what my Arab called the "Valley of Death and the Home of Hunger," a malarious level plain. Speke, whom I shall henceforth call my companion, was compelled by sickness to ride. The path, descending into a dense thicket of spear grass, bush, and thorny trees based on sand, was rough and uneven, but when I arrived at a ragged camping kraal, I found the water bad, and a smell of decay was emitted by the dark, dank ground. It was a most appalling day, and one I shall not lightly forget. From the black clouds driven before furious blasts pattered raindrops like musket bullets, splashing the already saturated ground. Tall, stiff trees groaned and bent before the gusts; birds screamed as they were driven from their resting-places; the asses stood with heads depressed, ears hung down, and shrinking tails turned to the wind; even the beasts of the wild seemed to have taken refuge in their dens.

Despite our increasing weakness, we marched on the following day, when we were interrupted by a body of about fifty Wazaramo, who called to us to halt. We bought them off with a small present of cloth and beads, and they stood aside to let us pass. I could not but admire the athletic and statuesque figures of the young warriors, and their martial attitudes, grasping in one hand their full-sized bows, and in the other sheaths of grinded arrows, whose black barbs and necks showed a fresh layer of poison.

Though handicapped by a very inadequate force, in eighteen days we accomplished, despite sickness and every manner of difficulty, a march of one hundred and eighteen miles, and entered K'hutu, the safe rendez-vous of foreign merchants, on July 14th. I found consolation in the thought that the expedition had passed without accident through the most dangerous part of the journey.

Resuming our march through the maritime region, on July 15th we penetrated into a thick and tangled jungle, with luxuriant and putrescent vegetation. Presently, however, the dense thicket opened out into a fine park country, peculiarly rich in game, where the giant trees of the seaboard gave way to mimosas, gums, and stunted thorns. Large gnus pranced about, pawing the ground and shaking their formidable manes; hartebeest and other antelopes clustered together on the plain. The homely cry of the partridge resounded from the brake, and the guinea-fowls looked like large bluebells upon the trees. Small land-crabs took refuge in pits and holes, which made the path a cause of frequent accidents, whilst ants of various kinds, crossing the road in close columns, attacked man and beast ferociously, causing the caravan to break into a halting, trotting hobble. The weather was a succession of raw mists, rain in torrents, and fiery sunbursts; the land appeared rotten, and the jungle smelt of death. At Kiruru I found a cottage and enjoyed for the first time an atmosphere of sweet, warm smoke. My companion would remain in the reeking, miry tent, where he partially laid the foundations of the fever which afterwards threatened his life in the mountains of Usagara.

Despite the dangers of hyenas, leopards, and crocodiles, we were delayed by the torrents of rain in the depths of the mud at Kiruru. We then resumed our march under most unpromising conditions. Thick grass and the humid vegetation rendered the black earth greasy and slippery, and the road became worse as we advanced. In three places we crossed bogs from a hundred yards to a mile in length, and admitting a man up to the knee. The porters plunged through them like laden animals, and I was obliged to be held upon the ass. At last we reached Dut'humi, where we were detained nearly a week, for malaria had brought on attacks of marsh fever, which, in my case, thoroughly prostrated me. I had during the fever fit, and often for hours afterwards, a queer conviction of divided identity, never ceasing to be two persons that generally thwarted and opposed each other. The sleepless nights brought with them horrid visions, animals of grisliest form, and hag-like women and men.

Dut'humi is one of the most fertile districts in K'hutu, and, despite its bad name as regards climate, Arabs sometimes reside here for some months for the purpose of purchasing slaves cheaply, and to repair their broken fortunes for a fresh trip into the interior. This kept up a perpetual feud amongst the chiefs of the country, and scarcely a month passed without fields being laid waste, villages burnt down, and the unhappy cultivators being carried off to be sold.

On July 24th, feeling strong enough to advance, we passed out of the cultivation of Dut'humi. Beyond the cultivation the road plunged into a jungle, where the European traveller realised every preconceived idea of Africa's aspect at once hideous and grotesque. The general appearance is a mingling of bush and forest, most monotonous to the eye. The black, greasy ground, veiled with thick shrubbery, supports in the more open spaces screens of tiger and spear grass twelve and thirteen feet high, with every blade a finger's breadth; and the towering trees are often clothed with huge creepers, forming heavy columns of densest verdure. The earth, ever rain-drenched, emits the odour of sulphuretted hydrogen, and in some parts the traveller might fancy a corpse to be hidden behind every bush. That no feature of miasma might be wanting to complete the picture, filthy heaps of the meanest hovels sheltered their miserable inhabitants, whose frames are lean with constant intoxication, and whose limbs are distorted with ulcerous sores. Such a revolting scene is East Africa from Central K'hutu to the base of the Usagara Mountains.

After a long, long tramp the next day through rice swamps, we came to the nearest outposts of the Zungomero district. Here were several caravans, with pitched tents, piles of ivory, and crowds of porters. The march had occupied us over four weeks, about double the usual time, and a gang of thirty-six Wanyamwezi native porters whom I had sent on in advance to Zungomero naturally began to suspect accident.

Zungomero was not a pleasant place, and though the sea breeze was here strong, beyond its influence the atmosphere was sultry and oppressive. It was the great centre of traffic in the eastern regions. Lying upon the main trunk road, it must be traversed by the up and down caravans, and during the travelling season, between June and April, large bodies of some thousand men pass through it every week. It was, therefore, a very important station, and the daily expenditure of large caravans being considerable, there was a good deal of buying and selling.

When we were ready to start from Zungomero, our whole party amounted to a total of one hundred and thirty-two souls, whom I need not, I think, describe in detail. We had plenty of cloth and beads for traffic with the natives, a good store of provisions, arms, and ammunition, a certain amount of camp furniture, instruments, such as chronometers, compasses, thermometers, etc., a stock of stationery, plenty of useful tools, clothing, bedding, and shoes, books and drawing materials, a portable domestic medicine chest, and a number of miscellaneous articles. As life at Zungomero was the acme of discomfort, I was glad enough to leave it.

On August 7th, 1857, our expedition left Zungomero to cross the East African ghauts in rather a pitiful plight. We were martyred by miasma; my companion and I were so feeble that we could hardly sit our asses, and we could scarcely hear. It was a day of severe toil, and we loaded with great difficulty.

From Central Zungomero to the nearest ascent of the Usagara Mountains is a march of five hours; and, after a painful and troublesome journey, we arrived at the frontier of the first gradient of the Usagara Mountains. Here we found a tattered kraal, erected by the last passing caravan, and, spent with fatigue, we threw ourselves on the short grass to rest. We were now about three hundred feet above the plain level, and there was a wondrous change of climate. Strength and health returned as if by magic; the pure sweet mountain air, alternately soft and balmy, put new life into us. Our gipsy encampment was surrounded by trees, from which depended graceful creepers, and wood-apples large as melons. Monkeys played at hide-and-seek, chattering behind the bolls, as the iguana, with its painted scale-armour, issued forth; white-breasted ravens cawed, doves cooed on well-clothed boughs, and the field cricket chirped in the shady bush. By night the view disclosed a peaceful scene, the moonbeams lying like sheets of snow upon the ruddy highlands, and the stars shone like glow-lamps in the dome above. I never wearied of contemplating the scene, and contrasting it with the Slough of Despond, unhappy Zungomero. We stayed here two days, and then resumed our upward march.

All along our way we were saddened by the sight of clean-picked skeletons and here and there the swollen corpses of porters who had perished by the wayside. A single large body passed us one day, having lost fifty of their number by smallpox, and the sight of their deceased comrades made a terrible impression. Men staggered on, blinded by disease; mothers carried infants as loathsome as themselves. He who once fell never rose again. No village would admit a corpse into its precincts, and they had to lie there until their agony was ended by the vulture, the raven, and the hyena. Several of my party caught the infection, and must have thrown themselves into the jungle, for when they were missed they could not be found. The farther we went on, the more we found the corpses; it was a regular way of death. Our Moslems passed them with averted faces, and with the low "La haul" of disgust.

When we arrived at Rufutah, I found that nearly all our instruments had been spoilt or broken; and one discomfort followed another until we arrived at Zonhwe, which was the turning-point of our expedition's difficulties.

As we went on, the path fell easily westwards through a long, grassy incline, cut by several water-courses. At noon I lay down fainting in the sandy bed of the Muhama, and, keeping two natives with me, I begged my companion to go on, and send me back a hammock from the halting-place. My men, who before had become mutinous and deserting, when they saw my extremity came out well; even the deserters reappeared, and they led me to a place where stagnant water was found, and said they were sorry. At two o'clock, as my companion did not send a hammock, I remounted, and passed through several little villages. I found my caravan halted on a hillside, where they had been attacked by a swarm of wild bees.

Our march presented curious contrasts of this strange African nature, which is ever in extremes. At one time a splendid view would charm me; above, a sky of purest azure, flecked with fleecy clouds. The plain was as a park in autumn, burnt tawny by the sun. A party was at work merrily, as if preparing for an English harvest home. Calabashes and clumps of evergreen trees were scattered over the scene, each stretching its lordly arms aloft. The dove, the peewit, and the guinea-fowl fluttered about. The most graceful of animals, the zebra and the antelope, browsed in the distance. Then suddenly the fair scene would vanish as if by enchantment. We suddenly turned into a tangled mass of tall, fœtid reeds, rank jungle, and forest. After the fiery sun and dry atmosphere of the plains, the sudden effect of the damp and clammy chill was overpowering. In such places one feels as if poisoned by miasma; a shudder runs through the frame, and cold perspiration breaks over the brow.

So things went on until September 4th, which still found us on the march. We had reached the basin of Inenge, which lies at the foot of the Windy Pass, the third and westernmost range of the Usagara Mountains. The climate is ever in extremes; during the day a furnace, and at night a refrigerator. Here we halted. The villagers of the settlements overlooking the ravine flocked down to barter their animals and grain.

The halt was celebrated by abundant drumming and droning, which lasted half the night; it served to raise the spirits of the men, who had talked of nothing the whole day but the danger of being attacked by the Wahumba, a savage tribe. The next morning there arrived a caravan of about four hundred porters, marching to the coast under the command of some Arab merchants. We interchanged civilities, and I was allured into buying a few yards of rope and other things, and also some asses. One of my men had also increased his suite, unknown to me at first, by the addition of Zawada – the "Nice Gift." She was a woman of about thirty, with black skin shining like a patent leather boot, a bulging brow, little red eyes, a wide mouth, which displayed a few long, scattered teeth, and a figure considerably too bulky for her thin legs. She was a patient and hardworking woman, and respectable enough in the acceptation of the term. She was at once married off to old Musangesi, one of the donkey-men, whose nose and chin made him a caricature of our old friend Punch. After detecting her in a lengthy walk, perhaps not a solitary one, he was guilty of such cruelty to her that I felt compelled to decree a dissolution of the marriage, and she returned safely to Zanzibar. At Inenge another female slave was added to our troop in the person of Sikujui – "Don't Know" – a herculean person with a virago manner. The channel of her upper lip had been pierced to admit a bone, which gave her the appearance of having a duck's bill. "Don't Know's" morals were frightful. She was duly espoused, in the forlorn hope of making her a respectable woman, to Goha, the sturdiest of the Wak'hutu porters; after a week she treated him with sublime contempt. She gave him first one and then a dozen rivals, and she disordered the whole caravan with her irregularities, in addition to breaking every article entrusted to her charge, and at last deserted shamelessly, so that her husband finally disposed of her to a travelling trader in exchange for a few measures of rice. Her ultimate fate I do not know, but the trader came next morning to complain of a broken head.

After Inenge we were in for a bad part of the journey, and great labour. Trembling with ague, with swimming heads, ears deafened by weakness, and limbs that would hardly support us, we contemplated with horrid despair the apparently perpendicular path up which we and our starving asses were about to toil.

On September 10th we hardened our hearts and began to breast the Pass Terrible. After rounding in two places wall-like sheets of

rock and crossing a bushy slope, we faced a long steep of loose white
soil and rolling stones, up which we could see the porters swarming
more like baboons than human beings, and the asses falling every
few yards. As we moved slowly and painfully forward, compelled to
lie down by cough, thirst, and fatigue, the sayhah, or war-cry, rang
loud from hill to hill, and Indian files of archers and spearmen
streamed like lines of black ants in all directions down the paths. The
predatory Wahumba, awaiting the caravan's departure, had seized
the opportunity of driving the cattle and plundering the village of
Inenge.

By resting every few yards, we reached, after about six hours, the
summit of the Pass Terrible, and here we sat down amongst aromatic
flowers and pretty shrubs to recover strength and breath.

On September 14th, our health much improved by the weather,
we left the hilltop and began to descend the counterslope of the
Usagara Mountains. For the first time since many days I had
strength enough to muster the porters and inspect their loads.
The outfit which had been expected to last a year had been
exhausted within three months. I summoned Said bin Salim, and
told him my anxiety. Like a veritable Arab, he declared we had
enough to last until we reached Unyamyembe, where we should
certainly be joined by reinforcements of porters.

"How do you know?" I inquired.

"Allah is all-knowing," said Said. "The caravan will come."

As the fatalism was infectious, I ceased to think upon the
subject.

The next day we sighted the plateau of Ugogo and its eastern
desert. The spectacle was truly impressive. The first aspect was stern
and wild – the rough nurse of rugged men. We went on the descent
from day to day until September 18th, when a final march of four
hours placed us on the plains of Ugogo. Before noon I sighted from a
sharp turn in the bed of a river our tent pitched under a huge
sycamore, on a level step. It was a pretty spot in the barren scene,
grassy, and grown with green mimosas, and here we halted for a
while. The second stage of our journey was accomplished.

After three days' sojourn at Ugogo to recruit the party and lay in
rations for four long desert marches, we set forth on our long march
through the province of Ugogo. Our first day's journey was over a
grassy country, and we accomplished it in comparative comfort. The
next day we toiled through the sunshine of the hot waste, crossing
plains over paths where the slides of elephants' feet upon the last
year's muddy clay showed that the land was not always dry. During
this journey we suffered many discomforts and difficulties. The orb

of day glowed like a fireball in our faces; then our path would take us through dense, thorny jungle, and over plains of black, cracked earth. Our caravan once rested in a thorny copse based upon rich red and yellow clay; once it was hurriedly dislodged by a swarm of wild bees, and the next morning I learnt that we had sustained a loss – one of our porters had deserted, and to his care had been committed one of the most valuable of our packages, a portmanteau containing "The Nautical Almanac," surveying books, and most of our papers, pen, and ink.

When we resumed our journey, the heat was awful. The sun burnt like the breath of a bonfire, warm siroccos raised clouds of dust, and in front of us the horizon was so distant that, as the Arabs expressed themselves, a man might be seen three marches off.

October 5th saw us in the centre of Kanyenye, a clearing in the jungle of about ten miles in diameter. The surface was of a red clayey soil dotted with small villages, huge calabashes, and stunted mimosas. Here I was delayed four days to settle blackmail with Magomba, the most powerful of the Wagogo chiefs. He was of a most avaricious nature. First of all I acknowledged his compliments with two cottons. On arrival at his headquarters, I was waited on by an oily Cabinet of Elders, who would not depart without their "respects" – four cottons. The next demand was made by his favourite, a hideous old Princess with more wrinkles than hair, with no hair black and no tooth white; she was not put right without a fee of six cottons. At last, accompanied by a mob of courtiers, appeared the chief *in magnifico*. He was the only chief who ever entered my tent in Ugogo – pride and a propensity for strong drink prevented such visits. He was much too great a man to call upon Arab merchants, but in our case curiosity mastered State considerations. Magomba was an old man, black and wrinkled, drivelling and decrepit. He wore a coating of castor-oil and a loincloth which grease and use had changed from blue to black. He chewed his quid, and expectorated without mercy; he asked many questions, and was all eyes to the main chance. He demanded, and received, five cloths, one coil of brass wire, and four blue cottons. In return he made me a present of the leanest of calves, and when it was driven into camp with much parade, his son, to crown all, put in a claim for three cottons. Yet Magomba, before our departure, boasted of his generosity – and indeed he was generous, for everything we had was in his hands, and we were truly in his power. It was, indeed, my firm conviction from first to last in this expedition that in case of attack or surprise by natives I had not a soul except my companion to stand by me, and all those who accompanied us would have either betrayed us or fled. We literally, therefore, carried our lives in our hands.

We toiled on and on, suffering severely from the heat by day and sometimes the cold by night, and troubled much with mutinous porters and fears of desertion, until at last we reached the heart of the great desert, or elephant ground, known as Fiery Field. On October 20th we began the transit of this Fiery Field. The waste here appeared in its most horrid phase; a narrow goat-path serpentined in and out of a growth of poisonous thorny jungle, with thin, hard grass straw growing on a glaring white and rolling ground. The march was a severe trial, and we lost on it three boxes of ammunition. By-and-by we passed over the rolling ground, and plunged into a thorny jungle, which seemed interminable, but which gradually thinned out into a forest of thorns and gums, bush and underwood, which afforded a broad path and pleasanter travelling. Unfortunately, it did not last long, and we again had a very rough bit of ground to go over. Another forest to pass through, and then we came out on October 27th into a clearing studded with large stockaded villages, fields of maize and millet, gourds and watermelons, and showing numerous flocks and herds. We had arrived at Unyamwezi, and our traverse of Ugogo was over.

The people swarmed from their abodes, young and old hustling one another for a better stare; the man forsook his loom and the girl her hoe, and we were welcomed and escorted into the village by a tail of screaming boys and shouting adults, the males almost nude, the women bare to the waist, and clothed only knee-deep in kilts. Leading the way, our guide, according to the immemorial custom of Unyamwezi, entered uninvited and *sans cérémonie* the nearest village; the long string of porters flocked in with bag and baggage, and we followed their example. We were placed under a wall-less roof, bounded on one side by the bars of the village palisade, and surrounded by a mob of starers, who relieved one another from morning to night, which made me feel like a wild beast in a menagerie.

We rested some days at Unyamwezi – the far-famed "Land of the Moon" – but I was urged to advance on the ground that the natives were a dangerous race, though they appeared to be a timid and ignoble people, dripping with castor and sesamum oil, and scantily attired in shreds of cotton or greasy goat-skins. The dangers of the road between Unyamwezi and Ujiji were declared to be great. I found afterwards that they were grossly exaggerated, but I set forth with the impression that this last stage of my journey would be the worst of all. The country over which we travelled varied very much from day to day, being sometimes opened and streaked with a thin forest of mimosas, and at other times leading us through jungly patches. Going through a thick forest, one of the porters, having imprudently lagged behind, was clubbed and cruelly bruised by three black robbers, who relieved him of his load. These highwaymen were not unusual in this part, and their raids formed one of the many dangers we had to guard against.

On November 7th, 1857, the one hundred and thirty-fourth day from the date of leaving the coast, we entered Kazeh, the principal village of Unyamwezi, much frequented by Arab merchants. I always got on well with the Arabs, and they gave me a most favourable reception. Striking indeed was the contrast between the open-handed hospitality and hearty goodwill of this truly noble race and the niggardliness of the savage and selfish Africans. Whatever I alluded to – onions, plantains, limes, vegetables, tamarinds, coffee, and other things, only to be found amongst the Arabs – were sent at once, and the very name of payment would have been an insult.

Kazeh is situated in Unyamyembe, the principal province of Unyamwezi, and is a great meeting-place of merchants and point of departure for caravans, which then radiate into the interior of Central Intertropical Africa. Here the Arab merchant from Zanzibar meets his compatriot returning from the Tanganyika and Uruwwa. Many of the Arabs settle here for years, and live comfortably, and even splendidly. Their houses, though single storied, are large, substantial, and capable of defence; their gardens are extensive and well planted. They receive regular supplies of merchandise, comforts, and luxuries from the coast; they are surrounded by troops of concubines and slaves; rich men have riding asses from Zanzibar, and even the poorest keep flocks and herds.

I was detained at Kazeh from November 8th until December 14th, and the delay was one long trial of patience. Nevertheless, on the morning of December 15th I started off afresh, charmed with the prospect of a fine open country, and delighted to get away from what had been to me a veritable imprisonment.

I will not describe the details of our march, which went on without a break. Christmas Day found us still marching, and so on day after day, if I except an enforced halt of twelve days at Msene. On January 10th, 1858, I left Msene, with considerable difficulty through the mutiny of porters; and so we pressed on, more or less with difficulty, until at last a formidable obstacle to progress presented itself. I had been suffering for some days; the miasmatic airs of Sorora had sown the seeds of a fresh illness. On the afternoon of January 18th, 1858, I was seized with an attack of fever, and then paralysis set in from the feet upwards, and I was completely *hors de combat*. There seemed nothing left for me but to lie down and die. One of my chief porters declared that the case was beyond his skill: it was one of partial paralysis, brought on by malaria, and he called in an Arab, who looked at me also. The Arab was more cheerful, and successfully predicted that I should be able to move in ten days. On the tenth I again mounted my ass, but the paralysis wore off very slowly, and prevented me from walking any distance for nearly a year. The sensation of numbness in my hands and feet disappeared even more slowly than that. I had, however, undertaken the journey in a "nothing like leather" frame of mind, and was determined to press on. So we pressed.

We had now left the "Land of the Moon" behind us, and entered upon a new district. The road before us lay through a howling wilderness, and the march lay along the right bank of a malarial river, and the mosquitoes feasted right royally upon our bodies, even in the daytime. A good deal of the ground was very swampy, and it then stretched over jungly and wooded hill-spires, with steep ascents and descents. Everywhere was thick, fœtid, and putrescent vegetation. The heaviness of this march caused two of our porters to levant and another four to strike work. It was, therefore, necessary for me to again mount ass ten days after an attack of paralysis. So we dragged on for the next week, throughout the early days of February, a weary toil of fighting through tiger and spear grass, over broken and slippery paths, and through thick jungle. But these difficulties were lightly borne, for we felt that we must be nearing the end of our journey.

On February 13th we resumed our travel through screens of lofty grass, which thinned out into a straggling forest. After about an hour's march, as we entered a small savannah, I saw our Arab leader running forward and changing the direction of the caravan. Presently he breasted a steep and stony hill, sparsely clad with thorny trees. Arrived at the summit with toil, for our fagged beasts now refused to proceed, we halted for a few minutes and gazed.

"What is that streak of light which lies below?" I inquired of Seedy Bombay, one of our porters.

"I am of opinion," quoth Seedy, "that is the water."

I gazed in dismay. The remains of my blindness, the veil of trees, and broad ray of sunshine illuminating but one reach of the lake, had shrunk its fair proportions. Prematurely I began to curse my folly in having risked life and health for so poor a prize, and even thought of proposing an immediate return with a view of exploring the Nyanza, or Northern Lake. Advancing, however, a few yards, the whole scene suddenly burst upon my view, filling me with wonder, admiration, and delight. My longing eyes beheld the Tanganyika Lake as it lay in the lap of the mountain, basking in the gorgeous tropical sunshine. Our journey had not been in vain.

A GLIMPSE OF LAKE VICTORIA

John Hanning Speke
(1827–64)

In July 1858, while returning from Lake Tanganyika with Burton, Speke made a solo excursion to the north in search of an even larger lake reported by an Arab informant. Although partially blind and unable to ascertain its extent, he named this lake "Victoria" and boldly declared it the long sought source of the White Nile. Burton scoffed at the idea and thus began exploration's bitterest controversy. Speke later substantiated his claim but died unaware of Baker's rival discovery of Lake Albert.

*13*th July, 1858   The caravan started at 6.30 a.m., and after travelling eight miles over an open, waving, well-cultivated country, stopped at the last village in Unyambéwa. The early morning before starting was wasted by the pagazis "striking" for more cloth, and refusing to move unless I complied with their demand. I peremptorily refused, and they then tried to wheedle me out of beads. In demanding cloth, they pretended that they were suffering from the chilling cold of night – a pretence too absurd to merit even a civil reply. I then explained to my head men that I would rather anything happened than listen to such imposture as this; for did the men once succeed by tricks of this sort, there would never be an end to their trying it on, and it would ultimately prove highly injurious to future travellers, especially to merchants. On the route we had nothing to divert attention, save a single Wasukuma caravan proceeding southwards to Unyanyembé. A sultana called Ungugu governs this district. She is the first and only female that we have seen in this position, though she succeeded to it after the custom of the country. I imagine she must have had a worthless husband, since every sultan can have as many wives as he pleases, and the whole could never have been barren. I rallied the porters for pulling up after so short a march, but could not induce them to go on. They declared that forests of such vast extent lay on ahead that it would be quite impossible to cross them before the night set in. In the evening I had a second cause for being vexed at this loss of time, when every mile and hour was of so much importance; for by our halt the sultana got news of my arrival, and sent a messenger to request the pleasure of my company at her house on the morrow. In vain I pleaded for permission to go and see her that moment, or to do so on my return from the N'yanza; her envoy replied that the day was so far spent I could not arrive at her abode till after dark, and she would not have the pleasure of seeing me sufficiently well. He therefore begged I would attend to the letter of her request, and not fail to visit her in the morning.

The lazy pagazis, smelling flesh, also aided the deputy in his endeavours to detain me, by saying that they could not oppose her majesty's will, lest at any future time, when they might want again to pass that way, she should take her revenge upon them. Though this might seem a very reasonable excuse, I doubt much, if their interests had lain the opposite way, whether they would have been so cautious. However, it was not difficult to detect their motives for bringing forward such an urgent reason against me, as it is a custom in this country that every wealthy traveller or merchant shall pay a passport-fee, according to his means, to the sultan of the country he travels through, who in return gives a cow or goat as a mark of amity, and this is always shared amongst the whole caravan.

14th   The sultana's house was reported to be near, so I thought to expedite the matter by visiting her in person, and thus perhaps gain an afternoon's march: otherwise to have sent the Jemadar with a present would have been sufficient, for these creatures are pure Mammonists. Vain hope, trying to do anything in a hurry in Negroland! I started early in the morning, unfortified within, and escorted by two Beluches, the Kirangozi, three porters, Bombay, and Mabruki.

After walking six miles over a well-cultivated plain, I felt anxious to know what they meant by "near," and was told, as usual, that the house was close at hand. Distrustful, but anxious to complete the business as speedily as possible (for to succeed in Africa one must do everything one's self), I followed the envoy across one of the waves that diversify the face of the country, descended into a well-cultivated trough-like depression, and mounted a second wave six miles farther on.

Here at last, by dint of perseverance, we had the satisfaction of seeing the palisadoed royal abode. We entered it by an aperture in the tall slender stakes which surround the dwellings and constitute the palisadoing, and after following up a passage constructed of the same material as the outer fence, we turned suddenly into a yard full of cows – a substitute for an anteroom. Arrived there, the negroes at once commenced beating a couple of large drums, half as tall as themselves, made something like a beer-barrel, covered on the top with a cow-skin stretched tightly over, by way of a drum-head. This drumming was an announcement of our arrival, intended as a mark of regal respect.

For ten minutes we were kept in suspense, my eyes the while resting upon the milk-pots which were being filled at mid-day, but I could not get a drop. At the expiration of that time a body of slaves came rushing in, and hastily desired us to follow them. They led us down the passage by which we entered, and then turned up another one similarly constructed, which brought us into the centre of the sultana's establishment – a small court, in which the common negro mushroom huts, with ample eaves, afforded us grateful shelter from the blazing sun. A cow-skin was now spread, and a wooden stool set for me, that I might assume a better state than my suite, who were squatted in a circle around me. With the usual precaution of African nobles, the lady's-maid was first sent to introduce herself – an ugly halting creature, very dirtily garbed, but possessing a smiling contented face. Her kindly mien induced me, starving and thirsty as I was after my twelve miles' walk, to ask for eggs and milk – great luxuries, considering how long I had been deprived of them. They were soon procured, and devoured with a voracity that must have astonished the bystanders.

The maid, now satisfied there was nothing to fear, whether from ghost, goblin, or white face, retired and brought her mistress, a short stumpy old dame, who had seen at least some sixty summers. Her nose was short, squat, and flabby at the end, and her eyes were bald of brows or lashes; but still she retained great energy of manner, and was blessed with an ever-smiling face. The dress she wore consisted of an old barsati, presented by some Arab merchant, and was if anything dirtier than her maid's attire. The large joints of all her fingers were bound up with small copper wire, her legs staggered under an immense accumulation of anklets made of brass wire wound round elephant's tail or zebra's hair; her arms were decorated with huge solid brass rings, and from other thin brass wire bracelets depended a great assortment of wooden, brazen, horn, and ivory ornaments, cut in every shape of talismanic peculiarity.

Squatting by my side, the sultana at once shook hands. Her nimble fingers first manipulated my shoes (the first point of notice in these barefooted climes), then my overalls, then my waistcoat, more particularly the buttons, and then my coat – this latter article being so much admired, that she wished I would present it to her, to wear upon her own fair person. Next my hands and fingers were mumbled, and declared to be as soft as a child's, and my hair was likened to a lion's mane. "Where is he going?" was the all-important query. This, without my understanding, was readily answered by a dozen voices, thus: "He is going to the Lake, to barter his cloth for large hippopotami teeth." Satisfied with this plausible story, she retired into privacy, and my slave, taking the hint, soon followed with the hongo (present or tax), duly presented it, and begged permission in my name to depart. But as she had always given a bullock to the Arabs who visited her, I also must accept one from her, though she could not realise the fact that so scurvy a present as mine could be intended for her, whose pretensions were in no way inferior to those of the Unyanyembé Sultan. An Arab could not have offered less, and this was a rich Mzungu!

Misfortunes here commenced anew: the bullock she was desirous of giving was out grazing, and could not be caught until the evening, when all the cattle are driven in together. Further, she could not afford to lose so interesting a personage as her guest, and volunteered to give me a shakedown for the night. I begged she would consider my position – the absolute necessity for my hurrying – and not insist on my acceptance of the bullock, or be offended by my refusing her kind offer to remain there, but permit our immediate departure. She replied that the word had gone forth, so the animal must be given; and if I still persisted in going, at any rate three porters could remain behind, and drive it on afterwards. To this I reluctantly consented, and only on the Kirangozi's promise to march the following morning. Then, with the usual farewell salutation, "Kuaheré, Mzungu," from my pertinacious hostess, I was not sorry to retrace my steps, a good five hours' walk. We re-entered camp at 7.20 p.m., which is long after dark in regions so near to the equator.

16th We started at 6 a.m., and travelled eleven miles to Ukamba, a village in the district of Msalala, which is held by a tribe called Wamanda. The first four miles lay over the cultivated plain of Ibanda, till we arrived at the foot of a ridge of hills, which, gradually closing from the right, intersects the road, and runs into a hilly country extending round the western side of the aforesaid plain. We now crossed the range, and descended into a country more closely studded with the same description of small hills, but highly cultivated in the valleys and plains that separate them. About twelve miles to the eastward of Ukamba live a tribe called Wasongo, and to the west, at twenty miles' distance, are the Waquanda. To-day was fully verified the absolute futility of endeavouring to march against time in these wild countries. The lazy pagazis finding themselves now, as it were, in clover, a country full of all the things they love, would not stir one step after 11 a.m. Were time of no consequence, and coloured beads in store, such travelling as this would indeed be pleasant. For the country here, so different from the Ujiji line, affords not only delightful food for the eyes, but abounds in flesh, milk, eggs, and vegetables in every variety. The son of the Mséné Sultan, who lives between Unyanyembé and Ujiji, and became great friends with us when travelling there, paid me a visit to-day. He caught me at work with my diary and instruments, and being struck with veneration at the sight of my twirling compass and literary pursuits, thought me a magician, and begged that I would cast his horoscope, divine the probable extent of his father's life, ascertain if there would be any wars, and describe the weather, the prospects of harvest, and what future state the country would lapse into. The shrewd Bombay replied, to save me trouble, that so great a matter required more days of contemplation than I could afford to give. Provisions were very dear when purchased with white beads, for they were not the fashion, and the people were indifferent to them. I paid him one loin-cloth for four fowls and nine eggs, though, had I had coloured beads, I might have purchased one hen per khete (or necklace). Had this been a cloth-wearing instead of a bead-decorating nation, I should have obtained forty fowls for one shukka (or loin-cloth), that being the equivalent value with beads, equal, according to Zanzibar money, to one dollar. It is always foolish to travel without an assortment of beads, in consequence of the tastes of the different tribes varying so much; and it is more economical in the long-run to purchase high-priced than low-priced beads when making up the caravan at Zanzibar, for every little trader buys the cheaper sorts, stocks the country with them, and thus makes them common.

17th   This day, like all the preceding ones, is delightful, and worthy of drawing forth an exclamation, like the Indian Griff's, of "What a fine day this is again!" We started at 7 a.m., and travelled thirteen miles, with fine bracing air, so cold in the morning that my fingers tingled with it. We were obliged here to diverge from the proper road *viâ* Sarengé, to avoid a civil war – the one before alluded to, and to escape which I had engaged the second guide – between two young chiefs, brothers of the Wamanda tribe, who were contending for the reins of government on the principle that might ought to give the right.

The whole country lies in long waves, crested with cropping little hills, thickly clad with small trees and brushwood. In the hollows of these waves the cultivation is very luxuriant. Here I unfortunately had occasion to give my miserable Goanese cook-boy a sound dressing, as the only means left of checking his lying, obstinate, destructive, wasteful, and injurious habit of intermeddling. This raised the creature's choler, and he vowed vengeance to the death, seconding his words with such a fiendish, murderous look, his eyes glistening like an infuriated tiger's, that I felt obliged to damp his temerity and freedom of tongue by further chastisement, which luckily brought him to a proper sense of his duty.

18th We left at 7 a.m., and travelled ten miles to Ukuni. The country still continues of the same rich and picturesque character, and retains daily the same unvarying temperature. On the road we met a party of Wayombo, who, taking advantage of the Wamanda disturbances, had lifted some forty or fifty head of their cattle in perfect security. I saw two albinos in this village, one an old woman with greyish eyes, and the other young, who ran away from fright, and concealed herself in a hut, and would not show again although beads were offered as an inducement for one moment's peep. The old lady's skin was of an unwholesome fleshy-pink hue, and her hair, eyebrows, and eyelashes were a light yellowish white. This march was shortened by two pagazis falling sick. I surmised this illness to be in consequence of their having gorged too much beef, to which they replied that everybody is sure to suffer pains in the stomach after eating meat, if the slayer of the animal happens to protrude his tongue and clench it with his teeth during the process of slaughtering. At last the white beads have been taken, but at the extravagant rate of two khetes for four eggs, the dearest I ever paid.

19th The caravan proceeded at 6 a.m., and, after going eight miles re-entered the Msalala district's frontier, where we put up in a village three miles beyond the border. The country throughout this march may be classed in two divisions, one of large and extensively cultivated plains, with some fine trees about; and the other of small irregularly-disposed hills, the prevailing granitic outcrops of the region. There is no direct line northwards here, so we had to track about, and hit upon the lines between the different villages, which enhanced our trouble and caused much delay. At this place I witnessed the odd operation of brother-making. It consists in the two men desirous of a blood-tie being seated face to face on a cow's hide, with their legs stretched out as wide to the front as their length will permit, one pair overlapping the other. They then place their bows and arrows across their thighs, and each holds a leaf: at the same time a third person, holding a pot of oil or butter, makes an incision above their knees, and requires each to put his blood on the other's leaf, and mix a little oil with it, when each anoints himself with the brother-salve. This operation over, the two brothers bawl forth the names and extent of their relatives, and swear by the blood to protect the other till death. Ugogo, on the highway between the coast and Ujiji, is a place so full of inhabitants compared with the other places on that line, that the coast people quote it as a wonderful instance of high population; but this district astonished all my retinue. The road to-day was literally thronged with a legion of black humanity so exasperatingly bold that nothing short of the stick could keep them from jostling me. Poor creatures! they said they had come a long way to see, and now must have a good long stare; for when was there ever a Mzungu here before?

20th   We broke ground at 6 a.m., and after travelling through high cultivation six miles, were suddenly stopped by a guard of Wamanda, sent by Kurua, a sultan of that tribe, and chief of the division we were marching in. Their business was to inform us that if we wished to travel to the Lake, the sultan would give directions to have us escorted by another route, as his eldest brother was disputing the rights of government with him along the line we were now pursuing; and added, that our intentions would be only known to him by the part we might choose to take. These constant interruptions were becoming very troublesome; so, as we were close to the confines of these two malcontents, I was anxious to force our way on, and agreed to do so with the Beluches. But the tiresome, lazy, flesh-seeking pagazis saw a feast in prospect by the sultan's arrangement, and would not move an inch. Further, the Kirangozi requested his discharge if I was otherwise than peacefully inclined. The guard then led us to Mgogua, the sultan's village, a little off the road.

Kurua is a young man, not very handsome himself, but he has two beautiful young wives. They secured me a comfortable house, showed many attentions, and sent me a bowl of fresh sweetmilk, the very extreme of savage hospitality. In the evening he presented me with a bullock. This I tried to refuse, observing that flesh was the prime cause of all my hindrances; but nothing would satisfy him;. I must accept it, or he would be the laughing-stock of everybody for inhospitality. If I gave nothing in return, he should be happy as long as his part of host was properly fulfilled. Salt, according to the sultan, is only to be found here in the same efflorescent state in which I saw it yesterday – a thin coating overspreading the ground, as though flour had been sprinkled there.

21st Halt. The quantity of cattle in Msalala surpasses anything I have seen in Africa. Large droves, tended by a few men each, are to be seen in every direction over the extensive plains, and every village is filled with them at night. The cultivation also is as abundant as the cattle are numerous, and the climate is delightful. To walk till breakfast, 9 a.m., every morning, I find a luxury, and from that time till noon I ride with pleasure; but the next three hours, though pleasant in a hut, are too warm to be agreeable under hard exertion. The evenings and the mornings, again, are particularly serene, and the night, after 10 p.m., so cold as to render a blanket necessary. But then it must be remembered that all the country about these latitudes, on this meridian, 33° east, is at an altitude of from 3500 to 4000 feet. My dinner to-day was improved by the addition of tomatos and the bird's-eye chili – luxuries to us, but which the negroes, so different from the Indians, never care about, and seldom grow.

22d After much groaning and grumbling, I got the sick men on their legs by 7 a.m., and we marched eight miles to Senagongo, the boma (palisade) of Sultan Kanoni, Kurua's second brother. These two younger brothers side together against the eldest. They are all by different mothers, and think the father's property should fairly be divided among them. It is a glaring instance of the bad effects of a plurality of wives; and being contrary to our constitutional laws of marriage, I declined giving an opinion as to who was right or wrong.

To avoid the seat of war my track was rather tortuous. On the east or right side the country was open, and afforded a spacious view; but on the west this was limited by an irregularly-disposed series of low hills. Cultivation and scrub-jungle alternated the whole way. The miserable Goanese, like a dog slinking off to die, slipped away behind the caravan, and hid himself in the jungle to suffer the pangs of fever in solitude. I sent men to look for him in vain: party succeeded party in the search, till at last night set in without his appearing. It is singular in this country to find how few men escape some fever or other sickness, who make a sudden march after living a quiet stationary life. It appears as if the bile got stirred, suffused the body, and, exciting the blood, produced this effect. I had to admonish a silly Beluch, who, foolishly thinking that power alone could not hurt a man, fired his gun off into a mass of naked human legs in order, as he said, to clear the court. The consequences was, that at least fifty pairs got covered with numerous small bleeding wounds, all dreadfully painful from the saltpetre contained in the powder. It was fortunate that the sultan was a good man, and was present at the time it occurred, else a serious row might have been the consequence of this mischievous trick.

23d Halt. We fired alarm-guns all night to no purpose; so at daybreak three different parties, after receiving particular orders how to scour the country, were sent off at the same time to search for Gaetano. Fortunately the Beluches obeyed my injunctions, and at 10 a.m., returned with the man, who looked for all the world exactly like a dog who, guilty of an indiscretion, is being brought in disgrace before his master to receive a flogging; for he knew I had a spare donkey for the sick, and had constantly warned the men from stopping behind alone in these lawless countries. The other two parties adopting, like true Easterns, a better plan of their own, spent the whole day ranging wildly over the country, fruitlessly exerting themselves, and frustrating any chance of my getting even an afternoon's march. Kanoni very kindly sent messengers all over his territory to assist in the search: he, like Kurua, has taken every opportunity to show me those little pleasing attentions which always render travelling agreeable. These Wamanda are certainly the most noisy set of beings that I ever met with: commencing their fêtes in the middle of the village every day at 3 p.m., with screaming, yelling, rushing, jumping, sham-fighting, drumming, and singing in one collective inharmonious noise, they seldom cease till midnight. Their villages, too, are everywhere much better protected by bomas (palisading) than is usual in Africa, arguing that they are a rougher and more warlike people than the generality. If shoved aside, or pushed with a stick, they show their savage nature by turning fiercely like a fatted pig upon whoever tries to poke it up.

24th The march commenced at 7 a.m.; and here we again left the direct road, to avoid a third party of belligerent Wamanda, situated in the northern extremity of the Msalala district, on the highway between Unyanyembé and the Lake. On bidding the sultan adieu, he was very urgent in his wishes that I should take a bullock from him. This I told him I should willingly have accepted, only that it would delay my progress; and he, more kindly than the other chief, excused me. Finding that none of our party knew the road, he advanced a short way with us, and generously offered to furnish us with a guide to the Lake and back, saying that he would send one of his own men after us to a place he appointed with my Kirangozi. I expressed my gratitude for his consideration, and we parted with warm regard for one another. Unfortunately, Bombay, who is not the clearest man in the world in expressing himself, stupidly bungled the sultan's arrangement, and we missed the man.

To keep the pagazis going was a matter of no little difficulty; after the fifth mile they persisted in entering every village that they came across, and, throwing down their loads, were bent upon making an easy day's work of it. I, on the contrary, was equally persistent in going on, and neither would allow the Beluches to follow them, nor enter the villages myself, until they, finding their game of no avail, quietly shouldered their loads and submitted to my orders. This day's journey was twelve miles over a highly-cultivated, waving country, at the end of which we took up our abode in a deserted village called Kahama.

25th We got under way at 7 a.m., and marched seven and a half hours, when we entered a village in the district of Nindo, nineteen miles distant. After passing through a belt of jungle three miles broad, we came upon some villages amidst a large range of cultivation. This passed, we penetrated a large wilderness of thorn and bush jungle, having sundry broad grassy flats lying at right angles to the road. Here I saw a herd of hartebeests, giraffes, and other animals, giving to the scene a truly African character. The tracks of elephants and different large beasts prove that this place is well tenanted in the season. The closeness of the jungle and evenness of the land prevented my taking any direct observations with the compass; but the mean oscillations of its card showed a course with northing again. This being a long stage, I lent my ass to a sick Beluch, and we accomplished the journey, notwithstanding the great distance, in a pleasant and spirited manner. This despatch may in part be attributable to there being so much desert, and the beloved "grub" and the village lying ahead of us luring the men on.

26th We broke ground at 7 a.m., and, after passing the village cultivation, entered a waterless wilderness of thorn and tree forest, with some long and broad plains of tall grass intersecting the line of march. These flats very much resemble some we crossed when travelling close to and parallel with the Malagarazi river; for the cracked and flawy nature of the ground, now parched up by a constant drought, shows that this part gets inundated in the wet season. Indeed, this peculiar grassy flat formation suggests the proximity of a river everywhere in Africa; and I felt sure, as afterwards proved true, that a river was not far from us. The existence of animal life is another warranty of water being near: elephants and buffaloes cannot live a day without it.

At the usual hour of departure this morning, the Kirangozi discovered that the pagazis' feet were sore from the late long marches, and declared that they could not walk. To this the Jemadar replied that the best asylum for such complaints was on ahead, where the sahib proposed to kill some goats and rest a day. The Kirangozi replied, "But the direct road is blocked up by wars: if a march must be made, I will show another route three marches longer round." "That," answered the Jemadar, "is not your business: if any troubles arise from marauders, we, the Beluches, are the fighting men – leave that to us." At last the Kirangozi, getting quite disconcerted, declared that there was no water on the way. "Then," quoth the energetic Jemadar, "were your gourds made for nothing? If you don't pack up at once, you and my stick shall make acquaintance." The party was then off in a moment.

29th We started at 6 a.m., and marched thirteen miles to a village at the northern extremity of the district. The face of the country is still very irregular, sometimes rising into hills, at other times dropping into dells, but very well cultivated in the lower portion; whilst the brown granite rocks, with trees and brushwood covering the upper regions, diversify the colouring, and form a pleasing contrast to the scene; added to this, large and frequent herds graze about the fields and amongst the villages, and give animation to the whole. Amongst the trees, palms take a prominent part. Indeed, for tropical scenery, there are few places that could equal this; and if the traveller, as he moves along, surrounded by the screeching, howling, inquisitive savages, running rudely about and boisterously jostling him, could only divest himself of the idea that he is a bear baited by a yelping pack of hounds, the journey would be replete with enjoyment.

Crossing some hills, the caravan sprang a covey of guinea-fowls, and at some springs in a valley I shot several couple of sand-grouse, darker in plumage than any I ever saw in Africa or India, and not quite so big as the Tibet bird. The chief of the village offered me a bullock; but as the beast did not appear until the time of starting, I declined it. Neither did I give him any cloth, being convinced in my mind that these and other animals have always been brought to me by the smaller chiefs at the instigation of the Kirangozi, and probably aided by the flesh-loving party in general. The Jemadar must have been particularly mortified at my way of disposing of the business, for he talked of nothing else but flesh and the animal from the moment it was sent for, his love for butcher-meat amounting almost to a frenzy. The sandstone in this region is highly impregnated with iron, and smelters do a good business; indeed, the iron for nearly all the tools and cutlery that are used in this division of Eastern Africa is found and manufactured here. It is the Brummagem of the land, and has not only rich but very extensive ironfields stretching many miles north, east, and west. I brought some specimens away. Cloth is little prized in this especially bead country, and I had to pay the sum of one dhoti kiniki for one pot of honey and one pot of ghee (clarified butter).

30th The caravan started at 6 a.m., and travelled four miles northwards, amidst villages and cultivation. From this point, on facing to the left, I could discern a sheet of water, about four miles from me, which ultimately proved to be a creek, and the most southern point of the N'yanza, which, as I have said before, the Arabs described to us as the Ukéréwé Sea.* We soon afterwards descended into a grassy and jungly depression, and arrived at a deep, dirty, viscid nullah (a watercourse that only runs in wet weather), draining the eastern country into the southern end of the creek. To cross this (which I shall name Jordan) was a matter of no small difficulty, especially for the donkeys, whose fording seemed quite hopeless, until the Jemadar, assisted by two other Beluches, with blows and threats made the lazy pagazis work, and dragged them through the mud by sheer force. This operation lasted so long that, after crossing, we made for the nearest village in the Uvira district, and completed a journey of eight miles. The country to the eastward appeared open and waving, but to the north and far west very hilly. The ground is fertile, and the flocks and herds very abundant. Hippopotami frequent the nullah at night, and reside there during the rainy season; but at this, the dry half of the year, they retreat to the larger waters of the creek. Rhinoceroses are said to pay nightly visits to fields around the villages, and commit sad havoc on the crops. The nullah, running from the south-east, drains the land in that direction; but a river, I hear, rising in the Msalala district, draws off the water from the lays we have recently been crossing, to the westward of our track, where its course lies, and empties it into the creek on the opposite side to where the nullah debouches.

31st On hearing that a shorter track than the Sukuma one usually frequented by the Arabs led to Muanza, the place Sheikh Snay advised my going to, I started by it at 8 a.m.; and after following it westward down the nullah's right bank a few miles, turned up northwards, and continued along the creek to a village, eight miles

---

* This, I maintain, was *the* discovery of the source of the Nile. Had the ancient kings and sages known that a rainy zone existed on the equator, they would not have puzzled their brains so long, and have wondered where those waters came from which meander through upwards of a thousand miles of scorching desert without a single tributary.

distant, at the farther end of the Urima district, where we took up
our quarters. The country has a mixed and large population of
smiths, agriculturists, and herdsmen, residing in the flats and depressions which lie between the scattered little hills. During the rainy
season, when the lake swells and the country becomes super-satu-
rated, the inundations are so great that all travelling becomes
suspended.

1st August This day's march, commenced at 6 a.m., differs but
little from the last. Following down the creek, which, gradually
increasing in breadth as it extended northwards, was here of very
considerable dimensions, we saw many little islands, well-wooded
elevations, standing boldly out of its waters, which, together with
the hill-dotted country around, afforded a most agreeable prospect.
Would that my eyes had been strong enough to dwell, unshaded,
upon such scenery! but my French grey spectacles so excited the
crowds of sable gentry who followed the caravan, and they were so
boisterously rude, stooping and peering underneath my wide-awake
to gain a better sight of my double eyes, as they chose to term them,
that it became impossible for me to wear them. I therefore pocketed
the instrument, closed my eyes, and allowed the donkey I was riding
to be quietly pulled along.

To-day's track lay for the first half of the way over a jungly
depression, where we saw ostriches, florikans, and the small Saltiana
antelopes; but as their shyness did not allow of an open approach, I
amused myself by shooting partridges. During the remainder of the
way, the caravan threaded between villages and cultivation lying in
small valleys, or crossed over low hills, accomplishing a total
distance of twelve miles. Here we put up at a village called Ukumbi,
occupied by the Walaswanda tribe.

2nd We set out at 6 a.m., and travelled thirteen miles by a tortuous
route, sometimes close by the creek, at other times winding between
small hills, the valleys of which were thickly inhabited by both
agricultural and pastoral people. Here some small perennial streams,
exuding from springs by the base of these hills, meander through the
valleys, and keep all vegetable life in a constant state of verdant
freshness. The creek still increases in width as it extends northward,
and is studded with numerous small rocky island-hills covered with
brushwood, which, standing out from the bosom of the deep-blue
waters, reminded me of a voyage I once had in the Grecian
Archipelago. The route also being so diversified with hills, afforded
fresh objects of attraction at every turn; and to-day, by good fortune,
the usually troublesome people have attended more to their harvest-
making, and left me to the enjoyment of the scenery. My trusty

Blissett made a florikan pay the penalty of death for his temerity in attempting a flight across the track. The day's journey lasted thirteen miles, and brought us into a village called Isamiro.

August 3rd The caravan, after quitting Isamiro, began winding up a long but gradually inclined hill – which, as it bears no native name, I shall call Somerset – until it reached its summit, when the vast expanse of the pale-blue waters of the N'yanza burst suddenly upon my gaze. It was early morning. The distant sea-line of the north horizon was defined in the calm atmosphere between the north and west points of the compass; but even this did not afford me any idea of the breadth of the lake, as an archipelago of islands, each consisting of a single hill, rising to a height of 200 or 300 feet above the water, intersected the line of vision to the left; while on the right the western horn of the Ukéréwé Island cut off any farther view of its distant waters to the eastward of north. A sheet of water – an elbow of the sea, however, at the base of the low range on which I stood – extended far away to the eastward, to where, in the dim distance, a hummock-like elevation of the mainland marked what I understood to be the south and east angle of the lake. The important islands of Ukéréwé and Mzita, distant about twenty or thirty miles, formed the visible north shore of this firth. The name of the former of these islands was familiar to us as that by which this long-sought lake was usually known. It is reported by the natives to be of no great extent; and though of no considerable elevation, I could discover several spurs stretching down to the water's edge from its central ridge of hills. The other island, Mzita, is of greater elevation, of a hog-backed shape, but being more distant, its physical features were not so distinctly visible.

In consequence of the northern islands of the Bengal Archipelago before mentioned obstructing the view, the western shore of the lake could not be defined: a series of low hill-tops extended in this direction as far as the eye could reach; while below me, at no great distance, was the debouchure of the creek, which enters the lake from the south, and along the banks of which my last three days' journey had led me. This view was one which, even in a well-known and explored country, would have arrested the traveller by its peaceful beauty. The islands, each swelling in a gentle slope to a rounded summit, clothed with wood between the rugged angular closely-cropping rocks of granite, seemed mirrored in the calm surface of the lake; on which I here and there detected a small black speck, the tiny canoe of some Muanza fisherman. On the gently shelving plain below me, blue smoke curled above the trees, which here and there partially concealed villages and hamlets, their brown thatched roofs contrasting with the emerald green of the beautiful milk-bush, the coral branches of which cluster in such profusion round the cottages, and form alleys and hedgerows about the villages as ornamental as any garden shrub in England. But the pleasure of the mere view vanished in the presence of those more intense and exciting emotions which are called up by the consideration of the commercial and geographical importance of the prospect before me.

I no longer felt any doubt that the lake at my feet gave birth to that interesting river, the source of which has been the subject of so much speculation, and the object of so many explorers. The Arabs' tale was proved to the letter. This is a far more extensive lake than the Tanganyika; "so broad you could not see across it, and so long that nobody knew its length."* I had now the pleasure of perceiving that a map I had constructed on Arab testimony, and sent home to the Royal Geographical Society before leaving Unyanyembé, was so substantially correct that in its general outlines I had nothing whatever to alter. Further, as I drew that map after proving their first statements about the Tanganyika, which were made before my going there, I have every reason to feel confident of their veracity relative to their travels north through Karagué, and to Kibuga in Uganda.

When Sheikh Snay told us of the Ukéréwé, as he called the N'yanza, on our first arrival at Kazé, proceeding westward from Zanzibar, he said, "If you have come only to see a large bit of water, you had better go northwards and see the Ukéréwé; for it is much greater in every respect than the Tanganyika"; and so, as far as I can ascertain, it is. Muanza, our journey's end, now lay at our feet. It is an open, well-cultivated plain on the southern end, and lies almost flush with the lake; a happy, secluded-looking corner, containing every natural facility to make life pleasant. After descending the hill, we followed along the borders of the lake, and at first entered Mahaya's Palace, when the absence of boats arousing my suspicions, made me inquire where the Arabs, on coming to Muanza, and wishing to visit Ukéréwé, usually resided. This, I heard, was some way farther on; so with great difficulty I persuaded the porters to come away and proceed at once to where they said an Arab was

---

* This magnificent sheet of water I have ventured to name VICTORIA, after our gracious Sovereign. Its length was not clearly understood by me, in consequence of the word Sea having been applied both to the Lake and to the Nile by my local informants; and there was no recent map of the Nile with the expedition by which I might have been guided.

actually living. It was a singular coincidence that, after Sheikh Snay's caution as to my avoiding Sultan Mahaya's Palace, by inquiring diligently about him yesterday, and finding no one who knew his name, the first person I should have encountered was himself, and that, too, in his own Palace. The reason of this was, that big men in this country, to keep up their dignity, have several names, and thus mystify the traveller.

I then proceeded along the shore of the lake in an easterly direction, and on the way shot a number of red Egyptian geese, which were very numerous; they are the same sort here as I once saw in the Somali country. Another goose, which unfortunately I could not kill, is very different from any I ever saw or heard of: it stands as high as the Canadian bird, or higher, and is black all over, saving one little white patch beneath the lower mandible. It was fortunate that I came on here, for the Arab in question, called Mansur bin Salim, treated me very kindly, and he had retainers belonging to the country, who knew as much about the lake as anybody, and were of very great assistance. I also found a good station for making observations on the lake. It was Mansur who first informed me of my mistake of the morning; but he said that the evil reports spread at Unyanyembé about Mahaya had no foundation; on the contrary, he had found him a very excellent and obliging person.

To-day we marched eight miles, and have concluded our journey northwards, a total distance of 226 miles from Kazé, which, occupying twenty-five days, is at the rate of nine miles per diem, halts inclusive.

THE RESERVOIR OF THE NILE

Samuel White Baker
(1821–93)

Amongst professional explorers and big game hunters, none was as successful as Baker. A bluff and plausible figure, wealthy and resourceful, he conducted his explorations on the grand scale, invariably reached his goal and invariably reaped the rewards, including a knighthood and the delectable Florence, his young Hungarian wife. In 1864, her golden tresses causing a sensation in darkest Africa, she shared his greatest triumph when together they left M'rooli in Uganda on the last leg of a two-year journey in search of the source of the White Nile.

The day of starting at length arrived; the chief and guide appeared, and we were led along the banks of the Kafoor for about a mile, until we arrived at a cluster of huts; here we were to wait for Kamrasi, who had promised to take leave of us. The sun was overpowering and we dismounted from our oxen, and took shelter in a blacksmith's shed. In about an hour Kamrasi arrived, attended by a considerable number of men, and took his seat in our shed. I felt convinced that his visit was simply intended to peel the last skin from the onion. I had already given him nearly all that I had, but he hoped to extract the whole before I should depart.

He almost immediately commenced the conversation by asking for a pretty yellow muslin Turkish handkerchief fringed with silver drops that Mrs. Baker wore upon her head: one of these had already been given to him, and I explained that this was the last remaining, and that she required it. . . . He "must" have it. . . . It was given. He then demanded other handkerchiefs. We had literally nothing but a few most ragged towels; he would accept no excuse, and insisted upon a portmanteau being unpacked, that he might satisfy himself by actual inspection. The luggage, all ready for the journey, had to be unstrapped and examined, and the rags were displayed in succession; but so wretched and uninviting was the exhibition of the family linen, that he simply returned them, and said "they did not suit him." Beads he must have, or I was "his enemy." A selection of the best opal beads was immediately given him. I rose from the stone upon which I was sitting, and declared that we must start immediately. "Don't be in a hurry," he replied; "you have plenty of time; but you have not given me that watch you promised me." . . . This was my only watch that he had begged for, and had been refused every day during my stay at M'rooli. So pertinacious a beggar I had never seen. I explained to him that, without the watch, my journey would be useless, but that I would give him all that I had except the watch when the exploration should be completed, as I should require nothing on my direct return to Gondokoro. At the same time, I repeated to him the arrangement for the journey that he had promised, begging him not to deceive me, as my wife and I should both die if we were compelled to remain another year in this country by losing the annual boats in Gondokoro. The understanding was this: he was to give me porters to the lake, where I was to be furnished with canoes to take me to Magungo, which was situated at the junction of the Somerset. From Magungo he told me that I should see the Nile issuing from the lake close to the spot where the Somerset entered, and that the canoes should take me down the river, and porters should carry my effects from the nearest point to Shooa, and deliver me at my old station without delay. Should he be faithful to this engagement, I trusted to procure porters from Shooa, and to reach Gondokoro in time for the annual boats. I had arranged that a boat should be sent from Khartoum to await me at Gondokoro early in this year, 1864; but I felt sure that should I be long delayed, the boat would return without me, as the people would be afraid to remain alone at Gondokoro after the other boats had quitted.

In our present weak state another year of Central Africa without quinine appeared to warrant death; it was a race against time, all was untrodden ground before us, and the distance quite uncertain. I trembled for my wife, and weighed the risk of another year in this horrible country should we lose the boats. With the self-sacrificing devotion that she had shown in every trial, she implored me not to think of any risks on her account, but to push forward and discover the lake – that she had determined not to return until she had herself reached the "M'wootan N'zigé."

I now requested Kamrasi to allow us to take leave, as we had not an hour to lose. In the coolest manner he replied, "I will send you to the lake and to Shooa, as I have promised; but, *you must leave your wife with me!*"

At that moment we were surrounded by a great number of natives, and my suspicions of treachery at having been led across the Kafoor river appeared confirmed by this insolent demand. If this were to be the end of the expedition I resolved that it should also be the end of Kamrasi, and, drawing my revolver quietly, I held it within two feet of his chest, and looking at him with undisguised contempt, I told him that if I touched the trigger, not all his men could save him: and that if he dared to repeat the insult I would shoot him on the spot. At the same time I explained to him that in my country such insolence would entail bloodshed, and that I looked upon him as an ignorant ox who knew no better, and that this excuse alone could save him. My wife, naturally indignant, had risen from her seat, and, maddened with the excitement of the moment, she made him a little speech in Arabic (not a word of which he understood), with a countenance almost as amiable as the head of Medusa. Altogether the *mise en scène* utterly astonished him; the woman Bacheeta, although savage, had appropriated the insult to her mistress, and she also fearlessly let fly at Kamrasi, translating as nearly as she could the complimentary address that "Medusa" had just delivered.

Whether this little *coup de théâtre* had so impressed Kamrasi with British female independence that he wished to be off his bargain, I cannot say, but with an air of complete astonishment, he said, "Don't be angry! I had no intention of offending you by asking for your wife; I will give you a wife, if you want one, and I thought you might have no objection to give me yours; it is my custom to give my visitors pretty wives, and I thought you might exchange. Don't make a fuss about it; if you don't like it, there's an end of it; I will never mention it again." This very practical apology I received very sternly, and merely insisted upon starting. He seemed rather confused at having committed himself, and to make amends he called his people and ordered them to carry our loads. His men ordered a number of women, who had assembled out of curiosity, to shoulder the luggage and carry it to the next village, where they would be relieved. I assisted my wife upon her ox, and with a very cold adieu to Kamrasi, I turned my back most gladly on M'rooli.

The country was a vast flat of grass land interspersed with small villages and patches of sweet potatoes; these were very inferior, owing to the want of drainage. For about two miles we continued on the banks of the Kafoor river; the women who carried the luggage

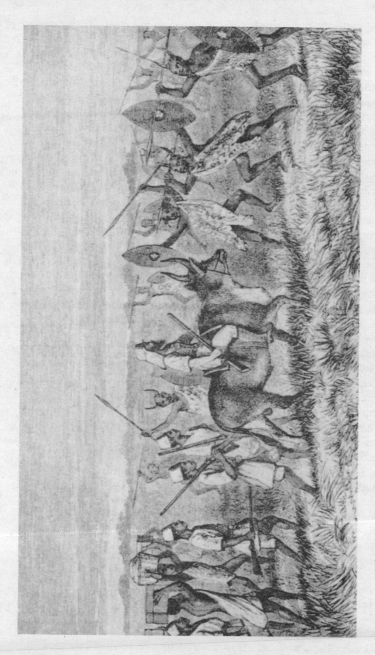

The start from M'rooli for the lake, with Kamrasi's escort. From *The Albert Nyanza, Great Basin of the Nile and Explorations of the Nile Sources*, London, 1867.

were straggling in disorder, and my few men were much scattered in their endeavours to collect them. We approached a considerable village; but just as we were nearing it, out rushed about six hundred men with lances and shields, screaming and yelling like so many demons. For the moment, I thought it was an attack, but almost immediately I noticed that women and children were mingled with the men. My men had not taken so cool a view of the excited throng that was now approaching us at full speed, brandishing their spears, and engaging with each other in mock combat. "There's a fight! – there's a fight!" my men exclaimed; "we are attacked! fire at them, Hawaga." However, in a few seconds I persuaded them that it was a mere parade, and that there was no danger. With a rush, like a cloud of locusts, the natives closed around us, dancing, gesticulating, and yelling before my ox, feigning to attack us with spears and shields, then engaging in sham fights with each other, and behaving like so many madmen. A very tall chief accompanied them; and one of their men was suddenly knocked down, and attacked by the crowd with sticks and lances, and lay on the ground covered with blood: what his offence had been I did not hear. The entire crowd were most grotesquely got up, being dressed in either leopard or white monkey skins, with cow's tails strapped on behind, and antelopes' horns fitted upon their heads, while their chins were ornamented with false beards, made of the bushy ends of cows' tails sewed together. Altogether, I never saw a more unearthly set of creatures; they were perfect illustrations of my childish ideas of devils – horns, tails, and all, excepting the hoofs; they were our escort! furnished by Kamrasi to accompany us to the lake.

We marched till 7 p.m. over flat, uninteresting country, and then halted at a miserable village which the people had deserted, as they expected our arrival. The following morning I found much difficulty in getting our escort together, as they had been foraging throughout the neighbourhood; these "devil's own" were a portion of Kamrasi's troops, who considered themselves entitled to plunder *ad libitum* throughout the march; however, after some delay, they collected, and their tall chief approached me, and begged that a gun might be fired as a curiosity. The escort had crowded around us, and as the boy Saat was close to me, I ordered him to fire his gun. This was Saat's greatest delight, and bang went one barrel unexpectedly, close to the tall chief's ear. The effect was charming. The tall chief, thinking himself injured, clasped his head with both hands, and bolted through the crowd, which, struck with a sudden panic, rushed away in all directions, the "devil's own" tumbling over each other, and utterly scattered by the second barrel which

Saat exultingly fired in derision as Kamrasi's warlike regiment dissolved before a sound. I felt quite sure, that in the event of a fight, one scream from the "Baby," with its charge of forty small bullets, would win the battle, if well delivered into a crowd of Kamrasi's troops.

That afternoon, after a march through a most beautiful forest of large mimosas in full blossom, we arrived at the morass that had necessitated this great *détour* from our direct course to the lake. It was nearly three-quarters of a mile broad, and so deep, that in many places the oxen were obliged to swim; both Mrs. Baker and I were carried across on our angareps by twelve men with the greatest difficulty; the guide, who waded before us to show the way, suddenly disappeared in a deep hole, and his bundle that he had carried on his head, being of light substance, was seen floating like a buoy upon the surface; after a thorough sousing, the guide reappeared, and scrambled out, and we made a circuit, the men toiling frequently up to their necks through mud and water. On arrival at the opposite side we continued through the same beautiful forest, and slept that night at a deserted village, M'Bazé.

The next day we were much annoyed by our native escort; instead of attending to us, they employed their time in capering and dancing about, screaming and gesticulating, and suddenly rushing off in advance whenever we approached a village, which they plundered before we could arrive. In this manner every place was stripped; nor could we procure anything to eat unless by purchasing it for beads from the native escort. We slept at Karché.

We were both ill, but were obliged to ride through the hottest hours of the sun, as our followers were never ready to start at an early hour in the morning. The native escort were perfectly independent, and so utterly wild and savage in their manner, that they appeared more dangerous than the general inhabitants of the country. My wife was extremely anxious, since the occasion of Kamrasi's "proposal," as she was suspicious that so large an escort as three hundred men had been given for some treacherous purpose, and that I should perhaps be waylaid to enable them to steal her for the king. I had not the slightest fear of such an occurrence, as sentries were always on guard during the night, and I was well prepared during the day.

On the following morning we had the usual difficulty in collecting porters, those of the preceding day having absconded, and others were recruited from distant villages by the native escort, who enjoyed the excuse of hunting for porters, as it gave them an opportunity of foraging throughout the neighbourhood. During this time we had to wait until the sun was high; we thus lost the cool hours of morning, and it increased our fatigue. Having at length started, we arrived in the afternoon at the Kafoor river, at a bend from the south where it was necessary to cross over in our westerly course. The stream was in the centre of a marsh, and although deep, it was so covered with thickly-matted water-grass and other aquatic plants, that a natural floating bridge was established by a carpet of weeds about two feet thick: upon this waving and unsteady surface the men ran quickly across, sinking merely to the ankles, although beneath the tough vegetation there was deep water. It was equally impossible to ride or to be carried over this treacherous surface; thus I led the way, and begged Mrs. Baker to follow me on foot as quickly as possible, precisely in my track. The river was about eighty yards wide, and I had scarcely completed a fourth of the distance and looked back to see if my wife followed close to me, when I was horrified to see her standing in one spot, and sinking gradually through the weeds, while her face was distorted and perfectly purple. Almost as soon as I perceived her, she fell, as though shot dead. In an instant I was by her side; and with the assistance of eight or ten of my men, who were fortunately close to me, I dragged her like a corpse through the yielding vegetation, and up to our waists we scrambled across to the other side, just keeping her head above the water: to have carried her would have been impossible, as we should all have sunk together through the weeds. I laid her under a tree, and bathed her head and face with water, as for the moment I thought she had fainted; but she lay perfectly insensible, as though dead, with teeth and hands firmly clenched, and her eyes open, but fixed. It was a *coup de soleil.*

Many of the porters had gone on ahead with the baggage; and I started off a man in haste to recall an angarep upon which to carry her, and also for a bag with a change of clothes, as we had dragged her through the river. It was in vain that I rubbed her heart, and the black women rubbed her feet, to endeavour to restore animation. At length the litter came, and after changing her clothes, she was carried mournfully forward as a corpse. Constantly we had to halt and support her head, as a painful rattling in the throat betokened suffocation. At length we reached a village, and halted for the night.

I laid her carefully in a miserable hut, and watched beside her. I opened her clenched teeth with a small wooden wedge, and inserted a wet rag, upon which I dropped water to moisten her tongue, which was dry as fur. The unfeeling brutes that composed the native escort were yelling and dancing as though all were well; and I ordered their chief at once to return with them to Kamrasi, as I would travel with them no longer. At first they refused to return; until at length I vowed that I would fire into them should they accompany us on the following morning. Day broke, and it was a relief to have got rid of the brutal escort. They had departed, and I had now my own men, and the guides supplied by Kamrasi.

There was nothing to eat in this spot. My wife had never stirred since she fell by the *coup de soleil*, and merely respired about five times in a minute. It was impossible to remain; the people would have starved. She was laid gently upon her litter, and we started forward on our funeral course. I was ill and broken-hearted, and I followed by her side through the long day's march over wild park-lands and streams, with thick forest and deep marshy bottoms; over undulating hills, and through valleys of tall papyrus rushes, which, as we brushed through them on our melancholy way, waved over the litter like the black plumes of a hearse. We halted at a village, and again the night was passed in watching. I was wet, and coated with mud from the swampy marsh, and shivered with ague; but the cold within was greater than all. No change had taken place; she had never moved. I had plenty of fat, and I made four balls of about half a pound, each of which would burn for three hours. A piece of a broken water-jar formed a lamp, several pieces of rag serving for wicks. So in solitude the still calm night passed away as I sat by her side and watched. In the drawn and distorted features that lay before me I could hardly trace the same face that for years had been my comfort through all the difficulties and dangers of my path. Was she to die? Was so terrible a sacrifice to be the result of my selfish exile?

Again the night passed away. Once more the march. Though weak and ill, and for two nights without a moment's sleep, I felt no fatigue, but mechanically followed by the side of the litter as though in a dream. The same wild country diversified with marsh and forest. Again we halted. The night came, and I sat by her side in a miserable hut, with the feeble lamp flickering while she lay as in death. She had never moved a muscle since she fell. My people slept. I was alone, and no sound broke the stillness of the night. The ears ached at the utter silence, till the sudden wild cry of a hyena made me shudder as the horrible thought rushed through my brain, that, should she be buried in this lonely spot, the hyena would . . . disturb her rest.

The morning was not far distant; it was past four o'clock. I had passed the night in replacing wet cloths upon her head and moistening her lips, as she lay apparently lifeless on her litter. I could do nothing more; in solitude and abject misery in that dark hour, in a country of savage heathens, thousand of miles away from a Christian land, I beseeched an aid above all human, trusting alone to Him.

The morning broke; my lamp had just burnt out, and, cramped with the night's watching, I rose from my low seat, and seeing that she lay in the same unaltered state, I went to the door of the hut to breathe one gasp of the fresh morning air. I was watching the first red streak that heralded the rising sun, when I was startled by the words, "Thank God," faintly uttered behind me. Suddenly she had awoke from her torpor, and with a heart overflowing I went to her bedside. Her eyes were full of madness! She spoke; but the brain was gone!

I will not inflict a description of the terrible trial of seven days of brain fever, with its attendant horrors. The rain poured in torrents, and day after day we were forced to travel, for want of provisions, not being able to remain in one position. Every now and then we shot a few guinea-fowl, but rarely; there was no game, although the country was most favourable. In the forests we procured wild honey, but the deserted villages contained no supplies, as we were on the frontier of Uganda, and M'tesé's people had plundered the district. For seven nights I had not slept, and although as weak as a reed, I had marched by the side of her litter. Nature could resist no longer. We reached a village one evening; she had been in violent convulsions successively – it was all but over. I laid her down on her litter within a hut; covered her with a Scotch plaid; and I fell upon my mat insensible, worn out with sorrow and fatigue. My men put a new handle to the pickaxe that evening, and sought for a dry spot to dig her grave!

The sun had risen when I woke. I had slept, and, horrified as the idea flashed upon me that she must be dead, and that I had not been with her, I started up. She lay upon her bed, pale as marble, and with that calm serenity that the features assume when the cares of life no longer act upon the mind, and the body rests in death. The dreadful thought bowed me down; but as I gazed upon her in fear, her chest gently heaved, not with the convulsive throbs of fever, but naturally. She was asleep; and when at a sudden noise she opened her eyes, they were calm and clear. She was saved! When not a ray of hope remained, God alone knows what helped us. The gratitude of that moment I will not attempt to describe.

Fortunately there were many fowls in this village; we found several nests of fresh eggs in the straw which littered the hut; these were most acceptable after our hard fare, and produced a good supply of soup.

Having rested for two days, we again moved forward, Mrs. Baker being carried on a litter. We now continued on elevated ground, on the north side of a valley running from west to east, about sixteen miles broad, and exceedingly swampy. The rocks composing the ridge upon which we travelled due west were all gneiss and quartz, with occasional breaks, forming narrow valleys, all of which were swamps choked with immense papyrus rushes, that made the march very fatiguing. In one of these muddy bottoms one of my riding oxen that was ill, stuck fast, and we were obliged to abandon it, intending to send a number of natives to drag it out with ropes. On arrival at a village, our guide started about fifty men for this purpose, while we continued our journey.

That evening we reached a village belonging to a headman, and very superior to most that we had passed on the route from M'rooli: large sugar-canes of the blue variety were growing in the fields, and I had seen coffee growing wild in the forest in the vicinity. I was sitting at the door of the hut about two hours after sunset, smoking a pipe of excellent tobacco, when I suddenly heard a great singing in chorus advancing rapidly from a distance towards the entrance of the courtyard. At first I imagined that the natives intended dancing, which was an infliction that I wished to avoid, as I was tired and feverish; but in a few minutes the boy Saat introduced a headman, who told me that the riding ox had died in the swamp where he had stuck fast in the morning, and that the natives had brought his body to me. "What!" I replied, "brought his body, the entire ox, to me?" "The entire ox as he died is delivered at your door," answered the headman; "I could not allow any of your property to be lost upon the road. Had the body of the ox not been delivered to you, we might have been suspected of having stolen it." I went to the entrance of the courtyard, and amidst a crowd of natives I found the entire ox exactly as he had died. They had carried him about eight miles on a litter, which they had constructed of two immensely long posts with cross-pieces of bamboo, upon which they had laid the body. They would not eat the flesh, and seemed quite disgusted at the idea, as they replied that "it had died."

It is a curious distinction of the Unyoro people, that they are peculiarly clean feeders, and will not touch either the flesh of animals that have died, neither of those that are sick; nor will they eat the crocodile. They asked for no remuneration for bringing their heavy load so great a distance; and they departed in good humour as a matter of course.

Never were such contradictory people as these creatures; they had troubled us dreadfully during the journey, as they would suddenly exclaim against the weight of their loads, and throw them down, and bolt into the high grass; yet now they had of their own free will delivered to me a whole dead ox from a distance of eight miles, precisely as though it had been an object of the greatest value.

The name of this village was Parkāni. For several days past our guides had told us that we were very near to the lake, and we were now assured that we should reach it on the morrow. I had noticed a lofty range of mountains at an immense distance west, and I had imagined that the lake lay on the other side of this chain; but I was now informed that those mountains formed the western frontier of the M'-wootan N'zigé, and that the lake was actually within a march of Parkāni. I could not believe it possible that we were so near the object of our search. The guide Rabonga now appeared, and declared that if we started early on the following morning we should be able to wash in the lake by noon!

That night I hardly slept. For years I had striven to reach the "sources of the Nile." In my nightly dreams during that arduous voyage I had always failed, but after so much hard work and perseverance the cup was at my very lips, and I was to *drink* at the mysterious fountain before another sun should set – at that great reservoir of Nature that ever since creation had baffled all discovery.

I had hoped, and prayed, and striven through all kinds of difficulties, in sickness, starvation, and fatigue, to reach that hidden source; and when it had appeared impossible, we had both determined to die upon the road rather than return defeated. Was it possible that it was so near, and that to-morrow we could say, "the work is accomplished?"

The 14th March   The sun had not risen when I was spurring my ox after the guide, who, having been promised a double handful of beads on arrival at the lake, had caught the enthusiasm of the moment. The day broke beautifully clear, and having crossed a deep valley between the hills, we toiled up the opposite slope. I hurried to the summit. The glory of our prize burst suddenly upon me! There, like a sea of quicksilver, lay far beneath the grand expanse of water, – a boundless sea horizon on the south and south-west, glittering in the noon-day sun; and on the west, at fifty or sixty miles' distance, blue mountains rose from the bosom of the lake to a height of about 7,000 feet above its level.

It is impossible to describe the triumph of that moment; – here was the reward for all our labour – for the years of tenacity with which we had toiled through Africa. England had won the sources of the Nile! Long before I reached this spot, I had arranged to give three cheers with all our men in English style in honour of the discovery, but now that I looked down upon the great inland sea lying nestled in the very heart of Africa, and thought how vainly mankind had sought these sources throughout so many ages, and reflected that I had been the humble instrument permitted to unravel this portion of the great mystery when so many greater than I had failed, I felt too serious to vent my feelings in vain cheers for victory, and I sincerely thanked God for having guided and supported us through all dangers to the good end. I was about 1,500 feet above the lake, and I looked down from the steep granite cliff upon those welcome waters – upon that vast reservoir which nourished Egypt and brought fertility where all was wilderness – upon that great source so long hidden from mankind; that source of bounty and of blessings to millions of human beings; and as one of the greatest objects in nature, I determined to honour it with a great name. As an imperishable memorial of one loved and mourned by our gracious Queen and deplored by every Englishman, I called this great lake "the Albert N'yanza." The Victoria and the Albert lakes are the two Sources of the Nile.

The zigzag path to descend to the lake was so steep and dangerous that we were forced to leave our oxen with a guide, who was to take them to Magungo and wait for our arrival. We commenced the descent of the steep pass on foot. I led the way, grasping a stout bamboo. My wife in extreme weakness tottered down the pass, supporting herself upon my shoulder, and stopping to rest every twenty paces. After a toilsome descent of about two hours, weak with years of fever, but for the moment strengthened by success, we gained the level plain below the cliff. A walk of about a mile through flat sandy meadows of fine turf interspersed with trees and bush, brought us to the water's edge. The waves were rolling upon a white pebbly beach: I rushed into the lake, and thirsty with heat and fatigue, with a heart full of gratitude, I drank deeply from the Sources of the Nile.

LAST DAYS

David Livingstone
(1813–73)

Livingstone, born in Blantyre near Glasgow, was nurtured in poverty and religious fervour. He reached southern Africa as a missionary doctor but, more suited to solitary exploration, edged north in a series of pioneering journeys into the interior. While exploring the headwaters of the Congo, which he thought must be those of the Nile, a massacre perpetrated by Arab slavers plus his failing health obliged him to return to Ujiji, his Tanganyikan base. The staccato entries of his last journals betray his physical and mental condition; declining to return with Stanley, he died on a subsequent foray from Ujiji.

20th July, 1871 I start back for Ujiji. All Dugumbé's people came to say good bye, and convoy me a little way. I made a short march, for being long inactive it is unwise to tire oneself on the first day, as it is then difficult to get over the effects.

21st July One of the slaves was sick, and the rest falsely reported him to be seriously ill, to give them time to negotiate for women with whom they had cohabited: Dugumbé saw through the fraud, and said "Leave him to me: if he lives, I will feed him; if he dies, we will bury him: do not delay for any one, but travel in a compact body, as stragglers now are sure to be cut off." He lost a woman of his party, who lagged behind, and seven others were killed besides, and the forest hid the murderers. I was only too anxious to get away quickly, and on the 22nd started off at daylight, and went about six miles to the village of Mañkwara, where I spent the night when coming this way. The chief Mokandira convoyed us hither: I promised him a cloth if I came across from Lomamé. He wonders much at the underground houses, and never heard of them till I told him about them. Many of the gullies which were running fast when

David Livingstone. From *The Last Journals of David Livingstone in Central Africa from 1865 to his Death*, London, 1874.

we came were now dry. Thunder began, and a few drops of rain fell.

23rd–24th July We crossed the River Kunda, of fifty yards, in two canoes, and then ascended from the valley of denudation, in which it flows to the ridge Lobango. Crowds followed, all anxious to carry loads for a few beads. Several market people came to salute, who knew that we had no hand in the massacre, as we are a different people from the Arabs. In going and coming they must have a march of 25 miles with loads so heavy no slave would carry them. They speak of us as "good": the anthropologists think that to be spoken of as wicked is better. Ezekiel says that the Most High put His comeliness upon Jerusalem: if He does not impart of His goodness to me I shall never be good: if He does not put of His comeliness on me I shall never be comely in soul, but be like these Arabs in whom Satan has full sway – the god of this world having blinded their eyes.

25th July We came over a beautiful country yesterday, a vast hollow of denudation, with much cultivation, interesected by a ridge some 300 feet high, on which the villages are built: this is Lobango. The path runs along the top of the ridge, and we see the fine country below all spread out with different shades of green, as on a map. The colours show the shapes of the different plantations in the great hollow drained by the Kunda. After crossing the fast flowing Kahembai, which flows into the Kunda, and it into Lualaba, we rose on to another intersecting ridge, having a great many villages burned by Matereka or Salem Mokadam's people, since we passed them in our course N.W. They had slept on the ridge after we saw them, and next morning, in sheer wantonness, fired their lodgings, – their slaves had evidently carried the fire along from their lodgings, and set fire to houses of villages in their route as a sort of horrid Moslem Nigger joke; it was done only because they could do it without danger of punishment: it was such fun to make the Mashensé, as they call all natives, houseless. Men are worse than beasts of prey, if indeed it is lawful to call Zanzibar slaves men. It is monstrous injustice to compare free Africans living under their own chiefs and laws, and cultivating their own free lands, with what slaves afterwards become at Zanzibar and elsewhere.

26th July Came up out of the last valley of denudation – that drained by Kahembai, and then along a level land with open forest. Four men passed us in hot haste to announce the death of a woman at their village to her relations living at another. I heard of several deaths lately of dysentery. Pleurisy is common from cold winds from N.W. Twenty-two men with large square black shields, capable of completely hiding the whole person, came next in a trot to receive the body of their relative and all her gear to carry her to her own home for burial: about twenty women followed them, and the men waited under the trees till they should have wound the body up and wept over her. They smeared their bodies with clay, and their faces with soot. Reached our friend Kama.

27th July Left Kama's group of villages and went through many others before we reached Kasongo's, and were welcomed by all the Arabs of the camp at this place. Bought two milk goats reasonably, and rest over Sunday. (*28th and 29th.*) They asked permission to send a party with me for goods to Ujiji; this will increase our numbers, and perhaps safety too, among the justly irritated people between this and Bambarré. All are enjoined to help me, and of course I must do the same to them. It is colder here than at Nyañgwé. Kasongo is off guiding an ivory or slaving party, and doing what business he can on his own account; he has four guns, and will be the first to maraud on his own account.

30th July They send thirty tusks to Ujiji, and seventeen Manyuema volunteers to carry thither and back: these are the very first who in modern times have ventured fifty miles from the place of their birth. I came only three miles to a ridge overlooking the River Shokoyé, and slept at village on a hill beyond it.

31st July Passed through the defile between Mount Kimazi and Mount Kijila. Below the cave with stalactite pillar in its door a fine echo answers those who feel inclined to shout to it. Come to Mangala's numerous villages, and two slaves being ill, rest on Wednesday.

1st August, 1871 A large market assembles close to us.

2nd August Left Mangala's, and came through a great many villages all deserted on our approach on account of the vengeance taken by Dugumbé's party for the murder of some of their people. Kasongo's men appeared eager to plunder their own countrymen: I had to scold and threaten them, and set men to watch their deeds. Plantains are here very abundant, good, and cheap. Came to Kittetté, and lodge in a village of Loembo. About thirty foundries were passed; they are very high in the roof, and thatched with leaves, from which the sparks roll off as sand would. Rain runs off equally well.

3rd August Three slaves escaped, and not to abandon ivory we wait a day, Kasongo came up and filled their places.

I have often observed effigies of men made of wood in Manyuema; some of clay are simply cones with a small hole in the top; on asking about them here, I for the first time obtained reliable information. They are called Bathata – fathers or ancients – and the name of each is carefully preserved. Those here at Kittetté were evidently the names of chiefs, Molenda being the most ancient, whilst Mbayo Yamba, Kamoanga, Kitambwé, Noñgo, Aulumba, Yengé Yengé, Simba Mayañga, Loembwé, are more recently dead. They were careful to have the exact pronunciation of the names. The old men told me that on certain occasions they offer goat's flesh to them: men eat it, and allow no young person or women to partake. The flesh of the parrot is only eaten by very old men. They say that if eaten by young men their children will have the waddling gait of the bird. They say that originally those who preceded Molenda came from Kongolakokwa, which conveys no idea to my mind. It was interesting to get even this little bit of history here.

4th August   Came through miles of villages all burned because the people refused a certain Abdullah lodgings! The men had begun to re-thatch the huts, and kept out of our way, but a goat was speared by some one in hiding, and we knew danger was near. Abdullah admitted that he had no other reason for burning them than the unwillingness of the people to lodge him and his slaves without payment, with the certainty of getting their food stolen and utensils destroyed.

5th and 6th August   Through many miles of palm-trees and plantains to a Boma or stockaded village, where we slept, though the people were evidently suspicious and unfriendly.

7th August   To a village, ill and almost every step in pain. The people all ran away, and appeared in the distance armed, and refused to come near – then came and threw stones at us, and afterwards tried to kill those who went for water. We sleep uncomfortably, the natives watching us all round. Sent men to see if the way was clear.

8th August   They would come to no parley. They knew their advantage, and the wrongs they had suffered from Bin Juma and Mohamad's men when they threw down the ivory in the forest. In passing along the narrow path with a wall of dense vegetation touching each hand, we came to a point where an ambush had been placed, and trees cut down to obstruct us while they speared us; but for some reason it was abandoned. Nothing could be detected; but by stooping down to the earth and peering up towards the sun, a dark shade could sometimes be seen: this was an infuriated savage, and a slight rustle in the dense vegetation meant a spear. A large spear from my right lunged past and almost grazed my back, and stuck firmly into the soil. The two men from whom it came appeared in an opening in the forest only ten yards off and bolted, one looking back over his shoulder as he ran. As they are expert with the spear I don't know how it missed, except that he was too sure of his aim and the good hand of God was upon me.

I was behind the main body, and all were allowed to pass till I, the leader, who was believed to be Mohamad Bogharib, or Kolokolo himself, came up to the point where they lay. A red jacket they had formerly seen me wearing was proof to them that I was the same that sent Bin Juma to kill five of their men, capture eleven women and children, and twenty-five goats. Another spear was thrown at me by an unseen assailant, and it missed me by about a foot in front. Guns were fired into the dense mass of forest, but with no effect, for nothing could be seen; but we heard the men jeering and denouncing us close by: two of our party were slain.

Coming to a part of the forest cleared for cultivation I noticed a gigantic tree, made still taller by growing on an anthill 20 feet high; it had fire applied near its roots, I heard a crack which told that the fire had done its work, but felt no alarm till I saw it come straight towards me: I ran a few paces back, and down it came to the ground one yard behind me, and breaking into several lengths, it covered me with a cloud of dust. Had the branches not previously been rotted off, I could scarcely have escaped.

Three times in one day was I delivered from impending death.

My attendants, who were scattered in all directions, came running back to me, calling out, "Peace! peace! you will finish all your work in spite of these people, and in spite of everything." Like them, I took it as an omen of good success to crown me yet, thanks to the "Almighty Preserver of men."

We had five hours of running the gauntlet, waylaid by spearmen, who all felt that if they killed me they would be revenging the death of relations. From each hole in the tangled mass we looked for a spear; and each moment expected to hear the rustle which told of deadly weapons hurled at us. I became weary with the constant strain of danger, and – as, I suppose, happens with soldiers on the field of battle – not courageous, but perfectly indifferent whether I were killed or not.

When at last we got out of the forest and crossed the Liya on to the cleared lands near the villages of Monanbundwa, we lay down to rest, and soon saw Muanampunda coming, walking up in a stately manner unarmed to meet us. He had heard the vain firing of my men into the bush, and came to ask what was the matter. I explained the mistake that Munangonga had made in supposing that I was Kolokolo, the deeds of whose men he knew, and then we went on to his village together.

In the evening he sent to say that if I would give him all my people who had guns, he would call his people together, burn off all the vegetation they could fire, and punish our enemies, bringing me ten goats instead of three milch goats I had lost. I again explained that the attack was made by a mistake in thinking I was Mohamad Bogharib, and that I had no wish to kill men: to join in his old feud would only make matters worse. This he could perfectly understand.

I lost all my remaining calico, a telescope, umbrella, and five spears, by one of the slaves throwing down the load and taking up his own bundle of country cloth.

9th August Went on towards Mamohela, now deserted by the Arabs. Monanponda convoyed me a long way, and at one spot, with grass all trodden down, he said, "Here we killed a man of Moezia and ate his body." The meat cut up had been seen by Dugumbé.

10th August In connection with this affair the party that came through from Mamalulu found that a great fight had taken place at Muanampunda's, and they saw the meat cut up to be cooked with bananas. They did not like the strangers to look at their meat, but said, "Go on, and let our feast alone," they did not want to be sneered at. The same Muanampunda or Monambonda told me frankly that they ate the man of Moezia: they seem to eat their foes to inspire courage, or in revenge. One point is very remarkable; it is not want that has led to the custom, for the country is full of food: nobody is starved of farinaceous food; they have maize, dura, pennisetum, cassava and sweet potatoes, and for fatty ingredients of diet, the palm-oil, ground-nuts, sessamum, and a tree whose fruit yields a fine sweet oil: the saccharine materials needed are found in the sugar-cane, bananas, and plantains.

Goats, sheep, fowls, dogs, pigs, abound in the villages, whilst the forest affords elephants, zebras, buffaloes, antelopes, and in the streams there are many varieties of fish. The nitrogenous ingredients are abundant, and they have dainties in palm-toddy, and tobacco or Bangé: the soil is so fruitful that mere scraping off the weeds is as good as ploughing, so that the reason for cannibalism does not lie in starvation or in want of animal matter, as was said to be the case with the New Zealanders. The only feasible reason I can discover is a depraved appetite, giving an extraordinary craving for meat which we call "high." They are said to bury a dead body for a couple of days in the soil in a forest, and in that time, owing to the climate, it soon becomes putrid enough for the strongest stomachs.

The Lualaba has many oysters in it with very thick shells. They are called *Makessi*, and at certain seasons are dived for by the Bagenya women: pearls are said to be found in them, but boring to string them has never been thought of.

The Manyuema are so afraid of guns, that a man borrows one to settle any dispute or claim: he goes with it over his shoulder, and quickly arranges the matter by the pressure it brings, though they all know that he could not use it.

A ball of hair rolled in the stomach of a lion, as calculi are, is a great charm among the Arabs: it scares away other animals, they say.

Lion's fat smeared on the tails of oxen taken through a country abounding in tsetse, or buñgo, is a sure preventive; when I heard of this, I thought that lion's fat would be as difficult of collection as gnat's brains or mosquito tongues, but I was assured that many lions are killed on the Basango highland, and they, in common with all beasts there, are extremely fat: so it is not at all difficult to buy a calabash of the preventive, and Banyamwezi, desirous of taking cattle to the coast for sale, know the substance, and use it successfully (?).

11th August   Came on by a long march of six hours across plains of grass and watercourses, lined with beautiful trees, to Kassessa's, the chief of Mamohela, who has helped the Arabs to scourge several of his countrymen for old feuds: he gave them goats, and then guided them by night to the villages, where they got more goats and many captives, each to be redeemed with ten goats more. During the last foray, however, the people learned that every shot does not kill, and they came up to the party with bows and arrows, and compelled the slaves to throw down their guns and powder-horns. They would have shown no mercy had Manyuema been thus in slave power; but this is a beginning of the end, which will exclude Arab traders from the country. I rested half a day, as I am still ill. I do most devoutly thank the Lord for sparing my life three times in one day. The Lord is good, a stronghold in the day of trouble, and He knows them that trust in Him.

12th August   Mamohela camp all burned off. We sleep at Mamohela village.

13th August   At a village on the bank of River Lolindi. I am suffering greatly. A man brought a young, nearly full-fledged, kite from a nest on a tree: this is the first case of their breeding, that I am sure of, in this country: they are migratory into these intertropical lands from the south, probably.

14th August   Across many brisk burns to a village on the side of a mountain range. First rains 12th and 14th, gentle; but near Luamo, it ran on the paths, and caused dew.

15th August   To Muanambonyo's. Golungo, a bush buck, with stripes across body, and two rows of spots along the sides (?).

16th August   To Luamo River. Very ill with bowels.

17th August   Cross river, and sent a message to my friend. Katomba sent a bountiful supply of food back.

18th August   Reached Katomba, at Moenemgoi's, and was welcomed by all the heavily-laden Arab traders. They carry their trade spoil in three relays. Kenyengeré attacked before I came, and 150 captives were taken and about 100 slain; this is an old feud of Moenemgoi, which the Arabs took up for their own gain. No news whatever from Ujiji, and M. Bogharib is still at Bambarré, with all my letters.

19th–20th August   Rest from weakness. (*21st August.*) Up to the

palms on the west of Mount Kanyima Pass. (*22nd August.*) Bambarré. (*28th August.*) Better and thankful. Katomba's party has
nearly a thousand frasilahs of ivory, and Mohamad's has 300
frasilahs.

29th August   Ill all night, and remain. (*30th August.*) Ditto, ditto;
but go on to Monandenda's on River Lombonda.

31st August   Up and half over the mountain range, (*1st September*)
and sleep in dense forest, with several fine running streams.

2nd September, 1871   Over the range, and down on to a marble-
capped hill, with a village on top.

3rd September   Equinoctial gales. On to Lohombo.

5th September   To Kasangangazi's. (*6th September.*) Rest. (*7th
September.*) Mamba's. Rest on 8th. (*9th September.*) Ditto ditto.
People falsely accused of stealing; but I disproved it to the confusion
of the Arabs, who wish to be able to say, "the people of the English
steal too." A very rough road from Kasangangazi's hither, and
several running rivulets crossed.

10th September   Manyuema boy followed us, but I insisted on his
father's consent, which was freely given: marching proved too hard
for him, however, and in a few days he left.

Down into the valley of the Kapemba through beautiful undulating country, and came to village of Amru: this is a common name,
and is used as "man," or "comrade," or "mate."

11th September   Up a very steep high mountain range Moloni or
Mononi, and down to a village at the bottom on the other side, of a
man called Molembu.

12th September   Two men sick. Wait, though I am now comparatively sound and well. Dura flour, which we can now procure, helps
to strengthen me: it is nearest to wheaten flour; maize meal is called
"cold," and not so wholesome as the *Holcus sorghum* or dura. A
lengthy march through a level country, with high mountain ranges
on each hand; along that on the left our first path lay, and it was very
fatiguing. We came to the Rivulet Kalangai. I had hinted to Mohamad that if he harboured my deserters, it might go hard with him;
and he came after me for two marches, and begged me not to think
that he did encourage them. They came impudently into the village,
and I had to drive them out: I suspected that he had sent them. I
explained, and he gave me a goat, which I sent back for.

13th September   This march back completely used up the Manyuema boy: he could not speak, or tell what he wanted cooked, when
he arrived. I did not see him go back, and felt sorry for the poor boy,
who left us by night. People here would sell nothing, so I was glad of
the goat.

14th September To Pyanamosindé's. (*15th September*.) To Kar-ungamagao's; very fine undulating green country. (*16th and 17th September*.) Rest, as we could get food to buy. (*18th September*.) To a stockaded village, where the people ordered us to leave. We complied, and went out half a mile and built our sheds in the forest: I like sheds in the forest much better than huts in the villages, for we have no mice or vermin, and incur no obligation.

19th September Found that Barua are destroying all the Manyue-ma villages not stockaded.

20th September We came to Kunda's on the River Katemba, through great plantations of cassava, and then to a woman chief's, and now regularly built our own huts apart from the villages, near the hot fountain called Kabila which is about blood-heat, and flows across the path. Crossing this we came to Mokwaniwa's, on the River Gombezé, and met a caravan, under Nassur Masudi, of 200 guns. He presented a fine sheep, and reported that Seyed Majid was dead – he had been ailing and fell from some part of his new house at Darsalam, and in three days afterwards expired. He was a true and warm friend to me and did all he could to aid me with his subjects, giving me two Sultan's letters for the purpose. Seyed Burghash succeeds him; this change causes anxiety. Will Seyed Burghash's goodness endure now that he has the Sultanate? Small-pox raged lately at Ujiji.

22nd September Caravan goes northwards, and we rest, and eat the sheep kindly presented.

23rd September We now passed through the country of mixed Barua and Baguha, crossed the River Loñgumba twice and then came near the great mountain mass on west of Tanganyika. From Mokwaniwa's to Tanganyika is about ten good marches through open forest. The Guha people are not very friendly; they know strangers too well to show kindness: like Manyuema, they are also keen traders. I was sorely knocked up by this march from Nyañgwé back to Ujiji. In the latter part of it, I felt as if dying on my feet. Almost every step was in pain, the appetite failed, and a little bit of meat caused violent diarrhœa, whilst the mind, sorely depressed, reacted on the body. All the traders were returning successful: I alone had failed and experienced worry, thwarting, baffling, when almost in sight of the end towards which I strained.

3rd October I read the whole Bible through four times whilst I was in Manyuema.

8th October The road covered with angular fragments of quartz was very sore to my feet, which are crammed into ill-made French shoes. How the bare feet of the men and women stood out, I don't know; it was hard enough on mine though protected by the shoes. We marched in the afternoons where water at this season was scarce. The dust of the march caused ophthalmia, like that which afflicted Speke: this was my first touch of it in Africa. We now came to the Lobumba River, which flows into Tanganyika, and then to the village Loanda and sent to Kasanga, the Guha chief, for canoes. The Loñgumba rises, like the Lobumba, in the mountains called Kabogo West. We heard great noises, as if thunder, as far as twelve days off, which were ascribed to Kabogo, as if it had subterranean caves into which the waves rushed with great noise, and it may be that the Loñgumba is the outlet of Tanganyika: it becomes the Luassé further down, and then the Luamo before it joins the Lualaba: the country slopes that way, but I was too ill to examine its source.

9th October   On to islet Kasengé. After much delay got a good canoe for three dotis, and on *15th October* went to the islet Kabiziwa.

18th October   Start for Kabogo East, and *19th* reach it 8 a.m.

20th October   Rest men.

22nd October   To Rombola.

23rd October   At dawn, off and go to Ujiji. Welcomed by all the Arabs, particularly by Moenyegheré. I was now reduced to a skeleton, but the market being held daily, and all kinds of native food brought to it, I hoped that food and rest would soon restore me, but in the evening my people came and told me that Shereef had sold off all my goods, and Moenyegheré confirmed it by saying, "We protested, but he did not leave a single yard of calico out of 3000, nor a string of beads out of 700 lbs." This was distressing. I had made up my mind, if I could not get people at Ujiji, to wait till men should come from the coast, but to wait in beggary was what I never contemplated, and I now felt miserable. Shereef was evidently a moral idiot, for he came without shame to shake hands with me, and when I refused, assumed an air of displeasure, as having been badly treated; and afterwards came with his "Balghere," good-luck salutation, twice a day, and on leaving said, "I am going to pray," till I told him that were I an Arab, his hand and both ears would be cut off for thieving, as he knew, and I wanted no salutations from him. In my distress it was annoying to see Shereef's slaves passing from the market with all the good things that my goods had bought.

24th October   My property had been sold to Shereef's friends at merely nominal prices. Syed bin Majid, a good man, proposed that they should be returned, and the ivory be taken from Shereef; but they would not restore stolen property, though they knew it to be stolen. Christians would have acted differently, even those of the lowest classes. I felt in my destitution as if I were the man who went down from Jerusalem to Jericho, and fell among thieves; but I could not hope for Priest, Levite, or good Samaritan to come by on either side, but one morning Syed bin Majid said to me, "Now this is the first time we have been alone together; I have no goods, but I have ivory; let me, I pray you, sell some ivory, and give the goods to you." This was encouraging; but I said, "Not yet, but by-and-bye." I had still a few barter goods left, which I had taken the precaution to deposit with Mohamad bin Saleh before going to Manyuema, in case of returning in extreme need. But when my spirits were at their lowest ebb, the good Samaritan was close at hand, for one morning Susi came running at the top of his speed and gasped out, "An Englishman! I see him!" and off he darted to meet him. The American flag at the head of a caravan told of the nationality of the stranger. Bales of goods, baths of tin, huge kettles, cooking pots, tents, &c., made me think "This must be a luxurious traveller, and not one at his wits' end like me." (28th October.) It was Henry Moreland Morton Stanley, the travelling correspondent of the *New York Herald*, sent by James Gordon Bennett, junior, at an expense of more than 4000*l.*, to obtain accurate information about Dr. Livingstone if living, and if dead to bring home my bones. The news he had to tell to one who had been two full years without any tidings from Europe made my whole frame thrill. The terrible fate that had befallen France, the telegraphic cables successfully laid in the Atlantic, the election of General Grant, the death of good Lord Clarendon – my constant friend, the proof that Her Majesty's Government had not forgotten me in voting 1000*l.* for supplies, and many other points of interest, revived emotions that had lain dormant in Manyuema. Appetite returned, and instead of the spare, tasteless, two meals a day, I ate four times daily, and in a week began to feel strong. I am not of a demonstrative turn; as cold, indeed, as we islanders are usually reputed to be, but this disinterested kindness of Mr. Bennett, so nobly carried into effect by Mr. Stanley, was simply overwhelming. I really do feel extremely grateful, and at the same time I am a little ashamed at not being more worthy of the generosity. Mr. Stanley has done his part with untiring energy; good judgment in the teeth of very serious obstacles. His helpmates turned out depraved blackguards, who, by their excesses at Zanzibar and elsewhere, had ruined their constitutions, and prepared their systems to be fit provender for the grave. They had used up their strength by wickedness, and were of

'Dr Livingstone I presume?' The meeting of Livingstone and Stanley.
From *How I found Livingstone, travels, adventures, and discoveries in Central Africa*, London, 1872.

next to no service, but rather downdrafts and unbearable drags to progress.

16th November, 1871   As Tanganyika explorations are said by Mr. Stanley to be an object of interest to Sir Roderick [Murchison], we go at his expense and by his men to the north of the Lake.

ENCOUNTERS ON THE UPPER CONGO

Henry Morton Stanley
(1841–1904)

Stanley made his name as an explorer by tracking down Livingstone in 1871. But obscure Welsh origins, plus the adoption of US citizenship and professional journalism, did not endear him to London's geographical establishment. His response was to out-travel all contemporaries, beginning with the first ever coast-to-coast crossing of equatorial Africa. Leaving Zanzibar, he had struck the headwaters of what proved to be the Congo (Zaire) by the end of 1876 and with Frank Pocock, his sole surviving companion, had now to run a gauntlet of hostility to the Atlantic.

*D*ec. 27. 1876 *Vinya-Njara.* In the evening, while sleep had fallen upon all save the watchful sentries in charge of the boat and canoes, Frank and I spent a serious time.

Frank was at heart as sanguine as I that we should finally emerge somewhere, but, on account of the persistent course of the great river towards the north, a little uneasiness was evident in his remarks.

"Before we finally depart, sir," said he, "do you really believe, in your inmost soul, that we shall succeed? I ask this because there are such odds against us – not that I for a moment think it would be best to return, having proceeded so far."

"Believe? Yes, I do believe that we shall all emerge into light again some time. It is true that our prospects are as dark as this night. Even the Mississippi presented no such obstacles to De Soto as this river will necessarily present to us. Possibly its islands and its forests possessed much of the same aspect, but here we are at an altitude of sixteen hundred and fifty feet above the sea. What conclusions can we arrive at? Either that this river penetrates a great distance north of the Equator, and, taking a mighty sweep

Henry Stanley, from a photograph taken in 1877. From *Through the Dark Continent*, London, 1878.

round, descends into the Congo – this, by the way, would lessen the chances of there being many cataracts in the river; – or that we shall shortly see it in the neighbourhood of the Equator, take a direct cut towards the Congo, and precipitate itself, like our Colorado river, through a deep cañon, or down great cataracts; or that it is either the Niger or the Nile. I believe it will prove to be the Congo; if the Congo then, there must be many cataracts. Let us only hope that the cataracts are all in a lump, close together.

"Any way, whether the Congo, the Niger, or the Nile, I am prepared, otherwise I should not be so confident. Though I love life as much as you do, or any other man does, yet on the success of this effort I am about to stake my life, my all. To prevent its sacrifice foolishly I have devised numerous expedients with which to defy wild men, wild nature, and unknown terrors. There is an enormous risk, but you know the adage, 'Nothing risked, nothing won.'

"I see us gliding down by tower and town, and my mind will not permit a shadow of doubt. Good night, my boy! Good night! and may happy dreams of the sea, and ships, and pleasure, and comfort, and success attend you in your sleep! To-morrow my lad, is the day we shall cry – 'Victory or death!'"

Dec. 28. Vinya-Njara The crisis drew nigh when the 28th December dawned. A grey mist hung over the river, so dense that we could not see even the palmy banks on which Vinya-Njara was situated. It would have been suicidal to begin our journey on such a gloomy morning. The people appeared as cheerless and dismal as the foggy day. We cooked our breakfasts in order to see if, by the time we had fortified the soul by satisfying the cravings of the stomach, the river and its shores might not have resumed their usual beautiful outlines, and their striking contrasts of light and shadow.

Slowly the breeze wafted the dull and heavy mists away until the sun appeared, and bit by bit the luxuriantly wooded banks rose up solemn and sad. Finally the grey river was seen, and at 9 a.m. its face gleamed with the brightness of a mirror.

"Embark, my friends! Let us at once away! and a happy voyage to us."

But, looking up, I saw the gleaming portal to the Unknown: wide open to us and away down for miles and miles, the river lay stretched with all the fascination of its mystery. I stood up and looked at the people. How few they appeared to dare the region of fable and darkness! They were nearly all sobbing. They were leaning forward, bowed, as it seemed, with grief and heavy hearts.

Then I urged my boat's crew, knowing that thus we should tempt the canoes to quicker pace. Three or four times Uledi, the coxswain, gallantly attempted to sing, in order to invite a cheery chorus, but his voice soon died into such piteous hoarseness that the very ludicrousness of the tones caused his young friends to smile even in the midst of their grief.

We knew that the Vinya-Njara district was populous from the numbers of natives that fought with us by land and water, but we had no conception that it was so thickly populated as the long row of villages we now saw indicated. I counted fourteen separate villages, each with its respective growth of elais palm and banana, and each separated from the other by thick bush.

Every three or four miles after passing Vinya-Njara, there were small villages visible on either bank, but we met with no disturbance, fortunately. At 5 p.m. we made for a small village called Kali-Karero, and camped there, the natives having retired peacefully. In half an hour they returned, and the ceremony of brotherhood was entered upon, which insured a peaceful night. The inhabitants of Rukura, opposite us, also approached us with confidence, and an interchange of small gifts served us as a healthy augury for the future.

On the morning of the 29th, accompanied by a couple of natives in a small fishing-canoe, we descended the river along the left bank, and, after about four miles, arrived at the confluence of the Kasuku, a dark-water stream of a hundred yards' width at the mouth. Opposite the mouth, at the southern end of Kaimba – a long wooded island on the right bank, and a little above the confluence – stands the important village of Kisanga-Sanga.

Below Kaimba Island and its neighbour, the Livingstone assumes a breadth of 1800 yards. The banks are very populous: the villages of the left bank comprise the district of Luavala. We thought for some time we should be permitted to pass by quietly, but soon the great wooden drums, hollowed out of huge trees, thundered the signal along the river that there were strangers. In order to lessen all chances of a rupture between us, we sheered off to the middle of the river, and quietly lay on our paddles. But from both banks at once, in fierce concert, the natives, with their heads gaily feathered, and armed with broad black wooden shields and long spears, dashed out towards us.

Tippu-Tib before our departure had hired to me two young men of Ukusu – cannibals – as interpreters. These were now instructed to cry out the word "Sennenneh!" ("Peace!"), and to say that we were friends.

But they would not reply to our greeting, and in a bold peremptory manner told us to return.

"But we are doing no harm, friends. It is the river that takes us down, and the river will not stop, or go back."

"This is our river."

"Good. Tell it to take us back, and we will go."

"If you do not go back, we will fight you."

"No, don't; we are friends."

"We don't want you for our friends; we will eat you."

But we persisted in talking to them, and as their curiosity was so great they persisted in listening, and the consequence was that the current conveyed us near to the right bank; and in such near neighbourhood to another district, that our discourteous escort

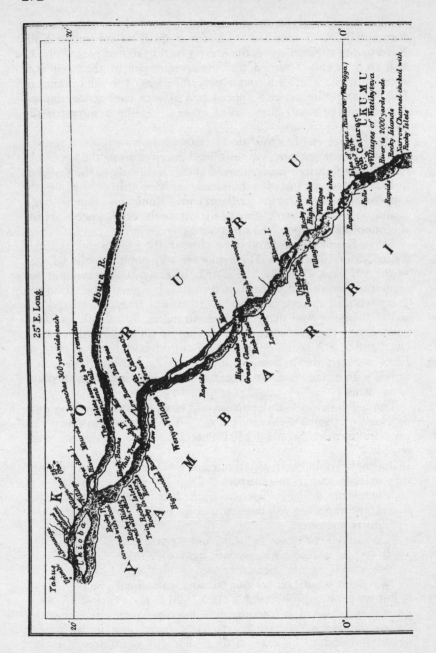

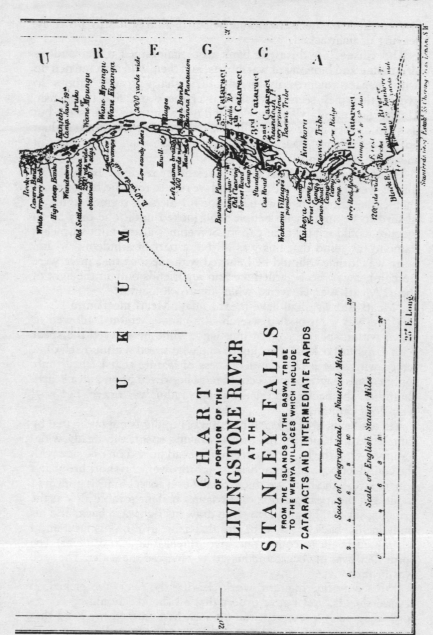

CHART
OF A PORTION OF THE
LIVINGSTONE RIVER
AT THE
STANLEY FALLS
FROM THE ISLANDS OF THE BASWA TRIBE
TO THE WENYA VILLAGES WHICH INCLUDE
7 CATARACTS AND INTERMEDIATE RAPIDS

had to think of themselves, and began to skurry hastily up river, leaving us unattacked.

The villages on the right bank also maintained a tremendous drumming and blowing of war-horns, and their wild men hurried up with menace towards us, urging their sharp-prowed canoes so swiftly that they seemed to skim over the water like flying fish. Unlike the Luavala villagers, they did not wait to be addressed, but as soon as they came within fifty or sixty yards they shot out their spears, crying out, "Meat! meat! Ah! ha! We shall have plenty of meat! Bo-bo-bo-bo, Bo-bo-bo-bo-o-o!"

Undoubtedly these must be relatives of the terrible "Bo-bo-bo's" above, we thought, as with one mind we rose to respond to this rabid man-eating tribe. Anger we had none for them. It seemed to me so absurd to be angry with people who looked upon one only as an epicure would regard a fat capon. Sometimes also a faint suspicion came to my mind that this was all but a part of a hideous dream. Why was it that I should be haunted with the idea that there were human beings who regarded me and my friends only in the light of meat? Meat! We? Heavens! what an atrocious idea!

"Meat! Ah! we shall have meat to-day. Meat! meat! meat!"

There was a fat-bodied wretch in a canoe, whom I allowed to crawl within spear-throw of me; who, while he swayed the spear with a vigour far from assuring to one who stood within reach of it, leered with such a clever hideousness of feature that I felt, if only within arm's length of him, I could have bestowed upon him a hearty thump on the back, and cried out applaudingly, "Bravo, old boy! You do it capitally!"

Yet not being able to reach him, I was rapidly being fascinated by him. The rapid movements of the swaying spear, the steady wide-mouthed grin, the big square teeth, the head poised on one side with the confident pose of a practised spear-thrower, the short brow and square face, hair short and thick. Shall I ever forget him? It appeared to me as if the spear partook of the same cruel inexorable look as the grinning savage. Finally, I saw him draw his right arm back, and his body incline backwards, with still that same grin on his face, and I felt myself begin to count, one, two, three, four – and *whizz*! The spear flew over my back, and hissed as it pierced the water. The spell was broken.

It was only five minutes' work clearing the river. We picked up several shields, and I gave orders that all shields should be henceforth religiously preserved, for the idea had entered my head that they would answer capitally as bulwarks for our canoes. An hour after this we passed close to the confluence of the Urindi – a stream

400 yards in width at the mouth, and deep with water of a light colour, and tolerably clear.

We continued down river along the right bank, and at 4 p.m. camped in a dense low jungle, the haunt of the hippopotamus and elephant during the dry season. When the river is in flood a much larger tract must be under water.

The left bank was between seventy and eighty feet high; and a point bearing from camp north-west was about one hundred and fifty feet high.

The traveller's first duty in lands infested by lions and leopards, is to build a safe corral, kraal, or boma, for himself, his oxen, horses, servants; and in lands infested like Usongora Meno and Kasera – wherein we now were – by human lions and leopards, the duty became still more imperative. We drew our canoes, therefore, halfway upon the banks, and our camp was in the midst of an impenetrable jungle.

On the high bluffs opposite was situated Vina-Kya. The inhabitants at once manned their drums and canoes, and advanced towards our camp. We could not help it. Here we were camped in a low jungle. How could the most captious, or the most cruel, of men find any cause or heart to blame us for resting on this utterly uninhabitable spot? Yet the savages of Vina-Kya did. Our interpreters were urged to be eloquent. And indeed they were, if I may judge by the gestures, which was the only language that was comprehensible to me. I was affected with a strange, envious admiration for those two young fellows, cannibals it is true, but endowed, none the less, with a talent for making even senseless limbs speak – and they appeared to have affected the savages of Vina-Kya also. At any rate, the wild natures relented for that day; but they promised to decapitate us early in the morning, for the sake of a horrid barbecue they intended to hold. We resolved not to wait for the entertainment.

At dawn we embarked, and descended about two miles, close to the right bank, when, lo! the broad mouth of the magnificent Lowwa, or Rowwa, river burst upon the view. It was over a thousand yards wide, and its course by compass was from the south-east, or east-south-east true. A sudden rain-storm compelled us to camp on the north bank, and here we found ourselves under the shadows of the primeval forest.

Judging from the height and size of these trees, I doubt whether the right bank of the Livingstone at the mouth of the Lowwa river was ever at any time inhabited. An impenetrable undergrowth consisting of a heterogeneous variety of ferns, young palms, date, doum, *Raphia vinifera*, and the *Mucuna pruriens* – the dread of the naked native for the tenacity with which its stinging sharp-pointed bristles attach themselves to the skin – masses of the capsicum plant, a hundred species of clambering vines, caoutchouc creepers, llianes, and endless lengths of rattan cane intermeshed and entangled, was jealously sheltered from sunlight by high, over-arching, and interlacing branches of fine grey-stemmed Rubiaceæ, camwood and bombax, teak, elais palms, ficus, with thick fleshy leaves, and tall gum-trees. Such is the home of the elephants which through this undergrowth have trodden the only paths available. In the forks of trees were seen large lumps, a spongy excrescence, which fosters orchids and tender ferns, and from many of the branches depended the Usneæ moss in graceful and delicate fringes. Along the brown clayey shores, wherever there is the slightest indentation in the banks and still water, were to be found the Cyperaceæ sedge, and in deeper recesses and shallow water the papyrus.

One hears much about "the silence of the forest" – but the tropical forest is not silent to the keen observer. The hum and murmur of hundreds of busy insect tribes make populous the twilight shadows that reign under the primeval growth. I hear the grinding of millions of mandibles, the furious hiss of a tribe just alarmed or about to rush to battle, millions of tiny wings rustling through the nether air, the march of an insect tribe under the leaves, the startling leap of an awakened mantis, the chirp of some eager and garrulous cricket, the buzz of an ant-lion, the roar of a bullfrog. Add to these the crackle of twigs, the fall of leaves, the dropping of nut and berry, the occasional crash of a branch, or the constant creaking and swaying of the forest tops as the strong wind brushes them or the gentle breezes awake them to whispers. Though one were blind and alone in the midst of a real tropical forest, one's sense of hearing would be painfully alive to the fact that an incredible number of minute industries, whose number one could never hope to estimate, were active in the shades. Silence is impossible in a tropical forest.

About ten o'clock, as we cowered in most miserable condition under the rude, leafy shelters we had hastily thrown up, the people of the wooded bluffs of Iryamba, opposite the Lowwa confluence, came over to see what strange beings were those who had preferred the secrecy of the uninhabited grove to their own loud roystering society. Stock still we sat cowering in our leafy coverts, but the mild reproachful voice of Katembo, our cannibal interpreter, was heard labouring in the interests of peace, brotherhood, and goodwill. The rain pattered so incessantly that I could from my position only faintly hear Katembo's voice pleading, earnestly yet mildly, with his unsophisticated brothers of Iryamba, but I felt convinced from the angelic tones that they would act as a sedative on any living creature except a rhinoceros or a crocodile. The long-drawn bleating sound of the word "Sen-nen-neh," which I heard frequently uttered by Katembo, I studied until I became quite as proficient in it as he himself.

Peace was finally made between Katembo on the one hand and the canoe-men of Iryamba on the other, and they drew near to gaze at their leisure at one of the sallow white men, who with great hollow eyes peered, from under the vizor of his cap, on the well-fed bronze-skinned aborigines.

After selling us ten gigantic plantains, 13 inches long and 3 inches in diameter, they informed us that we had halted on the shore of Luru, or Lulu, in the uninhabited portion of the territory of Wanpuma, a tribe which lived inland; that the Lowwa came from the east, and was formed of two rivers, called the Lulu from the north-east, and the Lowwa from the south-east; that about a day's journey up the Lowwa river was a great cataract, which was "very loud."

At 2 P.M. we left our camp in the forest of Luru, and pulled across to the Iryamba side of the Livingstone. But as soon as the rain had ceased, a strong breeze had risen, which, when we were in mid-river, increased to a tempest from the north, and created great heavy waves, which caused the foundering of two of our canoes, the drowning of two of our men, Farjalla Baraka and Nasib, and the loss of four muskets and one sack of beads. Half a dozen other canoes were in great danger for a time, but no more fatal accidents occurred.

I feared lest this disaster might cause the people to rebel and compel me to return, for it had shocked them greatly; but I was cheered to hear them remark that the sudden loss of their comrades had been ordained by fate, and that no precautions would have availed to save them. But though omens and auguries were delivered by the pessimists among us, not one hazarded aloud the belief that we ought to relinquish our projects; yet they were all evidently cowed by our sudden misfortune.

On the 31st, the last day of the year 1876, we resumed our voyage. The morning was beautiful, the sky blue and clear, the tall forest still and dark, the river flowed without a ripple, like a solid mass of polished silver. Everything promised fair. But from the island below, the confluence of the Lowwa and the Livingstone, the warning drum sounded loudly over the river, and other drums soon echoed the dull boom.

"Keep together, my men," I cried, "there may be hot work for us below."

We resolved to keep in mid-stream, because both the island and the left bank appeared to be extremely populous, and to paddle slowly and steadily down river. The canoes of the natives darted from either shore, and there seemed to be every disposition made for a furious attack; but as we drew near, we shouted out to them, "Friends, Sennenneh! Keep away from us. We shall not hurt you; but don't lift your spears, or we'll fight."

There was a moment's hesitation, wherein spears were clashed against shields, and some fierce words uttered, but finally the canoes drew back, and as we continued to paddle, the river with its stiff current soon bore us down, rapidly past the populous district and island.

The beginning of the new year, 1877, commenced, the first three hours after sunrise, with a delicious journey past an uninhabited tract, when my mind, wearied with daily solicitude, found repose in dwelling musingly upon the deep slumber of Nature. Outwardly the forest was all beauty, solemn peace, and soft dreamy rest, tempting one to sentiment and mild melancholy. Though it was vain to endeavour to penetrate with our eyes into the dense wall of forest – black and impervious to the sunlight which almost seemed to burn up the river – what could restrain the imagination? These were my calm hours, periods when my heart, oblivious of the dark and evil days we had passed, resolutely closed itself against all dismal forebodings, and revelled in the exquisite stillness of the uninhabited wilderness.

But soon after nine o'clock we discovered we were approaching settlements, both on islands and on the banks, and again the hoarse war-drums awaked the echoes of the forest, boomed along the river, and quickened our pulses.

We descend in close order as before, and steadily pursue our way. But, heading us off, about ten long canoes dart out from the shadow of palmy banks, and the wild crews begin to chant their war-songs, and now and then, in attitudes of bravado and defiance, raise spears and shields aloft and bring them downward with sounding clash.

As we approached them, we shouted out "Sen-nen-neh" – our Sesame and Shibboleth, our watchword and countersign. But they would not respond.

Hitherto they had called us Wasambye; we were now called Wajiwa (people of the sun?); our guns were called Katadzi, while before they were styled Kibongeh, or lightning. Katembo was implored to be eloquent, mild of voice, pacific in gesture.

They replied, "We shall eat Wajiwa meat to-day. Oho, we shall eat Wajiwa meat!" and then an old chief gave some word of command, and at once 100 paddles beat the water into foam, and the canoes darted at us. But the contest was short, and we were permitted to pursue our voyage.

The river, beyond these islands, expanded to a breadth of 3000 yards: the left bank being high, and the right low. At noon we were in south latitude 1° 10'.

Five miles below, the river narrowed to about 2800 yards, and then we floated down past an uninhabited stretch, the interval affording us rest, until, reaching the southern end of a large island, we camped, lest we might be plunged into hostilities once more.

The 2nd January was a lively day. We first ran the gauntlet past Kirembuka, an exciting affair, and next we were challenged by Mwana-Mara's fierce sons, who were soon joined by Mwana Vibondo's people, and about 10.30 a.m. we had to repulse an attack made by the natives of Lombo a Kiriro. We had fought for three hours almost without a pause, for the Kewanjawa and Watomba tribe from the left bank had joined in the savage mêlée, and had assisted the tribes of the right bank. Then for an hour we had rest; but after that we came to islands, which we afterwards discovered were called Kibombo, and, finding the tribe of Amu Nyam preparing for battle with animation, we took advantage of one of the group to see if we could not negotiate a peaceful passage before risking another fight. The latitude of this island was south 0° 52' 0".

Katembo, our interpreter, and his friend, were despatched in a canoe manned by eight men, halfway to the shore, to speak fair and sweet words of peace to the Amu Nyam. No verbal answer was given to them, but they had to retreat in a desperate hurry before a rapidly advancing crowd of canoes. The Amu Nyams had evidently not had time to be undeceived by their friends above, for they came up with a dauntless bearing, as though accustomed to victory. Yet we held out copper armlets and long strings of shells to them, vociferously shouting out "Sen-nen-neh," with appropriate and plausible gestures. They laughed at us; and one fellow, who had a mighty door-like shield painted black with soot, using his long spear as an index finger, asked us – if Katembo spoke correctly – if we thought we could disappoint them of so much meat by the presents of a few shells and a little copper.

Our canoes were lying broadside along the reedy island, and as soon as the first spears were thrown, the Wangwana received orders to reply to them with brass slugs, which created such a panic that a couple of shots from each man sufficed to drive them back in confusion. After a while they recovered, and from a distance began to fly their poisoned arrows; but the Sniders responded to them so effectually that they finally desisted, and we were again free from our meat-loving antagonists.

About 2 p.m. we dropped down river again a few miles, and at 4.30 p.m. halted to camp at an old clearing on the right bank. Had we dared, we might have continued our journey by night, but prudence forbade the attempt, as cataracts might have been more disastrous than cannibals.

Near sunset we were once more alarmed by finding arrows dropping into the camp. Of course there was a general rush to guns; but, upon noting the direction whence the arrows came, I ordered the people simply to go on about their duties as though nothing had occurred, while I sent twenty men in two canoes down the river with instructions to advance upon the enemy from behind, but by no means to fire unless they were overwhelmed in numbers.

Just at dark our canoes came back with three prisoners bound hand and foot. Except the poor dwarf at Ikondu up river, I had not seen any human creatures so unlovable to look at. I would not disturb them, however, that evening, but releasing their feet, and relaxing the bonds on their arms, appointed Katembo and his friend to keep them company and feed them, and Wadi Rehani to stimulate the keepers to be hospitable.

By the morning they were sociable, and replied readily to our questions. They were of the Wanongi – an inland tribe – but they had a small fishing village about an hour's journey below our camp called Katumbi. A powerful tribe called the Mwana Ntaba occupied a country below Katumbi, near some falls, which they warned us would be our destruction. On the left side of the river, opposite the Mwana Ntaba, were the Wavinza, south of a large river called the Rumami, or Lumami. The great river on which we had voyaged was known to them as the Lowwa.

As we stepped into our canoes we cut their bonds and permitted the unlovable and unsympathetic creatures to depart, a permission of which they availed themselves gladly.

The banks were from 10 to 30 feet high, of a grey-brown clay, and steep with old clearings, which were frequent at this part until below Katumbi. Half an hour afterwards we arrived at a channel which flowed in a sudden bend to the north-east, and, following it, we found ourselves abreast of a most populous shore, close to which we glided. Presently several large canoes appeared from behind an island to our right, and seemed to be hesitating as to whether they should retreat or advance.

The "Open Sesame" – "Sen-nen-neh!" – was loudly uttered by Katembo with his usual pathetic, bleating accent, and to our joy the word was repeated by over a hundred voices. "Sen-nen-neh! Sen-nenneh! Sennenneh!" – each voice apparently vying with the other in loudness. The river bore us down, and as they would not shorten the distance, we thought it better to keep this condition of things, lest the movement might be misconstrued, and we might be precipitated into hostilities.

For half an hour we glided down in this manner, keeping up a constant fire of smiling compliments and pathetic Sennennehs. Indeed, we were discovering that there was much virtue in a protracted and sentimental pronunciation of Sen-nen-neh! The men of the Expedition, who had previously ridiculed with mocking Ba-a-a-as, the absurd moan and plaintive accents of Sen-nen-neh, which Katembo had employed, now admired him for his tact. The good natives with whom we were now exchanging these suave, bleating courtesies proved to us that the true shibboleth of peace was to prolong each word with a quavering moan and melancholic plaint.

We came to a banana grove, of a delicious and luxuriant greenness which the shadowy black green of the antique forest behind it, only made more agreeable and pleasant. Beyond this grove, the bank was lined by hundreds of men and women, standing or sitting down, their eyes directed towards our approaching flotilla.

"Sen-nen-neh!" was delivered with happy effect by one of the boat-boys. A chorus of Sen-nen-nehs, long-drawn, loud, and harmonious, quickly following the notes of the last syllable, burst from the large assembly, until both banks of the great river re-echoed it with all its indescribable and ludicrous pathos.

The accents were peaceful, the bearing of the people and the presence of the women were unmistakably pacific, so the word was given to drop anchor.

The natives in the canoes, who had hitherto preceded us, were invited to draw near, but they shrugged their shoulders, and declined the responsibility of beginning any intercourse with the strangers. We appealed to the concourse on the banks, for we were not a hundred feet from them. They burst out into a loud laughter, yet with nothing of scorn or contempt in it, for we had been so long accustomed to the subtle differences of passion that we were by this

time adepts in discovering the nicest shades of feeling which wild
humanity is capable of expressing. We held out our hands to them
with palms upturned, heads sentimentally leaning on one side, and,
with a captivating earnestness of manner, begged them to regard us
as friends, strangers far from their homes, who had lost their way,
but were endeavouring to find it by going down the river.

The effect is manifest. A kind of convulsion of tenderness appears
to animate the entire host. Expressions of pity break from them, and
there is a quick interchange of sympathetic opinions.

"Ah," thought I, "how delighted Livingstone would have been
had he been here to regard this scene! Assuredly he would have been
enraptured, and become more firmly impressed than ever with the
innocence and guilelessness of true aborigines," and I am forced to
admit it is exceedingly pleasant, but – I wait.

We hold up long necklaces of beads of various colours to view:
blue, red, white, yellow, and black.

"Ah-h-h," sigh a great many, admiringly, and heads bend toward
heads in praise and delight of them.

"Come, my friends, let us talk. Bring one canoe here. These to
those who dare to approach us." There is a short moment of
hesitation, and then some forms disappear, and presently come
out again bearing gourds, chickens, bananas, and vegetables,
&c., which they place carefully in a small canoe. Two women step
in and boldly paddle towards us, while a deathly silence prevails
among my people as well as among the aborigines on the bank.

I observed one or two coquettish airs on the part of the two
women, but though my arm was getting tired with holding out so
long in one position those necklaces of glorious beads, I dared not
withdraw them, lest the fascination might be broken. I felt myself a
martyr in the cause of public peace, and the sentiment made me bear
up stoically.

"Boy," I muttered, in an undertone, to Mabruki, my gun-bearer,
"when the canoe is alongside, seize it firmly and do not let it
escape."

"Inshallah, my master."

Nearer the canoe came, and with its approach my blandness
increased, and further I projected my arm with those beads of
tempting colours.

At last the canoe was paddled alongside. Mabruki quietly grasped
it. I then divided the beads into sets, talking the while to Katembo –
who translated for me – of the happiness I felt at the sight of two
such beautiful women coming out to see the white chief, who was so
good, and who loved to talk to beautiful women. "There! these are

for you – and these are for you," I said to the steerswoman and her mate.

They clapped their hands in glee, and each woman held out her presents in view of the shore people; and hearty hand-claps from all testified to their grateful feelings.

The women then presented me with the gourds of malofu – palm-wine – the chickens, bananas, potatoes, and cassava they had brought, which were received by the boat's crew and the interested members of the Expedition with such a hearty clapping of hands that it sent the shore people into convulsions of laughter. Mabruki was told now to withdraw his hand, as the women were clinging to the boats themselves, and peace was assured. Presently the great native canoes drew near and alongside the boat, forming dense walls of strange humanity on either side.

"Tell us, friends," we asked, "why it is you are so friendly, when those up the river are so wicked?"

Then a chief said, "Because yesterday some of our fishermen were up the river on some islets near Kibombo Island, opposite the Amu-Nyam villages; and when we heard the war-drums of the Amu-Nyam we looked up, and saw your canoes coming down. You stopped at Kibombo Island, and we heard you speak to them, saying you were friends. But the Amu-Nyam are bad; they eat people, we don't. They fight with us frequently, and whomsoever they catch they eat. They fought with you, and while you were fighting our fishermen came down and told us that the Wajiwa" (we) "were coming; but they said that they heard the Wajiwa say that they came as friends, and that they did not want to fight. To-day we sent a canoe, with a woman and a boy up the river, with plenty of provisions in it. If you had been bad people, you would have taken that canoe. We were behind the bushes of that island watching you; but you said 'Sen-nen-neh' to them, and passed into the channel between the island and our villages. Had you seized that canoe, our drums would have sounded for war, and you would have had to fight us, as you fought the Amu-Nyam. We have left our spears on one of those islands. See, we have nothing."

It was true, as I had already seen, to my wonder and admiration. Here, then, I had opportunities for noting what thin barriers separated ferocity from amiability. Only a couple of leagues above lived the cannibals of Amu-Nyam, who had advanced towards us with evil and nauseous intentions; but next to them was a tribe which detested the unnatural custom of eating their own species, with whom we had readily formed a pact of peace and goodwill!

They said their country was called Kankoré, the chief of which was Sangarika, and that the village opposite to us was Maringa; and that three miles below was Simba-Simba; that their country was small, and only reached to the end of the islands; that after we had passed the islands we should come to the territory of the Mwana Ntaba, with whom we should have to fight; that the Mwana Ntaba people occupied the country as far as the falls; that below the falls were several islands inhabited by the Baswa, who were friends of the Mwana Ntaba. It would be impossible, they said, to go over the falls, as the river swept against a hill, and rolled over it, and tumbled down, down, down, with whirl and uproar, and we should inevitably get lost. It would be far better, they said, for us to return.

Having obtained so much information from the amiable Kankoré, we lifted our stone anchors and moved gently down stream. Before each village we passed groups of men and women seated on the banks, who gave a genial response to our peaceful greeting.

We were soon below the islands on our left, and from a course north by west the river gradually swerved to north by east, and the high banks on our right, which rose from 80 to 150 feet, towered above us, with grassy breaks here and there agreeably relieving the sombre foliage of groves.

About 2 p.m., as we were proceeding quietly and listening with all our ears for the terrible falls of which we had been warned, our vessels being only about thirty yards from the right bank, eight men with shields darted into view from behind a bush-clump, and, shouting their war-cries, launched their wooden spears. Some of them struck and dented the boat deeply, others flew over it. We shoved off instantly, and getting into mid-stream found that we had heedlessly exposed ourselves to the watchful tribe of Mwana Ntaba, who immediately sounded their great drums, and prepared their numerous canoes for battle.

Up to this time we had met with no canoes over 50 feet long, except that antique century-old vessel which we had repaired as a hospital for our small-pox patients; but those which now issued from the banks and the shelter of bends in the banks were monstrous. The natives were in full war-paint, one-half of their bodies being daubed white, the other half red, with broad black bars, the *tout ensemble* being unique and diabolical. There was a crocodilian aspect about these lengthy vessels which was far from assuring, while the fighting men, standing up alternately with the paddlers, appeared to be animated with a most ferocious cat-o'-mountain spirit. Horn-blasts which reverberated from bank to bank, sonorous drums, and a chorus of loud yells, lent a fierce éclat to the fight in which we were now about to be engaged.

We formed line, and having arranged all our shields as bulwarks for the non-combatants, awaited the first onset with apparent calmness. One of the largest canoes, which we afterwards found to be 85 feet 3 inches in length, rashly made the mistake of singling out the boat for its victim; but we reserved our fire until it was within 50 feet of us, and after pouring a volley into the crew, charged the canoe with the boat, and the crew, unable to turn her round sufficiently soon to escape, precipitated themselves into the river and swam to their friends, while we made ourselves masters of the *Great Eastern* of the Livingstone. We soon exchanged two of our smaller canoes and manned the monster with thirty men, and resumed our journey in line, the boat in front acting as a guide. This early disaster to the Mwana Ntaba caused them to hurry down river, blowing their horns, and alarming with their drums both shores of the river, until about forty canoes were seen furiously dashing down stream, no doubt bent on mischief.

At 4 p.m. we came opposite a river about 200 yards wide, which I have called the Leopold River, in honour of His Majesty Leopold II, King of the Belgians, and which the natives called either the Kankora, Mikonju, or Munduku. Perhaps, the natives were misleading me, or perhaps they really possessed a superfluity of names, but I think that whatever name they give it should be mentioned in connection with each stream.

Soon after passing by the confluence, the Livingstone, which above had been 2500 yards wide, perceptibly contracted, and turned sharply to the east-north-east, because of a hill which rose on the left bank about 300 feet above the river. Close to the elbow of the bend on the right bank we passed by some white granite rocks, from 1 to 6 feet above the water, and just below these we heard the roar of the First Cataract of the Stanley Falls series.

But louder than the noise of the falls rose the piercing yells of the savage Mwana Ntaba from both sides of the great river. We now found ourselves confronted by the inevitable necessity of putting into practice the resolution which we had formed before setting out on the wild voyage – to conquer or die. What should we do? Shall we turn and face the fierce cannibals, who with hideous noise drown the solemn roar of the cataract, or shall we cry out "Mambu Kwa Mungu" – "Our fate is in the hands of God" – and risk the cataract with its terrors!

A NOVICE AT LARGE

Joseph Thomson
(1858–95)

Barely twenty and just out of Edinburgh University, Thomson was unexpectedly employed on the Royal Geographical Society's 1878 expedition to the Central African lakes. Though later amongst the greatest African explorers, he retained the caution and humour of one who felt himself an inexperienced impostor. Unlike Burton he admired Africans; unlike Stanley he would not fight them. His motto – "he who goes slowly, goes safely; he who goes safely, goes far" – was never more seriously tested than when, just six weeks inland from Dar es Salaam, his first expedition lost Keith Johnston, its leader and Thomson's only European companion.

A s we had now arrived at the confines of the well cultivated and populous districts, it was necessary to be cautious in our movements, not pushing too hastily forward, but taking as our motto "be sure of every step before making it." As our guide was not certain about the best route for such a large caravan, so as to get food, we decided to send him forward a few marches to report upon the country. In the interval we enjoyed ourselves after various fashions; Johnston kept up incessant inquiries regarding the countries we would pass through, and spent the time in other profitable ways, while I wandered about hunting for beetles and butterflies, beasts, and crawling things of different kinds. But though I searched most assiduously the result was invariably disappointing. Everything animate seemed determined to keep out of my sight. Rarely did any living creature fall into my snares. Still, a lover of nature always finds something in these rambles interesting enough to draw him out. The great stillness of the forest and the entire novelty of his surroundings are of themselves sufficient to keep him from wearying.

One day, having nothing to do, we were suddenly taken with a

Joseph Thomson. From *To the Central African Lakes and Back*,
London, 1881.

fever for hunting. Wonderful stories had been told us of the
abundance of hippos in a small lake a few miles distant, which
did great damage to the crops. We resolved to become the bene-
factors of the natives and rid them of their ravagers. Fired with the
idea we at once seized our heavy rifles, and taking one or two men
and a guide set off for the field of action.

The men wanted to carry our rifles for us, but this we loftily
refused as derogatory to the dignity of sportsmen. For the same
reason we refused to be borne across a stream, and I dashing in got
a fine ducking, by tripping over a root in my haste to show that I
could rough it with impunity. I, however, only laughed, and
declared it to be the very best of fun. Pushing along for an hour,
we were overtaken with rain. The path disappeared, and the grass
became drenched with wet. Such little troubles were of course
beneath the notice of sportsmen! Then we entered a horrid miry

swamp, full of pitfalls and holes, which squirted mud over us till we looked the most blotched of individuals. We slipped and floundered about in the most wearisome manner, till at last, finding my rifle becoming rather heavy, I argued to myself that it would look more dignified if an attendant carried it. I should then be able to speak of "my gun-bearer!" This "happy thought" I at once acted upon, and Johnston, glad of such an example, also relieved himself of his gun. Another hour through swamp, jungle, and forest, and we emerged finally beside the so-called lake, followed by a crowd who were eager to witness our exploits, and whom we of course determined to astonish.

But where was the lake? A stretch of marshy-looking country spread out before us; and it was only after some investigation we made out that a body of water did lie at our feet, but hidden by a thick covering of floating vegetation, except at the centre, where we were told the hippos were to be found. This took us rather aback, as we would require to wade an indefinite distance by a hippos' track to reach the clear water. Our fervour for sport rather cooled at this prospect. Might there not be crocodiles or water-snakes hidden beneath the vegetation, ready to take a mean advantage and snap at us unseen?

We resorted to various plans in order to get a sight of the monsters. Trees were climbed and the treacherous edge of the mere was patiently investigated, but all to no purpose. The natives began to look disappointed, and evidently we were fast falling in their estimation. This rather nettled us. The idea of an ignominious retreat was anything but acceptable. Still the attempt to reach the open water seemed to mean an amount of trouble and discomfort out of all proportion to the value of the possible sport.

Chopfallen, we were therefore about to retire to our camp, when from the haunt of the hippos came three distinct grunts. We were fairly electrified. Were we to brook these notes of satiric triumph, and meekly accept our defeat? It was impossible! At once boots and coats were off, and in a minute Johnston dashed into the open track through the floating vegetation.

Struck with admiration, I stood and watched him. His footing seemed to be rather shaky from the way in which he moved forward, with "light springing footsteps." Further and further he boldly ventured. Deeper and deeper he got, while ever and anon the hippos grunted out defiance, and the mob shouted encouragement on the banks. The liquid mud reached his hip, then his waist, and gradually crept up till his armpits were reached, and still he had not attained the open water. It was a critical moment. He paused and looked back; then sternly making another step forward, he suddenly dropped out of sight, with only his gun above water. A few minutes later, he was hauled to the bank, covered with a thick integument of odoriferous mud, baffled and defeated; and loud rose the victorious grunt of the hippos.

While the men scraped off the obnoxious cuticle, I made an attempt in another direction, and returned in like manner to take my turn under the scraper. Johnston the while stood shivering and chilly. Feeling as if it would relieve us to indulge in a little strong language we commenced our return, crest-fallen, and in a most pitiable plight, thought before we once more re-entered Mkamba the pouring rain had pretty well washed the mud out of our clothes, and saved our washerman that trouble. We concluded that night that hippopotamus hunting was not exhilarating.

On the following morning, Johnston felt a pain in his back which he supposed to be rheumatic, and under that belief, took what he understood to be appropriate medicines. All too late, however, he found out that it was the commencement of a more deadly disease, as we shall see, in the course of our narrative.

Previous to this excursion, some capital observations were made, which fixed the latitude of Mkamba. From the very first day's march, Johnston had assiduously attempted to take meridian altitudes of various stars, but owing to the cloudy condition of the skies, had failed on every occasion.

On the third day after his departure, our guide returned from his reconnaissance of the country ahead, and brought a very unfavourable report. There would be eight days' march, in which no food could be got. Supplies would therefore require to be provided at Mkamba and a village two days further on. To this task, then, we immediately set ourselves. Men were despatched to every village to buy rice. In an hour, the camp when they returned, laden with bags of food.

On the following day, all the wooden mortars of the place were secured for husking the rice, and round these, animated groups pounded vigorously, keeping time to most peculiar chants. These mortars or "kinus" are wineglass-shaped blocks of wood, hollowed out to receive the rice, which is belaboured with a pole four feet long, struck vertically downwards. The process is very slow and laborious. The husks are removed by the horizontal motion of an almost flat basket, which separates the heavy grain from its light covering.

Having occasion here to flog one of the men for flagrant disobedience, I was greatly disgusted to see how much the others enjoyed the sight of the man's punishment. Yelling with laughter, they seized him with savage glee, had him down in a minute, turned him on his face, and held him as with a vice, while the punishment proceeded under the cane of Chuma.

There is, however, one good trait in the men's character. They never harbour any grudge or revengeful feeling if their punishment has been just. Half an hour after the ordeal they may be seen laughing and joking with the very men who held them. This of course may arise from the fact that no sense of degradation accompanies punishment, not even that of flogging; and being naturally lighthearted, and of a devil-may-care disposition, they soon forget.

While preparing for renewing our march, one of our porters disappeared, and suspecting that he had made direct for the coast, we despatched one of the headmen and a porter to hunt him up.

After this unpleasant detention, we with pleasure got once more *en route*, though Mr. Johnston was much pained by his illness; and the rain, which had never ceased during our stay, still continued with unabated violence, submerging all the low-lying tracts, and turning the footpaths in the higher ground into raging torrents, along which it was a weariness to struggle. Still these were pleasant days to us, when with robust frames and eager enthusiasm we only rejoiced in the troubles and hardships of our march. We had come prepared for all this; indeed, we should almost have felt disappointed if our route had proved easy and pleasant. Ridiculous as it may seem, we thought ourselves entirely unworthy of the honourable title of African travellers until we should have undergone such an apprenticeship of endurance and physical discipline. Disease and bad food had not then broken our spirits and undermined our constitutions. But that time came only too soon, and then one of us was added to a roll which in the sanguine hopefulness of good health we did not anticipate.

At Madodo, where we camped the first night after leaving Mkamba, we were astonished at the reappearance of our lost porter. He gave a most creditable account of himself. Hearing at Mkamba through some unknown source that his wife was very ill on the coast, he clandestinely went off to see her, fearing that, if we knew, he would not be allowed to go. In three days he traversed more than 120 miles, saw his wife, and returned like a faithful fellow to his work. Such a deed is worthy of honour in any land, but is especially noteworthy among such a race as the reviled Waswahili. During the night the men sent after the runaway returned, having followed him to the coast, marching night and day. There they heard the true version of the affair, and came back to find him safe in our camp.

Two more days' toil under the afore-mentioned wretched conditions brought us to the village of Msangapwani, where, as we had now reached the borders of the inhabited and populated district, we were compelled to halt to collect more food in anticipation of the desert marches.

When we arrived at Msangapwani neither of us had a single dry article of clothing, so little had the sun shone to give us an opportunity of freeing them from moisture. As one suit got wet another was put on, till at last we had to be content with a wet one. Even our blankets were damp and clammy, while the close steaming air was impregnated with malaria. The natural consequence of this was that Johnston became much worse. Here also he discovered, what he had not hitherto suspected, that it was dysentery, and not rheumatism with which he was troubled. Meanwhile I was likewise laid low with an attack of fever.

In these circumstances matters looked rather lugubrious and melancholy. We tried to joke feebly with each other on our ailments; but I could hardly hold my head erect, and Johnston was looking the agonies he would not express in words. While the men were employed collecting and preparing food, we resolved, after a council of war, to dismiss the guide we engaged at Zanzibar, as he clearly knew nothing about the road.

We had here a visit from an Mganga, or medicine man, fantastically dressed. He had with him an obscene image of a woman, clothed with beads, and looking like an absurd toy. Though he did not appear to have very much respect for his goddess, if such we might call it, yet he would not sell it under an exorbitant price. When using it, he irreverently shakes it in a bag, and, thus awakened, the oracle speaks, unheard, of course, by the materialistic ear of the mob, and declares its mind on whatever subject it may be consulted.

After a three days' enforced stay at Msangapwani, we once more got under weigh. We both presented a very pitiable and woe-begone aspect when we stepped out. We were by no means promising-looking leaders. As usual, I was in front, trying, like a drunken man, to assume some dignity of appearance, though I have no doubt the attempt was rather comical. Johnston was in the rear, even in a worse condition. Our march was, as before, made miserable by drenching rains, and we had to struggle successively through long grass, swamps, and deep swollen streams. At midday our efforts ended in a complete collapse. Johnston arrived an hour after me. As he appeared, I tried to look jolly, and to hail him with a consolatory remark, but his only response to my weak attempt was a groan, as he sank exhausted on the ground.

Two hours' rest and a cup of hot tea somewhat reinvigorated us, and as we could not camp where we were, we staggered on a little further to a more suitable locality in the forest. The tents were pitched, and a boma, or thorn fence formed, inside which the men made their huts. For three days we were confined in our tents *hors de combat*, and unable to do anything. Chuma, however, was equal to the occasion, and kept everything in order. It is under such circumstances that the value of a man like Chuma is understood. One with less influence and tact would be unable to keep down riot and disorder. One with less honesty would certainly take the opportunity to help himself in various ways. The worst of my attack was soon over, and I recovered with remarkable rapidity. Johnston also decidedly improved.

Our position in the forest was a somewhat awkward one, distant as we were from all food supplies, and it became necessary to move forward. Owing to the rains, the incompetency of our former guide, and the scarcity of food in the country, our progress had been exceedingly slow, and we got quite irritable in our anxiety to push ahead. As soon therefore as Johnston found himself able to rise, though still unable to walk, he determined, in spite of his illness, to set out once more. This was an unfortunate decision. He was improving rapidly, and a few days' more rest would have given him a fair chance of throwing off the dysentery. But in his eagerness to proceed there could be no rest for him, at least until we should have reached an important village, called Behobeho, which we had heard much of. As we unhappily were not supplied with a hammock or other convenience for carrying an invalid, we set to work, and with the aid of some of the men, we contrived to fix up a rude concern, which was certainly not of the most comfortable nature, but was the best we could produce with the materials at our command.

Resuming our journey, we kept in a south-westerly direction, entering the drainage basin of the Rufiji. The streams we had crossed as far as Mkamba form the head waters and tributaries of the Mzinga River, which, as we have already noticed, flows in a northerly direction to the Dar-es-Salaam creek. Between Mkamba and Msangapwani four considerable streams, with a number of minor ones, find their way directly east to the coast. At the point we had now reached the versant and drainage is towards the river Rufiji. The country maintained much of the general character which we have already described, only it was much more flat, spreading out like an immense plain. We missed the coast fruit-trees – the moisture-loving cocoa-nut, the luscious mango, and the stinking jack-fruit. No cultivated fields or inhabited villages met our eye. To add to the desolation of our surroundings, a great stillness pervaded the solitude, and nothing animate seemed to exist. There were no pretty chattering weaver-birds; no golden-vented thrush sent forth its joyous music; and the tooting of the tepe-tepe was hushed. Sunbirds, orioles, all were alike absent. Only occasionally from the surrounding forest was the cry of the hornbill, or of the omnipresent wood-pigeon heard, or it might be the caw of a parson crow.

In trudging along through some of the forest tracts, we were frequently in danger of broken legs, or sprained ankles, owing to the hundreds of deep grass-hidden pits from which the natives extract the gum-copal, of which all our best varnishes are made. As it was we several times got severe falls in very sudden and unexpected ways.

Having to occupy Mr. Johnston's place in the caravan during his illness, I began to learn what a dreadful nuisance the ordinary Unyamwesi donkey is. We had five of them bringing up the rear, each with a load equal to what would be carried by two men. Each one, however, required the services of a man to tug, swear at, and thrash him. So that a donkey was only equal after all to one man. But their value for purposes of transport sank into insignificance when one thought of the immense amount of trouble and delay they caused to the entire caravan. In a week the donkey-boys had lost all moral control of themselves, and indulged in nothing but profane language, till it was feared they would become insane from the amount of irritation they were subjected to. While loading in the morning it required about ten men to each beast, and success was only attained after a severe struggle. Once loaded they usually took the first opportunity to walk into the nearest thorny mass of scrub, where, madly and frequently successfully, they would strive to leave their loads behind. A quarter of an hour would then be spent in releasing them from their entanglements. Finally, all ready, off we would go, though with our moral balance very much upset. The donkey for a time would look like a lamb in its meekness, till, finding our vigilance relaxed, smash it would go against a tree-trunk, breaking girths and saddle-bags, and scattering the load on the pathway. Then, with unmitigated thumps and screams of rage, the donkey-boy, at his wit's end, would dance about shouting for help. Thus another half-hour would be wasted in mending the saddlebags and reloading.

When a stream had to be crossed more trouble and delay ensued. The loads required to be taken off and carried across by the men. Then a grand fight would commence to get the donkeys over to be reloaded again. In this manner a day's march in charge of the perverse brutes, became a weariness to the flesh, and left us little time to attend to anything else.

It was with a genuine feeling of relief we saw these weak creatures die off by some mysterious malady. What exactly was the occasion of their death one after the other it would be difficult to say. I do not think it was the tsetse; neither was it bad treatment, nor the want of food. The climate and the nature of the food seemed to be the chief causes. In the low swampy regions, covered with dense jungle-grass, neither bullock, horse, nor ass seems to thrive, except where the greatest care is taken of them. They require to be either fed on specially collected food, or allowed to stray only on parts which have been under cultivation, where the grass appears to become more wholesome.

Two marches from our camp in the forest brought us to the banks of the Rufiji River, at a village called Kimkumbi. These two long marches naturally told very severely upon Johnston, owing to the rude mode of conveyance at our command. The pain of his disease was much aggravated by the exceedingly unpleasant jolting trot of the carriers along slippery pathways, where a firm, steady footing was quite out of the question. On several occasions they nearly fell with their precious load. Moreover, to be carried under such a sun was of itself sufficient to knock up any one. His tortures under such circumstances were simply dreadful, and when we arrived at Kimkumbi he felt half dead. His body was stiff and swollen, and he was utterly unable to taste a particle of food. The only means by which he could sustain his waning energies was an occasional sip of brandy and water.

In order that he might recruit slightly, a day's halt was determined on. This I took advantage of to examine the river.

The Rufiji, notwithstanding its large size and apparent importance as a water-way to the interior, has as yet been little explored, owing to the difficulties attaching to its navigation, and the malarious nature of the bordering country. The sight which met my view was exceedingly disappointing. Instead of a noble river, winding along between well-defined banks, there seemed to be only a great swamp broken here and there by sandy islands, and huge sedgy tracts, the haunt of innumerable herons, storks, ducks, geese, king-fishers, ibises, and every variety of waterfowl to be found in

the tropics, along with the clumsy hippopotamus and the dangerous crocodile.

Somewhat improved by the day's rest, Johnston, despite my
anxious protestations, determined to start again. There should be
no more stoppage till Behobeho was reached!

The conditions of travelling had now, however, very much
changed. The rainy season was over, and from a clear cloudless
sky the sun beat down with withering effect. The change in the
appearance of the country was no less marked; swamps and
marshes were replaced by dry, burnt-up deserts, which were extremely painful to traverse, as the mud, during the rains, had been
cut up and wrinkled by the feet of wild game into a surface of the
greatest irregularity, which had then got baked and hardened by
the sun to the consistence of stone. Over this the men painfully
limped with their bare feet. Not a drop of running water was to be
got, and we had to be content with the slimy water of pits or small
ponds, befouled by rotting vegetation. The dense matted bush and
tall jungle-grass with which we have become acquainted in Uzaramo, gave place to open ground covered with scattered thorny
acacias. These proved to be a terrible nuisance to the bare feet and
legs of the porters. The fallen thorns on the pathways were
continually getting into their feet, and laming them in the most
painful manner.

The first day we marched for two hours along the banks of the
Rufiji; then striking away from them we traversed a shrivelled up
plain with small stunted trees, camping early at a village called
Mtemere. We found the country bordering the river here was
covered with deep lagoons and back-waters, where myriads of
wading and other aquatic birds found a congenial residence. As
the river could not be seen from the village I made an attempt to
reach it in a most extraordinary log of hollowed wood, which
rejoiced in the name of a canoe. It did not say much for the arboreal
growths of the neighbourhood that no better tree could be got than
one shaped like the letter S. Yet such was the elegant outline of the
craft in which I took passage. However, in the quiet lagoons, I
thought we could not be in much danger, and I squeezed myself in
accordingly. We failed to reach the Rufiji, but none the less enjoyed
the pleasant sail among the huge sedges, with their screaming
feathered inhabitants flying about in immense and varied flocks.

The next three marches led us still in the same direction (W.N.W.),
through the weary desert, so utterly devoid of all interest as to make
the sight of a herd of antelopes, or other large game, a matter of the
greatest excitement. At some times of the year this district must be

overrun with game, to judge from the way in which the ground is ploughed up with their feet. When we passed, however, they seemed to have shifted to more congenial parts. Occasionally a herd of antelope or quagga appeared in the distance, but carefully keeping out of gunshot; and as the open character of the ground and the abundance of dangerous thorns made stalking impossible, we had to be content with watching them a good way off.

By this time I had forgotten the humiliating result of our Mkamba hunting, and having camped one day at what seemed a promising place, I went out, taking with me the giant Beduè, to knock over, as I expected, a few nice antelopes. With the sporting fever still as strong within me as ever, off I started, full of sanguine hopes. The day was fast declining. We moved stealthily about for some time, like villains intent on mischief, peering eagerly here and there, and straining eyes and ears. As the shadows deepened, our imagination conjured up abundance of game. Like wary sportsmen, down we would drop on our knees, and suppressing heroically any interjections which might be suggested by the probing of the numerous thorns, we would carefully crawl up behind a bush, only to find that after all there was nothing to be seen. Darkness come on, and our toil was still unrewarded. We began to think of returning home, when suddenly, on emerging from a dense bush, we came upon a fine group of large antelopes. We saw each other simultaneously, and we exhibited mutual surprise. I was so struck with the fine pose of the figures and their look of alarm and astonishment, that I utterly forgot to put my gun to my shoulder; while they, paralyzed with fear, stood for a moment, uncertain what to do. Beduè, more practically minded, finally called out, "Piga, piga bunduki, Bwana!" (Shoot, shoot, master.) The words instantly broke the spell. With one grand bound they were into the forest, and lost in the darkness before I could raise my gun. We did not get another chance; and fearful of losing our way in the darkness, we returned, not without difficulty, to camp, heated and tired by our exertion, and withal disappointed with African sport, the only result being a bad cold, torn clothes, scratched skin, and general depression of spirits.

Small snakes are very common in this dry region, and we came frequently into unpleasant proximity. More than once did they glide over my foot, and I have frequently had my presence of mind upset by finding myself sitting down beside them. No accident happened, however, from their abundance, though there were many narrow escapes.

The horror with which the natives regard these venomous creatures is very great. I remember well on one occasion how I scattered a whole village, and my men besides, by coming amongst them holding by the neck a large green snake, eight feet long, which I had stunned and then picked up. It wriggled itself round my arm, and body, though of course it could not bite, and when I appeared in this fashion, the people broke and fled in astonishment and fear. Before I could disengage myself I had of course to kill it.

On the 20th of June we emerged from this dreary waste, and entered a more undulating piece of ground covered with quartz pebbles. We crossed a delicious crystal stream, flowing between richly clad banks, with a sandy bed, the first clear running water we had seen since leaving England. The vegetation in its rich and varied luxuriance reminded us by its creepers and fine trees of the Usambara mountains, and the whole country seemed to have put on a holiday dress to receive us, after the filthy swamps and marshes of Uzaramo, and the deserts of the Rufiji valley. We passed through rich fields of ripened or ripening grain, with natives busily preparing the virgin soil for a second crop. As we passed and repassed the small stream which waters the surrounding plain, we drank deep and repeatedly. Passing through a perfect tunnel in a tropical forest with its grateful shade, we stepped into an open space winding in a labyrinthine manner among the trees, and dotted with houses which formed the delightful village of Behobeho.

Johnston's eagerly anticipated haven was thus reached, and hope and pleasure beamed on his face as we laid him down under the cool shade of a native hut.

Behobeho well merits description, not only from the beauty of its surroundings, but also from the sorrowful event which marked our stay there.

Let the reader figure to himself a forest of the densest nature, formed of colossal trees, with deep green shady foliage, among which that prince of African trees the mparamusi or yellow-wood, with its silvery-grey trunk, rises prominently in stately grace. There are feathery acacias and mimosas, branching hyphene palms, and fan palms with their abnormally bulged trunks. A score of other species attract our attention, but their names were to me unknown. Fill up the intervening spaces between the trees with ivy-green shrubbery, until not a clear bit of ground is seen, and passage through the forest is rendered impossible. From tree to tree hang creepers of every description; slender leafy kinds, swaying gracefully in the breeze; giant forms thick as a man's thigh, gnarled and twisted, binding the tree-trunks as with bands of iron. The whole forms an impenetrable mass of vegetation, through which it is impossible even to see. Here and there, where a break occurs, the creepers may be perceived hanging snake-like from an overhanging branch, as if ready to strangle the unwary traveller, or forming light festooned bridges from tree to tree for gambolling monkeys to cross. The hoarse cry of the hornbill, or the bark of baboons, are the only sounds which are heard from the forest, though, when darkness sets in, crickets with their fairy chirp, and the weird warning voice of the owl, or the croak of the frogs, help to break the stillness.

Such is the forest of Behobeho. In the heart of this dense mass of vegetation there is a winding open space, dotted with trees, labyrinthine in its character, here opening into wider areas, there leading into deceptive *culs-de-sac*. This space is dotted over with native huts, regardless of order, which form the village. The dwellings are of a different style from any we have as yet seen. The quadrangular huts of the Wazaramo are represented here by simple circular ones, with low walls, huge conical roofs, and broad overhanging eaves. Few of them are more than eight feet in diameter, and as there are neither chimneys nor windows, the smoke of the fires must escape by the low doorway. Among these huts you may observe the natives at their several occupations, attired in scanty loin cloths, and with undressed hair.

Having thus reached Behobeho with such pleasant surroundings as these, new hope for our leader's recovery rose within us. Here surely were all the elements to please the eye, and by their charming novelty to infuse new vigour into mind and body! It soon, alas! became evident that we had come too late. We built a quadrangular hut for Mr. Johnston, as being more cool and commodious than the tent, and into this we removed him. He was, however, sinking fast, and little or no food passed his lips. To add to his agonies, a dreadful convulsive cough, the result of extreme exhaustion, rarely left him. We made but poor advisers. I myself had not the remotest acquaintance with illness of any kind, and could give no advice as to treatment, and I suppose I was but a rough nurse, though I did my best.

To employ some of my spare time during this detention, I made a short excursion to the prominent mountain occurring S.S.W. of Behobeho. Crossing the small stream which winds beside the village, we traversed a broken piece of country, passed over a high ridge of sandstone which lay in front of the mountain, and reached the base of the latter, where a small stream occurs flowing south to the Ruaha. Here I for the first time got a shot at a herd of antelopes. I have no doubt I missed, though at the time I flattered myself that I saw one looking rather shaky on its legs.

I was very much struck by the symmetrical appearance of the mountain, which rejoiced in the name of Mkulima-hatambula. It rose like some magnificent cyclopean monument. It is quadrangular in shape, the upper half sitting on the lower as a base, with a flat terrace round the bottom of the former. The sides of both the upper and the lower parts rise almost perpendicularly, and give the whole such an artificial appearance as to suggest the idea of a huge monument.

I attempted to ascend to the top, but became so sick that I had to give it up and return.

On examination the peculiar shape was seen to arise from its geological structure, which was that of a series of lava beds inter-calated between beds of fine chocolate-coloured sandstone in the lower part, and greyish-red coarse sandstone in the upper. The lava not being very decomposable, has resisted denuding influences longer than the sandstone, which has got worn away, till a broad, flat terrace of about half a mile lies between the base of the upper and the edge of the lower part. The sandstone which forms these hills belongs to the carboniferous system, and is found stretching along the coast from about the Equator to the Cape. The intercalated igneous rocks are volcanic, and contemporaneous, lying conform-able to the sandstone.

I have taken the liberty to substitute the name of Mount Johnston for the uncouth one of Mkulima-hatambula.

I at this time became subject to attacks of ague, which came on regularly at four o'clock in the afternoon.

On the night of the 22nd June the camp was thrown into an uproar by the arrival of men from Dar-es-Salaam, bringing our letters. It was a hard struggle for poor Johnston to get through his. To me there is something inexpressibly touching in the idea of a person situated as he was, trying with dazed eyes to read the many pleasant inquiries from friends at home, the hopes of a successful expedition, and that he was enjoying good health, and yet feeling that he was rapidly sinking into the grave, with his great work prematurely closed.

He now became frequently insensible, and gradually grew worse, until the 28th, when he finished his career. For the first time in my life I saw death, and I felt myself alone to take upon me the great responsibilities of leading what appeared to be a very forlorn hope.

One of the most promising of explorers who had ever set foot on African shores, Johnston has met his fate, and is numbered with the long list of geographical martyrs who have attempted to break through the barriers of disease and barbarism which make the interior almost impenetrable. It needs no words of mine to establish the fame of my late gallant leader, or to prove his unequalled qualification for the work laid out for him. These are well known to every one. But this I will say of him, that his whole soul was in his work, that not the slightest opportunity of adding to our exact knowledge of Africa was missed. Night and day he was ever on the alert, even when tortured by disease, and never satisfied except he himself saw everything done. Full of enthusiasm, and in every respect a scientific traveller, he would have led the Expedition in a clear, well-defined pathway. Without him the way seemed dark and uncertain indeed.

The position into which I was thus thrown was one of peculiar difficulty, and the question arose within me whether I should go forward or not. I was myself ill with fever. I was almost totally destitute of the special scientific knowledge of a geographical traveller; in fact, I knew little of anything that was most needful to know; and my age was but twenty-two. But though the question arose, it was soon disposed of. With my foot on the threshold of the unknown, I felt I must go forward, whatever might be my destiny. Was I not the countryman of Bruce, Park, Clapperton, Grant, Livingstone, and Cameron? Though the mantle of Mr. Johnston's knowledge could not descend upon me, yet Elijah-like he left behind him his enthusiasm for geographical research, and I resolved to carry out his designs as far as lay in my power.

It would not do to let the men imagine that there was any hesitation about my future movements, and I stepped from the hut with my purpose distinctly defined. A basket coffin was at once constructed, and a space cleared in the dense forest. On the day following our leader's death we laid him in his last resting-place, where his grave is now green, as his memory will ever be. He lies at the foot of a large tree festooned with graceful creepers, under an arbour of dense evergreen bushes. His name and the date of his death are carved on the bark of the tree, and the chief of the village has undertaken to keep the place clear – a contract, I have since heard, he is faithfully carrying out.

LANDFALL AT BOTANY BAY

James Cook
(1728–79)

The son of a Yorkshire farm labourer, Cook won distinction as a naval hydrographer but was still a controversial choice to command a voyage of scientific observation to the Pacific in 1768. Its results, including the first coastal surveys of New Zealand and eastern Australia, led to a second voyage to the south Pacific and a third to the north Pacific, during which he was killed in a fracas with the Hawaiians. It was a tragic end for one whose humble origins disposed him to respect indigenous peoples. "They are far happier than we Europeans", he noted of Australia's aborigines following a brief encounter at Botany Bay (Sydney), the first European landing on the Pacific coast, in 1770.

Saturday 28th April In the p.m. hoisted out the pinnace and yawl in order to attempt a landing but the pinnace took in the water so fast that she was obliged to be hoisted in again to stop her leakes. At this time we saw several people a shore four of whom were carrying a small boat or canoe which we imagined they were going to put into the water in order to come off to us but in this we were mistaken. Being now not above two miles from the shore Mr. Banks, Dr. Solander, Tupia and myself put off in the yawl and pull'd in for the land to a place where we saw four or five of the natives who took to the woods as we approached the shore, which disapointed us in the expectation we had of geting a near view of them if not to speak to them; but our disapointment was heighten'd when we found that we nowhere could effect a landing by reason of the great surff which beat every where upon the shore. We saw hauld up upon the beach 3 or 4 small canoes which to us appear'd not much unlike the small ones of New Zeland in the woods were several trees of the palm kind and no under wood and this was all we were able to observe from the boat after which we returned to the ship about 5 in the evening. At this time it fell calm and we were not above a mile and a half from shore in a II fathom water and within some breakers that lay to the southward of us, but luckily a light breeze came off from the land which carried us out of danger and with which we stood to the northward. At day light in the morning we discovered a bay which appeared to be tollerably well sheltered from all winds into which I resoloved to go with the ship and with this view sent the master in the pinnace to sound the entrance while we kept turning up with the ship haveing the wind right out. At noon the entrance bore NNW distance I mile.

Sunday 29th   In the p.m. winds southerly clear weather with which we stood into the bay and anchor'd under the south shore about 2 Mile within the entrence in 6 fathoms water, the south point bearing SE and the north point east. Saw as we came in on both points of the bay several of the natives and a few hutts, men, women and children on the south shore abreast of the ship, to which place I went in the boats in hopes of speaking with them accompanied by Mr. Banks, Dr. Solander and Tupia; as we approached the shore they all made

Capt. James Cook, from a painting by N. Dance. Courtesy of the Mansell Collection.

off except two men who seemed resolved to oppose our landing. As soon as I saw this I ordered the boats to lay upon their oars in order to speake to them but this was to little purpose for neither us nor Tupia could understand one word they said. We then threw them some nails, beeds etc. ashore which they took up and seem'd not ill pleased in so much that I thout that they beckon'd to us to come a shore; but in this we were mistaken, for as soon as we put the boat in they again came to oppose us upon which I fired a musket between the two which had no other effect than to make them retire back where bundles of their darts lay, and one of them took up a stone and threw at us which caused my fireing a second musquet load with small shott, and altho some of the shott struck the man yet it had no other effect than to make him lay hold of a shield or target to defend himself. Emmidiatly after this we landed which we had no sooner done than they throw'd two darts at us, this obliged me to fire a third shott soon after which they both made off, but not in such haste but what we might have taken one, but Mr. Banks being of opinion that the darts were poisoned, made me cautious how I advanced into the woods. We found here a few small hutts made of the bark of trees in one of which were four or five small children with whome we left some strings of beeds etc. A quantity of darts lay about the hutts these we took away with us. Three canoes lay upon the beach the worst I think I ever saw, they were about 12 or 14 feet long made of one peice of the bark of a tree drawn or tied up at each end and the middle kept open by means of peices of sticks by way of thwarts.

After searching for fresh water without success except a little in a small hole dug in the sand, we embarqued and went over to the north point of the bay where in coming in we saw several people, but when we now landed there were no body to be seen. We found here some fresh water which came trinkling down and stood in pools among the rocks; but as this was troblesome to come at I sent a party of men a shore in the morning to the place where we first landed to dig holes in the sand by which means and a small stream they found fresh water sufficient to water the ship. The strings of beeds etc. we had left with the children last night were found laying in the hut this morning, probably the natives were afraid to take them away. After breakfast we sent some empty casks a shore and a party of men to cut wood and I went my self in the pinnace to sound and explore the bay, in the doing of which I saw several of the natives but they all fled at my approach. I landed in two places one of which the people had but just left, as there were small fires and fresh muscles broiling upon them – here likewise lay vast heaps of the largest oyster shells I ever saw. *Monday 30th* As soon as the wooders and waterers were come on board to dinner 10 or 12 of the natives came to the watering place and took away there canoes that lay there but did not offer to touch any one of our casks that had been left ashore, and in the after noon 16 or 18 of them came boldly up to within 100 yards of our people at the watering place and there made a stand. Mr. Hicks who was the officer ashore did all in his power to entice them to him by offering them presents etc. but it was to no purpose, all they seem'd to want was for us to be gone. After staying a short time they went away. They were all arm'd with darts and wooden swords, the darts have each four prongs and pointed with fish bones, those we have seen seem to be intended more for strikeing fish than offensive weapons neither are they poisoned as we at first thought. After I had returnd from sounding the bay I went over to a cove on the north side where in 3 or 4 hauls with the saine we caught above 300 pounds weight of fish which I caused to be equally divided among the Ships Company. In the a.m. I went in the pinnace to sound and explore the north side of the bay where I neither met with inhabitants or any thing remarkable. Mr. Green took the suns meridion altitude a little with[in] the south entrence of the bay which gave the latitude 34°o′s. *Tuesday 1st May* Gentle breezes northerly. In the p.m. ten of the natives again visited the watering place. I being on board at this time went emmidiatly ashore but before I got there they were going away, I follow'd them alone and unarm'd some distance along the shore but they would not stop until they got farther off than I choose to trust myself; these were arm'd in the same manner as those that came yesterday. In the evening I sent some hands to haul the saine but they caught but a very few fish. A little after sun rise I found the variation to be 11°3′ east. Last night Torby Sutherland seaman departed this life and in the a.m. his body was buried ashore at the watering place which occasioned my calling the south point of this bay after his name. This morning a party of us went ashore to some hutts not far from the watering place where some of the natives are daly seen, here we left several articles such as cloth, looking glasses, combs, beeds nails etc. After this we made an excursion into the country which we found deversified with woods, lawns and marshes; the woods are free from under wood of every kind and the trees are at such a distance from one a nother that the whole country or at least great part of it might be cultivated without being oblig'd to cut down a single tree; we found the soil every where except in the marshes to be a light white sand and produccth a quantity of good grass which grows in little tufts about as big as one can hold in ones hand and pretty close to one another, in this manner the surface of the ground is coated in the woods between the trees. Dr. Solander had a bad sight of a small animal some thing like a rabbit and we found the dung of an animal which must feed upon grass and which we judged could not be less than a deer, we also saw the track of a dog or some such like animal. We met with some hutts and places where the natives had been and at our first seting out one of them was seen the others I suppose had fled upon our approach. I saw some trees that had been cut down by the natives with some sort of a blunt instrument and several trees that were barked the bark of which had been cut by the same instrument, in many of the trees, especialy the palms, were cut steps about 3 or 4 feet asunder for the conveniency of climeing them. We found 2 sorts of gum one sort of which is like Gum Dragon and is the same as I suppose Tasman took for gum lac, it is extracted from the largest tree in the woods.

Wednesday 2nd   Between 3 and 4 o'clock in the p.m. we returnd out of the country and after dinner went a shore to the watering place where we had not been long before 17 or 18 of the natives appear'd in sight. In the morning I had sent Mr. Gore with a boat up to the head of the bay to dridge for oysters; in his return to the ship he and another person came by land and met with these people who follow'd him at the distance of 19 or 20 yards; when ever Mr. Gore made a stand and face'd them they stood also and not withstanding they were all arm'd they never offerd to attack him, but after he had parted from them and they were met by Dr. Munkhouse and one or two more who upon makeing a sham retreat they throw'd 3 darts after them, after which they began to retire. Dr. Solander, I, and Tupia made all the haste we could after them but could by neither words nor actions prevail upon them to come near us. Mr. Gore saw some up the bay who by signs invited him ashore which he prudantly declined. In the a.m. had the wind at SE with rain which prevented me from makeing an excursion up to the head of the bay as I intended.

Thursday 3rd   Winds at the SE a gentle breeze and fair weather. In the p.m. I made a little excursion along the sea coast to the southward accompaned by Mr. Banks and Dr. Solander. At our first entering the woods we saw 3 of the natives who made off as soon as they saw us; more of them were seen by others of our people who likewise made off as soon as they found they were discover'd. In the a.m., I went in the pinnace to the head of the bay accompan'd by Dr. Solander and Munkhouse in order to examine the country and to try to form some connections with the natives: in our way theither we met with 10 or 12 of them fishing each in a small canoe who retired in to shoald water upon our approach, others again we saw at the first place we landed at who took to their canoes and fled before we came near them: after this we took water and went almost to the head of the inlet where we landed and travel'd some distance inland. We found the face of the country much the same as I have before described but the land much richer, for in stead of sand I found in many places a deep black soil which we thought was capable of produceing any kind of grain, at present it produceth besides timber as fine meadow as ever was seen. However we found it not all like this, some few places were very rocky but this I beleive to be uncommon; the stone is sandy and very proper for building etc. After we had sufficiently examined this part we return'd to the boat and seeing some smoke and canoes at a nother part we went theirther in hopes of meeting with the people but they made off as we approached. There were six canoes and six small fires near the shore and muscles roasting upon them and a few oysters laying near, from this we conjectured that there had been just six people who had been out each in his canoe picking up the shell fish and come a shore to eat them where each had made his fire to dress them by; we taisted of their cheer and left them in return strings of beeds etc. Near to this place at the foot of a tree was a small well or spring of water. The day being now far spent we set out on our return to the ship.

Friday 4th   Winds northerly serene weather. Upon my return to the ship in the evening I found that none of the natives had appear'd near the watering place but about 20 of them had been fishing in their canoes at no great distance from us. In the a.m., as the wind would not permit us to sail I sent out some parties into the country to try to form some connections with the natives. One of the midship-men met with a very old man and woman and two small children; they were close to the water side where several more were in their canoes gathering shell fish and he being alone was afraid to make any stay with the two old people least he should be discoverd by those in the canoes. He gave them a bird he had shott which they would not touch neither did they speak one word but seem'd to be much frighten'd, they were quite naked even the woman had nothing to cover her nuditie. Dr. Munkhouse and a nother man being in the woods not far from the watering place discovered six more of the natives who at first seemd to wait his coming but as he was going up to them had a dart thrown at him out of a tree which narrowly escaped him, as soon as the fellow had thrown the dart he descended the tree and made off and with him all the rest and these were all that were met with the course of this day.

Saturday 5th   In the p.m. I went with a party of men over to the north shore and while some hands were hauling the saine a party of us made an excursion of 3 or 4 miles into the country or rather along the sea coast. We met with nothing remarkable, great part of the

Cook's ship, the *Endeavour* in the South Seas. Courtesy of the Mansell Collection.

country for some distance in land from the sea coast is mostly a barren heath diversified with marshes and morasses. Upon our return to the boat we found they had caught a great number of small fish which the sailors call leather jackets on account of their having a very thick skin, they are known in the West Indias. I had sent the yawl in the morning to fish for *sting rays* who return'd in the evening with upwards of 4 hundred weight; one single one wieghd 240 lb exclusive of the entrails. In the a.m. as the wind still continued northerly I sent the yawl again afishing and I went with a party of men into the country but met with nothing extraordinary.

Sunday 6th   In the evening the yawl return'd from fishing having caught two sting rays weighing near 600 pounds. The great quantity of new plants etc. Mr. Banks & Dr. Solander collected in this place occasioned my giveing it the name of *Botany Bay*. It is situated in the latitude of 34°0's, longitude 208° 37′ west; it is capacious safe and commodious, it may be known by the land on the sea-coast which is of a pretty even and moderate height, rather higher than it is farther inland with steep rocky clifts next the sea and looks like a long island lying close under the shore: the entrance of the harbour lies about the middle of this land, in coming from the southward it is discovered before you are abreast of it which you cannot do in coming from the northward; the entrance is little more than a mile broad and lies in WNW. To sail into it keep the south shore on board until within a small bare island which lies close under the north shore, being within that island the deepest water is on that side 7, 6 and five fathom a good way up. There is shoal'd water a good way off from the south shore from the inner south point qu[i]te to the head of the harbour, but over towards the north and NW shore is a channell of 12 or 14 feet water at low water 3 or 4 leagues up to a place where there is 3 & 4 fathom but here I found very little fresh water. We anchord near the south shore about a mile within the entrance for the conveniency of sailing with a southerly wind and the getting of fresh water but I afterwards found a very fine stream of fresh water on the north shore in the first sandy cove within the Island before which a ship might lay almost land lock'd and wood for fuel may be got every where: altho wood is here in great plenty yet there is very little variety, the largest trees are as large or larger than our oaks in England and grows a good deal like them and yeilds a reddish gum, the wood itself is heavy hard and black like Lignum Vitae; another sort that grows tall and strait some thing like pines, the wood of this is hard and ponderous and something of the nature of American live oaks, these two are all the timber trees I met with. There are a few sorts of shrubs and several palm trees, and mangroves about the head of the harbour. The country is woody low and flat as far inland as we could see and I believe that the soil is in general sandy, in the wood are a variety of very boutifull birds such as cocatoo's, lorryquets, parrots etc. and crows exactly like those we have in England. Water fowl are no less plenty about the head of the harbour where there are large flats of sand and mud on which they seek their food, the most of these were unknown to us, one sort especialy which was black and white and as large as a goose but most like a pelican. On the sand and mud banks are oysters, muscles, cockles etc. which I believe are the chief support of the inhabitants, who go into shoald water with their little canoes and pick them out of the sand and mud with their hands and sometimes roast and eat them in the canoe, having often a fire for that purpose as I suppose, for I know no other it can be for. The natives do not appear to be numberous neither do they seem to live in large bodies but dispers'd in small parties along by the water side; those I saw were about as tall as Europeans, of a very dark brown colour but not black nor had they wooly frizled hair, but black and lank much like ours. No sort of cloathing or ornaments were ever seen by any of us upon any one of them or in or about any of their hutts, from which I conclude that they never wear any. Some we saw that had their faces and bodies painted with a sort of white paint or pigment. Altho I have said that shell fish is their chief support yet they catch other sorts of fish some of which we found roasting on the fire the first time we landed, some of these they strike with gigs and others they catch with hook and line; we have seen them strike fish with gigs and hooks and lines were found in their hutts. Sting rays I believe they do not eat because I never saw the least remains of one near any of their hutts or fire places. However we could know but very little of their customs as we never were able to form any connections with them, they had not so much as touch'd the things we had left in their hutts on purpose for them to take away. During our stay in this harbour I caused the English Colours to be display'd ashore every day and an inscription to be cut out upon one of the trees near the watering place seting forth the ships name, date etc. Having seen every thing this place afforded we at day light in the morning weigh'd with a light breeze at NW and put to sea and the wind soon after coming to the southward we steer'd along shore NNE and at noon we were by observation in the latitude of 33°50's about 2 or 3 miles from the land and abreast of a bay or harbour wherein there appered to be safe anchorage which I call'd *Port Jackson*. It lies 3 Leagues to the northward of Botany Bay. I had almost forgot to mention that it is high water in this bay at the full and change of the moon about 8 o'clock and rises and falls upon a perpendicular about 4 or 5 feet.

ESCAPE FROM THE OUTBACK

Charles Sturt
(1795–1869)

After pioneering journeys to the Darling and Murray rivers, Sturt in 1844–5 headed north for the heart of Australia. Since the continent appeared to have few seaward draining rivers it was assumed that, like Africa, it must boast an inland lake region; a boat was therefore included amongst the expedition's equipment. But Sturt failed to reach the geographical centre of the continent, and the largest stretch of water found was Coopers Creek, later to figure so prominently in the endeavours of Burke and Wills. Sturt's painful retreat during the hottest summer on record formed a fitting prelude to the Wills Saga.

B efore we finally left the neighbourhood where our hopes had so often been raised and depressed, I gave the name of Cooper's Creek to the fine watercourse we had so anxiously traced, as a proof of my great respect for Mr. Cooper, the Judge of South Australia. I am not conversant in the language of praise, but thus much will I venture to say, that whether in his public or private capacity, Mr. Cooper was equally entitled to this record of my feelings towards him. I would gladly have laid this creek down as a river, but as it had no current I did not feel myself justified in so doing. Had it been nearer the located districts of South Australia, its discovery would have been a matter of some importance. As it is we know not what changes or speculations may lead the white man to its banks. Purposes of utility were amongst the first objects I had in view in my pursuit of geographical discovery; nor do I think that any country, however barren, can be explored without the attainment of some good end. Circumstances may yet arise to give a value to my recent labours, and my name may be remembered by after generations in Australia, as the first who tried to penetrate to its

Charles Sturt, from a painting by Crossland. From Mrs Napier Charles Sturt, *Life of Charles Sturt*. London, 1889.

centre. If I failed in that great object, I have one consolation in the retrospect of my past services. My path amongst savage tribes has been a bloodless one, not but that I have often been placed in situations of risk and danger, when I might have been justified in shedding blood, but I trust I have ever made allowances for human timidity, and respected the customs and prejudices of the rudest people. I hope, indeed, that in this my last expedition, I have not done discredit to the good opinion Sir C. Napier, an officer I knew not, was pleased to entertain of me. Most assuredly in my intercourse with the savage, I have endeavoured to elevate the character of the white man. Justice and humanity have been my guides, but while I have the consolation to know that no European will follow my track into the Desert without experiencing kindness from its tenants, I have to regret that the progress of civilized man into an uncivilized region, is almost invariably attended with misfortune to its original inhabitants.

I struck Cooper's Creek in lat. 27° 44', and in long. 140° 22', and traced it upwards to lat. 27° 56', and long. 142° 00'. There can be no doubt but that it would support a number of cattle upon its banks, but its agricultural capabilities appear to me doubtful, for the region in which it lies is subject evidently to variations of temperature and seasons that must, I should say, be inimical to cereal productions; nevertheless I should suppose its soil would yield sufficient to support any population that might settle on it.

By half past eleven of the 9th November we had again got quietly settled, and I then found leisure to make such arrangements as might suggest themselves for our further retreat. To insure the safety of the animals as much as possible, I determined to leave all my spare provisions and weightier stores behind, and during the afternoon we were engaged making the loads as compact and as light as we could.

It was not, however, the fear of the water in Strzelecki's Creek having dried up, that was at this moment the only cause of anxiety to me, for I thought it more than probable that Mr. Browne had been obliged to retreat from Fort Grey, in which case I should still have a journey before me to the old Depot of 170 miles or more, under privations, to the horses at least, of no ordinary character; and I had great doubts as to the practicability of our final retreat upon the Darling. The drought had now continued so long, and the heat been so severe, that I apprehended we might be obliged to remain another summer in these fearful solitudes. The weather was terrifically hot, and appeared to have set in unusually early.

Under such circumstances, and with so many causes to render my mind anxious, the reader will believe I did not sleep much. The men were as restless as myself, so that we commenced our journey before the sun had risen on the morning of the 10th of November, to give the horses time to take their journey leisurely. Slowly we retraced our steps, nor did I stop for a moment until we had got to within five miles of our destination, at which distance we saw a single native running after us, and taking it into my head that he might be a messenger from Mr. Browne, I pulled up to wait for him, but curiosity alone had induced him to come forward. When he got to within a hundred yards, he stopped and approached no nearer. This little delay made it after sunset before we reached the upper pool (not the one Mr. Browne and I had discovered), and were relieved from present anxiety by finding a thick puddle still remaining in it, so that I halted for the night. Slommy, Bawley, and the colt had hard work to keep up with the other horses, and it really grieved me to see them so reduced. My own horse was even now beginning to give way, but I had carried a great load upon him.

As we approached the water, three ducks flew up and went off down the creek southwards, so I was cheered all night by the hope that water still remained at the lower pool, and that we should be in time to benefit by it. On the 11th, therefore, early we pushed on, as I intended to stop and breakfast at that place before I started for the Depot. We had scarcely got there, however, when the wind, which had been blowing all the morning hot from the N. E., increased to a heavy gale, and I shall never forget its withering effect. I sought shelter behind a large gum-tree, but the blasts of heat were so terrific, that I wondered the very grass did not take fire. This really was nothing ideal: every thing, both animate and inanimate, gave way before it; the horses stood with their backs to the wind, and their noses to the ground, without the muscular strength to raise their heads; the birds were mute, and the leaves of the trees, under which we were sitting, fell like a snow shower around us. At noon I took a thermometer, graduated to 127°, out of my box, and observed that the mercury was up to 125°. Thinking that it had been unduly influenced, I put it in the fork of a tree close to me, sheltered alike from the wind and the sun. In this position I went to examine it about an hour afterwards, when I found that the mercury had risen to the top of the instrument, and that its further expansion had burst the bulb, a circumstance that I believe no traveller has ever before had to record. I cannot find language to convey to the reader's mind an idea of the intense and oppressive nature of the heat that prevailed. We had reached our destination however before the worst of the hot wind set in; but all the water that now remained in the once broad and capacious pool to which I have had such frequent occasion to call the attention of the reader, was a shining patch of mud nearly in the centre. We were obliged to dig a trench for the water to filter into during the night, and by this means obtained a scanty supply for our horses and ourselves.

About sunset the wind shifted to the west, a cloud passed over us, and we had heavy thunder; but a few drops of rain only fell. They partially cooled the temperature, and the night was less oppressive than the day had been. We had now a journey of 86 miles before us: to its results I looked with great anxiety and doubt. I took every precaution to fortify the horses, and again reduced the loads, keeping barely a supply of flour for a day or two. Before dawn we were up, and drained the last drop of water, if so it could be called, out of the little trench we had made, and reserving a gallon for the first horse that should fall, divided the residue among them

Just as the morning was breaking, we left the creek, and travelled for 36 miles. I then halted until the moon should rise, and was glad to see that the horses stood it well. At seven we resumed the journey, and got on tolerably well until midnight, when poor Bawley, my favourite horse, fell; but we got him up again, and abandoning his saddle, proceeded onwards. At a mile, however, he again fell, when I stopped, and the water revived him. I now hoped he would struggle on, but in about an hour he again fell. I was exceedingly fond of this poor animal, and intended to have purchased him at the sale of the remnants of the expedition, as a present to my wife. We sat down and lit a fire by him, but he seemed fairly worn out. I then determined to ride on to the Depot, and if Mr. Browne should still be there, to send a dray with water to the relief of the men. I told them, therefore, to come slowly on, and with Mr. Stuart pushed for the camp. We reached the plain just as the sun was descending, without having dismounted from our horses for more than fifteen hours, and as we rode down the embankment into it, looked around for the cattle, but none were to be seen. We looked towards the little sandy mound on which the tents had stood, but no white object there met our eye; we rode slowly up to the stockade, and found it silent and deserted. I was quite sure that Mr. Browne had had urgent reasons for retiring. I had indeed anticipated the measure: I hardly hoped to find him at the Fort, and had given him instructions on the subject of his removal, yet a sickening feeling came over me when I saw that he was really gone; not on my own account, for, with the bitter feelings of disappointment with which I was returning home, I could calmly have laid my head on that desert, never to raise it again. The feeling was natural, and had no mixture whatever of reproach towards my excellent companion.

We dismounted and led our horses down to water before I went to the tree under which I had directed Mr. Browne to deposit a letter for me. A good deal of water still remained in the channel, but nevertheless a large pit had been dug in it as I had desired. I did not drink, nor did Mr. Stuart, the surface of the water was quite green, and the water itself was of a red colour, but I believe we were both thinking of any thing but ourselves at the moment. As soon as we had unsaddled the horses, we went to the tree and dug up the bottle into which, as agreed upon, Mr. Browne had put a letter; informing me that he had been most reluctantly obliged to retreat; the water at the Depot having turned putrid, and seriously disagreed with the men; he said that he should fall back on the old Depot along the same line on which we had advanced, and expressed his fears that the water in Strzelecki's Creek would have dried, on the permanence of which he knew our safety depended. Under present circumstances the fate of poor Bawley, if not of more of our horses, was sealed. Mr. Stuart and I sat down by the stockade, and as night closed in lit a fire to guide Morgan and Mack on their approach to the plain. They came up about 2 p.m. having left Bawley on a little stony plain, and the Colt on the sand ridges nearer to us, and in the confusion and darkness had left all the provisions behind; it therefore became necessary to send for some, as we had not had anything for many hours. The horses Morgan and Mack had ridden were too knocked up for further work, but I sent the latter on my own horse with a leather bottle that had been left behind by the party, full of water for poor Bawley, if he should still find him alive. Mack returned late in the afternoon, having passed the Colt on his way to the Depot, towards which he dragged himself with difficulty, but Bawley was beyond recovery; he gave the poor animal the water, however, for he was a humane man, and then left him to die.

We had remained during the day under a scorching heat, but could hardly venture to drink the water of the creek without first purifying it by boiling, and as we had no vessel until Mack should come up we had to wait patiently for his arrival at 7 p.m. About 9 we had a damper baked, and broke our fast for the first time for more than two days.

While sitting under a tree in the forenoon Mr. Stuart had observed a crow pitch in the little garden we had made, but which never benefited us, since the sun burnt up every plant the moment it appeared above the ground. This bird scratched for a short time in one of the soft beds, and then flew away with something in his bill. On going to the spot Mr. Stuart scraped up a piece of bacon and some suet, which the dogs of course had buried. These choice morsels were washed and cooked, and Mr. Stuart brought me a small piece of bacon, certainly not larger than a dollar, which he assured me had been cut out of the centre and was perfectly clean. I had not tasted the bacon since February, nor did I now feel any desire to do so, but I ate it because I thought I really wanted it in the weak state in which I was.

Perhaps a physician would laught at me for ascribing the pains I felt the next morning to so trifling a cause, but I was attacked with pains at the bottom of my heels and in my back. Although lying down I felt as if I was standing balanced on stones; these pains increased during the day, insomuch that I anticipated some more violent attack, and determined on getting to the old Depot as soon as possible; but as the horses had not had sufficient rest, I put off my journey to 5 p.m. on the following day, when I left Fort Grey with

Mr. Stuart, directing Mack and Morgan to follow at the same hour on the following day, and promising that I would send a dray with water to meet them. I rode all that night until 3 p.m. of the 17th, when we reached the tents, which Mr. Browne had pitched about two miles below the spot we had formerly occupied. If I except two or three occasions on which I was obliged to dismount to rest my back for a few minutes we rode without stopping, and might truly be said to have been twenty hours on horseback.

Sincere I believe was the joy of Mr. Browne, and indeed of all hands, at seeing us return, for they had taken it for granted that our retreat would have been cut off. I too was gratified to find that Mr. Browne was better, and to learn that everything had gone on well. Davenport had recently been taken ill, but the other men had recovered on their removal from the cause of their malady.

When I dismounted I had nearly fallen forward. Thinking that one of the kangaroo dogs in his greetings had pushed me between the legs, I turned round to give him a slap, but no dog was there, and I soon found out that what I had felt was nothing more than strong muscular action brought on by hard riding.

As I had promised I sent Jones with a dray load of water to meet Morgan and Mack, who came up on the 19th with the rest of the horses.

Mr. Browne informed me that the natives had frequently visited the camp during my absence. He had given them to understand that we were going over the hills again, on which they told him that if he did not make haste all the water would be gone. It now behoved us therefore to effect our retreat upon the Darling with all expedition. Our situation was very critical, for the effects of the drought were more visible now than before the July rain, – no more indeed had since fallen, and the water in the Depot creek was so much reduced that we had good reason to fear that none remained anywhere else. On the 18th I sent Flood to a small creek, between us and the Pine forest, but he returned on the following day with information that it had long been dry. Thus then were my fears verified, and our retreat to the Darling apparently cut off. About this time too the very elements, against which we had so long been contending, seemed to unite their energies to render our stay in that dreadful region still more intolerable. The heat was greater than that of the previous summer; the thermometer ranging between 110° and 123° every day; the wind blowing heavily from N.E. to E.S.E. filled the air with impalpable red dust, giving the sun the most foreboding and lurid appearance as we looked upon him. The ground was so heated that our matches falling on it, ignited; and, having occasion to make a night signal, I found the whole of our rockets had been rendered useless, as on being lit they exploded at once without rising from the ground.

I had occasion – in the first volume of this work – to remark that I should at a future period have to make some observations on the state of the vegetation at this particular place; there being about a month or six weeks difference between the periods of the year when we first arrived at, and subsequently returned to it. When we first arrived on the 27th of January, 1845, the cereal grasses had ripened their seed, and the larger shrubs were fast maturing their fruit; the trees were full of birds, and the plains were covered with pigeons – having nests under every bush. At the close of November of the same year – that is to say six weeks earlier – not an herb had sprung from the ground, not a bud had swelled, and, where the season before the feathered tribes had swarmed in hundreds on the creek, scarcely a bird was now to be seen. Our cattle wandered about in search for food, and the silence of the grave reigned around us day and night.

Was it instinct that warned the feathered races to shun a region in which the ordinary course of nature had been arrested, and over which the wrath of the Omnipotent appeared to hang? Or was it that a more genial season in the country to which they migrate, rendered their desertion of it at the usual period unnecessary? Most sincerely do I hope that the latter was the case, and that a successful destiny will await the bold and ardent traveller* who is now crossing those regions.

On the 20th I sent Flood down the creek to ascertain if water remained in it or the farther holes mentioned by the natives, thinking that in such a case we might work our way to the eastward; but on the 23rd he returned without having seen a drop of water from the moment he left us. The deep and narrow channel I had so frequently visited, and which I had hoped might still contain water, had long been dry, and thus was our retreat cut off in that quarter also. There was apparently no hope for us – its last spark had been extinguished by this last disappointment; but the idea of a detention in that horrid desert was worse than death itself.

On the morning of the 22nd the sky was cloudy and the sun obscure, and there was every appearance of rain. The wind was somewhat to the south of west, the clouds came up from the north, and at ten a few drops fell; but before noon the sky was clear, and a strong and hot wind was blowing from the west:

* Dr. Leichhardt had started to cross the Continent some time before

the dust was flying in clouds around us, and the flies were insupportable.

At this time Mr. Stuart was taken ill with pains similar to my own, and Davenport had an attack of dysentery.

On the 23rd it blew a fierce gale and a hot wind from west by north, which rendered us still more uncomfortable: nothing indeed could be done without risk in such a temperature, and such a climate. The fearful position in which we were placed, caused me great uneasiness; the men began to sicken, and I felt assured that if we remained much longer, the most serious consequences might be apprehended.

On the 24th, Mr. Browne went with Flood to examine a stony creek about 16 miles to the south, and on our way homewards. We had little hope that he would find any water in it, but if he did, a plan had suggested itself, by which we trusted to effect our escape. It being impossible to stand the outer heat, the men were obliged to take whatever things wanted repair, to our underground room, and I was happy to learn from Mr. Stuart, who I sent up to superinted them, that the natives had not in the least disturbed Mr. Poole's grave.

On the 25th Mr. Browne returned, and returned unsuccessful: he could find no water any where, and told me it was fearful to ride down the creeks and to witness their present state.

We were now aware that there could be no water nearer to us than 118 miles, i.e. at Flood's Creek, and even there it was doubtful if water any longer remained. To have moved the party on the chance of finding it would have been madness: the weather was so foreboding, the heat so excessive, and the horses so weak, that I did not dare to trust them on such a journey, or to risk the life of any man in such an undertaking. I was myself laid up, a helpless being, for I had gradually sunk under the attack of scurvy which had so long hung upon me. The day after I arrived in camp I was unable to walk: in a day or two more, my muscles became rigid, my limbs contracted, and I was unable to stir; gradually also my skin blackened, the least movement put me to torture, and I was reduced to a state of perfect prostration. Thus stricken down, when my example and energies were so much required for the welfare and safety of others, I found the value of Mr. Browne's services and counsel. He had already volunteered to go to Flood's Creek to ascertain if water was still to be procured in it, but I had not felt justified in availing myself of his offer. My mind, however, dwelling on the critical posture of our affairs, and knowing and feeling as I did the value of time, and that the burning sun would lick up any shallow pool that might be left exposed, and that three or four days might determine our captivity or our release, I sent for Mr. Browne, to consult with him as to the best course to be adopted in the trying situation in which we were placed, and a plan at length occurred by which I hoped he might venture on the journey to Flood's Creek without risk. This plan was to shoot one of the bullocks, and to fill his hide with water. We determined on sending this in a dray, a day in advance, to enable the bullock driver to get as far as possible on the road, we then arranged that Mr. Browne should take the light cart, with 36 gallons of water, and one horse only; that on reaching the dray, he should give his horse as much water as he would drink from the skin, leaving that in the cart untouched until he should arrive at the termination of his second day's journey, when I proposed he should give his horse half the water, and leaving the rest until the period of his return, ride the remainder of the distance he had to go. I saw little risk in this plan, and we accordingly acted upon it immediately: the hide was prepared, and answered well, since it easily contained 150 gallons of water. Jones proceeded on the morning of the 27th, and on the 28th Mr. Browne left me on this anxious and to us important journey, accompanied by Flood. We calculated on his return on the eighth day, and the reader will judge how anxiously those days passed. On the day Mr. Browne left me, Jones returned, after having deposited the skin at the distance of 32 miles.

On the eighth day from his departure, every eye but my own was turned to the point at which they had seen him disappear. About 3 p.m., one of the men came to inform me that Mr. Browne was crossing the creek, the camp being on its left bank, and in a few minutes afterwards he entered my tent. "Well, Browne," said I, "what news? Is it to be good or bad?" "There is still water in the creek," said he, "but that is all I can say. What there is is as black as ink, and we must make haste, for in a week it will be gone." Here then the door was still open, – a way to escape still practicable, and thankful we both felt to that Power which had directed our steps back again ere it was finally closed upon us; but even now we had no time to lose.

DEATH AT COOPERS CREEK

William John Wills
(1834–61)

In early 1861 Robert O'Hara Burke, William Wills and John King reached Australia's northern coast on the Gulf of Carpentaria, thus completing the first transcontinental crossing. Returning the way they had come, after four months of appalling hardship they staggered into Sturt's Coopers Creek where men and supplies had been left to await their return. They were just eight hours too late; the relief party, despairing of their return, had left that very morning. One of exploration's most poignant moments was followed by one of its most protracted tragedies as the expedition tried to extricate itself, failed, faded, and died. Only King survived; three months later he was discovered living with the aborigines; Wills's heartbreaking journal was found lying beside his skeleton.

*S*unday, April 21   Arrived at the depôt this evening, just in time to find it deserted. A note left in the plant by Brahe communicates the pleasing information that they have started today for the Darling; their camels and horses all well and in good condition. We and our camels being just done up, and scarcely able to reach the depôt, have very little chance of overtaking them. Brahe has fortunately left us ample provisions to take us to the bounds of civilization. These provisions, together with a few horse-shoes and nails and some odds and ends, constitute all the articles left, and place us in a very awkward position in respect to clothing. Our disappointment at finding the depôt deserted may easily be imagined; – returning in an exhausted state, after four months of the severest travelling and privation, our legs almost paralysed, so that each of us found it a most trying task only to walk a few yards. Such a leg-bound feeling I never before experienced, and hope I never shall again. The exertion required to get up a slight piece of rising ground, even without any load, induces an indescribable sensation of pain and helplessness, and the general lassitude makes one unfit for anything. Poor Gray must have suffered very much many times when we thought him shamming. It is most fortunate for us that these symptoms, which so early affected him, did not come on us until we were reduced to an exclusively animal diet of such an inferior description as that offered by the flesh of a worn out and exhausted horse. We were not long in getting out the grub that Brahe had left, and we made a good supper off some oatmeal porridge and sugar. This, together with the excitement of finding ourselves in such a peculiar and almost unexpected position, had a wonderful effect in removing the stiffness from our legs. Whether it is possible that the vegetables can so have affected us, I know not; but both Mr. Burke and I remarked a most decided relief and a strength in the legs greater than we had had for several days. I am inclined to think that but for the abundance of portulac that we obtained on the journey, we should scarcely have returned to Cooper's Creek at all.

[The advance party of the Victorian Exploring Expedition, consisting of Burke, Wills, and King (Gray being dead), having returned from Carpentaria on the 21st April in an exhausted and weak state, and finding that the depôt party left at Cooper's Creek had started for the Darling, with their horses and camels fresh and in good condition, deemed it useless to attempt to over-take them, having only two camels, both done up, and being so weak themselves as to be unable to walk more than four or five miles a day. Finding also that the provisions left at the depôt for them would scarcely take them to Menindie, started down Cooper's Creek for Adelaide, *viâ* Mount Hopeless, on the morning of the 23rd April, intending to follow as nearly as possible the route taken by Gregory; by so doing they hoped to be able to recruit themselves and the camels, whilst sauntering slowly down the creek, and to have sufficient provisions left to take them comfortably, or at least without risk, to some station in South Australia.]

Tuesday, April 23   From Depôt. – Having collected together all the odds and the ends that seemed likely to be of use to us, in addition to provisions left in the plant, we started at a quarter past nine a.m., keeping down the southern bank of the creek. We only went about five miles, and camped at half past eleven on a billibong, where the feed was pretty good. We find the change of diet already making a great improvement in our spirits and strength.

Wednesday, April 24   From Camp No. 1. – As we were about to start this morning some blacks came by, from whom we were fortunate enough to get about twelve pounds of fish for a few pieces of straps and some matches, &c. This is a great treat for us, as well as a valuable addition to our rations. We started at a quarter past eight p.m. on our way down the creek, the blacks going in the opposite direction – little thinking that in a few miles they would be able to get lots of pieces for nothing, better than those they had obtained from us. To Camp No. 2.

Thursday, April 25   From Camp No. 2. – Awoke at five o'clock, after a most refreshing night's rest. The sky was beautifully clear and the air rather chilly. We had scarcely finished breakfast when our friends the blacks, from whom we obtained the fish, made their appearance with a few more, and seemed inclined to go with us and keep up the supply. We gave them some sugar, with which they were greatly pleased. They are by far the most well-behaved blacks we have seen on Cooper's Creek. We did not get away from the camp until half-past nine a.m., continuing our course down the most southern branch of the creek, which keeps a general S.W. course. We passed across the stony point which abuts on one of the largest waterholes in the creek, and camped at half-past twelve about a mile below the most dangerous part of the rocky path. At this latter place we had an accident that might have resulted badly for us. One of the camels fell while crossing the worst part, but we fortunately got him out with only a few cuts and bruises. The waterhole at this camp is a very fine one, being several miles long.

Friday, April 26   From Camp No. 3. – Last night was beautifully calm, and comparatively warm, although the sky was very clear. Reloaded the camels by moonlight this morning, and started at a quarter to six. Striking off to the south of the creek, we soon got on a native path, which leaves the creek just below the stony ground, and takes a course nearly west across a piece of open country, bounded on the south by sand-ridges, and on the north by the scrubby ground which flanks the bank of the creek at this part of its course. Leaving the path on the right at a distance of three miles, we turned up a small creek which passes down between some sand-hills; and finding a nice patch of feed for the camels at a waterhole, we halted at fifteen minutes past seven for breakfast. We started again at fifty minutes past nine a.m. Continuing our westerly course along the path we crossed to the S. of the watercourse above the water, and proceeded over the most splendid saltbush country that one could wish to see, bounded on the left by sand-hills, whilst to the right the peculiar-looking flat-topped sandstone ranges form an extensive amphitheatre, through the far side of the arena of which may be traced the dark line of creek timber. At twelve o'clock we camped in the bed of the creek. This comparative rest, and the change in diet, have also worked wonders, however; the leg-tied feeling is now entirely gone, and I believe that in less than a week we shall be fit to undergo any fatigue whatever. The camels are improving, and seem capable of doing all that we are likely to require of them. To Camp No. 4.

Saturday, April 27 We started at six o'clock, and, following the native path, which at about a mile from our camp takes a southerly direction, we soon came to the high sandy alluvial deposit, which separates the creek at this point from the stony rises. Here we struck off from the path, keeping well to the S. of the creek, in order that we might mess in a branch of it that took a southerly direction. At twenty minutes past nine we came in on the creek again where it runs due south, and halted for breakfast at a fine waterhole, with fine fresh feed for the camels. Here we remained until noon, when we moved on again, and camped at one o'clock on a general course; having been throughout the morning S.W. eight miles. The weather is most agreeable and pleasant; nothing could be more favourable for us up to the present time. To Camp No. 5.

Sunday, April 28 From Camp No. 5. – Morning fine and calm, but rather chilly. Started at a quarter to five a.m., following down the bed of a creek in a westerly direction, by moonlight. Our stage was, however, very short, for about a mile one of the camels (Landa) got bogged by the side of a waterhole, and although we tried every means in our power, we found it impossible to get him out. All the ground beneath the surface was a bottomless quicksand, through which the beast sank too rapidly for us to get bushes or timber fairly beneath him, and being of a very sluggish stupid nature, he could never be got to make sufficiently strenuous efforts towards extricating himself. In the evening, as a last chance, we let the water in from the creek, so as to buoy him up and at the same time soften the ground about his legs, but it was of no avail. The brute lay quietly in it as if he quite enjoyed his position. To Camp No. 6.

Monday, April 29 – From Camp No. 6. – Finding Landa still in the hole, we made a few attempts at extricating him, and then shot him; and after breakfast commenced cutting off what flesh we could get at, for jerking.

Tuesday, April 30 Camp No. 6. – Remained here to-day for the purpose of drying the meat, for which process the weather is not very favourable.

Wednesday, May 1 From Camp No. 6. – Started at twenty minutes to nine, having loaded our only camel, Rajah, with the most necessary and useful articles, and packed up a small swag each of bedding and clothing for our own shoulders. We kept on the right bank of the creek for about a mile, and then crossed over at a native camp to the left, where we got on a path running due west, the creek having turned to the N. Following the path, we crossed an open plain, and then sand-ridges, whence we saw the creek straight ahead of us, running nearly S. again. The path took us to the southernmost point of the bend, in a distance of about two and a-half miles from where we had crossed the creek, thereby saving us from three to four miles, as it cannot be less than six miles round by the creek. To Camp No. 7.

Thursday, May 2 Camp No. 7. – Breakfasted by moonlight, and started at half-past six. Following down the left bank of the creek in a westerly direction, we came, at a distance of six miles, on a lot of natives, who were camped on the bed of a creek. They seemed to have just breakfasted, and were most liberal in the presentations of fish and cake. We could only return the compliment by some fish-hooks and sugar. About a mile further on, we came to a separation of the creek, where what looked like the main branch looked towards the south. This channel we followed, not, however, without some misgivings as to its character, which were soon increased by the small and unfavourable appearance that the creek assumed. On our continuing along it a little further, it began to improve, and widened out, with fine waterholes of considerable depth. The banks were very steep, and a belt of scrub lined it on either side. This made it very inconvenient for travelling, especially as the bed of the creek was full of water for considerable distances. At eleven a.m., we halted until half past one p.m., and then moved on again, taking a S.S.W. course for about two miles, when, at the end of a very long waterhole, it breaks into billibongs, which continue splitting into sandy channels until they are all lost in the earthy soil of a box forest. Seeing little chance of water ahead, we turned back to the end of the long waterhole, and camped for the night. On our way back, Rajah showed signs of being done up. He had been trembling greatly all the morning. On this account his load was further lightened to the amount of a few pounds, by the doing away with the sugar, ginger, tea, cocoa, and two or three tin-plates. To camp No. 8.

Friday, May 3 Camp No. 8. – Started at seven a.m., striking off in a northerly direction for the main creek. At a mile and a-half came to a branch which (left unfinished.) To camp No. 9.

Saturday, May 4 Junction from Camp No. 9. – Night and morning very cold. Sky clear, almost calm; occasionally a light breath of air from south. Rajah appears to feel the cold very much. He was so stiff this morning as to be scarcely able to get up with his load. Started to return down the creek at 6.45, and halted for breakfast at nine a.m., at the same spot as we breakfasted at yesterday. Proceeding from there down the creek, we soon found a repetition of the features that were exhibited by the creek examined on Thursday. At a mile and a-half we came to the last water-hole, and below that the channel became more sandy and shallow, and continued to send off billibongs to the south and west, slightly changing its course each time until it disappeared altogether in a north-westerly direction. Leaving King with the camel, we went on a mile or two to see if we could find water, and being unsuccessful, we were obliged to return to where we had break-fasted, as being the best place for feed and water.

Sunday, May 5 To Camp No. 10. – Started by myself to recon-noitre the country in a southerly direction, leaving Mr. Burke and King with the camel at Camp No. 10. Travelled S. W. by S. for two hours, following the course of the most southerly billibongs. Found the earthy soil becoming more loose and cracked up, and the box-track gradually disappearing. Changed course to west, for a high sand ridge, which I reached in one hour and a half, and continuing in the same direction to one still higher, obtained from it a good view of the surrounding country. To the north were the extensive box forests bounding the creek on either side. To the east earthy plains inter-sected by water-courses and lines of timber, and bounded in the distance by sand-ridges. To the south the projection of the sand-ridge partially intercepted the view; the rest was composed of earthy plains, apparently clothed with chrysanthemums. To the westward, another but smaller plain was bounded also by high sand-ridges, running nearly parallel with the one on which I was standing. This dreary prospect offering no encouragement for me to proceed, I returned to Camp 10 by a more direct and better route than I had come, passing over some good saltbush land, which borders on the billibongs to the westward.

Monday, May 6 From Camp No. 10 back to Camp No. 9. – Moved up the creek again to Camp No. 9, at the junction, to breakfast, and remained the day there. The present state of things is not calculated to raise our spirits much. The rations are rapidly diminishing; our clothing especially the boots, are all going to pieces, and we have not the materials for repairing them properly; the camel is completely done up, and can scarcely get along, although he has the best of feed, and is resting half his time. I suppose this will end in our having to live like the blacks for a few months.

Tuesday, May 7 Camp No. 9. – Breakfasted at daylight, but when about to start, found that the camel would not rise, even without any load on his back. After making every attempt to get him up, we were obliged to leave him to himself. Mr. Burke and I started down the creek to reconnoitre. At about eleven miles we came to some blacks fishing. They gave us some half-a-dozen fish each for luncheon, and intimated that if we would go to their camp, we should have some more, and some bread. I tore in two a piece of macintosh stuff that I had, and Mr. Burke gave one piece, and I the other. We then went on to their camp, about three miles further. They had caught a considerable quantity of fish, but most of them were small.

On our arrival at the camp, they led us to a spot to camp on, and soon afterwards brought a lot of fish and bread, which they call nardoo. The lighting a fire with matches delights them, but they do not care about having them. In the evening, various members of the tribe came down with lumps of nardoo and handfuls of fish, until we were positively unable to eat any more. They also gave us some stuff they call bedgery, or pedgery. It has a highly intoxicating effect, when chewed even in small quantities. It appears to be the dried stems and leaves of some shrub.

Wednesday, May 8 Left the blacks' camp at half-past seven, Mr. Burke returning to the junction, whilst I proceeded to trace down the creek. This I found a shorter task than I had expected, for it soon showed signs of running out, and at the same time kept considerably to the north of west. There were several fine waterholes within about four miles of the camp I had left, but not a drop all the way beyond that, a distance of seven miles. Finding that the creek turned greatly towards the north, I returned to the blacks' encampment; and, as I was about to pass, they invited me to stay. So I did so, and was even more hospitably entertained than before, being on this occasion offered a share of a gunyah, and supplied with plenty of fish and nardoo, as well as a couple of nice fat rats. The latter I found most delicious. They were baked in the skins. Last night was clear and calm, but unusually warm. We slept by a fire, just in front of the blacks' camp. They were very attentive in bringing us firewood, and keeping the fire up during the night.

Thursday, May 9 Parted from my friends, the blacks, at half-past seven, and started for Camp No.9.

Friday, May 10 Camp No.9. – Mr. Burke and King employed in jerking the camel's flesh, whilst I went out to look for the nardoo seed, for making bread. In this I was unsuccessful, not being able to find a single tree of it in the neighbourhood of the camp. I however tried boiling the large kind of bean which the blacks call padlu; they boil easily, and when shelled are very sweet, much resembling in taste the French chesnut. They are to be found in large quantities nearly everywhere.

Saturday, May 11   Camp No.9. – To-day Mr. Burke and King started down the creek for the blacks' camp, determined to ascertain all particulars about the nardoo. I have now my turn at the meat jerking, and must divise some means for trapping the birds and rats, which is a pleasant prospect after our dashing trip to Carpentaria, having to hang about Cooper's Creek, living like the blacks.

Sunday, May 12   Mr. Burke and King returned this morning, having been unsuccessful in their search for the blacks, who, it seems, have moved over to the other branch of the creek. Decided on moving out on the main creek tomorrow, and then trying to find the natives of the creek.

Monday, May 13   Shifted some of the things, and brought them back again, Mr. Burke thinking it better for one to remain here with them for a few days, so as to eat the remains of the fresh meat, whilst the others went in search of the blacks and nardoo.

Tuesday, May 14   Mr. Burke and King gone up the creek to look for blacks, with four days' provisions. Self employed in preparing for a final start on their return. This evening Mr. Burke and King returned, having been some considerable distance up the creek, and found no blacks. It is now settled that we plant the things, and all start together the day after tomorrow. The weather continues very fine; the nights calm, clear, and cold, and the days clear, with a breeze generally from S., but to-day from E., for a change. This makes the first part of the day rather cold. When clouds appear they invariably move from W. to E.

Wednesday, May 15   Camp 9. – Planting the things, and preparing to leave the creek for Mount Hopeless.

Thursday, May 16   Having completed our planting, &c., started up the creek to the second blacks' camp, a distance of about eight miles. Finding our loads rather too heavy, we made a small plant here of such articles as could best be spared.

Friday, May 17   Nardoo. – Started this morning on a blacks' path, leaving the creek on our left, our intention being to keep a south-easterly direction until we should cut some likely-looking creek, and then to follow it down. On approaching the foot of the first sand-hill King caught sight in the flat of some nardoo seeds, and we soon found that the flat was covered with them. This discovery caused somewhat of a revolution in our feelings, for we considered that with the knowledge of this plant we were in a position to support ourselves, even if we were destined to remain on the creek and wait for assistance from town. Crossing some sand-ridges running N. and S., we struck into a creek which runs out of Cooper's Creek, and followed it down. At about five miles we came to a large waterhole, beyond which the watercourse runs out on extensive flats and earthy plains. Calm night; sky cleared towards morning, and it became very cold. A slight easterly breeze sprang up at sunrise, but soon died away again. The sky again became overcast, and remained so throughout the day. There was occasionally a light breeze from south, but during the greater portion of the day it was quite calm. Fine halo around the sun in the afternoon.

Saturday, May 18   Camp No. 16. Calm night, sky sometimes clear and sometimes partially overcast with veil clouds.

Tuesday, May 21   Creek.

Wednesday, May 22   Cooper's Creek.

Friday, May 24   Started with King to celebrate the Queen's birthday by fetching from Nardoo Creek what is now to us the staff of life. Returned at a little after two p.m., with a fair supply, but find the collecting of the seed a slower and more troublesome process than could be desired. Whilst picking the seed, about eleven o'clock a.m., both of us heard distinctly the noise of an explosion, as if of a gun, at some considerable distance. We supposed it to have been a shot fired by Mr. Burke; but on returning to the camp found that he had not fired nor had heard the noise. The sky was partially overcast with high cum. str. clouds, and a light breeze blew from the east, but nothing to indicate a thunderstorm in any direction.

Monday, May 27   Started up the creek this morning for the depôt, in order to deposit journals and a record of the state of affairs here. On reaching the sand-hills below where Landa was bogged I passed some blacks on a flat collecting nardoo seed. Never saw such an abundance of the seed before. The ground in some parts was quite black with it. There were only two or three gins and children, and they directed me on, as if to their camp, in the direction I was before going; but I had not gone far over the first sand-hill when I was overtaken by about twenty blacks, bent on taking me back to their camp, and promising any quantity of nardoo and fish. On my going with them, one carried the shovel, and another insisted on taking my swag, in such a friendly manner that I could not refuse them. They were greatly amused with the various little things I had with me. In the evening they supplied me with abundance of nardoo and fish; and one of the old men, Poko Tinnamira, shared his gunyah with me . . . The night was very cold, but, by the help of several fires —

Tuesday, May 28 Left the blacks' camp, and proceeded up the creek. Obtained some mussels near where Landa died, and halted for breakfast. Still feel very unwell from the effects of the constipation of the bowels. The stools are exceedingly painful. After breakfast, travelled on to our third camp coming down.

Wednesday, May 29 Started at seven o'clock, and went on to the duck-holes, where we breakfasted coming down. Halted there at thirty minutes past nine for a feed, and then moved on. At the stones saw a lot of crows quarrelling about something near the water. Found it to be a large fish, of which they had eaten a considerable portion. Finding it quite fresh and good, I decided the quarrel by taking it with me. It proved a most valuable addition to my otherwise scanty supper of nardoo porridge. This evening I camped very comfortably in a mia-mia, about eleven miles from the depôt. The night was very cold, although not entirely cloudless. A brisk easterly breeze sprang up in the morning, and blew freshly all day. In the evening the sky clouded in, and there were one or two slight showers, but nothing to wet the ground.

Thursday, May 30 Reached the depôt this morning, at eleven o'clock. No traces of any one except blacks having been here since we left. Deposited some journals, and a notice of our present condition. Started back in the afternoon, and camped at the first waterhole. Last night being cloudy, was unusually warm and pleasant.

Friday, May 31 Decamped at thirty minutes past seven, having first breakfasted. Passed between the sand-hills at nine, and reached the blanket mia-mias at twenty minutes to eleven; from there proceeded on to the rocks, where I arrived at half-past one, having delayed about half-an-hour on the road in gathering some portuloc. It had been a fine morning, but the sky now became overcast, and threatened to set in for a steady rain; and as I felt very weak and tired I only moved on about a mile further, and camped in a sheltered gully, under some bushes. Night clear and very cold.

Saturday, June 1 Started at a quarter to eight a.m. Passed the duck-holes at ten a.m., and my second camp up at two p.m., having rested in the meantime about forty-five minutes. Thought to have reached the blacks' camp, or at least where Landa was bogged, but found myself altogether too weak and exhausted; in fact, had extreme difficulty in getting across the numerous little gullies, and was at last obliged to camp, from sheer fatigue. Night ultimately clear and cloudy, with occasional showers.

Sunday, June 2 Started at half-past six, thinking to breakfast at the blacks' camp, below Landa's grave; found myself very much fogged, and did not arrive at their camp until ten a.m., and then found myself disappointed as to a good breakfast, the camp being deserted. Having rested awhile, and eaten a few fish-bones, I moved down the creek, hoping by a late march to be able to reach our own camp, but I soon found, from my extreme weakness, that that would be out of the question. A certain amount of good luck, however, still stuck to me, for, on going along by a large waterhole, I was so fortunate as to find a large fish, about a pound and a-half in weight, which was just being choked by another which it had tried to swallow, but which had stuck in its throat. I soon had a fire lit, and both of the fish cooked and eaten. The large one was in good condition. Moving on again after my late breakfast, I passed Camp 67 of the journey to Carpentaria, and camped for the night under some polygonum bushes.

Monday, June 3 Started at seven o'clock, and, keeping on the south bank of the creek, was rather encouraged, at about three miles, by the sound of numerous crows a-head; presently fancied I could see smoke, and was shortly afterwards set at my ease by hearing a cooey from Pitchery, who stood on the opposite bank, and directed me around the lower end of the waterhole, continually repeating his assurance of abundance of fish and bread. Having with some considerable difficulty managed to ascend the sandy path that led to the camp, I was conducted by the chief to a fire, where a large pile of fish were just being cooked in the most approved style. These I imagined to be for the general consumption of the half a dozen natives gathered around, but it turned out that they had already had their breakfast. I was expected to dispose of this lot – a task which, to my own astonishment, I soon accomplished, keeping two or three blacks pretty steadily at work extracting the bones for me. The fish being disposed of, next came a supply of nardoo cake and water, until I was so full as to be unable to eat any more, when Pitchery allowing me a short time to recover myself, fetched a large bowl of the raw nardoo flour, mixed to a thin paste – a most insinuating article, and one that they appear to esteem a great delicacy. I was then invited to stop the night there, but this I declined, and proceeded on my way home.

Tuesday, June 4 Started for the blacks' camp, intending to test the practicability of living with them, and to see what I could learn as to their ways and manners.

Wednesday, June 5 Remained with the blacks. Light rain during the greater part of the night, and more or less throughout the day, in showers. Wind blowing in squalls from S.

Thursday, June 6 Returned to our own camp, found that

Mr. Burke and King had been well supplied with fish by the blacks. Made preparation for shifting our camp nearer to their's on the morrow.

Friday, June 7 Started in the afternoon for the blacks' camp with such things as we could take; found ourselves all very weak, in spite of the abundant supply of fish that we have lately had. I myself could scarcely get along, although carrying the lightest swag – only about thirty pounds. Found that the blacks had decamped, so determined on proceeding to-morrow up to the next camp, near the nardoo field.

Saturday, June 8 With the greatest fatigue and difficulty we reached the nardoo camp. No blacks, greatly to our disappointment. Took possession of their best mia mia, and rested for the remainder of the day.

Sunday, June 9 King and I proceeded to collect nardoo, leaving Mr. Burke at home.

Monday, June 10 Mr. Burke and King collecting nardoo; self at home, too weak to go out. Was fortunate enough to shoot a crow.

Tuesday, June 11 King out for nardoo. Mr. Burke up the creek to look for the blacks.

Wednesday, June 12 King out collecting nardoo. Mr. Burke and I at home, pounding and cleaning. I still feel myself, if anything, weaker in the legs, although the nardoo appears to be more thoroughly (?) digested.

Thursday, June 13 Last night the sky was pretty clear, and the air rather cold, but nearly calm. Mr. Burke and King out for nardoo. Self weaker than ever, scarcely able to go to the water hole for water.

Friday, June 14 Night alternately clear and cloudy, no wind, beautifully mild for the time of year; in the morning some heavy clouds on the horizon. King out for nardoo; brought in a good supply. Mr. Burke and I at home, pounding and cleaning seed. I feel weaker than ever, and both Mr. B. and King are beginning to feel very unsteady in the legs.

Saturday, June 15 Night clear, calm, and cold; morning very fine, with a light breath of air from N.E. King out for nardoo; brought in a fine supply. Mr. Burke and I pounding and cleaning. He finds himself getting very weak, and I am not a bit stronger. I have determined on beginning to chew tobacco and eat less nardoo, in hopes that it may induce some change in the system. I have never yet recovered from the effects of the constipation, and the passage of the stools is always exceedingly painful.

Sunday, June 16 Wind shifted to N., clouds moving from W. to E.;

thunder audible two or three times to the southward; sky becoming densely overcast, with an occasional shower about nine a.m. We finished up the remains of the Rajah for dinner yesterday. King was fortunate enough to shoot a crow this morning. The rain kept all hands in pounding and cleaning seed during the morning. The weather cleared up towards the middle of the day, and a brisk breeze sprang up in the south, lasting till near sunset, but rather irregular in its force. Distant thunder was audible to westward and southward frequently during the afternoon.

Monday, June 17 Night very boisterous and stormy. Northerly wind blowing in squalls, and heavy showers of rain, with thunder in the north and west. Heavy clouds moving rapidly from north to south; gradually clearing up during the morning, the wind continuing equally during the day from W. and N. W. King out in the afternoon for nardoo.

Tuesday, June 18 Exceedingly cold night. Sky clear, slight breeze, very chilly, and changeable; very heavy dew.

Wednesday, June 19 Night calm; sky during first part overcast most of which cleared away towards morning, leaving the air much colder, but the sky remained more or less hazy all night, and it was not nearly as cold as last night. About eight o'clock a strong southerly wind sprung up, which enabled King to blow the dust out of our nardoo seeds, but made me too weak to render him any assistance.

Thursday, June 20 Night and morning very cold, sky clear. I am completely reduced by the effects of the cold and starvation. King gone out for nardoo. Mr. Burke at home pounding seed; he finds himself getting very weak in the legs. King holds out by far the best; the food seems to agree with him pretty well. Finding the sun come out pretty warm towards noon, I took a sponging all over, but it seemed to do little good beyond the cleaning effects, for my weakness is so great that I could not do it with proper expedition. I cannot understand this nardoo at all; it certainly will not agree with me in any form. We are now reduced to it alone, and we manage to get from four to five pounds per day between us. The stools it causes are enormous, and seem greatly to exceed the quantity of bread consumed, and is very slightly altered in appearance from what it was when eaten.

Friday, June 21 Last night was cold and clear, winding up with a strong wind from N.E. in the morning. I feel much weaker than ever, and can scarcely crawl out of the mia-mia. Unless relief comes in some form or other, I cannot possibly last more than a fortnight. It is a great consolation, at least, in this position of ours, to know that we have done all we could, and that our deaths will rather be the result of the mismanagement of others than of any rash acts of our own. Had we come to grief elsewhere, we could only have blamed ourselves; but here we are, returned to Cooper's Creek, where we had every reason to look for provisions and clothing; and yet we have to die of starvation, in spite of the explicit instructions given by Mr. Burke, that the depôt party should await our return, and the strong recommendation to the committee that we should be followed up by a party from Menindie.

Saturday, June 22   Night cloudy and warm. Every appearance of rain. Thunder once or twice during the night. Clouds moving in an easterly direction. Lower atmosphere perfectly calm. There were a few drops of rain during the night, and in the morning, about nine a.m., there was every prospect of more rain until towards noon, when the sky cleared up for a time. Mr. Burke and King out for nardoo. The former returned much fatigued. I am so weak to-day as to be unable to get on my feet.

Sunday, June 23   All hands at home. I am so weak as to be incapable of crawling out of the mia-mia. King holds out well, but Mr. Burke finds himself weaker every day.

Monday, June 24   A fearful night. At about an hour before sunset, a southerly gale sprang up and continued throughout the greater portion of the night; the cold was intense, and it seemed as if one would be shrivelled up. Towards morning, it fortunately lulled a little, but a strong cold breeze continued till near sunset, after which it became perfectly calm. King went out for nardoo, in spite of the wind, and came in with a good load, but he himself terribly cut up. He says that he can no longer keep up the work, and as he and Mr. Burke are both getting rapidly weaker, we have but a slight chance of anything but starvation, unless we can get hold of some blacks.

Tuesday, June 23 (sic)   Night calm, clear, and intensely cold, especially towards morning. Near daybreak, King reported seeing a moon in the E., with a haze of light stretching up from it, he declared it to be quite as large as the moon, and not dim at the edges. I am so weak that any attempt to get a sight of it was out of the question; but I think it must have been Venus in the zodiacal light that he saw, with a corona around her. Mr. Burke and King remain at home cleaning and pounding seed. They are both getting weaker every day. The cold plays the deuce with us, from the small amount of clothing we have. My wardrobe consists of a wide-a-awake, a merino shirt, a regatta shirt without sleeves, the remains of a pair of flannel trousers, two pairs of socks in rags, and a waistcoat of which

I have managed to keep the pockets together. The others are no better off. Besides these we have between us for bedding, two small camel pads, some horsehair, two or three little bits of a rag, and pieces of oilcloth saved from the fire. The day turned out nice and warm.

Wednesday, June 24 (sic) Calm night; sky overcast with hazy clouds. An easterly breeze sprang up towards morning, making the air much colder. Mr. Burke and King are preparing to go up the creek in search of the blacks. They will leave me some nardoo, wood and water, with which I must do the best I can until they return. I think this is almost our only chance. I feel myself, if anything, rather better, but I cannot say stronger. The nardoo is beginning to agree better with me; but without some change I see little chance for any of us. They have both shown great hesitation and reluctance with regard to leaving me, and have repeatedly desired my candid opinion in the matter. I could only repeat, however, that I considered it our only chance, for I could not last long on the nardoo, even if a supply could be kept up.

Thursday, June 25 (sic) Cloudy, calm, and comparatively warm night, clouds almost stationary. In the morning a gentle breeze from east. Sky partially cleared up during the day, making it pleasantly warm and bright, it remained clear during the afternoon and evening, offering every prospect of a clear cold night.

Friday, June 26 (sic) Clear cold night, slight breeze from the E., day beautifully warm and pleasant. Mr. Burke suffers greatly from the cold, and is getting extremely weak; he and King start to-morrow up the creek, to look for the blacks – it is the only chance we have of being saved from starvation. I am weaker than ever although I have a good appetite, and relish the nardoo much, but it seems to give us no nutriment, and the birds here are so shy as not to be got at. Even if we got a good supply of fish, I doubt whether we could do much work on them and the nardoo alone. Nothing now but the greatest good luck can now save any of us; and as for myself, I may live four or five days if the weather continues warm. My pulse are at forty-eight, and very weak, and my legs and arms are nearly skin and bone. I can only look out, like Mr. Micawber, "for something to turn up;" but starvation on nardoo is by no means very unpleasant, but for the weakness one feels, and the utter inability to move oneself, for as far as appetite is concerned, it gives me the greatest satisfaction. Certainly, fat and sugar would be more to one's taste, in fact, those seem to me to be the great stand by for one in this extraordinary continent; not that I mean to depreciate the farinacious food, but the want of sugar and fat in all substances obtainable here is so great that they become almost valueless to us as articles of food, without the addition of something else.

(Signed)   W. J. WILLS.

TO SEE THE SEA

John McDouall Stuart
(1815–66)

Modest, dedicated, immensely tough and thoroughly congenial, Stuart was very much an explorer's explorer. With little support or fuss he began probing north from Adelaide in the late 1850s. In 1860 he was the first to reach the centre of the continent, thus completing the work of Sturt whom he had accompanied in 1844–5. Although Burke and Wills just beat him in the race to cross the continent, Stuart's 1862 route was much longer and more difficult; and he did actually reach the sea (down the Adelaide river in Arnhem Land). He was also to return alive.

*S*aturday, 19th July, Lily Marsh, Adelaide River Started at 9.10., course 20° east of north. At three miles crossed some stony rises and broad alluvial grassy valleys; at four miles met the river, had to go half a mile to the south-east to round it. Again changed to my first course; at seven miles and a half crossed a creek with water. The country to this is good, with occasionally a little ironstone and gravel, timber of stringy-bark, and a little low gum scrub. Having crossed this creek, we ascended a sandy table land with an open forest of stringy bark (good timber), palms, gums, other trees and bushes; it has been lately burnt, but the roots of the grass abound. This continued for about three miles. There is a small stony range of hills to the west, which at the end of the three miles dropped into a grassy plain of a beautiful black alluvial soil, covered with lines and groves of the cabbage palm trees, which give it a very picturesque appearance; its dip is towards the river; in two miles crossed it, and again ascended low table land of the very same description as the other. At fourteen miles struck another creek with water, and camped. The country gone over to-day, though not all of the very best description, has plains in it of the very finest kind – even

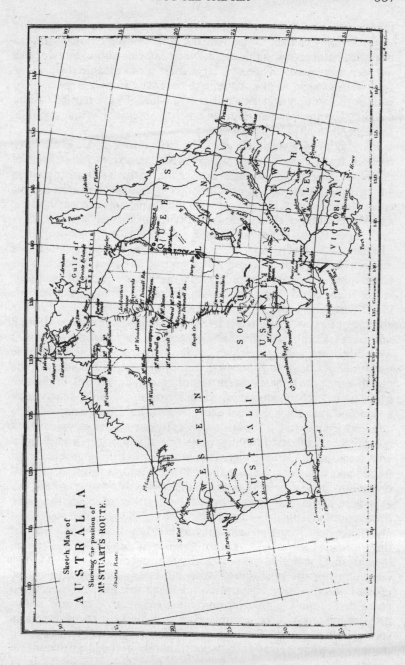

Sketch Map of
AUSTRALIA
Showing the position of
Mr STUART'S ROUTE.

Stuart's Route

the sandy table-land bears an abundant crop of grass. The trees are so thick that I can get no view of the surrounding country; the tall beautiful palm grows in this creek. Native smoke about, but we have not seen any natives. There are large masses of volcanic rock on the sides of this creek. At about a mile to the eastward is a large body of springs that supply water to this creek, which I have named "Anna Creek." Camped at ten minutes to three o'clock. Wind variable. Latitude, 12° 39′ 7″.

Sunday, 20th July, Anna Creek   The mosquitoes at this camp have been most annoying; scarcely one of us has been able to close his eyes in sleep during the whole night: I never found them so bad anywhere – night and day they are at us. The grass in, and on the banks of, this creek is six feet high; to the westward there are long reaches of water, and the creek very thickly timbered with melaleuca, gum, stringy-bark, and palms. Wind, south-east.

Monday, 21st July, Anna Creek and Springs   Again passed a miserable night with the mosquitoes. Started at eight o'clock; course, north-north-west. At three miles came upon another extensive fresh-water marsh, too boggy to cross. There is rising ground to the north-west and north; the river seems to run between. I can see clumps of bamboos and trees, by which I suppose it runs at about a mile to the north-north-west. The ground for the last three miles is of a sandy nature, and light-brown colour, with ironstone gravel on the surface, volcanic rock occasionally cropping out. The borders of the marsh are of the richest description of black alluvial soil, and when the grass has sprung after it has been burnt, it has the appearance of a rich and very thick crop of green wheat. I am now compelled to alter my course to 30° south of east, to get across a water creek coming into the marsh, running deep, broad and boggy, and so thick with trees, bushes, and strong vines interwoven throughout it, that it would take a day to cut a passage through. At three miles we crossed the stream, and proceeded again on the north-north-west course, but at a mile and a half were stopped by another creek of the same description. Changed to east, and at half a mile was able to cross it also, and again went on my original bearing. Continued on it for three miles, when we were again stopped by another running stream, but this one I was able to cross without going far out of my course. Proceeded on the north-north-west course, passing over elevated ground of the same description as the first three miles. At seventeen miles came upon a thick clump of trees, with beautiful palms growing amongst them; examined it and found it to have been a spring, but now dry. Proceeded on another mile, and was again stopped by what seemed to be a continuation of the large marsh; we now appeared to have got right into the middle of it. It was to be seen to the south-west, north-east, and south-east of us. Camped on a point of rising ground running into it. The timber on the rises between the creeks is stringy-bark, small gums, and in places a nasty scrub, very sharp, which tore a number of our saddle-bags: it is a very good thing the patches of it are not broad. The grass, where it has not been burned, is very thick and high – up to my shoulder when on horseback. About a mile from here, to the west, I can see what appears to be the water of the river, running through clumps of trees and bamboos, beyond which, in the distance, are courses of low rising ground, in places broken also with clumps of trees; the course of the river seems to be north-north-west. On the east side of the marsh is also rising ground; the marsh in that direction seems to run five or six miles before it meets the rising ground, and appears after that to come round to the north. Nights cool. Latitude, 12° 28′ 19″. Wind, south-east.

Tuesday, 22nd July, Fresh-water Marsh As the marsh seems to run so much to the east, and not knowing how much further I shall have to go to get across the numerous creeks that appear to come into it, I shall remain here to-day and endeavour to find a road through it to the river, and follow up the banks if I can. I have a deal of work to do to the plan, and our bags require mending. After collecting the horses, Thring tried to cross the marsh to the river, and succeeded in reaching its banks, finding firm ground all the way; the breadth of the river here being about a hundred yards, very deep, and running with some velocity, the water quite fresh. He having returned with this information, I sent him, King, and Frew, mounted on the strongest horses, to follow the banks of the river till noon, to see if there is any obstruction to prevent my travelling by its banks. In two hours they returned with the sad tidings that the banks were broken down by watercourses, deep, broad, and boggy; this is a great disappointment, for it will take me a day or two longer than I expected in reaching the sea-coast, in consequence of having to go a long way round to clear the marsh and creeks. The edge of the marsh was still of the same rich character, and covered with luxuriant grass. The rise we are camped on is also the same, with ironstone gravel on the surface; this seems to have been a favourite camping-place for a large number of natives. There is a great quantity of fish bones, mussel, and turtle shells, at a little distance from the camp, close to where there was some water. There are three poles fixed in the ground, forming an equilateral triangle, on the top of which was a frame-work of the same figure, over which were placed bars of wood; its height from the ground eight feet. This has apparently been used by them for smoke-drying a dead blackfellow. We have seen no natives since leaving the Roper, although their smoke is still round about us. On and about the marsh are large flocks of geese, ibis, and numerous other aquatic birds; they are so wild that they will not allow us to come within shot of them. Mr. Kekwick has been successful in shooting a goose; it has a peculiar-shaped head, having a large horny lump on the top resembling a topknot, and only a very small web at the root of his toes. The river opposite this, about a yard from the bank, is nine feet deep. Wind variable. Night cool.

Wednesday, 23rd July, Fresh-water Marsh   Started at 7.40, course 22° east of south, one mile, to round the marsh; thence one mile south-east; thence east for six miles, when we struck a large creek, deep and long reaches; thence three quarters of a mile south before we could cross it. This I have named "Thring Creek," in token of my approbation of his conduct throughout the journey; thence east, one mile and a half; thence north for nine miles, when I again struck the large marsh. Thring Creek has been running nearly parallel with the north course until it empties itself into the marsh. The country gone over to-day, after leaving the side of the marsh, as well as the banks of the creek, and also some small plains, is of the same rich description of soil covered with grass; the other parts are slightly elevated, the soil light with a little sand on the surface of a brown colour; timber, mixture of stringybark and gums, with many others; also, a low thick scrub, which has lately been burnt in many places, the few patches that have escaped abounding in grass. I have come twelve miles to the eastward to try to round the marsh, but have not been able to do so; the plains that were seen from the river by those who came up it in boats is the marsh; it is covered with luxuriant grass, which gives it the appearance of extensive grassy plains. I have camped at where the Thring spreads itself over a portion of the marsh. There is rising ground to the north-west, on the opposite side, which I suppose to be a continuation of the elevated ground I passed before crossing the creek, and the same that I saw bearing north from the last camp. I suppose it runs in towards the river. Wind, south. Latitude, 13° 22' 30".

Thursday, 24th July, Thring Creek, Entering the Marsh   Started at 7.40, course north. I have taken this course in order to make the sea-coast, which I suppose to be distant about eight miles and a half, as soon as possible; by this I hope to avoid the marsh. I shall travel along the beach to the north of the Adelaide. I did not inform any of the party, except Thring and Auld, that I was so near to the sea, as I wished to give them a surprise on reaching it. Proceeded through a light soil, slightly elevated, with a little ironstone on the surface, the volcanic rock cropping out occasionally; also some flats of black alluvial soil. The timber much smaller and more like scrub, showing that we are nearing the sea. At eight miles and a half came upon a broad valley of black alluvial soil, covered with long grass; from this I can hear the wash of the sea. On the other side of the valley, which is rather more than a quarter of a mile wide, is growing a line of thick heavy bushes, very dense, showing that to be the boundary of the beach. Crossed the valley, and entered the scrub, which was a complete network of vines. Stopped the horses to clear a way, whilst I advanced a few yards on to the beach, and was gratified and delighted to behold the water of the Indian Ocean in Van Diemen Gulf, before the party with the horses knew anything of its proximity. Thring, who rode in advance of me, called out "The Sea!" which so took them all by surprise, and they were so astonished, that he had to repeat the call before they fully understood what was meant. Then they immediately gave three long and hearty cheers. The beach is covered with a soft blue mud. It being ebb tide, I could see some distance; found it would be impossible for me to take the horses along it; I therefore kept them where I had halted them, and allowed half the party to come on to the beach and gratify themselves by a sight of the sea, while the other half remained to watch the horses until their return. I dipped my feet, and washed my face and hands in the sea, as I promised the late Governor Sir Richard McDonnell I would do if I reached it. The mud has nearly covered all the shells; we got a few, however. I could see no sea-weed. There is a point of land some distance off, bearing 70°. After all the party had had some time on the beach, at which they were much pleased and gratified, they collected a few shells; I returned to the valley, where I had my initials (J. M. D. S.) cut on a large tree, as I did not intend to put up my flag until I arrived at the mouth of the Adelaide. Proceeded, on a course of 302°, along the valley; at one mile and a half, coming upon a small creek, with running water, and the valley being covered with beautiful green grass, I have camped to give the horses the benefit of it. Thus have I, through the instrumentality of Divine Providence, been led to accomplish the great object of the expedition, and take the whole party safely as witnesses to the fact, and through one of the finest countries man could wish to behold – good to the coast, and with a stream of running water within half a mile of the sea. From Newcastle Water to the sea-beach, the main body of the horses have been only one night without water, and then got it within the next day. If this country is settled, it will be one of the finest Colonies under the Crown, suitable for the growth of any and everything – what a splendid country for producing cotton! Judging from the number of the pathways from the water to the beach, across the valley, the natives must be very numerous; we have not seen any, although we have passed many of their recent tracks and encampments. The cabbage and fan palm-trees have been very plentiful during to-day's journey down to this valley. This creek I named "Charles Creek," after the eldest son of John Chambers, Esq.: it is one by which some large bodies of springs discharge their surplus water into Van Diemen Gulf; its banks are of soft mud, and boggy. Wind, south. Latitude, 12° 13' 30".

Friday, 25th July, Charles Creek, Van Diemen Gulf I have sent Thring to the south-west to see if he can get round the marsh. If it is firm ground I shall endeavour to make the mouth of the river by that way. After a long search he has returned and informs me that it is impracticable, being too boggy for the horses. As the great object of the expedition is now attained, and the mouth of the river already well known, I do not think it advisable to waste the strength of my horses in forcing them through, neither do I see what object I should gain by doing so; they have still a very long and fatiguing journey in recrossing the continent to Adelaide, and my health is so bad that I am unable to bear a long day's ride. I shall, therefore, cross this creek and see if I can get along by the sea-beach or close to it. Started and had great difficulty in getting the horses over, although we cut a large quantity of grass, putting it on the banks and on logs of wood which were put into it. We had a number bogged, and I was nearly losing one of my best horses, and was obliged to have him pulled out with ropes; after the loss of some time we succeeded in getting them all over safely. Proceeded on a west-north-west course over a firm ground of black alluvial soil. At two miles came upon an open part of the beach, went on to it, and again found the mud quite impassable for horses; in the last mile we have had some rather soft ground. Stopped the party, as this travelling is too much for the horses, and, taking Thring with me, rode two miles to see if the ground was any firmer in places; found it very soft where the salt water had covered it, in others not so bad. Judging from the number of shells banked up in different places, the sea must occasionally come over this. I saw at once that this would not do for the weak state in which my horses were, and I therefore returned to where I had left the party, resolving to recross the continent to the City of Adelaide. I now had an open place cleared, and selecting one of the tallest trees, stripped it of its lower branches, and on its highest branch fixed my flag, the Union Jack, with my name sewn in the

Planting the flag on the shores of the Indian Ocean. From *The Journals of John McDouall Stuart during the years 1858, 1859, 1860, 1861, and 1862*, London, 1864.

centre of it. When this was completed, the party gave three cheers, and Mr. Kekwick then addressed me, congratulating me on having completed this great and important undertaking, to which I replied. Mr. Waterhouse also spoke a few words on the same subject, and concluded with three cheers for the Queen and three for the Prince of Wales. At one foot south from the foot of the tree is buried, about eight inches below the ground, an air-tight tin case, in which is a paper with the following notice:-

South Australian Great Northern Exploring Expedition.

The exploring party, under the command of John McDouall Stuart, arrived at this spot on the 25th day of July, 1862, having crossed the entire Continent of Australia from the Southern to the Indian Ocean, passing through the centre. They left the City of Adelaide on the 26th day of October, 1861, and the most northern station of the Colony on 21st day of January, 1862. To commemorate this happy event, they have raised this flag bearing his name. All well. God save the Queen!

[Here follow the signatures of myself and party.]

As this bay has not been named, I have taken this opportunity of naming it "Chambers Bay," in honour of Miss Chambers, who kindly presented me with the flag which I have planted this day, and I hope this may be the first sign of the dawn of approaching civilization. Exactly this day nine months the party left North Adelaide. Before leaving, between the hours of eleven and twelve o'clock, they had lunch at Mr. Chambers' house; John Bentham Neals, Esq., being present, proposed success to me, and wished I might plant the flag on the north-west coast. At the same hour of the day, nine months after, the flag was raised on the shores of Chambers Bay, Van Diemen Gulf. On the bark of the tree on which the flag is placed is cut – DIG ONE FOOT – S. We then bade farewell to the Indian Ocean, and returned to Charles Creek, where we had again great difficulty in getting the horses across, but it was at last accomplished without accident. We have passed numerous and recent tracks of natives to-day; they are still burning the country at some distance from the coast. Wind, south-east. Latitude, 12° 14′ 50″.

FIRST CROSSING OF AMERICA

Alexander Mackenzie
(c.1755–1820)

"Endowed by nature with an acquisitive mind and an enterprising spirit", Mackenzie, a Scot engaged in the Canadian fur trade, resolved, as he put it "to test the practicability of penetrating across the continent of America". In 1789 he followed a river (the Mackenzie) to the sea; but it turned out to be the Arctic Ocean. He tried again in 1793 and duly reached the Pacific at Queen Charlotte Sound in what is now British Columbia. Although this was the first recorded overland crossing of the continent, Mackenzie was not given to trumpeting his achievement. In his narrative it passes without celebration and very nearly without mention.

July 1793 At one in the afternoon we embarked, with our small baggage, in two canoes, accompanied by seven of the natives. The stream was rapid, and ran upwards of six miles an hour. We proceeded at a very great rate for about two hours and an half, when we were informed that we must land, as the village was only at a short distance. I had imagined that the Canadians who accompanied me were the most expert canoe-men in the world, but they are very inferior to these people, as they themselves acknowledged, in conducting those vessels.

Some of the Indians ran before us, to announce our approach, when we took our bundles and followed. We had walked along a well-beaten path, through a kind of coppice, when we were informed of the arrival of our couriers at the houses, by the loud and confused talking of the inhabitants. As we approached the edge of the wood, and were almost in sight of the houses, the Indians who were before me made signs for me to take the lead, and that they would follow. The noise and confusion of the natives now seemed to increase, and when we came in sight of

Alexander Mackenzie. From George Bryce *The Makers of Canada: Mackenzie, Selkirk, Simpson*, London, 1905.

the village, we saw them running from house to house, some armed with bows and arrows, others with spears, and many with axes, as if in a state of great alarm. This very unpleasant and unexpected circumstance, I attributed to our sudden arrival, and the very short notice of it which had been given them. At all events, I had but one line of conduct to pursue, which was to walk resolutely up to them, without manifesting any signs of apprehension at their hostile appearance. This resolution produced the desired effect, for as we approached the houses, the greater part of the people laid down their weapons, and came forward to meet us. I was, however, soon obliged to stop from the number of them that surrounded me. I shook hands, as usual with such as were the nearest to me, when an elderly man broke through the crowd, and took me in his arms; another then came, who turned him away without the least ceremony, and paid me the same compliment. The latter was followed by a young man, whom I understood to be his son. These embraces, which at first rather surprised me, I soon found to be marks of regard and friendship. The crowd pressed with so much violence and contention to get a view of us, that we could not move in any direction. An opening was at length made to allow a person to approach me, whom the old man made me understand was another of his sons. I instantly stepped forward to meet him, and presented my hand, whereupon he broke the string of a very handsome robe of sea-otter skin, which he had on, and covered me with it. This was as flattering a reception as I could possibly receive, especially as I considered him to be the eldest son of the chief. Indeed it appeared to me that we had been detained here for the purpose of giving him time to bring the robe with which he had presented me.

The chief now made signs for us to follow him, and he conducted us through a narrow coppice, for several hundred yards, till we came to an house built on the ground, which was of larger dimensions, and formed of better materials than any I had hitherto seen; it was his residence. We were no sooner arrived there, than he directed mats to be spread before it, on which we were told to take our seats, when the men of the village, who came to indulge their curiosity, were ordered to keep behind us. In our front other mats were placed, where the chief and his counsellors took their feats. In the intervening space, mats, which were very clean, and of a much neater workmanship than those on which we sat were also spread, and a small roasted salmon placed before each of us. When we had satisfied ourselves with the fish, one of the people who came with us from the last village approached, with a kind of ladle in one hand, containing oil, and in the other something that resembled the inner rind of the cocoa-nut, but of a lighter colour; this he dipped in the oil, and, having eat it, indicated by his gestures how palatable he thought it. He then presented me with a small piece of it, which I chose to taste in its dry state, though the oil was free from any unpleasant smell. A square cake of this was next produced, when a man took it to the water near the house, and having thoroughly soaked it, he returned, and, after he had pulled it to pieces like oakum, put it into a well-made trough, about three feet long, nine inches wide, and five deep; he then plentifully sprinkled it with salmon oil, and manifested by his own example that we were to eat of it. I just tasted it, and found the oil perfectly sweet, without which the other ingredient would have been very insipid. The chief partook of it with great avidity, after it had received an additional quantity of oil. This dish is considered by those people as a great delicacy; and on examination, I discovered it to consist of the inner rind of the hemlock tree, taken off early in summer, and put into a frame, which shapes it into cakes of fifteen inches long, ten broad, and half an inch thick; and in this form I should suppose it may be preserved for a great length of time. This discovery satisfied me respecting the many hemlock trees which I had observed stripped of their bark.

In this situation we remained for upwards of three hours, and not one of the curious natives left us during all that time, except a party of ten or twelve of them, whom the chief ordered to go and catch fish, which they did in great abundance, with dipping nets, at the foot of the weir.

At length we were relieved from the gazing crowd, and got a lodge erected, and covered in for our reception during the night. I now presented the young chief with a blanket, in return for the robe with which he had favoured me, and several other articles, that appeared to be very gratifying to him. I also presented some to his father, and amongst them was a pair of scissors, whose use I explained to him, for clipping his beard, which was of great length; and to that purpose he immediately applied them. My distribution of similar articles was also extended to others, who had been attentive to us. The communication, however, between us was awkward and inconvenient, for it was carried on entirely by signs, as there was not a person with me who was qualified for the office of an interpreter.

We were all of us very desirous to get some fresh salmon, that we might dress them in our own way, but could not by any means obtain that gratification, though there were thousands of that fish strung on cords, which were fastened to stakes in the river. They were even averse to our approaching the spot where they clean and prepare them for their own eating. They had, indeed, taken our kettle from us, lest we should employ it in getting water from the river; and they assigned as the reason for this precaution, that the salmon dislike the smell of iron. At the same time they supplied us with wooden boxes, which were capable of holding any fluid. Two of the men that went to fish, in a canoe capable of containing ten people, returned with a full lading of salmon, that weighed from six to forty pounds, though the far greater part of them were under twenty. They immediately strung the whole of them, as I have already mentioned, in the river.

When we were surrounded by the natives on our arrival, I counted sixty-five men, and several of them may be supposed to have been absent; I cannot, therefore, calculate the inhabitants of this village at less than two hundred souls.

The people who accompanied us hither, from the other village, had given the chief a very particular account of everything they knew concerning us: I was, therefore, requested to produce my astronomical instruments; nor could I have any objection to afford them this satisfaction, as they would necessarily add to our importance in their opinion.

Friday 19 Soon after I had retired to rest last night, the chief paid me a visit to insist on my going to his bed-companion, and taking my place himself; but, notwithstanding his repeated entreaties, I resisted this offering of his hospitality.

At an early hour this morning I was again visited by the chief, in company with his son. The former complained of a pain in his breast; to relieve his suffering, I gave him a few drops of Turlington's Balsam on a piece of sugar; and I was rather surprised to see him take it without the least hesitation. When he had taken my medicine, he requested me to follow him, and conducted me to a shed, where several people were assembled round a sick man, who was another of his sons. They immediately uncovered him, and shewed me a violent ulcer in the small of his back, in the foulest state that can be imagined. One of his knees was also afflicted in the same manner. This unhappy man was reduced to a skeleton, and, from his appearance, was drawing near to an end of his pains. They requested that I would touch him, and his father was very urgent with me to administer medicine; but he was in such a dangerous state, that I thought it prudent to yield no further to the importunities than to give the sick person a few drops of Turlington's balsam in some water. I therefore left them, but was soon called back by the loud lamentations of the women, and was rather apprehensive that some inconvenience might result from my compliance with the chief's request. On my return I found the native physicians busy in practising their skill and art on the patient. They blew on him, and then whistled; at times they pressed their extended fingers, with all their strength on his stomach; they also put their forefingers doubled into his mouth, and spouted water from their own with great violence into his face. To support these operations the wretched sufferer was held up in a sitting posture; and when they were concluded, he was laid down and covered with a new robe made of the skin of a lynx. I had observed that his belly and breast were covered with scars, and I understood that they were caused by a custom prevalent among them, of applying pieces of lighted touchwood to their flesh, in order to relieve pain or demonstrate their courage. He was now placed on a broad plank, and carried by six men into the woods; where I was invited to accompany them. I could not conjecture what would be the end of this ceremony, particularly as I saw one man carry fire, another an axe, and a third dry wood. I was, indeed, disposed to suspect that, as it was their custom to burn the dead, they intended to relieve the poor man from his pain, and perform the last sad duty of surviving affection. When they had advanced a short distance into the wood, they laid him upon a clear spot, and kindled a fire against his back, when the physician began to scarify the ulcer with a very blunt instrument, the cruel pain of which operation the patient bore with incredible resolution. The scene afflicted me and I left it.

On my return to our lodge, I observed before the door of the chief's residence, four heaps of salmon, each of which consisted of between three and four hundred fish. Sixteen women were employed in cleaning and preparing them. They first separate the head from the body, the former of which they boil; they then cut the latter down the back on each side of the bone, leaving one third of the fish adhering to it, and afterwards take out the guts. The bone is roasted for immediate use, and the other parts are dressed in the same manner, but with more attention, for future provision. While they are before the fire, troughs are placed under them to receive the oil. The roes are also carefully preserved, and form a favourite article of their food.

After I had observed these culinary preparations, I paid a visit to the chief, who presented me with a roasted salmon; he then opened one of his chests, and took out of it a garment of blue cloth, decorated with brass buttons; and another of a flowered cotton, which I supposed were Spanish; it had been trimmed with leather fringe, after the fashion of their own cloaks. Copper and brass are in great estimation among them, and of the former they have great plenty: they point their arrows and spears with it, and work it up into personal ornaments; such as collars, ear-rings, and bracelets, which they wear on their wrists, arms, and legs. I presume they find it the most advantageous article of trade with the more inland tribes. They also abound in iron. I saw some of their twisted collars of that metal which weighed upwards of twelve pounds. It is generally beat into bars of fourteen inches in length, and one inch three quarters wide. The brass is in thin squares: their copper is in larger pieces, and some of it appeared to be old stills cut up. They have various trinkets; but their iron is manufactured only into poniards and daggers. Some of the former have very neat handles, with a silver coin of a quarter or eighth of a dollar fixed on the end of them. The blades of the latter are from ten to twelve inches in length, and about four inches broad at the top, from which they gradually lessen into a point.

When I produced my instruments to take an altitude, I was desired not to make use of them. I could not then discover the cause of this request, but I experienced the good effect of the apprehension which they occasioned, as it was very effectual in hastening my departure. I had applied several times to the chief to prepare canoes and people to take me and my party to the sea, but very little attention had been paid to my application till noon; when I was informed that a canoe was properly equipped for my voyage, and that the young chief would accompany me. I now discovered that they had entertained no personal fear of the instruments, but were apprehensive that the operation of them might frighten the salmon from that part of the river. The observation taken in this village gave me 52.25.52 North latitude.

In compliance with the chief's request I desired my people to take their bundles, and lay them down on the bank of the river. In the mean time I went to take the dimensions of his large canoe, in which, it was signified to me, that about ten winters ago he went a considerable distance towards the mid-day sun, with forty of his people, when he saw two large vessels full of such men as myself, by whom he was kindly received: they were, he said, the first white people he had seen. They were probably the ships commanded by Captain Cook. This canoe was built of cedar, forty-five feet long, four feet wide, and three feet and a half in depth. It was painted black and decorated with white figures of fish of different kinds. The gunwale, fore and aft, was inlaid with the teeth of the sea-otter.

When I returned to the river, the natives who were to accompany us, and my people, were already in the canoe. The latter, however, informed me, that one of our axes was missing. I immediately applied to the chief, and requested its restoration; but he would not understand me till I sat myself down on a stone, with my arms in a state of preparation, and made it appear to him that I should not depart till the stolen article was restored. The village was immediately in a state of uproar, and some danger was apprehended from the confusion that prevailed in it. The axe, however, which had been hidden under the chief's canoe, was soon returned. Though this internment was not, in itself, of sufficient value to justify a dispute with these people, I apprehended that the suffering them to keep it, after we had declared its loss, might have occasioned the loss of everything we carried with us, and of our lives also. My people were dissatisfied with me at the moment; but I thought myself right then, and, I think now, that the circumstances in which we were involved, justified the measure which I adopted.

At one in the afternoon we renewed our voyage in a large canoe with four of the natives. The navigation of the river now became more difficult, from the numerous channels into which it was divided, without any sensible diminution in the velocity of its current. We soon reached another house of the common size, where we were well received.

The inhabitants of the last house accompanied us in a large canoe. They recommended us to leave ours here, as the next village was but at a small distance from us, and the water more rapid than that which we had passed. They informed us also, that we were approaching a cascade. I directed them to shoot it, and proceeded myself to the foot thereof, where I re-imbarked, and we went on with great velocity, till we came to a fall, where we left our canoe, and carried our luggage along a road through a wood for some hundred yards, when we came to a village, consisting of six very large houses, erected on pallisades, rising twenty-five feet from the ground, which differed in no one circumstance from those already described, but the height of their elevation. They contained only four men and their families. The rest of the inhabitants were with us and in the small houses which we passed higher up the river. These people do not seem to enjoy the abundance of their neighbours, as the men who returned from fishing had no more than five salmon; they refused to sell one of them, but gave me one roasted of a very indifferent kind. In the houses there were several chests or boxes containing different articles that belonged to the people whom we had lately passed. If I were to judge by the heaps of filth beneath these buildings, they must have been erected at a more distant period than any which we had passed. From these houses I could perceive the termination of the river, and its discharge into a narrow arm of the sea.

As it was now half past six in the evening and the weather cloudy, I determined to remain here for the night, and for that purpose we possessed ourselves of one of the unoccupied houses. The remains of our last meal, which we brought with us, served for our supper, as we could not procure a single fish from the natives. The course of the river is about West, and the distance from the great village upwards of thirty-six miles. There we had lost our dog, a circumstance of no small regret to me.

Saturday 20   We rose at a very early hour this morning, when I proposed to the Indians to run down our canoe, or procure another at this place. To both these proposals they turned a deaf ear, as they imagined that I should be satisfied with having come in sight of the sea. Two of them peremptorily refused to proceed; but the other two having consented to continue with us, we obtained a larger canoe than our former one, and though it was in a leaky state we were glad to possess it.

At about eight we got out of the river, which discharges itself by various channels into an arm of the sea. The tide was out, and had left a large space covered with sea-weed. The surrounding hills were involved in fog. The wind was at West, which was ahead of us, and very strong; the bay appearing to be from one to three miles in breadth. As we advanced along the land we saw a great number of sea-otters. We fired several shots at them, but without any success from the rapidity with which they plunge under the water. We also saw many small porpoises or divers. The white-headed eagle, which is common in the interior parts; some small gulls, a dark bird which is inferior in size to the gull, and a few small ducks, were all the birds which presented themselves to our view.

At two in the afternoon the swell was so high, and the wind, which was against us, so boisterous, that we could not proceed with our leaky vessel, we therefore landed in a small cove on the right side of the bay. Opposite to us appeared another small bay, in the mouth of which is an island, and where, according to the information of the Indians, a river discharges itself that abounds in salmon.

When it was dark the young chief returned to us, bearing a large porcupine on his back. He first cut the animal open, and having disencumbered it of the entrails, threw them into the sea; he then singed its skin, and boiled it in separate pieces, as our kettle was not sufficiently capacious to contain the whole: nor did he go to rest, till, with the assistance of two of my people who happened to be awake, every morsel of it was devoured.

I had flattered myself with the hope of getting a distance of the moon and stars, but the cloudy weather continually disappointed me, and I began to fear that I should fail in this important object; particularly as our provisions were at a very low ebb, and we had, as yet, no reason to expect any assistance from the natives. Our stock was, at this time, reduced to twenty pounds weight of pemmican, fifteen pounds of rice, and six pounds of flour, among ten half-starved men, in a leaky vessel, and on a barbarous coast. Our course from the river was about West-South-West, distance ten miles.

As I could not ascertain the distance from the open sea, and being uncertain whether we were in a bay or among inlets and channels of islands, I confined my search to a proper place for taking an observation. We steered, therefore, along the land on the left, West-North-West a mile and an half; then North-West one fourth of a mile, and North three miles to an island, the land continuing to run North-North-West, then along the island, South-South-West half a mile, West a mile and an half, and from thence directly across to the land on the left, (where I had an altitude,) South-West three miles.* From this position a channel, of which the island we left appeared to make a cheek, bears North by East.

Under the land we met with three canoes, with fifteen men in them, and laden with their moveables, as if proceeding to a new situation, or returning to a former one. They manifested no kind of mistrust or fear of us, but entered into conversation with our young man, as I supposed, to obtain some information concerning us. It did not appear that they were the same people as those we had lately seen, as they spoke the language of our young chief, with a different accent. They then examined everything we had in our canoe, with an air of indifference and disdain. One of them in particular made me understand, with an air of insolence, that a large canoe had lately been in this bay, with people in her like me, and that one of them, whom he called *Macubah*, had fired on him and his friends, and that *Benfins* had struck him on the back, with the flat part of his sword. He also mentioned another name, the articulation of which I could not determine. At the same time he illustrated these circumstances by the assistance of my gun and sword; and I do not doubt but he well deserved the treatment which he described. He also produced several European articles, which could not have been long in his possession. From his conduct and appearance, I wished very much to be rid of him, and flattered myself that he would prosecute his voyage, which appeared to be in an opposite direction to our course. However, when I prepared to part from them, they turned their canoes about, and persuaded my young man to leave me, which I could not prevent.

We coasted along the land at about West-South-West for six miles, and met a canoe with two boys in it, who were dispatched to summon the people on that part of the coast to join them. The troublesome fellow now forced himself into my canoe, and pointed out a narrow channel on the opposite shore, that led to his village, and requested us to steer towards it, which I accordingly ordered. His importunities now became very irksome, and he wanted to see everything we had, particularly my instruments, concerning which he must have received information from my young man. He asked for my hat, my handkerchief, and, in short, everything that he saw about me. At the same time he frequently repeated the unpleasant

* The Cape or Point Menzies of Vancouver.

intelligence that he had been shot at by people of my colour. At some distance from the land a channel opened to us, at South-West by West, and pointing that way, he made me understand that *Macubah* came there with his large canoe. When we were in mid-channel, I perceived some sheds, or the remains of old buildings, on the shore; and as, from that circumstance, I thought it probable that some Europeans might have been there, I directed my steersman to make for that spot. The traverse is upwards of three miles North-West.

We landed, and found the ruins of a village, in a situation calculated for defence. We were soon followed by ten canoes, each of which contained from three to six men. They informed us that we were expected at the village, where we should see many of them. From their general deportment I was very apprehensive that some hostile design was meditated against us, and for the first time I acknowledged my apprehensions to my people. I accordingly desired them to be very much upon their guard, and to be prepared if any violence was offered to defend themselves to the last.

We had no sooner landed, than we took possession of a rock, where there was not space for more than twice our number, and which admitted of our defending ourselves with advantage, in case we should be attacked. The people in the three first canoes, were the most troublesome, but, after doing their utmost to irritate us, they went away. They were, however, no sooner gone, than an hat, an handkerchief, and several other articles, were missing. The rest of our visitors continued their pressing invitations to accompany them to their village, but finding our resolution to decline them was not to be shaken, they, about sun-set relieved us from all further importunities, by their departure . . .

The natives having left us, we made a fire to warm ourselves, and as for supper, there was but little of that, for our whole daily allowance did not amount to what was sufficient for a single meal. The weather was clear throughout the day, which was succeeded by a fine moon-light night. I directed the people to keep watch by two in turn, and laid myself down in my cloak.

Monday 22 This morning the weather was clear and pleasant; nor had anything occurred to disturb us throughout the night. One solitary Indian, indeed, came to us with about half a pound of boiled seal's flesh, and the head of a small salmon, for which he asked an handkerchief, but afterwards accepted a few beads. As this man came alone, I concluded that no general plan had been formed among the natives to annoy us, but this opinion did not altogether calm the apprehensions of my people.

Soon after eight in the morning, I took five altitudes for time, and the mean of them was 36° 48′ at six in the afternoon, 58. 34. time, by the watch, which makes the achrometer show apparent time $1^h 21^m 44'$.

Two canoes now arrived from the same quarter as the rest, with several men, and our young Indian along with them.

These Indians were of a different tribe from those which I had already seen, as our guide did not understand their language. I now mixed up some vermillon in melted grease, and inscribed, in large characters, on the South-East face of the rock on which we had slept last night, this brief memorial – "Alexander Mackenzie, from Canada, by land, the twenty-second of July, one thousand seven hundred and ninety-three."

MEETING THE SHOSHONEE

Meriwether Lewis
(1774–1809)

As Thomas Jefferson's personal secretary, Lewis was chosen to lead the US government's 1804–5 expedition to explore (and to establish US interests) from the Mississipi to the Pacific. Travelling up the Missouri river to the continental divide in Montana, Lewis left the main party under his colleague William Clark, and scouted ahead. With everything now dependent on securing the goodwill of the formidable Shoshonee, he showed admirable caution; but the issue was eventually decided by a fortuitous reunion between the Indian wife of one of his men and her long-lost brethren.

S unday, August 11 Captain Lewis again proceeded on early, but had the mortification to find that the track which he followed yesterday soon disappeared. He determined, therefore, to go on to the narrow gate or pass of the river which he had seen from the camp, in hopes of being able to recover the Indian path. For this purpose he waded across the river, which was now about twelve yards wide and barred in several places by the dams of the beaver, and then went straight forward to the pass, sending one man along the river to his left and another on the right, with orders to search for the road, and if they found it to let him know by raising a hat on the muzzle of their guns. In this order they went along for about five miles, when Captain Lewis perceived, with the greatest delight, a man on horseback at the distance of two miles coming down the plain towards them. On examining him with the glass, Captain Lewis saw that he was of a different nation from any Indians we had hitherto met; he was armed with a bow and a quiver of arrows; mounted on an elegant horse without a saddle, and a small string attached to the under jaw answered as a bridle. Convinced that he was a Shoshonee, and knowing how much of our success depended

Meriwether Lewis. Courtesy of the Mary Evans Picture Library.

on the friendly offices of that nation, Captain Lewis was full of anxiety to approach without alarming him, and endeavour to convince him that he was a white man. He therefore proceeded on towards the Indian at his usual pace. When they were within a mile of each other the Indian suddenly stopt; Captain Lewis immediately followed his example, took his blanket from his knapsack, and holding it with both hands at the two corners, threw it above his head and unfolded it as he brought it to the ground as if in the act of spreading it. This signal, which originates in the practice of spreading a robe or a skin, as a seat for guests to whom they wish to show a distinguished kindness, is the universal sign of friendship among the Indians on the Missouri and the Rocky mountains. As usual, Captain Lewis repeated this signal three times; still the Indian kept his position, and looked with an air of suspicion on Drewyer and Shields who were now advancing on each side. Captain Lewis was afraid to make any signal for them to halt, lest he should increase the suspicions of the Indian, who began to be uneasy, and they were too distant to hear his voice. He therefore took from his pack some beads, a looking-glass, and a few trinkets, which he had brought for the purpose, and leaving his gun, advanced unarmed towards the Indian. He remained in the same position till Captain Lewis came within two hundred yards of him, when he turned his horse, and began to move off slowly. Captain Lewis then called out to him, in as loud a voice as he could, repeating the words, tabba bone! which in the Shoshonee language means white man. The Indian suffered him to advance within one hundred paces, then suddenly turned his horse, and giving him the whip, leaped across the creek and disappeared in an instant among the willow bushes; with him vanished all the hopes which the sight of him had inspired of a friendly introduction to his countrymen. Though sadly disappointed Captain Lewis determined to make the incident of some use, and therefore calling the men to him they all set off after the track of the horse, which they hoped might lead them to the camp of the Indian who had fled, or if he had given the alarm to any small party, their track might conduct them to the body of the nation. They now fixed a small flag of the United States on a pole, which was carried by one of the men as a signal of their friendly intentions, should the Indians observe them as they were advancing. The route lay across an island formed by a nearly equal division of the creek in the bottom; after reaching the open grounds on the right side of the creek, the track turned towards some high hills about three miles distant. Presuming that the Indian camp might be among these hills, and that by advancing hastily he might be seen and alarm them, Captain Lewis sought an elevated situation near the creek, had a fire made of willow brush, and took breakfast. At the same time he prepared a small assortment of beads, trinkets, awls, some paint, and a looking-glass, and placed them on a pole near the fire, in order that if the Indians returned they might discover that the party were white men and friends. Whilst making these preparations a very heavy shower of rain and hail came on, and wet them to the skin; in about twenty minutes it was over, and Captain Lewis then renewed his pursuit, but as the rain had made the grass which the horse had trodden down rise again, his track could with difficulty be distinguished. As they went along they passed several places where the Indians seemed to have been digging roots to-day, and saw the fresh track of eight or ten horses, but they had been wandering about in so confused a manner that he could not discern any particular path, and at last, after pursuing it about four miles along the valley to the left under the foot of the hills, he lost the track of the fugitive Indian. Near the head of the valley they had passed a large bog covered with moss and tall grass, among which were several springs of pure cold water; they now turned a little to the left along the foot of the high hills, and reached a small creek, where they encamped for the night, having made about twenty miles, though not more than ten in a direct line from their camp of last evening.

Monday, 12th This morning, as soon as it was light, Captain Lewis sent Drewyer to reconnoitre if possible the route of the Indians; in about an hour and a half he returned, after following the tracks of the horse which we had lost yesterday to the mountains, where they ascended and were no longer visible. Captain Lewis now decided on making the circuit along the foot of the mountains which formed the cove, expecting by that means to find a road across them, and accordingly sent Drewyer on one side and Shields on the other. In this way they crossed four small rivulets near each other, on which were some bowers or conical lodges of willow brush, which seemed to have been made recently. From the manner in which the ground in the neighbourhood was torn up, the Indians appeared to have been gathering roots; but Captain Lewis could not discover what particular plant they were searching for, nor could he find any fresh track, till at the distance of four miles from his camp he met a large plain Indian road which came into the cove from the northeast, and wound along the foot of the mountains to the southwest, approaching obliquely the main stream he had left yesterday. Down this road he now went towards the southwest; at the distance of five miles it crossed a large run or creek, which is a principal branch of the main stream into which it falls, just above the high cliffs or gates observed yesterday, and which they now saw below them; here they halted and breakfasted on the last of the deer, keeping a small piece of pork in reserve against accident; they then continued through the low bottom along the main stream, near the foot of the mountains on their right. For the first five miles the valley continues towards the southwest from two to three miles in width; then the main stream, which had received two small branches from the left in the valley, turns abruptly to the west through a narrow bottom between the mountains. The road was still plain, and as it led them directly on towards the mountain the stream gradually became smaller, till after going two miles it had so greatly diminished in width that one of the men in a fit of enthusiasm, with one foot on each side of the river, thanked God that he had lived to bestride the Missouri. As they went along their hopes of soon seeing the waters of the Columbia arose almost to painful anxiety; when, after four miles from the last abrupt turn of the river, they reached a small gap formed by the high mountains which recede on each side, leaving room for the Indian road. From the foot of one of the lowest of these mountains, which rises with a gentle ascent of about half a mile, issues the remotest water of the Missouri. They had now reached the hidden sources of that river, which had never yet been seen by civilized man; and as they quenched their thirst at the chaste and icy fountain, – as they sat down by the brink of that little rivulet, which yielded its distant and modest tribute to the parent ocean, – they felt themselves rewarded for all their labours and all their difficulties. They left reluctantly this interesting spot, and pursuing the Indian road through the interval of the hills, arrived at the top of a ridge, from which they saw high mountains partially covered with snow still to the west of them. The ridge on which they stood formed the dividing line between the waters of the Atlantic and Pacific oceans. They followed a descent much steeper than that on the eastern side, and at the distance of three-quarters of a mile reached a handsome bold creek of cold clear water running to the westward. They stopped to taste for the first time the waters of the Columbia; and after a few minutes followed the road across steep hills and low hollows, till they reached a spring on the side of a mountain; here they found a sufficient quantity of dry willow brush for fuel, and therefore halted for the night; and having killed nothing in the course of the day, supped on their last piece of pork, and trusted to fortune for some other food to mix

with a little flour and parched meal, which was all that now
remained of their provisions.

Tuesday, 13th Very early in the morning Captain Lewis resumed
the Indian road, which led him in a western direction, through an
open broken country; on the left was a deep valley at the foot of a
high range of mountains running from southeast to northwest, with
their sides better clad with timber than the hills to which we have
been for some time accustomed, and their tops covered in part with
snow.

They proceeded along a waving plain parallel to this valley for
about four miles, when they discovered two women, a man, and
some dogs, on an eminence at the distance of a mile before them.
The strangers first viewed them apparently with much attention for
a few minutes, and then two of them sat down as if to await
Captain Lewis's arrival. He went on till he reached within about
half a mile, then ordered his party to stop, put down his knapsack
and rifle, and unfurling the flag advanced alone towards the
Indians. The females soon retreated behind the hill, but the man
remained till Captain Lewis came within a hundred yards from
him, when he, too, went off, though Captain Lewis called out tabba
bone! loud enough to be heard distinctly. He hastened to the top of
the hill, but they had all disappeared. The dogs, however, were less
shy, and came close to him; he therefore thought of tying a
handkerchief with some beads round their necks, and then let
them loose to convince the fugitives of his friendly disposition,
but they would not suffer him to take hold of them, and soon left
him. He now made a signal to the men, who joined him, and then
all followed the track of the Indians, which led along a continuation of the same road they had been already travelling. It was dusty,
and seemed to have been much used lately both by foot passengers
and horsemen. They had not gone along it more than a mile when
on a sudden they saw three female Indians, from whom they had
been concealed by the deep ravines which intersected the road, till
they were now within thirty paces of each other; one of them, a
young woman, immediately took to flight; the other two, an elderly
woman and a little girl, seeing we were too near for them to escape,
sat on the ground, and holding down their heads seemed as if
reconciled to the death which they supposed awaited them. Captain
Lewis instantly put down his rifle, and advancing towards them,
took the woman by the hand, raised her up, and repeated the words
tabba bone! at the same time stripping up his shirt sleeve to prove
that he was a white man, for his hands and face had become by
constant exposure quite as dark as their own. She appeared

immediately relieved from her alarm, and Drewyer and Shields now coming up, Captain Lewis gave them some beads, a few awls, pewter mirrors, and a little paint, and told Drewyer to request the woman to recall her companion who had escaped to some distance, and by alarming the Indians might cause them to attack him without any time for explanation. She did as she was desired, and the young woman returned, almost out of breath; Captain Lewis gave her an equal portion of trinkets, and painted the tawny cheeks of all three of them with vermilion, a ceremony which among the Shoshonees is emblematic of peace. After they had become composed, he informed them by signs of his wish to go to their camp in order to see their chiefs and warriors; they readily obeyed, and conducted the party along the same road down the river. In this way they marched two miles, when they met a troop of nearly sixty warriors, mounted on excellent horses, riding at full speed towards them. As they advanced Captain Lewis put down his gun, and went with the flag about fifty paces in advance. The chief, who, with two men, were riding in front of the main body, spoke to the women, who now explained that the party was composed of white men, and showed exultingly the presents they had received. The three men immediately leaped from their horses, came up to Captain Lewis and embraced him with great cordiality, putting their left arm over his right shoulder and clasping his back; applying at the same time their left cheek to his, and frequently vociferating ah hi e! ah hi e! "I am much pleased, I am much rejoiced." The whole body of warriors now came forward, and our men received the caresses, and no small share of the grease and paint, of their new friends. After this fraternal embrace, of which the motive was much more agreeable than the manner, Captain Lewis lighted a pipe and offered it to the Indians, who had now seated themselves in a circle around the party. But before they would receive this mark of friendship they pulled off their moccasins, a custom, as we afterwards learnt, which indicates the sacred sincerity of their professions when they smoke with a stranger, and which imprecates on themselves the misery of going barefoot forever if they are faithless to their words, a penalty by no means light to those who rove over the thorny plains of their country. After smoking a few pipes, some trifling presents were distributed amongst them, with which they seemed very much pleased, particularly with the blue beads and the vermilion. Captain Lewis then informed the chief that the object of his visit was friendly, and should be explained as soon as he reached their camp; but that in the meantime, as the sun was oppressive and no water near, he wished to go there as soon as possible. They now put on their moccasins, and their chief, whose name was Cameahwait, made a short speech to the warriors. Captain Lewis then gave him the flag, which he informed him was among white men the emblem of peace and now that he had received it was to be in future the bond of union between them. The chief then moved on, our party followed him, and the rest of the warriors, in a squadron, brought up the rear. After marching a mile they were halted by the chief, who made a second harangue, on which six or eight young men rode forward to their camp, and no further regularity was observed in the order of march. At the distance of four miles from where they had first met they reached the Indian camp, which was in a handsome level meadow on the bank of the river. Here they were introduced into an old leathern lodge which the young men who had been sent from the party had fitted up for their reception. After being seated on green boughs and antelope skins, one of the warriors pulled up the grass in the centre of the lodge so as to form a vacant circle of two feet diameter, in which he kindled a fire. The chief then produced his pipe and tobacco, the warriors all pulled off their moccasins, and our party was requested to take off their own. This being done, the chief lighted his pipe at the fire within the magic circle, and then retreating from it began a speech several minutes long, at the end of which he pointed the stem towards the four cardinal points of the heavens, beginning with the east and concluding with the north.

The ceremony of smoking being concluded, Captain Lewis explained to the chief the purposes of his visit, and as by this time all the women and children of the camp had gathered around the lodge to indulge in a view of the first white man they had ever seen, he distributed among them the remainder of the small articles he had brought with him. It was now late in the afternoon, and our party had tasted no food since the night before. On apprising the chief of this circumstance, he said that he had nothing but berries to eat, and presented some cakes made of serviceberry and chokecherries which had been dried in the sun. On these Captain Lewis made a hearty meal, and then walked down towards the river. He found it a rapid clear stream, forty yards wide and three feet deep; the banks were low and abrupt, like those of the upper part of the Missouri, and the bed formed of loose stones and gravel. Its course, as far as he could observe it, was a little to the north of west, and was bounded on each side by a range of high mountains, of which those on the east are the lowest and most distant from the river.

Captain Lewis returned from the river to his lodge, and on his way an Indian invited him into his bower and gave him a small morsel of boiled antelope and a piece of fresh salmon roasted. This was the first salmon he had seen, and perfectly satisfied him that he was now on the waters of the Pacific. On reaching this lodge he resumed his conversation with the chief, after which he was entertained with a dance by the Indians. It now proved, as our party had feared, that the men whom they had first met this morning had returned to the camp and spread the alarm that their enemies, the Minnetarees of fort de Prairie, whom they call Pahkees, were advancing on them. The warriors instantly armed themselves and were coming down in expectation of an attack, when they were agreeably surprised by meeting our party. The greater part of them were armed with bows and arrows and shields, but a few had small fusils, such as are furnished by the north-west company traders, and which they had obtained from the Indians on the Yellowstone, with whom they are now at peace. They had reason to dread the approach of the Pahkees, who had attacked them in the course of this spring and totally defeated them. On this occasion twenty of their warriors were either killed or made prisoners, and they lost their whole camp except the leathern lodge which they had fitted up for us, and were now obliged to live in huts of a conical figure made with willow brush. The music and dancing, which was in no respect different from those of the Missouri Indians, continued nearly all night; but Captain Lewis retired to rest about twelve o'clock, when the fatigues of the day enabled him to sleep, though he was awaked several times by the yells of the dancers.

Wednesday, 14th In order to give time for the boats to reach the forks of Jefferson river, Captain Lewis determined to remain here and obtain all the information he could collect with regard to the country. Having nothing to eat but a little flour and parched meal, with the berries of the Indians, he sent out Drewyer and Shields, who borrowed horses from the natives, to hunt for a few hours. About the same time the young warriors set out for the same purpose. There are but few elk or black-tailed deer in this neighbourhood, and as the common red deer secrete themselves in the bushes when alarmed, they are soon safe from the arrows, which are but feeble weapons against any animals which the huntsmen cannot previously run down with their horses. Soon after they returned, our two huntsmen came in with no better success. Captain Lewis therefore made a little paste with the flour, and the addition of some berries formed a very palatable repast. Having now secured the good will of Cameahwait, Captain Lewis informed him of his wish that he would speak to the warriors and endeavour to engage them to accompany him to the forks of Jefferson river, where by this time another chief with a large party of white men were waiting his return; that it would be necessary to take about thirty horses to transport the merchandize; that they should be well rewarded for their trouble; and that when all the party should have reached the Shoshonee camp they would remain some time among them, and trade for horses, as well as concert plans for furnishing them in future with regular supplies of merchandize. He readily consented to do so, and after collecting the tribe together he made a long harangue, and in about an hour and a half returned, and told Captain Lewis that they would be ready to accompany him in the morning.

Thursday, 15th   Captain Lewis rose early, and having eaten nothing yesterday except his scanty meal of flour and berries, felt the inconveniences of extreme hunger. On inquiry he found that his whole stock of provisions consisted of two pounds of flour. This he ordered to be divided into two equal parts, and one-half of it boiled with the berries into a sort of pudding; and after presenting a large share to the chief, he and his three men breakfasted on the remainder. Cameahwait was delighted at this new dish; he took a little of the flour in his hand, tasted and examined it very narrowly, asking if it was made of roots; Captain Lewis explained the process of preparing it, and he said it was the best thing he had eaten for a long time.

This being finished, Captain Lewis now endeavoured to hasten the departure of the Indians, who still hesitated and seemed reluctant to move, although the chief addressed them twice for the purpose of urging them; on inquiring the reason, Cameahwait told him that some foolish person had suggested that he was in league with their enemies the Pahkees, and had come only to draw them into ambuscade, but that he himself did not believe it. Captain Lewis felt uneasy at this insinuation; he knew the suspicious temper of the Indians, accustomed from their infancy to regard every stranger as an enemy, and saw that if this suggestion were not instantly checked it might hazard the total failure of the enterprise. Assuming therefore a serious air, he told the chief that he was sorry to find they placed so little confidence in him, but that he pardoned their suspicions because they were ignorant of the character of white men, among whom it was disgraceful to lie or entrap even an enemy by falsehood; that if they continued to think thus meanly of us they might be assured no white men would ever come to supply them with arms and merchandize; that there was at this moment a party of white men waiting to trade with them at the forks of the river; and that if the greater part of the tribe entertained any suspicion, he hoped there were still among them some who were men, who would go and see with their own eyes the truth of what he said, and who, even if there was any danger, were not afraid to die. To doubt the courage of an Indian is to touch the tenderest string of his mind, and the surest way to rouse him to any dangerous achievement. Cameahwait instantly replied that he was not afraid to die, and mounting his horse, for the third time harangued the warriors; he told them that he was resolved to go if he went alone, or if he were sure of perishing; that he hoped there were among those who heard him some who were not afraid to die, and who would prove it by mounting their horses and following him. This harangue produced an effect on six or eight only of the warriors, who now joined their chief. With these Captain Lewis smoked a pipe, and then, fearful of some change in their capricious temper, set out immediately. It was about twelve o'clock when his small party left the camp, attended by Cameahwait and the eight warriors; their departure seemed to spread a gloom over the village; those who would not venture to go were sullen and melancholy, and the women were crying and imploring the Great Spirit to protect their warriors as if they were going to certain destruction. Yet such is the wavering inconstancy of these savages that Captain Lewis's party had not gone far when they were joined by ten or twelve more warriors, and before reaching the creek which they had passed on the morning of the 13th, all the men of the nation and a number of women had overtaken them, and had changed from the surly ill temper in which they were two hours ago to the greatest cheerfulness and gayety. When they arrived at the spring on the side of the mountain where the party had encamped on the 12th, the chief insisted on halting to let the horses graze; to which Captain Lewis assented, and smoked with them. They are excessively fond of the pipe, in which, however, they are not able to indulge much, as they do not cultivate tobacco themselves, and their rugged country affords them but few articles to exchange for it. Here they remained for about an hour, and on setting out, by engaging to pay four of the party, Captain Lewis obtained permission for himself and each of his men to ride behind an Indian; but he soon found riding without stirrups more tiresome than walking, and therefore dismounted, making the Indian carry his pack. About sunset they reached the upper part of the level valley in the cove through which he had passed, and which they now called Shoshonee cove. The grass being burned on the north side of the river they crossed over to the south, and encamped

about four miles above the narrow pass between the hills noticed as
they traversed the cove before. The river was here about six yards
wide, and frequently dammed up by the beaver. Drewyer had been
sent forward to hunt, but he returned in the evening unsuccessful,
and their only supper therefore was the remaining pound of flour,
stirred in a little boiling water, and then divided between the four
white men and two of the Indians.

16th Friday   As neither our party nor the Indians had anything to
eat, Captain Lewis sent two of his hunters ahead this morning to
procure some provision; at the same time he requested Cameahwait
to prevent his young men from going out, lest by their noise they
might alarm the game. But this measure immediately revived their
suspicions; it now began to be believed that these men were sent
forward in order to apprise the enemy of their coming, and as
Captain Lewis was fearful of exciting any further uneasiness, he
made no objection on seeing a small party of Indians go on each
side of the valley under pretence of hunting, but in reality to watch
the movements of our two men; even this precaution, however, did
not quiet the alarms of the Indians, a considerable part of whom
returned home, leaving only twenty-eight men and three women.
After the hunters had been gone about an hour, Captain Lewis
again mounted with one of the Indians behind him, and the whole
party set out; but just as they passed through the narrows they saw
one of the spies coming back at full speed across the plain; the chief
stopped and seemed uneasy, the whole band were moved with
fresh suspicions, and Captain Lewis himself was much disconcerted, lest by some unfortunate accident some of their enemies
might have perhaps straggled that way. The young Indian had
scarcely breath to say a few words as he came up, when the whole
troop dashed forward as fast as their horses could carry them; and
Captain Lewis, astonished at this movement, was borne along for
nearly a mile before he learnt with great satisfaction that it was all
caused by the spy's having come to announce that one of the white
men had killed a deer. Relieved from his anxiety, he now found the
jolting very uncomfortable; for the Indian behind him, being afraid
of not getting his share of the feast, had lashed the horse at every
step since they set off; he therefore reined him in and ordered the
Indian to stop beating him. The fellow had no idea of losing time in
disputing the point, and jumping off the horse ran for a mile at full
speed. Captain Lewis slackened his pace, and followed at a
sufficient distance to observe them. When they reached the place
where Drewyer had thrown out the intestines, they all dismounted
in confusion and ran tumbling over each other like famished dogs;

each tore away whatever part he could, and instantly began to eat it; some had the liver, some the kidneys, in short no part on which we are accustomed to look with disgust escaped them; one of them who had seized about nine feet of the entrails was chewing at one end, while with his hand he was diligently clearing his way by discharging the contents at the other; yet though suffering with hunger they did not attempt, as they might have done, to take by force the whole deer, but contented themselves with what had been thrown away by the hunter. Captain Lewis now had the deer skinned, and after reserving a quarter of it gave the rest of the animal to the chief to be divided among the Indians, who immediately devoured nearly the whole of it without cooking. They now went forward towards the creek where there was some brushwood to make a fire, and found Drewyer, who had killed a second deer; the same struggle for the entrails was renewed here, and on giving nearly the whole deer to the Indians, they devoured it, even to the soft part of the hoofs. A fire being made, Captain Lewis had his breakfast, during which Drewyer brought in a third deer; this, too, after reserving one quarter, was given to the Indians, who now seemed completely satisfied and in good humour. At this place they remained about two hours to let the horses graze, and then continued their journey, and towards evening reached the lower part of the cove, having on the way shot an antelope, the greater part of which was given to the Indians. As they were now approaching the place where they had been told by Captain Lewis they would see the white men, the chief insisted on halting; they therefore all dismounted, and Cameahwait, with great ceremony, and as if for ornament, put tippets or skins round the necks of our party, similar to those worn by themselves. As this was obviously intended to disguise the white men, Captain Lewis, in order to inspire them with more confidence, put his cocked hat and feather on the head of the chief, and as his own over-shirt was in the Indian form, and his skin browned by the sun, he could not have been distinguished from an Indian; the men followed his example, and the change seemed to be very agreeable to the Indians.

In order to guard, however, against any disappointment, Captain Lewis again explained the possibility of our not having reached the forks in consequence of the difficulty of the navigation, so that if they should not find us at that spot they might be assured of our not being far below. They again all mounted their horses and rode on rapidly, making one of the Indians carry their flag, so that we might recognise them as they approached us; but to the mortification and disappointment of both parties on coming within two miles of the forks no canoes were to be seen. Uneasy lest at this moment he should be abandoned, and all his hopes of obtaining aid from the Indians be destroyed, Captain Lewis gave the chief his gun, telling him that if the enemies of his nation were in the bushes he might defend himself with it; that for his own part he was not afraid to die, and that the chief might shoot him as soon as they discovered themselves betrayed. The other three men at the same time gave their guns to the Indians, who now seemed more easy, but still wavered in their resolutions. As they went on towards the point, Captain Lewis, perceiving how critical his situation had become, resolved to attempt a stratagem which his present difficulty seemed completely to justify. Recollecting the notes he had left at the point for us, he sent Drewyer for them with an Indian who witnessed his taking them from the pole. When they were brought, Captain Lewis told Cameahwait that on leaving his brother chief at the place where the river issues from the mountains, it was agreed that the boats should not be brought higher than the next forks we should meet; but that if the rapid water prevented the boats from coming on as fast as they expected, his brother chief was to send a note to the first forks above him to let him know where the boats were; that this note had been left this morning at the forks, and mentioned that the canoes were just below the mountains, and coming slowly up in consequence of the current. Captain Lewis added that he would stay at the forks for his brother chief, but would send a man down the river, and that if Cameahwait doubted what he said, one of their young men would go with him whilst he and the other two remained at the forks. This story satisfied the chief and the greater part of the Indians, but a few did not conceal their suspicions, observing that we told different stories, and complaining that the chief exposed them to danger by a mistaken confidence. Captain Lewis now wrote by the light of some willow brush a note to Captain Clark, which he gave to Drewyer, with an order to use all possible expedition in ascending the river, and engaged an Indian to accompany him by a promise of a knife and some beads. At bedtime the chief and five others slept round the fire of Captain Lewis, and the rest hid themselves in different parts of the willow brush to avoid the enemy, who they feared would attack them in the night. Captain Lewis endeavoured to assume a cheerfulness he did not feel, to prevent the despondency of the savages; after conversing gayly with them he retired to his musquitoe bier, by the side of which the chief now placed himself; he lay down, yet slept but little, being in fact scarcely less uneasy than his Indian companions. He was apprehensive that, finding the ascent of the river impracticable, Captain Clark might have stopped below the Rattlesnake bluff, and the messenger would not meet him. The consequence of disappointing the Indians at this moment would most probably be, that they would retire and secrete themselves in the mountains, so as to prevent our having an opportunity of recovering their confidence; they would also spread a panic through all the neighbouring Indians, and cut us off from the supply of horses so useful and almost so essential to our success.

Saturday, August 17 Captain Lewis rose very early and despatched Drewyer and the Indian down the river in quest of the boats. Shields was sent out at the same time to hunt, while M'Neal prepared a breakfast out of the remainder of the meat. Drewyer had been gone about two hours, and the Indians were all anxiously waiting for some news, when an Indian who had straggled a short distance down the river returned with a report that he had seen the white men, who were only a short distance below, and were coming on. The Indians were all transported with joy, and the chief in the warmth of his satisfaction renewed his embrace to Captain Lewis, who was quite as much delighted as the Indians themselves. The report proved most agreeably true. On setting out at seven o'clock, Captain Clark, with Chaboneau and his wife, walked on shore; but they had not gone more than a mile before Captain Clark saw Sacajawea, who was with her husband one hundred yards ahead, begin to dance and show every mark of the most extravagant joy, turning round him and pointing to several Indians, whom he now saw advancing on horseback, sucking her fingers at the same time to indicate that they were of her native tribe. As they advanced Captain Clark discovered among them Drewyer dressed like an Indian, from whom he learnt the situation of the party. While the boats were performing the circuit he went towards the forks with the Indians, who, as they went along, sang aloud with the greatest appearance of delight. We soon drew near to the camp, and just as we approached it a woman made her way through the crowd towards Sacajawea, and recognising each other, they embraced with the most tender affection. The meeting of these two young women had in it something peculiarly touching, not only in the ardent manner in which their feelings were expressed, but from the real interest of their situation. They had been companions in childhood; in the war with the Minnetarees they had both been taken prisoners in the same battle, they had shared and softened the rigours of their captivity, till one of them had escaped from the Minnetarees, with scarce a hope of ever seeing her friend relieved from the hands of her enemies. While Sacajawea was renewing among the women the friendships of former days, Captain Clark went on, and was received by Captain Lewis and the chief, who, after the first embraces and salutations were over, conducted him to a sort of circular tent or shade of willows. Here he was seated on a white robe, and the chief immediately tied in his hair six small shells resembling pearls, an ornament highly valued by these people, who procured them in the course of trade from the seacoast. The moccasins of the whole party were then taken off, and after much ceremony the smoking began. After this the conference was to be opened, and glad of an opportunity of being able to converse more intelligibly, Sacajawea was sent for; she came into the tent, sat down, and was beginning to interpret, when in the person of Cameahwait she recognised her brother; she instantly jumped up and ran and embraced him, throwing over him her blanket and weeping profusely; the chief was himself moved, though not in the same degree. After some conversation between them she resumed her seat, and attempted to interpret for us, but her new situation seemed to overpower her, and she was frequently interrupted by her tears. After the council was finished, the unfortunate woman learnt that all her family were dead except two brothers, one of whom was absent, and a son of her eldest sister, a small boy, who was immediately adopted by her. The canoes arriving soon after, we formed a camp in a meadow on the left side, a little below the forks, took out our baggage, and by means of our sails and willow poles formed a canopy for our Indian visitors. About four o'clock the chiefs and warriors were collected, and after the customary ceremony of taking off the moccasins and smoking a pipe, we explained to them in a long harangue the purposes of our visit, making themselves one conspicuous object of the good wishes of our government, on whose strength as well as its friendly disposition we expatiated. We told them of their dependance on the will of our government for all future supplies of whatever was necessary either for their comfort or defence; that as we were sent to discover the best route by which merchandize could be conveyed to them, and no trade would be begun before our return, it was mutually advantageous that we should proceed with as little delay as possible; that we were under the necessity of requesting them to furnish us with horses to transport our baggage across the mountains, and a guide to show us the route, but that they should be amply remunerated for their horses, as well as for every other service they should render us. In the meantime our first wish was, that they should immediately collect as many horses as were necessary to transport our baggage to their village, where, at our leisure, we would trade with them for as many horses as they could spare.

The speech made a favourable impression; the chief in reply thanked us for our expressions of friendship towards himself and his nation, and declared their willingness to render us every service.

EATING DIRT IN VENEZUELA

Alexander von Humboldt
(1769–1859)

Geographer, geologist, naturalist, anthropologist, physician and philosopher, Baron von Humboldt brought to exploration a greater range of enquiry than any contemporary. Also an indomitable traveller, particularly in the Orinoco/Amazon basin (1799–1804), he often invited danger but always in the cause of scientific observation. The interest of his narratives therefore lies primarily in the author's insatiable curiosity and in the erudition that allowed him to generalize from his observations. A classic example is his ever deadpan disquisition on earth-eating. It occurs in the middle of a hair-raising account of descending the Orinoco in Venezuela.

This spot displayed one of the most extraordinary scenes of nature, that we had contemplated on the banks of the Orinoco. The river rolled its waters turbulently over our heads. It seemed like the sea dashing against reefs of rocks; but at the entrance of the cavern we could remain dry beneath a large sheet of water that precipitated itself in an arch from above the barrier. In other cavities, deeper, but less spacious, the rock was pierced by the effect of successive filtrations. We saw columns of water, eight or nine inches broad, descending from the top of the vault, and finding an issue by clefts, that seemed to communicate at great distances with each other.

The cascades of Europe, forming only one fall, or several falls close to each other, can never produce such variety in the shifting landscape. This variety is peculiar to rapids, to a succession of small cataracts several miles in length, to rivers that force their way across rocky dikes and accumulated blocks of granite. We had the opportunity of viewing this extraordinary sight longer than we wished. Our boat was to coast the eastern bank of a narrow island, and to take us in again after a long circuit. We passed an hour and a half in vain expectation of it. Night approached, and with it a tremendous storm. It rained with violence. We began to fear that our frail bark had been wrecked against the rocks, and that the Indians, conformably to their habitual indifference for the evils of others, had returned tranquilly to the mission. There were only three of us: we were completely wet, and uneasy respecting the fate of our boat: it appeared far from agreeable to pass, without sleep, a long night of the torrid zone, amid the noise of the Raudales. M. Bonpland proposed to leave me in the island with Don Nicolas Soto, and to swim across the branches of the river, that are separated by the granitic dikes. He hoped to reach the forest, and seek assistance at Atures from Father Zea. We dissuaded him with difficulty from undertaking this hazardous enterprise. He knew little of the labyrinth of small channels, into which the Orinoco is divided. Most of them have strong whirlpools, and what passed before our eyes, while we were deliberating on our situation, proved sufficiently, that the natives had deceived us respecting the absence of crocodiles in the cataracts. The little monkeys which we had carried along with us for months, were deposited on the point of our island. Wet by the rains, and sensible of the least lowering of the temperature, these delicate animals sent forth plaintive cries, and attracted to the spot two crocodiles, the size and leaden colour of which denoted their great age. Their unexpected appearance made us reflect on the danger we had incurred by bathing, at our first passing by the mission of Atures, in the middle of the Raudal. After long waiting, the Indians at length arrived at the close of day. The natural coffer-dam, by which they had endeavoured to descend, in order to make the circuit of the island, had become impassable, owing to the shallowness of the water. The pilot sought long for a more accessible passage in this labyrinth of rocks and islands. Happily our canoe was not damaged, and in less than half an hour our instruments, provision, and animals, were embarked.

We pursued our course during a part of the night, to pitch our tent again in the island of Panumana. We recognized with pleasure the spots where we had botanized when going up the Orinoco. We examined once more on the beach of Guachaco that small formation of sandstone, which reposes directly on granite. Its position is the same as that of the sandstone which Burckhardt observed at the entrance of Nubia, superimposed on the granite of Syene. We passed, without visiting it, the new mission of San Borga, where (as we learned with regret a few days after) the little colony of Guahibos had fled *al monte*, from the chimerical fear that we should carry them off, to sell them as *poitos*, or slaves. After having passed the rapids of Tabaje, and the Raudal of Cariven, near the mouth of the great Rio Meta, we arrived without accident at Carichana. The missionary received us with that kind hospitality which he extended to us on our first passage. The sky was unfavourable for astronomical observations; we had obtained some new ones in the two Great Cataracts; but thence, as far as the mouth of the Apure, we were obliged to renounce the attempt. M. Bonpland had the satisfaction at Carichana of dissecting a manati more than nine feet long. It was a female, and the flesh appeared to us not unsavoury. I have spoken in another place of the manner of catching this herbivorous cetacea. The Piraoas, some families of whom inhabit the mission of Carichana, detest this animal to such a degree, that they hid themselves, to avoid being obliged to touch it, whilst it was being conveyed to our hut. They said, that the people of their tribe die infallibly, when they eat of it. This prejudice is the more singular, as the neighbours of the Piraoas, the Guamos and the Ottomacs, are very fond of the flesh of the manati. The flesh of the crocodile is also an object of horror to some tribes, and of predilection to others.

Our stay at Carichana was very useful in recruiting our strength after our fatigues. M. Bonpland bore with him the germs of a cruel malady; he needed repose; but as the delta of the tributary streams included between the Horeda and Paruasi is covered with a rich vegetation, he made long herbalizations, and was wet through several times in a day. We found, fortunately, in the house of the missionary, the most attentive care; we were supplied with bread made of maize flour, and even with milk. The cows yield milk plentifully enough in the lower regions of the torrid zone, wherever good pasturage is found. I call attention to this fact, because local circumstances have spread through the Indian during Archipelago the prejudice of considering hot climates as repugnant to the secretion of milk. We may conceive the indifference of the inhabitants of the New World for a milk diet, the country having been originally destitute of animals capable of furnishing it; but how can we avoid being astonished at this indifference in the immense Chinese population, living in great part beyond the tropics, and in the same latitude with the nomad and pastoral tribes of central Asia? If the Chinese have ever been a pastoral people, how have they lost the tastes and habits so intimately connected with that state, which precedes agricultural institutions? These questions are interesting with respect both to the history of the nations of oriental Asia, and to the ancient communications that are supposed to have existed between that part of the world and the north of Mexico.

We went down the Orinoco in two days, from Carichana to the mission of Uruana, after having again passed the celebrated strait of Baraguan. We stopped several times to determine the velocity of the river, and its temperature at the surface, which was 27.4°. The velocity was found to be two feet in a second (sixty-two toises in 3'6"), in places where the bed of the Orinoco was more than twelve thousand feet broad, and from ten to twelve fathoms deep. The slope of the river is in fact extremely gentle from the Great Cataracts to Angostura; and, if a barometric measurement were wanting, the difference of height might be determined by approximation, by measuring from time to time the velocity of the stream, and the extent of the section in breadth and depth. We had some observations of the stars at Uruana. I found the latitude of the mission to be 7°8'; but the results from different stars left a doubt of more than 1'. The stratum of mosquitos, which hovered over the ground, was so thick that I could not succeed in rectifying properly the artificial horizon. I tormented myself in vain; and regretted that I was not provided with a mercurial horizon.

The situation of the mission of Uruana is extremely picturesque. The little Indian village stands at the foot of a lofty granitic mountain. Rocks everywhere appear in the form of pillars above the forest, rising higher than the tops of the tallest trees. The aspect of the Orinoco is nowhere more majestic, than when viewed from the hut of the missionary, Fray Ramon Bueno. It is more than two thousand six hundred toises broad, and it runs without any winding, like a vast canal, straight toward the east. Two long and narrow islands (*Isla de Uruana* and *Isla vieja de la Manteca*) contribute to give extent to the bed of the river; the two banks are parallel, and we cannot call it divided into different branches. The mission is inhabited by the Ottomacs, tribe in the rudest state, and presenting one of the most extraordinary physiological phenomena. They eat earth; that is, they swallow every day, over several months, very considerable quantities, to appease hunger, and this practice does not appear to have any injurious effect on their health. Though we could stay only one day at Urana, this short space of time sufficed to make us acquainted with the preparation of the *poya*, or balls of earth. I also found some traces of this vitiated appetite among the Guamos; and between the confluence of the Meta and the Apure, where everybody speaks of dirt-eating as of a thing anciently known. I shall here confine myself to an account of what we ourselves saw or heard from the missionary, who had been doomed to live for twelve years among the savage and turbulent tribe of the Ottomacs.

The inhabitants of Uruana belong to those nations of the savannahs called wandering Indians (Indios andantes), who, more difficult to civilize than the nations of the forest (Indios del monte), have a decided aversion to cultivate the land, and live almost exclusively by hunting and fishing. They are men of very robust constitution; but ill-looking, savage, vindictive, and passionately fond of fermented liquors. They are omnivorous *animals* in the highest degree; and therefore the other Indians, who consider them as barbarians, have a common saying, "nothing is so loathsome but that an Ottomac will eat it." While the waters of the Orinoco and its tributary streams are low, the Ottomacs subsist on fish and turtles. The former they kill with surprising dexterity, by shooting them with an arrow when they appear at the surface of the water. When the rivers swell fishing almost entirely ceases. It is then very difficult to procure fish, which often fails the poor missionaries, on fast-days as well as flesh-days, though all the young Indians are under the obligation of "fishing for the convent." During the period of these inundations, which last two or three months, the Ottomacs swallow a prodigious quantity of earth. We found heaps of earth-balls in their huts, piled up in pyramids three or four feet high. These balls were five or six inches in diameter. The earth which the Ottomacs eat, is a very fine and unctuous clay, of a yellowish grey colour; and, when being slightly baked at the fire, the hardened crust has a tint inclining to red, owing to the oxide of iron which is mingled with it. We brought away some of this earth, which we took from the winter-provision of the Indians; and it is a mistake to suppose that it is steatitic, and that it contains magnesia. Vauquelin did not discover any traces of that substance in it: but he found that it contained more silex than alumina, and three or four per cent of lime.

The Ottomacs do not eat every kind of clay indifferently; they choose the alluvial beds or strata, which contain the most unctuous earth, and the smoothest to the touch. I inquired of the missionary whether the moistened clay were made to undergo that peculiar decomposition which is indicated by a disengagement of carbonic acid and sulphuretted hydrogen, and which is designated in every language by the term of *putrefaction*; but he assured us, that the natives neither cause the clay to *rot*, nor do they mingle it with flour of maize, oil of turtle's eggs, or fat of the crocodile. We ourselves examined, both at the Orinoco and after our return to Paris, the balls of earth which we brought away with us, and found no trace of the mixture of any organic substance, whether oily or farinaceous. The savage regards every thing as nourishing that appeases hunger: when, therefore, you inquire of an Ottomac on what he subsists during the two months when the river is at its highest flood he shows you his balls of clayey earth. This he calls his principal food at the period when he can seldom procure a lizard, a root of fern, or a dead fish swimming at the surface of the water. If necessity force the Indians to eat earth during two months (and from three quarters to five quarters of a pound in twenty-four hours), he eats it from choice during the rest of the year. Every day in the season of drought, when fishing is most abundant, he scrapes his balls of *poya*, and mingles a little clay with his other aliment. It is most surprising that the Ottomacs do not become lean by swallowing such quantities of earth: they are, on the contrary, extremely robust. The missionary Fray Ramon Bueno asserts, that he never remarked any alteration in the health of the natives at the period of the great risings of the Orinoco.

The Ottomacs during some months eat daily three-quarters of a pound of clay slightly hardened by fire, but which they moisten before swallowing it. It has not been possible to verify hitherto with precision how much nutritious vegetable or animal matter they take in a week at the same time; but they attribute the sensation of satiety which they feel, to the clay, and not to the wretched aliments which they take with it occasionally.

No physiological phenomenon being entirely insulated, it may be interesting to examine several analogous phenomena, which I have been able to collect. I observed everywhere within the torrid zone, in a great number of individuals, children, women, and sometimes even full-grown men, an inordinate and almost irresistible desire of swallowing earth; not an alkaline or calcareous earth, to neutralize (as it is said) acid juices, but a fat clay, unctuous, and exhaling a strong smell. It is often found necessary to tie the children's hands or to confine them, to prevent their eating earth when the rain ceases to fall. At the village of Banco, on the bank of the river Magdalena, I saw the Indian women who make pottery continually swallowing great pieces of clay. These women were not in a state of pregnancy; and they affirmed, that earth is an aliment which they do not find hurtful. In other American tribes, people soon fall sick, and waste away, when they yield too much to this mania of eating earth. We found at the mission of San Borja an Indian child of the Guahiba nation, who was as thin as a skeleton. The mother informed us that the little girl was reduced to this lamentable state of atrophy in consequence of a disordered appetite, she having refused during four months to take almost any other food than clay. Yet San Borja is only twenty-five leagues distant from the mission of Uruana, inhabited by that tribe of the Ottomacs, who, from the effect no doubt of a habit progressively acquired, swallow the *poya* without experiencing any pernicious effects. Father Gumilla asserts, that the Ottomacs take as an aperient, oil, or rather the melted fat of the crocodile, when they feel any gastric obstructions; but the missionary whom we found among them was little disposed to confirm this assertion. It may be asked, why the mania of eating earth is much more rare in the frigid and temperate than in the torrid zones; and why in Europe it is found only among women in a state of pregnancy, and sickly children. This difference between hot and temperate climates arises perhaps only from the inert state of the functions of the stomach, caused by strong cutaneous perspiration. It has been supposed to be observed, that the inordinate taste for eating earth augments among the African slaves, and becomes more pernicious, when they are restricted to a regimen purely vegetable and deprived of spirituous liquors.

The negroes on the coast of Guinea delight in eating a yellowish earth, which they call *caouac*. The slaves who are taken to America endeavour to indulge in this habit; but it proves detrimental to their health. They say, that the earth of the West Indies is not so easy of digestion as that of their country. Thibaut de Chanvalon, in his Voyage to Martinico, expresses himself very judiciously on this pathological phenomenon. "Another cause," he says, "of this pain in the stomach is, that several of the negroes, who come from the coast of Guinea, eat earth; not from a depraved taste, or in consequence of disease, but from a habit contracted at home in Africa, where they eat, they say, a particular earth, the taste of which they find agreeable, without suffering any inconvenience. They seek in our islands for the earth most similar to this, and prefer a yellowish red volcanic tufa. It is sold secretly in our public markets; but this is an abuse which the police ought to correct. The negroes who have this habit are so fond of *caouac*, that no chastisement will prevent their eating it."

In the Indian Archipelago, at the island of Java, Labillardière saw, between Surabaya and Samarang, little square and reddish cakes exposed for sale. These cakes called *tanaampo*, were cakes of clay, slightly baked, which the natives eat with relish. The attention of physiologists, since my return from the Orinoco, having been powerfully directed to these phenomena of *geophagy*, M. Leschenault, (one of the naturalists of the expedition to the Antarctic regions under the command of captain Baudin) has published some curious details on the *tanaampo, or ampo,* of the Javanese. "The reddish and somewhat ferruginous clay," he says "which the inhabitants of Java are fond of eating occasionally, is spread on a plate of iron, and baked, after having been rolled into little cylinders in the form of the bark of cinnamon. In this state it takes the name of *ampo* and is sold in the public markets. This clay has a peculiar taste, which is owing to the baking: it is very absorbent, and adheres to the tongue, which it dries. In general it is only the Javanese women who eat the *ampo,* either in the time of pregnancy, or in order to grow thin; the absence of plumpness being there regarded as a kind of beauty. The use of this earth is fatal to health; the women lose their appetite imperceptibly, and take only with relish a very small quantity of food; but the desire of becoming thin, and of preserving a slender shape, induces them to brave these dangers, and maintains the credit of the *ampo.*" The savage inhabitants of New Caledonia also, to appease their hunger in times of scarcity, eat great pieces of a friable *Lapis ollaris.* Vauquelin analysed this stone, and found in it, beside magnesia and silex in equal portions, a small quantity of oxide of copper. M. Goldberry had seen the negroes in Africa, in the islands of Bunck and Los Idolos, eat earth of which he had himself eaten, without being incommoded by it, and which also was a white and friable steatite. These examples of earth-eating in the torrid zone appear very strange. We are struck by the anomaly of finding a taste, which might seem to belong only to the inhabitants of the most sterile regions, prevailing among races of rude and indolent men, who live in the finest and most fertile countries on the globe. We saw at Popayan, and in several mountainous parts of Peru, lime reduced to a very fine powder, sold in the public markets to the natives among other articles of food. This powder, when eaten, is mingled with *coca,* that is, with the leaves of the Erythroxylon peruvianum. It is well known, that Indian messengers take no other aliment for whole days than lime and *coca*: both excite the secretion of saliva, and of the gastric juice; they take away the appetite, without affording any nourishment to the body. In other parts of South America, on the coast of Rio de la Hacha, the Guajiros swallow lime alone, without adding any vegetable matter to it. They carry with them a little box filled with lime, as we do snuff-boxes, and as in Asia people carry a betel-box. This American custom excited the curiosity of the first Spanish navigators. Lime blackens the teeth; and in the Indian Archipelago, as among several American hordes, to blacken the teeth is to beautify them. In the cold regions of the kingdom of Quito, the natives of Tigua eat habitually from choice, and without any injurious consequences, a very fine clay, mixed with quartzose sand. This clay, suspended in water, renders it milky. We find in their huts large vessels filled with this water, which serves as a beverage, and which the Indians call *agua* or *leche de llanka*.*

When we reflect on these facts, we perceive that the appetite for clayey, magnesian, and calcareous earth is most common among the people of the torrid zone; that it is not always a cause of disease; and that some tribes eat earth from choice, whilst others (as the Ottomacs in America, and the inhabitants of New Caledonia, in the Pacific) eat it from want, and to appease hunger. A great number of physiological phenomena prove that a temporary cessation of hunger may be produced though the substances that are submitted to the organs of digestion may not be, properly speaking, nutritive. The earth of the Ottomacs, composed of alumine and silex, furnishes probably nothing, or almost nothing, to the composition of the organs of man. These organs contain lime and magnesia in the bones, in the lymph of the thoracic duct, in the colouring matter of the blood, and in white hairs; they afford very small quantities of silex in black hair; and, according to Vauquelin, but a few atoms of alumine in the bones, though this is contained abundantly in the greater part of those vegetable substances which form part of our nourishment. It is not the same with man as with animated beings placed lower in the scale of organization. In the former, assimilation is exerted only on those substances that enter essentially into the composition of the bones, the muscles, and the medullary matter of the nerves and the brain. Plants, on the contrary, draw from the soil the salts that are found accidentally mixed in it; and their fibrous texture varies according to the nature of the earths that predominate in the spots which they inhabit. An object well worthy of research, and which has long fixed my attention, is the small number of simple substances (earthy and metallic) that enter into the composition of animated beings, and which alone appear fitted to maintain what we may call the chemical movement of vitality.

* Water or milk of clay. *Llanka* is a word of the general language of the Incas, signifying fine clay.

IRON RATIONS IN AMAZONIA

Henry Savage Landor
(1867–1924)

Bar Antartica, Everest and the Empty Quarter, twentieth-century explorers have largely had to contrive their challenges. Landor went one better and contrived the hazards. From Japan, Korea, Central Asia, Tibet, and Africa he returned, always alone, with ever more improbable claims and ever more extravagant tales. The climax came in 1911 with Across Unknown South America, *the sort of book that gave exploration a bad name. His route, irrelevant and seldom "unknown", nevertheless demanded superhuman powers of endurance as when the expedition marched without food for fifteen days.*

We started once more across the virgin forest, directing our steps due west. Filippe this time undertook to open the *picada*, while I, compass in hand, marched directly behind him, Benedicto following me. If I had let him go, he would have described circle after circle upon himself instead of going in a straight line.

From that point our march across the forest became tragic. Perhaps I can do nothing better than reproduce almost word by word the entries in my diary.

We ate that morning what little there remained of the *mutum* we had shot the previous evening. Little we knew then that we were not to taste fresh meat again for nearly a month from that date.

During September 3rd we made fairly good progress, cutting our way through incessantly. We went that day 20 kil. We had no lunch, and it was only in the evening that we opened the last of the three small boxes of sardines, our entire dinner consisting of three and a half sardines each.

On September 4th we were confronted, soon after our departure, with a mountainous country with deep ravines and furrows, most trying for us owing to their steepness. We went over five ranges of hills from 100 to 300 ft. in height, and we crossed five streamlets in the depressions between those successive ranges.

Filippe was again suffering greatly from an attack of fever, and I had to support him all the time, as he had the greatest difficulty in walking. Benedicto had that day been entrusted with the big knife for cutting the *picada*.

We went some 20 kil. that day, with nothing whatever to eat, as we had already finished the three boxes of sardines, and I was reserving the box of anchovies for the moment when we could stand hunger no longer.

On September 5th we had another very terrible march over broken country, hilly for a good portion of the distance, but quite level in some parts.

The man Benedicto, who was a great eater, now collapsed altogether, saying that he could no longer carry his load and could not go on any farther without food.

The entire day our eyes had roamed in all directions, trying to discover some wild fruit which was edible, or some animal we might shoot, but there was the silence of death all around us. Not a branch, not a leaf was moved by a living thing; no fruit of any kind was to be seen anywhere.

Our appetite was keen, and it certainly had one good effect – it stopped Filippe's fever and, in fact, cured it altogether.

The two men were tormenting me the whole day, saying they had no faith in the compass: how could a brass box – that is what they called it – tell us where we could find *feijão*? It was beyond them to understand it. They bemoaned themselves incessantly, swearing at the day they had been persuaded to come along with me and leave their happy homes in order to die of starvation in the forest with a mad Englishman! And why did we go across the forest at all, where there was no trail, when we could have gone down by the river on a trading boat?

On September 6th it was all I could do to wake up my men. When they did wake, they would not get up, for they said the only object in getting up was to eat, and as there was nothing to eat there was no use in getting up. They wanted to remain there and die.

I had to use a great deal of gentle persuasion, and even told them a big story – that my *agulha* or needle (the compass) was telling me that morning that there was plenty of *feijão* ahead of us.

We struggled on kilometre after kilometre, one or another of us collapsing under our loads every few hundred metres. We went over very hilly country, crossing eight hill ranges that day with steep ravines between. In fact, all that country must once have been a low tableland which had been fissured and then eroded by water, leaving large cracks. At the bottom of each we found brooks and streamlets of delicious water. Of the eight rivulets found that day one only was fairly large. It fell in little cascades over rock. We could see no fish in its waters.

The forest was fairly clean underneath, and we had no great difficulty in getting through, a cut every now and then with the knife being sufficient to make a passage for us. I had by that time entirely given up the idea of opening a regular *picada*, over which I could eventually take the men and baggage I had left behind.

We found that day a palm with a bunch of small nuts which Benedicto called *coco do matto*; he said they were delicious to eat, so we proceeded to cut down the tall palm tree. When we came to split open the small *cocos* our disappointment was great, for they merely contained water. There was nothing whatever to eat inside the hard shells. We spent some two hours that evening cracking the *cocos* – some two hundred of them – each nut about the size of a cherry. They were extremely hard to crack, and our expectant eyes were disappointed two hundred times in succession as we opened every one and found nothing whatever to eat in them.

We were beginning to feel extremely weak, with a continuous feeling of emptiness in our insides. Personally, I felt no actual pain. The mental strain, perhaps, was the most trying thing for me, for I had no idea when we might find food. I was beginning to feel more than ever the responsibility of taking those poor fellows there to suffer for my sake. On their side they certainly never let one moment go by during the day or night without reminding me of the fact.

On September 7th I had the greatest difficulty in getting the men out of their hammocks. They were so exhausted that I could not rouse them. We had had a terrific storm during the night, which had added misery to our other sufferings. Innumerable ants were now causing us a lot of damage. Filippe's coat, which had dropped out of his hammock, was found in the morning entirely destroyed. Those miniature demons also cut the string to which I had suspended my shoes in mid-air, and no sooner had they fallen to the ground than the ants started on their mischievous work. When I woke up in the morning all that remained of my shoes were the two leather soles, the upper part having been completely destroyed.

Going through the forest, where thorns of all sizes were innumerable, another torture was now in store for me. With pieces of string I turned the soles of the shoes into primitive sandals, but when I started on the march I found that they hurt me much more than if I walked barefooted. After marching a couple of kilometres, my renovated foot-gear hurt me so much in going up and down the steep ravines that I took off the sandals altogether and flung them away.

That day we went over eleven successive hill ranges and crossed as many little streamlets between them. My men were terribly down-hearted. We had with us a Mauser and two hundred cartridges, but although we did nothing all day long but look for something to kill we never heard a sound of a living animal. Only one day at the beginning of our fast did I see a big *mutum* – larger than a big turkey. The bird had never seen a human being, and sat placidly perched on the branch of a tree, looking at us with curiosity, singing gaily. I tried to fire with the Mauser at the bird, which was only about seven or eight metres away, but cartridge after cartridge missed fire. I certainly spent not less than twenty minutes constantly replenishing the magazine, and not a single cartridge went off. They had evidently absorbed so much moisture on our many accidents in the river and in the heavy rain-storms we had had of late, that they had become useless.

While I was pointing the gun the bird apparently took the greatest interest in my doings, looked at me, stooping down gracefully each time that the rifle missed fire, singing dainty notes almost as if it were laughing at me. The funny part of it all was that we eventually had to go away disappointed, leaving the bird perched on that very same branch.

As the days went by and we could find nothing to eat, my two men lost their courage entirely. They now refused to suffer any longer. They said they had not the strength to go back, so they wanted to lie down and die. Many times a day did I have to lift them up again and persuade them gently to come on another few hundred metres or so. Perhaps then we might find the great river Madeira, where we should certainly meet traders from whom we could get food.

Late in the afternoon of September 7th, as we were on a high point above the last range of hills met that day, a large panorama opened before us, which we could just see between the trees and foliage of the forest.

To obtain a full view of the scenery it was necessary to climb up a tree. I knew well that we could not yet have reached the river we were looking for, but perhaps we were not far from some large tributary of the Madeira, such as the Secundury.

Climbing up trees in the Brazilian forest was easier said than done, even when you possessed your full strength. So many were the ants of all sizes which attacked you with fury the moment you embraced the tree, that it was not easy to get up more than a few feet.

When we drew lots as to whom of us should climb the tree, Benedicto was the one selected by fate. Benedicto was certainly born under an unlucky star; when anything nasty or unpleasant happened to anybody it was always to poor Benedicto. After a lot of pressing he proceeded to go up the tree, uttering piercing yells as every moment great *sauba* ants bit his arms, legs or body. He was brave enough, and slowly continued his way up until he reached a height of some 30 ft. above the ground, from which eminence he gave us the interesting news that there were some high hills standing before us to the west, while to the north-west was a great flat surface covered by dense forest.

No sooner had Benedicto supplied us with this information from his high point of vantage than we heard an agonising yell and saw him spread flat on the ground, having made a record descent.

Filippe and I, although suffering considerably, were in fits of laughter at Benedicto, who did not laugh at all, but pawed himself all over, saying he must have broken some bones. When I proceeded to examine him I found upon his body over a hundred *sauba* ants clinging to his skin with their powerful clippers.

Aching all over, poor Benedicto got up once more. I put the load upon his back and we resumed our journey, making a precipitous descent almost *à pic* down the hill side. Our knees were so weak that we fell many times and rolled down long distances on that steep incline. At last we got to the bottom, rejoicing in our hearts that we had no more hills to climb, as I had made up my mind that I would now march slightly to the north-west, so as to avoid the hilly region which Benedicto had discovered to the west.

My men had an idea that the great river we were looking for must be in that plain. For a few hours they seemed to have regained their courage. We heard some piercing shrieks, and we at once proceeded in their direction, as we knew they came from monkeys. In fact we found an enormously high tree, some 5 ft. in diameter. Up on its summit some beautiful yellow fruit stared us in the face. Four tiny monkeys were busy eating the fruit. Benedicto, who had by that time become very religious, joined his hands and offered prayers to the Virgin that the monkeys might drop some fruit down, but they went on eating while we gazed at them from below. We tried to fire at them with the Mauser, but again not a single cartridge went off. Eventually the monkeys dropped down the empty shells of the fruit they had eaten. With our ravenous appetite we rushed for them and with our teeth scraped off the few grains of sweet substance which remained attached to the inside of the shells. We waited and waited under that tree for a long time, Filippe now joining also in the prayers. Each time a shell dropped our palates rejoiced for a few moments at the infinitesimal taste we got from the discarded shells. It was out of the question to climb up such a big tree or to cut it down, as we had no strength left.

We went on until sunset; my men once more having lost heart. Brazilians lose heart very easily. At the sight of small hills before them, a steep descent, or a deep river to cross, they would lie down and say they wanted to remain there and die. Filippe and Benedicto did not carry more than 20 lb. each of my own baggage, but their hammocks weighed some 20 lb. each, so that their loads weighed altogether about 40 lb.

We went on, crossing five more streamlets that afternoon, of which one, 2 m. wide, had beautifully limpid water. We nevertheless went on, until eventually after sunset we had to camp near a stream of filthy water.

As we had now been four entire days without eating anything at all, I thought it was high time to open the valuable tin of anchovies – the only one in our possession. We had a terrible disappointment when I opened the tin. I had purchased it in S. Manoel from Mr. Barretto. To our great distress we discovered that instead of food it contained merely some salt and a piece of slate. This was a great blow to us. The box was a Brazilian counterfeit of a tin of anchovies. How disheartening to discover the fraud at so inopportune a moment! I had reserved the tin until the last as I did not like the look of it from the outside. We kept the salt – which was of the coarsest description.

On September 8th we were slightly more fortunate, as the country was flatter. I was steering a course of 290° b. m. (N. W.). I found that farther south we would have encountered too mountainous a country.

We crossed several streamlets, the largest 3 m. wide, all of which flowed south. We had no particular adventure that day, and considering all things, we marched fairly well – some 20 kil. Towards the evening we camped on a hill. When we got there we were so exhausted that we made our camp on the summit, although there was no water near.

On September 9th, after marching for half an hour we arrived at a stream 15 m. wide, which I took at first to be the river Secundury, a tributary of the Madeira River. Near the banks of that stream we found indications that human beings had visited that spot – perhaps the Indians we had heard so much about. The marks we found, however, were, I estimated, about one year old. Although these signs should have given us a little courage to go on, we were so famished and exhausted that my men sat down on the river bank and would not proceed. By that time we had got accustomed even to the fierce bites of the ants. We had no more strength to defend ourselves. In vain we strained our eyes all the time in search of wild fruit. In the river we saw plenty of fish; we had a fishing-line with us, but no bait whatever that we could use. There are, of course, no worms underground where ants are so numerous. We could not make snares in the river, as it was much too deep. So we sat with covetous eyes, watching the fish go by. It was most tantalising, and made us ten times more hungry than ever to be so near food and not be able to get it.

It is curious how hunger works on your brain. I am not at all a glutton, and never think of food under ordinary circumstances. But while I was starving I could see before me from morning till night, in my imagination, all kinds of delicacies – caviare, Russian soups, macaroni au gratin, all kinds of refreshing ice-creams, and plum pudding. Curiously enough, some days I had a perfect craving for one particular thing, and would have given anything I possessed in the world to obtain a morsel of it. The next day I did not care for that at all, in my imagination, but wanted something else very badly. The three things which I mostly craved for while I was starving were caviare, galantine of chicken, and ice-cream – the latter particularly.

People say that with money you can do anything you like in the world. I had at that time on my person some £6,000 sterling, of which £4,000 was in actual cash. If anybody had placed before me a morsel of any food I would gladly have given the entire sum to have it. But no, indeed; no such luck! How many times during those days did I vividly dream of delightful dinner and supper parties at the Savoy, the Carlton, or the Ritz, in London, Paris, and New York! How many times did I think of the delicious meals I had had when a boy in the home of my dear father and mother! I could reconstruct in my imagination all those meals, and thought what an idiot I was to have come there out of my own free will to suffer like that. My own dreams were constantly interrupted by Benedicto and Filippe, who also had similar dreams of the wonderful meals they had had in their own houses, and the wonderful ways in which their *feijãozinho* – a term of endearment used by them for their beloved beans – had been cooked at home by their sweathearts or their temporary wives.

"Why did we leave our *feijãozinho*" – and here they smacked their lips – "to come and die in this rotten country?"

All day I heard them talk of *feijãozinho, feijãozinho*, until I was wearied to distraction by that word – particularly as, even when starving, I had no desire whatever to eat the beastly stuff.

The negro Filippe and Benedicto were really brave in a way. I tried to induce them all the time to march as much as we could, so as to get somewhere; but every few moments they sat or fell down, and much valuable time was wasted.

As the days went by and our strength got less and less every hour, I decided not to cut the forest any more, but to go through without that extra exertion. As I could not trust my men with the big knife, I had to carry it myself, as occasionally it had to be used – especially near streams, where the vegetation was always more or less entangled.

That evening (September 9th) we had halted at sunset – simply dead with fatigue and exhaustion. The *sauba* ants had cut nearly all the strings of Filippe's hammock; while he was resting peacefully on it the remainder of the strings broke, and he had a bad fall. He was so exhausted that he remained lying on the ground, swarming all over with ants and moaning the whole time, having no strength to repair the hammock.

When Filippe eventually fell into a sound slumber I had a curious experience in the middle of the night. I was sleeping in my improvised hammock, when I felt two paws resting on my body and something sniffing in my face. When I opened my eyes I found a jaguar, standing up on its hind paws, staring me straight in the face. The moment I moved, the astonished animal, which had evidently never seen a human being before, leapt away and disappeared.

I find that people have strange ideas about wild animals. It is far from true that wild beasts are vicious. I have always found them as gentle as possible. Although I have seen nearly every wild beast that it is possible for man to see in the world, I have never once been attacked by them, although on dozens of occasions I have come into close contact with them. I invariably found all wild animals – expect the African buffalo – quite timid and almost gentle, unless, of course, they have been worried or wounded. These remarks do not apply to wild animals in captivity.

On September 10th – that was the seventh day of our involuntary fast – we had another dreary march, again without a morsel of food. My men were so down-hearted that I really thought they would not last much longer. Hunger was playing on them in a curious way. They said that they could hear voices all round them and people firing rifles. I could hear nothing at all. I well knew that their minds were beginning to go, and that it was a pure hallucination. Benedicto and Filippe, who originally were both atheists of an advanced type, had now become extremely religious, and were muttering fervent prayers all the time. They made a vow that if we escaped alive they would each give £5 sterling out of their pay to have a big mass celebrated in the first church they saw.

At this place I abandoned the few cartridges we had, as they were absolutely useless. They were Mauser cartridges which I had bought in Rio de Janeiro, and it is quite possible that they were counterfeits.

Taking things all round, my men behaved very well, but these were moments of the greatest anxiety for me, and I myself was praying fervently to God to get us out of that difficulty. My strength was failing more and more daily, and although I was suffering no actual pain, yet the weakness was simply appalling. It was all I could do to stand up on my legs. What was worse for me was that my head was still in good working order, and I fully realised our position all the time.

The country we were travelling over was fairly hilly, up and down most of the time, over no great elevations. We passed two large tributaries of the main stream we had found before, and a number of minor ones. The main stream was strewn with fallen trees, and was not navigable during the dry season. The erosion of the banks by the water had caused so many trees to fall down across it that no canoe could possibly go through.

I noticed in one or two places along the river traces of human beings having been there some years before.

In the afternoon we again wasted much energy in knocking down two palm-trees on the summit of which were great bunches of *coco do matto*. Again we had a bitter disappointment. One after the other we split the nuts open, but they merely contained water inside shells that were much harder to crack than wood. My craving for food was such that in despair I took two or three *sauba* ants and proceeded to eat them. When I ground them under my teeth their taste was so acidly bitter that it made me quite ill. Not only that, but one *sauba* bit my tongue so badly that it swelled up to a great size, and remained like that for several days.

On September 11th we had another terrible march, the forest being very dense and much entangled along the stream. We had great trouble in getting through, as there were many palms and ferns, and we had no more strength to cut down our way. We came to a big tree, which was hollow inside up to a great height, and round which were millions of bees.

Benedicto, who was a great connoisseur in such matters, said that high up inside the tree there must be honey. The bees round that tree were unfortunately stinging bees. We drew lots as to who should go inside the tree to get the honey. It fell to Benedicto. We took off most of our clothes and wrapped up his head and legs so that he might proceed to the attack. The job was not an easy one, for in the first reconnaissance he made with his head inside the tree he discovered that the honey must be not less than 20 ft. above the ground, and it was necessary to climb up to that height inside the tree before he could get it. In order to hasten matters – as Benedicto was reluctant in carrying out the job – I tried my hand at it, but I was stung badly by hundreds of bees behind my head, on my eyelids, on my arms and legs. When I came out of the tree I was simply covered with angry bees, which stung me all over. So I told Benedicto that, as Fate had called upon him to do the work, he had better do it.

Benedicto was certainly very plucky that day. All of a sudden he dashed inside the tree and proceeded to climb up. We heard wild screams for some minutes; evidently the bees were protecting their home well. While Filippe and I were seated outside, smiling faintly at poor Benedicto's plight, he reappeared. We hardly recognized him when he emerged from the tree, so badly stung and swollen was his face, notwithstanding the protection he had over it. All he brought back was a small piece of the honeycomb about as large as a florin. What little honey there was inside was quite putrid, but we divided it into three equal parts and devoured it ravenously, bees and all. A moment later all three of us were seized with vomiting, so that the meagre meal was worse than nothing to us.

We were then in a region of innumerable liane, which hung from the trees and caught our feet and heads, and wound themselves round us when we tried to shift them from their position. Nearly all the trees in that part had long and powerful spikes. Then near water there were huge palms close together, the sharp-edged leaves of which cut our hands, faces and legs as we pushed our way through.

A violent storm broke out in the afternoon. The rain was torrential, making our march extremely difficult. It was just like marching under a heavy shower-bath. The rain lasted for some three hours. We crossed one large stream flowing west into the Secundury, and also two other good-sized streamlets.

We had a miserable night, drenched as we were and unable to light a fire, the box of matches having got wet and the entire forest being soaked by the torrential storm. During the night another storm arrived and poured regular buckets of water upon us.

On September 12th we drowsily got up from our hammocks in a dejected state. By that time we had lost all hope of finding food, and no longer took the trouble to look round for anything to eat. We went on a few hundred metres at a time, now Benedicto fainting from exhaustion, then Filippe, then myself. While one or another was unconscious much time was wasted. Marching under those conditions was horrible, as either one or other of us collapsed every few hundred metres.

Another violent storm broke out, and we all lay on the ground helpless, the skin of our hands and feet getting shrivelled up with the moisture.

My feet were much swollen owing to the innumerable thorns which had got into them while walking barefooted. It was most painful to march, as I was not accustomed to walk without shoes.

We went only ten kilometres on September 12th. We crossed two small rivers and one large, flowing west and south, evidently into the Secundury.

On September 13th we had another painful march, my men struggling along, stumbling and falling every little while. They were dreadfully depressed. Towards the evening we came to a big tree, at the foot of which we found some discarded shells, such as we had once seen before, of fruit eaten by monkeys. My men and I tried to scrape with our teeth some of the sweet substance which still adhered to the shells. We saw some of the fruit, which was fit to eat, at a great height upon the tree, but we had not the strength to climb up or cut down that enormous tree.

All the visions of good meals which I had had until then had now vanished altogether on that tenth day of fasting, and I experienced a sickly feeling in my inside which gave me an absolute dislike for food of any kind. My head was beginning to sway, and I had difficulty in collecting my ideas. My memory seemed to be gone all of a sudden. I could no longer remember in what country I was travelling, nor could I remember anything distinctly. Only some lucid intervals came every now and then, in which I realised our tragic position; but those did not last long, all I could remember being that I must go to the west. I could not remember why nor where I intended to come out.

Everything seemed to be against us. We were there during the height of the rainy season. Towards sunset rain came down once more in bucketfuls and lasted the entire night, the water dripping from our hammocks as it would from a small cascade. We were soaked, and shivering, although the temperature was not low. I had my maximum and minimum thermometers with me, but my exhaustion was such that I had not the strength to unpack them every night and morning and set them.

We crossed two streamlets flowing west. Benedicto and Filippe were in such a bad way that it was breaking my heart to look at them. Every time they fell down in a faint I never knew whether it was for the last time that they had closed their eyes. When I felt their hearts with my hand they beat so faintly that once or twice I really thought they were dead. That day I myself fainted, and fell with the left side of my face resting on the ground. When I recovered consciousness some time later, I touched my face, which was hurting me, and found that nearly the whole skin of my cheek had been eaten up by small ants, the lower lid of the eye having suffered particularly. A nasty sore remained on my face for some two months after that experience, the bites of those ants being very poisonous.

Bad as they were, there is no doubt that to a great extent we owed our salvation to those terrible ants. Had it not been for them and the incessant torture they inflicted on us when we fell down upon the ground, we should have perhaps lain there and never got up again.

I offered Benedicto and Filippe a large reward if they continued marching without abandoning the precious loads. Brazilians have a great greed for money, and for it they will do many things which they would not do otherwise.

On September 14th we made another most painful march of 20 kil., again up and down high hills, some as much as 300 ft. above the level land of that country, and all with steep, indeed, almost vertical, sides, extremely difficult for us to climb in our exhausted condition. We saw several streamlets flowing west. When evening came we had before us a high hill, which we ascended. When we reached the top we just lay upon the ground like so many corpses, and, ants or no ants biting us, we had not the energy to get up again. Once more did the rain come down in torrents that night, and to a certain extent washed the ants from our bodies.

My surprise was really great the next morning when I woke up. I felt myself fading away fast. Every time I closed my eyes I expected never to open them again.

On September 15th we made another trying march, collapsing under our loads every few hundred metres. My men were constantly looking for something to eat in all directions, but could find nothing. Benedicto and Filippe were now all the time contemplating suicide. The mental strain of perpetually keeping an eye on them was great.

We were sitting down, too tired to get up, when Filippe amazed me considerably by the following words, which he spoke in a kind of reverie:

"It would be very easy," he said, "now that you have no more strength yourself, for us two to get the big knife and cut your throat. We know that you have a big, big sum of money upon you, and if we robbed you we would be rich for ever. But we do not want to do it. It would not be much use to us, as we could not get out of the forest alone. I believe we shall all die together, and all that money will go to waste."

Filippe said this in quite a good-natured manner. The two poor fellows were so depressed that one had to forgive them for anything they said.

As the river seemed to describe a big loop, I had left it three days before, seeing plainly by the conformation of the country that we should strike it again sooner or later. We were marching once more by compass. My men, who had no faith whatever in the magnetic needle, were again almost paralysed with fear that we might not encounter the stream again. A thousand times a day they accused me of foolishness in leaving the river, as they said it would have been better to follow its tortuous course – notwithstanding the trouble we had in following it, owing to the dense vegetation near the water – rather than strike once more across country. They were beginning to lose heart altogether, when I told them I could see by the vegetation that we were once more near the water. Anybody accustomed as I am to marching through the forest could tell easily by the appearance of the vegetation some miles before actually getting to a stream.

I reassured my companions, saying that within a few hours we should certainly meet the "big water" again. In fact, not more than half an hour afterwards we suddenly found ourselves once more on the large stream – at that point 70 metres wide.

My men were so amazed and delighted that they embraced me and sobbed over my shoulders for some time. From that moment their admiration for the compass was unbounded; they expected me to find anything with it.

THE DISCOVERY OF MACHU PICCHU

Hiram Bingham
(1875–1956)

Just when it seemed as if all the "forbidden cities" had been entered and the "lost civilizations" found, there occurred one of the most sensational discoveries in the history of travel. Hiram Bingham, the son of missionary parents in Hawaii, was a lecturer in Latin American history at Yale and Berkeley who devoted his vocations to retracing the routes of Spanish conquest and trade in Columbia and Peru. He was drawn to the high Andes near Cuzco and to the awesome gorges of the Urubamba River by rumours about the existence there of the lost capital and last retreat of the Incas. Machu Picchu was neither; but it richly rewarded his heroic endeavour in reaching it. After excavation by Bingham in 1912 and 1915, it was revealed as the best preserved of the Inca cities and South America's most impresssive site.

I t was in July, 1911, that we first entered that marvellous canyon of the Urubamba, where the river escapes from the cold regions near Cuzco by tearing its way through gigantic mountains of granite. From Torontoy to Colpani the road runs through a land of matchless charm. It has the majestic grandeur of the Canadian Rockies, as well as the startling beauty of the Nuuanu Pali near Honolulu, and the enchanting vistas of the Koolau Ditch Trail on Maui. In the variety of its charms and the power of its spell, I know of no place in the world which can compare with it. Not only has it great snow peaks looming above the clouds more than two miles overhead; gigantic precipices of many-coloured granite rising sheer for thousands of feet above the foaming, glistening, roaring rapids; it has also, in striking contrast, orchids and tree ferns, the delectable beauty of luxurious vegetation, and the mysterious witchery of the jungle. One is drawn irresistibly onward by ever-recurring surprises through a deep, winding gorge, turning and twisting past overhanging cliffs of incredible height. Above all, there is the fascination of finding here and there under the swaying vines, or perched on top of a beetling crag, the rugged masonry of a bygone race; and of trying to understand the bewildering romance of the ancient builders who ages ago sought refuge in a region which appears to have been expressly designed by Nature as a sanctuary for the oppressed, a place where they might fearlessly and patiently give expression to their passion for walls of enduring beauty. Space forbids any attempt to describe in detail the constantly changing panorama, the rank tropical foliage, the countless terraces, the towering cliffs, the glaciers peeping out between the clouds.

We had camped at a place near the river, called Mandor Pampa. Melchor Arteaga, proprietor of the neighbouring farm, had told us of ruins at Machu Picchu.

The morning of July 24th dawned in a cold drizzle. Arteaga shivered and seemed inclined to stay in his hut. I offered to pay him well if he would show me the ruins. He demurred and said it was too hard a climb for such a wet day. When he found that we were willing to pay him a *sol*, three or four times the ordinary daily wage in this vicinity, he finally agreed to guide us to the ruins. No one supposed that they would be particularly interesting. Accompanied by Sergeant Carrasco I left camp at ten o'clock and went some distance upstream. On the road we passed a venomous snake which recently had been killed. This region has an unpleasant notoriety for being the favourite haunt of "vipers". The lance-headed or yellow viper, commonly known as the fer-de-lance, a very venomous serpent capable of making considerable springs when in pursuit of its prey, is common hereabouts. Later two of our mules died from snake-bite.

After a walk of three-quarters of an hour the guide left the main road and plunged down through the jungle to the bank of the river. Here there was a primitive "bridge" which crossed the roaring rapids at its narrowest part, where the stream was forced to flow between two great boulders. The bridge was made of half a dozen very slender logs, some of which were not long enough to span the distance between the boulders. They had been spliced and lashed together with vines. Arteaga and Carrasco took off their shoes and crept gingerly across, using their somewhat prehensile toes to keep from slipping. It was obvious that no one could have lived for an instant in the rapids, but would immediately have been dashed to pieces against granite boulders. I am frank to confess that I got down on hands and knees and crawled across, six inches at a time. Even after we reached the other side I could not help wondering what

would happen to the "bridge" if a particularly heavy shower should
fall in the valley above. A light rain had fallen during the night. The
river had risen so that the bridge was already threatened by the
foaming rapids. It would not take much more rain to wash away the
bridge entirely. If this should happen during the day it might be very
awkward. As a matter of fact, it did happen a few days later and the
next explorers to attempt to cross the river at this point found only
one slender log remaining.

Leaving the stream, we struggled up the bank through a dense
jungle, and in a few minutes reached the bottom of a precipitous
slope. For an hour and twenty minutes we had a hard climb. A good
part of the distance we went on all fours, sometimes hanging on by
the tips of our fingers. Here and there, a primitive ladder made from
the roughly hewn trunk of a small tree was placed in such a way as to
help one over what might otherwise have proved to be an impassable
cliff. In another place the slope was covered with slippery grass
where it was hard to find either handholds or footholds. The guide
said that there were lots of snakes here. The humidity was great, the
heat was excessive, and we were not in training.

Shortly after noon we reached a little grass-covered hut where
several good-natured Indians, pleasantly surprised at our unexpected arrival, welcomed us with dripping gourds full of cool,
delicious water. Then they set before us a few cooked sweet
potatoes, called here *cumara*, a Quichua word identical with the
Polynesian *kumala*, as has been pointed out by Mr Cook.

Apart from the wonderful view of the canyon, all we could see
from our cool shelter was a couple of small grass huts and a few
ancient stone-faced terraces. Two pleasant Indian farmers, Richarte
and Alvarez, had chosen this eagle's nest for their home. They said
they had found plenty of terraces here on which to grow their crops
and they were usually free from undesirable visitors. They did not
speak Spanish, but through Sergeant Carrasco I learned that there
were more ruins "a little farther along". In this country one never
can tell whether such a report is worthy of credence. "He may have
been lying" is a good footnote to affix to all hearsay evidence.
Accordingly, I was not unduly excited, nor in a great hurry to move.
The heat was still great, the water from the Indian's spring was cool
and delicious, and the rustic wooden bench, hospitably covered
immediately after my arrival with a soft, woollen poncho, seemed
most comfortable. Furthermore, the view was simply enchanting.
Tremendous green precipices fell away to the white rapids of the
Urubamba below. Immediately in front, on the north side of the
valley, was a great granite cliff rising 2000 feet sheer. To the left was

the solitary peak of Huayna Picchu, surrounded by seemingly inaccessible precipices. On all sides were rocky cliffs. Beyond them cloud-capped mountains rose thousands of feet above us.

The Indians said there were two paths to the outside world. Of one we had already had a taste; the other, they said, was more difficult – a perilous path down the face of a rocky precipice on the other side of the ridge. It was their only means of egress in the wet season, when the bridge over which we had come could not be maintained. I was not surprised to learn that they went away from home only "about once a month".

Richarte told us that they had been living here four years. It seems probable that, owing to its inaccessibility, the canyon had been unoccupied for several centuries, but with the completion of the new government road settlers began once more to occupy this region. In time somebody clambered up the precipices and found on the slopes of Machu Picchu, at an elevation of 9000 feet above the sea, an abundance of rich soil conveniently situated on artificial terraces, in a fine climate. Here the Indians had finally cleared off some ruins, burned over a few terraces, and planted crops of maize, sweet and white potatoes, sugar cane, beans, peppers, tree tomatoes, and gooseberries. At first they appropriated some of the ancient houses and replaced the roofs of wood and thatch. They found, however, that there were neither springs nor wells near the ancient buildings. An ancient aqueduct which had once brought a tiny stream to the citadel had long since disappeared beneath the forest, filled with earth washed from the upper terraces. So, abandoning the shelter of the ruins, the Indians were now enjoying the convenience of living near some springs in roughly built thatched huts of their own design.

Without the slightest expectation of finding anything more interesting than the stone-faced terraces of which I already had a glimpse, and the ruins of two or three stone houses such as we had encountered at various places on the road between Ollantaytambo and Torontoy, I finally left the cool shade of the pleasant little hut and climbed farther up the ridge and around a slight promontory. Arteaga had "been here once before", and decided to rest and gossip with Richarte and Alvarez in the hut. They sent a small boy with me as a guide.

Hardly had we rounded the promontory when the character of the stonework began to improve. A flight of beautifully constructed terraces, each two hundred yards long and ten feet high, had been recently rescued from the jungle by the Indians. A forest of large trees had been chopped down and burned over to make a clearing for agricultural purposes. Crossing these terraces, I entered the untouched forest beyond, and suddenly found myself in a maze of beautiful granite houses! They were covered with trees and moss and the growth of centuries, but in the dense shadow, hiding in bamboo thickets and tangled vines, could be seen, here and there, walls of white granite ashlars most carefully cut and exquisitely fitted together. Buildings with windows were frequent. Here at least was a "place far from town and conspicuous for its windows".

Under a carved rock the little boy showed me a cave beautifully lined with the finest cut stone. It was evidently intended to be a Royal Mausoleum. On top of this particular boulder a semicircular building had been constructed. The wall followed the natural curvature of the rock and was keyed to it by one of the finest examples of masonry I have ever seen. This beautiful wall, made of carefully matched ashlars of pure white granite, especially selected for its fine grain, was the work of a master artist. The interior surface of the wall was broken by niches and square stone-pegs. The exterior surface was perfectly simple and unadorned. The lower courses, of particularly large ashlars, gave it a look of solidity. The upper courses, diminishing in size towards the top, lent grace and delicacy to the structure. The flowing lines, the symmetrical arrangement of the ashlars, and the gradual gradation of the courses, combined to produce a wonderful effect, softer and more pleasing than that of the marble temples of the Old World. Owing to the absence of mortar, there are no ugly spaces between the rocks. They might have grown together.

The elusive beauty of this chaste, undecorated surface seems to me to be due to the fact that the wall was built under the eye of a master mason who knew not the straight edge, the plumb rule, or the square. He had no instruments of precision, so he had to depend on his eye. He had a good eye, an artistic eye, an eye for symmetry and beauty of form. His product received none of the harshness of mechanical and mathematical accuracy. The apparently rectangular blocks are not really rectangular. The apparently straight lines of the courses are not actually straight in the exact sense of that term.

To my astonishment I saw that this wall and its adjoining semicircular temple over the cave were as fine as the finest stone-work in the far-famed Temple of the Sun in Cuzco. Surprise followed surprise in bewildering succession. I climbed a marvellous great stairway of large granite blocks, walked along a *pampa* where the Indians had a small vegetable garden, and came into a little clearing. Here were the ruins of two of the finest structures I have ever seen in Peru. Not only were they made of selected blocks of beautifully grained white granite; their walls contained ashlars of Cyclopean size, ten feet in length, and higher than a man. The sight held me spellbound.

Each building had only three walls and was entirely open on the side towards the clearing. The principal temple was lined with exquisitely made niches, five high up at each end, and seven on the back wall. There were seven courses of ashlars in the end walls. Under the seven rear niches was a rectangular block fourteen feet long, probably a sacrificial altar. The building did not look as though it had ever had a roof. The top course of beautifully smooth ashlars was not intended to be covered.

The other temple is on the east side of the *pampa*. I called it the Temple of the Three Windows. Like its neighbour, it is unique among Inca ruins. Its eastern wall, overlooking the citadel, is a massive stone framework for three conspicuously large windows, obviously too large to serve any useful purpose, yet most beautifully made with the greatest care and solidity. This was clearly a ceremonial edifice of peculiar significance. Nowhere else in Peru, so far as I know, is there a similar structure conspicuous as "a masonry wall with three windows".

These ruins have no other name than that of the mountain on the slopes of which they are located. Had this place been occupied uninterruptedly, like Cuzco and Ollantaytambo, Machu Picchu would have retained its ancient name, but during the centuries when it was abandoned, its name was lost. Examination showed that it was essentially a fortified place, a remote fastness protected by natural bulwarks, of which man took advantage to create the most impregnable stronghold in the Andes. Our subsequent excavations and the clearing made in 1912, has shown that this was the chief place in Uilcapampa.

It did not take an expert to realize, from the glimpse of Machu Picchu on that rainy day in July, 1911, when Sergeant Carrasco and I first saw it, that here were most extraordinary and interesting ruins. Although the ridge had been partly cleared by the Indians for their fields of maize, so much of it was still underneath a thick jungle growth – some walls were actually supporting trees ten and twelve inches in diameter – that it was impossible to determine just what would be found here. As soon as I could get hold of Mr Tucker, who was assisting Mr Hendriksen, and Mr Lanius, who had gone down the Urubamba with Dr Bowman, I asked them to make a map of the ruins. I knew it would be a difficult undertaking and that it was essential for Mr Tucker to join me in Arequipa not later than the first of October for the ascent of Coropuna. With the hearty aid of Richarte and Alvarez, the surveyors did better than I expected. In the ten days while they were at the ruins they were able to secure data from which Mr Tucker afterwards prepared a map which told better than could any words of mine the importance of this site and the necessity for further investigation.

With the possible exception of one mining prospector, no one in Cuzco had seen the ruins of Machu Picchu or appreciated their importance. No one had any realization of what an extraordinary place lay on top of the ridge. It had never been visited by any of the planters of the lower Urubamba Valley who annually passed over the road which winds through the canyon two thousand feet below.

It seems incredible that this citadel, less than three days' journey from Cuzco, should have remained so long undescribed by travellers and comparatively unknown even to the Peruvians themselves. If the *conquistadores* ever saw this wonderful place, some reference to it surely would have been made; yet nothing can be found which clearly refers to the ruins of Machu Picchu. Just when it was first seen by a Spanish-speaking person is uncertain. When the Count de Sartiges was at Huadquiña in 1834 he was looking for ruins; yet, although so near, he heard of none here. From a crude scrawl on the walls of one of the finest buildings, we learned that the ruins were visited in 1902 by Lizarraga, lessee of the lands immediately below the bridge of San Miguel. This is the earliest local record. Yet some one must have visited Machu Picchu long before that; because in 1875, as has been said, the French explorer Charles Wiener heard in Ollantaytambo of their being ruins at "Huaina-Picchu or Matcho-Picchu". He tried to find them. That he failed was due to there being no road through the canyon of Torontoy and the necessity of making a wide detour through the pass of Panticalla and the Lucumayo Valley, a route which brought him to the Urubamba River at the bridge of Chuquichaca, twenty-five miles below Machu Picchu.

It was not until 1890 that the Peruvian Government, recognizing the needs of the enterprising planters who were opening up the lower valley of the Urubamba, decided to construct a mule trail along the banks of the river through the grand canyon to enable the much-desired *coca* and *aguardiente* to be shipped from Huadquiña, Maranura, and Santa Ana to Cuzco more quickly and cheaply than formerly. This road avoids the necessity of carrying the precious cargoes over the dangerous snowy passes of Mt Veronica and Mt Salcantay, so vividly described by Raimondi, de Sartiges, and others. The road, however, was very expensive, took years to build, and still requires frequent repair. In fact, even today travel over it is often suspended for several days or weeks at a time, following some tremendous avalanche. Yet it was this new road which had led Melchor Arteaga to build his hut near the arable land at Mandor Pampa, where he could raise food for his family and offer rough shelter to passing travellers. It was this new road which brought Richarte, Alvarez, and their enterprising friends into this little-known region, gave them the opportunity of occupying the ancient terraces of Machu Picchu, which had lain fallow for centuries, encouraged them to keep open a passable trail over the precipices, and made it feasible for us to reach the ruins. It was this new road which offered us in 1911 a virgin field between Ollantaytambo and Huadquiña and enabled us to learn that the Incas, or their predecessors, had once lived here in the remote fastnesses of the Andes, and had left stone witnesses of the magnificence and beauty of their ancient civilization, more interesting and extensive than any which have been found since the days of the Spanish Conquest of Peru.

FOUR YEARS IN THE ICE

John Ross
(1777–1856)

*Discredited for his report of an imaginary mountain range blocking
the most likely access to the North West Passage, in 1829 a crusty
Ross returned to Canada's frozen archipelago to vindicate his
reputation. He rounded the north of Baffin Island and entered what
he named the Gulf of Boothia. Here the* Victory, *his eccentric
paddle-steamer, became frozen into the ice. Through three tantaliz-
ingly brief summers the expedition tried to find a way out and
through four long winters they endured the worst of Arctic conditions in a makeshift camp. In July 1832, with the ship long since
abandoned, Ross made what must be their last bid to reach open
water.*

July 7   The shooting of fifty dovekies [guillemots] yesterday gave
the men a good Sunday's dinner; and the last divine service we
trusted ever to attend in this house, was performed. It was the
commencement of a farewell which all hoped would be eternal; but
every one must answer for the feelings under which he, for the
expected last time, repeated the Lord's prayer, and heard himself
dismissed in those words which promise, to those who deserve it,
that peace which passes all understanding. I trust there were few
who did not recollect to return their own private thanksgiving for so
long a preservation amid such dangers and privation and who did
not put up their own prayers for help in the great undertaking now
impending, on the success or failure of which must turn the event of
life or death to all.

On Monday, every thing was ready, and we too were as prepared
as we were anxious to quit this dreary place, as we hoped, for ever.
Yet, with those hopes, there were mingled many fears: enough to
render it still but too doubtful in all our minds whether we might not

Captain West's interview with the Esquimaux.

yet be compelled to return; to return once more to despair, and
perhaps, to return but to die. To have been able, confidently, to say,
Adieu for ever, would have been indeed to render this a delightful
parting; when even the shelter which we had received was insufficient to balance all the miseries which we had suffered; miseries to
have extinguished every sense of regret that we could have felt in
pronouncing those two words, which, it is said, have never yet,
under any circumstances, been pronounced without pain. This may
be true; I almost believe that it would have been true even in our
case, though in parting from our miserable winter house of timber
and snow, we left nothing behind us but misery and the recollection
of misery; since, in the comparison with what might have been, it
was, heaven knows, a shelter from evils far greater, from death itself;
and, such home as it was, a Home; that strange entity from which
man never parts, bad as it may be, without reluctance, and never
leaves but with some strange longing to see it again. But true as may
be the pain of an adieu, or the fancy of leaving for ever a home, or
true as may be, reversely the pleasure of quitting for ever the scene of
past miseries, neither the pleasure nor the pain was ours. Scarcely the
feeling of a farewell, for hope or regret, for pain or for pleasure, was
in any mind, when we coldly departed in the evening with our three
sledges, to encounter such fate as Providence might have in store for
us.

The sick, who formed our great difficulty, bore the first journey
well, and we reached our first station before mid-day. It was a fine
day, and the warmest that had yet occurred; the temperature being
48°. In the afternoon, at three, we proceeded again, with infinite
toil, through nearly impassable ways, which were rendered more
difficult to us by the care which the sick required and so hard was
the labour, that even here, and at night we were obliged to work in
our shirts. We gained but two miles by midnight and were glad to
rest.

July 10   We recommenced with all the baggage labouring through
ways as bad, or worse, under a sun that was occasionally very hot
and at nine, reached the third position at the cascade, which was
now pouring down abundantly into a pool filled with kittiwakes
where we procured some sorrel. We found that the bears had upset a
cask full of skins which we had left here but they could not contrive
to open it.

On the next day we brought forward the sick whom we could not
move together with the baggage, and then proceeded to the third
position, after a very fatiguing journey backward and forwards,
of twenty-four miles. We had lately obtained a good supply of

dovekies, and could now afford every one a good breakfast; which was not less necessary than agreeable, emaciated as most of us were, and nevertheless compelled to endure this constant labour. In the afternoon, the road on the shore being better we contrived to take most of our stores, the sick included: but it was not, finally till after many difficulties in avoiding and traversing bad ice, that we reached the boats in Batty bay, at eight in the morning.

We found that the bears and foxes had committed considerable depredations on our stores, by destroying a cask of bread, some oil, and some sugar, and also all the leather shoes and boots they could find. The weather was very fine, and the dovekies being numerous, we killed some for our provision. Even at midnight the thermometer was now 48°: it was a great revolution in the weather, and it had been a sudden one; unexpected, but not undue. Two light sledges to-day [July 13] brought up the few things which we had been obliged to leave at the last place, together with some sorrel for the sick; while we obtained thirty dovekies.

July 14 Sunday was made a day of rest. They who walked found the land quite destitute of vegetation, and a considerable river running into the head of the bay. On the following day the ice was examined from the hills, but was not yet breaking in the offing: the weather being calm and fine, but sometimes foggy. The men were employed in repairing the boats, and in preparations for embarking. The ice moved on the sixteenth; but the large creek was still filled, and impassable. On the two next days it rained almost constantly, and we were prisoners. About a hundred dovekies were killed, so that our supply of fresh meat was respectable, if not great.

On the twentieth, the weather became fine again; the ice continued to move, and the caulking of the boats was continued. An easterly wind made the thermometer fall to 38°. On Sunday the ice was reported to be broken up in the offing; but after three days, without any thing material to note, except the killing of fifty dovekies, it remained close packed on the shore, so that it was impossible for us to move. The weather, from this time, continued variable, with occasional rain and wind, together with fogs, till the thirtieth; as the only events worth noticing, were the improvement of the sick, and the killing of some more birds for our table.

We had now seen the ice leave the shore at last, but had yesterday been prevented from embarking, by a heavy fog. This ending in rain and sleet, with an adverse east wind, on the last morning of the month, we did not load the boats till mid-day; but as it proved, in vain, since it came to blow and rain so heavily all the afternoon and evening, that it was impossible to embark. In every way it was desirable to quit this place; as the stones had now begun to fall from the cliffs, in consequence of which two men experienced severe contusions, and one narrowly escaped with his life. Thus ended July.

Of that month, any summary is superseded by the preceding journal; it is almost sufficient to note that the mean temperature had been 36°, and the extremes 28° and 50° plus. It had not been an unfavourable one to our prospects, on the whole while we had no right to expect an open sea in these regions at so early a period, far less in a strait which had exhibited such perseverance in preserving its ice through the whole summer during the preceding years. That the sick had improved was a very consoling circumstance; while our situation was, at least, one of joint exertion and hope.

Between the first and the fifteenth of the month of August, the changes of the wind and the vacillations in the nature of the weather were such as I have often recorded during the past two; while the general result is all that is here worthy of notice. The prevailing nature of the former was north-easterly: and the consequence was, to block up the shore with ice, and to keep us closely imprisoned to our beach and our boats. On the third, indeed, we made an attempt to move round the southern point of the bay: but being unable to effect this, and finding the blockade of this headland so heavy that the bay must open sooner, so as to give us notice where we might possibly pass it, we returned, as there was nothing to gain by this project.

But even this fruitless labour was not without its use. The result of it was to do something: and, to do, even what was useless, was to keep up the spirits and hopes of the people, as it also interrupted that uniformity of idle wakefulness which led them to brood over their present condition, and to indulge in evil anticipations. The Highland squire who makes Boswell haul on the backstay in a gale of wind, displays more knowledge than a landsman has any right to possess.

I know not what we should have done, what would have "become of us," as the phrase is, had we not made work when we had ceased to find it. "The men," as they are called, are not much given to thinking, it is certain; though seamen of the present day (and I am sorry to say it), think much more than they did in the days of my junior service, and, most assuredly and certainly, are "all the worse" for it. Let my fraternity in command say whether this be true or not; and they are the bold men who will so say, despite of the paltry, fantastical, and pretending, ultra philanthropy of these days of ruinous folly. But that is an over serious matter to discuss at present. "An idle man is a pillow for the devil," says a Spanish or Italian proverb; it was no good that our men should have been pillowed in this manner: better was it that they should work themselves into utter weariness, that they should so hunger as to think only of their stomachs, fall asleep and dream of nothing but a better dinner, as they awoke to hope and labour for it, and that their sleep should be, not on the pillow of the proverb, but on a couch of snow, sufficient to impede all reflections but the wish for a better bed after a better supper and the gnawing desire of more and better on the following day.

The shooting of waterfowl furnished indeed some occupation to those who were worthy of being trusted with powder and shot; but I believe the best occupation, to a set of such starved wretches as we were, was to eat the game, not to shoot it. Every morning now rose on the hopes of a good supper: if that came, it was more than welcome; and when it did not, why then there was the chance of one to-morrow. I do not say that the supper which was missed was equivalent to the one that was eaten; since hope or expectation will not, more than wishing, fill a man's stomach; but it is certain that the sick recovered rapidly, and the well improved in strength; nor could I doubt that their present state of mind was, in this, scarcely less efficacious than the broiled ducks and the dovekie sea-pies.

To look out from the top of the hill, for the state of the ice, was another occupation for any one that chose; and it was exercise, while it served to waste the time. It was not, like Behring's unhappy men, to watch for the ship that was destined never to appear, and, when the day closed, to retire once more to darkness and despair. The day of relief might be delayed, but it was long yet before it would be time to fear that it was not to arrive; while, in every change of a breeze, in every shower of rain, and in every movement of the ice, however minute, there was sufficient to maintain hope, and to render all anxious for the to-morrow; as each, on retiring for the night, felt inclined to say, yet not under the same motives as the wretches in the Castle of Indolence, "Thank God, the day is done."

It was on the fourteenth that hope became anxiety, when a lane of water was for the first time seen, leading to the northward; and not many, I believe, slept, under the anticipations of what the next day might bring. On this, all were employed in cutting the ice which obstructed the shore, as early as four o'clock in the morning; and the tide having risen soon after, with a fine westerly breeze, we launched the boats, embarked the stores and the sick, and, at eight o'clock, were under way.

We really were under way at last; and it was our business to forget that we had been in the same circumstances, the year before, in the same place; to feel that the time for exertion was now come, and those exertions to be at length rewarded; to exchange hope for certainty, and to see, in the mind's eye, the whole strait open before us, and our little fleet sailing with a fair wind through that bay which was now, in our views, England and home.

We soon rounded the north cape of Batty bay, and, finding lane of water, crossed Elwin's bay at midnight; reaching, on the sixteenth, that spot to the north of it where we had pitched our tents on the twenty-eighth of August in the preceding year. I know not if all were here quite free of recollections to damp our new hopes. The difference in time was but twelve days; and should those days pass as they had done in the former, it might still be our fate to return to our last winter's home and there to end our toils as it was but too easy to anticipate; the first whose fortune it should be, in a frozen grave, and the last in the maws of bears and foxes.

We found here no passage to the eastward, but the lane of water still extended towards the north; so that our stay was of no longer duration than was indispensable for rest. As we proceeded, the open water increased in breadth; and, at eight in the evening, we reached our former position at the north-eastern cape of America. A view from the hill here, showed that the ice to the northward and north-eastward was in such a state as to admit of sailing through it; but as it blew too hard to venture among it in the night, we pitched our tents for rest.

At three in the morning we embarked once more, leaving an additional note of our proceedings, in the same place where the former was concealed. It was calm, and we held on to the eastward by rowing, until, at noon, we reached the edge of the packed ice, through many streams of floating pieces; when we found that its extremity was but a mile to the northward. A southerly breeze then springing up, enabled us to round it: when, finding the water open, we stood on through it, and reached the eastern shore of the strait at three in the afternoon. In a few hours we had at length effected that for which we had formerly waited in vain so many days, and which, it is likely, could not have been effected in any of the years that we had been imprisoned in this country.

Accustomed as we were to the ice, to its caprices, and to its sudden and unexpected alterations, it was a change like that of magic, to find that solid mass of ocean which was but too fresh in our memories, which we had looked at for so many years as if it was fixed for ever in a repose which nothing could hereafter disturb, suddenly converted into water; navigable, and navigable to us, who had almost forgotten what it was to float at freedom on the seas. It was at times scarcely to be believed: and he who dozed to awake again, had for a moment to renew the conviction that he was at length a seaman on his own element, that his boat once more rose on the waves beneath him, and that when the winds blew, it obeyed his will and his hand.

Thus we ran quickly along the shore as the breeze increased; and, passing Eardly point, were at length compelled, by the rising of this breeze to a gale accompanied by hard squalls, to take shelter on a beach twelve miles west of Cape York; having made, on this day, a run of seventy-two miles.

The wind moderating, and it at length becoming calm, we were obliged, in the morning, to take to the oars; and finding no ice to obstruct us, rowed along to the eastward, and by midnight rested for a short time at the cape to the east of Admiralty inlet. On the next day, the weather being the same, we were halfway between this place and that termed Navy-board inlet, by eight in the morning; when, the men being exhausted with nearly twenty hours rowing, we stopped on the beach and pitched our tents. The weather had not yet become warm, clear as the water might be; since the night temperature had never exceeded 35°, nor that of the day 40°.

We were soon driven from this exposed place by the coming on of an easterly wind; and thus, taking once more to the oars, we rowed along among icebergs, till we arrived at an excellent harbour, receiving a considerable stream, where we were protected by these heavy masses, while we could, if necessary, haul the boats into a pool at the mouth of the river. We had thus gained five miles more; and being six or seven to the west of Navy-board inlet, were within eighty of Possession bay.

It began to blow hard last night with a north-east wind, and a heavy sea, which continued this day; blocking us up completely, but allowing us to haul up the boats for repair. Growing worse at length, we brought them into the inner harbour which the pool formed; when, increasing to a violent gale, all the icebergs which had arranged themselves into an outer one, broke away and disappeared. There was, with this storm, a steady fall of mixed rain and snow, and the thermometer subsided to 34°.

August 22   It had become prudent to reduce ourselves, once more, to a two-thirds allowance; and thus were we imprisoned on the twenty-third and twenty-fourth, by a continuance of the gale, with fog and rain; the thermometer falling to 29°; a degree of cold which was severely felt by the sick people.

The wind at length abated, and the sea came down, so that we launched the boats; and it being by that time calm, we rowed to the eastward across Navy-board inlet, passing through several streams of ice; when, the men being exhausted by twelve hours' labour, we found a harbour after a progress of ten miles, and pitched our tents at the mouth of another river; there resting, and repairing the boats, which were not in the best condition.

August 26 At four in the morning, when all were asleep, the look-out man, David Wood, thought he discovered a sail in the offing, and immediately informed Commander Ross, who, by means of his glass, soon saw that it was, in reality, a ship. All hands were immediately out of their tents and on the beach, discussing her rig, quality, and course; though there were still some despairers who maintained that it was only an iceberg.

No time was however lost: the boats were launched, and signals made by burning wet powder; when, completing our embarkation, we left our little harbour at six o'clock. Our progress was tedious, owing to alternate calms, and light airs blowing in every direction; yet we made way towards the vessel, and had it remained calm where she was, should soon have been alongside. Unluckily, a breeze just then sprang up, and she made all sail to the south-eastward; by which means the boat that was foremost was soon left astern, while the other two were steering more to the eastward, with the hopes of cutting her off.

About ten o'clock we saw another sail to the northward, which appeared to be lying to for her boats; thinking, at one time, when she hove to, that she had seen us. That, however, proved not to be the case, as she soon bore up under all sail. In no long time it was apparent that she was fast leaving us; and it was the most anxious moment that we had yet experienced, to find that we were near to no less than two ships, either of which would have put an end to all our fears and all our toils, and that we should probably reach neither.

It was necessary, however, to keep up the courage of the men, by assuring them, from time to time, that we were coming up with her; when, most fortunately, it fell calm, and we really gained so fast, that, at eleven o'clock we saw her heave to with all sails aback, and lower down a boat, which rowed immediately towards our own.

She was soon alongside, when the mate in command addressed us, by presuming that we had met with some misfortune and lost our ship. This being answered in the affirmative, I requested to know the name of his vessel, and expressed our wish to be taken on board. I was answered that it was "the Isabella of Hull, once commanded by Captain Ross"; on which I stated that I was the identical man in question, and my people the crew of the *Victory*. That the mate, who commanded this boat, was as much astonished at this information as he appeared to be, I do not doubt; while, with the usual blunderheadedness of men on such occasions, he assured me that I had been dead two years. I easily convinced him, however, that what ought to have been true, according to his estimate, was a somewhat premature conclusion; as the bear-like form of the whole set of us might have shown him, had he taken time to consider, that we were certainly not whaling gentlemen, and that we carried tolerable evidence of our being "true men, and no impostors," on our backs, and in our starved and unshaven countenances. A hearty congratulation followed of course, in the true seaman style, and, after a few natural inquiries, he added that the *Isabella* was commanded by Captain Humphreys; when he immediately went off in his boat to communicate his information on board; repeating that we had long been given up as lost, not by them alone, but by all England.

As we approached slowly after him, to the ship, he jumped up the side, and in a minute the rigging was manned; while we were saluted with three cheers as we came within cable's length, and were not long in getting on board of my old vessel, where we were all received by Captain Humphreys with a hearty seaman's welcome.

Though we had not been supported by our names and characters, we should not the less have claimed, from charity, the attentions that we received, for never was seen a more miserable-looking set of wretches; while, that we were but a repulsive-looking people, none of us could doubt. If, to be poor, wretchedly poor, as far as all our present property was concerned, was to have a claim on charity, no one could well deserve it more; but if, to look so, be to frighten away the so called charitable, no beggar that wanders in Ireland could have outdone us in exciting the repugnance of those who have not known what poverty can be. Unshaven since I know not when, dirty, dressed in the rags of wild beasts instead of the tatters of civilization, and starved to the very bones, our gaunt and grim looks, when contrasted with those of the well-dressed and well-fed men around us, made us all feel, I believe for the first time, what we really were, as well as what we seemed to others. Poverty is without half its mark, unless it be contrasted with wealth: and what we might have known to be true in the past days, we had forgotten to think of, till we were thus reminded of what we truly were, as well as seemed to be.

But the ludicrous soon took place of all other feelings; in such a crowd and such confusion, all serious thought was impossible, while the new buoyancy of our spirits made us abundantly willing to be amused by the scene which now opened. Every man was hungry and was to be fed, all were ragged and were to be clothed, there was not one to whom washing was not indispensable, nor one whom his beard did not deprive of all English semblance. All, every thing, too, was to be done at once; it was washing, dressing, shaving, eating, all intermingled, it was all the materials of each jumbled together; while, in the midst of all, there were interminable questions to be asked and answered on all sides: the adventures of the *Victory*, our own escapes, the politics of England, and the news which was now four years old. But all subsided into peace at last. The sick were accommodated, the seamen disposed of, and all was done, for all of us, which care and kindness could perform. Night at length brought quiet and serious thoughts; and I trust there was not one man among us who did not then express, where it was due, his gratitude for that interposition which had raised us all from a despair which none could now forget, and had brought us from the very borders of a not distant grave, to life and friends and civilization.

Long accustomed, however, to a cold bed on the hard snow or the bare rock, few could sleep amid the comfort of our new accommodations. I was myself compelled to leave the bed which had been kindly assigned me, and take my abode in a chair for the night, nor did it fare much better with the rest. It was for time to reconcile us to this sudden and violent change, to break through what had become habit, and to inure us once more to the usages of our former days.

LIVING OFF LICHEN AND LEATHER

John Franklin
(1786–1847)

In 1845, looking again for the North West Passage, two well-crewed ships under Franklin's command sailed into the Canadian Arctic and were never seen again. There began the most prolonged search ever mounted for an explorer. For Franklin had been lost before and yet had survived. In 1821, returning from an overland reconnaissance of the Arctic coast north of Great Slave Lake, he and Dr. John Richardson, with two Lieutenants and about a dozen voyageurs (mostly French), had run out of food and then been overtaken by the Arctic winter. Franklin's narrative of what is probably the grisliest journey on record omits unpalatable details, like the cannibalism of one of his men, the murder of Lieut. Hood, and Richardson's summary shooting of the murderer; but it well conveys the debility of men forced to survive on leather and lichen (tripe de roche) plus that sense of demoralization and disintegration that heralds the demise of an expedition.

T hose in advance made, as usual, frequent halts, yet being unable from the severity of the weather to remain long still, they were obliged to move on before the rear could come up, and the party, of course, straggled very much.

About noon Samandrè coming up, informed us that Crédit and Vaillant could advance no further. Some willows being discovered in a valley near us, I proposed to halt the party there, whilst Dr. Richardson went back to visit them. I hoped too, that when the sufferers received the information of a fire being kindled at so short a distance they would be cheered, and use their utmost efforts to reach it, but this proved a vain hope. The Doctor found Vaillant about a mile and a half in the rear, much exhausted with cold and fatigue. Having encouraged him to advance to

Franklin's passage over the ice at Point Lata. Courtesy of the
Mansell Collection.

the fire, after repeated solicitations he made the attempt, but fell
down amongst the deep snow at every step. Leaving him in this
situation, the Doctor went about half a mile farther back, to the
spot where Crédit was said to have halted, and the track being
nearly obliterated by the snow drift, it became unsafe for him to
go further. Returning he passed Vaillant, who having moved only
a few yards in his absence, had fallen down, was unable to rise, and
could scarcely answer his questions. Being unable to afford him any
effectual assistance, he hastened on to inform us of his situation.
When J. B. Belanger had heard the melancholy account, he went
immediately to aid Vaillant, and bring up his burden. Respecting
Crédit, we were informed by Samandrè, that he had stopped a short
distance behind Vaillant, but that his intention was to return to the
encampment of the preceding evening.

When Belanger came back with Vaillant's load, he informed us
that he had found him lying on his back, benumbed with cold, and
incapable of being roused. The stoutest men of the party were now
earnestly entreated to bring him to the fire, but they declared
themselves unequal to the task; and, on the contrary, urged me
to allow them to throw down their loads, and proceed to Fort
Enterprise with the utmost speed. A compliance with their desire

would have caused the loss of the whole party, for the men were totally ignorant of the course to be pursued, and none of the officers, who could have directed the march, were sufficiently strong to keep up at the pace they would then walk; besides, even supposing them to have found their way, the strongest men would certainly have deserted the weak. Something, however, was absolutely necessary to be done, to relieve them as much as possible from their burdens, and the officers consulted on the subject. Mr. Hood and Dr. Richardson proposed to remain behind, with a single attendant, at the first place where sufficient wood and *tripe de roche* should be found for ten days' consumption; and that I should proceed as expeditiously as possible with the men to the house, and thence send them immediate relief. They strongly urged that this arrangement would contribute to the safety of the rest of the party, by relieving them from the burden of a tent, and several other articles; and that they might afford aid to Crédit, if he should unexpectedly come up. I was distressed beyond description at the thought of leaving them in such a dangerous situation, and for a long time combated their proposal; but they strenuously urged, that this step afforded the only chance of safety for the party, and I reluctantly acceded to it. The ammunition, of which we had a small barrel, was also to be left with them, and it was hoped that this deposit would be a strong inducement for the Indians to venture across the barren grounds to their aid. We communicated this resolution to the men, who were cheered at the slightest prospect of alleviation to their present miseries, and promised with great appearance of earnestness to return to those officers, upon the first supply of food.

The party then moved on; Vaillant's blanket and other necessaries were left in the track, at the request of the Canadians, without any hope, however, of his being able to reach them. After marching till dusk without seeing a favourable place for encamping, night compelled us to take shelter under the lee of a hill, amongst some willows, with which, after many attempts, we at length made a fire. It was not sufficient, however, to warm the whole party, much less to thaw our shoes; and the weather not permitting the gathering of *tripe de roche*, we had nothing to cook. The painful retrospection of the melancholy events of the day banished sleep, and we shuddered as we contemplated the dreadful effects of this bitterly cold night on our two companions, if still living. Some faint hopes were entertained of Crédit's surviving the storm, as he was provided with a good blanket, and had leather to eat.

The weather was mild next morning. We left the encampment at nine, and a little before noon came to a pretty extensive thicket of small willows, near which there appeared a supply of *tripe de roche* on the face of the rocks. At this place Dr. Richardson and Mr. Hood determined to remain, with John Hepburn, who volunteered to stop with them. The tent was securely pitched, a few willows collected, and the ammunition and all other articles were deposited, except each man's clothing, one tent, a sufficiency of ammunition for the journey, and the officers' journals. I had only one blanket, which was carried for me, and two pair of shoes. The offer was now made for any of the men, who felt themselves too weak to proceed, to remain with the officers, but none of them accepted it. Michel alone felt some inclination to do so. After we had united in thanksgiving and prayers to Almighty God, I separated from my companions, deeply afflicted that a train of melancholy circumstances should have demanded of me the severe trial of parting, in such a condition, from friends who had become endeared to me by their constant kindness and co-operation, and a participation of numerous sufferings. This trial I could not have been induced to undergo, but for the reasons they had so strongly urged the day before, to which my own judgment assented, and for the sanguine hope I felt of either finding a supply of provision at Fort Enterprise, or meeting the Indians in the immediate vicinity of that place, according to my arrangements with Mr. Wentzel and Akaitcho. Previously to our starting, Peltier and Benoit repeated their promises, to return to them with provision, if any should be found at the house, or to guide the Indians to them, if any were met.

Greatly as Mr. Hood was exhausted, and indeed, incapable as he must have proved, of encountering the fatigue of our very next day's journey, so that I felt his resolution to be prudent, I was sensible that his determination to remain was chiefly prompted by the disinterested and generous wish to remove impediments to the progress of the rest. Dr. Richardson and Hepburn, who were both in a state of strength to keep pace with the men, besides this motive which they shared with him, were influenced in their resolution to remain, the former by the desire which had distinguished his character, throughout the Expedition, of devoting himself to the succour of the weak, and the latter by the zealous attachment he had ever shown towards his officers.

We set out without waiting to take any of the *tripe de roche*, and walking at a tolerable pace, in an hour arrived at a fine group of pines, about a mile and a quarter from the tent. We sincerely regretted not having seen these before we separated from our companions, as they would have been better supplied with fuel here, and there appeared to be more *tripe de roche* than where we had left them.

Descending afterwards into a more level country, we found the snow very deep, and the labour of wading through it so fatigued the whole party, that we were compelled to encamp, after a march of four miles and a half. Belanger and Michel were left far behind, and when they arrived at the encampment appeared quite exhausted. The former, bursting into tears, declared his inability to proceed, and begged me to let him go back next morning to the tent, and shortly afterwards Michel made the same request. I was in hopes they might recover a little strength by the night's rest, and therefore deferred giving any permission *until* morning. The sudden failure in the strength of these men cast a gloom over the rest, which I tried in vain to remove, by repeated assurances that the distance to Fort Enterprise was short, and that we should, in all probability, reach it in four days. Not being able to find any *tripe de roche*, we drank an infusion of the Labrador tea plant (*ledum palustre*), and ate a few morsels of burnt leather for supper. We were unable to raise the tent, and found its weight too great to carry it on, we, therefore, cut it up, and took a part of the canvass for a cover. The night was bitterly cold, and though we lay as close to each other as possible, having no shelter, we could not keep ourselves sufficiently warm to sleep. A strong gale came on after midnight, which increased the severity of the weather. In the morning Belanger and Michel renewed their request to be permitted to go back to the tent, assuring me they were still weaker than on the preceding evening, and less capable of going forward; and they urged, that the stopping at a place where there was a supply of *tripe de roche* was their only chance of preserving life; under these circumstances, I could not do otherwise than yield to their desire. I wrote a note to Dr. Richardson and Mr. Hood, informing them of the pines we had passed, and recommending their removing thither. Having found that Michel was carrying a considerable quantity of ammunition, I desired him to divide it among my party, leaving him only ten balls and a little shot, to kill any animals he might meet on his way to the tent. This man was very particular in his inquiries respecting the direction of the house, and the course we meant to pursue; he also said, that if he should be able, he would go and search for Vaillant and Crédit; and he requested my permission to take Vaillant's blanket, if he should find it, to which I agreed, and mentioned it in my notes to the officers.

Scarcely were these arrangements finished, before Perrault and Fontano were seized with a fit of dizziness, and betrayed other

symptoms of extreme debility. Some tea was quickly prepared for
them, and after drinking it, and eating a few morsels of burnt
leather, they recovered, and expressed their desire to go forward;
but the other men, alarmed at what they had just witnessed,
became doubtful of their own strength, and, giving way to absolute
dejection, declared their inability to move. I now earnestly pressed
upon them the necessity of continuing our journey, as the only
means of saving their own lives, as well as those of our friends at
the tent; and, after much entreaty, got them to set out at ten a.m.:
Belanger and Michel were left at the encampment, and proposed to
start shortly afterwards. By the time we had gone about two
hundred yards, Perrault became again dizzy, and desired us to
halt, which we did, until he, recovering, offered to march on. Ten
minutes more had hardly elapsed before he again desired us to
stop, and, bursting into tears, declared he was totally exhausted,
and unable to accompany us further. As the encampment was not
more than a quarter of a mile distant, we recommended that he
should return to it, and rejoin Belanger and Michel, whom we
knew to be still there, from perceiving the smoke of a fresh fire;
and because they had not made any preparation for starting when
we quitted them. He readily acquiesced in the proposition, and
having taken a friendly leave of each of us, and enjoined us to
make all the haste we could in sending relief, he turned back,
keeping his gun and ammunition. We watched him until he was
nearly at the fire, and then proceeded. During these detentions,
Augustus becoming impatient of the delay had walked on, and we
lost sight of him. The labour we experienced in wading through the
deep snow induced us to cross a moderate-sized lake, which lay in
our track, but we found this operation far more harassing. As the
surface of the ice was perfectly smooth, we slipped at almost every
step, and were frequently blown down by the wind, with such
force as to shake our whole frames.

Poor Fontano was completely exhausted by the labour of this
traverse, and we made a halt until his strength was recruited, by
which time the party was benumbed with cold. Proceeding again, he
got on tolerably well for a little time; but being again seized with
faintness and dizziness, he fell often, and at length exclaimed that he
could go no further. We immediately stopped, and endeavoured to
encourage him to persevere, until we should find some willows to
encamp; he insisted, however, that he could not march any longer
through this deep snow; and said, that if he should even reach our
encampment this evening, he must be left there, provided *tripe de
roche* could not be procured to recruit his strength. The poor man

was overwhelmed with grief, and seemed desirous to remain at that spot. We were about two miles from the place where the other men had been left, and as the track to it was beaten, we proposed to him to return thither, as we thought it probable he would find the men still there; at any rate, he would be able to get fuel to keep him warm during the night; and, on the next day, he could follow their track to the officer's tent; and, should the path be covered by the snow, the pines we had passed yesterday would guide him, as they were yet in view.

I cannot describe my anguish on the occasion of separating from another companion under circumstances so distressing. There was, however, no alternative. The extreme debility of the rest of the party put the carrying him quite out of the question, as he himself admitted; and it was evident that the frequent delays he must occasion if he accompanied us, and did not gain strength, would endanger the lives of the whole. By returning he had the prospect of getting to the tent where *tripe de roche* could be obtained, which agreed with him better than with any other of the party, and which he was always very assiduous in gathering. After some hesitation, he determined on going back, and set out, having bid each of us farewell in the tenderest manner. We watched him with inexpressible anxiety for some time, and were rejoiced to find, though he got on slowly, that he kept on his legs better than before. Antonio Fontano was an Italian, and had served many years in De Meuron's regiment. He had spoken to me that very morning, and after his first attack of dizziness, about his father; and had begged, that should he survive, I would take him with me to England, and put him in the way of reaching home.

The party was now reduced to five persons, Adam, Peltier, Benoit, Samandrè, and myself. Continuing the journey, we came, after an hour's walk, to some willows, and encamped under the shelter of a rock, having walked in the whole four miles and a half. We made an attempt to gather some *tripe de roche*, but could not, owing to the severity of the weather. Our supper, therefore, consisted of tea and a few morsels of leather.

Augustus did not make his appearance, but we felt no alarm at his absence, supposing he would go to the tent if he missed our track. Having fire, we procured a little sleep. Next morning the breeze was light and the weather mild, which enabled us to collect some *tripe de roche*, and to enjoy the only meal we had had for four days. We derived great benefit from it, and walked with considerably more ease than yesterday. Without the strength it supplied, we should certainly have been unable to oppose the strong breeze we met in the afternoon. After walking about five miles, we came upon the borders of Marten Lake, and were rejoiced to find it frozen, so that we could continue our course straight for Fort Enterprise. We encamped at the first rapid in Winter River amidst willows and alders; but these were so frozen, and the snow fell so thick, that the men had great difficulty in making a fire. This proving insufficient to warm us, or even thaw our shoes, and having no food to prepare, we crept under our blankets. The arrival in a well-known part raised the spirits of the men to a high pitch, and we kept up a cheerful conversation until sleep overpowered us. The night was very stormy, and the morning scarcely less so; but, being desirous to reach the house this day, we commenced our journey very early. We were gratified by the sight of a large herd of rein-deer on the side of the hill near the track, but our only hunter, Adam, was too feeble to pursue them. Our shoes and garments were stiffened by the frost, and we walked in great pain until we arrived at some stunted pines, at which we halted, made a good fire, and procured the refreshment of tea. The weather becoming fine in the afternoon, we continued our journey, passed the Dog-rib Rock, and encamped among a clump of pines of considerable growth, about a mile further on. Here we enjoyed the comfort of a large fire, for the first time since our departure from the sea-coast; but this gratification was purchased at the expense of many severe falls in crossing a stony valley, to get at these trees. These was no *tripe de roche*, and we drank tea and ate some of our shoes for supper. Next morning, after taking the usual repast of tea, we proceeded to the house. Musing on what we were likely to find there, our minds were agitated between hope and fear, and, contrary to the custom we had kept up, of supporting our spirits by conversation, we went silently forward.

At length we reached Fort Enterprise, and to our infinite disappointment and grief found it a perfectly desolate habitation. There was no deposit of provision, no trace of the Indians, no letter from Mr. Wentzel to point out where the Indians might be found. It would be impossible to describe our sensations after entering this miserable abode, and discovering how we had been neglected: the whole party shed tears, not so much for our own fate, as for that of our friends in the rear, whose lives depended entirely on our sending immediate relief from this place.

I found a note, however, from Mr. Back, stating that he had reached the house two days before, and was going in search of the Indians, at a part where St. Germain deemed it probable they might be found. If he was unsuccessful, he purposed walking to Fort

Providence, and sending succour from thence; but he doubted whether either he or his party could perform the journey to that place in their present debilitated state. It was evident that any supply that could be sent from Fort Providence would be long in reaching us, neither could it be sufficient to enable us to afford any assistance to our companions behind, and that the only relief for them must be procured from the Indians. I resolved, therefore, on going also in search of them; but my companions were absolutely incapable of proceeding, and I thought by halting two or three days they might gather a little strength, whilst the delay would afford us the chance of learning whether Mr. Back had seen the Indians.

We now looked round for the means of subsistence, and were gratified to find several deer skins, which had been thrown away during our former residence. The bones were gathered from the heap of ashes; these with the skins, and the addition of *tripe de roche*, we considered would support us tolerably well for a time. As to the house, the parchment being torn from the windows, the apartment we selected for our abode was exposed to all the rigour of the season. We endeavoured to exclude the wind as much as possible, by placing loose boards against the apertures. The temperature was now between 15° and 20° below zero. We procured fuel by pulling up the flooring of the other rooms, and water for cooking, by melting the snow. Whilst we were seated round the fire, singeing the deer-skin for supper, we were rejoiced by the unexpected entrance of Augustus. He had followed quite a different course from ours, and the circumstance of his having found his way through a part of the country he had never been in before, must be considered a remarkable proof of sagacity. The unusual earliness of this winter became manifest to us from the state of things at this spot. Last year at the same season, and still later, there had been very little snow on the ground, and we were surrounded by vast herds of rein-deer; now there were but few recent tracks of these animals, and the snow was upwards of two feet deep. Winter River was then open, now it was frozen two feet thick.

When I arose the following morning, my body and limbs were so swollen that I was unable to walk more than a few yards. Adam was in a still worse condition, being absolutely incapable of rising without assistance. My other companions happily experienced this inconvenience in a less degree, and went to collect bones, and some *tripe de roche*, which supplied us with two meals. The bones were quite acrid, and the soup extracted from them excoriated the mouth if taken alone, but it was somewhat milder when boiled with *tripe de roche*, and we even thought the mixture palatable, with the addition of salt, of which a cask had been fortunately left here in the spring. Augustus to-day set two fishing lines below the rapid. On his way thither he saw two deer, but had not strength to follow them.

On the 13th the wind blew violently from south-east, and the snow drifted so much that the party were confined to the house. In the afternoon of the following day Belanger arrived with a note from Mr. Back, stating that he had seen no trace of the Indians, and desiring further instructions as to the course he should pursue. Belanger's situation, however, required our first care, as he came in almost speechless, and covered with ice, having fallen into a rapid, and, for the third time since we left the coast, narrowly escaped drowning. He did not recover sufficiently to answer our questions, until we had rubbed him for some time, changed his dress, and given him some warm soup. My companions nursed him with the greatest kindness, and the desire of restoring him to health, seemed to absorb all regard for their own situation. I witnessed with peculiar pleasure this conduct so different from that which they had recently pursued, when every tender feeling was suspended by the desire of self-preservation. They now no longer betrayed impatience or despondency, but were composed and cheerful, and had entirely given up the practice of swearing, to which the Canadian voyagers are so addicted.

I undertook the office of cooking, and insisted they should eat twice a day whenever food could be procured; but as I was too weak to pound the bones, Peltier agreed to do that in addition to his more fatiguing task of getting wood. We had a violent snow storm all the next day, and this gloomy weather increased the depression of spirits under which Adam and Samandrè were labouring. Neither of them would quit their beds, and they scarcely ceased from shedding tears all day; in vain did Peltier and myself endeavour to cheer them. We had even to use much entreaty before they would take the meals we had prepared for them. Our situation was indeed distressing, but in comparison with that of our friends in the rear, we thought it happy. Their condition gave us unceasing solicitude, and was the principal subject of our conversation.

Though the weather was stormy on the 26th, Samandrè assisted me to gather *tripe de roche*. Adam, who was very ill, and could not now be prevailed upon to eat this weed, subsisted principally on bones, though he also partook of the soup. The *tripe de roche* had hitherto afforded us our chief support, and we naturally felt great uneasiness at the prospect of being deprived of it, by its being so frozen as to render it impossible for us to gather it.

We perceived our strength decline every day, and every exertion began to be irksome; when we were once seated the greatest effort was necessary in order to rise, and we had frequently to lift each other from our seats; but even in this pitiable condition we conversed cheerfully, being sanguine as to the speedy arrival of the Indians. We calculated indeed that if they should be near the situation where they had remained last winter, our men would have reached them by this day. Having expended all the wood which we could procure from our present dwelling, without danger of its fall, Peltier began this day to pull down the partitions of the adjoining houses. Though these were only distant about twenty yards, yet the increase of labour in carrying the wood fatigued him so much, that by the evening he was exhausted. On the next day his weakness was such, especially in the arms, of which he chiefly complained, that he with difficulty lifted the hatchet; still he persevered, while Samandrè and I assisted him in bringing in the wood, but our united strength could only collect sufficient to replenish the fire four times in the course of the day. As the insides of our mouths had become sore from eating the bone-soup, we relinquished the use of it, and now boiled the skin, which mode of dressing we found more palatable than frying it, as we had hitherto done.

On the 29th, Peltier felt his pains more severe, and could only cut a few pieces of wood. Samandrè, who was still almost as weak, relieved him a little time, and I aided them in carrying in the wood. We endeavoured to pick some *tripe de roche*, but in vain, as it was entirely frozen. In turning up the snow, in searching for bones, I found several pieces of bark, which proved a valuable acquisition, as we were almost destitute of dry wood proper for kindling the fire. We saw a herd of rein-deer sporting on the river, about half a mile from the house; they remained there a long time, but none of the party felt themselves strong enough to go after them, nor was there one of us who could have fired a gun without resting it.

Whilst we were seated round the fire this evening, discoursing about the anticipated relief, the conversation was suddenly interrupted by Peltier's exclaiming with joy, "*Ah! le monde!*" imagining that he heard the Indians in the other room; immediately afterwards, to his bitter disappointment, Dr. Richardson and Hepburn entered, each carrying his bundle. Peltier, however, soon recovered himself enough to express his delight at their safe arrival, and his regret that their companions were not with them. When I saw them alone my own mind was instantly filled with apprehensions respecting my friend Hood, and our other companions, which were immediately confirmed by the Doctor's melancholy communication, that

Mr. Hood and Michel were dead. Perrault and Fontano had neither reached the tent, nor been heard of by them. This intelligence produced a melancholy despondency in the minds of my party, and on that account the particulars were deferred until another opportunity. We were all shocked at beholding the emaciated countenances of the Doctor and Hepburn, as they strongly evidenced their extremely debilitated state. The alteration in our appearance was equally distressing to them, for since the swellings had subsided we were little more than skin and bone. The Doctor particularly remarked the sepulchral tone of our voices, which he requested us to make more cheerful if possible, unconscious that his own partook of the same key.

Hepburn having shot a partridge, which was brought to the house, the Doctor tore out the feathers, and having held it to the fire a few minutes divided it into six portions. I and my three companions ravenously devoured our shares, as it was the first morsel of flesh any of us had tasted for thirty-one days, unless, indeed, the small grizzly particles which we found occasionally adhering to the pounded bones may be termed flesh. Our spirits were revived by this small supply, and the Doctor endeavoured to raise them still higher by the prospect of Hepburn's being able to kill a deer next day, as they had seen, and even fired at, several near the house. He endeavoured, too, to rouse us into some attention to the comfort of our apartment, and particularly to roll up, in the day, our blankets, which (expressly for the convenience of Adam and Samandrè) we had been in the habit of leaving by the fire where we lay on them. The Doctor having brought his prayer book and testament, some prayers and psalms, and portions of scripture, appropriate to our situation, were read, and we retired to bed.

Next morning the Doctor and Hepburn went out early in search of deer; but though they saw several herds and fired some shots, they were not so fortunate as to kill any, being too weak to hold their guns steadily. The cold compelled the former to return soon, but Hepburn persisted until late in the evening.

My occupation was to search for skins under the snow, it being now our object immediately to get all that we could, but I had not strength to drag in more than two of those which were within twenty yards of the house, until the Doctor came and assisted me. We made up our stock to twenty-six, but several of them were putrid, and scarcely eatable, even by men suffering the extremity of famine. Peltier and Samandrè continued very weak and dispirited, and they were unable to cut fire-wood. Hepburn had in consequence that laborious task to perform after he came back. The Doctor having scarified the swelled parts of Adam's body, a large quantity of water flowed out, and he obtained some ease, but still kept his bed.

After our usual supper of singed skin and bone soup, Dr. Richardson acquainted me with the afflicting circumstances attending the death of Mr. Hood and Michel, and detailed the occurrences subsequent to my departure from them, which I shall give from his own journal, in his own words; but I must here be permitted to express the heart-felt sorrow with which I was overwhelmed at the loss of so many companions; especially of my friend Mr. Hood, to whose zealous and able co-operation I had been indebted for so much invaluable assistance during the Expedition, whilst the excellent qualities of his heart engaged my warmest regard. His scientific observations, together with his maps and drawings (a small part of which only appear in this work), evince a variety of talent, which, had his life been spared, must have rendered him a distinguished ornament to his profession, and which will cause his death to be felt as a loss to the service.

ADRIFT ON AN ARCTIC ICE FLOE

Fridtjof Nansen
(1861–1930)

Norwegian patriot, natural scientist, and Nobel laureate, Nansen caught the world's imagination when he almost reached the North Pole in 1895. The attempt was made on skis from a specially reinforced vessel which, driven into the ice, was carried from Siberia towards Greenland. The idea stemmed from his first expedition, an 1888 crossing of Greenland. Then too he had used skis and then too, unwittingly and nearly disastrously, he had taken to the ice. Arrived off Greenland's inhospitable east coast, he had ordered his five-man party to spare their vessel by crossing the off-shore ice floe in rowing boats. A task which he expected to take a few hours turned into an involuntary voyage down the coast of twelve days.

The last touches were given to our despatches and home letters; and if any of us had a specially dear friend to whom he wished to send a final farewell, it was sent, I take it, for it was not quite certain when the next meeting would be. But my companions seemed in a particularly cheerful humour, and there was no consciousness to be seen in the little band of preparation for a serious struggle. Nor was this to be wondered at, seeing that after six weeks of waiting and longing the hour of release was now at hand. The sensation which the sight of land that morning gave me was nothing short of delicious. As I then wrote to a friend, our prospects looked brighter than I had ever dared to hope. I had a sense of elasticity, as when one is going to a dance and expecting to meet the choice of one's heart. A dance indeed we had, but not on the floor of roses which we could have wished, and our heart's choice certainly kept us a long time waiting.

Towards seven o'clock in the evening everything is ready for our start. Sermilikfjord lies now straight in front of us. According to the results of cross-bearings taken from points on shore we ought to be about nine miles from its mouth. I go up to the mast-head for the last time to see where the ice looks easiest and what will be our best course. The reflection of open water beyond the ice is now more clearly visible than before. In a line somewhat west of Kong Oscars Havn the ice seems most open, and I determine to take that course.

More confident than ever I descend to the deck, and now the hour of departure is at hand. The whole of the "Jason's" crew were assembled. In spite of our joy at the prospect of a successful start, I think it was with somewhat strange feelings that we bid farewell to these brave sea-folk, with whom we had now spent six weeks, and among whom we had each of us found many a faithful friend, who at this moment assumed a doubtful air or turned away his head with an expressive shake. No doubt they thought they would never see us again. We shook hands with Captain Jakobsen last of all, and in his calm, quiet way this typical Norwegian sailor bid us a kind farewell and wished us God-speed.

Then down the ladder we went, and into the boats. I took charge of our "Jason" boat with Dietrichson and Balto at the oars, while Sverdrup steered the other with Ravna and Kristiansen.

"Ready? Give way then!" And as the boats rush through the dark water before the first vigorous strokes, the air rings with three lusty cheers from sixty-four voices, and then come two white clouds of smoke as the "Jason's" guns send us her last greeting. The report rolls heavily out into the thick, saturated air, proclaiming to the silent, solemn world of ice around us that we have broken the last bridge which could take us back to civilisation. Henceforth we shall follow our own path. Then good-bye! and our boats glide with regular strokes into the ice to meet the first cold embrace of that nature which for a while is to give us shelter. All of us had the most implicit faith in our luck; we knew that exertion and danger awaited us, but we were convinced that we must and should get the better of them.

When we had got some way into the ice a boat and twelve men in charge of the second mate overtook us. They had been sent by Captain Jakobsen to help us as far as they could the first part of the way by dragging our boats or forcing a passage. They kept with us for a while, but when I saw they could be of very little use to us, as we worked our way through as fast as they did, I thanked them for their kindness and sent them back. We then reach a long stretch of slack ice, wave farewell to the boat, and push on with unabated courage.

At first we advanced quickly. The ice was open enough to let us row our way to a great extent among the floes, though now and then we had to force a passage by the help of crowbars and axes. There were few places where we had to drag our boats over the ice, and then the floes were small. It had begun to rain a little before we left the "Jason"; it now grew heavier, and the sky darkened and assumed a curiously tempestuous look. It was an odd and striking sight to see these men in their dark-brown waterproofs, with their pointed hoods, like monks' cowls, drawn over their heads, working their way surely and silently on in the two boats, one following close in the other's wake, amid the motionless white ice-floes, which contrasted strangely with the dark and stormy sky. Over the jagged peaks by Sermilikfjord black banks of cloud had gathered. Now and again the mass would break, and we could see as if through rents in a curtain far away to a sky still glowing with all the lingering radiance of an Arctic sunset, and reflecting a subdued and softer warmth upon the edges of the intercepting veil. Then in a moment the curtain was drawn close again, and it grew darker than ever, while we, stroke upon stroke, pushed indefatigably on, the rain beating in our faces. Was this an image of our own fate that we had seen, to have all this radiance revealed to us and then hidden and cut off by a veil of thick, impenetrable cloud? It could scarcely be so, but the soul of man is fanciful and superstitious, ready to see tokens on all sides of him, and willing to believe that the elements and the universe revolve on the axis of his own important self.

The ice now gave us rather more difficulty, and we had often to mount a hummock to look out for the best way. From the top of one of these look-outs I waved a last farewell to the "Jason" with our flag, which she answered by dipping hers. Then we start off again, and quickly, as we have no time to spare.

From the first we had had a big iceberg far to the west of us, but now for a long time we had been astonished to see how much nearer we were getting to it, though we were not working in its direction, as our course lay considerably to the east. We saw it must be the current which was taking us west. And so it was; we were being carried along with irresistible force, and it soon became plain that we could not pass to the east of this iceberg, but would have to go under its lee. Just here, however, we drift suddenly into a tearing mill-race which is driving the floes pell-mell, jamming them together and piling them one upon another. Both our boats are in danger of destruction. Sverdrup drags his up on to a floe, and is safe enough. We take ours on towards an open pool, though every moment in danger of getting it crushed. The only course is to keep a sharp look-out, and clear all the dangerous points by keeping our boat always over the so-called "foot," or projecting base of the floe, or in a recess or inlet in its side, when a nip is threatened. This is not easy in these irresistible currents, but by our united efforts we succeed, and reach a large open pool to the lee of the iceberg, and are for the time secure. Now comes Sverdrup's turn; I signal to him to follow us, and he succeeds, keeping his boat in calmer water than we had.

We now find many good lanes of open water on our way inwards. The ice jams only once or twice, especially when the current carries us against one of the icebergs which lie stranded round about us, but it soon opens again, and we pass on. Our prospects are good, and our hearts are light. The weather is better too: it has ceased to rain, and the king of day is just rising behind the jagged background of Sermilikfjord, setting the still clouded heaven in a blaze and lighting his beacons on the mountain tops.

Long stretches of water lie in front of us, and I already fancy I can see from the boat the open water beyond the ice. We are very near the land to the west of Sermilikfjord, and I can clearly and distinctly see the stones and details of the rocks and mountain side. It does not seem possible that anything can stop us, and prevent our landing, and we are so self-confident that we already begin to discuss where and when we shall take our boats ashore. Just at this moment the ice packs, and we are obliged to find a place of safety for our boats, and drag them up. This we do, Sverdrup a little way off us. We have not secured a very desirable harbour for our boat, as the approach is too narrow, and when the floes part again and we are taking her out, a sharp edge of ice cuts through a plank in her side. She would no longer float, and there was nothing to be done but unload her and pull her up on to the floe for repairs. Sverdrup and Kristiansen took her in hand and mended her again with really masterly skill, and with little loss of time, considering the wretched implements they had to use. We had nothing to give them but a bit of deal which had formed the bottom board of one of the boats, some nails, a hatchet, and a wooden mallet. This broken boat, however, settled our fate. While we were at work the ice had packed again, the clouds had gathered, and the rain began to pour down in torrents, enveloping all around in gloom and mist. The only thing to be done was to get up tent and wait.

It is now ten o'clock on the morning of the 18th of July. The best thing we can do is to crawl into our sleeping-bags and take the rest which is not unwelcome to us after fifteen hours' hard and continuous work in the ice.

Before we turned in, it grew a little clearer sea wards, and through a break we caught sight of the "Jason" far away. She was just getting up full steam, and a while later she disappeared in the distance, no doubt comfortably believing that we were now safe on shore. This was our last glimpse of her.

"When Ravna saw the ship for the last time," writes Balto, "he said to me: 'What fools we were to leave her to die in this place. There is no hope of life; the great sea will be our graves.' I answered that it would not have been right for us two Lapps to turn back. We should not have been paid, and perhaps the Norwegian consul would have had to send us to Karasjok out of the poor rates. This would have been a great disgrace."

While we were asleep it was necessary for one of us to keep watch in order to turn the others out, in case the ice should open enough to let us make further progress. Dietrichson at once volunteered for the first watch. But the ice gave little or no sign of opening. Only once had I to consider the possibility of setting to work again, but the floes closed up immediately. Dragging our boats over this ice was not to be thought of; it was too rough, and the floes were too small. So, while the rain continues we have more time for sleep and rest than we care for.

In fact, we were already in the fatal current. With irresistible force it first carried us westwards into the broader belt of ice beyond Sermilikfjord. Here it took a more southerly direction and bore us straight away from shore, at a pace that rendered all resistance on our part completely futile. Had we not been detained by our broken boat, we should probably have been able to cross the zone where the current ran strongest and get into quieter water nearer shore. As it was, the critical time was wasted and we were powerless to recover it.

The force of the current into which we had thus fallen was considerably greater than had been previously supposed. That a current existed was well known, and I had taken measures accordingly, but, had I had a suspicion of its real strength, I should certainly have gone to work in a different way. I should in that case have taken to the ice considerably further to the east, and just off Cape Dan, and had we then worked inwards across the line of the stream we should probably have got through the ice before we were driven so far west, *i.e.* past the mouth of Sermilikfjord, and into the broader belt of ice where the current turns southwards. Then we should, as we had expected, have reached shore all well on July 19, and chosen our landing-place where we had pleased. But now it was our fate to see how well we might have managed. We had seen the open water under the shore, we had seen the rocks on the beach; a couple of hours of easy work, and we should have been there. But Paradise was barred in our faces; it was the will of Destiny that we should land many miles to the south.

Meanwhile the rain is descending in streams, and we are constantly at work keeping our tent-floor clear of the pools of water which finds its way in through the lace-holes. After we have spent nearly twenty-four hours in the tent, mainly engaged in this occupation, the ice opens enough to tempt us to continue our efforts to reach land with renewed courage and restored vigour. This was at six o'clock on the morning of July 19.

The rain has abated somewhat, and through an opening in the fog we can see land somewhere near Sermilikfjord. We are much more than double as far distant from it as we had been – some twenty miles, in fact; but we look trustfully forward to the future. For even if we did not reach shore at Inigsalik, as we had hoped, we can still do so further south at Pikiudtlek. All we have to do is to work resolutely across the current, and we must get to shore sooner or later. As far as we could see, this was plain and simple reasoning and gave us no ground for apprehension, but experience was to show us that our premises were not altogether in accordance with fact. The main factor in the calculation, the strength of the current, was unfortunately an extremely uncertain quantity.

However, determination and courage were not wanting. We worked with glee, got to the lee of a huge iceberg, found lanes of open water stretching far inwards, and pushed a good way on towards land.

Then the ice packs again, and we have to take refuge on a floe once more. The sun now finds its way through the clouds from time to time, so we pull our boats right up on to the floe, set up our tent and settle down as comfortably as we can, get a change of clothes on, and dry a few of our wet things. This was a process I had especial need of, as in the course of our day's work I had fallen into the water owing to the breaking of the edge of a floe as I was jumping into the boat. An involuntary bath of this kind was, however, an almost daily experience to one or other member of the expedition. Later on in the day the sun comes out altogether, and we pass a really pleasant afternoon. We do thorough justice to the tins of provisions sent us from the Stavanger Preserving Factory, and we have no lack of drink. Had we had no more beer in our keg, we could have found plenty of the most delightful drinking-water in pools on the floes.

Our keg, I may say, belonged to the boat the "Jason" had handed over to us. All the small boats attached to the sealers are provided with a keg of beer and a chest of bread and bacon. The keg and chest the captain had let us carry off well supplied, much to our present comfort.

We now for the first time can hear rather clearly the sound of breakers on the edge of the ice towards the sea, but pay no particular attention to the fact. We seem to be drifting straight away from land, and the tops of the mountains by Sermilikfjord gradually diminish.

That evening I sit up late, long after the others have crept into their bags, to take some sketches. It is one of those glorious evenings with the marvellously soft tones of colour which seem to steal so caressingly upon one, and with that dreamy, melancholy light which soothes the soul so fondly and is so characteristic of the northern night. The wild range of jagged peaks in the north by Sermilikfjord stands out boldly against the glowing sky, while the huge expanse of the "Inland ice" bounds the horizon far away to the west, where its soft lines melt gently into the golden background.

The evening was lovely, and the "Inland ice" lay temptingly and enticingly just before me. Strange that a narrow strip of drifting floes should be able to divide us so hopelessly from the goal of our desires! Is not this often the case in life? The land of enchantment looks so alluring and so near. One spring would take us there, it seems. There is but one obstacle in our way, but that one is enough.

As I sit and sketch and meditate I notice a rumbling in the ice, the sound of a growing swell which has found its way in to us. I turn seawards, where it looks threatening, and, thinking that there is a storm brewing out there, but that that is of small consequence to us, I go at last to join my slumbering comrades in the bags to sleep the sleep of the just.

Next morning, July 20, I was roused by some violent shocks to the floe on which we were encamped, and thought the motion of the sea must have increased very considerably. When we get outside we discover that the floe has split in two not far from the tent. The Lapps, who had at once made for the highest points of our piece of ice, now shout that they can see the open sea. And so it is; far in the distance lies the sea sparkling in the morning sunshine. It is a sight we have not had since we left the "Jason."

I may here reproduce the entries in my diary for this and the following day: –

"The swell is growing heavier and heavier and the water breaking over our floe with ever-increasing force. The blocks of ice and slush, which come from the grinding of the floes together, and are thrown up round the edges of our piece, do a good deal to break the violence of the waves. The worst of it all is that we are being carried seawards with ominous rapidity. We load our sledges and try to drag them inwards towards land, but soon see that the pace we are drifting at is too much for us. So we begin again to look around us for a safer floe to pitch our camp on, as our present one seems somewhat shaky. When we first took to it it was a good round flat piece about seventy yards across, but it split once during the night, and is now preparing to part again at other places, so that we shall soon not have much of it left. Close by us is a large strong floe, still unbroken, and thither we move our camp.

"Meanwhile the breakers seem to be drawing nearer, their roar grows louder, the swell comes rolling in and washes over the ice all round us, and the situation promises before long to be critical.

"Poor Lapps! they are not in the best of spirits. This morning they had disappeared, and I could not imagine what had become of them, as there were not many places on our little island where any of us could hide ourselves away. Then I noticed that some tarpaulins had been carefully laid over one of the boats. I lifted a corner gently and saw both the Lapps lying at the bottom of the boat. The younger, Balto, was reading aloud to the other out of his Lappish New Testament. Without attracting their attention I replaced the cover of this curious little house of prayer which they had set up for themselves. They had given up hope of life, and were making ready for death. As Balto confided to me one day long afterwards, they had opened their hearts to one another here in the boat and mingled their tears together, bitterly reproaching themselves and others because they had ever been brought to leave their homes. This is not to be wondered at, as they have so little interest in the scheme.

"It is glorious weather, with the sun so hot and bright that we must have recourse to our spectacles. We take advantage of this to get an observation, our bearings showing us to be in 65°8′N. and 38°20′W., i.e. 30 minutes or about 35 miles from the mouth of Sermilikfjord, and from 23 to 25 minutes or about 30 miles from the nearest land.

"We get our usual dinner ready, deciding, however, in honour of the occasion, to treat ourselves to pea-soup. This is the first time we have allowed ourselves to cook anything. While the soup is being made the swell increases so violently that our cooking apparatus is on the point of capsizing over and over again.

"The Lapps go through their dinner in perfect silence, but the rest of us talk and joke as usual, the violent rolls of our floe repeatedly giving rise to witticisms on the part of one or other of the company, which in spite of ourselves kept our laughing muscles in constant use. As far as the Lapps were concerned, however, these jests fell on anything but good ground, for they plainly enough thought that this was not at all the proper time and place for such frivolity.

"From the highest point on our floe we can clearly see how the ice is being washed by the breakers, while the columns of spray thrown high into the air look like white clouds against the background of blue sky. No living thing can ride the floes out there as far as we can see. It seems inevitable that we must be carried thither, but, as our floe is thick and strong, we hope to last for a while. We have no idea of leaving it before we need, but when it comes to that, and we can hold on no longer, our last chance will be to try and run our boats out through the surf. This will be a wet amusement, but we are determined to do our best in the fight for life. Our provisions, ammunition, and other things are divided between the two boats, so that if one is stove in and sinks we shall have enough to keep us alive in the other. We should probably be able to save our lives in that case, but of course the success of the expedition would be very doubtful.

"To run one of our loaded boats into the water through the heavy surf and rolling floes without getting her swamped or crushed will perhaps be possible, as we can set all our hands to work, but it will be difficult for the crew of the remaining boat to get their ship launched. After consideration we come to the conclusion that we must only put what is absolutely necessary into one boat, and keep it as light as possible, so that in case of extremity we can take to it alone. For the rest, we shall see how things look when we actually reach the breakers.

"We have scarcely half a mile left now, and none of us have any doubt but that before another couple of hours are passed we shall find ourselves either rocking on the open sea, making our way along the ice southwards, or sinking to the bottom.

"Poor Ravna deserves most sympathy. He is not yet at all accustomed to the sea and its caprices. He moves silently about, fiddling with one thing or another, now and again goes up on to the highest points of our floe, and gazes anxiously out towards the breakers. His thoughts are evidently with his herd of reindeer, his tent, and wife and children far away on the Finmarken mountains, where all is now sunshine and summer weather.

"But why did he ever leave all this? Only because he was offered money? Alas! what is money compared with happiness and home, where all is now sun and summer? Poor Ravna!

"It is but human at such moments to let the remembrance dwell on what has been fairest in life, and few indeed can have fairer memories to look back upon than yours of the mountain and reindeerherd.

"But here, too, the sun is shining as kindly and peacefully as elsewhere, down on the rolling sea and thundering surf, which is boiling round us. The evening is glorious, as red as it was yesterday, and as no doubt it will be to-morrow and ever after, setting the western sky on fire, and pressing its last long passionate kiss on land and ice and sea before it disappears behind the barrier of the 'Inland ice.' There is not a breath of wind stirring, and the sea is rolling in upon us ruddy and polished as a shield under the light of the evening sky.

"Beautiful it is, indeed, with these huge long billows coming rolling in, sweeping on as if nothing could withstand them. They fall upon the white floes, and then, raising their green, dripping breasts, they break and throw fragments of ice and spray far before them on to the glittering snow, or high above them into the blue air. But it seems almost strange that such surroundings can be the scene of death. Yet death must come one day, and the hour of our departure could scarcely be more glorious.

"But we have no time to waste; we are getting very near now. The swell is so heavy that when we are down in the hollows we can see nothing of the ice around us, nothing but the sky above. Floes crash together, break, and are ground to fragments all about us, and our own has also split. If we are going to sea we shall need all our strength in case we have to row for days together in order to keep clear of the ice. So all hands are ordered to bed in the tent, which is the only thing we have not yet packed into the boats. Sverdrup, as the most experienced and cool-headed among us, is to take the first watch and turn us out at the critical moment. In two hours Kristiansen is to take his place.

"I look in vain for any sign which can betray fear on the part of my comrades, but they seem as cool as ever, and their conversation is as usual. The Lapps alone show some anxiety, though it is that of a calm resignation, for they are fully convinced that they have seen the sun set for the last time. In spite of the roar of the breakers we are soon fast asleep, and even the Lapps seem to be slumbering quietly and soundly. They are too good children of nature to let anxiety spoil their sleep. Balto, who, not finding the tent safe enough, is lying in one of the boats, did not even wake when some time later it was almost swept by the waves, and Sverdrup had to hold it to keep it on the floe.

"After sleeping for a while, I do not know how long, I am woke by the sound of the water rushing close by my head and just outside the wall of the tent. I feel the floe rocking up and down like a ship in a heavy sea, and the roar of the surf is more deafening than ever. I lay expecting every moment to hear Sverdrup call me or to see the tent filled with water, but nothing of the kind happened. I could distinctly hear his familiar steady tread up and down the floe between the tent and the boats. I seemed to myself to see his sturdy form as he paced calmly backwards and forwards, with his hands in his pockets and a slight stoop in his shoulders, or stood with his calm and thoughtful face gazing out to sea, his quid now and again turning in his cheek – I remember no more, as I dozed off to sleep again.

"I did not wake again till it was full morning. Then I started up in astonishment, for I could hear nothing of the breakers but a distant thunder. When I got outside the tent I saw that we were a long way off the open sea. Our floe, however, was a sight to remember. Fragments of ice, big and little, had been thrown upon it by the waves till they formed a rampart all round us, and the ridge on which our tent and one of the boats stood was the only part the sea had not washed.

"Sverdrup now told us that several times in the course of the night he had stood by the tent-door prepared to turn us out. Once he actually undid one hook, then waited a bit, took another turn to the boats, and then another look at the surf, leaving the hook unfastened in case of accidents. We were then right out at the extreme edge of the ice. A huge crag of ice was swaying in the sea close beside us and threatening every moment to fall upon our floe. The surf was washing us on all sides, but the rampart that had been thrown up round us did us good service, and the tent and one of the boats still stood high and dry. The other boat, in which Balto was asleep, was washed so heavily that again and again Sverdrup had to hold it in its place.

"Then matters got still worse. Sverdrup came to the tent-door again, undid another hook, but again hesitated and waited for the next sea. He undid no more hooks, however. Just as things looked worst, and our floe's turn had come to ride out into the middle of the breakers, she suddenly changed her course and with astonishing speed we were once more sailing in towards land. So marvellous was the change that it looked as if it were the work of an unseen hand. When I got out we were far inside and in a good harbour, though the roar of the breakers was still audible enough to remind us of the night. Thus for this time we were spared the expected trial of the seaworthiness of our boats and our own seamanship."

THE POLE IS MINE

Robert Edwin Peary
(1856–1920)

Born in Pennsylvania and latterly a commander in the US navy, Peary had set his sights on claiming the North Pole from childhood. It was not just an obsession but a religion, his manifest destiny. Regardless of cost, hardship, and other men's sensibilities, he would be Peary of the Pole, and the Pole would be American. Critics might carp over the hundreds of dogs that were sacrificed to his ambition, over the chain of supply depots that would have done credit to a military advance, and over the extravagance of Peary's ambition, but success, in 1909, came only after a catalogue of failures; and even then it would be disputed. Under the circumstances his triumphalism is understandable and, however distasteful, not unknown amongst other Polar travellers.

T he last march northward ended at ten o'clock of the forenoon of April 6. I had now made the five marches planned from the point at which Bartlett turned back, and my reckoning showed that we were in the immediate neighbourhood of the goal of all our striving. After the usual arrangements for going into camp, at approximate local noon, on the Columbia meridian, I made the first observation at our polar camp. It indicated our position as 89° 57'.

We were now at the end of the last long march of the upward journey. Yet with the Pole actually in sight I was too weary to take the last few steps. The accumulated weariness of all those days and nights of forced marches and insufficient sleep, constant peril and anxiety, seemed to roll across me all at once. I was actually too exhausted to realize at the moment that my life's purpose had been achieved. As soon as our igloos had been completed, and we had eaten our dinner and double-rationed the dogs, I turned in for a few

Robert E. Peary. From *The North Pole* London, 1910.

hours of absolutely necessary sleep, Henson and the Eskimos having unloaded the sledges and got them in readiness for such repairs as were necessary. But, weary though I was, I could not sleep long. It was, therefore, only a few hours later when I woke. The first thing I did after awaking was to write these words in my diary: "The Pole at last. The prize of three centuries. My dream and goal for twenty years. Mine at last! I cannot bring myself to realize it. It seems all so simple and commonplace."

Everything was in readiness for an observation at 6 p.m., Columbia meridian time, in case the sky should be clear, but at that hour it was, unfortunately, still overcast. But as there were indications that it would clear before long, two of the Eskimos and myself made ready a light sledge carrying only the instruments, a tin of pemmican, and one or two skins; and drawn by a double team of dogs, we pushed on an estimated distance of ten miles. While we travelled, the sky cleared, and at the end of the journey, I was able to get a satisfactory series of observations at Columbia meridian midnight. These observations indicated that our position was then beyond the Pole.

Nearly everything in the circumstances which then surrounded us seemed too strange to be thoroughly realized, but one of the strangest of those circumstances seemed to me to be the fact that, in a march of only a few hours, I had passed from the western to the eastern hemisphere and had verified my position at the summit of the world. It was hard to realize that, on the first miles of this brief march, we had been travelling due north, while, on the last few miles of the same march, we had been travelling south, although we had all the time been travelling precisely in the same direction. It would be difficult to imagine a better illustration of the fact that most things are relative. Again, please consider the uncommon circumstance that, in order to return to our camp, it now became necessary to turn and go north again for a few miles and then to go directly south, all the time travelling in the same direction.

As we passed back along that trail which none had ever seen before or would ever see again, certain reflections intruded themselves which, I think, may fairly be called unique. East, west, and north had disappeared for us. Only one direction remained and that was south. Every breeze which could possibly blow upon us, no matter from what point of the horizon, must be a south wind. Where we were, one day and one night constituted a year, a hundred such days and nights constituted a century. Had we stood in that spot during the six months of the Arctic winter night, we should have seen every star of the northern hemisphere circling the sky at the same distance from the horizon, with Polaris (the North Star) practically in the zenith.

All during our march back to camp the sun was swinging around in its ever-moving circle. At six o'clock on the morning of April 7, having again arrived at Camp Jesup, I took another series of observations. These indicated our position as being four or five miles from the Pole, towards Behring Strait. Therefore, with a double team of dogs and a light sledge, I travelled directly towards the sun an estimated distance of eight miles. Again I returned to the camp in time for a final and completely satisfactory series of observations on April 7 at noon, Columbia meridian time. These observations gave results essentially the same as those made at the same spot twenty-four hours before.

I had now taken in all thirteen single, or six and one-half double, altitudes of the sun, at two different stations, in three different directions, at four different times. All were under satisfactory conditions, except for the first single altitude on the sixth. The temperature during these observations, had been from minus 11° Farhrenheit to minus 30° Fahrenheit, with clear sky and calm weather (except as already noted for the single observation on the sixth).

In traversing the ice in these various directions as I had done, I had allowed approximately ten miles for possible errors in my observations, and at some moment during these marches and counter-marches, I had passed over or very near the point where north and south and east and west blend into one.

Of course there were some more or less informal ceremonies connected with our arrival at our difficult destination, but they were not of a very elaborate character. We planted five flags at the top of the world. The first one was a silk American flag which Mrs. Peary gave me fifteen years ago. That flag has done more travelling in high latitudes than any other ever made. I carried it wrapped about my body on every one of my expeditions northward after it came into my possession, and I left a fragment of it at each of my successive "farthest norths": Cape Morris K. Jesup, the northernmost point of land in the known point of Jesup Land, west of Grant land; Cape Columbia, the northernmost point of North American lands; and my farthest north in 1906, latitude 87° 6′ in the ice of the polar sea. By the time it actually reached the Pole, therefore, it was somewhat worn and discoloured.

A broad diagonal section of this ensign would now mark the

farthest goal of earth – the place where I and my dusky companions stood.

It was also considered appropriate to raise the colours of the Delta Kappa Epsilon fraternity, in which I was initiated a member while an undergraduate student at Bowdoin College, the "World's Ensign of Liberty and Peace," with its red, white, and blue, in a field of white, the Navy League flag, and the Red Cross flag.

After I had planted the American flag in the ice, I told Henson to time the Eskimos for three rousing cheers, which they gave with the greatest enthusiasm. Thereupon, I shook hands with each member of the party – surely a sufficiently unceremonious affair to meet with the approval of the most democratic. The Eskimos were childishly delighted with our success. While, of course, they did not realize its importance fully, or its world-wide significance, they did understand that it meant the final achievement of a task upon which they had seen me engaged for many years.

Then, in a space between the ice blocks of a pressure ridge, I deposited a glass bottle containing a diagonal strip of my flag and records of which the following is a copy:

> 90 N. Lat., North Pole,
> April, 6, 1909.

Arrived here to-day, 27 marches from C. Columbia.

I have with me 5 men, Matthew Henson, coloured, Oo-tah, E-ging-wah, See-gloo, and Oo-ke-ah, Eskimos; 5 sledges and 38 dogs. My ship, the S. S. *Roosevelt*, is in winter quarters at C. Sheridan, 90 miles east of Columbia.

The expedition under my command which has succeeded in reaching the Pole, is under the auspices of the Peary Arctic Club of New York City, and has been fitted out and sent north by the members and friends of the club for the purpose of securing this geographical prize, if possible, for the honour and prestige of the United States of America.

The officers of the club are Thomas H. Hubbard, of New York, President; Zenas Crane, of Mass., Vice-president; Herbert L. Bridgman, of New York, Secretary and Treasurer.

I start back for Cape Columbia to-morrow.

> ROBERT E. PEARY,
> *United States Navy.*

> 90 N. Lat., North Pole,
> April 6, 1909.

I have to-day hoisted the national ensign of the United States of America at this place, which my observations indicate to be the North Polar axis of the earth, and have formally taken possession of the entire region, and adjacent, for and in the name of the President of the United States of America.

I leave this record and United States flag in possession.

ROBERT E. PEARY,
United States Navy.

If it were possible for a man to arrive at 90° north latitude without being utterly exhausted, body and brain, he would doubtless enjoy a series of unique sensations and reflections. But the attainment of the Pole was the culmination of days and weeks of forced marches, physical discomfort, insufficient sleep, and racking anxiety. It is a wise provision of nature that the human consciousness can grasp only such degree of intense feeling as the brain can endure, and the grim guardians of earth's remotest spot will accept no man as guest until he has been tried and tested by the severest ordeal.

Perhaps it ought not to have been so, but when I knew for a certainty that we had reached the goal, there was not a thing in the world I wanted but sleep. But after I had a few hours of it, there succeeded a condition of mental exaltation which made further rest impossible. For more than a score of years that point on the earth's surface had been the object of my every effort. To attain it my whole being, physical, mental, and moral, had been dedicated. Many times my own life and the lives of those with me had been risked. My own material and forces and those of my friends had been devoted to this object. This journey was my eighth into the Arctic wilderness. In that wilderness I had spent nearly twelve years out of the twenty-three between my thirtieth and my fifty-third year, and the intervening time spent in civilized communities during that period had been mainly occupied with preparations for returning to the wilderness. The determination to reach the Pole had become so much a part of my being that, strange as it may seem, I long ago ceased to think of myself save as an instrument for the attainment of that end. To the layman this may seem strange, but an inventor can understand it, or an artist, or any one who has devoted himself for years upon years to the service of an idea.

But though my mind was busy at intervals during those thirty hours spent at the Pole with the exhilarating thought that my dream had come true, there was one recollection of other times that, now and then, intruded itself with startling distinctness. It was the recollection of a day three years before, April 21, 1906, when after making a fight with ice, open water, and storms, the expedition which I commanded had been forced to turn back from

87° 6′ north latitude because our supply of food would carry us no further. And the contrast between the terrible depression of that day and the exaltation of the present moment was not the least pleasant feature of our brief stay at the Pole. During the dark moments of that return journey in 1906, I had told myself that I was only one in a long list of Arctic explorers, dating back through the centuries, all the way from Henry Hudson to the Duke of the Abruzzi, and including Franklin, Kane, and Melville – a long list of valiant men who had striven and failed. I told myself that I had only succeeded at the price of the best years of my life in adding a few links to the chain that led from the parallels of civilization towards the polar centre, but that, after all, at the end the only word I had to write was failure.

But now, while quartering the ice in various directions from our camp, I tried to realize that, after twenty-three years of struggles and discouragement, I had at last succeeded in placing the flag of my country at the goal of the world's desire. It is not easy to write about such a thing, but I knew that we were going back to civilization with the last of the great adventure stories – a story the world had been waiting to hear for nearly four hundred years, a story which was to be told at last under the folds of the Stars and Stripes, the flag that during a lonely and isolated life had come to be for me the symbol of home and everything I loved – and might never see again.

The thirty hours at the Pole, what with my marchings and counter-marchings, together with the observations and records, were pretty well crowded. I found time, however, to write to Mrs. Peary on a United States postal card which I had found on the ship during the winter. It had been my custom at various important stages of the journey northward to write such a note in order that, if anything serious happened to me, these brief communications might ultimately reach her at the hands of survivors. This was the card, which later reached Mrs. Peary at Sydney:

> 90 North Latitude, April 7th   .
>
> My dear Jo,
>   I have won out at last. Have been here a day. I start for home and you in an hour. Love to the "kidsies."
>
> BERT.

In the afternoon of the 7th, after flying our flags and taking our photographs, we went into our igloos and tried to sleep a little, before starting south again.

I could not sleep and my two Eskimos, Seegloo and Egingwah, who occupied the igloo with me, seemed equally restless. They turned from side to side, and when they were quiet I could tell from their uneven breathing that they were not asleep. Though they had not been specially excited the day before when I told them that we had reached the goal, yet they also seemed to be under the same exhilarating influence which made sleep impossible for me.

Finally I rose, and telling my men and the three men in the other igloo, who were equally wakeful, that we would try to make our last camp, some thirty miles to the south, before we slept, I gave orders to hitch up the dogs and be off. It seemed unwise to waste such perfect travelling weather in tossing about on the sleeping platforms of our igloos.

Neither Henson nor the Eskimos required any urging to take to the trail again. They were naturally anxious to get back to the land as soon as possible – now that our work was done. And about four o'clock on the afternoon of the 7th of April we turned our backs upon the camp at the North Pole.

Though intensely conscious of what I was leaving, I did not wait for any lingering farewell of my life's goal. The event of human beings standing at the hitherto inaccessible summit of the earth was accomplished, and my work now lay to the south, where four hundred and thirteen nautical miles of ice floes and possibly open leads still lay between us and the north coast of Grand Land. One backward glance I gave – then turned my face toward the south and toward the future.

FARTHEST SOUTH

Ernest Henry Shackleton
(1874–1922)

Born in Ireland, Shackleton joined the merchant navy before being recruited for Captain Scott's 1901 expedition to Antarctica. He was with Scott on his first attempt to reach the South Pole and, though badly shaken by the experience, realized that success was now feasible. In 1907, with a devoted team but little official support, he launched his own expedition. A scientific programme gave it respectability but Shackleton was essentially an adventurer, beguiled alike by the challenge of the unknown and the reward of celebrity. His goal was the Pole, 90 degrees south, and by Christmas 1908 his four-man team were already at 85 degrees.

D ecember 25   Christmas Day. There has been from 45° to 48° of frost, drifting snow and a strong biting south wind, and such has been the order of the day's march from 7 a.m. to 6 p.m. up one of the steepest rises we have yet done, crevassed in places. Now, as I write, we are 9500 ft. above sea-level, and our latitude at 6 p.m. was 85° 55′ South. We started away after a good breakfast, and soon came to soft snow, through which our worn and torn sledge-runners dragged heavily. All morning we hauled along and at noon had done 5 miles 250 yards. Sights gave us latitude 85° 51′ South. We had lunch then, and I took a photograph of the camp with the Queen's flag flying and also our tent flags, my companions being in the picture. It was very cold, the temperature being minus 16° Fahr., and the wind went through us. All the afternoon we worked steadily uphill, and we could see at 6 p.m. the new land plainly trending to the south-east. This land is very much glaciated. It is comparatively bare of snow, and there are well-defined glaciers on the side of the range, which seems to end up in the south-east with a large mountain like a keep. We have called it "The Castle." Behind these the mountains have more gentle slopes and are more rounded. They seem to fall away to the south-east, so that, as we are going south, the angle opens and we will soon miss them. When we camped at 6 p.m. the wind was decreasing. It is hard to understand this soft snow with such a persistent wind, and I can only suppose that we have not yet reached the actual plateau level, and that the snow we are travelling over just now is on the slopes, blown down by the south and south-east wind. We had a splendid dinner. First came hoosh, consisting of pony ration boiled up with pemmican and some of our emergency Oxo and biscuit. Then in the cocoa water I boiled our little plum pudding, which a friend of Wild's had given him. This, with a drop of medical brandy, was a luxury which Lucullus himself might have envied; then came cocoa, and lastly cigars and a spoonful of *creme de menthe* sent us by a friend in Scotland. We are full to-night, and this is the last time we will be for many a long day. After dinner we discussed the situation, and we have decided to still further reduce our food. We have now nearly 500 miles, geographical, to do if we are to get to the Pole and back to the spot where we are at the present moment. We have one month's food, but only three weeks' biscuit, so we are going to make each week's food last ten days. We will have one biscuit in the morning, three at mid-day, and two at night. It is the only thing to do. To-morrow we will throw away everything except the most absolute necessities. Already we are, as regards clothes, down to the limit, but we must trust to the old sledge-runners and dump the spare ones. One must risk this. We are very far away from all the world, and home thoughts have been much with us to-day, thoughts interrupted by pitching forward into a hidden crevasse more than once. Ah, well, we shall see all our own people when the work here is done. Marshall took our temperatures to-night. We are all two degrees sub normal, but as fit as can be. It is a fine open-air life and we are getting south.

December 26 Got away at 7 a.m. sharp, after dumping a lot of gear. We marched steadily all day except for lunch, and we have done 14 miles 480 yards on an uphill march, with soft snow at times and a bad wind. Ridge after ridge we met, and though the surface is better and harder in places, we feel very tired at the end of ten hours' pulling. Our height to-night is 9590 ft. above sea-level according to the hypsometer. The ridges we meet with are almost similar in appearance. We see the sun shining on them in the distance, and then the rise begins very gradually. The snow gets soft, and the weight of the sledge becomes more marked. As we near the top the soft snow gives place to a hard surface, and on the summit of the ridge we find small crevasses. Every time we reach the top of a ridge we say to ourselves: "Perhaps this is the last," but it never is the last; always there appears away ahead of us another ridge. I do not think that the land lies very far below the ice-sheet, for the crevasses on the summits of the ridges suggest that the sheet is moving over land at no great depth. It would seem that the descent towards the glacier proper from the plateau is by a series of terraces. We lost sight of the land to-day, having left it all behind us, and now we have the waste of snow all around. Two more days and our maize will be finished. Then our hooshes will be more woefully thin than ever. This shortness of food is unpleasant, but if we allow ourselves what, under ordinary circumstances, would be a reasonable amount, we would have to abandon all idea of getting far south.

December 27 If a great snow plain, rising every seven miles in a steep ridge, can be called a plateau, then we are on it at last, with an altitude above the sea of 9820 ft. We started at 7 a.m. and marched till noon, encountering at 11 a.m. a steep snow ridge which pretty well cooked us, but we got the sledge up by noon and camped. We are pulling 150 lb. per man. In the afternoon we had good going till 5 p.m. and then another ridge as difficult as the previous one, so that our backs and legs were in a bad way when we reached the top at 6 p.m., having done 14 miles 930 yards for the day. Thank heaven it has been a fine day, with little wind. The temperature is minus 9 Fahr. This surface is most peculiar, showing layers of snow with little sastrugi all pointing south-south-east. Short food makes us think of plum puddings, and hard half-cooked maize gives us indigestion, but we are getting south. The latitude is 86° 19′ South to-night. Our thoughts are with the people at home a great deal.

December 28 If the Barrier is a changing sea, the plateau is a changing sky. During the morning march we continued to go up hill steadily, but the surface was constantly changing. First there was soft snow in layers, then soft snow so deep that we were well over our ankles, and the temperature being well below zero, our feet were cold through sinking in. No one can say what we are going to find next, but we can go steadily ahead. We started at 6.55 a.m., and had done 7 miles 200 yards by noon, the pulling being very hard. Some of the snow is blown into hard sastrugi, some that look perfectly smooth and hard have only a thin crust through which we break when pulling; all of it is a trouble. Yesterday we passed our last crevasse, though there are a few cracks or ridges fringed with crystals shining like diamonds, warning us that the cracks are open. We are now 10,199 ft. above sea-level, and the plateau is gradually flattening out, but it was heavy work pulling this afternoon. The high altitude and a temperature of 48° of frost made breathing and work difficult. We are getting south – latitude 86° 31' South to-night. The last sixty miles we hope to rush, leaving everything possible, taking one tent only and using the poles of the other as marks every ten miles, for we will leave all our food sixty miles off the Pole except enough to carry us there and back. I hope with good weather to reach the Pole on January 12, and then we will try and rush it to get to Hut Point by February 28. We are so tired after each hour's pulling that we throw ourselves on our backs for a three minutes' spell. It took us over ten hours to do 14 miles 450 yards to-day, but we did it all right. It is a wonderful thing to be over 10,000 ft. up, almost at the end of the world. The short food is trying, but when we have done the work we will be happy. Adams had a bad headache all yesterday, and to-day I had the same trouble, but it is better now. Otherwise we are all fit and well. I think the country is flattening out more and more, and hope to-morrow to make fifteen miles, at least.

December 29   Yesterday I wrote that we hoped to do fifteen miles to-day, but such is the variable character of this surface that one cannot prophesy with any certainty an hour ahead. A strong south-erly wind, with from 44° to 49° of frost, combined with the effect of short rations, made our distance 12 miles 600 yards instead. We have reached an altitude of 10,310 ft., and an uphill gradient gave us one of the most severe pulls for ten hours that would be possible. It looks serious, for we must increase the food it we are to get on at all, and we must risk a depot at seventy miles off the Pole and dash for it then. Our sledge is badly strained, and on the abominably bad surface of soft snow is dreadfully hard to move. I have been suffering from a bad headache all day, and Adams also was worried by the cold. I think that these headaches are a form of mountain sickness, due to our high altitude. The others have bled from the nose, and that must relieve them. Physical effort is always trying at a high altitude, and we are straining at the harness all day, sometimes slipping in the soft snow that overlies the hard sastrugi. My head is very bad. The sensation is as though the nerves were being twisted up with a corkscrew and then pulled out. Marshall took our temperature to-night, and we are all at about 94°, but in spite of this we are getting south. We are only 198 miles off our goal now. If the rise would stop the cold would not matter, but it is hard to know what is man's limit. We have only 150 lb. per man to pull, but it is more severe work than the 250 lb. per man up the glacier was. The Pole is hard to get

December 30   We only did 4 miles 100 yards to-day. We started at 7 a.m., but had to camp at 11 a.m., a blizzard springing up from the south. It is more than annoying. I cannot express my feelings. We were pulling at last on a level surface, but very soft snow, when at about 10 A.M. the south wind and drift commenced to increase, and at 11 A.M. it was so bad that we had to camp. And here all day we have been lying in our sleeping-bags trying to keep warm and listening to the threshing drift on the tent-side. I am in the cooking-tent, and the wind comes through, it is so thin. Our precious food is going and the time also, and it is so important to us to get on. We lie here and think of how to make things better, but we cannot reduce food now, and the only thing will be to rush all possible at the end. We will do and are doing all humanly possible. It is with Providence to help us.

December 31   The last day of the old year, and the hardest day we have had almost, pushing through soft snow uphill with a strong head wind and drift all day. The temperature is minus 7° Fahr., and our altitude is 10,477 ft. above sea-level. The altitude is trying. My head has been very bad all day, and we are all feeling the short food, but still we are getting south. We are in latitude 86° 54' South to-night, but we have only three weeks' food and two weeks' biscuit to do nearly 500 geographical miles. We can only do our best. Too tired to write more to-night. We all get iced-up about our faces, and are on the verge of frost-bite all the time. Please God the weather will be fine during the next fourteen days. Then all will be well. The distance to-day was eleven miles.

NOTE If we had only known that we were going to get such cold weather as we were at this time experiencing, we would have kept a pair of scissors to trim our beards. The moisture from the condensation of one's breath accumulated on the beard and trickled down on to the Burberry blouse. Then it froze into a sheet of ice inside, and it became very painful to pull the Burberry off in camp. Little troubles of this sort would have seemed less serious to us if we had been able to get a decent feed at the end of the day's work, but we were very hungry. We thought of food most of the time. The chocolate certainly seemed better than the cheese, because the two spoonfuls of cheese per man allowed under our scale of diet would not last as long as the two sticks of chocolate. We did not have both at the same meal. We had the bad luck at this time to strike a tin in which the biscuits were thin and overbaked. Under ordinary circumstances they would probably have tasted rather better than the other biscuits, but we wanted bulk. We soaked them in our tea so that they would swell up and appear larger, but if one soaked a biscuit too much, the sensation of biting something was lost, and the food seemed to disappear much too easily.

January 1, 1909   Head too bad to write much. We did 11 miles 900 yards (statute) to-day, and the latitude at 6 p.m. was 87° 6½ ′ South, so we have beaten North and South records. Struggling uphill all day in very soft snow. Every one done up and weak from want of food. When we camped at 6 p.m. fine warm weather, thank God. Only 172½ miles from the Pole. The height above sea-level, now 10,755 ft., makes all work difficult. Surface seems to be better ahead. I do trust it will be so to-morrow.

January 2   Terribly hard work to-day. We started at 6.45 a.m. with a fairly good surface, which soon became very soft. We were sinking in over our ankles, and our broken sledge, by running sideways, added to the drag. We have been going uphill all day, and to-night are 11,034 ft. above sea-level. It has taken us all day to do 10 miles 450 yards, though the weights are fairly light. A cold wind, with a temperature of minus 14° Fahr., goes right through us now, as we are weakening from want of food, and the high altitude makes every movement an effort, especially if we stumble on the march. My head is giving me trouble all the time. Wild seems the most fit of us. God knows we are doing all we can, but the outlook is serious if this surface continues and the plateau gets higher, for we are not travelling fast enough to make our food spin out and get back to our depot in time. I cannot think of failure yet. I must look at the matter sensibly and consider the lives of those who are with me. I feel that if we go on too far it will be impossible to get back over this surface, and then all the results will be lost to the world. We can now definitely locate the South Pole on the highest plateau in the world, and our geological work and meteorology will be of the greatest use to science; but all this is not the Pole. Man can only do his best, and we have arrayed against us the strongest forces of nature. This cutting south wind with drift plays the mischief with us, and after ten hours of struggling against it one pannikin of food with two biscuits and a cup of cocoa does not warm one up much. I must think over the situation carefully to-morrow, for time is going on and food is going also.

January 3   Started at 6.55 a.m., cloudy but fairly warm. The temperature was minus 8° Fahr. at noon. We had a terrible surface all the morning, and did only 5 miles 100 yards. A meridian altitude gave us latitude 87° 22′ South at noon. The surface was better in the afternoon, and we did six geographical miles. The temperature at 6 p.m. was minus 11° Fahr. It was an uphill pull towards the evening, and we camped at 6.20 p.m., the altitude being 11,220 ft. above the sea. To-morrow we must risk making a depot on the plateau, and make a dash for it, but even then, if this surface continues, we will be two weeks in carrying it through.

January 4 The end is in sight. We can only go for three more days at the most, for we are weakening rapidly. Short food and a blizzard wind from the south, with driving drift, at a temperature of 47° of frost, have plainly told us to-day that we are reaching our limit, for we were so done up at noon with cold that the clinical thermometer failed to register the temperature of three of us at 94°. We started at 7.40 a.m., leaving a depot on this great wide plateau, a risk that only this case justified, and one that my comrades agreed to, as they have to every one so far, with the same cheerfulness and regardlessness of self that have been the means of our getting as far as we have done so far. Pathetically small looked the bamboo, one of the tent poles, with a bit of bag sewn on as a flag, to mark our stock of provisions, which has to take us back to our depot, one hundred and fifty miles north. We lost sight of it in half an hour, and are now trusting to our footprints in the snow to guide us back to each bamboo until we pick up the depot again. I trust that the weather will keep clear. To-day we have done 12½ geographical miles, and with only 70 lb. per man to pull it is as hard, even harder, work than the 100 odd lb. was yesterday, and far harder than the 250 lb. were three weeks ago, when we were climbing the glacier. This, I consider, is a clear indication of our failing strength. The main thing against us is the altitude of 11,200 ft. and the biting wind. Our faces are cut, and our feet and hands are always on the verge of frost-bite. Our fingers, indeed, often go, but we get them round more or less. I have great trouble with two fingers on my left hand. They had been badly jammed when we were getting the motor up over the ice face at winter quarters, and the circulation is not good. Our boots now are pretty well worn out, and we have to halt at times to pick the snow out of the soles. Our stock of sennegrass is nearly exhausted, so we have to use the same frozen stuff day after day. Another trouble is that the lamp-wick with which we tie the finnesko is chafed through, and we have to tie knots in it. These knots catch the snow under our feet, making a lump that has to be cleared every now and then. I am of the opinion that to sledge even in the height of summer on this plateau, we should have at least forty ounces of food a day per man, and we are on short rations of the ordinary allowance of thirty-two ounces. We depoted our extra underclothing to save weight about three weeks ago, and are now in the same clothes night and day. One suit of underclothing, shirt and guernsey, and our thin Burberries, now all patched. When we get up in the morning, out of the wet bag, our Burberries become like a coat of mail at once, and our heads and beards get iced-up with the moisture when breathing on the march. There is half a gale blowing dead in our teeth all the time. We hope to reach within 100 geographical miles of the Pole; under the circumstances we can expect to do very little more. I am confident that the Pole lies on the great plateau we have discovered, miles and miles from any outstanding land. The temperature tonight is minus 24° Fahr.

January 5 To-day head wind and drift again, with 50° of frost, and a terrible surface. We have been marching through 8 in, of snow, covering sharp sastrugi, which plays havoc with our feet, but we have done 13⅓ geographical miles, for we increased our food, seeing that it was absolutely necessary to do this to enable us to accomplish anything. I realise that the food we have been having has not been sufficient to keep up our strength, let alone supply the wastage caused by exertion, and now we must try to keep warmth in us, though our strength is being used up. Our temperatures at 5 a.m. were 94° Fahr. We got away at 7 a.m. sharp and marched till noon, then from 1 p.m. sharp till 6 p.m. All being in one tent makes our campwork slower, for we are so cramped for room, and we get up at 4.40 a.m. so as to get away by 7 a.m. Two of us have to stand outside the tent at night until things are squared up inside, and we find it cold work. Hunger grips us hard, and the food-supply is very small. My head still gives me great trouble. I began by wishing that my worst enemy had it instead of myself, but now I don't wish even my worst enemy to have such a headache; still, it is no use talking about it. Self is a subject that most of us are fluent on. We find the utmost difficulty in carrying through the day, and we can only go for two or three more days. Never once had the temperature been above zero since we got on to the plateau, though this is the height of summer. We have done our best, and we thank God for having allowed us to get so far.

January 6 This must be our last outward march with the sledge and camp equipment. To-morrow we must leave camp with some food, and push as far south as possible, and then plant the flag. To-day's story is 57° of frost, with a strong blizzard and high drift; yet we marched 13 geographical miles through soft snow, being helped by extra food. This does not mean full rations, but a bigger ration than we have been having lately. The pony maize is all finished. The most trying day we have yet spent, our fingers and faces being frost-bitten continually. To-morrow we will rush south with the flag. We are at 88°7' South to-night. It is our last outward march. Blowing hard to-night. I would fail to explain my feelings if I tried to write them down, now that the end has come. There is only one thing that lightens the disappointment, and that is the feeling that we have done all we could. It is the forces of nature that have prevented us from going right through. I cannot write more.

January 7 A blinding, shrieking blizzard all day, with the temperature ranging from 60° to 70° of frost. It has been impossible to leave the tent, which is snowed up on the lee side. We have been lying in our bags all day, only warm at food time, with fine snow making through the walls of the worn tent and covering our bags. We are greatly cramped. Adams is suffering from cramp every now and then. We are eating our valuable food without marching. The wind has been blowing eighty to ninety miles an hour. We can hardly sleep. To-morrow I trust this will be over. Directly the wind drops we march as far south as possible, then plant the flag, and turn homeward. Our chief anxiety is lest our tracks may drift up, for to them we must trust mainly to find our depot; we have no land bearings in this great plain of snow. It is a serious risk that we have taken, but we had to play the game to the utmost, and Providence will look after us.

January 8 Again all day in our bags, suffering considerably physically from cold hands and feet, and from hunger, but more mentally, for we cannot get on south, and we simply lie here shivering. Every now and then one of our party's feet go, and the unfortunate beggar has to take his leg out of the sleeping-bag and have his frozen foot nursed into life again by placing it inside the shirt, against the skin of his almost equally unfortunate neighbour. We must do something more to the south, even though the food is going, and we weaken lying in the cold, for with 72° of frost the wind cuts through our thin tent, and even the drift is finding its way in and on to our bags, which are wet enough as it is. Cramp is not uncommon every now and then, and the drift all round the tent has made it so small that there is hardly room for us at all. The wind has been blowing hard all day; some of the gusts must be over seventy or eighty miles an hour. This evening it seems as though it were going to ease down, and directly it does we shall be up and away south for a rush. I feel that this march must be our limit. We are so short of food, and at this high altitude, 11,600 ft., it is hard to keep any warmth in our bodies between the scanty meals. We have nothing to read now, having depoted our little books to save weight, and it is dreary work lying in the tent with nothing to read, and too cold to write much in the diary.

January 9 Our last day outwards. We have shot our bolt, and the tale is latitude 88° 23′ South, longitude 162° East. The wind eased down at 1 a.m., and at 2 a.m. we were up and had breakfast. At 4 a.m. started south, with the Queen's Union Jack, a brass cylinder containing stamps and documents to place at the furthest south point, camera, glasses, and compass. At 9 a.m. we were in 88° 23′ South, half running and half walking over a surface much hardened by the recent blizzard. It was strange for us to go along without the nightmare of a sledge dragging behind us. We hoisted Her Majesty's flag and the other Union Jack afterwards, and took possession of the plateau in the name of His Majesty. While the Union Jack blew out stiffly in the icy gale that cut us to the bone, we looked south with our powerful glasses, but could see nothing but the dead white snow plain. There was no break in the plateau as it extended towards the Pole, and we feel sure that the goal we have failed to reach lies on this plain. We stayed only a few minutes, and then, taking the Queen's flag and eating our scanty meal as we went, we hurried back and reached our camp about 3 p.m. We were so dead tired that we only did two hours' march in the afternoon and camped at 5.30 p.m. The temperature was minus 19° Fahr. Fortunately for us, our tracks were not obliterated by the blizzard; indeed, they stood up, making a trail easily followed. Homeward bound at last. Whatever regrets may be, we have done our best.

THE POLE AT LAST

Roald Amundsen
(1872–1928)

Amundsen's 1903–6 voyage through the North West Passage had heralded a new era in exploration. The route by then was tolerably well known and its environs explored. His vessel was a diminutive fishing smack, his crew a group of Norwegian friends, and his object simply to be the first to have sailed through. He did it because it had not been done and "because it was there". The same applied to his 1911 conquest of the South Pole. Shackleton had shown the way and Amundsen drew the right conclusions. The Pole was not a scientist's playground nor a mystic's dreamland; it was simply a physical challenge. Instead of officers, gentlemen and scientists, he took men who could ski and dogs that could pull; if need be, the former could eat the latter. The only real anxiety was whether they would forestall Scott.

W e had a great piece of work before us that day: nothing less than carrying our flag farther south than the foot of man had trod. We had our silk flag ready; it was made fast to two ski-sticks and laid on Hanssen's sledge. I had given him orders that as soon as we had covered the distance to 88° 23′ S., which was Shackleton's farthest south, the flag was to be hoisted on his sledge. It was my turn as forerunner, and I pushed on. There was no longer any difficulty in holding one's course; I had the grandest cloud-formations to steer by, and everything now went like a machine. First came the forerunner for the time being, then Hanssen, then Wisting, and finally Bjaaland. The forerunner who was not on duty went where he liked; as a rule he accompanied one or other of the sledges. I had long ago fallen into a reverie – far removed from the scene in which I was moving; what I thought about I do not remember now, but I was so preoccupied that I had entirely forgotten my surroundings. Then suddenly I was roused from my dreaming by a jubilant shout, followed by ringing cheers. I turned round quickly to discover the reason of this unwonted occurrence, and stood speechless and overcome.

I find it impossible to express the feelings that possessed me at this moment. All the sledges had stopped, and from the foremost of them the Norwegian flag was flying. It shook itself out, waved and flapped so that the silk rustled; it looked wonderfully well in the pure, clear air and the shining white surroundings. 88° 23′ was past; we were farther south than any human being had been. No other moment of the whole trip affected me like this. The tears forced their way to my eyes; by no effort of will could I keep them back. It was the flag yonder that conquered me and my will. Luckily I was some way in advance of the others, so that I had time to pull myself together and master my feelings before reaching my comrades. We all shook hands, with mutual congratulations; we had won our way far by holding together, and we would go farther yet – to the end.

We did not pass that spot without according our highest tribute of admiration to the man, who – together with his gallant companions – had planted his country's flag so infinitely nearer to the goal than any of his precursors. Sir Ernest Shackleton's name will always be written in the annals of Antarctic exploration in letters of fire. Pluck and grit can work wonders, and I know of no better example of this than what that man has accomplished.

The cameras of course had to come out, and we got an excellent photograph of the scene which none of us will ever forget. We went on a couple of miles more, to 88°25′, and then camped. The weather had improved, and kept on improving all the time. It was now almost perfectly calm, radiantly clear, and, under the circumstances, quite summer-like: –0.4° F. Inside the tent it was quite sultry. This was more than we had expected.

After much consideration and discussion we had come to the conclusion that we ought to lay down a depot – the last one – at this spot. The advantages of lightening our sledges were so great that we should have to risk it. Nor would there be any great risk attached to it, after all, since we should adopt a system of marks that would lead even a blind man back to the place. We had determined to mark it not only at right angles to our course – that is, from east to west – but by snow beacons at every two geographical miles to the south.

We stayed here on the following day to arrange this depot. Hanssen's dogs were real marvels, all of them; nothing seemed to have any effect on them. They had grown rather thinner, of course, but they were still as strong as ever. It was therefore decided not to lighten Hanssen's sledge, but only the two others; both Wisting's and Bjaaland's teams had suffered, especially the latter's. The reduction in weight that was effected was considerable – nearly 110 pounds on each of the two sledges; there was thus about 220 pounds in the depot. The snow here was ill-adapted for building, but we put up quite a respectable monument all the same. It was dog's pemmican and biscuits that were left behind; we carried with us on the sledges provisions for about a month. If, therefore, contrary to expectation, we should be so unlucky as to miss this depot, we should nevertheless be fairly sure of reaching our depot in 86° 21′ before supplies ran short. The cross-marking of the depot was done with sixty splinters of black packingcase on each side, with 100 paces between each. Every other one had a shred of black cloth on the top. The splinters on the east side were all marked, so that on seeing them we should know instantly that we were to the east of the depot. Those on the west had no marks.

The warmth of the past few days seemed to have matured our frost-sores, and we presented an awful appearance. It was Wisting, Hanssen, and I who had suffered the worst damage in the last south-east blizzard; the left side of our faces was one mass of sore, bathed in matter and serum. We looked like the worst type of tramps and ruffians, and would probably not have been recognized by our nearest relations. These sores were a great trouble to us during the latter part of the journey. The slightest gust of wind produced a sensation as if one's face were being cut backwards and forwards with a blunt knife. They lasted a long time, too; I can remember Hanssen removing the last scab when we were coming into Hobart – three months later. We were very lucky in the weather during this depot work; the sun came out all at once, and we had an excellent opportunity of taking some good azimuth observations, the last of any use that we got on the journey.

December 9 arrived with the same fine weather and sunshine. True, we felt our frost-sores rather sharply that day, with –18.4°F. and a little breeze dead against us, but that could not be helped.

Every step we now took in advance brought us rapidly nearer the goal; we could feel fairly certain of reaching it on the afternoon of the 14th. It was very natural that our conversation should be chiefly concerned with the time of arrival. None of us would admit that he was nervous, but I am inclined to think that we all had a little touch of that malady. What should we see when we got there? A vast, endless plain, that no eye had yet seen and no foot yet trodden; or –

No, it was an impossibility; with the speed at which we had travelled, we must reach the goal first, there could be no doubt about that. And yet – and yet – Wherever there is the smallest loophole, doubt creeps in and gnaws and gnaws and never leaves a poor wretch in peace. "What on earth is Uroa scenting?" It was Bjaaland who made this remark, on one of these last days, when I was going by the side of his sledge and talking to him. "And the strange thing is that he's scenting to the south. It can never be – " Mylius, Ring, and Suggen, showed the same interest in the southerly direction; it was quite extraordinary to see how they raised their heads, with every sign of curiosity, put their noses in the air, and sniffed due south. One would really have thought there was something remarkable to be found there.

From 88° 25' S. the barometer and hypsometer indicated slowly but surely that the plateau was beginning to descend towards the other side. This was a pleasant surprise to us; we had thus not only found the very summit of the plateau, but also the slope down on the far side. This would have a very important bearing for obtaining an idea of the construction of the whole plateau. On December 9 observations and dead reckoning agreed within a mile. The same result again on the 10th: observation 2 kilometres behind reckoning. The weather and going remained about the same as on the preceding days: light south-easterly breeze, temperature –18.4° F. The snow surface was loose, but ski and sledges glided over it well. On the 11th, the same weather conditions. Temperature –13° F. Observation and reckoning again agreed exactly. Our latitude was 89° 15' S. On the 12th we reached 89° 30', reckoning 1 kilometre behind observation. Going and surface as good as ever. Weather splendid – calm with sunshine. The noon observation on the 13th gave 89° 37' S. Reckoning 89° 38.5' S. We halted in the afternoon, after going eight geographical miles, and camped in 89° 45', according to reckoning.

The weather during the forenoon had been just as fine as before; in the afternoon we had some snow-showers from the south-east. It was like the eve of some great festival that night in the tent. One could feel that a great event was at hand. Our flag was taken out again and lashed to the same two ski-sticks as before. Then it was rolled up and laid aside, to be ready when the time came. I was awake several times during the night, and had the same feeling that I can remember as a little boy on the night before Christmas Eve – an intense expectation of what was going to happen. Otherwise I think we slept just as well that night as any other.

On the morning of December 14 the weather was of the finest, just as if it had been made for arriving at the Pole. I am not quite sure, but I believe we despatched our breakfast rather more quickly than usual and were out of the tent sooner, though I must admit that we always accomplished this with all reasonable haste. We went in the usual order – the forerunner, Hanssen, Wisting, Bjaaland, and the reserve forerunner. By noon we had reached 89° 53' by dead reckoning, and made ready to take the rest in one stage. At 10 a.m. a light breeze had sprung up from the south-east, and it had clouded over, so that we got no noon altitude; but the clouds were not thick, and from time to time we had a glimpse of the sun through them. The going on that day was rather different from what it had been; sometimes the ski went over it well, but at others it was pretty bad. We advanced that day in the same mechanical way as before; not much was said, but eyes were used all the more, Hanssen's neck grew twice as long as before in his endeavour to see a few inches farther. I had asked him before we started to spy out ahead for all he was worth, and he did so with a vengeance. But, however keenly he stared, he could not descry anything but the endless flat plain ahead of us. The dogs had dropped their scenting, and appeared to have lost their interest in the regions about the earth's axis.

At three in the afternoon a simultaneous "Halt!" rang out from the drivers. They had carefully examined their sledge-meters, and they all showed the full distance – our Pole by reckoning. The goal was reached, the journey ended. I cannot say – though I know it would sound much more effective – that the object of my life was attained. That would be romancing rather too bare facedly. I had better be honest and admit straight out that I have never known any man to be placed in such a diametrically opposite position to the goal of his desires as I was at that moment. The regions around the North Pole – well, yes, the North Pole itself – had attracted me from childhood, and here I was at the South Pole. Can anything more topsy-turvy be imagined?

We reckoned now that we were at the Pole. Of course, every one of us knew that we were not standing on the absolute spot; it would be an impossibility with the time and the instruments at our disposal to ascertain that exact spot. But we were so near it that the few miles which possibly separated us from it could not be of the slightest importance. It was our intention to make a circle round this camp, with a radius of twelve and a half miles (20 kilometres), and to be satisfied with that. After we had halted we collected and congratulated each other. We had good grounds for mutual respect in what had been achieved, and I think that was just the feeling that was expressed in the firm and powerful grasps of the fist that were exchanged. After this we proceeded to the greatest and most solemn act of the whole journey – the planting of our flag. Pride and affection shone in the five pairs of eyes that gazed upon the flag, as it unfurled itself with a sharp crack, and waved over the Pole. I had determined that the act of planting it – the historic event – should be equally divided among us all. It was not for one man to do this; it was for *all* who had staked their lives in the struggle, and held together through thick and thin. This was the only way in which I could show my gratitude to my comrades in this desolate spot. I could see that they understood and accepted it in the spirit in which it was offered. Five weather-beaten, frost-bitten fists they were that grasped the pole, raised the waving flag in the air, and planted it as the first at the geographical South Pole. "Thus we plant thee, beloved flag, at the South Pole, and give to the plain on which it lies the name of King Haakon VII's Plateau." That moment will certainly be remembered by all of us who stood there.

One gets out of the way of protracted ceremonies in those regions – the shorter they are the better. Everyday life began again at once. When we had got the tent up, Hanssen set about slaughtering Helge, and it was hard for him to have to part from his best friend. Helge had been an uncommonly useful and good-natured dog; without making any fuss he had pulled from morning to night, and had been a shining example to the team. But during the last week he had quite fallen away, and on our arrival at the Pole there was only a shadow of the old Helge left. He was only a drag on the others, and did absolutely no work. One blow on the skull, and Helge had ceased to live. "What is death to one is food to another," is a saying that can scarcely find a better application than these dog meals. Helge was portioned out on the spot, and within a couple of hours there was nothing left of him but his teeth and the tuft at the end of his tail. This was the second of our eighteen dogs that we had lost. The Major, one of Wisting's fine dogs, left us in 88° 25' S., and never returned. He was fearfully worn out, and must have gone away to die. We now had sixteen dogs left, and these we intended to divide into two equal teams, leaving Bjaaland's sledge behind.

Of course, there was a festivity in the tent that evening – not that champagne corks were popping and wine flowing – no, we contented ourselves with a little piece of seal meat each, and it tasted well and did us good. There was no other sign of festival indoors. Outside we heard the flag flapping in the breeze. Conversation was lively in the tent that evening, and we talked of many things. Perhaps, too, our thoughts sent messages home of what we had done.

Everything we had with us had now to be marked with the words "South Pole" and the date, to serve afterwards as souvenirs. Wisting proved to be a first-class engraver, and many were the articles he had to mark. Tobacco – in the form of smoke – had hitherto never made its appearance in the tent. From time to time I had seen one or two of the others take a quid, but now these things were to be altered. I had brought with me an old briar pipe, which bore inscriptions from many places in the Arctic regions, and now I wanted it marked "South Pole." When I produced my pipe and was about to mark it, I received an unexpected gift: Wisting offered me tobacco for the rest of the journey. He had some cakes of plug in his kit-bag, which he would prefer to see me smoke. Can anyone grasp what such an offer meant at such a spot, made to a man who, to tell the truth, is very fond of a smoke after meals? There are not many who can understand it fully. I accepted the offer, jumping with joy, and on the way home I had a pipe of fresh, fine-cut plug every evening. Ah! that Wisting, he spoiled me entirely. Not only did he give me tobacco, but every evening – and I must confess I yielded to the temptation after a while, and had a morning smoke as well – he undertook the disagreeable work of cutting the plug and filling my pipe in all kinds of weather.

But we did not let our talk make us forget other things. As we had got no noon altitude, we should have to try and take one at midnight. The weather had brightened again, and it looked as if midnight would be a good time for the observation. We therefore crept into our bags to get a little nap in the intervening hours. In good time – soon after 11 p.m. – we were out again, and ready to catch the sun; the weather was of the best, and the opportunity excellent. We four navigators all had a share in it, as usual, and stood watching the course of the sun. This was a labour of patience, as the difference of altitude was now very slight. The result at which we finally arrived was of great interest; as it clearly shows how unreliable and valueless a single observation like this is in these regions. At 12.30 a.m. we put our instruments away, well satisfied with our work, and quite convinced that it was the midnight altitude that we had observed. The calculations which were carried out immediately afterwards gave us 89° 56′ S. We were all well pleased with this result.

The arrangement now was that we should encircle this camp with a radius of about twelve and a half miles. By encircling I do not, of course, mean that we should go round in a circle with this radius; that would have taken us days, and was not to be thought of. The encircling was accomplished in this way: Three men went out in three different directions, two at right angles to the course we had been steering, and one in continuation of that course. To carry out this work I had chosen Wisting, Hassel, and Bjaaland. Having concluded our observations, we put the kettle on to give ourselves a drop of chocolate; the pleasure of standing out there in rather light attire had not exactly put warmth into our bodies. As we were engaged in swallowing the scalding drink, Bjaaland suddenly observed: "I'd like to tackle this encircling straight away. We shall have lots of time to sleep when we get back." Hassel and Wisting were quite of the same opinion, and it was agreed that they should start the work immediately. Here we have yet another example of the good spirit that prevailed in our little community. We had only lately come in from our day's work – a march of about eighteen and a half miles – and now they were asking to be allowed to go on another twenty-five miles. It seemed as if these fellows could never be tired. We therefore turned this meal into a little breakfast – that is to say, each man ate what he wanted of his bread ration, and then they began to get ready for the work. First, three small bags of light windproof stuff were made, and in each of these was placed a paper, giving the position of our camp. In addition, each of them carried a large square flag of the same dark brown material, which could be easily seen at a distance. As flag-poles we elected to use our spare sledge-runners, which were both long – 12 feet – and strong, and which we were going to take off here in any case, to lighten the sledges as much as possible for the return journey.

Thus equipped, and with thirty biscuits as an extra ration, the three men started off in the directions laid down. Their march was by no means free from danger, and does great honour to those who undertook it, not merely without raising the smallest objection, but with the greatest keenness.

The first thing we did – Hanssen and I – was to set about arranging a lot of trifling matters; there was something to be done here, something there, and above all we had to be ready for the series of observations we were to carry out together, so as to get as accurate a determination of our position as possible. The first observation told us at once how necessary this was. For it turned out that this, instead of giving us a greater altitude than the midnight observation, gave us a smaller one, and it was then clear that we had gone out of the meridian we thought we were following. Now the first thing to be done was to get our north and south line and latitude determined, so that we could find our position once more. Luckily for us, the weather looked as if it would hold. We measured the sun's altitude at every hour from 6 a.m. to 7 p.m., and from these observations found, with some degree of certainty, our latitude and the direction of the meridian.

By nine in the morning we began to expect the return of our comrades; according to our calculation they should then have covered the distance – twenty-five miles. It was not till ten o'clock that Hanssen made out the first black dot on the horizon, and not long after the second and third appeared. We both gave a sigh of relief as they came on; almost simultaneously the three arrived at the tent. We told them the result of our observations up to that time; it looked as if our camp was in about 89° 54′ 30″ S., and that with our encircling we had therefore included the actual Pole. With this result we might very well have been content, but as the weather was so good and gave the impression that it would continue so, and our store of provisions proved on examination to be very ample, we decided to go on for the remaining ten kilometres (five and a half geographical miles), and get our position determined as near to the Pole as possible. Meanwhile the three wanderers turned in – not so much because they were tired, as because it was the right thing to do – and Hanssen and I continued the series of observations.

In the afternoon we again went very carefully through our provision supply before discussing the future. The result was that we had food enough for ourselves and the dogs for eighteen days. The surviving sixteen dogs were divided into two teams of eight each, and the contents of Bjaaland's sledge were shared between Hanssen's and Wisting's. The abandoned sledge was set upright in the snow, and proved to be a splendid mark. The sledge-meter was screwed to the sledge, and we left it there; our other two were quite sufficient for the return journey; they had all shown themselves very accurate. A couple of empty provision cases were also left behind. I wrote in pencil on a piece of case the information that our tent – "Polheim" – would be found five and a half geograph-ical miles north-west quarter west by compass from the sledge. Having put all these things in order the same day, we turned in, very well satisfied.

Early next morning, December 16, we were on our feet again. Bjaaland, who had now left the company of the drivers and been received with jubilation into that of the forerunners, was immedi-ately entrusted with the honourable task of leading the expedition forward to the Pole itself. I assigned this duty, which we all regarded as a distinction, to him as a mark of gratitude to the gallant Telemarkers for their pre-eminent work in the advancement of ski sport. The leader that day had to keep as straight as a line, and if possible to follow the direction of our meridian. A little way after Bjaaland came Hassel, then Hanssen, then Wisting, and I followed a good way behind. I could thus check the direction of the march very accurately, and see that no great deviation was made. Bjaaland on this occasion showed himself a matchless forerunner; he went perfectly straight the whole time. Not once did he incline to one side or the other, and when we arrived at the end of the distance, we could still clearly see the sledge we had set up and take its bearing. This showed it to be absolutely in the right direction.

It was 11 a.m. when we reached our destination. While some of us were putting up the tent, others began to get everything ready for the coming observations. A solid snow pedestal was put up, on which the artificial horizon was to be placed, and a smaller one to rest the sextant on when it was not in use.

Observations were now taken every hour through the whole twenty-four. It was very strange to turn in at 6 p.m., and then on turning out again at midnight to find the sun apparently still at the same altitude, and then once more at 6 a.m. to see it still no higher. The altitude had changed, of course, but so slightly that it was imperceptible with the naked eye. To us it appeared as though the sun made the circuit of the heavens at exactly the same altitude.

On December 17 at noon we had completed our observations, and it is certain that we had done all that could be done. In order if possible to come a few inches nearer to the actual Pole, Hanssen and Bjaaland went out four geographical miles (seven kilometres) in the direction of the newly found meridian.

Bjaaland astonished me at dinner that day. Speeches had not hitherto been a feature of this journey, but now Bjaaland evidently thought the time had come, and surprised us all with a really fine oration. My amazement reached its culmination when, at the conclusion of his speech, he produced a cigar-case full of cigars and offered it round. A cigar at the Pole! What do you say to that? But it did not end there. When the cigars had gone round, there were still four left. I was quite touched when he handed the case and cigars to me with the words: "Keep this to remind you of the Pole." I have taken good care of the case, and shall preserve it as one of the many happy signs of my comrades' devotion on this journey. The cigars I shared out afterwards, on Christmas Eve, and they gave us a visible mark of that occasion.

When this festival dinner at the Pole was ended, we began our preparations for departure. First we set up the little tent we had brought with us in case we should be compelled to divide into two parties. It had been made by our able sailmaker, Rönne, and was of very thin windproof gabardine. Its drab colour made it easily visible against the white surface. Another pole was lashed to the tent-pole, making its total height about 13 feet. On the top of this a little Norwegian flag was lashed fast, and underneath it a pennant, on which "Fram" was painted. The tent was well secured with guy-ropes on all sides. Inside the tent, in a little bag, I left a letter, addressed to H.M. the King, giving information of what we had accomplished. The way home was a long one, and so many things might happen to make it impossible for us to give an account of our expedition. Besides this letter, I wrote a short epistle to Captain Scott, who, I assumed, would be the first to find the tent. Other things we left there were a sextant with a glass horizon, a hyps-ometer case, three reindeerskin foot-bags, some kamiks and mits.

When everything had been laid inside, we went into the tent, one by one, to write our names on a tablet we had fastened to the tent-pole. On this occasion we received the congratulations of our companions on the successful result, for the following messages were written on a couple of strips of leather, sewed to the tent: "Good luck," and "Welcome to 90°." These good wishes, which we suddenly discovered, put us in very good spirits. They were signed by Beck and Rönne. They had good faith in us. When we had finished this we came out, and the tent-door was securely laced together, so that there was no danger of the wind getting a hold on that side.

And so good-bye to Polheim. It was a solemn moment when we bared our heads and bade farewell to our home and our flag. And then the travelling tent was taken down and the sledges packed. Now the homeward journey was to begin – homeward, step by step, mile after mile, until the whole distance was accomplished. We drove at once into our old tracks and followed them. Many were the times we turned to send a last look to Polheim. The vaporous, white air set in again, and it was not long before the last of Polheim, our little flag, disappeared from view.

IN EXTREMIS

Robert Falcon Scott
(1868–1912)

Scott was chosen to lead the 1900–4 British National Antarctic Expedition. Its considerable achievements seemed to vindicate the choice of a naval officer more noted for integrity and courage than any polar experience and, following Shackleton's near success, in 1910 Scott again sailed south intending to combine a busy scientific programme with a successful bid for the South Pole. On 17 January 1912 he and four others duly reached the Pole, indeed they sighted a real pole and it bore a Norwegian flag; Amundsen had got there 34 days ahead of them. Bitterly disappointed, soon overtaken by scurvy and bad weather, and still dragging sledges laden with geological specimens, they trudged back. The tragedy which then unfolded eclipsed even Amundsen's achievement and won them an immortality beyond the dreams of any explorer.

*T*hursday, January 23   There is no doubt Evans is a good deal run down – his fingers are badly blistered and his nose is rather seriously congested with frequent frost bites. He is very much annoyed with himself, which is not a good sign. I think Wilson, Bowers and I are as fit as possible under the circumstances. Oates gets cold feet. One way and another, I shall be glad to get off the summit! We are only about 13 miles from our "Degree and half" Depot and should get there to-morrow. The weather seems to be breaking up. Pray God we have something of a track to follow to the Three Degree Depot – once we pick that up we ought to be right. *Wednesday, January 24*   Lunch Temp. –8°. Things beginning to look a little serious. A strong wind at the start has developed into a full blizzard at lunch, and we have had to get into our sleeping-bags. It was a bad march, but we covered 7 miles. At first Evans, and then Wilson went ahead to scout for tracks. Bowers guided the sledge

Scott's team pictured at the South Pole. From *Scott's Last Expedition*, London, 1913.

alone for the first hour, then both Oates and he remained alongside it; they had a fearful time trying to make the pace between the soft patches. At 12.30 the sun coming ahead made it impossible to see the tracks further, and we had to stop. By this time the gale was at its height and we had the dickens of a time getting up the tent, cold fingers all round. We are only 7 miles from our depot, but I made sure we should be there to-night. This is the second full gale since we left the Pole. I don't like the look of it. Is the weather breaking up? If so, God help us, with the tremendous summit journey and scant food. Wilson and Bowers are my standby. I don't like the easy way in which Oates and Evans get frostbitten.

Thursday, January 25 Temp. Lunch – 11°, Temp. night –16°. Thank God we found our Half Degree Depot. After lying in our bags yesterday afternoon and all night, we debated breakfast; decided to have it later and go without lunch. At the time the gale seemed as bad as ever, but during breakfast the sun showed and there was light enough to see the old track. It was a long and terribly cold job digging out our sledge and breaking camp, but we got through and on the march without sail, all pulling. This was about 11, and at about 2.30, to our joy, we saw the red depot flag. We had lunch and left with 9½ days' provisions, still following the track – marched till 8 and covered over 5 miles, over 12 in the day. Only 89 miles (geogr.) to the next depot, but it's time we cleared off this plateau. We are not without ailments: Oates suffers from a very cold foot; Evans' fingers and nose are in a bad state, and to-night Wilson is suffering tortures from his eyes. Bowers and I are the only members of the party without troubles just at present. The weather still looks unsettled, and I fear a succession of blizzards at this time of year; the wind is strong from the south and this afternoon has been very helpful with the full sail. Needless to say I shall sleep much better with our provision bag full again. The only real anxiety now is the finding of the Three Degree Depot. The tracks seem as good as ever so far; sometimes for 30 or 40 yards we lose them under drifts, but then they reappear quite clearly raised above the surface. If the light is good there is not the least difficulty in following. Blizzards are our bug-bear, not only stopping our marches, but the cold damp air takes it out of us.

Wednesday, February 14 Lunch Temp. 0°; Supper Temp. –1°. A fine day with wind on and off down the glacier, and we have done a fairly good march. We started a little late and pulled on down the moraine. At first I thought of going right, but soon, luckily, changed my mind and decided to follow the curving lines of the moraines. This course had brought us well out on the glacier. Started on crampons; one hour after, hoisted sail; the combined efforts produced only slow speed, partly due to the sandy snow-drifts similar to those on summit, partly to our torn sledge runners. At lunch these were scraped and sand-papered. After lunch we got on snow, with ice only occasionally showing through. A poor start, but the gradient and wind improving, we did 6½ miles before night camp.

There is no getting away from the fact that we are not going strong. Probably none of us: Wilson's leg still troubles him and he doesn't like to trust himself on ski; but the worst case is Evans, who is giving us serious anxiety. This morning he suddenly disclosed a huge blister on his foot. It delayed us on the march, when he had to have his crampon readjusted. Sometimes I fear he is going from bad to worse, but I trust he will pick up again when we come to steady work on ski like this afternoon. He is hungry and so is Wilson. We can't risk opening out our food again, and as cook at present I am serving something under full allowance. We are inclined to get slack and slow with our camping arrangements, and small delays increase. I have talked of the matter to-night and hope for improvement. We cannot do distance without the ponies. The next depot some 30 miles away and nearly 3 days' food in hand.

Thursday, February 15 R. 29. Lunch Temp. –10°; Supper Temp. –4°. 13.5 miles. Again we are running short of provision. We don't know our distance from the depôt, but imagine about 20 miles. Heavy march – did 13¾ (geo.). We are pulling for food and not very strong evidently. In the afternoon it was overcast; land blotted out for a considerable interval. We have reduced food, also sleep; feeling rather done. Trust 1½ days or 2 at most will see us at depot.

Friday, February 16 12.5 m. Lunch Temp. –6.1°; Supper Temp. –7°. A rather trying position. Evans has nearly broken down in brain, we think. He is absolutely changed from his normal self-reliant self. This morning and this afternoon he stopped the march on some trivial excuse. We are on short rations with not very short food; spin out till to-morrow night. We cannot be more than 10 or 12 miles from the depot, but the weather is all against us. After lunch we were enveloped in a snow sheet, land just looming. Memory should hold the events of a very troublesome march with more troubles ahead. Perhaps all will be well if we can get to our depot to-morrow fairly early, but it is anxious work with the sick man. But it's no use meeting troubles half way, and our sleep is all too short to write more.

Saturday, February 17 A very terrible day. Evans looked a little better after a good sleep, and declared, as he always did, that he was quite well. He started in his place on the traces, but half an hour later worked his ski shoes adrift, and had to leave the sledge. The surface was awful, the soft recently fallen snow clogging the ski and runners at every step, the sledge groaning, the sky overcast, and the land hazy. We stopped after about one hour, and Evans came up again, but very slowly. Half an hour later he dropped out again on the same plea. He asked Bowers to lend him a piece of string. I cautioned him to come on as quickly as he could, and he answered cheerfully as I thought. We had to push on, and the remainder of us were forced to pull very hard, sweating heavily. Abreast the Monument Rock we stopped, and seeing Evans a long way astern, I camped for lunch. There was no alarm at first, and we prepared tea and our own meal, consuming the latter. After lunch, and Evans still not appearing, we looked out, to see him still afar off. By this time we were alarmed, and all four started back on ski. I was first to reach the poor man and shocked at his appearance; he was on his knees with clothing disarranged, hands uncovered and frostbitten, and a wild look in his eyes. Asked what was the matter, he replied with a slow speech that he didn't know, but thought he must have fainted. We got him on his feet, but after two or three steps he sank down again. He showed every sign of complete collapse. Wilson, Bowers, and I went back for the sledge, whilst Oates remained with him. When we returned he was practically unconscious, and when we got him into the tent quite comatose. He died quietly at 12.30 a.m. On discussing the symptoms we think he began to get weaker just before we reached the Pole, and that his downward path was accelerated first by the shock of his frostbitten fingers, and later by falls during rough travelling on the glacier, further by his loss of all confidence in himself. Wilson thinks it certain he must have injured his brain by a fall. It is a terrible thing to lose a companion in this way, but calm reflection shows that there could not have been a better ending to the terrible anxieties of the past week. Discussion of the situation at lunch yesterday shows us what a desperate pass we were in with a sick man on our hands at such a distance from home.

At 1 a.m. we packed up and came down over the pressure ridges, finding our depot easily.

Tuesday, February 21 R. 35. Lunch Temp. 9½ °; Supper Temp. –11°. Gloomy and overcast when we started; a good deal warmer. The marching almost as bad as yesterday. Heavy toiling all day, inspiring gloomiest thoughts at times. Rays of comfort when we picked up tracks and cairns. At lunch we seemed to have missed the way, but an hour or two after we passed the last pony walls, and since, we struck a tent ring, ending the march actually on our old pony-tracks. There is a critical spot here with a long stretch between cairns. If we can tide that over we get on the regular cairn route, and with luck should stick to it; but everything depends on the weather. We never won a march of 8½ miles with greater difficulty, but we can't go on like this. We are drawing away from the land and perhaps may get better things in a day or two. I devoutly hope so.

Wednesday, February 22 R. 36. Supper Temp. –2°. There is little doubt we are in for a rotten critical time going home, and the lateness of the season may make it really serious. Shortly after starting to-day the wind grew very fresh from the S.E. with strong surface drift. We lost the faint track immediately, though covering ground fairly rapidly. Lunch came without sight of the cairn we had hoped to pass. In the afternoon, Bowers being sure we were too far to the west, steered out. Result, we have passed another pony camp without seeing it. Looking at the map to-night there is no doubt we are too far to the east. With clear weather we ought to be able to correct the mistake, but will the weather get clear? It's a gloomy position, more especially as one sees the same difficulty returning even when we have corrected the error. The wind is dying down to-night and the sky clearing in the south, which is hopeful. Meanwhile it is satisfactory to note that such untoward events fail to damp the spirit of the party. To-night we had a pony hoosh so excellent and filling that one feels really strong and vigorous again.

Friday, March 2 Lunch. Misfortunes rarely come singly. We marched to the (Middle Barrier) depot fairly easily yesterday afternoon, and since that have suffered three distinct blows which have placed us in a bad position. First we found a shortage of oil; with most rigid economy it can scarce carry us to the next depot on this surface (71 miles away). Second, Titus Oates disclosed his feet, the toes showing very bad indeed, evidently bitten by the late temperatures. The third blow came in the night, when the wind, which we had hailed with some joy, brought dark overcast weather. It fell below −40° in the night, and this morning it took 1½ hours to get our foot gear on, but we got away before eight. We lost cairn and tracks together and made as steady as we could N. by W., but have seen nothing. Worse was to come – the surface is simply awful. In spite of strong wind and full sail we have only done 5½ miles. We are in a *very* queer street since there is no doubt we cannot do the extra marches and feel the cold horribly.

Saturday, March 3 Lunch. We picked up the track again yesterday, finding ourselves to the eastward. Did close on 10 miles and things looked a trifle better; but this morning the outlook is blacker than ever. Started well and with good breeze; for an hour made good headway; then the surface grew awful beyond words. The wind drew forward; every circumstance was against us. After 4½ hours things so bad that we camped, having covered 4½ miles. (R. 46.) One cannot consider this a fault of our own – certainly we were pulling hard this morning – it was more than three parts surface which held us back – the wind at strongest, powerless to move the sledge. When the light is good it is easy to see the reason. The surface, lately a very good hard one, is coated with a thin layer of woolly crystals, formed by radiation no doubt. These are too firmly fixed to be removed by the wind and cause impossible friction on the runners. God help us, we can't keep up this pulling, that is certain. Amongst ourselves we are unendingly cheerful, but what each man feels in his heart I can only guess. Pulling on foot gear in the morning is getting slower and slower, therefore every day more dangerous.

Sunday, March 4 Lunch. Things looking *very* black indeed. As usual we forgot our trouble last night, got into our bags, slept splendidly on good hoosh, woke and had another, and started marching. Sun shining brightly, tracks clear, but surface covered with sandy frost-rime. All the morning we had to pull with all our strength, and in 4½ hours we covered 3½ miles. Last night it was overcast and thick, surface bad; this morning sun shining and surface as bad as ever. One has little to hope for except perhaps strong dry wind – an unlikely contingency at this time of year. Under the immediate surface crystals is a hard sastrugi surface, which must have been excellent for pulling a week or two ago. We are about 42 miles from the next depot and have a week's food, but only about 3 to 4 days' fuel – we are as economical of the latter as one can possibly be, and we cannot afford to save food and pull as we are pulling. We are in a very tight place indeed, but none of us despondent *yet*, or at least we preserve every semblance of good cheer, but one's heart sinks as the sledge stops dead at some sastrugi behind which the surface sand lies thickly heaped. For the moment the temperature is on the −20° – an improvement which makes us much more comfortable, but a colder snap is bound to come again soon. I fear that Oates at least will weather such an event very poorly. Providence to our aid! We can expect little from man now except the possibility of extra food at the next depot. It will be really bad if we get there and find the same shortage of oil. Shall we get there? Such a short distance it would have appeared to us on the summit! I don't know what I should do if Wilson and Bowers weren't so determinedly cheerful over things.

Monday, March 5 Lunch. Regret to say going from bad to worse. We got a slant of wind yesterday afternoon, and going on 5 hours we converted our wretched morning run of 3½ miles into something over 9. We went to bed on a cup of cocoa and pemmican solid with the chill off. (R. 47.) The result is telling on all, but mainly on Oates, whose feet are in a wretched condition. One swelled up tremendously last night and he is very lame this morning. We started march on tea and pemmican as last night – we pretend to prefer the pemmican this way. Marched for 5 hours this morning over a slightly better surface covered with high moundy sastrugi. Sledge capsized twice; we pulled on foot, covering about 5½ miles. We are two pony marches and 4 miles about from our depot. Our fuel dreadfully low and the poor Soldier nearly done. It is pathetic enough because we can do nothing for him; more hot food might do a little, but only a little, I fear. We none of us expected these terribly low temperatures, and of the rest of us Wilson is feeling them most;

mainly, I fear, from his self-sacrificing devotion in doctoring Oates' feet. We cannot help each other, each has enough to do to take care of himself. We get cold on the march when the trudging is heavy, and the wind pierces our warm garments. The others, all of them, are unendingly cheerful when in the tent. We mean to see the game through with a proper spirit, but it's tough work to be pulling harder than we ever pulled in our lives for long hours, and to feel that the progress is so slow. One can only say "God help us!" and plod on our weary way, cold and very miserable, though outwardly cheerful. We talk of all sorts of subjects in the tent, not much of food now, since we decided to take the risk of running a full ration. We simply couldn't go hungry at this time.

Tuesday, March 6   Lunch. We did a little better with help of wind yesterday afternoon, finishing 9½ miles for the day, and 27 miles from depot. (R.48.) But this morning things have been awful. It was warm in the night and for the first time during the journey I overslept myself by more than an hour; then we were slow with foot gear; then, pulling with all our might (for our lives) we could scarcely advance at rate of a mile an hour; then it grew thick and three times we had to get out of harness to search for tracks. The result is something less than 3½ miles for the forenoon. The sun is shining now and the wind gone. Poor Oates is unable to pull, sits on the sledge when we are track-searching – he is wonderfully plucky, as his feet must be giving him great pain. He makes no complaint, but his spirits only come up in spurts now, and he grows more silent in the tent. We are making a spirit lamp to try and replace the primus when our oil is exhausted. It will be a very poor substitute and we've not got much spirit. If we could have kept up our 9-mile days we might have got within reasonable distance of the depot before running out, but nothing but a strong wind and good surface can help us now, and though we had quite a good breeze this morning, the sledge came as heavy as lead. If we were all fit I should have hopes of getting through, but the poor Soldier has become a terrible hindrance, though he does his utmost and suffers much I fear.

Wednesday, March 7   A little worse I fear. One of Oates' feet *very* bad this morning; he is wonderfully brave. We still talk of what we will do together at home.

We only made 6½ miles yesterday. (R. 49.) This morning in 4½ hours we did just over 4 miles. We are 16 from our depot. If we only find the correct proportion of food there and this surface continues, we may get to the next depot [Mt. Hooper, 72 miles farther] but not to One Ton Camp. We hope against hope that the dogs have been to

Mt. Hooper; then we might pull through. If there is a shortage of oil again we can have little hope. One feels that for poor Oates the crisis is near, but none of us are improving, though we are wonderfully fit considering the really excessive work we are doing. We are only kept going by good food. No wind this morning till a chill northerly air came ahead. Sun bright and cairns showing up well. I should like to keep the track to the end.

Thursday, March 8 Lunch. Worse and worse in morning; poor Oates' left foot can never last out, and time over foot gear something awful. Have to wait in night foot gear for nearly an hour before I start changing, and then am generally first to be ready. Wilson's feet giving trouble now, but this mainly because he gives so much help to others. We did 4½ miles this morning and are now 8½ miles from the depot – a ridiculously small distance to feel in difficulties, yet on this surface we know we cannot equal half our old marches, and that for that effort we expend nearly double the energy. The great question is, What shall we find at the depot? If the dogs have visited it we may get along a good distance, but if there is another short allowance of fuel, God help us indeed. We are in a very bad way, I fear, in any case.

Saturday, March 10 Things steadily downhill. Oates' foot worse. He has rare pluck and must know that he can never get through. He asked Wilson if he had a chance this morning, and of course Bill had to say he didn't know. In point of fact he has none. Apart from him, if he went under now, I doubt whether we could get through. With great care we might have a dog's chance, but no more. The weather conditions are awful, and our gear gets steadily more icy and difficult to manage. At the same time of course poor Titus is the greatest handicap. He keeps us waiting in the morning until we have partly lost the warming effect of our good breakfast, when the only wise policy is to be up and away at once; again at lunch. Poor chap! it is too pathetic to watch him; one cannot but try to cheer him up.

Yesterday we marched up the depot, Mt. Hooper. Cold comfort. Shortage on our allowance all round. I don't know that anyone is to blame. The dogs which would have been our salvation have evidently failed.

This morning it was calm when we breakfasted, but the wind came from the W.N.W. as we broke camp. It rapidly grew in strength. After travelling for half an hour I saw that none of us could go on facing such conditions. We were forced to camp and are spending the rest of the day in a comfortless blizzard camp, wind quite foul. (R. 52.)

Sunday, March 11   Titus Oates is very near the end, one feels. What we or he will do, God only knows. We discussed the matter after breakfast; he is a brave fine fellow and understands the situation, but he practically asked for advice. Nothing could be said but to urge him to march as long as he could. One satisfactory result to the discussion; I practically ordered Wilson to hand over the means of ending our troubles to us, so that any one of us may know how to do so. Wilson had no choice between doing so and our ransacking the medicine case. We have 30 opium tabloids apiece and he is left with a tube of morphine. So far the tragical side of our story. (R. 53.)

The sky completely overcast when we started this morning. We could see nothing, lost the tracks, and doubtless have been swaying a good deal since – 3.1 miles for the forenoon – terribly heavy dragging – expected it. Know that 6 miles is about the limit of our endurance now, if we get no help from wind or surfaces. We have 7 days' food and should be about 55 miles from One Ton Camp to-night, 6 × 7 = 42, leaving us 13 miles short of our distance, even if things get no worse. Meanwhile the season rapidly advances.

Monday, March 12   We did 6.9 miles yesterday under our necessary average. Things are left much the same, Oates not pulling much, and now with hands as well as feet pretty well useless. We did 4 miles this morning in 4 hours 20 min. – we may hope for 3 this afternoon, 7 × 6 = 42. We shall be 47 miles from the depot. I doubt if we can possibly do it. The surface remains awful, the cold intense, and our physical condition running down. God help us! Not a breath of favourable wind for more than a week, and apparently liable to head winds at any moment.

Wednesday, March 14   No doubt about the going downhill, but everything going wrong for us. Yesterday we woke to a strong northerly wind with temp. –37°. Couldn't face it, so remained in camp (R. 54) till 2, then did 5¼ miles. Wanted to march later, but party feeling the cold badly as the breeze (N.) never took off entirely, and as the sun sank the temp. fell. Long time getting supper in dark. (R. 55.)

This morning started with southerly breeze, set sail and passed another cairn at good speed; half-way, however, the wind shifted to W. by S. or W.S.W., blew through our wind clothes and into our mits. Poor Wilson horribly cold, could not get off ski for some time. Bowers and I practically made camp, and when we got into the tent at last we were all deadly cold. Then temp. now midday down –43° and the wind strong. We *must* go on, but now the making of every camp must be more difficult and dangerous. It must be near the end, but a pretty merciful end. Poor Oates got it again in the foot. I shudder to think what it will be like to-morrow. It is only with greatest pains rest of us keep off frostbites. No idea there could be temperatures like this at this time of year with such winds. Truly awful outside the tent. Must fight it out to the last biscuit, but can't reduce rations.

Friday, March 16 or Saturday 17 Lost track of dates, but think the last correct. Tragedy all along the line. At lunch, the day before yesterday, poor Titus Oates said he couldn't go on; he proposed we should leave him in his sleeping-bag. That we could not do, and induced him to come on, on the afternoon march. In spite of its awful nature for him he struggled on and we made a few miles. At night he was worse and we knew the end had come.

Should this be found I want these facts recorded. Oates' last thoughts were of his Mother, but immediately before he took pride in thinking that his regiment would be pleased with the bold way in which he met his death. We can testify to his bravery. He has borne intense suffering for weeks without complaint, and to the very last was able and willing to discuss outside subjects. He did not – would not – give up hope to the very end. He was a brave soul. This was the end. He slept through the night before last, hoping not to wake; but he woke in the morning – yesterday. It was blowing a blizzard. He said, "I am just going outside and may be some time." He went out into the blizzard and we have not seen him since.

I take this opportunity of saying that we have stuck to our sick companions to the last. In case of Edgar Evans, when absolutely out of food and he lay insensible, the safety of the remainder seemed to demand his abandonment, but Providence mercifully removed him at this critical moment. He died a natural death, and we did not leave him till two hours after his death. We knew that poor Oates was walking to his death, but though we tried to dissuade him, we knew it was the act of a brave man and an English gentleman. We all hope to meet the end with a similar spirit, and assuredly the end is not far.

I can only write at lunch and then only occasionally. The cold is intense, – 40° at midday. My companions are unendingly cheerful but we are all on the verge of serious frostbites, and though we constantly talk of fetching through I don't think any one of us believes it in his heart.

We are cold on the march now, and at all times except meals. Yesterday we had to lay up for a blizzard and to-day we move dreadfully slowly. We are at No. 14 pony camp, only two pony marches from One Ton Depot. We leave here our theodolite, a camera, and Oates' sleeping-bags. Diaries, &c., and geological specimens carried at Wilson's special request, will be found with us or on our sledge.

Sunday, March 18 To-day, lunch, we are 21 miles from depot. Ill fortune presses, but better may come. We have had more wind and drift from ahead yesterday; had to stop marching; wind N.W., force 4, temp. –35°. No human being could face it, and we are worn out *nearly*.

My right foot has gone, nearly all the toes – two days ago I was proud possessor of best feet. These are the steps of my downfall. Like an ass I mixed a small spoonful of curry powder with my melted pemmican – it gave me violent indigestion. I lay awake and in pain all night; woke and felt done on the march; foot went and I didn't know it. A very small measure of neglect and have a foot which is not pleasant to contemplate. Bowers takes first place in condition, but there is not much to choose after all. The others are still confident of getting through – or pretend to be – I don't know! We have the last *half* fill of oil in our primus and a very small quantity of spirit – this alone between us and thirst. The wind is fair for the moment, and that is perhaps a fact to help. The mileage would have seemed ridiculously small on our outward journey.

Monday, March 19 Lunch. We camped with difficulty last night and were dreadfully cold till after our supper of cold pemmican and biscuit and a half a pannikin of cocoa cooked over the spirit. Then, contrary to expectation, we got warm and all slept well. To-day we started in the usual dragging manner. Sledge dreadfully heavy. We are 15½ miles from the depot and ought to get there in three days. What progress! We have two day's food but barely a day's fuel. All our feet are getting bad – Wilson's best, my right foot worst, left all right. There is no chance to nurse one's feet till we can get hot food into us. Amputation is the least I can hope for now, but will the trouble spread? That is the serious question. The weather doesn't give us a chance – the wind from N. to N. W. and – 40° temp, to-day.

Wednesday, March 21 Got within 11 miles of depot Monday night; had to lay up all yesterday in severe blizzard. To-day forlorn hope, Wilson and Bowers going to depot for fuel.

Thursday, March 22 and 23 Blizzard bad as ever – Wilson and Bowers unable to start – to-morrow last chance – no fuel and only one or two of food left – must be near the end. Have decided it shall be natural – we shall march for the depot with or without our effects and die in our tracks.

Thursday, March 29 Since the 21st we have had a continuous gale from W. S. W. and S. W. We had fuel to make two cups of tea a piece and bare food for two days on the 20th. Every day we have been ready to start for our depot *11 miles* away, but outside the door of the tent it remains a scene of whirling drift. I do not think we can hope for any better things now. We shall stick it out to the end, but we are getting weaker, of course, and the end cannot be far.

It seems a pity, but I do not think I can write more.

R. SCOTT

For God's sake look after our people.

Wilson and Bowers were found in the attitude of sleep, their sleeping-bags closed over their heads as they would naturally close them.

Scott died later. He had thrown back the flaps of his sleeping-bag and opened his coat. The little wallet containing the three notebooks was under his shoulders and his arm flung across Wilson. So they were found eight months later.

With the diaries in the tent were found the following letters:

To Mrs. E. A. Wilson

My dear Mrs. Wilson,

If this letter reaches you Bill and I will have gone out together. We are very near it now and I should like you to know how splendid he was at the end – everlastingly cheerful and ready to sacrifice himself for others, never a word of blame to me for leading him into this mess. He is not suffering, luckily, at least only minor discomforts.

His eyes have a comfortable blue look of hope and his mind is peaceful with the satisfaction of his faith in regarding himself as part of the great scheme of the Almighty. I can do no more to comfort you than to tell you that he died as he lived, a brave, true man – the best of comrades and staunchest of friends.

My whole heart goes out to you in pity,

Yours,

R. SCOTT.

To Mrs. Bowers

My dear Mrs. Bowers,

I am afraid this will reach you after one of the heaviest blows of your life.

I write when we are very near the end of our journey, and I am finishing it in company with two gallant, noble gentlemen. One of these is your son. He had come to be one of my closest and soundest friends, and I appreciate his wonderful upright nature, his ability and energy. As the troubles have thickened his dauntless spirit ever shone brighter and he has remained cheerful, hopeful, and indomitable to the end.

The ways of Providence are inscrutable, but there must be some reason why such a young, vigorous and promising life is taken.

My whole heart goes out in pity for you.

Yours,

R. SCOTT.

To the end he has talked of you and his sisters. One sees what a happy home he must have had and perhaps it is well to look back on nothing but happiness.

He remains unselfish, self-reliant and splendidly hopeful to the end, believing in God's mercy to you.

To Sir J. M. Barrie

My dear Barrie,

We are pegging out in a very comfortless spot. Hoping this letter may be found and sent to you, I write a word of farewell . . . More practically I want you to help my widow and my boy – your godson. We are showing that Englishmen can still die with a bold spirit, fighting it out to the end. It will be known that we have accomplished our object in reaching the Pole, and that we have done everything possible, even to sacrificing ourselves in order to save sick companions. I think this makes an example for Englishmen of the future, and that the country ought to help those who are left behind to mourn us. I leave my poor girl and your godson, Wilson leaves a widow, and Edgar Evans also a widow in humble circumstances. Do what you can to get their claims recognised. Goodbye. I am not at all afraid of the end, but sad to miss many a humble pleasure which I had planned for the future on our long marches. I may not have proved a great explorer, but we have done the greatest march ever made and come very near to great success. Goodbye, my dear friend,

Yours,

R. SCOTT.

We are in a desperate state, feet frozen, &c. No fuel and a long way from food, but it would do your heart good to be in our tent, to hear our songs and the cheery conversation as to what we will do when we get to Hut Point.

Later. – We are very near the end, but have not and will not lose our good cheer. We have four days of storm in our tent and nowhere's food or fuel. We did intend to finish ourselves when things proved like this, but we have decided to die naturally in the track.

As a dying man, my dear friend, be good to my wife and child. Give the boy a chance in life if the State won't do it. He ought to have good stuff in him. . . . I never met a man in my life whom I admired and loved more than you, but I never could show you how much your friendship meant to me, for you had much to give and I nothing.

SOURCES AND ACKNOWLEDGMENTS

George William Steller: Reprinted from American Geographical Society Research Series No 2, 1925. Translated by Leonhard Stejneger

John Dundas Cochrane: Taken from *A Pedestrian Journey Through Russia & Siberian Tartary to the Frontiers of China, The Frozen Sea, and Kamtchatka*, Constable & Co., 1829

Alexander Burnes: Taken from *Travels into Bokhara*, John Murray, 1839

John Wood: Taken from *A Journey to the Source of the River Oxus*, John Murray, 1872

Regis-Evariste Huc: Taken from *Lamas of the Western Heavens*, translated by Charles de Salis, © The Folio Society Ltd., 1982

Henri Mouhot: Taken from *Travels in the Central Parts of Indo-China, Cambodia & Laos*, John Murray, 1864

Francis Edward Younghusband: Taken from *Among The Celestials*, John Murray, 1898

Ekai Kawaguchi: Taken from *Three Years in Tibet*, Theosophical Publishing Society, 1909

Sven Hedin: Taken from *Trans-Himalaya*, MacMillan & Co., 1909

Edmund Hillary: Taken from 'The Ascent of Mount Everest' by Col John Hunt in *Geographical Journal* CXIX(4) pp. 385–99, Dec. 1953, RGS, London

William Gifford Palgrave: Taken from *A Year's Journey through Central and Eastern Arabia*, MacMillan & Co., 1871

Charles Montagu Doughty: Taken from *Wanderings in Arabia*, Duckworth, 1923

Harry St John Bridger Philby: Taken from *The Empty Quarter*, Constable & Co., London, 1933

Wilfred Thesiger: Taken from *Arabian Sands*, Longman Green, London, 1959, repr Penguin 1964, by kind permission of Curtis Brown

Mungo Park: Taken from *Travels in the Interior of Africa*, Adam & Charles Black, 1860

Hugh Clapperton: Taken from *Narrative of Travels & Discoveries in Northern & Central Africa*, John Murray, 1826

Richard Lander: Taken from *Journal of an Expedition to Explore the Course and Termination of the Niger*, Thomas Tegg, 1845

Heinrich Barth: Taken from *Travels & Discoveries in North and Central Africa*, Longman Brown, 1858

Mary Kingsley: Taken from *Travels in West Africa*, MacMillan & Co., 1897

James Bruce: Taken From *Travels to Discover the Source of the Nile*, Constable & Co., 1804

Richard Francis Burton: Taken from *Wanderings in Three Continents*, Hutchinson, 1901

John Hanning Speke: Taken from *What Led to the Discovery of the Source of the Nile*, Blackwood & Sons, 1864

Samuel White Baker: Taken from *The Albert N'yanza, Great Basin of the Nile and Explorations of the Nile Sources*, MacMillan, 1867

David Livingstone: Taken from *The Last Journals of David Livingstone*, John Murray, 1874

Henry Morton Stanley: Taken from *Through the Dark Continent*, Sampson Low, 1878

Joseph Thomson: Taken from *To the Central African Lakes and Back*, Frank Cass, 1968

James Cook: Taken from *The Journals of Captain James Cook*, Hakluyt Society

Charles Sturt: Taken from *Narrative of an Expedition into Central Australia*, T & W Boone, 1849

William John Wills: Taken from *An Account of the Crossing the Continent of Australia*, Wilson & MacKinnon, 1861

John McDonald Stuart: Taken from *The Journals of John MCDouall Stuart*, Saunders, Otley & Co., 1864

Alexander Mackenzie: Taken from *Voyages from Montreal on the River St Laurence through the Continent of North America to the Frozen and Pacific Oceans*, Cadell & Davies, 1801

Meriwether Lewis: Taken from *History of the Expedition of Captains Lewis and Clark*, A. C. McClurg, 1903

Alexander von Humboldt: Taken from *Personal Narrative of Travels to the Equinoctial Regions of America*, George Routledge & Sons

Henry Savage Landor: Taken from *Across Unknown South America*, Hodder & Stoughton

Hiram Bingham: Taken from *Inca Land: Explorations in the Highlands of Peru*, London, Constable & Co., 1922

John Ross: Taken from *Narrative of a Second Voyage in Search of a North-West Passage*, A. W. Webster, 1835

John Franklin: Taken from *Narrative of a Journey to the Shores of The Polar Sea*, John Murray, 1823

Fridtjof Nansen: Taken from *The First Crossing of Greenland*, Longmans, Green & Co., 1890

Robert Edwin Peary: Taken from *The North Pole*, Hodder & Stoughton, 1910

Ernest Henry Shackleton: Taken from *The Heart of the Antarctic*, Heinemann, 1910

Roald Amundsen: Taken from *The South Pole*, John Murray, 1912

Robert Falcon Scott: Taken from *Scott's Last Expedition*, Smith Elder & Co., 1913